Human Rights

Human Rights
Politics and Practice

EDITED BY

Michael Goodhart

OXFORD
UNIVERSITY PRESS

OXFORD

UNIVERSITY PRESS

Great Clarendon Street, Oxford OX2 6DP

Oxford University Press is a department of the University of Oxford.

It furthers the University's objective of excellence in research, scholarship,
and education by publishing worldwide in

Oxford New York

Auckland Cape Town Dar es Salaam Hong Kong Karachi
Kuala Lumpur Madrid Melbourne Mexico City Nairobi
New Delhi Shanghai Taipei Toronto

With offices in

Argentina Austria Brazil Chile Czech Republic France Greece
Guatemala Hungary Italy Japan Poland Portugal Singapore
South Korea Switzerland Thailand Turkey Ukraine Vietnam

Oxford is a registered trade mark of Oxford University Press
in the UK and in certain other countries

Published in the United States
by Oxford University Press Inc., New York

British Library Cataloguing in Publication Data

Data available

Library of Congress Cataloging in Publication Data
Human rights: politics and practice/edited by Michael Goodhart.
p. cm.
ISBN 978-0-19-954084-6
1. Human rights. I. Goodhart, Michael E., 1969-
JC571.H769685 2009
323—dc22

2009002099

Typeset by Laserwords Private Ltd, Chennai, India
Printed in Italy by
L.E.G.O. S.p.A., Lavis (TN)

ISBN 978-0-19-954084-6

5 7 9 10 8 6 4

For my parents, who gave me a love of learning.

Acknowledgements

This book is the result of many people's hard work. First, and most fundamentally, the authors of the chapters have contributed their knowledge and expertise. I am grateful to all of them for their participation in this project and for their collegial good cheer in working with me to tight deadlines, despite everything else happening in their lives. Second, I owe many thanks to Ruth Anderson, until recently at OUP, who conceived the idea for this book and persuaded me to undertake the challenge of putting it together. She provided tremendous support and guidance while giving me broad intellectual freedom—the ideal editor. I wish her all the best in her new endeavours. Following Ruth's departure, Helen Tyas has stepped in ably to shepherd the project to completion. I am very grateful to her for making what might have been a disruptive transition effectively invisible to me. Thanks also go to Julie Harris, who did outstanding work in copy-editing the text, making it more accurate, more precise, and more readable.

Many friends and colleagues (especially in the Political Science department at the University of Pittsburgh) have contributed in ways large and small to this effort. I cannot thank each of them, but I want to thank them all. I also want to acknowledge the institutional support I have received from my department and my university, support which makes projects like this one possible. Work on the book was completed at the Hertie School of Governance in Berlin, where I am spending the 2008–9 academic year as a Visiting Professor. This opportunity was made possible by a generous research fellowship from the Alexander von Humboldt Foundation, and I am grateful to both the Hertie School and the Humboldt Foundation for their support as well. In addition, Susan Hoppe deserves special mention and thanks for her innumerable and invaluable contributions.

I owe a tremendous debt to the group of human rights scholars I have been privileged to know and work with in recent years. I count many of them as mentors and friends, and I am deeply appreciative of their confidence in my work and of the many opportunities they have kindly provided me. The work they do continues to teach and inspire me. In particular, I want to thank those involved with the University of Connecticut Human Rights Institute, the American Political Science Association human rights section, and the Columbia University Human Rights Seminar. Finally, I want to thank my students, whose optimism, enthusiasm, and activism have encouraged me in thinking that studying human rights matters, even when the state of the world might seem to suggest otherwise.

Guided Tour of the Textbook Features

This text is enriched with a range of learning tools to help you navigate the text material and reinforce your knowledge of human rights. This guided tour shows you how to get the most out of your textbook package.

Chapter Contents

This feature provides a concise overview of the subjects covered in the chapter.

Reader's Guide

This feature at the beginning of every chapter sets the scene for upcoming themes and issues and indicates the scope of coverage within each chapter.

Reader's guide

The chapter provides a general overview of the purpose, challenges, and types of human rights measures. It covers the main content of human rights that ought to be measured, including the different categories (civil, political, economic, social, and cultural) and dimensions (respect, protect, and fulfil) of human rights. It outlines the different ways that human rights have been measured using different kinds of data and measurement strategies. It concludes by identifying the remaining challenges for this sub-tradition in the field of human rights, including the need for more measures of economic and social rights and better measures of civil and political rights.

Introduction

The introduction opens each chapter and succinctly presents the main themes, issues, and controversies.

Introduction

Many commentators have observed the fact that human rights frameworks have become an integral part of a new, more hierarchical, international order, undermining UN Charter restrictions on the use of military force and justifying new, more coercive forms of international regulation and intervention in the post-colonial world. To view these consequences of human rights claims and discourses as the ideological backed by law. Declarations of the 'rights of man' were no more than rhetorical fancies and collections of pious wishes that were not worth the paper they were written on. The idea that we were born with universal equal rights simply because we were human made no sense to Bentham. Firstly, we are born into a relationship of dependency rather than equality, and are not considered as moral or legal equals until we reach maturity

Boxes

Boxes are interspersed throughout the chapters and provide further insight into specific topics and issues.

published collections and reviews of human rights measures produced by academics and NGOs (Claude, 1976; Jabine and Claude, 1992) and efforts to collate and assess the quality of human rights measures continue to be carried out (see, for example, Green, 2001; Landman and Häusermann, 2003; Landman, 2004, 2006b; Landman and Carvalho, to appear).

Since the publication of *Human Rights and Statistics* (Jabine and Claude, 1992), there have been an increasing number of efforts to measure more and different categories of human rights (e.g. the Cingranelli and Richards Human Rights Data Project), and there have been a

Box 3.1 The Behavioural Revolution

The behavioural revolution began in the 1930s and 1940s, primarily in the United States. It putatively moved political science away from normative questions and 'value-based' research, and concentrated on *observable* and *measurable* attributes of human beings and human societies in an effort to uncover empirical regularities and provide 'law-like' generalizations that had universal applicability. Research in this tradition involves hypothesis testing using quantitative measures on individuals and states and the research design in such studies is one very much beholden to the natural

Key Points

Key points follow each main section in every chapter and summarize the key issues to reinforce learning.

has risen on the international agenda. Internal displacement can be caused by conflict, environmental
disaster, economic change, or large-scale development
projects. Like refugees, IDPs have been displaced from
their homes, suffer many of the same deprivations and
human rights violations as refugees do, and are in need
of protection. However, they do not receive the same
rights and opportunities as refugees. While there has
been a relatively clear legal and institutional framework
regulating refugee protection, the IDP issue was rarely
recognized or debated until the end of the 1980s. The
international regime governing IDP protection and
assistance has only recently begun to take shape. Since

KEY POINTS

Individuals fleeing persecution who cross borders to seek
safety and protection in the territory of another state are
considered to be refugees. IDPs are persons in a refugee-
like situation who have not crossed the borders of their
country.

The majority of refugee and IDP movements are caused by
war, persecution and ethnic strife, weak institutions, and
sharp socio-economic inequalities, or a combination of
these factors.

Refugees can suffer further human rights violations while

Conclusion

The conclusion provides a review of each chapter and reinforces its main points.

Conclusion

The aspiration to improve children's lives globally is
important. However, there are questions over whether
children's rights are capable of empowering children
and the extent to which legal approaches may address
the problems faced by children globally. Moreover,
children's rights advocacy risks inverting civil rights
and democratic freedoms. There are further contradictions in contemporary global children's rights.

historical understanding risk distracting the development of analysis and action essential to realize a more
humane world. Norms of a secure childhood cannot be
globalized without universally transforming the material conditions of childhood. Post-industrial norms of
childhood cannot be realized in non-industrial conditions. The fundamental interdependence between
material advancement and social advancement needs

Questions

Individual study questions at the end of each chapter test your understanding and help you to track your progress. Group discussion questions spark debate and additional reflection.

QUESTIONS

INDIVIDUAL STUDY QUESTIONS

1. How are forced migrants a human rights issue?
2. What is a refugee? Does the 1951 Refugee Convention adequately define a refugee? How has the
   term refugee been widened over the past sixty years beyond its narrow legal definition?
3. What are the differences between the ways that refugees and internally displaced persons are treated
   by the international community? What special problems do IDPs present?
4. What are the major constraints facing the UNHCR in fulfilling its role of protecting and assisting
   refugees? What does this tell us about the problems of governance in a world in which the interests

Further Reading

This end-of-chapter feature recommends key texts on important issues and provides short summaries of each, helping you quickly survey the key academic literature in the field.

FURTHER READING

Black, M. (1996). *Children First: The Story of UNICEF*. Oxford: Oxford University Press.
An informative account of UNICEF changing child policies. Black explains why UNICEF was initially opposed to
children's rights and why UNICEF came to adopt a children's rights approach.
Burman, E. (1994). Innocents abroad: Western fantasies of childhood and the iconography of emergencies.
Disasters, **18**/3, 238–253.
One of various insightful articles by Burman, which discusses how Western disaster aid responses construct
recipient countries as children and a form of 'disaster pornography'.
Detrick, S. (ed.) (1992). *The United Nations Convention on the Rights of the Child: A Guide to the 'Travaux
Preparatoires'*. Dordrecht: Martinus Nijhoff.
Provides very useful insights into the drafting process of the CRC and the concerns of developing countries

Web Links

Each chapter provides web links to data, reports, organizations, and other information related to the themes and debates covered in the chapter.

WEB LINKS

http://www.freedomhouse.org Freedom House: two standards-based scales on civil and political rights from
1972, updated annually.
http://www.politicalterrorscale.org Political terror scale: standards-based scale on personal integrity rights
from 1976 to 2006, updated occasionally.
http://www.humanrightsdata.com Cingranelli and Richards human rights data: large collection of standards-
based data on seventeen different human rights from 1980 to 2006, updated occasionally.
http://www.hrdag.org Human Rights Data Analysis Group: world-leading organization in the production and
analysis of events-based data on human rights.

Glossary

A glossary provides concise definitions of key terms highlighted throughout the text.

Abrogation of rights The failure to honour rights.
Accession or accretion The acquisition of territory that has
emerged from the action of the forces of nature.
Alien Torts Claims Act (ATCA) An act of the US Congress
passed in 1789 that provides jurisdiction in federal courts over
lawsuits by aliens for torts committed either in violation of
international law or of treaties to which the United States is a
party. It has been used successfully by torture victims and their
families to bring civil suits against torturers residing in the
United States.
Amnesty Immunity from prosecution, often granted through
legislation as part of a peace agreement.

aims were to help rebuild the shattered post-War world
economy and to promote international economic cooperation.
The original Bretton Woods agreement also included plans
for an International Trade Organization (ITO), but these lay
dormant until the **World Trade Organization** (WTO) was
created in the early 1990s. The creation of the World Bank and
the IMF came at the end of the Second World War as a central
feature of a multilateral framework established to overcome
the destabilizing effects of the previous global economic
depression and trade battles.
Brown v. Board of Education of Topeka, Kansas The
landmark 1954 ruling by the US Supreme Court that
overturned previously restrictive laws segregating blacks and

Guided Tour of the Online Resource Centre

 www.oxfordtextbooks.co.uk/orc/goodhart/

Written by Marco Larizza, the Online Resource Centre that accompanies this book provides lecturers and students with ready-to-use teaching and learning materials. Dr Marco Larizza is Visiting Fellow, Department of Government, University of Essex.

LECTURER RESOURCES

A test bank with 10 multiple-choice, true-or-false and fill-in-the-blank questions for each chapter provides lecturers with a wide range of testing options.

PowerPoints complement each chapter and are a useful resource for preparing lectures and handouts. These fully customizable slides include key concepts, ideas, and theories enabling teaching flexibility.

STUDENT RESOURCES

Flashcard glossary allows students to test their understanding of the terminology.

Two types of web link allow students to easily research pertinent topics. The first type, drawn from each chapter, connects students to various organizations, reports, and other relevant discussions. The second type is a topically organized list of links to key documents and more.

Brief Contents

Detailed Contents

● Part II   Human Rights in Practice

Notes on Contributors

John Barry is a Reader in Politics in the School of Politics, International Studies, and Philosophy at Queen's University Belfast. He has written extensively on green political theory, green political economy, governance and policy for sustainability and the environment, and the relationship between green theory, citizenship, and republicanism. His works include *Rethinking Green Politics: Nature, Virtue and Progress* (1999, London: Sage)—winner of the Political Studies Association prize for best book published in political science—and *Environment and Social Theory* (2007, 2nd edn, London: Routledge). His co-edited work includes *The Nation-State and the Global Ecological Crisis* (with Robyn Eckersley; 2005, Cambridge, MA: MIT Press) and *The International Encyclopedia of Environmental Politics* (with Gene Frankland; 2001, London: Routledge).

Andrea Bertone is the Director of http://HumanTrafficking.org at the Academy for Educational Development in Washington, DC. She has been researching the issue of human trafficking for the last decade.

Sonia Cardenas is Associate Professor of Political Science and Director of the Human Rights Program at Trinity College in Connecticut. She is the author of, among other publications, *Conflict and Compliance: State Responses to International Human Rights Pressure* (2007, Philadelphia, PA: University of Pennsylvania). Her current research focuses on the global rise of national human rights institutions.

David Chandler is Professor of International Relations at the Centre for the Study of Democracy, University of Westminster, London. He is the editor of the journal *Intervention and Statebuilding* and author of several books including *From Kosovo to Kabul (and Beyond): Human Rights and International Intervention* (2006, 2nd edn, London: Pluto) and *Empire in Denial: The Politics of State-building* (2006, London: Pluto).

Christian Davenport is Professor of Peace Studies and Political Science at the Kroc Institute, University of Notre Dame, as well as Director of the Radical Information Project (RIP) and Stop Our States (SOS). Primary research interests include political conflict (e.g. human rights violations, genocide/politicide, torture, political surveillance/covert repressive action, civil war, and social movements), measurement, and racism. Prof. Davenport is the author of *State Repression and the Promise of Democratic Peace* (2007, Comparative Politics, Cambridge: Cambridge University Press) and *Media Bias and State Repression* (to appear, Contentious Politics, Cambridge: Cambridge University Press). For more information, please refer to the following webpage: http://www.christiandavenport.com.

Tim Dunne is Professor of International Relations and Head of Humanities and Social Sciences at the University of Exeter. His most recent book is *Foreign Policy: Actors, Issues, Cases* (2008, Oxford: Oxford University Press), edited with Steve Smith and Amelia Hadfield. He is currently an associate editor of the *European Journal of International Relations*.

Sakiko Fukuda-Parr is Professor of International Affairs at the New School, New York. She was director of the UNDP's annual *Human Development Reports* from 1995 to 2004. Her research focuses on the nexus of human rights, poverty, and violent conflict, and on global technology.

Ronald D. Gelleny is Assistant Professor of Political Science at the University of Akron. He specializes in the areas of comparative and international politics. His research focuses on political economy, human rights, and cross-national political behaviour. His research has been published in the *Canadian Journal of Political Science, European Union Politics, International Studies Quarterly, Journal of Peace Research*, and *Political Research Quarterly*.

Marlies Glasius is a Lecturer in International Relations at the University of Amsterdam and a visiting fellow at the Centre for the Study of Global Governance, London School of Economics and Political Science. She is author of *The International Criminal Court: A Global Civil Society Achievement* (2005, London: Routledge) and a founding editor of the *Global Civil Society Yearbook*.

Michael Goodhart is Associate Professor of Political Science and Women's Studies at the University of Pittsburgh (http://www.pitt.edu/~goodhart). He is the author of *Democracy as Human Rights: Freedom and Equality in the Age of Globalization* (2005, New York: Routledge) and of numerous articles on democracy, democratization, and human rights in the context of globalization. His current research focuses on injustice, governance, and democracy in the global economy.

Marianne Hanson is a Reader in International Relations at the University of Queensland, Brisbane, Australia, where she also teaches courses in peace and conflict studies. She received her D.Phil. from Oxford University in 1993, and has written widely on human rights issues (following on from her doctoral dissertation on the Helsinki process) as well as on nuclear arms control and disarmament.

Paul Havemann is Professor of Law at James Cook University, Australia. He has held academic posts in the UK, Canada, and New Zealand. Publications he has contributed to include *Law and Order for Canada's Indigenous Peoples* (1984, Ottawa: Solicitor General of Canada), *Indigenous Peoples' Rights in Australia, Canada and New Zealand* (1999, Oxford: Oxford University Press), and *Miner's Canary* (2002, UN World Summit on Sustainable Development), a submission concerning Indigenous peoples' rights. His recent research concerns Indigenous people and placelessness, the law relating to traditional use of marine resource agreements on the Great Barrier Reef, and Indigenous community-based approaches to the conservation of dugongs and turtles in the Torres Strait.

Alan J. Kuperman is Associate Professor at the LBJ School of Public Affairs, University of Texas at Austin. He is author of *The Limits of Humanitarian Intervention: Genocide in Rwanda* (2001, Washington, DC: Brookings) and co-editor of *Gambling on Humanitarian Intervention: Moral Hazard, Rebellion and Civil War* (with Timothy Crawford; 2006, New York: Routledge). Prior to his academic career, he served as legislative director for Congressman Charles Schumer (D-NY). He holds a Ph.D. in political science from MIT (2002).

Todd Landman is a Reader in the Department of Government at the University of Essex. He has numerous publications on comparative methods and human rights, and he has carried out a variety of international consultancy appointments relating to the measurement of human rights.

Anthony J. Langlois is a Senior Lecturer in the School of Political and International Studies at Flinders University, Adelaide, Australia (http:socsci.flinders.edu.au/spis/staff/langlois.php). He was educated at the University of Tasmania and the Australian National University. Langlois is the author of *The Politics of Justice and Human Rights: Southeast Asia and Universalist Theory* (2001, Cambridge: Cambridge University Press) and co-editor of *Global Democracy and its Difficulties* (2008, London: Routledge). He has published many scholarly articles.

Gil Loescher is a Visiting Professor at the Refugee Studies Centre, University of Oxford and Professor Emeritus at the University of Notre Dame. He is the author, co-author and co-editor of numerous books on refugee policy including *UNHCR and World Politics* (2001, New York: Oxford University Press), *UNHCR: The Politics and Practice of Refugee Protection into the 21st Century* (2008, London: Routledge), and *Protracted Refugee Situations: Political, Security and Human Rights Implications* (with James Milner; 2008, London: Routledge). He is the Co-Director of The PRS Project: Towards Solutions for Protracted Refugee Situations based at the University of Oxford.

Vanessa Pupavac is a Lecturer in the School of Politics and International Relations at the University of Nottingham. She trained as a lawyer and has previously worked for the United Nations. She has published widely on international aid policy and human rights. In 2003 she received the Otto Klineberg Intercultural and International Relations Award.

Joanna R. Quinn is Assistant Professor of Political Science at The University of Western Ontario, where she teaches courses in international human rights, transitional justice, and genocide. She has published widely in the area of transitional justice in Uganda.

David L. Richards is Assistant Professor of Political Science at the University of Memphis and Co-Director of the Cingranelli–Richards (CIRI) Human Rights Data Project (http://www.humanrightsdata.org). He is the author of numerous journal articles and book chapters on human rights measurement and government respect for human rights in the contexts of economic globalization and democratic institutions. His most recent work examines the distribution and formation of citizen attitudes toward human rights.

William F. Schulz, Senior Fellow at the Center for American Progress, in Washington, DC, and Adjunct Professor of Public Administration at the Wagner School of Public Service at New York University, served as Executive Director of Amnesty International USA from 1994 to 2006. He is the author of *In Our Own Best Interest: How Defending Human Rights Benefits Us All* (2001, Boston, MA: Beacon) and *Tainted Legacy: 9/11 and the Ruin of Human Rights* (2003, New York: Nation Books), and the contributing editor of *The Phenomenon of Torture: Readings and Commentary* (2007, Philadelphia, PA: University of Pennsylvania Press) and *The Future of Human Rights: US Policy for a New Era* (2008, Philadelphia, PA: University of Pennsylvania Press).

Damien Short is a Senior Lecturer in Human Rights at the International Centre for Human Rights, Institute for Commonwealth Studies, School of Advanced Study, University of London (http://commonwealth.sas.ac.uk/) and Convenor of the MA Understanding and Securing Human Rights (http://commonwealth.sas.ac.uk/ma_human.htm). He has published several articles on Indigenous peoples and reconciliation, and on the social construction of 'native title' land rights. A monograph titled *Reconciliation and Colonial Power: Indigenous Rights in Australia* (2008, Aldershot: Ashgate) was published in March 2008. He is currently working on a new monograph titled *Genocides?* for Zed Books.

Rhona K. M. Smith is Professor of International Human Rights in the School of Law at Northumbria University, Newcastle, UK. She has authored various books on international human rights including *Textbook on International Human Rights* (2007, 3rd edn, Oxford University Press) and *Text and Materials on International Human Rights* (2007, London: Routledge-Cavendish). She has also worked with the Nordic human rights centres and institutes, most recently on human rights capacity building projects in China.

Scott Straus is Associate Professor of Political Science at the University of Wisconsin, Madison. He is the author of *The Order of Genocide: Race, Power, and War in Rwanda* (2006, Ithaca, NY: Cornell University Press). His current research is on the comparative study of genocide and mass violence.

Kerri Woods is a British Academy postdoctoral Fellow in the Department of Politics at the University of York, UK. She has written on green political theory and on human rights and environmental justice.

Introduction: Human Rights in Politics and Practice

Michael Goodhart

Chapter Contents

Reader's Guide

This chapter aims to provide the historical and conceptual background necessary for informed critical engagement with the ideas and arguments presented throughout this book. It begins by considering why human rights have emerged as a particularly powerful and important moral and political discourse since the middle of the twentieth century, stressing their modernity, their invention, and their revolutionary character. It examines the work that human rights do in politics, explaining them as value claims with powerful social, political, and economic implications. Next, it shows why this political character means that human rights play out in complex and divergent ways in practice. This makes human rights difficult to study, as they are inherently multi-faceted and necessarily interdisciplinary. This introduction concludes with a brief overview of the aims, structure, and objectives of the book.

Consider the following political events: an authoritarian government silences a critical independent media; rural villagers and the urban poor endure sickness caused by the lack of clean water; criminal networks traffic women and girls for sex; transnational corporations shift manufacturing jobs to low-wage countries with lax labour standards; gay men and women organize to win the right to marry and found families; refugees fleeing tribal or religious violence are denied asylum in nearby wealthy countries; suspected terrorists are captured and detained without trial or review; reformers organize resistance to a repressive military regime; a bombing campaign halts attacks on local populations by ethnic militias; a campaign eliminates school fees and makes education available for all. What do such disparate events have in common? It would be difficult to talk about any of them without invoking human rights.

The decades since the Universal Declaration of Human Rights (UDHR) was approved by the United Nations General Assembly in 1948 have witnessed what one writer aptly calls 'the rise and rise of human rights'.[1] Human rights have become so pervasive that it is hard to imagine making sense of, or even talking about, the political world without them.

Why Human Rights?

The advancement of human rights to the forefront of global politics has been as remarkable as it has been improbable. The UDHR, an abstract and non-binding collection of noble words and sentiments, has engendered a vast and growing body of international law that is challenging the ideal of sovereignty and transforming relations among states. This transformation includes the creation and development of a diverse array of international institutions concerned with human rights monitoring, compliance, and, increasingly, enforcement. Human rights have inspired domestic and transnational social movements that have toppled repressive regimes and won protection for oppressed and marginalized people; these movements have emerged as powerful political actors in their own right. While the idea of human rights has provoked sometimes sharp controversy, it has nonetheless become the dominant normative or moral discourse of global politics and a major standard of international legitimacy. Why?

Although this text focuses on the post-War era of human rights and on their study within the discipline of politics, understanding the contemporary state of human rights politics and practice requires some sense of their logic and appeal. It would be impossible to summarize the history of human rights here; instead, in the following sections I shall focus on several essential features of human rights that help to explain their emergence and their success, as well as some of the controversies surrounding them. The point of doing so is to provide the historical and conceptual background necessary for informed critical engagement with the ideas and arguments presented throughout this book. Three related features of human rights deserve special emphasis in this respect:

- human rights are distinctively modern;
- human rights are a political invention;
- human rights are inherently revolutionary.

The Modernity of Human Rights

To say that human rights are distinctively modern is not to deny the long history of the values that animate them. Human rights are closely tied historically to notions of justice and human dignity that are as old as human social interaction itself. To stress the modernity of human rights is rather to stress two important contrasts, one with the corporate conception of rights that dominated medieval Europe and many other premodern societies, the other with notions of justice and dignity based in religious cosmology.

Medieval conceptions of rights were anchored in social status. Rights pertained to classes or categories of persons rather than to individuals, and they were strongly supportive of hierarchical notions of social organization. The rights one had depended upon and varied with one's status or social position. Rights and duties defined the social roles that constituted society; they were in this sense conservative (norm-preserving) and stabilizing (order-preserving) features of society. Rights were often also anchored in cosmological conceptions or religious views that interpreted the existing social order as divinely orchestrated, or at least sanctioned. That is, the organization of society, including the rights and duties of different groups of persons, was seen as reflecting a divine will or plan.

In Western Europe, where the idea of human rights first emerged in its modern form, this way of viewing society and social organization underwent a profound and sustained transformation beginning as early as the twelfth and thirteenth centuries. The transformation entailed economic development, artistic and literary renaissance, religious reformation, and intellectual flowering. Together, these trends fostered *humanism* (an emphasis on the achievements and potential of human beings), *rationalism* (an emphasis on reason and science rather than on belief or superstition), and *individualism* (a focus on persons, rather than on groups or classes, as the fundamental constituents of society).

Modern human rights reflect and embody these humanist, rationalist, and individualist sensibilities. In describing a set of rights that belongs to everyone they make a powerful statement about human capabilities and potential and assert a far-reaching normative programme for protecting and respecting people's ability to exercise those capabilities and realize that potential. In relying on reason as a foundation or justification, human rights make an appeal to universality that transcends—and thus threatens—traditional values and beliefs. Finally, in ascribing the same rights to all persons, the modern conception of rights challenges conventional understandings of social and political order.

Human Rights as a Political Invention

This radicalism indicates that human rights were less the product of evolution than invention (see Minogue, 1979). The idea of rights in Europe can be traced back to its origins and meanings in Roman law (Tuck, 1979), but in seventeenth-century England it became a radical and disruptive notion. This development would have horrified one of the key figures responsible for this change, the political philosopher Thomas Hobbes

(1588–1679). Hobbes was a devoted monarchist who tried to develop a justification for royal absolutism that would be more persuasive than the divine right of kings, which was increasingly under challenge from theologians and rebellious Parliamentarians. Hobbes's key innovation was to suggest that, in a hypothetical 'state of nature' before the creation of society, all individuals should be considered free and equal. Hobbes believed that this natural freedom and equality would result in chaos and war, to which an all-powerful ruler was the logical and best solution (see Hobbes, 1968).

Although Hobbes used freedom and equality to justify absolute authority, others quickly saw the potential to put them to other, very different purposes. The most famous and important of them was the philosopher and Whig revolutionary John Locke (1632–1704). Locke saw that Hobbes's arguments about natural freedom and equality had the potential to justify political revolution by making authority depend on the consent of the governed (Locke, 1960). Locke understood this freedom and equality in terms of natural or human rights enshrined in natural law. Government was established, in Locke's view, to provide means to interpret, judge, and execute this natural law—in other words, to protect rights. When it lacked consent or failed to respect and protect rights, Locke argued, government made itself illegitimate and the people had the right to replace it.

The Revolutionary Character of Human Rights

The revolutionary character is the third feature essential for understanding the politics and practice of human rights and the success and controversy they have generated. By the close of the eighteenth century, rights had become a moral standard for assessing the legitimacy of governmental authority and the battle cry of revolutionaries in the United States, France, and Haiti. This revolutionary character is inherent in the logic of rights themselves. As Carole Pateman (1988, pp. 39–40) has argued, the simple premise of natural freedom and equality undermines justifications for natural authority and subjection: 'the doctrine of natural individual freedom and equality was revolutionary precisely because it swept away, in one fell swoop, all the grounds through which the subordination of some individuals, groups or categories of people to others had been justified.'

This is what Kenneth Minogue (1979, p. 11) meant in describing human rights as the leading edge of the axe of rationalism that toppled monarchies and cleared the ground for democracy. The great revolutions of the eighteenth and nineteenth centuries marched under the banner of human rights precisely because of the power of this argument against monarchy and aristocracy. Yet these human rights revolutions were at best partial and incomplete. Women, labourers, slaves, and 'natives' in areas subjected to European rule were denied the very 'universal' rights that the revolutions themselves proclaimed (see Pateman, 1988; Mills, 1997; Goodhart, 2005).

This was as the early proponents of 'the rights of man' had always intended. Their cause was narrowly political, about the empowerment of a small class of landowning gentry chafing under a hereditary monarchy and aristocracy. The logic of consent and natural rights justified their revolution, but in the end it justified much more besides. The logic of human rights extended much further than Locke or his contemporaries could have imagined or endorsed, and over time the axe of rationalism came more to resemble a double-edged sword, as those excluded from enjoyment of their rights used the logic of universality to challenge their subjection and the hypocrisy that supported it. It is this revolutionary potential and emancipatory logic that make human rights particularly appealing to people struggling against domination and oppression and that explain a large part of their 'rise and rise'.

Appeal and Criticisms

Yet the universal aspiration of human rights is itself double-sided. The failure of human rights in practice to live up to their universal promise has been the source of much of the criticism lodged against them, and this criticism has often been justified. It was perfectly obvious for a long time that who qualified as 'human' in most conceptions of human rights was a fairly narrow group of wealthy European males. The origins of modern human rights in a particular Western social context has fuelled the criticism that they are an essentially Western concept, one at odds with cultural and philosophical traditions elsewhere. This criticism has gained credence thanks to the invocation of human rights in justifying all sorts of domination—from colonialism and imperialism to patriarchy, preventive war, and the global neoliberal economic order.

Yet human rights have been and remain integral to struggles against sexism, racism, and poverty, and in resistance to colonial and authoritarian rule—precisely because they challenge any arbitrary or non-consensual grounds for subordination. It is precisely their incompatibility with traditional cultures and philosophies that explains their appeal to those chafing under domination and oppression—as much in the West as elsewhere. As this suggests, human rights are inherently political, and attention to their political character and the politics surrounding them is central to understanding their place in our world.

The Politics of Human Rights

To assert a human right is to make a fundamentally political claim: that one is entitled to equal moral respect and to the social status, support, and protection necessary to achieve that respect. This explains why human rights resonate with notions of justice and human dignity that are ancient and global. Yet human rights are not simply equivalent with human dignity or justice; they represent a certain kind of dignity or justice, one incompatible with subordination. This is why, as the images of the axe and the double-edged sword suggest, human rights imply the levelling of traditional forms of status and hierarchy.

Another way of saying this is that human rights are values claims. They express a certain set of political convictions and aspirations concerning the freedom and equality of all people. This makes the politics or ideology of human rights incompatible with any system of values that regards some persons as naturally or divinely subordinate to others. This point is vital: when opponents of human rights argue that they clash with traditional values or cultures they are perfectly correct.

To deny or downplay this clash is to miss what is happening politically when human rights get invoked: power is being challenged, domination contested, authority questioned. The issue is not whether human rights are compatible with existing beliefs and practices around the world; in many instances they are not. The issue is rather whether one endorses the values expressed through human rights or the values underlying beliefs and practices that might conflict with human rights.

Human rights can also be asserted, as I alluded to earlier, as rhetorical or ideological cover for political choices motivated by other considerations. Examples of such behaviour are familiar: European powers justified colonial enterprises as 'civilizing missions'; American politicians cite human rights abuses in launching 'pre-emptive' military attacks. The rejection of human rights often works in a similar way, as when authoritarian rulers decry human rights as cultural imperialism to secure their grip on power. The important point here is that it is impossible to understand the advantage to be gained from trumpeting or denouncing human rights without understanding what various actors are doing *politically* when they claim or reject them—namely, taking sides.

The Practice of Human Rights

Human rights are inherently political; they are values claims, and they are embraced or contested to the extent that those doing the embracing or contesting approve of or benefit from the values they embody. I began this introduction by arguing that human rights have in effect become the coin of the realm in global politics, the dominant normative discourse, and a benchmark for legitimate authority. If politics represents the face of that coin, its flip side is the long record of human rights practice that has developed over the past four centuries and accelerated dramatically in recent decades. One can no more understand human rights purely as an abstract political idea than one can understand football by reading the rulebook without watching a match.

This practice is evident in the history of social movements, legal developments, political argumentation, institutional consolidation, and public discourse. It represents the real world of human rights, the empirical record of their use by all kinds of people in varied contexts through time. Regardless of what one might think of the philosophical arguments in favour of human rights, there exists this legacy of their actual use and effects in the world that must be reckoned with. Just as it is perfectly possible to be an atheist and still recognize that religion exists and has a real and significant impact on social life, one need not find the moral or philosophical arguments for human rights conclusive or even persuasive to acknowledge that human rights practice is a significant political phenomenon in our world.

How widely or narrowly one reads this history of human rights is itself probably determined in large part by where one's ideological sympathies lie (for a very broad reading see Ishay (2004)). Was the democratic political revolution that began with seventeenth-century opposition to monarchy and aristocracy a human rights movement? What about the struggles for labourers and for abolition? Women's rights? Resistance to colonial rule? One way to answer these questions is to try to determine the rhetoric and beliefs of the participants. Another is to argue that what the actors said or thought is less important than the thrust and logic of their arguments. Still another is to focus on outcomes, assessing how these movements contributed to the realization of human rights as we understand them today. There is no correct answer to these questions, because the answers one gives have themselves real political consequences. This is, at least in part, what makes human rights so challenging, so important, and so rewarding to study.

Human Rights as an Object of Enquiry

Human rights are an amazingly rich and complex object of political enquiry. Their study involves normative, empirical, and critical approaches and has historical, sociological, anthropological, comparative, and international dimensions.

The discipline of politics or political science is concerned with the theory as well as the practice of human rights, with the normative as well as the empirical. Normative political theorists primarily concern themselves with philosophical and policy questions, while empirical political scientists focus primarily on trying to understand how human rights work in the world. Both are crucially important, and they are much more closely related than many people seem to realize.

In fact, one of the chief difficulties in the study of human rights is that the normative and the empirical often become blurred. Consider human rights' status as a global standard of legitimacy. Political theorists might be concerned with the appropriateness of this standard and with what exactly it entails. These normative questions are distinct from, but closely related to, empirical questions about how human rights came to function as a global standard in the first place and how effectively they work. These questions can be answered in part by tracing the history of the laws and institutions that have evolved over time and of the social actors and movements that advocated their development. Here things get confusing, as such questions direct us back to considerations about what these actors thought they were doing; why, politically, they wanted to do it; the resulting norms to which their actions contributed; and, whether they were right to take up this cause in the first place.

Despite these difficulties, some generalizations can be made. Empirical studies of human rights, both qualitative and quantitative, aim to help us understand the reality of human rights politics and practice. These studies might focus on laws, movements, or institutions, or on levels of achievement or violation of human rights standards, trying to uncover the factors that contribute to them. Alternatively, they might seek to trace how the discourse of human rights works to socialize political actors through a combination of pressure and persuasion. Or, they might study the politics of human rights within a particular country or region, trying to explain why certain policies or practices have emerged. They might also focus on how states and other international actors use human rights politically—as a tool of foreign policy, a condition on aid, and so on.

Normative studies of human rights aim to understand the philosophical bases of human rights. They focus on the justifications given for human rights and

TABLE I.1 Human rights as an object of enquiry.

	Empirical	Normative
Scope of analysis	*What is*; the practice of human rights in the world	*What ought to be*; moral, philosophical, or conceptual questions about human rights
Objects of analysis	*Real-world phenomena*, e.g. treaties and conventions, institutions, violations, enforcement, social movements, historical records, interviews, opinion surveys, statistical measures	*Concepts*, e.g. democracy, freedom, obligation, rights *Arguments*, e.g. freedom requires X; one should do Y if Z applies
Aims of analysis	*Description* or observation of what is actually going on	*Clarification* of key concepts and definitions
	Explanation of what accounts for the patterns and relationships in our observations or predicts what is likely to occur	*Justification* or moral arguments that support human rights
		Moral critique or critical evaluation of existing laws, policies, and practices on moral grounds

on the values that human rights claims embody. Normative studies might track the intellectual development of human rights arguments, clarify concepts (such as freedom), or try to justify a particular way of understanding the human rights or the obligations they entail. They might also critique (endorse or criticize) past or present practice on moral grounds (see Table I.1).

Legal and policy approaches draw on the normative and the empirical. One can study the law from an empirical point of view, emphasizing its content, development, and enforcement, or from a normative perspective, emphasizing its moral character and its interpretation. Similarly, one can try to understand the effects of existing policy or predict the effects of a new policy by relying on empirical analysis, and one can argue for or recommend new policies because of their moral virtues or effects. In practice elements of the normative and the empirical are combined in much of the research on human rights.

About this Book

This book attempts to provide a comprehensive introduction to the politics and practice of human rights from a political perspective. It has two principal aims:

- to introduce students to human rights, both within the discipline of political science and in the politics and practice of our world;
- to provide detailed treatment of some key issues in contemporary human rights in ways that simultaneously illuminate those issues and illustrate the approaches that political scientists use in studying them.

The book is divided into two parts that reflect these complementary objectives. Part I comprises seven chapters showcasing the 'state of the art' of the study of human rights within political science. These chapters introduce the main approaches to the study of human rights as a political phenomenon and survey the key findings they have yielded. These chapters also highlight the primary challenges and controversies involved in the study of human rights.

Part II comprises thirteen thematic chapters written to investigate important topics in contemporary human rights politics and practice. Through the use of varied and extensive case studies, these chapters provide fresh insights into important issues while also providing students with clear examples of how scholars undertake research on human rights. The chapters were all purpose-written for this text by an impressive group of international scholars of human rights. These chapters are representative; they address important themes and issues in the contemporary study of human rights, but they do not exhaust the list of important issues and themes.

The chapters reflect a variety of perspectives on human rights; there has been no attempt to have the authors rely on a standard definition of human rights and no requirement that they hold any particular views about them. The chapters also contain significant overlap, with numerous themes, cases, treaties, and institutions being mentioned in several chapters. This diversity and overlap are intentional and serve an important pedagogical purpose, illustrating that there is no one way to understand human rights or to study them.

NOTE

1. Kirsten Sellars (2002). *The Rise and Rise of Human Rights*. Stroud, UK: Sutton Publishing.

ONLINE RESOURCE CENTRE

 Visit the Online Resource Centre that accompanies this book for updates and a range of other resources:

http://www.oxfordtextbooks.co.uk/orc/goodhart/

PART 1

Human Rights and Politics

Normative and Theoretical Foundations of Human Rights

1

Anthony J. Langlois

Chapter Contents

Reader's Guide

Human rights have come to provide a powerful basis for an ethical critique of international politics and policy. This chapter examines the theoretical basis for the normative ideas advanced by those who offer critiques using the language of human rights. It recognizes that the idea of human rights has a philosophical and a political history, a history that emerges out of political liberalism, and one that resonates still in many of the contemporary controversies surrounding the development and use of human rights. The rhetoric of human rights declares the idea to be universal; in this chapter we look at the various ways in which this claim may be interpreted, including the views of cultural relativists and others who deny the universality of human rights. The chapter concludes by emphasizing the way in which the human rights agenda is deeply political: it privileges a certain set of normative commitments that its proponents hope will become, in time, the ethical constitution of the international system.

Introduction

Understanding the history of the human rights idea is essential to understanding the debates and problems that arise when we try to theorize human rights. Despite the rhetoric of human rights—that they are universal, inalienable, inherent, and so on—the contemporary usage of rights is a very recent affair, emergent out of the history of the West. Neither Socrates nor Jesus, neither Confucius nor the Buddha, would have claimed—in the face of injustices they experienced—that their universal human rights were being abused. Today, however, the language of human rights has become globally recognized as a response to injustice. The way in which we think about this transition, the emergence and spread of the idea of rights, is important for the way in which we seek to justify and theorize human rights.

The Emergence of Rights Language

Rights language did not appear out of a vacuum, but developed gradually through Western political history, reaching its first golden age in the European Enlightenment. Prior to the Enlightenment, social, moral, and political values were spoken of in relation to the right—that is, in relation to an objective moral order that stood over and above all people. This order was conceptualized as the natural law, which, after the rise of Christianity, became associated with the Church. Under the natural law, people had duties to one another and to God; rights were derived from the duties we owed one another under God. The practice of claiming modern secular rights, rights that have as their focus the subjective freedoms and liberties of individuals rather than *objective right* (the divinely sanctioned moral order of the day), is associated with the long development of the idea of individual liberty, culminating in the Enlightenment.

The rights claimed in the Enlightenment made sense to the people of that period because they had been preceded by the development of specific conceptions of society, individuality, freedom, liberty, government, and religion. These conceptions lay the groundwork for human rights—or, as they were called at the time, the rights of man. As these subversive ideas gained critical influence, they began to appear in the political documents known as rights declarations.

These documents, the most important of which were drafted in the final decades of the 1700s, are the early rhetorical and legal masterpieces of rights politics (Fields, 2003, p. 22). They were created under the influence of both a long chain of political events and the intellectual ferment of the Enlightenment. The former included crucial historical events, such as the illegal and confused but fabulously daring trial of King Charles I of England, in 1649 (Kamenka, 1978). With this trial, the English Monarch's rights were made a function of the rights of the people. These same rights were to be discussed and promoted by a host of Enlightenment *philosophes* over the ensuing 130 years. Despite their differences with one another, these thinkers demanded individual freedom from absolutist control.

The Revolutionary Uses of Human Rights

It was this demand for freedom that led American colonists to revolt against their British masters, a revolt that led to the creation of the first grand document of the 'age of rights': the US Declaration of Independence of 1776 (see Box 1.1). While not the first American rights document (there had been a Bill of Rights in

---

Box 1.1 **Revolutionary Statements of Human Rights**

From the United States *Declaration of Independence (1776).*

We hold these truths to be self-evident, that all men are created equal, that they are endowed by their Creator with certain unalienable Rights, that among these are Life, Liberty and the pursuit of Happiness. . . . That to secure these rights, Governments are instituted among Men, deriving their just powers from the consent of the governed, . . . That whenever any Form of Government becomes destructive of these ends, it is the Right of the People to alter or to abolish it, and to institute new Government, laying its foundation on such principles and organizing its powers in such form, as to them shall seem most likely to effect their Safety and Happiness.

From the French *Declaration of the Rights of Man and of the Citizen* ***(1789).***

The representatives of the French people, organized as a National Assembly, believing that the ignorance, neglect, or contempt of the rights of man are the sole cause of public calamities and of the corruption of governments, have determined to set forth in a solemn declaration the natural, unalienable, and sacred rights of man, in order that this declaration, being constantly before all the members of the Social body, shall remind them continually of their rights and duties; in order that the acts of the legislative power, as well as those of the executive power, may be compared at any moment with the objects and purposes of all political institutions and may thus be more respected, and, lastly, in order that the grievances of the citizens, based hereafter upon simple and incontestable principles, shall tend to the maintenance of the constitution and redound to the happiness of all. Therefore the National Assembly recognizes and proclaims, in the presence and under the auspices of the Supreme Being, the following rights of man and of the citizen:

Article 1: Men are born and remain free and equal in rights. Social distinctions may be founded only upon the general good.

Article 2: The aim of all political association is the preservation of the natural and imprescriptable rights of man. These rights are liberty, property, security, and resistance to oppression.

1774 in the First Continental Congress; and the state of Virginia also declared a Bill of Rights on 12 June 1776), the Declaration of Independence penned by Thomas Jefferson (1743–1826) gave poetic and radical voice to the claim that all men (*sic*) should be free to live independently and with equality (Lauren, 1998, p. 17). Jefferson argued that people are entitled to a bill of rights to guard their freedoms against all governments. Americans subsequently gained these entitlements through the US Constitution (1789) and its first ten amendments, which constitute the Bill of Rights (1791).

In France, too, revolution against a despotic monarch and regime led to the creation of that other grand rights document: The Declaration of the Rights of Man and of the Citizen (1789—see Box 1.1). The French were inspired by the Americans—indeed, key French citizens had fought in the American Revolutionary War—and they sought to secure rights, not just for their countrymen, but for everyone: '*all men* are born free and equal in rights' (Article 1, emphasis added).

These Declarations encapsulate what we now call liberal democracy. They do not merely set out an action plan for short-term political goals; rather, they articulate a philosophical account of what it means to have legitimate government (Kamenka, 1978). Central to this is an egalitarian philosophy of what it means to be human.

Philosophical Questions

The political consequences of these rights declarations continue to escalate today. But ever since these rights were first mooted, they have been dogged by philosophical questioning. Natural and imprescriptable rights had their critics; and even those who wished to embrace such rights had questions.

Philosophical Foundations

The difficulty concerned the underlying philosophy from which the notion of rights was derived. The rights described in the Declarations are moral ideas known as **natural rights**, derived from the natural law, which in Christian civilization had to do with the moral character given by God to his creation. This is very clear, for example, when one reads the work of John Locke (1632–1704), who laid the foundation for much of the subsequent enthusiasm about rights. However, this period in which the early rights theorizing occurred was also the period in which Christian theism gradually lost its hold on the allegiance of the *philosophes*. The reason of man came to replace the word of God as the highest authority, fracturing the logic of natural law and duty that lay behind the Christian natural rights framework (Waldron, 1987). New theories were developed—by Hugo Grotius (1583–1645) and Thomas Hobbes (1588–1679), for example—that sought to derive rights, not from the natural law (ordained by God), but from our basic humanity. While these theories were for a time quelled by powerful restatements of natural law theories (such as Samuel Pufendorf's (1632–1694)), they nonetheless added to the cultural shift that highlighted the moral autonomy of the individual, undermined the derivative natural law–duty–rights structure, and

focused the popular imagination on the idea of basic, inalienable, rights—natural rights that could be derived from our natural humanity, not from God's natural law (Haakonssen, 1991, p. 61). Over time, the natural rights idea became more and more politically efficacious; it also became more philosophically tenuous. If natural rights were no longer justified by direct appeal to God via the natural law, how were they to be justified? Nature by itself evinced a bewildering array of values, with no consensus about which were the correct ones. It seemed that the fate of natural rights was to be a political idea that came too late to be awarded philosophical respectability (Waldron, 1987, p. 13).

Early Critics of Rights

By the time of the Rights Declarations, key philosophers were forcefully attacking the idea of natural rights. These attacks came from across the philosophical spectrum—from conservatives, liberals (particularly utilitarians), and socialists (see Box 1.2).

Box 1.2 **The Philosophers on the Rights of Man**

Bentham (1748–1832)

How stands the truth of things? That there are no such things as natural rights—no such things as rights anterior to the establishment of government—no such things as natural rights opposed to, in contradistinction to, legal: that the expression is merely figurative; that when used, in the moment you attempt to give it a literal meaning it leads to error, and to that sort of error that leads to mischief—to the extremity of mischief. ('Anarchical Fallacies', see Bentham (1843))

Burke (1729–1797)

As to the share of power, authority, and direction which each individual ought to have in the management of the state, that I must deny to be amongst the direct original right of man in civil society; for I have in my contemplation the civil social man, and no other. It is a thing to be settled by convention. (*Reflections on the Revolution in France*, see Burke (1971))

Marx (1818–1883)

Thus none of the so called rights of man goes beyond egoistic man, man as he is in civil society, namely an individual withdrawn behind his private interests and whims and separated from the community. Far from the rights of man conceiving of man as a species-being . . . The

only bond that holds them together is natural necessity, need and private interest, the conservation of their property and egoistic person. ('On "the Jewish Question" ', see Marx (1987))

Hobbes (1588–1679)

The Right of Nature . . . is the Liberty each man hath, to use his own power, as he will himselfe, for the preservation of his own nature; that is to say, of his own Life; and consequently, of doing any thing, which in his own Judgement, and Reason, hee shall conceive to be the aptest means thereunto. (*Leviathan*, see Hobbes (1968))

Locke (1632–1704)

Men being . . . by nature all free, equal, and independent, no one can be put out of his estate and subjected to the political power of another without his consent. (*The Second Treatise of Government*, see Locke (1952))

Kant (1724–1804)

So act that the maxim of your will can at the same time be a universal law . . . Treat all humans as ends in themselves rather than as mere means . . . Conduct yourself as a member of a kingdom of ends. (*Groundwork for the Metaphysics of Morals*, see Kant (2002))

(Edmundson, 2004)

Conservatives are most famously represented by Edmund Burke (1729–1797), author of *Reflections on the Revolution in France* (Burke, 1971); here, the French Declaration of the Rights of Man and of the Citizen is denounced in strong terms. Burke's denunciation concerned the basis on which people were thought to have rights. He did not reject rights as such, but rejected the idea that rights were natural, that they existed as an 'Archimedean point' beyond government by which government could be judged. Such abstractions were wrong headed, he argued. Rather, man had rights because of the organic traditions and institutions of his society. Rights were the rights of *Englishmen* or *Frenchmen*, not of *man*. Different political communities may construct different rights, he argued. The attempt to impose one list of abstract rights on all men would issue in the breakdown of social bonds, the eruption of chaos, and eventually tyranny—expectations that for Burke were vindicated by subsequent events in France.

Liberals, in the form of utilitarians, also attacked natural rights. Jeremy Bentham (1748–1832) declared in 'Anarchical Fallacies' (Bentham, 1843): '*Natural rights is simple nonsense: natural and imprescriptable rights, rhetorical nonsense—nonsense upon stilts.*' Natural rights were 'unreal metaphysical phenomena', unreal rights that stemmed from an unreal law, the natural law, which itself was dismissed due to the absence of a divine lawgiver. If one wanted to advance liberal democracy, one should speak of the reform of actual rights and laws—positive rights and laws—not fanciful ones.

Radicals criticized the rights of man for being the rights of bourgeois man. Rights to liberty, property, and personal security gave the entrepreneur a relatively free hand in his capitalist occupations. The economic well-being of the masses would remain of little concern. Karl Marx's (1818–1883) passion was the emancipation of the proletariat or wage workers, to be achieved via revolution with the backing of rigorous science. In practice, rights were part of the general capitalist system of domination that stood in the way of the achievement of equality and well-being for all human persons.

The great irony of the rights revolution, then, is that, just when the language of natural rights became extraordinarily efficacious in dealing with social and political issues, the main currents of political and philosophical thought became ambivalent about the idea (Langlois, 2001, Chapter 3).

KEY POINTS

The foundation for rights is a puzzling philosophical question.

The early natural law foundation for rights became vulnerable during the Enlightenment because of the decline of Christian theism.

At the same time the idea of rights became more politically effective.

Conservatives, liberals, and radicals all criticized the idea of natural rights.

Modern Human Rights

This was all changed by the Second World War (1939–1945). The horror of total war and, in particular, the atrocities of the Jewish Holocaust 'outraged the conscience of mankind'—to cite the language of the UN's Universal Declaration of Human Rights (UDHR; see Box 1.3). In moral shock, the response of the collective Western social imagination was to return to the natural law. Members of the Nazi leadership were charged and tried at the Nuremberg Tribunal (1945–1949), under the auspices of the natural law, with crimes against humanity. This charge was not extant in any formal international document or law, but was one that, so it

would be held, was patently clear and known to any reasonable person *because* it was a part of the natural law. The point here—one to which we shall return—is that positive law, be it domestic or international, is held to account by a higher moral standard. Natural law, then, was invoked as the legal basis for the indictments against the Nazis and as the moral foundation for liberal democracy and human rights.

Human rights standards were placed centrally in the United Nations Charter (1945), and in 1948 the UN promulgated its Universal Declaration. The UDHR has a preamble and thirty articles, the first of which declares that 'all human beings are born free and equal in dignity and rights.' A quick perusal of the Declaration is sufficient for the reader to recognize all the main elements of liberal political theory expressed in the idioms of first and second generation rights (see Box 1.4): the emphasis on freedom and liberty, dignity, and equality; the importance of the rule of law, freedom from slavery and torture, and the presumption of inno-cence; the ownership of private property, freedom of religion and expression, and the right to take part in the government of one's country (first generation rights); and, more controversially, rights to adequate standards of living, education, and cultural participation (second generation rights).

This modern account of human rights contains philosophical tensions. The whole underlying *structure* of the human rights idea is linked to ideas of natural law and natural right that, as we have seen, were philosophically problematic. The *content* of the new human rights represented a very specific philosophical account of human society: that of liberal political thought. Thus, the new universal human rights were highly *particularistic*: they emerged out of Western philosophy and politics, and they embodied a distinct ideological position. The sense in which these ideas are universal has neither to do with their history (which is one thread in the larger history of the West) nor with any form of global empirical reality (modern human rights are not found indigenously occurring in all human societies). Instead, the universality of these rights derived from their proponents' belief that human sociability *should* be articulated (at least in part) by the use of rights language, and that these particular rights *should* be the moral norms by which human behaviour is judged and evaluated.

Box 1.4 **Three Generations of Rights**

The idea of generations of rights was coined by Karel Vasak in the 1970s. Vasak adopted the rallying cry of the French Revolution—Liberty, Equality, Fraternity—as his template for organizing our understandings of human rights. Vasak's template has become commonplace, despite being unsatisfactory either as a theoretical or as a chronological account of human rights.

Liberty rights are the first generation rights. These civil and political rights were the first to be established historically, and have often been viewed as the basis or core of any possible rights system. These rights emerged to protect the interests and negative liberties of the individual against the power and encroachment of states, and include freedom of speech, religion, and association, rights to a fair trial, and voting rights, among others. They are codified in the UN's **International Covenant on Civil and Political Rights**.

The second generation rights, equality rights in Vasak's scheme, recognize that certain basic goods should be equally available to all people; that a certain set of political and economic circumstances are needed for human flourishing. Included are rights to basic levels of economic subsistence, education, work, housing, and health care, among others. They are found in the UN's **International Covenant on Economic, Social and Cultural Rights**. These rights are often called positive rights, as opposed to the negative rights of the first generation, because they require rights providers to act, rather than to refrain from interfering. This distinction is itself subject to much criticism (see Shue, 1980).

Third generation rights, known as fraternity, solidarity, or group rights, attends to communal aspects of human being. These rights extend the reach of human rights to matters such as the recognition of minority groups, social identity, and cultural issues. These rights are often provided for by dedicated UN human rights instrumentalities such as the Declarations on the Right of Peoples to Peace, or the Right to Development. This category of rights is the most controversial and least institutionalized.

Box 1.5 **Jacques Maritain on the Justification of Rights**

I am fully convinced that my way of justifying the belief in the rights of man [sic] and the ideal of liberty, equality, fraternity, is the only one which is solidly based on truth. That does not prevent me from agreeing in these practical tenets with those who are convinced that their way of justifying them, entirely different from mine, or even opposed to mine in its theoretical dynamism, is likewise the only one that is based on truth. Assuming they both believe in the democratic charter, a Christian and a rationalist will nevertheless give justifications that are incompatible with each other, to which their souls, their minds and their blood are committed, and about these justifications they will fight. And God keep me from saying that it is not important to know which of the two is right! That is essentially important. They remain, however, in agreement on the practical affirmation of that charter, and they can formulate common principles of action. (Maritain, J. (1947). The possibilities for co-operation in a divided world. Inaugural address to the Second International Conference of UNESCO, 6 November)

The Moral Basis of Human Rights

We see, then, that for proponents, human rights are viewed as a set of moral demands, demands that should be institutionalized in our corporate political life—within states and internationally. How is it that these moral demands are justified? The UDHR powerfully articulates the moral urgency that energized the world after the Second World War. Crucially, however, the UN document makes no attempt at explanation, justification, or philosophical defence. This was a deliberate strategy (see Box 1.5). The Human Rights Commission, the body given the responsibility to draft the UDHR, was well aware of the differences that would have to be managed. Its strategy was to focus on norms or rules, leaving aside questions of justification (Morsink, 2000).

Much has been written in the years since the Declaration's promulgation about how to reconcile the specificity of the political and moral claims made in the name of human rights with the multiplicity of human ethical, religious, philosophical, cultural, and social traditions. The dilemma is this: the UDHR engages a universalist rhetoric to present a particular position, that of the liberal rights tradition. This position is

normatively universal, to be sure; but it is not shared universally by all human persons, and the traditions and communities in which they live.

Much of the subsequent controversy associated with arguments about universalism and relativism has been complicated by the failure of rights proponents either to be clear about or to properly understand the liberal nature of the political project in which they are involved. In the same way that believers in natural law and rights often claimed that these ideas were self-evident, so too, for many believers in human rights, the liberal values that they articulate are held to be universal, values of the common human sense. But, in fact, they are not common or universal, despite the desire of many of us that they be so. And it is this that makes the philosophical justification of human rights so important: the proponents of human rights need to have good reasons with which to defend human rights, and by which to attempt to persuade others to support human rights.

One might argue that the difficult task of philosophical justification has been superseded by the creation of the international human rights regime. It may be observed that we have had sixty years of the development and implementation of human rights law, both domestically within states and internationally; that human rights have 'worldwide acceptance' and 'global legitimacy'; that, by signing on to the UN Charter, the UDHR, and subsequent human rights instruments, states have ceded some measure of their sovereignty and may legitimately and legally be held accountable for their behaviour in relation to human rights standards. It may be argued: given that the political philosophers were unable to persuade the world of the veracity of rights before the Second World War, perhaps the defence of human rights is rightly given to the international lawyers and diplomats who have made such progress in expanding the remit of human rights in the decades since. We have human rights now, and they are protected because of the laws and institutions these people established and maintained.

The technical description of this approach is 'the argument from legal positivism' (Langlois, 2004). The main fault in the argument is that it risks equating or *reducing* human rights to legal rights. The potential danger in this approach is clear: it would mean that human rights *only* exist where there are actual laws or agreements or institutions that say they exist. Take these away, and you no longer have human rights. Clearly this is a perilous doctrine, one that runs against the thrust of the human rights movement. The historical development of human rights has depended on the conviction that rights exist as *moral demands* that need to be translated into legal and institutional contexts in order to be effectively protected and policed. These moral demands stand behind any laws, agreements, or institutions, and are the impetus for the creation of such. The ability to claim or argue for rights is often most important to us when we *do not* in fact have a well-functioning legal and institutional context by which to claim them—what Jack Donnelly (1989) terms the 'possession paradox' (see Box 1.6). This ability is dependent upon people being able to understand and identify with certain moral requirements—one of the goals of philosophical justification.

The Philosophical Justification of Modern Human Rights

We have seen that the idea of human rights emerged out of the political history of the West and, in particular, out of liberal political theory. There are many varieties of liberalism, but they are all fundamentally linked by their regard for the individual human subject. In Immanuel Kant's (1724–1804) phrase, individuals are always to be regarded as an ends, not a means. All individuals are to be considered of equal moral worth and standing. But exactly how this is understood varies between different proponents of liberalism. Here, I will briefly indicate some alternative contemporary philosophical approaches to the justification of rights within liberalism.

Human dignity

The rights that people possess have often been argued to be grounded in the basic dignity of the human person. Within the Western tradition, the principle historical source for this idea of human dignity is the Christian idea that man is made in the image of God—in the *imago dei*. Liberal rights and freedoms are derived from the dignity of man, which rests on the character of God—the ultimate source of value. The human dignity approach to rights justification has been significantly effective in making rights approaches understood in non-Western political and religious traditions. (See Perry, 2000.)

Reason

More commonly, liberal approaches stress human characteristics, rather than divine ones. So, for example, the human capacity for rationally purposive agency is determined to be the distinguishing characteristic of human beings, and the prerequisite conditions for fulfilling this activity are considered to be entitlements. Thus, humans have entitlements to well-being and freedom as these are required for us to engage in purposive activities; this in turn becomes the basis for a fuller doctrine of human rights. (See Gewirth, 1996.)

Autonomy

The self-directed or self-authored life is considered to be the human ideal. Autonomy and choice are fundamental ingredients in any valuable life, and rights are derived from the conditions—the liberties and freedoms—that are needed in order to sustain such a life. (See Raz, 1986.)

Equality

The idea of political equality can mean the right to equal treatment, or the right to treatment as an equal. The former refers to goods and opportunities, and is commonly granted in Western democracies in relation to civil and political rights (such as the right to one vote per person); it has had little acceptance in relation to goods. These treatments of equality rest fundamentally on the notion of treatment as an equal—that each individual has equal moral worth and should be accorded this by equal respect in a political community's political processes. (See Dworkin, 1977.)

Box 1.6 **The Possession Paradox**

'Having' a right is . . . of most value precisely when one does not 'have' the object of the right–that is, when one is denied direct, objective enjoyment of the right. I call this 'the possession paradox' of rights: 'having' and 'not having' a right at the same time, the 'having' being particularly important precisely when one *does not* 'have' it. This possession paradox is characteristic of all rights . . . We must distinguish between *possession* of a right, the *respect* it receives and the ease or frequency of *enforcement* . . . It is the ability to claim the right if necessary–the special force this gives to the demand and the special social practices it brings into play–that make having rights so valuable and that distinguishes having a right from simply enjoying the benefit of being the (right-less) beneficiary of someone else's obligation. (Donnelly, 1989: 11–12)

Needs

All human beings have certain basic needs—the most obvious ones being to do with security and subsistence. The universality of these needs contributes to the case for seeing them as basic rights. But the requirements for fulfilling these needs also links them theoretically to the concept of rights, because the fulfilment of these needs is dependent on the availability of certain freedoms—such as freedom of movement, freedom of association, and freedom of information. Without effective control over these freedoms, people cannot be guaranteed their basic needs. (See Shue, 1980.)

Capabilities

This neo-Aristotelian approach focuses on what people are capable of being and doing: it is oriented toward human potential and fulfilment. Capabilities themselves are defined as the general goods that are required to live a life of dignity, and are seen by proponents as the more fundamental normative basis upon which rights regimes must rest. This approach is argued to provide a more pluralistic justification for human rights, and has often been deployed as a corrective in arguments over gender justice. (See Sen, 1999; Nussbaum, 2000.)

Consensus

This pragmatic approach is reluctant to be too specific about a particular grounding or foundation for human rights, focusing instead on areas of agreement among diverse people, and using this agreement as the basis for legitimating rights. This approach has the advantage of being pluralistic, but the disadvantage of only functioning well where there is already substantial agreement, either philosophically or institutionally, and generally trades on a background liberal culture. (See Rawls, 1971, 1993, 1999.)

KEY POINTS

The Second World War was the catalyst for the modern re-deployment of the idea of the rights of man, now called Human Rights.

The United Nation's Universal Declaration of Human Rights was promulgated in 1948.

While the rights in the new Declaration emerge out of the liberal political tradition, no philosophical justification is formally given for the rights declared because of the variability of human belief systems. Individuals and groups are left to expound their own justifications for the rights in the Declaration.

Liberal justifications for human rights have been presented on the following grounds: human dignity, our ability to reason, the autonomy of individuals, the equality of all persons, our common needs, the capabilities of the human person, and the consensus of diverse parties on key beliefs.

The Universalism of Human Rights

A key difficulty is the UDHR's claim to have *universal* application. Some people simply reject the idea of human rights, or the idea that such rights might be universal. Others advance modified approaches to human rights.

Rejecting Human Rights

The challenge against the universalism of human rights comes in a number of different forms. The most extreme is the rejection of human rights altogether. Commonly, this rejection of human rights is put in one of two related ways (Freeman, 2002, Chapter 6). The first is the argument from cultural relativism, a conceptual rejection of rights that states that norms are only appropriate for the cultures out of which they emerge, and that therefore the norms of human rights emergent out of the West only apply in the West. Related to this is the argument from *imperialism*, which—often using cultural relativism as a supporting argument—states that, far from being about the protection of all people everywhere, human rights is a political tool that has been used to promote and defend Western interests. The argument from imperialism suggests that the 'truths' of human rights are disguised forms of power, part of a complex system of global political manipulation.

Cultural Relativism

The cultural relativist often criticizes the human rights doctrine for not being respectful of different cultural, religious, and philosophical traditions, and therefore, ultimately, of not respecting peoples' identities. *Tolerance* and respect are the key values here; the irony is supposed to be that liberals, in the form of human rights proponents, are being *illiberal* by expecting everyone else to become liberals. However, this is an inconsistent use of the cultural relativist argument, precisely because it is not relative *enough*.

A consistent relativist is refuted by her own doctrine: by claiming that all truths are relative, she proclaims the relativism of her own truths, and the incoherence of her position. A consistent relativist cannot prioritize any values at all. A relativist has no basis on which to hold that tolerance or respect are *universal* values that can be used to discredit the supposed interference of specific liberal values (note the double irony that tolerance and respect, along with an appreciation of pluralism, are liberal values anyway: the so-called relativist may simply be a confused liberal). All that a consistent cultural relativist can do in politics is to note that people have different values: the relativist has no basis for ordering or prioritizing these values, and is thus reduced to political quietism and irrelevance.

A quite common source of this inconsistency is a failure to differentiate between the theoretical claims of cultural relativism and the empirical fact of cultural relativity. The former undermines any attempt to establish a basis for universal human rights; the latter simply recognizes that people (as individuals and groups) are different from one another. What one does with this recognition will depend entirely on one's broader philosophical approach.

Human Rights Imperialism

A similar confusion is played out by those who charge human rights universalists with being imperialistic. Ironically, the anti-imperialism of the human rights challengers must also appeal to a universal principle—a universal principle of anti-imperialism. This principle must either be a principle of freedom, a principle of tolerance, or a principle of equality. It would suggest that people should be free to believe what they like or belong to whichever culture they like; or, people should tolerate the differences of others and respect their right to be different; or, people should regard other people's capacity to belong to a culture and to have beliefs as equal to their own such capacity. In any of these cases,

the argument of the cultural imperialists seems to reduce into an argument along these lines: 'we *do not* agree with you imposing your will on us, because we *do* agree with you that we have certain rights to liberty of action and belief.' The anti-imperialist's argument, like that of the confused relativist's, seems to be a form of nascent liberalism.

There is a crucial question that must be addressed to political leaders who engage in the human rights challenging rhetoric of anti-imperialism: Are the cultural beliefs and practices that they defend using the rhetoric of anti-imperialism consistent with the principles that are logically required to frame that anti-imperialism? In all too many of the political disputes over human rights in international politics, those taking the anti-imperialist line against human rights fail to apply the principles that support their anti-imperialism *within* the jurisdictions over which they have authority. Strongman authoritarian leaders argue against human rights on the basis of universal principles that give state leaders freedom, autonomy, and equal respect in the community of sovereign states, and then impose policies that deprive their citizens of that same freedom, tolerance, and equality within the domestic polity. Or, similarly, religious leaders demand freedom of belief, tolerance, and equal treatment for their religious values and practices, and then proceed to deny freedom, tolerance, and equal treatment to members of their communities who may have minority or dissenting opinions. The anti-imperialist rhetoric is useful for drawing our attention to the universal principles we use to frame our responses to injustice; however, rather than succeeding as a critique of the liberalism that grounds human rights, this rhetoric's failures and inconsistencies serve to further support liberalism's claim to be a more adequate safeguard against imperialism.

Modifying Human Rights

Some challengers value human rights but question the justifications used by contemporary liberal theorists. The criticism is that the reasoning from which the universality derives is a very particular way of thinking about what it is to be human, which might not legitimately apply to all human persons. The approach is criticized for being foundationalist and essentialist. It proposes a certain foundation for moral thinking, a foundation that is characterized as universal; the criticism is, however, that this foundation only stands if one agrees with the philosophical premises on which it is based, and that there is in turn no knock-down argument to guarantee the veracity of those premises. Similarly, it is essentialist, in that it claims that certain qualities or capacities (reason, autonomy, for example) are essential to what it means to be human, or to how we determine the nature of morality and ethics; in turn, there is no final agreement on what qualities or capacities are central to our 'humanness'. Therefore, to proclaim a set of *universal* rights on the basis of such *particular* assumptions is to claim too much; it also excludes from consideration a range of other ways of thinking and feeling about the human condition and how we should respond to it.

The Feminist Challenge

This form of criticism of the universality of human rights has often been taken up by feminist thinkers. Their argument has often been that 'the rights of man' were precisely that: rights afforded to men. They argue that historically women were thought of quite differently from the way in which men were conceptualized. For example, the 'right reason', autonomy, and equality that were used to characterize the essential qualities of what it meant to be human within the liberal tradition were not considered to be characteristics properly assumed by women. Women were not understood to be rational or autonomous, and while they may have been considered to have equal moral worth with men, they certainly did not have equal status or place in society. The feminist movement has been successful in bringing many of these issues to attention and in changing both social views and institutions. By the time of the creation of the UN, feminists had gained sufficient influence to have the rights of women included in the UN Charter, a move that was central to the increased institutional recognition of women's rights at the international level. Key milestones here were the Decade for Women (1975–1985) and the adoption in 1979 of the *Convention on the Elimination of all forms of Discrimination Against Women* (CEDAW).

But there is still a long way to go. Theoretical issues continue to play an important role in the debates about women's rights (see Okin, 1999; Nussbaum, 2000; Gould,

2004). A key example here is the debate over the way in which we divide the social world into a private sphere and a public sphere. Traditionally, liberals have argued that this division, which is designed to protect citizens' private lives from the power of the state, plays a crucial role in protecting women from rights violations. However, many feminists will argue in turn that it is precisely in the private sphere that women are most vulnerable to rights abuse by powerful men, so that sanctioning the distinction is tantamount to ignoring the most egregious and systematic denial of women's rights. It is in the private sphere that sexual violence, reproductive rights, child rearing, and many other issues are faced by women each day. The concern is that many of these problems are not adequately addressed by the received understanding of rights. On the one hand, the theoretical structures used to explain and justify rights values appear to be significantly disconnected from both the concerns and experiences of women; on the other hand, the institutions that have emerged out of the received rights politics fail to adequately address the way in which women suffer rights abuses, primarily because their default setting is to address the rights abuses experienced by men. For some feminists, this is the basis for a reform agenda. For others, the deficiencies of the present framework are so serious that they de-legitimize the framework altogether, requiring a more radical solution.

Religious Challenges

The evolution of modern rights in the West went hand in hand with increased challenges to Christian religious orthodoxy; but the values that were to be articulated as rights were nonetheless deeply shaped by those same patterns of religious belief. At the global level, however, there are many different forms of religion. These in turn are structured around many different values systems, which may or may not be compatible with modern human rights—both in form and substance. For example, the autonomy and equality that is so privileged by Western liberalism has often been directly challenged by religious leaders from other traditions. This is a challenge both to the underlying philosophical framework of human rights, and to specific rights as articulated in the UDHR and other human rights documents.

The responses to global religious diversity by human rights theorists and proponents are many and varied. Some take the view that, because human rights are to be universal, the introduction of specific or particularistic values drawn from religions will undermine the universalism of rights. For others the only way for human rights to be universal is to translate them through the particularistic traditions of human beings. So, for Muslims or Hindus (as two examples) to be able to embrace human rights, they must be able to give justifications for the values expressed by the human rights movement; but these justifications must also be genuinely integral to their own tradition as well.

Some religious communities reject human rights completely, seeing them as alien and incompatible with their way of being. Others have moved from rejection to embrace—the Roman Catholic Church being the key example here. Many religious communities view human rights as consonant with their own traditions. Still others have been persuaded that there is a need to reinterpret their own tradition in the light of human rights, seeing this as an opportunity for the revitalization and rejuvenation of belief structures at risk of ossification.

Group Rights

The idea of group rights poses a fascinating challenge to rights universalism, a challenge that emerges out of the success of human rights (Kymlicka, 2007). Proponents of group rights argue that for certain groups of people it may be legitimate to invoke specific rights, or specific interpretations of rights, which do not apply universally. Access to these rights is dependent on membership of a group. These groups may be of a religious, social, cultural, indigenous, gender, sexual orientation, or other minority issue nature.

Universalists have significant concerns about group rights (Jones, 1999). One concern rests on whether such rights are understood as the rights of individuals that arise from membership of a group, or whether they are understood as rights that accrue to the group itself (however the identity or nature of this group might be understood, itself a vexed question). If group rights are the rights that accrue to the group, liberals have concerns about how individuals within such groups will be treated. Will they, for example, have a right to speak, or crucially, to exit, if they disagree with the behaviour of the group? And how would such an exit right be adjudicated against the group's right to ensure its survival and growth?

The rights of minorities and groups are without doubt significant political issues. Many of these rights have been realized or bolstered because of the influence of the now global human rights regime. There is a grave concern, however, that the values of some groups may undermine those of the universal human rights regime. The liberal account of rights that informs the human rights regime is premised fundamentally on the well-being of individuals. Group rights are of use to human rights when they bolster those groups of individuals whose human rights are inadequately supported by universal regimes. But what this suggests strongly is that group rights should always be derivative from human rights—understood, as they are in the UDHR, as the rights of individuals. This sets up a permanent tension between the proponents of human rights and others who do not place so much value on the liberal individualism that structures the human rights movement. Awareness of this tension in turn helps us to see the quintessentially *political* nature of the human rights project (Jones, 2008).

KEY POINTS

Cultural relativists criticize human rights for illegitimately privileging one set of values over others; rights defenders respond that it is the relativists whose views are inconsistent and that there are very good reasons for privileging rights values.

Human rights are criticized for being the exercise of an imperialist politics; however, those who make this argument are shown to be inconsistent and not genuinely concerned with protecting the victims of authoritarian rule.

Feminists argue that the international human rights regime is inadequate to satisfy woman's rights. Some argue for reform, others for more radical solutions.

Some religious groups reject the liberal rights tradition; others adopt it wholeheartedly. Some religious groups reinterpret human rights through their own traditions; others explicitly use human rights to reform their own tradition.

Group rights are invoked as a way of protecting the rights of minorities who belong to identifiable groups. These rights are politically very controversial, not least because in some forms they can undermine the protections of the more general human rights regime.

Human Rights as a Political Project

The rhetoric of human rights can sometimes obscure the many ways in which the human rights movement is a *political* movement. The talk of universalism, of common standards for human kind, and of inalienable and self-evident rights, can give the impression that all the big questions about human rights are settled. As even a cursory investigation of the history of the human rights idea shows, however, the greater part of what we appeal to when we appeal to human rights is controversial and contested. There are four levels at which the political nature of human rights is important.

The first level has to do with the normative tradition out of which human rights historically emerges. The normative under-girdings of human rights are from liberal political theory and, before that, from the natural law tradition. In our contemporary world, the language of human rights is being spoken by people who work in a great variety of other traditions, and the confluence of these traditions with that of the liberal one produces contestation, dispute, and disagreement. The claim that the liberal approach should continue to be the arbiter or referee in the continued development of human rights as they go global is deeply controversial. Similarly, any change to the existing human rights corpus brought on by adopting values from other traditions is also deeply controversial. There are no fixed answers about how to resolve these conflicts.

A second level at which human rights are political concerns rights declarations—quintessentially the UDHR, but also its precursors, and the subsequent human rights instruments created through the UN and regionally. Human rights declarations are usually the product of a committee appointed by a political authority. What goes into a declaration and what is left out is determined by those involved in the drafting. None of these people have clear and pristine access to human reason or religious revelation; the rights that they declare are heavily contingent on the historical and political framework in which they work. However good or bad a particular rights declaration may be, it is always a political outcome, a compromise, or a diplomatic resolution of competing interests. Rights declarations, then, must also be recognized as political instruments.

The implementation of a rights regime is the third level at which rights are political. The decision to describe certain states of being as human rights abuses, the decision to use state power to change circumstances or to detain or free individuals in the name of human rights—these are all profoundly political decisions, and they are decisions that of necessity are engaged with in a local context. The diversity of human communities may well mean that behaviour that in one place is considered a rights abuse is routinely accepted somewhere else. There is no settled means for universal resolution of these differences.

The fourth level at which human rights are political is the most familiar: rights emerged within the Western tradition as a way of preserving the freedoms and liberties of individuals and groups against the powers of the state. The political project of human rights is a strategy for fighting against existing power structures in the hope of creating a social environment that is more nearly just. Local context is everything in this equation, and where that local context is inhospitable to the principles embedded in received human rights norms, the struggle can be interminable and disheartening.

What is common across these four areas is the way in which the normative agenda pursued by human rights practitioners is both displayed and questioned, challenged and interrogated (Langlois, 2001; Baxi, 2006). Whether one is explaining a normative tradition, declaring a right, applying some aspect of a rights regime, or defending the rights of the abused against powerful interests, one is asserting a set of political beliefs about the value of human beings and the way in which they should be treated. Defending those convictions is an essential part of the human rights project and is ultimately what we are doing when we engage in debates about the normative and theoretical justification of human rights.

KEY POINTS	
Human rights are political in the following four senses.	The implementation of any established human rights regime is subject to interpretation, political context, and local circumstances.
Human rights are political because they embody a set of norms that emerged out of the tradition of political liberalism, with which not all identify.	The pursuit of human rights translates into local engagement, and quite often bitter confrontation, with prevailing unjust power structures.
Specific human rights regimes are created by groups of people who have their own political agendas and constituencies, and who must make decisions about what to include and exclude that cannot satisfy everyone.	

Conclusion

The language of human rights is fundamentally a normative or ethical language, one that emerges out of the political liberalism of the Enlightenment, and one that leads to a very distinctive form of political engagement. In our modern period, the Universal Declaration of Human Rights is the defining text of the human rights movement; but behind the rights that are declared in that document are layers of history and philosophy. These in turn are present in many of the debates in contemporary global politics over the meaning, usefulness, and effective implementation of human rights. This chapter has shown that understanding the history and philosophy of human rights is essential to being able to navigate the complex political debates surrounding the desirability and normative content of human rights reform in the international system.

QUESTIONS

INDIVIDUAL STUDY QUESTIONS

1. Why is the history of the human rights idea important today?
2. Why do the rights of international human rights law need philosophical or moral foundations?
3. What are the strengths and limitations of Jacques Maritain's position on the justification of rights?
4. Explain why having a right is most important when we lack the object of that right?
5. What are the common elements of the various liberal justifications for rights?
6. What appear to be the key differences between the three generations of rights?

GROUP DISCUSSION QUESTIONS

1. Examine the Universal Declaration of Human Rights and explore how its key words and phrases embody the ideals of political liberalism.
2. Why are the cultural relativists and imperialists wrong to dismiss human rights?
3. Discuss the different approaches of feminists to human rights.
4. In what ways do religious traditions relate to human rights?
5. Why and in what senses are human rights political?

FURTHER READING

Baxi, U. (2006). *The Future of Human Rights*. Oxford: Oxford University Press.
The author connects the sometimes complacent arguments about human rights theory with the lives of those suffering human rights abuse and considers the new challenges facing human rights today.

Freeman, M. (2002). *Human Rights: An Interdisciplinary Approach*. Cambridge: Polity.
A useful introductory text, covering the history of human rights, key theoretical issues, and contemporary challenges such as globalization.

Griffin, J. (2008). *On Human Rights*. Cambridge: Cambridge University Press.
A state-of-the-art attempt to provide a substantive theory of human rights.

Herbert, G. B. (2002). *A Philosophical History of Rights*. Piscataway, NJ: Transaction Publishers.
A comprehensive philosophical survey of the history of the idea of rights.

Ignatieff, M. (2001). *Human Rights as Politics and Idolatry*. Princeton, NJ: Princeton University Press.
In two highly accessible essays Ignatieff sets out all the major issues to do with human rights in contemporary international politics; his views are then interrogated by a number of eminent commentators.

Langlois, A. J. (2001). *The Politics of Justice and Human Rights*. Cambridge: Cambridge University Press.
This book considers the questions of universalism and pluralism through an examination of the so-called Asian Values Debate of the 1990s.

Lauren, P. G. (1998). *The Evolution of International Human Rights: Visions Seen*. Philadelphia, PA: University of Pennsylvania Press.
A comprehensive historical account of the rise of human rights.

Mahoney, J. (2007). *The Challenge of Human Rights*. Oxford: Blackwell Publishing.
Traces the rise of human rights as a resource for ethical reasoning in politics.

WEB LINKS

http://plato.stanford.edu/entries/rights-human/ The human rights entry in the online Stanford Encyclopedia of Philosophy, which provides valuable discussion and useful links to related topics.

http://europa.eu/pol/rights/index_en.htm The European Union Human Rights website provides a discussion of the role of human rights in the EU, including legislation and other activities.

http://www.rightsphilosophyforum.org/index.html The Rights Philosophy Forum provides biographies, learning guides, and other resources for those interested in studying human rights.

http://www.natsiew.nexus.edu.au/lens/udhr/index.html An annotated Universal Declaration of Human Rights provided by the Australian National Aboriginal and Torres Straight Islander Education website. It provides links under each article of the UDHR to the websites of organizations concerned with the rights expressed in that article.

ONLINE RESOURCE CENTRE

Visit the Online Resource Centre that accompanies this book for updates and a range of other resources:

http://www.oxfordtextbooks.co.uk/orc/goodhart/

Human Rights in International Law

Rhona K. M. Smith

2

Chapter Contents

Reader's Guide

This chapter introduces the international legal context of human rights. It complements the preceding chapter by outlining the practical (rather than theoretical) framework for human rights. In summary, this chapter will consider where to find human rights (in law) and how to ensure those rights and freedoms are respected by states. From an initial focus on the principal instruments (treaties), the institutional framework will be considered, explaining the mechanisms for monitoring and enforcing human rights. Neither politics nor law can be considered in isolation: political will is needed to secure the drafting and adoption of international instruments; political will is also a factor in monitoring and enforcing international human rights. However, without law, international human rights would undoubtedly be a less tangible, measurable, and enforceable concept than is the case today.

Introduction

International human rights are now an integral part of public international law. Indeed, there is a strong argument for human rights being regarded as a distinct branch of international law as respect for human rights is not primarily a characteristic of inter-state obligations, but rather a reflection of the state's undertakings in respect of its population. Acceptance of human rights is a manifestation of a state's acknowledgement of the pre-eminence of the rule of law. This chapter introduces the international legal context of human rights. It thus complements the preceding chapter by outlining the practical legal (rather than theoretical) framework for human rights promotion and protection (see Box 2.1).

All states profess to respect certain international human rights, many of which are explored in detail elsewhere in this book. These rights are normally tabulated in a legal binding format as a treaty, thus easily ascertainable. While their existence (in tangible legal form) is beyond question, their content remains hotly disputed. Every state claims to promote respect for key human rights and fundamental freedoms within their territory, but not all states accept all the tabulated rights and freedoms. Given that there are hundreds of instruments of varying legal force that purport to enumerate human rights, this is not entirely surprising. From a legal perspective, the most enforceable human rights are expressed in treaties, primarily multilateral treaties,

---

Box 2.1 **Finding International Human Rights Law Online**

In the twenty-first century, engaging fully with international human rights law demands the use of online sources. All primary sources are freely available online in several languages. Once familiarity with the principal websites is achieved, it is possible to research any aspect of basic human rights. Space constraints restrict this guide to two websites that students find particularly useful.

http://www.ohchr.org
The main website is that of the UN Office of the High Commissioner for Human Rights. Information can be found through a variety of routes—the following is a simple approach to finding information on key areas of this important portal.

From the home page, note the following from the top banner.

Your human rights
This links to *International law*, which in turn has a link to *The core international human rights instruments*, a hyperlinked list of full text of all the principal UN human rights treaties, instruments, codes, and guidelines. A quick link to *Human rights instruments* is also available at the right-hand side of the home page. It links to the same page. This is the main primary source that you will require.

Countries
This links through *Human rights in the world* to a map and an alphabetical list of member states. For each country, you can obtain information on contracting status (ratifications, reservations, and derogations) as well as recent Special

Procedures reports and concluding observations of treaty monitoring bodies.

Human rights bodies
This links to a portal for all the UN Charter and treaty monitoring bodies. It also has a link to the material on treaty body reform. Each treaty monitoring body has its own page from which you can access the relevant treaty, reporting guidelines, committee information, the reports of each state to the committee, the concluding observations of the committee thereon (through *Sessions*), and general comments and recommendations of the committee.

Publications and resources
This links to *Publications* that give access to a variety of useful electronic publications on human rights, including *Fact sheets* and *Special issue* papers.

http://www.bayefsky.com
Professor Ann Bayefsky's portal for UN human rights contains a useful search engine. UN materials can be searched by state, treaty article, or particularly helpfully, by theme or subject matter. The latter opens to an A–Z list of human rights issues on which you can search for treaty articles, concluding observations (across all states), and jurisprudence (if available). Only relevant excerpts are provided, but with the UN Document number provided, the entire document can easily be obtained from the ohchr.org website's treaty body database (located at the left column under all of the treaty bodies).

i.e. international treaties with many states participating. Nevertheless, there are many examples of human rights that predate such multilateral treaties—these too can be enforceable against states. Moreover, many of these rights are now contained in treaties.

This chapter starts by exploring the origins of human rights law, considering the implications inherent in creating international human rights law. The seismic shift this reflects (and caused) in the conceptualization of international law will be highlighted. Tragic events around the world have frequently proved to be the prompt for articulating international human rights. Such a manifestation of political will is a crucial factor in ensuring the success of human rights: without consensus, no treaty can become 'law', be embedded into normal state practice, or be internationally monitored or enforced.

Following this overview of the evolution on international human rights law, the emphasis will move to elaborating the principal sources of international human rights law. The various forms of expressing human rights will be considered before identifying the core international human rights instruments. As will be apparent, even when a state accepts a particular human rights treaty, it can still avoid full legal responsibility by a variety of legal means. These are important as they impact, sometimes considerably, on the extent of a state's obligations.

While articulating lists of human rights has some merit in itself, ensuring that the rhetoric of the law is transformed into a practical reality is a major issue. Accordingly, attention will then move to the institutional framework, identifying the mechanisms for monitoring and enforcing human rights. Once more, political will is a factor in monitoring and enforcing international human rights. Are human rights enforceable in law? Most importantly, can an individual actually claim that a state has infringed his or her human rights? Subsequent chapters explore specific rights that states accept.

Historical Evolution of International Human Rights Law

This section will outline the evolution of human rights, particularly charting the reincarnation of philosophical ideals as international laws (treaties). The next section will then consider the sources of contemporary international human rights law. There is evidence of laws and policies that ensure respect for some rights of individuals many centuries ago. Most religious texts promulgate certain rights and freedoms of followers, assuming they adhere to the codes for life enshrined in the tenets of faith. Enlightenment philosophers also contributed toward the development of human rights theories (see Chapter 1), although there are many examples of non-Christian philosophical contributions that help rebalance the alleged Eurocentricity of human rights' origins. Human rights have a long history, much of which is rarely discussed today (Burgers, 1992). What is beyond doubt is that the majority of legally binding instruments (treaties) that form the body of modern human rights law emerged during the twentieth century—although these were not the first treaties on international human rights. Early examples of 'human rights' instruments focused on the abolition of slavery, humanitarian law, and minority protection guarantees.

Following this brief review of early examples of human rights agreements, contemporary international human rights instruments will be discussed later in the text.

Abolition of Slavery

Slavery is now universally condemned, all states having outlawed it by the end of the last century. Its prohibition is an obligation owed by all states to the entire international community (on such obligations, see Barcelona Traction Case (*Belgium* v. *Spain* (1970), ICJ Reps 32)). Some two hundred years ago, the UK and the USA claimed to begin the end of the slave trade by enacting national legislation prohibiting trade in people. Over the next sixty years, a series of bilateral treaties, legally binding agreements between two countries, were concluded between the UK and other states by which the two states involved agreed to prevent their subjects from engaging in the slave trade (see Martinez, 2008). In 1815, the international Congress of Vienna deemed the slave trade repugnant. Under the auspices of the League of Nations, a Slavery Commission was established and a 1926 Slavery Convention adopted (League of Nations, 1926). This was followed in 1956 by the Supplementary Convention on the Abolition of Slavery, the Slave Trade, and Institutions and Practices similar to Slavery. Despite this, modern incarnations of slavery remain, with human trafficking and forced labour being the most obvious examples. Human trafficking in particular appears to be a growth industry which various modern treaties and transnational initiatives seek to suppress in the twenty-first century (see Chapter 12).

Humanitarian Law and the Laws of War

Humanitarian law, agreements on the conduct of hostilities, also emerged comparatively early in the history of international human rights law. These have as their goal the 'civilization' of conflict by ensuring only enemy agents could be targeted, and civilians thus protected. Agreements also related to the types of killing to be deployed (humane deaths). Today, this body of law is still in existence. The Hague 1907 laws of war and the Geneva Conventions and Protocols of 1949 and 1977, respectively, are the most famous examples; more recent agreements include a ban on landmines, and the Convention on Cluster Munitions, which was opened for signature in December 2008.

Individual legal responsibility arises for those who fail to respect the rights of combatants under these treaties. This was evidenced in the *Tokyo Tribunal* and the Nuremberg Tribunal following the Second World War. Those defeated leaders found responsible for mass violations of human rights were tried and sentenced (usually to death). Following a spate of special courts and *ad hoc* tribunals focusing on criminal justice, the International Criminal Court (ICC) was established in terms of a treaty—the Rome Statute on the International Criminal Court of 1998, which entered into force in 2002. It has competence to investigate and consider war crimes and violations of humanitarian law when the national courts are unable or unwilling to do so. Violations of other human rights, in contrast, cannot be prosecuted in the court (see later). Although closely related, humanitarian law and international human rights have evolved as discrete areas of law and policy. Human rights apply generally: the state is required to respect the declared and accepted human rights of all. Humanitarian laws, in contrast, are essentially minimum rights that must be respected during proclaimed emergencies/conflicts (see Chapter 19). Violations of international humanitarian law may result in individual prosecutions, whereas violations of general human rights will not as liability rests with the state.

Minority and Labour Rights

There are also historic minority protection regimes—for example, the 1878 Treaty of Berlin accorded special status in law to specified religious groups. Prior to this 'aliens' (foreigners) were only accorded minimum rights and freedoms, based on the idea that an injury to an individual was tantamount to an injury to the individual's state of nationality. Reparations, or remedies for loss or damage suffered, could be sought. In the early twentieth century, there was a focus on ensuring the peaceful coexistence of peoples within states in the wake of the First World War—hence the minority guarantee treaty regimes instigated by the League of Nations and the creation of the International Labour Organization (ILO). The former sought to ensure respect for those religious or linguistic minorities who found themselves in a 'foreign' state due to the redrawing of Europe's boundaries and/or the redistribution of the overseas territories of the defeated countries. The latter sought to regulate labour, assisting with rebuilding economies of countries decimated by war and ensuring fair working conditions for all.

In the aftermath of the collapse of the League of Nations and the Second World War, the international community had to rethink its approach to the maintenance of peace, law, and order. Although the ILO survived intact from this tumultuous period between the two World Wars, the minority protection system was discontinued; the newly established United Nations elected to focus on universal human rights, thereby obviating (it was hoped) the need for special minority guarantees. Despite the change in focus, minority groups (whether ethnic, religious, linguistic, or other) are all too often in a weaker position than majority groups in any given state. With the emphasis on equality in international human rights, remedies may be available for such individuals.

Contemporary human rights law has early antecedents, traces of which survive to the present day. The following section will examine the mechanisms for establishing binding obligations on states to protect human rights, thereafter the parameters of modern human rights law will be outlined.

KEY POINTS

There are early examples of international agreements on human rights issues dating back more than two centuries.

Efforts to abolish all forms of slavery today focus on proscribing those practices analogous to slavery.

International humanitarian law and the laws of war have very early origins. The formal laws were negotiated between the warring states and governed hostilities. Today, these laws are found in the Hague and Geneva conventions and associated instruments, and apply to most conflicts.

Minority rights seek to respect the culture of minorities in a state. Developed under the League of Nations, they remain contentious today.

Sources of International Human Rights Law

As with any area of law, it is necessary to establish what the building blocks are, to know 'where to find the law'. International law is a little different from national law in this respect—there is no single legislature passing laws that must be obeyed. Rather, there are various organizations from which treaties emanate and various other agreements made by states of their own volition. On top of this, there is a mass of additional materials that outlines and informs international law. In this section we will consider the key sources of international human rights law.

Treaties

Treaties are probably the closest thing to recognizable (in the national sense) law in international law. They are, for the purposes of human rights, written down and agreed by states. In this way, treaties are most obviously 'international legislation'. States have to 'agree' to treaties. They indicate their agreement through signature (generally a political act) followed by ratification (the legal act). For students, the most comprehensive guide to treaty law is the partial codification (collation of existing laws and practices) and partial progressive development (evolution of new law) of the pre-existing law found in the Vienna Convention on the Law of Treaties 1969. This treaty contains detailed (technical) guidance on the creation, dissolution, meaning, and enforcement of treaties. Not all states agree to its terms, but many do, and parts of the treaty represent customary international law (discussed below).

Treaties contain statements of law. They can be broadly compared to legislative acts. The treaty specifies the legal obligation of the state, an obligation that can be enforced. Not all obligations are negative, requiring states simply to refrain from doing something; some are positive, with states obliged to actively do something to respect the right in question—passing homicide and assault laws to help ensure respect for the right to life is an obvious example. The state would not be directly at fault if an individual killed another individual, but, nevertheless, attracts responsibility if there is no national homicide law that can be invoked. For example, in *Ng v. Canada* (UN Doc. CCPR/C/49/D/469/1991—Human Rights Committee), the USA requested the extradition of Ng to stand trial for various counts of capital murder and other crimes in California. Although the Canadian Supreme Court considered extradition not to infringe Canada's obligations, the *UN Human Rights Committee* (that monitors implementation of the International Covenant on Civil and Political Rights (ICCPR)) concluded that the resultant execution by gas asphyxiation, which he would inevitably be subjected to if convicted, was cruel and inhuman treatment in violation of Article 7. Canada clearly was not directly responsible for this, but its decision to extradite had a foreseeable consequence (an infringement of human rights). Such positive obligations have significant consequences for states when contemplating extradition, deportation, or asylum. Undertakings not to torture an individual or not to impose the death penalty are often required in advance.

Obviously treaties can have far-ranging consequences for states. They are legal obligations that should not be undertaken lightly. States, in effect, contract out of respect for their territorial sovereignty through treaties (e.g. Advisory Opinion on *Nationality Decrees Issued in Tunis and Morocco* (1922), PCIJ Series B, No. 4). This is noteworthy as many states claim international human rights law impinges on their internationally protected (e.g. under the UN Charter) and virtually sacrosanct national sovereignty. There are, however, many (non-law and non-sovereignty related) reasons why states agree to treaties. Irrespective of the reason, states agreeing to international human rights law have agreed to any limitation on their sovereignty flowing therefrom. How does a state indicate acceptance of a treaty's terms? Why do states accept these obligations? Can a state avoid treaty obligations?

How does a state signify acceptance of a treaty's terms?

Just as with contracts under national law, states must agree to be bound by a treaty (see Fig. 2.1). Treaties are concluded in writing: thus a state has to indicate its consent to be bound by the signature of the Head of State or appropriately authorized representative. At this stage, the state is a signatory to the treaty. Often there are signing ceremonies when the main protagonists are photographed signing the treaty. Article 18 of the Vienna Convention on the Law of Treaties stipulates that states should act in accordance with the terms of a treaty during the period between signature and ratification. That is not, however, the end of the matter. Generally, a state confirms its consent by ratification or acceptance of the treaty. This usually follows state-specific national procedures. The instrument of ratification should be deposited with the specified body, usually the UN Sec-

retary General's office, for communication to other contracting states. The modern process is complicated by the numbers of states involved. Some international human rights treaties have over 190 states parties. However, modern communications aid the process of keeping all parties or ratifying states informed as to who has accepted any treaty. Treaties usually specify a minimum number of ratifications necessary for the treaty to enter into force.

As commentators such as Bayefsky (2001) note, some states may ratify a treaty as a political act, rather than to guarantee human rights to all individuals within their territory—that is, they might ratify to enhance their reputation or placate critics without having any intention of complying fully. The use of reservations (see below) aids this. Hathaway (2007, p. 592) identifies the potential for domestic legal enforcement of the terms of the treaty (i.e. not through an international court) and the positive political collateral consequences of the decision to ratify as key incentives for states when electing to commit to international human rights treaties.

Reservations and declarations after ratification

Even if a state does elect to ratify a human rights treaty, there are a number of legal ways in which a state can avoid responsibility for its terms. States may enter reservations and declarations either upon ratification or at any time thereafter. These are statements of intent entered by the state and communicated to other parties to the treaty. In effect, they provide a mechanism for a state to opt out of the provision in question, either partly or in whole. A simple reservation may exclude liability for a specific article of the treaty. More controversial are those that seek to pervade the entire treaty—for example, Saudi Arabia's statement on ratification of the *Convention on the Elimination of all Forms of Discrimination Against Women* that, in the event of a conflict between the Convention and Islamic law, the Kingdom would not be obliged to follow the Convention. Although objected to by a number of European states, the Saudi reservation remains in force.

International law treats reservations that are incompatible with the object and purpose of the treaty as void (ineffective). This view is derived from the opinion of the International Court of Justice (ICJ or World

FIGURE 2.1 Creating a treaty—simplified outline.

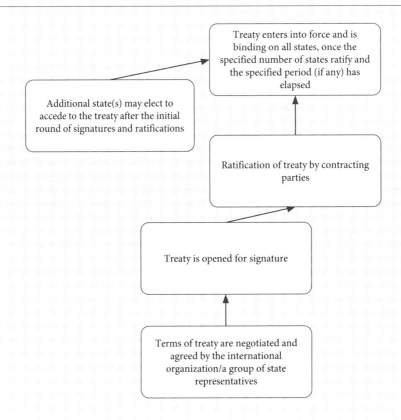

Court) in the Genocide Case (1951, ICJ Reps 15) and the Human Rights Committee (1994). While the argument that states should not be able to opt out of fundamental human rights has merits, for states, the process can be more complicated. Thus the USA's reservation transmitted on ratification of the ICCPR: 'That article 20 does not authorize or require legislation or other action by the United States that would restrict the right of free speech and association protected by the Constitution and laws of the United States.' This reservation is potentially problematic as Article 20 provides that any propaganda for war shall be prohibited by law and any advocacy of national, racial, or religious hatred that constitutes incitement to discrimination, hostility, or violence shall be prohibited by law. However, for the USA the freedoms protected by its Constitution are pre-eminent in law.

States can also make declarations upon ratification, or subsequently. These may simply be a political statement regarding, for example, non-recognition of certain states that have ratified the treaty (e.g. the statement made by China upon ratifying the International Covenant on Economic, Social and Cultural Rights (ICESCR) regarding Taiwan: 'the signature that the Taiwan authorities affixed, by usurping the name of "China", to the [said Covenant] on 5 October 1967, is illegal and null and void').

The terminology employed is irrelevant; it is the effect of the statement that is important (Human Rights Committee, 1994, paragraph 3). This was famously demonstrated in a communication before the Human Rights Committee brought after France had 'declared' that it did not recognize minorities and thus a claim of a linguistic minority person could not be considered by the Committee (*Guedson* v. *France*, UN Doc. CCPR/C/39/D/219/1986).

Reservations constitute a significant problem for proponents of universal human rights. While states will sign and ratify treaties, the efficacy of their actions can be undermined by reservations entered to negate key provisions. Although the concept of reservations appears inconsistent with that of human rights treaties, little action is taken against states entering and maintaining reservations other than to encourage a re-evaluation of the reservation's necessity. This is a perennial problem with a consensus-based system such as international law—it is generally regarded as preferable to have states at least try to conform to the international standard than to have states withdraw from the framework of international monitoring. Since international treaty law is basically consensual, the goal of universal ratification of core international human rights instruments is perhaps unrealistic without the benefit of reservations (see Box 2.2).

Derogations during a state emergency

Derogations allow states to avoid all responsibility for violations of certain human rights during emergency situations. Most importantly, there are some human rights from which states may never derogate—non-derogable rights include freedom of thought, conscience, and religion and the prohibition on torture (see, for example,

Article 4(2), ICCPR). Each treaty stipulates whether derogation is possible and, if so, from which provision(s). Some treaties do not permit derogations (e.g. ICESCR, due to the nature of those rights—see below; African Charter on Human and Peoples' Rights).

Measures justifying derogation must be of a temporary and exceptional nature. Generally, the emergency must pose a genuine threat to the existence or stability of the state and the state must have legally proclaimed a state of emergency. The UK has a notable history of entering lengthy derogations. For example, it derogated from the International Covenant on Civil and Political Rights in 1976, and was urged to consider withdrawing the derogation by the Human Rights Committee (UN Doc. CCPR/C/79/Add.55, paragraph 23) and did so (noted UN Doc. CCPR/CO/73/UK, paragraph 4). The UK instituted a semi-permanent derogation for much of its UN membership last century, matched by derogations entered under the regional mechanism, the Council of Europe (see, for example, *Brannigan & McBride* v. *United Kingdom* (1993), Series A, No.258-B). The UK's justification was the perceived threat from terrorists in Ireland and Northern Ireland.

The power to derogate should be limited to extreme situations. It is not a way for states to avoid human rights obligations. Moreover, even in emergency situations, human rights remain crucially important and international humanitarian law still applies. In times

---

Box 2.2 **Perspectives on Universal Ratification of the Core Human Rights Treaties**

For a great many states ratification has become an end in itself, a means to easy accolades for empty gestures. The problem has arisen in part because of a deliberate emphasis on ratification.

The primary goal of the UN community has been to achieve universal ratification of the human rights treaties. The underlying belief is that once universal ratification is realized, the implementation techniques can be strengthened. Once committed to participation, states will find it difficult to pull out and will find themselves ensnared in an ever-expanding network of international supervision and accountability.

In the meantime, ratification by human rights adversaries is purchased at a price, namely, diminished obligations, lax supervision, and few adverse consequences from non-compliance. The cost of membership has been deliberately minimized. (Bayefsky, 1996)

The emphasis upon promoting universal ratification is an essential one in order to strengthen and consolidate the universalist foundations of the United Nations human

rights regime. Despite the fears of some critics, the quest for universal ratification need not have any negative consequences for the treaty regime as a whole. (Alston, 1997, Paragraph 23)

There is clear evidence . . . that states with strong domestic institutions and poor human rights records are less likely to join human rights treaties than states with weaker domestic institutions that have similar records. That is true even though democracies as a whole—which realize more domestic collateral benefits from membership than non-democracies, because the constituencies favouring human rights treaties tend to be stronger—are more likely to join human rights treaties. Moreover, consistent with the prediction that collateral incentives are at work, newer regimes, which stand to gain larger collateral benefits from treaty membership, have a higher likelihood of joining human rights treaties. Also consistent with the approach, states in regions with higher levels of human rights treaty commitment are themselves consistently more likely to join those treaties. (Hathaway, 2007, p. 613) of war and other emergencies, human rights are more likely to be threatened and respect for them should therefore be regarded as more not less important.

Toward an international, interdependent, and indivisible system of human rights

Having outlined the process of becoming bound by a treaty, it is now appropriate to identify the legal obligations assumed by the states under the key international human rights treaties and to consider why there are so many treaties and other instruments.

At present, there are nine core international human rights instruments, concluded under the auspices of the United Nations (see Box 2.3). Of these, the two main treaties are the 'twin' Covenants—the ICCPR and the ICESCR. Together they enshrine the content of the Universal Declaration on Human Rights (UDHR) in a legally binding format. Accordingly, they contain the range of rights and freedoms that the international community wishes to enforce. However, the treaty with virtually universal acceptance is the *Convention on the Rights of the Child*. Every UN member state, save the

---

Box 2.3 **Principal International Human Rights Instruments (UN)**

UN Nine Core Human Rights Treaties

1. International Convention on the Elimination of All Forms of Racial Discrimination 1965.

2. International Covenant on Civil and Political Rights 1966.

2a. Optional Protocol to the International Covenant on Civil and Political Rights 1966.

2b. Second Optional Protocol to the International Covenant on Civil and Political Rights, aiming at the abolition of the death penalty 1989.

3. International Covenant on Economic, Social, and Cultural Rights 1966.

4. Convention on the Elimination of All Forms of Discrimination against Women 1979.

4a. Optional Protocol to the Convention on the Elimination of Discrimination against Women 1999.

5. Convention against Torture and Other Cruel, Inhuman, or Degrading Treatment or Punishment 1984.

5a. Optional Protocol to the Convention against Torture and Other Cruel, Inhuman, or Degrading Treatment or Punishment 2002.

6. Convention on the Rights of the Child 1989.

6a. Optional protocol to the Convention on the Rights of the Child on the involvement of children in armed conflict 2000.

6b. Optional protocol to the Convention on the Rights of the Child on the sale of children, child prostitution, and child pornography 2000.

7. International Convention on the Protection of the Rights of All Migrant Workers and Members of Their Families 1990.

8. Convention on the Rights of Persons with Disabilities 2006.

8a. Optional Protocol to the Convention on the Rights of Persons with Disabilities 2006.

9. International Convention for the Protection of All Persons from Enforced Disappearances 2006.

Other Key United Nations Instruments

Convention relating to the status of refugees 1951 and 1967 protocol.

Standard Minimum Rules for the Treatment of Prisoners (ECOSOC) 1957.

Code of Conduct for Law Enforcement Officials 1979 (GA Resolution 34/169).

Declaration on the Right to Development (GA Resolution 41/128).

Declaration on the Rights of Indigenous Peoples 2007 (GA Resolution 61/295).

The International Labour Organisation's Eight Fundamental Treaties

Convention No. 29 on forced labour 1930.

Convention No. 87 on freedom of association and protection of the right to organize 1948.

Convention No. 98 on the right to organize and collective bargaining 1949.

Convention No. 100 addresses the issue of equal remuneration 1951.

Convention No. 105 on the abolition of forced labour 1957.

Convention No. 111 on discrimination (employment and occupation) 1958.

Convention No. 138 on minimum age 1973.

Convention No. 182 on worst forms of child labour 1999.

USA and Somalia, has ratified it (on the USA and non-ratification, see also Chapter 13). Of the nine core treaties, only the International Convention for the Protection of All Persons from Enforced Disappearances has yet to attract sufficient ratifications to enter into force.

Even in the era of the United Nations, drafting international human rights instruments proved initially to be a tortuous process. While agreement on punishing genocide was relatively easily reached as details emerged of the Holocaust in Europe during the Second World War, agreement on universal human rights proved more problematic. The former Commission on Human Rights made great progress in drafting the Universal Declaration of Human Rights 1948, an aspirational tabulation of the fundamental rights and freedoms of all. Although the United Nations had only 56 member states in 1948, there are now 192 member states, all of whom profess adherence to the UDHR. It is truly a universal declaration today.

The initial plan was for the 'blueprint' set out in the Declaration to be translated into treaty obligations binding on states. Unfortunately, international politics intervened and consensus could not be reached. As the Cold War set in, a devastating polarization of attitudes toward human rights emerged. Communist states and many developing states considered that rights pertaining to existence, such as rights to adequate food, shelter, education, and work were pre-eminent, while Western democracies emphasized civil and political rights such as free speech, the right to fair trials, etc. As a result of the tension, the decision was taken to pursue two separate instruments, one focusing on economic, social, and cultural rights, the other on civil and political rights. Different obligations characterize these treaties. The ICESCR requires states to progressively realize the rights, to the maximum of their available resources (Article 2(1)), while the ICCPR demands instant respect for its rights and provision of national remedies for violations (Article 2).

However, irrespective of the designation accorded to any given right, human rights are, above all, interdependent, indivisible, and universal. One cannot exercise rights of political participation without benefiting from the economic, social, and cultural right to education, to facilitate an informed choice. Similarly, the civil right to life is devoid of meaning if there is no food or clean water (economic, social, and cultural rights). It is the two Covenants that combine to entrench the breadth of rights and freedoms espoused in the UDHR. Arguably, most of the other treaties and instruments simply elaborate their application.

Other Sources: Customary International Law and 'Soft' Law

Customary international law is the term applied to the body of rules and regulations that represent accepted state practice. Customary international law is usually agreed by most or all states, their agreement being signified by compliance, rather than written agreement. Some aspects of human rights arguably reflect customary international law. The prohibition on torture and, more especially, the prohibition on slavery are examples. All states accept that slavery is contrary to international law. They are bound to prohibit slavery irrespective of whether or not they have ratified the anti-slavery treaties. More difficult is torture—although all states ostensibly prohibit it, state practice sadly seems to condone varying degrees of torture and related practices (see Chapter 17). It is thus more problematic to consider its prohibition as accepted custom. Other issues arise with definitions—there is no customary law definition of 'torture' and the treaty definition (e.g. Article 1, Convention Against Torture and Other Cruel, Inhuman, or Degrading Treatment or Punishment) cannot be imported to obligations of non-contracting states. There continues to be debate over the existence of and legal enforceability of customary international law. Given that so few disputes reach the ICJ, which could provide a definitive answer, a satisfactory resolution is not imminent. Moreover, with most states now party to some of the main international human rights treaties, there is less need to rely on customary international law to prove a legal obligation enforceable against the state.

In addition to the foregoing, human rights may also be found in soft law. Soft law is the term used to contrast with 'hard' (treaty/customary) law that produces legally binding obligations. It includes a variety of different instruments concluded under the auspices of international organizations. These instruments are not technically legally binding but do enshrine principles agreed by states. Breaching soft law is not necessarily without consequences. Political ramifications may ensue. As Shelton (2000) notes, non-binding measures are an increasing feature on the international stage. Examples include the Declaration on the Right to Development and the Standard Rules for the Treatment of Prisoners. Frequently, 'soft law' instruments precede 'hard' law—thus the Universal Declaration was subsequently legally expressed in the twin covenants, the Declaration of the Elimination of Discrimination against Women (1967) was followed by the Convention on the Elimination of All Forms of Discrimination against Women (CEDAW) in 1979.

Soft law informs the obligations of states but does not define them. Forsyth (2006, p. 13) notes the importance of the full range of human rights 'soft law' in helping realize non-governmental organizations (NGO) and foreign policy objectives. The end of apartheid in South Africa and Communism in Europe are given as two such examples, albeit controversial ones.

KEY POINTS	
Treaties are the most common source of international human rights law. They are concluded in writing and states must actively agree to their terms.	'Soft law' constitutes another important source of international human rights insofar as it reflects the practice and opinion of states. It can also indicate prevailing international opinion prior to the adoption of a treaty on the topic. Soft law can be influential but is not legally enforceable.
States can avoid certain parts of treaty obligations through reservations, declarations, and derogations. However, reservations should not negate the object and purpose of the treaty. Derogations should only be used when the state genuinely feels the requisite level of threat exists.	Human rights are interdependent and indivisible. Most human rights are co-dependent on other human rights. Human rights thus form a cohesive web of rights and freedoms.
Customary international law is a source of international human rights insofar as certain rights and freedoms are now regarded as being so widely accepted that every state is bound by them.	

Monitoring and Enforcing International Human Rights Law

A system of human rights law, as outlined above, will clearly be of benefit in delineating the parameters of human rights protection and enshrining the entitlements of individuals (and occasionally groups). However, any benefit of having human rights is seriously eroded if those rights cannot be enforced. This section will thus examine the existing mechanisms for monitoring and enforcing human rights. The international system will be outlined first in this section, followed by regional and national systems. Inevitably, less recourse is available for the aggrieved individual at international level than at national level.

The International (United Nations) System for Monitoring and Enforcing Human Rights

In this section, the UN organs and bodies will be considered first, then the treaty monitoring bodies that oversee the implementation of the nine core human rights treaties. Other UN systems for monitoring human rights will then be outlined. Finally, a brief review of a major growth area of international activity—criminal and transitional justice—will complete this section.

The United Nations is clearly the most important source of human rights law. Most of the major treaties are adopted under the auspices of the United Nations or by organizations linked to the United Nations (such as UN Economic, Scientific, and Cultural Organization (UNESCO), the World Health Organization (WHO), or the ILO). More pertinently, the United Nations system has developed a system of monitoring compliance with human rights (see Fig. 2.2). Every single member state of the United Nations is monitored by these systems, as will be explained. However, as Tomuschat (2003, p. 7) notes, 'international protection of human rights is a chapter of legal history that has begun at a relatively late stage in the history of humankind.' Moreover, it is a system that exemplifies consensual diplomacy, with all that entails. States will only actively participate when they feel it benefits them (politically, economically, or diplomatically). If a state feels victimized by the system, it is free to withdraw. There is thus a political undercurrent of trying to achieve effective monitoring while not alienating any state from the process. Inclusivity is important.

Primary (charter) bodies

The UN Charter and associated legislation includes machinery for monitoring compliance with international human rights law. The principal body with responsibility for monitoring compliance with human rights is the **Human Rights Council (HRC)**, which was established in 2006 (see, for example, Oberleitner, 2007) following the dissolution of the much-derided Commission on Human Rights, a functional commission of the Economic and Social Council (see Article 61, UN Charter). Principal criticisms against the Commission included that it was biased and secretive (e.g. Franck, 1984; Boekle, 1995; Annan, 2002, 2005).

FIGURE 2.2 United Nations human rights system—a simplified version.

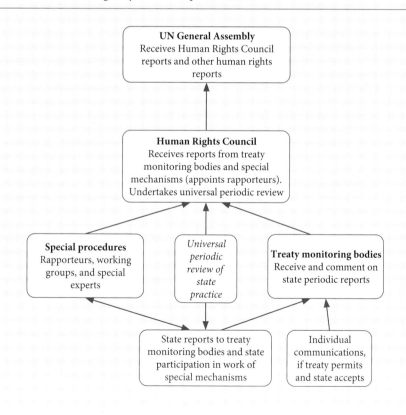

The Human Rights Council is a subsidiary body of the United Nations General Assembly to which it reports. It comprises forty-seven elected states and is 'responsible for promoting universal respect for the protection of all human rights and fundamental freedoms for all, without any distinction of any kind and in a fair and equal manner' (GA Resn 60/251 at 2; see United Nations, 2006). It is imbued with power to undertake a universal periodic review of the fulfilment by each state of its human rights obligations and commitments. States will be specifically reviewed while serving as members of the Council, though all states will be reviewed by the end of a four-year cycle, commencing in 2008. This system is heralded as complementing the work of the treaty monitoring bodies (see below) and not 'overly burdensome' to those involved (Human Rights Council Resolution 5/1 at 3(f)+(h)). The entire process will be reviewed after the completion of the first full cycle. This review will address international human rights law and, perhaps more controversially, international humanitarian law. As for the information to be consulted: states will submit reports; the United Nations Office of the High Commissioner for Human Rights (OHCHR) will compile relevant reports of treaty bodies and special procedures; and additional credible and reliable information provided by 'other relevant stakeholders' summarized by the OHCHR may be used.

The HRC also has competence to receive complaints addressing 'consistent patterns of gross and reliably attested violations' of human rights and freedoms. This procedure draws heavily on its predecessor (the former Commission's 1253/1503 procedure). Human Rights Council Resolution 5/1 of 2007 provides information on the new process that has three sequential stages: an initial admissibility review by a working group of independent experts; consideration of situations by a working group that is drawn from Council members; and review and/or action by the HRC. No information on the nature of the complaints or the discussions of the Council will be made public (unless the state consents).

The ILO and UNESCO both have distinct systems for ensuring the protection of rights protected by treaties concluded under their auspices. UNESCO also operates a system for considering communications concerning rights within its jurisdiction—primarily, the rights to education and to participate freely in cultural life and rights related to freedom of expression and information. Decision 104, EX/3.3 by UNESCO (1978) examines the procedures that should be followed in the examination of cases and questions that might be submitted to UNESCO concerning the exercise of human rights in the spheres of its competence. These proceedings are generally confidential.

Article 24 of the Constitution of the International Labour Organization 1919 allows for complaints by industrial associations of employers/workers who are claiming that any of the members has failed to secure effective observance of any convention. This is part of the ILO system for monitoring compliance with its human (workers') rights.

Undoubtedly, there are few remedies available to the individual under the primary international mechanisms. This is perhaps inevitable in an organization focused on the obligations that states owe each other. The confidential nature of the various systems is consonant with respect for national sovereignty and a reluctance to risk alienating states. All states are encouraged to participate, with a 'light touch' enforcement style being the inevitable consequence.

Secondary (treaty) bodies

In addition to the foregoing, each of the principal treaties includes a mechanism for monitoring compliance with human rights. This is a secondary system as it is based on the principal treaties and thus only applies to those states that have ratified the treaty in question. All the treaty bodies are centred and serviced in Geneva, home of the OHCHR. The composition of each committee, its powers, and functions are specified in the salient treaty (e.g. for Committee on the Rights of the Child, see the Convention on the Rights of the Child, Articles 43–45).

Each treaty receives and considers self-evaluative state reports at intervals specified in the relevant treaty or by the Committee. Concluding Observations issued in response to the state reports and deliberations thereon detail good practice and assess state compliance with their obligations. Non-compliance engages no sanction. All reports are public and available online. Many committees are competent to receive complaints of violations of human rights from one state against another. However, for obvious diplomatic reasons (not least the fear of retribution) these procedures are not utilized.

Some committees may undertake visits to states (e.g. Committee against Torture visits detention facilities). Many of the treaties also contain an individual complaints system. States must agree expressly, either contemporaneously with ratification or subsequently, to accept this competence and allow the relevant committee to hear individual complaints. Indeed, some of these procedures are contained in separate instruments (usually protocols) explicitly to emphasize a distinction from the scope of normal treaty obligations. In a conscious attempt to render the complaint system acceptable to states, non-legalistic terms are deployed. Thus communications are transmitted to a committee that considers the material submitted to it and issues an opinion thereon. Considering the number of assenting states, and especially in comparison to the regional systems (see below), there are very few complaints by individuals. Yet surely no one can argue that this reflects predominant good state practice and contented individuals enjoying the full range of rights and freedoms to which their state has acquiesced!

The international system is often regarded as 'toothless': there are a plethora of international bodies that monitor compliance by states with accepted international human rights but no real mechanisms for forcing states to fully honour their treaty obligations within their territory. Attempts are being made to streamline the system of reporting, rendering it less onerous on states (e.g. a core report with all the general information supported by treaty-specific information where required rather than repeating information to different committees). Countering common state complaints should render the monitoring system more efficient. Alston (1997), Annan (2005), and Hathaway (2007), among others, suggest that, with universal ratification of many instruments approaching, improving the effectiveness of treaty obligations is the next hurdle to securing human rights. Political will has been expressed, the rhetoric must now become a reality.

Criminal justice mechanisms

Despite the idealistic and uniform statements on securing international peace and security that characterized the formative years of the United Nations, there have been civil wars and international conflicts. During many of these, human rights have been violated. Although international human rights law imposes obligations on states, it is usually individuals who actually infringe rights and freedoms. This is most apparent when war crimes, etc. are committed. Can these individuals be held to account for their actions?

Following the tragedies of Rwanda and Yugoslavia in the 1990s, demands for ascribing criminal responsibility strengthened. *Ad hoc* international tribunals were established by resolutions of the United Nations Security Council to try those involved in the atrocities. This was replicated in various self-funded tribunals and courts (e.g. Sierra Leone, Cambodia, and Indonesia) with varying degrees of involvement of the United Nations. Ultimately, the international community established a permanent International Criminal Court, with jurisdiction to prosecute individuals allegedly involved in violations of international criminal law (see Cassesse, 2003). The relevant treaty (Rome Statute of the International Criminal Court) only applies to those states accepting its jurisdiction (currently 106 countries have ratified the treaty). The Rome Statute details all crimes within the jurisdiction of the court—Chapters 16 (Genocide) and 17 (Torture) in this book address two examples. Cases can be referred to it by the Security Council of the United Nations (e.g. Sudan) and by states themselves when they are unable (or unwilling) to prosecute. It is effectively a last resort for bringing to justice individuals committing specified heinous crimes. The first trial should commence soon, so it is too early to assess its effectiveness. Still, the Court's very existence represents a significant achievement and addition to international humanitarian and human rights laws.

The emphasis in the international courts and tribunals is on prosecuting those higher up the chain of command. Slobodan Milosevic (former President of Yugoslavia) was on trial for genocide and other war crimes at the *ad hoc* International Criminal Tribunal for the Former Yugoslavia when he died in 2006 (*Prosecutor* v. *Milosevic*, Case IT-02-54, incomplete). Previously, in Arusha, Tanzania the former Prime Minister of Rwanda, Jean Kambanda, was the first senior official convicted on counts of genocide (*Prosecutor* v. *Kambanda*, 4 September 1998, Case ICTR 97-23-S, upheld *Kambanda* v. *Prosecutor*, 19 October 2000, Case ICTR 97-23-A). More recently, the ICC issued an arrest warrant for the Sudanese Humanitarian Affairs Minister, Ahmed Haroun, in connection with events in Darfur.

Regional Human Rights Systems for Monitoring and Enforcement

Alongside the UN human rights system are a number of regional human rights systems. These are international systems, created by treaties and agreed by states. Even the rights and freedoms contained in the regional treaties bear striking similarities to those articulated in the UDHR and subsequent instruments. According to their proponents, there are many advantages to regional human rights arrangements. 'Peer pressure' is more likely to prompt a state to comply with human rights obligations within a smaller regional setting (though, as some regional systems have over fifty members, that is perhaps an increasingly moot point). Furthermore, the regional systems can enshrine a system of rights and freedoms that reflects regional characteristics. Nevertheless, similar rights appear in each instrument, although the African system uniquely includes collective 'peoples' rights as well. Africa, the Americas, and Europe have adopted numerous treaties on human rights—the following brief discussion merely highlights the key arrangements of the principal regional systems.

The Organization of American States (OAS) is one of the oldest regional organizations. Its American Convention on Human Rights was, however, only adopted in 1969. This establishes a court to adjudicate on disputes and allows the pre-existing American Commission on Human Rights to consider human rights infringements. The Commission can also be seized of complaints brought by individuals against states that have not ratified the Convention (e.g. *Mary & Carry Dann* v. *United States of America* (2002), Report 75/02).

The Council of Europe was established in 1949, after the OAS, and adopted its Convention for the Protection of Human Rights and Fundamental Freedoms in 1950. The treaty is restricted to a narrow band of civil and political rights, although the Council later adopted a Social Charter listing social and economic rights. Today, a European Court of Human Rights sits permanently with competence to consider individual complaints brought by individuals against member states concerning any of the rights and freedoms in the European Convention (not Charter) and associated Protocols. It has heard two inter-state complaints (*Ireland* v. *UK* (1979), Series A, No. 25 and *Cyprus* v. *Turkey* [2001], ECHR 331) and over 100 000 individual complaints. The European

Court officially supervises national conformity with human rights (another organ oversees observance of the Court's judgements). While national courts and governments retain primary responsibility for enforcing human rights, the jurisprudence of the Court is widely complied with by governments and is influential worldwide.

The *African Charter on Human and Peoples' Rights* (1981), more than any of the other regional systems, claims to reflect a distinctive regional set of values, giving an African 'spin' to pre-existing human rights. The Charter initially established a Commission to monitor compliance and had competence to receive individual and group complaints. These powers are being extended to a new Court created under the auspices of the African Union (which succeeded the Organization of African Unity).

The newest regional system covers countries of the League of Arab States. Its revised Arab Charter on Human Rights entered into force in 2008 and envisages a Committee receiving reports on progress made toward realizing human rights.

National Human Rights Systems for Monitoring and Enforcing Human Rights

States, as signatories of international human rights treaties, have primary responsibility for ensuring those rights and freedoms within their territory. The obligation to protect human rights thus falls clearly on the state, but enforcement of human rights at the regional and international level remains open to criticism. States are all too often reluctant to accept the jurisdiction of international and regional bodies to receive complaints from individuals. However, some succour may be gleaned from national laws. It is ideal if individuals enjoy successful recourse to national law when human rights are infringed as the state can/should be able to swiftly remedy the raised problem. National courts can also be used in the prosecution of violations of certain serious human rights.

National courts: universal jurisdiction and rights of action

In terms of the core human rights treaties, states undertake to ensure the human rights specified in the treaty are secured and guaranteed for all citizens within their jurisdiction. Most states have written constitutions, many of which enshrine human rights. An early example is the French Constitution of 1791, which included the 1789 Declaration of the Rights of Man and of the Citizen as its preamble. More recent examples are the Canadian Charter of Rights and the South African Constitution. There is usually a court empowered to review the compatibility of national law and policies with human rights. States may adopt a monist or dualist approach to treaties whereby treaties are, respectively, automatically part of national law or treated as external to national law. Creating a system whereby individuals can enforce international and regional human rights at the national level is imperative to the success of international human rights law when the international systems appear impotent and some regional systems overburdened.

Additionally, violations of some human rights (e.g. torture, slavery, and genocide) are universal crimes and subject to universal jurisdiction—that is to say, the perpetrators can be tried anywhere in the world, irrespective of his or her nationality, that of the victim, or the state in which the violation occurred. Faryadi Zardad, an Afghan warlord, was convicted in the UK of conspiring to torture and kidnap in Afghanistan under the Taliban regime (first instance unreported, on appeal *R* v. *Zardad* [2007], All ER (D) 90). The USA has also expressed willingness to consider torture under national law (see *Filartiga* v. *Pena-Irala* 1980F. 2d 876 (2d cir) and Chapter 17). There should be no hiding place for those perpetrating atrocities.

National human rights institutions

Given the lack of mechanisms available at the UN level and the costs and difficulties involved in engaging with the regional systems, it should be no surprise that the system of international human rights is predicated on the concept of national human rights institutions. These institutions, commissions, units, etc. should be independent of the government and capable of monitoring the plight of human rights within the country concerned. The emphasis should be on promoting and protecting human rights, ensuring that all nationals benefit fully from the human rights regime that the state has signed up to. The *Paris Principles* (see

General Assembly, 1993; OHCHR, 1993) guide the international community as to what the powers, functions, and composition of a national human rights institution should be (see Box 2.4).

The systems which exist for protecting and promoting international human rights law are clearly fallible. However, in little over fifty years, a dramatic new web of mechanisms for monitoring and enforcing rights has created a paradigm shift in how individuals are viewed on the international stage.

KEY POINTS

No set of laws (international, regional, or national) can be developed and enforced without the will of the states concerned. State consent is vital to the development of the law and state willingness is a precursor to successful enforcement.

The United Nations has created a comprehensive system of bodies with responsibility for monitoring compliance with international human rights law. Their effectiveness depends on state cooperation in various 'constructive dialogue' processes.

The Human Rights Council has significant powers to review all state activities under its universal periodic review process. Treaty monitoring bodies have evolved over the years to become more proactive proponents of human rights, though are dependent on the enabling treaty for their powers.

Criminal justice poses a new challenge for the international community. The International Criminal Court is one mechanism that seeks to ensure that those who violate serious human rights can be held to account.

Regional systems operate alongside, not instead of, international human rights systems, in Europe, the Americas, Africa, and the Arab States. Regional systems can be more successful at ensuring compliance with human rights as several have courts and/or commissions with competence to receive individual complaints against states.

National human rights institutions are often regarded as the 'great salvation' of international human rights law. The emphasis is on ensuring appropriate function and powers. To ensure remedies for individuals, disputes are best resolved at the national level rather than pursuing a complaint to the regional or international level.

Box 2.4 **Paris Principles on National Human Rights Institutions**

3. A national institution shall, *inter alia*, have the following responsibilities:

   (a) To submit to the government, parliament and any other competent body, on an advisory basis either at the request of the authorities concerned or through the exercise of its power to hear a matter without higher referral, opinions, recommendations, proposals and reports on any matters concerning the protection and promotion of human rights. The national institution may decide to publicize them. These opinions, recommendations, proposals and reports, as well as any prerogative of the national institution, shall relate to the following areas:

      (i) Any legislative or administrative provisions, as well as provisions relating to judicial organization, intended to preserve and extend the protection of human rights. In that connection, the national institution shall examine the legislation and administrative provisions in force, as well as bills and proposals, and shall make such recommendations as it deems appropriate in order to ensure that these provisions conform to the fundamental principles of human rights. It shall, if necessary, recommend the adoption of new legislation, the amendment of legislation in force and the adoption or amendment of administrative measures;

      (ii) Any situation of violation of human rights which it decides to take up;

      (iii) The preparation of reports on the national situation with regard to human rights in general, and on more specific matters;

      (iv) Drawing the attention of the government to situations in any part of the country where

   human rights are violated and making proposals to it for initiatives to put an end to such situations and, where necessary, expressing an opinion on the positions and reactions of the government;

   (b) To promote and ensure the harmonization of national legislation, regulations and practices with the international human rights instruments to which the State is a party, and their effective implementation;

   (c) To encourage ratification of the above-mentioned instruments or accession to those instruments, and to ensure their implementation;

   (d) To contribute to the reports which States are required to submit to United Nations bodies and committees, and to regional institutions, pursuant to their treaty obligations, and, where necessary, to express an opinion on the subject, with due respect for their independence;

   (e) To cooperate with the United Nations and any other agency in the United Nations system, the regional institutions and the national institutions of other countries which are competent in the areas of the protection and promotion of human rights;

   (f) To assist in the formulation of programmes for the teaching of, and research into, human rights and to take part in their execution in schools, universities and professional circles;

   (g) To publicize human rights and efforts to combat all forms of discrimination, in particular racial discrimination, by increasing public awareness, especially through information and education and by making use of all press organs.

Conclusion

As this chapter has demonstrated, states generally indicate their acceptance of international human rights law by agreeing to treaties. However, there are a number of ways in which states can avoid the full impact of such legal obligations: reservations; derogations; and declarations. Politically, states find adopting human rights a positive experience; legally, there are many ways they can avoid full legal responsibility for the rights and freedoms accepted. The existing mechanisms for monitoring human rights adopt a 'light' touch, encouraging states to comply with treaties through a constructive dialogue rather than forcing them through any court process. In contrast, individuals committing war crimes can be prosecuted anywhere. The 'common standard of achievement for all peoples and all nations' proclaimed sixty years ago in the Universal Declaration of Human Rights is not yet a reality. Nevertheless, without law, international human rights would be a less tangible, measurable, and enforceable concept than it is today.

QUESTIONS

INDIVIDUAL STUDY QUESTIONS

1. What is the process followed for a state wishing to be bound to the provisions of a treaty?

2. What are the benefits of listing human rights in treaties?

3. What is the effect of a reservation on a state's legal obligations under a treaty? Can you find examples of reservations that seek to defeat the object and purpose of the treaty?

4. What is meant by interdependent and indivisible rights? Can you give some examples of this interdependence?

5. What is the role of the Human Rights Council?

6. Why are the principal UN human rights treaties monitored via committees rather than courts? What benefits does such a system bring?

7. Research your state's ratification record, regional, and national human rights arrangements. What treaties have been ratified? Are there significant reservations or declarations? Is there a body that conforms to the Paris Principles? Can you directly action infringements of international human rights in national courts?

GROUP DISCUSSION QUESTIONS

1. Does the current situation regarding world terrorism justify derogations from human rights treaties, and if so, which provisions; if not, why not?

2. To what extent should the enforceability of treaties be prioritized over securing a high number of ratifications? (This is a debate that Alston and Bayefsky instigated in the 1990s.)

3. Should human rights be aspirational standards of achievement for states to strive for, or should they be clearly articulated and enforceable against each and every state under national and/or international law?

4. Examine news reports over a set period of time. Identify human rights stories. Are the human rights issues correctly identified and appropriately explored?

FURTHER READING

Alfredsson, G. and **Eide**, A. (eds) (1999). *The Universal Declaration of Human Rights—A Common Standard of Achievement*. The Hague: Martinus Nijhoff.
This text comprises a series of chapters in which experts analyse the impact of each of the rights and freedoms contained in the Universal Declaration.

Buergenthal, T., **Shelton**, D., and **Stewart**, D. (2002). *International Human Rights in a Nutshell* (3rd edn). St Paul, MN: West Group.
This is a very good introduction to international human rights law and the international regime.

Hathaway, O. (2002). Do treaties make a difference? Human rights treaties and the problem of compliance. *Yale Law Journal*, **111**, 1932–2042.
Qualitative analysis of the relationship between human rights treaties and state practice.

Lijnzaad, L. (1995). *Reservations to UN Human Rights Treaties, Ratify and Ruin?* The Hague: Martinus Nijhoff.
Expert monograph on the concept of reservations and their impact on international human rights law.

Shelton, D. (1999). *Remedies in International Human Rights Law*. Oxford: Oxford University Press.
The principal book reviewing remedies available for infringements of human rights.

Smith, R. (2007). *Textbook on International Human Rights* (3rd edn). Oxford: Oxford University Press.
A basic introduction to international human rights law.

Steiner, H., **Alston**, P., and **Goodman**, R. (2007). *International Human Rights in Context: Law, Politics, Morals*.
Oxford: Oxford University Press.
Comprehensive reader, with interpretation, on international human rights focused primarily on legal and related philosophical issues.

Symonides, J. (ed.) (2003). *Human Rights: International Protection, Monitoring, Enforcement*. Aldershot: Ashgate and Burlington, VT: UNESCO.
Expert essays on the problems and processes of monitoring international human rights law.

WEB LINKS

http://www.ohchr.org The website of the United Nations Office of the High Commissioner for Human Rights (OHCHR) provides access to all UN human rights treaties as well as the texts of all Committee (treaty monitoring body) reports. It is easy to navigate around and contains copious links to additional materials.

http://www.bayefsky.com Professor Bayefsky's website focuses on the work of the treaty monitoring bodies of the United Nations. It has a particularly useful thematic search facility.

http://www.icc-cpi.int The website of the International Criminal Court provides access to the documentation surrounding the current warrants, and pre-trial and trial proceedings.

http://www.echr.coe.int The website of the European Court of Human Rights includes a search engine facilitating access to the jurisprudence of the Court. This website is included as the European Court has produced the greatest volume of regional jurisprudence.

http://www.hrea.org The website of an NGO supporting human rights training and providing useful resource material.

ONLINE RESOURCE CENTRE

Visit the Online Resource Centre that accompanies this book for updates and a range of other resources:

http://www.oxfordtextbooks.co.uk/orc/goodhart/

Measuring Human Rights

3

Todd Landman

Chapter Contents

Reader's Guide

The chapter provides a general overview of the purpose, challenges, and types of human rights measures. It covers the main content of human rights that ought to be measured, including the different categories (civil, political, economic, social, and cultural) and dimensions (respect, protect, and fulfil) of human rights. It outlines the different ways that human rights have been measured using different kinds of data and measurement strategies. It concludes by identifying the remaining challenges for this sub-tradition in the field of human rights, including the need for more measures of economic and social rights and better measures of civil and political rights.

Introduction

The measurement and monitoring of human rights has been a mainstay activity of human rights non-governmental organizations (NGOs) and has become increasingly important among political scientists. Human rights NGOs, such as Amnesty International and Human Rights Watch, use monitoring systems to track the degree to which international human rights treaties have been implemented, to alert the international community about egregious violations of human rights, to mobilize different constituencies around particular human rights issues, and to advocate for additional standard setting in the international law of human rights. Political science, particularly since the behavioural revolution (see Box 3.1), has sought to measure and analyse political *violence* from state and non-state actors, an effort that has, since the 1980s, turned to systematic analysis of the *causes and consequences of cross-national variation in human rights protection around the world* (e.g. McCamant, 1981; Mitchell and McCormick, 1988; Landman, 2005a). Complementing these developments, scholars have published collections and reviews of human rights measures produced by academics and NGOs (Claude, 1976; Jabine and Claude, 1992) and efforts to collate and assess the quality of human rights measures continue to be carried out (see, for example, Green, 2001; Landman and Häusermann, 2003; Landman, 2004, 2006b; Landman and Carvalho, to appear).

Since the publication of *Human Rights and Statistics* (Jabine and Claude, 1992), there have been an increasing number of efforts to measure more and different categories of human rights (e.g. the Cingranelli and Richards Human Rights Data Project), and there have been a variety of international conferences and workshops on human rights measurement, sponsored by professional academic organizations (e.g. the 2004 Chicago workshop organized by the Human Rights Section of the American Political Science Association, and the 2005 conference on economic and social rights organized by the Human Rights Institute at the University of Connecticut in Storrs) and international organizations (e.g. the 2000 conference on human rights and statistics in Montreux, followed by similar summits in ensuing years in Merida, Munich, and Brussels). The most cutting-edge advances in human rights measurement,

however, have come from the non-governmental sector, particularly those organizations working with truth commissions around the world. In particular, the work of the Human Rights Data Analysis Group (HRDAG) at the American Association for the Advancement of Science in Washington, DC (and now the Benetech Initiative in Palo Alto, California) has been instrumental in developing systematic techniques for the measurement and analysis of large-scale human rights violations across a range of different country contexts.

The increasing provision and availability of human rights measures has led to a new demand within the international human rights and donor communities, such as the *United Nations*, the World Bank, and the aid ministries in the USA (USAID), UK (DFID), Sweden (SIDA), Canada (CIDA), and Denmark (DANIDA), to integrate human rights assessment into overall policy formulation and aid allocation strategies. Donors such as DFID in the UK use human rights assessment in their aid programming to find ways in which

---

Box 3.1 **The Behavioural Revolution**

The behavioural revolution began in the 1930s and 1940s, primarily in the United States. It putatively moved political science away from normative questions and 'value-based' research, and concentrated on *observable* and *measurable* attributes of human beings and human societies in an effort to uncover empirical regularities and provide 'law-like' generalizations that had universal applicability. Research in this tradition involves hypothesis testing using quantitative measures on individuals and states and the research design in such studies is one very much beholden to the natural science model of knowledge accumulation typically found in books such as Hempel's (1966) *The Philosophy of Natural Science*. Where human rights featured in the early years of this research tradition, if at all, was in the focus on political violence and state repression, as found, for example in Ted Robert Gurr's (1970) seminal book, *Why Men Rebel*. But this research did not adopt the language of rights to frame its research questions or its policy implications. It did, however, initiate the attempt to measure state and non-state violence in ways that would prove crucial to the development in human rights measures in the years to come.

different aid modalities can address particular needs within partner countries to improve the human rights situation, while at the same time addressing larger questions of poverty reduction. In contrast, the Millennium Challenge Account in the USA uses human rights measures as an incentive to allocate aid to those countries that can demonstrate improvements in their human rights performance. In addition, the *Office of the High Commissioner for Human Rights* in Geneva has been engaged in a long-term process of consultation with international experts to provide matrices of human rights indicators for use in state party reports to the treaty monitoring bodies, while the United Nations Development Programme's (UNDP) Oslo Governance Centre has produced guides on measures of good governance and human rights for use in their own country

offices and within the wider donor community (see UNDP, 2004, 2006).

This chapter locates and discusses these developments in the context of broader historical shifts in the discipline of political science and shows that, at present, significant progress has been made in providing different kinds of measures of human rights for an increasingly larger set of rights. It does so through consideration of the purpose of measurement, the challenges to measurement, the types of measures, and the remaining lacunae in the field. Taken together, the measurement and monitoring of human rights is marked out as a distinct subfield within the discipline of political science as well as an increasingly important activity among international and domestic governmental and non-governmental organizations.

The Purpose of Measuring Human Rights

Human rights measures serve a variety of important and inter-related functions across the academic and non-academic sectors of the human rights community. First, they allow for *contextual description and documentation*, which provide the raw information for monitoring, carried out primarily by NGOs, as well as for developing and deriving standardized measures of human rights. Second, they help efforts at *classification*, which allow for the differentiation of rights violations across their different categories and dimensions, and for grouping states and regimes into different categories, such as authoritarian, personal dictatorship, fragile states, unconsolidated or weak democracies, and one-party dominant regimes. Third, they can be used for *monitoring* the degree to which states respect, protect, and fulfil the various rights set out in the different treaties to which they may be a party. Fourth, they can be used for *mapping and pattern recognition*, which provide time series and spatial information on the broad patterns of violations within and across different countries, as well as within different groups of countries (e.g. human rights performance within less developed countries). Fifth, they are essential for *secondary analysis*, including hypothesis testing, prediction, and impact assessment, the inferences from which can be fed into the policy-making process. Finally, human rights measures can serve as important

advocacy tools at the domestic and international level by showing the improvement or deterioration in rights practices around the world. The accumulation of information on human rights protection in the world and the results of systematic analysis can serve as the basis for the continued development of human rights policy, advocacy, and education (Rubin and Newberg, 1980, p. 268; Claude and Jabine, 1992).

Traditionally, organizations such as Amnesty International and Human Rights Watch have used various indicators for depicting the human rights situation in different countries, which provides in depth information on developments with respect to particular rights problems. Human rights measures add weight to an assessment of a country situation and serve to enhance any effort in advocating for the international community to action on behalf of individuals or groups that are suffering. Increasingly, human rights organizations are using more sophisticated forms of measurement and analysis to enhance the types of international argument and dialogue needed to bring about progressive change in human rights. For example, the Centre for Economic and Social Rights has begun a new project that compares the relative ability and effort of states for the progressive realization of social and economic rights, the World Organization Against Torture carried out a large-scale project that analysed the causes of violence that used cross-national human rights measures, and the International Council for Human Rights Policy carried out a project and consultation that examined the causes and consequences of corruption and their implication for human rights policy and advocacy.

In the academic world, the use of human rights measures has allowed social scientists to compare and contrast the human rights performance of countries over time and across space in an effort to explain why some countries have a better record at protecting human rights (see Chapter 5). The analysis has concentrated on social and political variables, such as the level of economic development, the level of democracy, involvement in civil war and international war, and various international factors, such as trade with other countries, the level of interdependence, and the degree to which a country takes part in the international regime for the protection of human rights. These studies are important in identifying the underlying reasons for why countries have different levels of human rights protection and provide guidance to political leaders, international governmental, and international non-governmental

organizations for the types of issues that need to be addressed in order to improve the protection of human rights. One seminal study carried out by Steve Poe and Neal C. Tate (1994) argued that the three issue areas that most needed attention from the international community included the promotion of economic development, democracy, and conflict resolution.

KEY POINTS

Human rights can and should be measured.

The measurement of human rights has six main purposes:
- contextual description and documentation;
- classification;
- monitoring;
- mapping and pattern recognition;
- secondary analysis;
- advocacy tools and political dialogue.

Analysis of human rights measures helps increase their protection worldwide.

Challenges to Measuring Human Rights

There are significant theoretical and methodological challenges to measuring human rights. Theoretically, there is both an absence of agreed philosophical foundations for human rights and the ongoing contestation over the meaning of human rights and the core content of human rights. Together these make the *operationalization* (or translation of these definitions into measurable concepts) for political science research problematic. Many of the methodological challenges to human rights measurement are related to the theoretical challenges in the sense that efforts to measure rights necessarily draw on theoretical attempts to define human rights in general terms and to provide 'systematized' definitions that can be operationalized for political science research (see Adcock and Collier, 2001). There are additional methodological challenges relating to the nature and extent to which human rights problems can be observed and then measured in any systematic fashion, and the degree to which information about human rights is necessarily biased, uneven, and highly incomplete (see Bollen, 1992, p. 198).

At a theoretical level there are two broad sets of responses to the absence of agreed philosophical foundations. *Legal responses* cite the growth and proliferation in human rights norms, instruments, and declarations as evidence that there is an emerging global consensus on the need to promote and protect human rights (Freeman, 2001), as well as a 'language of commitment' from state and non-state actors in the international community (Boyle, 1995, p. 81). *Social and political responses* argue that rights 'made' initially through domestically-based struggles in the eighteenth, nineteenth, and early twentieth centuries have been joined by international advocacy efforts at standard setting and implementation, which created the international human rights system as we now know it (see, for example, Marshall, 1963; Tilly *et al.*, 1975; Claude, 1976; Barbalet, 1988; Foweraker and Landman, 1997; Ishay, 2004). This 'making' of rights has led to more general and pragmatic claims that human rights represent 'bulwarks against the permanent threat of human evil' (Mendus, 1995, pp. 23–24), 'necessary legal guarantees for the exercise of human agency' (Ignatieff, 2001), or an 'important political lever for the realization of global justice' (Falk, 2000). And it is these pragmatic functions and dimensions of human rights that have provided important starting points for the measurement of human rights.

Categories and Dimensions of Human Rights

But even if the legal and socio-political arguments hold, there remains considerable disagreement on the meaning of different types of human rights, which continues to complicate the attempts to measure them. It is probably unfair to say that human rights are 'essentially contested' (Gallie, 1956), since the international law of human rights and its associated jurisprudence has made great strides in clarifying the content of human rights in ways that have not been done for other contested concepts (see Chapter 2). Still, for purposes of social scientific research, there remain definitional problems that present significant obstacles for their operationalization. The international instruments have in many ways established both *categories* and *dimensions* of human rights that ought to be protected. The categories are well known and range across civil, political, economic, social, and cultural rights. The notion of human rights *dimensions* has evolved from understanding human rights in

'positive' and 'negative' terms to 'generations' of rights, to a more useful formulation that comprises the separate dimensions of respect, protection, and fulfilment, which arise from the legal obligations of states party to international human rights instruments (e.g. E/C.12/1999/5).[1]

The obligation to *respect* human rights requires the state and all its organs and agents to abstain from carrying out, sponsoring, or tolerating any practice, policy, or legal measure violating the integrity of individuals or impinging on their freedom to access resources to satisfy their needs. It also requires that legislative and administrative codes take account of guaranteed rights. The obligation to *protect* requires the state and its agents to prevent the violation of rights by other individuals or non-state actors. Where violations do occur, the state must guarantee access to legal remedies.

The obligation to *fulfil* involves issues of advocacy, public expenditure, governmental regulation of the economy, the provision of basic services and related infrastructure, and redistributive measures. The duty of fulfilment comprises those active measures necessary for guaranteeing opportunities to access entitlements (see UNDP, 2006, p. 4).

Combining these categories and dimensions produces a simple matrix of the scope of human rights, and provides a good starting point from which to operationalize human rights for social science analysis (see Table 3.1). To date in the social sciences, more attention has been given to civil and political rights

TABLE 3.1 The categories and dimensions of human rights.

Dimensions of human rights

		Respect No interference in the exercise of the right	**Protect** Prevent violations from third parties	**Fulfil** Provision of resources and the outcomes of policies
Categories of human rights	Civil and political	1 Torture, extra-judicial killings, disappearances, arbitrary detention, unfair trials, electoral intimidation, and disenfranchisement	2 Measure to prevent non-state actors from committing violations, such as militias, uncivil movements, or private sector firms and organisations	3 Investment in judiciaries, prisons, police forces, electoral authorities, and resource allocations to ability
	Economic, social, and cultural	4 Ethnic, racial, gender, or linguistic discrimination in health, education, and welfare, and resource allocations below ability	5 Measures to prevent non-state actors from engaging in discriminatory behaviour that limits access to services and conditions	6 Progressive realization: investment in health, education, and welfare, and resource allocations to ability

Source: Adapted from UNDP (2006, p. 5).

across the two dimensions of respect and protect. Such attempts can be seen as a function of larger ideological and methodological reasons that go beyond the scope of this chapter (but see Landman, 2005a).

Other Methodological Challenges

While this matrix provides a good overview of what is to be measured in terms of the different categories and dimensions of human rights, there are many remaining methodological challenges to providing *valid* (i.e. the measure measures what it purports to measure), *meaningful* (i.e. it actually measures something that matters), and *reliable* (i.e. that the measure can be produced in other contexts and by other people consistently) measures that fill the different cells in the matrix. Human rights are a class of social phenomena that are often unreported, misreported, under-reported, or over-reported in ways that make their systematic measurement highly problematic. Over the years, political science has moved away from straight *event counting*, the counting of how often particular rights are violated based on a select number of newspapers, to the use of multiple sources of information that are coded more systematically and reliably. But there remain significant trade-offs in the types of data available that measure human rights directly and the types of political science analysis that can be carried out with them. On the one hand, there are very good but limited collections of highly disaggregated forms of human rights events data available for a handful of countries that have experienced prolonged authoritarianism, foreign occupation, or civil war (see Jabine and Claude, 1992; Ball *et al.*, 2000, Ball *et al.*, 2003; Landman, 2006a, 2006b). These data are on gross violations and are coded using multiple sources of information, such as statements collected by official truth commissions, monitoring systems developed by non-governmental organizations, analysis of morgue records (e.g. Haiti) and cemeteries (e.g. East Timor), or some form of retrospective survey instrument (e.g. East Timor) (see Landman, 2006b, pp. 107–125).

On the other hand, there are more extensive collections of human rights data for many countries ($150 < N < 194$) over time ($25 < T < 36$) that are of a more general nature and capture broad trends in the protection of certain human rights (see Jabine and Claude, 1992; Landman, 2002, 2006b). These data are coded from a variety of sources (some of which are not explicitly reported[2]) in which some form of a standardized scale is derived from a deep reading of narrative accounts on general trends in different categories of human rights. By and large, these have relied on the annual reports produced by either the US State Department or Amnesty International (see below).

Like other trade-offs in political science, scholars are thus faced with engaging in research using either form of data, while recognizing the different types of inferences made possible through the analysis of different samples of countries. To date, the published political science literature engages in either the statistical analysis of pooled cross-national time-series (PCTS) data sets or small-N comparative and single case studies that make little use of available events data. PCTS data sets comprise measures of human rights and other variables across a large number of countries and over long periods of time. Events data are simply not yet available for many countries in the world, which precludes this kind of analysis being carried out. For those countries where these kinds of data have been gathered, it is possible to conduct a comparative analysis that seeks to explain the similarities and differences that are present across a selection of countries, such as Brockett's (2005) comparison of human rights data in El Salvador and Guatemala. While events data on human rights are most suited for single-country analyses that focus in much greater detail on the specific features of countries, few studies have yet to take full advantage of these data.

Nevertheless, efforts to develop systems for human rights measurement have advanced both within the discipline of political science and among other human rights scholars and practitioners, covering more categories and dimensions of human rights using a variety of measurement strategies. It is to these different types of human rights measures that the discussion now turns.

KEY POINTS
Human rights have different categories and dimensions that can be measured.
Some categories and dimensions have been measured more than others.
There are many methodological challenges to measuring human rights that are being overcome.
Political scientists use measures to compare many countries or a few countries, and to carry out an analysis of single countries.

Types of Human Rights Measures

Despite the continued problems with definition and operationalization, five main types of measures have been developed that serve as direct measures of human rights or as significant proxy measures for different dimensions of human rights. *Events-based* data count and chart the reported acts of violation committed against groups and individuals. *Standards-based* data establish how often and to what degree violations occur, and then translate such judgements into quantitative scales that are designed to achieve commensurability by coding narrative information on human rights conditions into a standardized scale. *Survey-based* data use random samples of country populations to ask a series of standard questions on the perception of rights protection and/or experiences with human rights violations. Increasingly, *socio-economic and administrative statistics* have been used to measure in a more indirect fashion state efforts to respect, protect, and fulfil human rights. Finally, some efforts at measurement have *combined* different types of data to measure human rights or compare human perceptions to the human rights

performance of different countries (e.g. see Anderson *et al.*, 2005; Richards, 2006) (see Box 3.2).

Events-Based Data

Events-based data answer the important questions of what happened, when it happened, and who was involved, and then report descriptive and numerical summaries of the events. Counting such events and violations involves identifying the various acts of commission and omission that constitute or lead to human rights violations, such as extra-judicial killings, arbitrary arrest, or torture. Such data tend to be disaggregated to the level of the violation itself, which may have related data units such as the perpetrator, the victim, and the witness (Ball *et al.*, 2000; Landman, 2006b, pp. 82–83). Events-based data analysis has a long tradition, where one of the first applications of statistics to the study of violence analysed the distribution of more than 15 000 'quasi-judicial' executions carried out during the height of the Reign of Terror (March 1793 to August 1794) after the French Revolution. Using the archived documents of the tribunals that sentenced people to death, Greer (1935) analyses the patterns of sentencing and executions over time, space, and by social class (nobles, upper middle class, lower middle class, clergy, working class, and peasants). Similar analyses have been carried out for the more contemporary cases of Guatemala (Ball, 2000), Peru (Ball *et al.*, 2003), Kosovo (Ball *et al.*, 2002), and Colombia (Guzmán *et al.*, 2007), as well as a global comparison of violations committed against human rights defenders (see Box 3.3). Highly-disaggregated forms of violations data can be used to estimate the total number of violations that have occurred (usually extra-judicial killings and **disappearances**), the temporal and spatial patterns in the data, and any ethno-political dimensions that might demonstrate that particular groups suffered disproportionately. In his comparison of El Salvador and Guatemala, for example, Brockett (2005) uses time-series events data on social protest and patterns of state repression to show how state violence in Guatemala virtually eliminated a popular rural movement, while in El Salvador similar levels of state violence did not.

Box 3.2 **Combining Measures of Human Rights**

The World Bank has devised measures of 'good governance' that maximize the use of a broad range of available indicators on good governance through a data reduction technique that combines up to 300 disparate indicators of good governance into six separate indices. These separate indices include:

voice and accountability;

political instability and violence;

government effectiveness;

regulatory burden;

rule of law;

graft.

Many of these categories of good governance have significant overlaps with many human rights principles and standards, and focus almost exclusively on the protection of civil and political rights. The governance measures are now available for a large number of countries for over ten years of time. See http://www.govindicators.org.

Box 3.3 **Events-Based Data on Human Rights Defenders**

Using the annual reports produced by the International Federation of Human Rights Leagues for the period between 1997 and 2003, Landman (2006b) counted abuses committed against human rights defenders across more than seventy countries, such as harassment, threats, smear campaigns, arbitrary detention, torture, and extra-judicial killings. The coding of events allows for analysis of the breakdown of abuses that have been committed across different types of perpetrators. Table 3.2 shows this breakdown. Further analysis can be conducted that explains the cross-national variation in these abuses and how they may be related to socio-economic and political conditions, as well as major developments in the international sphere.

TABLE 3.2 Main abuses committed against human rights defenders by type of perpetrator.

	Arbitrary arrest/detention	Threats	Harassment	Summary execution	Judicial investigation	Total
Police	75.00	5.51	14.41	1.27	3.81	100
	(177)	(13)	(34)	(3)	(9)	(236)
Unknown	2.11	52.82	9.86	35.21		100
	(3)	(75)	(14)	(50)		(142)
Judiciary	25.49		9.80		64.71	100
	(13)		(5)		(33)	(51)
State agents	16.98	35.85	37.74		9.43	100
	(9)	(19)	(20)		(5)	(53)
Security services	54.39	14.04	28.07	1.75	1.75	100
	(31)	(8)	(16)	(1)	(1)	(57)
Total	43.23	21.34	16.51	10.02	8.91	100
	(233)	(115)	(89)	(54)	(48)	(539)

Note: Percentages reported with *N* abuses in parentheses: $x^2 = 583.96$ (p < 0.001); l = 0.34 (p < 0.001).

Source: Adapted from Landman (2006b, p. 132).

Standards-based measures

Standards-based measures of human rights are one level removed from event counting and violation reporting, and merely apply an ordinal scale to qualitative information, where the resulting scale is derived from determining if the reported human rights situation reaches particular threshold conditions. The most dominant examples include the Freedom House scales of civil and political liberties (Gastil, 1978, 1980, 1988, 1990; http://www.freedomhouse.org), the 'political terror scale' (Mitchell *et al.*, 1986; Poe and Tate, 1994; Gibney and Stohl, 1998), a scale of torture (Hathaway, 2002), and a series of seventeen different rights measures collected by Cingranelli and Richards (http://www.humanrightsdata.com). Freedom House has a standard checklist that it uses to code civil and political rights based on press reports and country sources about state practices and then derives two separate scales for each category of rights on a scale that ranges from 1 (full protection) to 7 (full violation). The political terror scale ranges from 1 (full protection) to 5 (full violation) for state practices that include torture, political imprisonment, unlawful killing, and disappearance. Information for these scales comes from the US State Department and Amnesty International country reports. Using this information, teams of coders apply a code to countries for each year using the following criteria (Zanger, 2000, p. 218; Landman, 2005b, pp. 46–47).

Level 1: 'Countries ... under a secure rule of law, people are not imprisoned for their views, and torture is rare or exceptional ... political murders are extremely rare.'

Level 2: 'There is a limited amount of imprisonment for non-violent political activity. However, few persons are affected, torture and beating are exceptional ... political murder is rare.'

Level 3: 'There is extensive political imprisonment, or a recent history of such imprisonment. Execution or other political murders and brutality may be common. Unlimited detention, with or without trial, for political views is accepted.'

Level 4: 'The practices of [Level 3] are expanded to larger numbers. Murders, disappearances are a common part of life ... In spite of its generality, on this level terror affects primarily those who interest themselves in politics or ideas.'

Level 5: 'The terror of [Level 4] ha[s] been expanded to the whole population ... The leaders of these societies place no limits on the means or thoroughness with which they pursue personal or ideological goals.'

The coding teams need to determine if a country has reached the different threshold conditions listed here and then assign a score. The coding effort then yields a collection of data with annual scores for a large number of countries whose human rights practices can be compared (see Box 3.4). In similar fashion, Hathaway (2002) measures torture on a 1 to 5 scale using information from the US State Department and has devised

---

Box 3.4 **Standards-Based Measures of Human Rights**

Standards-based measures code country performances on the protection of human rights using a variety of source materials, including the annual reports published by Amnesty International and the US State Department. Figure 3.1 shows the average score per year across five different standards-based measures for the period between 1976 and 2000.

FIGURE 3.1 Five standards-based measures of human rights, 1976–2000.

Note: Measures are the political terror scale (Amnesty and State Department), Freedom House (Civil and Political Liberties), and the torture scale (Hathaway, 2002).

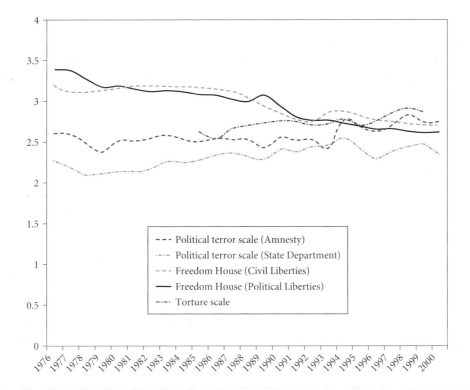

a set of coding criteria based on the relative degree to which torture is practised and/or tolerated within different countries. The Cingranelli and Richards human rights data code similar sets of rights on scales from 0 to 2, and 0 to 3, with some combined indices ranging from 0 to 8, where higher scores denote better rights protections. Again, they use a set of coding criteria, coding teams, and test for the reliability of their scales by using multiple coding teams and comparing their scores. In addition to a series of civil and political rights, Cingranelli and Richards also provide measures for such rights as women's economic, social, and political rights, worker rights, and religious rights.

While these scales have been primarily developed to measure the *de facto* realization of human rights, other scholars have used standards-based measures to code the *de jure* commitment of states to the promotion and protection of human rights. In this application, the scale denotes the degree to which a state *signs*, ratifies, and files reservations to the various international human rights treaties that have been negotiated since the 1948 Universal Declaration of Human Rights. In these coding schemes, countries are rewarded for treaty ratification and punished for the degree to which their reservations undermine the object and purpose of the treaty. Camp Keith (1999), Hathaway (2002), Neumayer (2005), and Hafner-Burton and Tsutsui (2005, 2007) use a simple dummy variable for ratification, while Landman (2005b) uses a trichotomous variable that takes into account state signature and combines the variable with a four-point scale that weights the ratification for reservations. The weighting criteria are as follows (Landman, 2005b, pp. 42–43).

(4): *Given to countries that have no reservations with regard to said treaty, interpretive declarations that do not modify obligations, or non-substantial declarations.* This would include declarations such as criticism of the treaty not being open to all states, or political non-recognition of other states.

(3): *Given to countries whose reservations could have some but not major impact on their obligations.* This would include reservations to certain aspects of a specific right but not nullifying it completely, or to whole articles that are procedural (such as articles allowing one-sided referral to the International Court of Justice, ICJ).

(2): *Given to countries whose reservations have noticeable effect on their obligations under the treaty* to a whole article, nullifying or leaving open the possibility not to abide by a whole article. This score would also be given for reservations that do not limit a whole right or article, but nevertheless contain the core obligation of the article or right.

(1): *Given to countries whose reservations can have significant and severe effects on the treaty obligations.* This would include reservations that show disregard for the object and purpose, or for rules of customary international law. Reservations that subject the whole treaty to national or religious legislation would receive this score.

This weighting is arguably more subjective in nature and requires a legal judgment on the degree to which a country's reservation undermines the object and purpose of any given human rights treaty, but when combined with the more objective ratification score, it adds valuable information to a country score that more accurately captures its legal intentions.

Survey Data

Survey data have been less used in social scientific research on human rights than either events-based or standards-based measures. They have usually featured more often in research on the support for democracy (e.g. Kaase and Newton, 1995), trust and social capital (e.g. Whiteley, 1999, 2000), patterns of corruption (http://www.transparency.org), or as components of larger indices of 'post-material' values (see Inglehart, 1997). But increasingly, household surveys have been used to provide measures for popular attitudes about rights and to uncover direct and indirect experiences of human rights violations. Some of the most notable work has been carried out by the NGO Physicians for Human Rights, which conducts surveys of 'at risk' populations (e.g. internally displaced people or women in conflict) to determine the nature and degree of human rights violations. The 'minorities at risk' project certainly captures the degree to which communal groups and other national minorities suffer different forms of discrimination. In addition, the truth commission in East Timor carried out a retrospective household mortality survey on all lives, deaths, and illnesses within the country during the period of Indonesian occupation between 1974 and 1999. The survey data were then matched with other kinds of data collected from statements given to the truth commission and from a census of all graveyards. These multiple sources of data were then used to estimate the total number of people who had died during the occupation using a log–linear method of estimation common in biological and epidemiological research (see International Working Group for Disease Monitoring and Forecasting, 1995; Ball *et al.*, 2003).

Survey analysis and public opinion research has also begun to explore the degree to which citizen attitudes and perceptions about human rights are in line with the actual human rights situation in countries. This research combines the standards-based indicators of human rights outlined above with random sample surveys that ask questions about respect for human rights, where typical response categories include such terms as 'a lot', 'some respect', 'not much respect', and 'no respect at all' (see Anderson *et al.*, 2005; Richards, 2006). The research effort is then to compare the perceptions of the human rights situation to the general trends in the protection of different categories of human rights either for the world (Richards, 2006), or broken down for particular regions (Anderson *et al.*, 2005; Richards, 2006). The global comparisons reveal that citizens have multiple rights referents when they formulate assessments of the human rights situation in their own countries, and that there is a moderate congruence between public opinion about the human rights situation and the actual human rights situation, which is further differentiated across regions (Richards, 2006, pp. 28–31). Across the post-communist states of Central and Eastern Europe, there is a high congruence between perceptions of human rights and actual human rights practices, but this congruence tends to be stronger for more highly educated citizens (Anderson *et al.*, 2005). Both studies represent the application of cross-cultural analysis using perceptions as a main subjective variable of interest as it relates to more objective human rights conditions.

Administrative and Socio-Economic Statistics

Administrative and socio-economic statistics produced by national statistical offices or recognized international governmental organizations have been increasingly seen as useful sources of data for the indirect measure of human rights, or as indicators for rights-based approaches to different sectors, such as justice, health, education, and welfare. Government statistical agencies and inter-governmental organizations produce a variety of socio-economic statistics that can be used to approximate measures of human rights. For example, academic and policy research has used aggregate measures of development as proxy measures for the progressive realization of social and economic rights. Such aggregate measures include the **Physical Quality of Life Index (PQLI)** and the **Human Development Index (HDI)**.[3] The PQLI is a 0 to 100 scale derived from combining equally weighted measures of the literacy rate, infant mortality, and life expectancy. In similar fashion, the HDI is a 0 to 1 scale that combines differently weighted measures of life expectancy, literacy rate, gross enrolment ratio, and per capita GDP. These two measures are highly correlated with each other and with per capita GDP, where the HDI has a higher correlation since per capita GDP is one of its components.

In both cases, the indices have been used to track both the level of development and the change in development, which are then linked to the notion of *fulfilling* social and economic rights. The PQLI represents a measure of subsistence rights (Milner *et al.*, 1999), since it captures the fundamental aspects of an individual's life and those basic requirements for human existence. For Cingranelli and Richards (2007) the PQLI can be compared to other measures in ways that capture a state's achievement in the area of economic and social rights. Accordingly, they regress the PQLI onto per capita GDP (a rough measure of ability to fulfil these rights) and Landman's (2005b) standards-based scale of ratification for the International Covenant on Economic, Social and Cultural Rights, and then save the residual, which reflects the overall level of achievement on these rights as a function of ability and willingness. Their measure is thus derived from a socio-economic statistic and a standard-based measure, which captures the idea of 'government effort to respect economic rights' (Cingranelli and Richards, 2007, p. 224).

In any such application, however, these measures are imperfect since they provide little information on the degree to which different groups in society enjoy the benefits of development. There are aggregate measures of macro-economic performance, and in the absence of a breakdown by gender, ethnicity, religion, and other social categories traditionally associated with exclusion, such measures do not yet capture a full rights dimension. Other measures, such as the percentage of women or other minority groups in society that achieve levels of literacy and/or education and the breakdown of households with access to available housing, health, and other social welfare services, can serve as indicators for the presence of possible discrimination against certain groups in the exercise of their social and economic rights. It is typical of national statistical offices to collect on an annual basis a variety of socio-economic indicators that in principle should be disaggregated by gender, age, income, and geography in ways that can provide proxy indicators for economic and social rights, but, owing to capacity issues and limited resources, sample sizes make it difficult to disaggregate the data.

KEY POINTS

There are four main ways in which human rights have been measured.

- Events-based measures count the number of human rights violations that occur within a country.

- Standards-based measures apply an overall score to countries for the relative degree to which certain human rights are protected.

- Survey-based measures capture experiences and perceptions of rights protections within countries.

- Socio-economic and administrative statistics can be used as 'proxy' measures for different categories and dimensions of human rights.

Political scientists have tended to use standards-based measures in their published research since such measures allow for the comparison of a large number of countries over time.

NGOs have been in the lead for the development of events-based measures.

Conclusion

This brief overview of the purpose, challenges, and examples of human rights measurement and monitoring shows that human rights scholars and practitioners have made great advances since the measurement agenda turned its attention to human rights. Political scientists, sociologists, statisticians, geographers, demographers, health professionals, and activists from non-governmental organizations have all contributed to the general increase in the availability of human rights measures or indicators that can be used for rights-based approaches. Despite these impressive developments, however, there remain distinct lacunae in this field. The different cells in Table 3.1 have not been filled equally with sets of valid, meaningful, and reliable indicators of human rights. There has been a bias toward the production of indicators for the respect dimension of civil and political rights (Cell 1) with events-based, standards-based, and survey-based data that cover a wide geographical and temporal range. There are aggregate measures of fulfilment of economic rights that cover a wide range of countries (Cell 6) (e.g. Cingranelli and Richards, 2007), but there is a dearth of measures for

the respect and protect dimensions for social and economic rights (Cells 4 and 5), and very little has been done on the protect and fulfil dimensions of civil and political rights (Cells 2 and 3).

These gaps in data provision are a function of ideological and theoretical biases toward civil and political rights within political science and methodological issues surrounding the measurement of economic and social rights. Increasingly, however, attempts have been made to explore the possibility of violations approaches to economic and social rights (Chapman, 1996) that will make them amenable to similar kinds of measurement strategies adopted for civil and political rights, and there has been a recognition that the protection of civil and political rights also relies on the fiscal capacity of states (Holmes and Sunstein 1999) and thus can be measured using strategies adopted for economic and social rights.

There is now an increasing demand for the provision of human rights measures from within both the academic and policy community. Political scientists have played a large part in the development, analysis, and improvement of human rights measures and will continue to do so in the future. This effort can only be enhanced through the exchange of ideas and experiences from governmental, non-governmental, and inter-governmental organizations around the world. Work will continue on the provision of events-based, standards-based, survey-based, and socio-economic and administrative statistics to capture the full picture of human rights within countries around the world.

The future for human rights measurement and monitoring will involve greater attention to all dimensions of all human rights, disaggregation of measures to assess the enjoyment of human rights within countries and among the world's most vulnerable groups, and more open communication and transparency about the ways in which different measures have been developed. These developments and the continued demand for more and better human rights measures suggest that this particular sub-tradition within the human rights field will continue to prosper in ways that can only be fruitful to the long-term goal of enhancing human dignity worldwide.

QUESTIONS

INDIVIDUAL STUDY QUESTIONS

1. Why is it important to measure human rights?
2. Who wants to develop and use human rights measures?
3. Why is it difficult to measure human rights?
4. What is the full scope of human rights that ought to be measured?
5. What are the different categories of human rights?
6. What are the different dimensions of human rights?
7. What is an events-based measure of human rights?
8. What is a standards-based measure of human rights?
9. What is a survey-based measure of human rights?
10. Why are socio-economic and administrative statistics useful for measuring human rights?

GROUP DISCUSSION QUESTIONS

a. How do the 'post-behavioural' approaches described here compare with the normative and legal approaches discussed in the previous chapters? What are the advantages and drawbacks of each?
b. Are people's perceptions of human rights different from the actual human rights condition in a country? What might be some reasons for this?
c. Why is there a tendency for less-developed countries to have worse records at protecting human rights? And is it fair to compare these countries to more wealthy countries in the Global North?
d. What are the remaining challenges for human rights measurement?

FURTHER READING

Ball, P. B., **Asher**, J., **Sulmont**, D., and **Manrique**, D. (2003). *How Many Peruvians Have Died?* Washington, DC: American Association for the Advancement of Science (AAAS). http://shr.aaas.org/peru/aaas_peru_5.pdf.
Best example of the estimation of events-based human rights data using the case of Peru 1980–2000.

Green, M. (2001). What we talk about when we talk about indicators: Current approaches to human rights measurement. *Human Rights Quarterly*, **23**, 1062–1097.
Good overview of conceptual and methodological issues surrounding the measurement of human rights.

Hafner-Burton, E. and **Ron**, J. (2007). Special issue on human rights. *Journal of Peace Research*, **44**/4.
Excellent illustration of the use of standards-based measures of human rights in political science research.

Hertel, S. and **Minkler**, L. (eds) (2007). *Economic Rights: Conceptual, Measurement and Policy Issues.*
Cambridge: Cambridge University Press.
Excellent review of the conceptual and methodological issues surrounding the measurement of economic and social rights.

Jabine, T. B. and **Claude**, R. P. (eds) (1992). *Human Rights and Statistics: Getting the Record Straight.*
Philadelphia, PA: University of Pennsylvania Press.
Great overview of human rights measurement, including theoretical and methodological issues.

Landman, T. (2004). Measuring human rights: Principle, practice, and policy. *Human Rights Quarterly*, **26**
(November), 906–931.
Comprehensive review with examples of the ways in which human rights are measured.

WEB LINKS

http://www.freedomhouse.org Freedom House: two standards-based scales on civil and political rights from 1972, updated annually.

http://www.politicalterrorscale.org Political terror scale: standards-based scale on personal integrity rights from 1976 to 2006, updated occasionally.

http://www.humanrightsdata.com Cingranelli and Richards human rights data: large collection of standards-based data on seventeen different human rights from 1980 to 2006, updated occasionally.

http://www.hrdag.org Human Rights Data Analysis Group: world-leading organization in the production and analysis of events-based data on human rights.

NOTES

1. While this ethical and analytic framework applies to civil and political rights, obligations to respect, protect, and fulfil are not yet legally recognized in connection with those rights. (Note added by editor.)

2. Freedom House relies on a large number of sources, but does not list which ones in particular are used for the production of its two scales of civil and political rights.

3. There is no single source for the PQLI as it is derived from other measures available from various international sources. In contrast, the UNDP provides annual HDI figures; see http://hdr.undp.org/statistics/. See also the statistical databases available from the United Nations http://unstats.un.org/unsd/.

ONLINE RESOURCE CENTRE

Visit the Online Resource Centre that accompanies this book for updates and a range of other resources:

http://www.oxfordtextbooks.co.uk/orc/goodhart/

Human Rights in International Relations

Tim Dunne and Marianne Hanson

Contents

Reader's Guide

Human rights have become firmly enmeshed in both the practice and study of international relations. Dominant theories of international relations explain the role of such rights in significantly different ways, and it is evident that their major claims carry persuasive arguments, indicating an uneasy juxtaposition of state sovereignty with ideas of a universal moral order. While the Cold War prevented the immediate focus on human rights that the United Nations system warranted, the growth of the UN's international human rights regime and the rise of international non-governmental organizations and human rights activists enabled a closer insertion of human rights into state diplomatic practices, a development that revealed the existence of human rights contestation itself as part of the Cold War. The ending of the Cold War heralded a 'springtime' for human rights and liberalism, but the advent of the 'war on terror' has also shown that the cascade of human rights norms might also be open to reversion, as particular states reinterpret or reject previously espoused principles. These developments raise important questions about state practice and human rights. While some norm reversion is occurring, it remains the case that states continue to be confronted with human rights challenges and display, to varying degrees, evidence of human rights protection at home and promotion abroad. Although much attention is rightly focused on changes to the internalization of such norms (such as reinterpretations of the Convention Against Torture or the restrictions of civil liberties in domestic arenas), we are also seeing an important evolution of concepts and practices on protecting human rights at the international level. This is visible in formulations such as the responsibility to protect and its attendant focus on intervention to protect human rights, and also in the recognition that the prevention of human rights abuses is vitally important.

Introduction

The prevalence of human rights in contemporary debates about world politics presents something of a puzzle to many academicians working in international relations (IR). In a geopolitical world that is dominated by states' claims to exclusive authority in their domain, human rights are a polite fiction. At least, such is the claim by political realists who have been the dominant voice in IR since the emergence of the discipline.

As we show in the first section of the chapter, realists do not have it all their own way. Liberal thinking in IR argues that it is rational for states to pursue policies congruent with human rights principles. Constructivists are also critical of realism, although for different reasons. According to them, states pursue human rights goals for reasons to do with their identity and status. The fact that there is a lively debate among the main theories of IR as to what human rights are and why actors promote them reveals an important philosophical issue about the difference between 'reality' and our theories that interpret and explain it.[1]

The second section of this chapter focuses on key controversies over human rights as understood in the discipline of IR. The first of these concerns the mismatch between the importance attached to human rights at the declaratory level and the prevalence of human rights abuses in reality. What explanation can be given for this double standard? One set of answers relates to the weak monitoring and enforcement mechanisms in the international human rights regime. Another takes us back to the question of state sovereignty, particularly the unrelenting tendency on the part of elites to support narrow national and class-based interests over universal values of justice and fairness. These controversies are discussed in accordance with the development of human rights norms in modern international society.

The third section follows organically from the narrative about the human rights story in international relations. If we are to take seriously the claim that there is a global human rights culture, then we are entitled to ask what duties that imposes upon states and other actors to protect the rights of others when they are being systematically denied. The discussion will focus on two dimensions of international responsibility. The first is the duty of protection that is incumbent on all states in light of their obligations under the various human rights covenants. In this discussion, protection applies to the 'internal' dimension of the norm of sovereignty as responsibility. The second dimension of international responsibility relates to the duty that falls on states to act as humanitarian rescuers in instances where a state is collapsing or a regime is committing gross violations of human rights.

Theoretical Issues and Context

It is commonplace in the mainstream study of IR to claim that the subject matter is 'the world of sovereign states'. It is also commonplace in mainstream IR to treat states as rational actors who seek to maximize their power or security. Both assumptions follow from what IR scholars call the assumption of *anarchy*. By this term, what is being signified is not a permanent state of war but rather the absence of an 'international state' that has the power and the authority to impose a just peace.

A good illustration of the problem of anarchy can be gleaned from Hobbes's description of how order emerges from a state of nature. In his famous book *Leviathan*, written in 1651, just as the states system was beginning to take hold in Europe, Hobbes argued that a state was a necessary condition for a durable domestic political order. The state was justified in terms of a bargain between the government, whose duty it was to provide security, and the people, who consented to obey the will of the sovereign.

Hobbes rightly argued that states did not stand in relation to one another in the same way that individuals related to one another in a state of nature. To begin with, they were fewer in number, and the vast inequality between the strongest and the weakest meant that conflicts would be short lived. Despite these differences, the Hobbesian world view is a continual reminder of the limits to cooperation—and the ever present possibility of conflict—in a decentralized system where there is no 'global Leviathan' to watch over sovereign states.

Realism

If we accept this as a starting point, then the landscape of world politics immediately seems inhospitable to human rights. The realist world is one where rules are regularly broken, and agreements last only as long as they benefit the contracting parties. As Hobbes put the problem with characteristic clarity, treaties that are not imposed by force 'are but words'.

Today's realists continue to believe that, for the most part, the diplomacy of human rights is just talk. They understand that human rights are part of the vocabulary of modern international society: after all, no state leader openly challenges the principles underpinning the human rights regime. The realist contention is that, when push comes to shove, human rights are very low on the list of national policy goals. This explains the prevalence of *double standards* in international diplomacy, whereby political leaders pay lip service to protecting human rights while at the same time allowing these principles to be undermined by the pursuit of other goals. In other words, in the final analysis, unless the promotion of human rights is in the *national interest* why would it be rational for states to pursue such goals?

The condition of international anarchy and the pursuit of the national interest are two significant reasons why realists are sceptical about human rights. A third reason is an ethical objection to the assumption of a universal morality that is in many ways the bedrock of the existing human rights regime. As the great realists of the early part of the twentieth century argued (Carr, 1946; Morgenthau, 1948), exhortations to obey the universal moral law are simply techniques to hide the pursuit of narrow selfish interests. All great powers in history have articulated universal claims: we should not be surprised if such measures benefited the dominant power. Such a convenient linkage between universal morality and the national interest was evident in the justifications for colonial possessions made by the European imperial powers in the nineteenth century, just as democracy promotion consolidated US hegemony in the modern

era. Likewise, those living outside the 'greater West' today often complain that human rights are a tool wielded by the powerful to secure various goals such as favourable terms of trade or even a change of regime.

Liberalism

Liberalism is historically the main challenger to realism in international relations. At the level of ideas, liberalism develops out of a Western tradition of thinking in which the individual has rights that public authorities must respect. While there are varieties of liberal thinking, the central idea is that individual persons have basic rights to free speech, fair treatment in terms of judicial process, and political equality enshrined in a political constitution. While Hobbes and Machiavelli are invoked by realists to justify the promotion of national self-interest, liberals look to Locke and Kant as their lodestars. Kant's pamphlet 'Perpetual Peace' (Kant, 1991) builds a theory of international liberalism in which all individuals have equal moral worth, and in which an abuse of rights in one part of the world is 'felt everywhere'.

It is easy to dismiss liberalism as being utopian. The history of statecraft from the mid-seventeenth century onwards is more readily understood in terms of conflict and aggression. But, as liberals point out, moral universalism has continued to insert itself into the practice of international politics. From the birth of the **Enlightenment** onwards, states have made significant advances in terms of meeting universal principles central to liberalism. Western states have, over time, enshrined the rights of citizens in legal constitutions, ended the trade in slaves and then the institution of slavery, agreed to protect the condition of workers, and advanced international **humanitarian law** to protect wounded or captured soldiers and to criminalize the targeting of civilians. Many of these advances that took place between the mid-nineteenth and the early twentieth centuries became codified in the internationalization of human rights in the UN system after 1945 (see Chapters 1 and 2).

As will become apparent in the following section, the implementation of human rights standards in the twentieth century has been chequered. Liberals recognize that the division of global humanity into separate sovereign states presents particular problems when it comes to embedding universal moral principles. Two kinds of responses are triggered by this dilemma. The first is the attempt to expand the liberal 'zone' such that there are fewer authoritarian states in the world; the second is to strengthen international institutions in the expectation that they can alter the incentives of member states in ways that enhance respect for human rights and human dignity.

Constructivism

Constructivism differs from realism and liberalism in that it is not a theory of human rights *per se*. What it offers students of IR is a way of thinking about the relationship between norms and interests. Unlike realists and liberals, constructivists argue that there is no necessary tension between the interests of sovereign states and the moral principles associated with the promotion and protection of human rights. The important theoretical point here concerns the constitutive nature of international political reality, specifically how states create—and are created by—shared norms and values.

The development of human rights needs to be understood according to this dynamic. As is often the case in social life, the international realm is made up of many contending sets of expectations and rules as to how actors ought to behave. While the historically dominant realist logic suggests one form of international conduct, constructivists argue that this inter-state order has been transformed by the emergence of universal values. The protection of human rights therefore becomes 'integral to the moral purpose of the modern state, to the dominant rationale that licences the organization of power and authority into territorially defined sovereign units'

(Reus-Smit, 2001, p. 520). Constructivists argue that if states reject universal values outright, they will have to pay a price: this could take the form of condemnation, exclusion, or possibly coercive measures aimed at enforcing the new standard of legitimate statehood. (Realist, liberal, and constructivist views of human rights are summarized in Table 4.1.)

KEY POINTS

While they do not deny the existence of human rights, proponents of the various theories of IR examined here (realism, liberalism, and constructivism) view the role and promotion of human rights in world politics in very different ways.

The clash between the division of the world into separate sovereign states and claims for universal moral principles is felt most keenly by realist scholars, for whom national interest will always trump calls for inserting human rights into foreign policy formulation.

Liberals view human rights as having an increasingly important role in IR and point to the spread of liberal democracy as well as the establishment of a global human rights regime as evidence of this; constructivists, for their part, note that respect for human rights can have an important effect on the forming of state identities, noting that some states seek to practise a foreign policy that is both pragmatic and principled.

Constructivists argue that, in practice, human rights should not be regarded in opposition to state sovereignty but rather as an emergent standard for legitimate statehood.

Key Controversies

Human Rights in the Cold War—Organized Hypocrisy?

Liberal histories of human rights regard the 1948 Universal Declaration of Human Rights (UDHR) as a founding document that had been brought into being because of the horrendous destructive capacity of modern states. Eleanor Roosevelt, one of its main advocates, said that it had 'set up a common standard of achievement for all people and all nations' (cited in

Risse and Sikkink, 1999, p. 1). Defenders of human rights believe the UDHR signalled a normative shift away from the absolute sovereignty presumed by states and toward the idea that all individuals should have rights by virtue of their common humanity.

The persistence of two sets of rival normative claims—one based on the rights of sovereign states and the other on the rights of individuals as members of a natural universal community—is one that IR scholars trace back many centuries. Theologians in the Columbian period

TABLE 4.1 Dimensions of human rights (HR) according to main IR theories.

| IR theories | Sectors | | |
	Moral basis of human rights	Status of institutions	Human rights in foreign policy
Realism	The logic of self-help in an anarchic system means HR are a luxury that states cannot afford. Claims to universal values mask the play of national interest.	Institutions are powerless—HR are left to the will of states. State leaders pay lip service to human rights standards.	HR can be a useful tool if they enhance the relative power of a state; the moment they work against the state's vital security interests, they must be abandoned. Using force to uphold HR values is almost always reckless and self-interested.
Liberalism	HR are an extension of natural and inalienable rights. States have a duty to protect rights—if they fail to do this their sovereign status is in question.	HR regimes (the informal rules) and institutions (e.g. the HR commission) are vital for monitoring compliance. If institutions are weak, states will 'cheat'. Legalization within the EU has meant that obligations are legally binding.	The promotion of HR is inextricably linked to the promotion of democracy and good governance. Unless HR values are embedded in state-based institutions, they will not be durable.
Constructivism	The basis of HR is the overlapping consensus that exists among actors and institutions in international and world society. It is not a 'natural' virtue but an inter-subjectively generated commitment.	Institutions matter, but the 'norm cascade' enables the researcher to track the process of socialization. Transnational social movements assist with the compliance problem by cajoling and shaming.	The realist claim about the primacy of the national interest is problematized by constructivists. Interests, they argue, are a product of the identity and values of a state or region. Therefore, we should expect rights-protecting states at home to promote HR abroad.

debated the rights of the aborigines in the Americas (see Chapter 15); peacemakers at Westphalia in 1648 included minority rights in the final treaties; and the period of British hegemony in the nineteenth century witnessed the emergence of an anti-slavery norm—albeit coexisting with the practice of colonialism, which was anything but human rights-friendly.

The contemporary struggle between the universal and particular is brought into sharp relief by the doctrine of human rights. After the euphoria of the UN General Assembly's proclamation of the UDHR, human rights advocates had to wait a further three decades before such principles began significantly to constrain the behaviour of states. In the intervening period, the call for states to live up to respecting universal rights was muted by two factors: first, the priority accorded to national security by the leading protagonists (and their allies) during the Cold War; and second, the fact that states did not allow multilateral monitoring of their human rights practices. This last point was nicely illustrated by the first session of the UN Commission

on Human Rights (in early 1947), which noted that it had 'no power to take any action in regard to any complaints concerning human rights' (Donnelly, 2003, p. 73). In other words, from the outset, human rights were overshadowed by systemic factors to do with great power rivalry and the preference by members of international society to view human rights as standards and not as enforceable commitments. With the exception of the limited group of states who were signatories to the European Convention of Human Rights, the general picture from 1945 to 1973 was one in which there was a yawning gap between standards and delivery.

Several factors converged in the mid-1970s that together signalled a step-change in the power of the human rights regime. These can be grouped into the following themes (examined in turn below): the growing legalization of human rights norms; the emergence of human rights INGOs (international non-governmental organizations); and the increased priority accorded to human rights in the foreign policies of key Western states.

Development of legal norms

In 1976 the two international human rights covenants came into force. With no little historical irony, the Czechoslovak parliament ratified the two covenants in the knowledge that this would enable the International Covenant on Civil and Political Rights (ICCPR) to come into effect. Over and above the internationalization of what Jack Donnelly calls 'an international bill of rights', other institutional changes had an important impact. The UN Commission on Human Rights became more active, in part helped by its expanded membership and the inclusion of states committed to making a difference. While the work of the Commission is largely that of information gathering and sharing, its role raises the status of human rights in the UN system. The appointment of a UN High Commissioner for Human Rights in 1993 took the profile to an even higher level.

Emergence of human rights INGOs

The 1970s also saw the emergence of INGOs committed to deepening state compliance with human rights law. Dismissed by Soviet diplomats in 1969 as 'weeds in the field' (Foot, 2000, p. 38), INGO activity was beginning to have a significant impact on state–society relations in all corners of the globe. Amnesty International (AI) is a good example. Its mission is to campaign for internationally recognized human rights (http://www.amnesty.org). Originally set up around a clutch of activists in 1961, it had over 150,000 members in more than 100 countries by 1977; today, the membership is close to 2 million with subscribers in over 150 states.

INGOs like Amnesty perform two vital functions. They act as information networks with a capacity to communicate evidence of human rights violations to their membership and the global media. If INGOs are believed to be authoritative and independent, as Amnesty is, then this information is taken seriously both by UN bodies entrusted with monitoring human rights and by other actors in global civil society. In 1977, Amnesty won the Nobel Peace Prize, and seven years later it was highly influential in the drafting of the 1984 Convention Against Torture. The second key function that human rights INGOs play in world politics is one of monitoring governments' records in complying with the treaties they have signed. Significant in this respect is the annual Amnesty International Report that documents non-compliance in countries throughout the world—a practice that other leading INGOs, such as Human Rights Watch, have emulated. When systematic non-compliance has been exposed, human rights INGOs are skilful at using print and digital media to embarrass those public bodies whose word is not as good as their bond, a technique known as naming and shaming.

Insertion of human rights into diplomacy

Of the three dynamics for change that became evident in the 1970s, probably the most significant was the intrusion of human rights into the diplomacy of Western states. In the USA, Congress was increasingly minded to pass legislation linking aid and trade to human rights. And when Jimmy Carter became president, the cause of human rights found a passionate advocate—in sharp contrast to the Nixon–Kissinger era, when they were thought to complicate the achievement of more important goals in the economic and security domains. In Western Europe, Norway and the Netherlands were becoming more activist in promoting human rights in their own foreign policies. Within the European Community (EC), and after 1993 the European Union (EU), respect for human rights had always been a condition for membership. Individuals in many European states could also bring human rights complaints against their governments through the European Court of Human Rights (ECHR), indicating a much higher level of institutionalization than is the case in the UN system (which in some instances allows for individual complaint but in which the views of the treaty bodies are not binding).

The signing of the Helsinki Accords in 1975 illustrates each type of agency at work. This agreement was the culmination of three years of negotiation among thirty-five states involved in the *Conference on Security and Cooperation in Europe* (CSCE). The Eastern bloc countries were desperate to normalize relations with the rest of Europe and have the Cold War division of Europe recognized in an international treaty. The West Europeans were pushing hard for shared commitments to fundamental human rights: while this was resisted by communist states, they eventually yielded in order to realize their gains in other issue-areas. The Accords set out ten 'guiding principles for relations among European states', including 'respect for human rights and fundamental freedom, including the freedom of thought, conscience, religion or belief' (Conference on

Security and Cooperation in Europe, Final Act, 1975). While the communist elites chose to emphasize other articles in the final declaration that underscored the principle of non-intervention in their internal affairs, activists inside their societies began a period of intense mobilization that did untold damage to the stability of communist rule. 'Less than a year after the Helsinki Final Act,' Daniel Thomas argues (see Thomas, 1999, p. 214), 'the combination of domestic mobilization and transnational networking had rendered the international normative environment inhospitable to the political status quo in Eastern Europe—precisely the opposite of what the Warsaw Pact elites intended when they called for a European security conference.' The novel feature of repeat meetings and robust and critical 'follow up' among Helsinki states, a process not found in the UN human rights system at the time, was also instrumental in the reinforcement of these human rights norms (Hanson, 1994; see Box 4.1).

The CSCE process reminds us that the Cold War, while it was preoccupied with security concerns, nuclear parity, a divided Europe, and other dominant factors, was, at its heart, also a debate about human

rights. From the Western viewpoint, the ideological divisions between East and West were not restricted to territorial contests and competing economic systems, but were also inherently about the relationship between governments and the rights they afforded their citizens. And even if Western outrage about the plight of dissidents and others in the Soviet bloc was not paramount in diplomatic discussions, neither had it been totally subsumed or forgotten in the need to avoid nuclear confrontation. Writing in 1986, R. J. Vincent reminded us that 'the history of East–West relations' was 'in an important sense the history of a dispute about human rights' (Vincent, 1986, p. 61).

After the Cold War: springtime for human rights?

By the mid-to-late 1990s, the international human rights norm had diffused widely. One key driver here was the rapid increase in the number of liberal democratic states. With the fall of communism, and countries transitioning to democracy in Latin America and Asia, it is now the case that a far larger proportion of the world's population live in what could broadly be described as liberal democratic states. (The Polity IV Project records approximately 20 states as democracies in 1945; by 2006, this number had risen to well over 90.) Such regime types are naturally hospitable to protecting individual rights; on those occasions when citizens' rights are being curtailed by excessive presidential/executive authority, liberal states contain important countervailing legal mechanisms to protect individuals.

A second key driver was the growing acquiescence of non-liberal states into the human rights regime. The 1993 Vienna World Conference on Human Rights was an important signifier of the unchallenged status of the standard, as was the signing of the ICCPR by China in 1998. These tipping points illustrate the progressive socialization of states into a framework where their internal behaviour is subject to the scrutiny of other states as well as international public opinion. Constructivist thinkers in IR talk about this process of socialization in terms of a 'norm cascade' (see Box 4.2).

Simply glancing at the website of a leading pro-democracy INGO such as Freedom House reveals how successful democratic socialization has been since 1990. Empirical data, however, is not in itself an explanation for how and why a norm of 'democratic entitlement' (Franck, 2000) emerged. Was it a triumph

---

Box 4.1 **Gorbachev's Adherence to the Helsinki Process**

Mikhail Gorbachev, leader of the Soviet Union from 1985 until its demise in 1991, cited the Helsinki Final Act as a major influence on his decision to promote human rights in the Soviet Union in the late 1980s, saying that 'what we are seeing is the unfolding of the Helsinki process in its concrete, contemporary forms' (Gorbachev, 1989). Unlike his predecessors, Gorbachev decided that the human rights provisions contained in the Helsinki Final Act and subsequent CSCE documents would be taken seriously by his government. Gorbachev had relied on Western powers to conclude urgently needed arms control agreements and this placed pressure on him to observe human rights in the Soviet Union; demands were also mounting from the many human rights NGOs operating inside the Soviet bloc and outside it. But Gorbachev believed in the importance of human rights. He also cited the Helsinki Final Act's agreement that borders in Europe could be changed, but by peaceful means only, in 1989. The end result of Moscow's adherence to all these factors was the peaceful revolutions in Eastern Europe and the Soviet Union that ultimately brought about the end of the Cold War.

Box 4.2 **The 'Norm Cascade'**

Constructivists are interested in how beliefs about human rights are translated into global norms. This issue leads directly to the relationship between domestic political practices and international standards of right conduct. Drawing on sociological theory, constructivists have developed a model of norm socialization that is referred to as a 'norm cascade'. The cascade has five phases. *Phase one* is the repression of opposition groups and the effective blocking of the influence of transnational networks. *Phase two* is where advocacy groups begin to scrutinize the activity of governments that violate the basic rights of their citizens. The reaction of the target state is one of denial, i.e. a refusal to accept that the international human rights standards invoked by INGOs are legitimate. *Phase three* is where forces of resistance are mobilized in the target state,

aided and supported by the global human rights movement; the government is inclined to make a tactical concession hoping that the problem will go away. In reality, such governments are prone to self-entrapment; in other words, they begin to take seriously opposition groups and in doing so provide them with a degree of legitimacy. *Phase four* is where governments make an effort to improve their human rights practices, recording and regarding external standards as something they ought to aspire to; however, non-compliance continues despite recognition of the validity of the international bill of rights. Finally, *phase five* occurs when the institutions of the state see themselves as being guardians of human rights; conformity to the norm becomes automatic, making its operation difficult to discern.

of political ideology (Fukuyama, 1992), a triumph of marketization, or a triumph of United States' hegemony (Ikenberry, 2001)? In complex ways, all of these accounts overlap; what matters at this juncture is to point out that the landscape of international relations looked much more hospitable to human rights in the 1990s than it had ever done before. The decision by the North Atlantic Treaty Organization (NATO) in March 1999 to use force against the Federal Republic of Yugoslavia in an attempt to end human rights abuses against Kosovo Albanians was the apogee—it seemed that power and principle were at last converging.

After 9/11: the challenge to the Torture Convention

The previous narrative about an ever-expanding zone of peace in which the rights of ordinary citizens remain sacrosanct appears, from the vantage point of today, to be something of an anachronism. Whereas the challenge to human rights during the Cold War originated from societies built on a collectivist ideology, the challenge to the human rights regime post-9/11 has been taken up by leading liberal states such as the United States and the United Kingdom.

The most graphic representation of the retreat of human rights is the haunting images of naked prisoners, first aired on CBS news in April 2004. The official reaction of the Bush Administration to the Abu Ghraib scandal was that these incidents were committed by 'a few bad apples'. Such complacency is unfounded given

that the USA has, since 9/11, systematically sought to reinterpret key articles of the International Bill of Rights, specifically in relation to the treatment of prisoners. The Secretary of Defence called for stronger interrogation techniques to be used against so-called high-value detainees. Far from refraining from cruel and degrading treatment, the Administration raised the bar for what counts as torture such that it was equated with the infliction of lasting pain commensurate with 'serious physical injury such as death or organ failure' (Bybee, 2005).

The context of the threat posed by al-Qaeda-inspired suicide bombers prompted voices inside the liberal establishment to question whether certain human rights commitments were in tension with national security. In relation to the Torture Convention, both Michael Ignatieff (2004) and Alan Dershowitz (2004) have argued that the threat of apocalyptic terrorism is such that certain exceptions to the convention ought to be permissible (see Chapter 17). The former argues that human rights infringements ought to be seen as a lesser evil, while the latter believes **torture warrants** should be considered as a way of regulating the practice. Needless to say, the response from the broadly international legal establishment has been one of horror (Greenberg and Datel, 2005).

While liberal intellectuals slug it out, governments around the world are quickly curtailing the rights of terror suspects—often so widely defined as to include political opposition movements. The general retreat from certain core human rights commitments after 9/11 reminds us that compliance to human rights norms is contingent and reversible. Moreover, human wrongs norms can 'cascade' throughout global politics just as quickly as human rights norms.

The preceding discussion has endorsed Vincent's observation that 'there is an inescapable tension between human rights and foreign policy' (Vincent, 1986, p. 129). What is also evident is that this tension has not gone away, despite the best hopes of liberal internationalists after the fall of communism. All three background theories of human rights have important contributions to make to understanding how this controversy is played out. 'Realists' remind us of the grip of state sovereignty, with its claim to absolute jurisdiction on the 'inside' and the necessity of promoting the national interest on the 'outside'. 'Liberals' remind us that the moral basis of community is not artificial sovereign states but relations between individuals, and that respecting fundamental rights is a means to furthering the wider goal of promoting what Kant described as 'a universal kingdom of ends'. 'Constructivists' highlight the mutuality of these rival normative arguments: the debate about human rights has changed what is understood by the term 'state sovereignty'.

> **KEY POINTS**
>
> Although developed as part of the 1945 UN system, the international human rights regime was marginalized by the Cold War. Yet human rights concerns had always been part of this confrontation, and came to be incorporated into East–West diplomacy from the late 1970s, thanks largely to the mobilization of transnational human rights NGOs.
>
> ---
>
> The end of the Cold War and the subsequent spread of 'zones of peace and liberal democracy' created new hopes that human rights would gain ever greater importance in international relations. Paradoxically, however, this same period also saw some of the worst abuses of human rights, in states such as Somalia, Rwanda, Bosnia, and East Timor. These represented a serious challenge to states and international organizations that were still coming to grips with how to respond to such tragedies effectively.
>
> ---
>
> The onset of the 'war on terror' has refocused attention on the human rights practices of the USA, Britain, and other states that had previously been seen as human rights champions. It is not yet clear what the full impact of this 'roll-back' of human rights principles might mean for international relations.
>
> ---
>
> Primary elements of the theories of IR remain compelling: for realists, state sovereignty has not been subsumed by alleged universal principles, while liberals will note the persistence of moral issues in international relations, notwithstanding any weakening on the part of some individual states.

Findings: Human Rights and State Practice

In this section we illustrate the impact of human rights on state sovereignty in three key respects: first, the process by which human rights standards are internalized; and second, the development of an external human rights policy in which 'a state has explicit mechanisms for integrating human rights concerns into foreign policy' (Sikkink, 1993, 143). This leads into a discussion about the Responsibility to Protect doctrine, which emerged as a response to the claim on the part of some states that there is a right of humanitarian intervention in cases of clear and widespread violations of human rights, and the new emphasis on the need to prevent atrocities—a subtle shift away from the largely reactive approach to human rights protection evident until recently.

Internalization

There is a tendency in the IR literature to focus on the narrow question of the promotion of human rights in foreign policy—often narrowing still further to the question of the forcible promotion of human rights. The danger here is that the spotlight falls on those states in the world that have the military capacity to respond to humanitarian emergencies. Instead, the spotlight should be directed more widely on all of the 150-plus signatories to the ICCPR. Remember that, for the most part, the protection of human rights begins at 'home'. It is noteworthy that former UN Secretary General Kofi Annan recognized the primacy of national human rights institutions. These institutions will, 'in the long run', ensure that 'human rights are protected', he argued.

The 'norm cascade' featured in Box 4.2 provides an analytical device for examining how far a particular state or region has progressed in terms of developing a comprehensive human rights policy. In broader terms, the first requirement for states to be able to claim that they take human rights seriously is 'to surrender a degree of sovereignty' and permit some degree of international scrutiny (Sikkink, 1993, p. 142). Such an injunction requires a detailed analysis of treaty ratification, or the mechanism by which human rights standards are embedded in domestic law.

The question of ratification leads inexorably to the discussion of variations in domestic legal orders. Paradoxically, authoritarian states find the process of ratification easier given that the Head of State retains supreme power to enact domestic laws. Democracies find the process of ratification to be longer and more complex. The adoption of a treaty in the United States, for example, requires a two-thirds vote in the Senate, rendering the process vulnerable to partisan politics. In the case of regional human rights regimes, the pattern is similar: standards are set regionally but it is left largely to domestic institutions to monitor and enforce. The one partial exception is the European Convention on Human Rights, which empowers a court to preside over petitions from states but also from individuals.

The post-9/11 period has refocused attention on the role of national courts in challenging the claim by the executive branch of government to exercise a rule of 'exception' in relation to the rights of suspected terrorists. The defeats of the executive branch of government by the United States Supreme Court and the UK High Court are indicative. In July 2004, the Supreme Court ruled that detainees at Camp Delta in Guantanamo Bay, Cuba, can take their allegation of wrongful imprisonment to an American court. The rationale offered by the Court was the ancient principle of habeas corpus, which compels the holder of the prisoner to bring him or her to trial. The Supreme Court dealt the Bush Administration another blow on 29 June 2006 when it ruled—by a 5-3 majority—that the executive had over-reached its authority in seeking to try suspects by military tribunal. In the UK, the case of unlawful detention at Camp Delta was also heard. Lawyers working for detainee Ferroz Abbassi claimed that his imprisonment was in breach of the ICCPR and that the British government

had a duty to protect those rights. Set against the government's position that it can have no meaningful view about matters of United States jurisdiction, Nicholas Blake QC dismantled this argument, referring to it as 'an old view which takes no account of modern developments in international law and human rights' (Sands, 2006, pp. 165–166). These illustrations suggest that it is not just international non-governmental organizations such as Amnesty International that monitor and shame state leaders. Box 4.3 discusses the importance of individuals and institutions outside government being prepared to make a 'noise' about human rights.

Externalization—Promoting Human Rights in Foreign Policy

The other dimension to having a comprehensive human rights policy is the incorporation of internationalist values in a country's (or conceivably a region's) foreign policy. For it to be said that a state actor has an external human rights policy, two aspects need to be present. First, the pursuit of human rights values and policies must be given strategic importance—not simply a 'desk' in a foreign ministry that regards its main business as maximizing trade and security interests. Second, there must be explicit policy instruments, as well as mechanisms for advocacy and scrutiny inside the governments of other states.

Box 4.3 Doing Something about Human Rights Abuses—The Need for 'Noise'

At the time of the Rwandan genocide in March/April 1994, Anthony Lake was a member of President Clinton's National Security Council. In retrospect, he argues that the Administration he served never seriously addressed the problem of how to effectively respond to the bloodletting that cost the lives of up to one million Rwandan citizens. From a policy perspective, the problem was that 'nobody was for it'. Lake argues that those outside of government who believed intervention would have succeeded should have created 'more noise' that would have helped people like him inside government. 'Noise means television interviews. Noise means newspaper articles. Noise can even mean peaceful demonstrations, etc.' (From PBS documentary, 'Ghosts of Rwanda'. http://www.pbs.org/wgbh/pages/frontline/shows/ghosts/interviews/lake.html. Cited in Michael Barnett (2008, pp. 198–199))

The remainder of the chapter focuses on an aspect of human rights that brings together these internal and external dimensions. Especially after 1989, key Western states recognized that the liberal values that defeated communism were *universal* values. The so-called 'King's peace', by which states turned a blind eye to what was going on inside other countries' borders, was no longer tolerable. Having a comprehensive human rights policy meant insisting on the legitimate appraisal of the internal conduct of all states (Vincent, 1986, p. 152). For states to be in conformity with the new standard of civilization, they had to not only protect human rights inside their own borders, but also actively support basic rights externally (Reus-Smit, 2001).

This duty to 'do something' was being championed by norm entrepreneurs inside several key states, driven in part by the horrific abuses witnessed in Somalia and Rwanda, in the Balkan wars, and in East Timor. By the end of the century, however, inconsistency in its application—or worse, inaction in the face of genocide in the case of Rwanda—triggered an important debate about the circumstances in which it is right to engage in armed intervention in the affairs of other sovereign states without their consent.

The Canadian government was particularly supportive of a new initiative to tackle the conceptual, legal, moral, and operational challenges of reconciling intervention with state sovereignty. This initiative, the International Commission on Intervention and State Sovereignty (ICISS) grappled with the need to keep alive the case for humanitarian intervention in a world that was not always receptive to the idea, and which was rapidly coming to be dominated by the major Western powers' emphasis on the war on terrorism. This state-sponsored Commission's task was to find a way to bridge the international community's responsibility to act when faced with clear violations of humanitarian norms, while still respecting the perennial issue of the sovereign rights of states. As one observer claimed, this was the 'problem from hell' (Evans, 2007). A new orientation evolved from these discussions, utilizing the term the responsibility to protect (or R2P as it has come to be known). The extensive deliberations of the ICISS firmly placed the responsibility to uphold human rights and protect citizens primarily on the state itself. All countries had a responsibility to protect their citizens from genocide, war crimes, ethnic cleansing, and crimes against humanity. But where a state manifestly failed to do this, the international

community would now share a collective responsibility to respond. Thus, only in the event that a state would not or could not protect its people would outside intervention be considered; a respect for sovereignty was therefore coupled with a clearly articulated *responsibility* of the international community to respond appropriately in the event that a state failed to live up to its duties.

This formulation did much to strengthen the view that the responsibility to protect human rights lies first and foremost with individual governments. In doing so, it continues the elaboration of the notion of 'sovereignty as responsibility' articulated by Deng *et al.* (1996), which no longer sees sovereignty as a protection against intervention but rather as a notion and practice that carries with it undeniable obligations to citizens to whom a sovereign government is accountable. The implication here is far-reaching: sovereignty as an entitlement is conditional upon the promotion and protection of the rights of citizens. Further, accountability is due, not only to a state's domestic population, but to an international community also (Thakur, 2002; Etzioni, 2006). Similar notions of sovereignty were elaborated in the United Nations (2004) publication 'A more secure world', the commissioned report of the High Level Panel on Threats, Challenges, and Change, and these various reports have now come to influence academic thinking on human rights to a substantial degree. (There is also a resonance here with the conceptual and operational elements of the International Criminal Court, which also places responsibility primarily on the relevant state to prosecute its citizens who have violated international norms. Again, where a state fails or is unable to do this, the responsibility to do so falls on external bodies.)

The Responsibility to Protect, the Responsibility to Prevent

The International Commission on Intervention and State Sovereignty (ICISS, 2001) report 'The Responsibility to Protect' has come to be seen as a pivotal document on the place of human rights in IR. It iterated a number of basic principles: first among these was the view (outlined above) that state sovereignty implies responsibility and that primary responsibility for the protection of its people clearly lies with the state itself; where clear evidence shows a state unable or unwilling to act to protect its people from serious harm, the principle of sovereignty yields to the international responsibility to protect. This made it clear that the 'debate about intervention . . . should focus not on the "right to intervene" but on the "responsibility to protect" ' and that 'the change in terminology' signalled also a 'change in perspective'. The report notes that its foundations lie clearly within, first, the obligations 'inherent in the concept of sovereignty' itself, and then in the specific legal obligations enshrined in human rights and humanitarian law, in the deliberations of the United Nations Security Council, and in the developing practice of states.

The report identifies three main elements of the R2P formulation: the responsibility to *prevent* atrocities and other abuses of human rights, the responsibility to *react* in the event that these abuses occur, and finally, the responsibility to *rebuild* the structures and institutions of a community after an intervention so as to prevent a recurrence of such violations. Of these three, prevention has been accorded the highest priority, distancing the report from any alleged association with a 'rush to intervene' (see Chapter 19). Prevention is to include measures for building state capacity, assistance supporting the operation of the rule of law, and mechanisms for remedying grievances. As Evans (2008) stressed, 'non-intrusive and non-coercive measures are always to be preferred, at both the prevention and reaction stages, to more intrusive and coercive ones.' Additionally, and conscious of the problems that plagued (to varying degrees) the interventions of the 1990s, the report suggests a broad range of interventionary measures—political, diplomatic, economic, legal, and in the last resort, military. The ethical and strategic contexts of any intervention also require attention, and here the report stipulates guidelines that address the just cause threshold, the precautionary principles that must be applied, the question of right authority, and operational principles.

That the challenges of responding to human rights violations remained paramount in international relations was demonstrated when, in 2005, the UN World Summit and, importantly, the UN Security Council adopted the responsibility to protect as a new doctrine, in theory, at least, removing the difficulties associated with sovereignty and the external application of human rights. The Co-Chair of the ICISS noted that:

The international community has too often in the past stood paralysed between the competing imperatives of intervention to protect human rights catastrophically at risk, and that of non-intervention in the internal affairs of sovereign states. Throughout the 1990s there was fundamental disagreement between those—mainly in the global North—arguing for a 'right to humanitarian intervention', and those, mainly in the global South, who feared that any recognition of such a 'right' would mean a revival of old imperialist habits and put often newly-won and still-fragile independence at risk. It was necessary to cut through that deadlock, and 'R2P' did that, by using language which clearly changed the emphasis from 'right' to 'responsibility', by approaching the issue from the perspective of the victims rather than any potential intervener. (Evans, 2008)

The position of human rights in IR has been receiving attention in other forums also, reinforcing an analysis that the externalization of human rights norms is a growing trend. The increasing focus on *conflict prevention* as a key tool in protecting human rights anticipated the emphasis on preventing atrocities, and its terminology resonates with R2P. Early warning mechanisms and conflict prevention are not only relatively new areas of study in the disciplines of IR and peace and conflict resolution, but have also been adopted as essential elements in the practice of human rights protection and humanitarian projects. Examples include the ongoing work of the Organization for Security and Cooperation in Europe (OSCE), the EU, and the Organization of African Unity (now the African Union), the latter of which established in 1993 a Mechanism for Conflict Prevention, Management, and Settlement. In turn, the Economic Community of West Africa States (ECOWAS) established in 2000 a Mechanism for Conflict Prevention, Management, Resolution, Peace, and Security, clearly signalling a shift away from reactive responses toward global and regional proactive initiatives to protect populations.

The area of development studies in IR is also replete with the intrusion of human rights into its agenda (see Chapter 10). While a rights-based approach might have been implicit in early formulations of development practice, the argument now is that it should be explicitly and firmly embedded in discourses of poverty reduction and on the operations of institutions such as the World Bank and the International Monetary Fund (Nelson and Dorsey, 2003; Gready and Ensor, 2005; Uvin 2007).

Do these new areas of discussion move us significantly forward in being able to uphold human rights in the practice of international politics? Has a new formulation on the responsibility to protect, an emphasis on conflict prevention, and the insertion of rights-based approaches into development theory and practice moved us any further? There are at least two criticisms that can be placed at the door of these innovations in thinking about human rights in international relations. The first is that they might foster expectations of protection that are unrealizable in reality. The second and related factor is that, while these formulations might have provided useful conceptual tools for addressing the worst kinds of human rights abuse, and even go so far as to specify guidelines for intervention, they have not been put to the test in practical terms. The widespread violation of fundamental human rights in Darfur continues, and so does poverty at an unacceptable level.

Human rights and state practice coexist at a complicated and uneasy level, but—if recent developments are to be believed—also a workable level. International human rights regimes are slowly evolving to make symbolic, if not yet actually substantive, progress, as demonstrated by the Prosecutor of the International Criminal Court's July 2008 move to charge Sudan President Omar Bashir with genocide, crimes against humanity, and war crimes. These are the first charges of genocide and the first charge against a head of state to be brought before the Court. And while the enormity of the Darfur tragedy reminds us of the inability of international institutions to put a quick end to this conflict, the 'Human Security Report' (2005) documents that there has nevertheless been a significant decrease in the number and intensity of such conflicts worldwide. Many of these conflicts, as Darfur clearly shows, have in the past typically allowed violations of human rights and mass atrocities. All this would indicate that an emphasis on peacekeeping and conflict prevention might be a key element in avoiding human rights abuses in the future.

If this section has shown us anything, it has shown that, even if there has been a reverse cascade of human rights norms in some instances—for example, regarding torture, rendition, and the curtailing of civil liberties in some states—the slow weaving of human rights threads into the fabric of international politics continues.

But neither is this cause for complacency; just as in the Cold War we did not see an absence of the championing of human rights, so too in the arguably more liberal and progressive period of global history following the Cold War do we see that rights can easily be reinterpreted and even jettisoned.

These contrasting developments remind us of the complex nature of the relationship between sovereignty, power, and norms. On the one hand, evidence of a 'reverse norm cascade' when we see practices of torture might lead us to conclude that human rights have not progressed greatly since the end of the Cold War (just as it is interesting to note that, even during the Cold War, human rights as an issue was well and truly alive). On the other hand, recent years have seen some important conceptual reformulations and the growing allocation of resources for peacekeeping and conflict prevention that have brought about decreases in conflict, especially in the region of Africa. In other words, at a day-to-day level, much is going on in terms of promoting human rights in international relations, even if what is most visible to us is the focus on Abu Ghraib and Guantanamo Bay.

KEY POINTS

Two elements of human rights protection in the practice of states need to be present in any claims that norm cascades are successfully occurring: first is the internalization of human rights norms where the rights of citizens are enshrined in domestic legal and social practices; the second, an externalization of these norms, can be seen as a commitment to international human rights regimes and an acceptance of a responsibility to protect human rights where abuses are evident in other states.

The formulation of the responsibility to protect assists in this second element of externalization. At the same time that it endows sovereignty with primacy—but also with responsibility—it focuses attention on the need for states to act *outside* their borders and sometimes against other states, in order, as Nicholas Wheeler has put it, to 'save strangers'.

State practice has also recognized the need to engage in early warning and conflict prevention, and this is a growing area of study in IR.

Conclusion

The nexus between human rights and mainstream IR is both productive and at the same time troublesome. It is productive in the sense that the normative choice about where to begin—with a world of individuals or a world of states—ineluctably leads the researcher to consider the impact of the actors on the other side of the ledger. It only takes a moment's reflection about the daily life of human rights fieldworkers to illustrate how embedded their role is in the inter-state order: their work is conditional on the consent of the host government, their employer will require recognition by its 'home' government and in some cases direct funding from it, and their likelihood of success depends on whether the regional and international conditions are conducive to some kind of progress on furthering human rights goals.

This productive tension can also be troublesome at times. It requires advocates to be aware of the complexities of the world political system and the plain but uncomfortable truth that there are often competing justice claims on the part of different actors. No simple appeal to universal rights on the part of one constituency is likely to be the basis of an adequate resolution.

The example of Indigenous peoples' rights is instructive here (see Chapter 15). Often with just cause, Indigenous groups claim a special category of rights related to their common experience of violent dispossession and social deprivation. But who has a responsibility to redress these wrongs? Is it ordinary settlers who have built their lives on the land that once belonged to the first nation peoples? Or is it the regional or federal government who has a duty of care? Even more distantly, it could be argued that the imperial politics of the old European empires was the underlying cause of the condition in which Indigenous peoples find themselves. The chapter has demonstrated that these questions can only be answered in the context of theoretical understandings of what human rights are and how they relate to other moral and political goals. As the debate between security and liberty after 9/11 illustrates, the choice is seldom a straightforward one in which values can be pitted against interests. Rather, as Weber put it over a century ago, the choice is often between irreconcilable moral values.

QUESTIONS

INDIVIDUAL STUDY QUESTIONS

1. Why has the study of international relations not focused on human rights until relatively recently?
2. In what way might realists, who argue that human rights have no place in foreign policy, share views with those who claim that universal human rights are 'a Western imposition'?
3. What are the elements of a liberal approach to human rights in IR?
4. How might we best explain the emergence of a universal human rights regime?
5. What kinds of mechanisms and processes might enable human rights norms to 'cascade'?
6. What role did human rights activists play in ending the Cold War?

GROUP DISCUSSION QUESTIONS

1. Has the universal human rights regime been irredeemably damaged by the practices of certain Western states in the 'war against terror'?
2. Can the responsibility to protect mean anything more than words?
3. Can states like the USA, Britain, and Australia (the main actors in the 2003 invasion of Iraq) legitimately continue to raise human rights concerns in other states?
4. Are human rights issues 'here to stay' in international relations?

FURTHER READING

Donnelly, J. (2003). *Universal Human Rights in Theory and Practice* (2nd edn). Ithaca, NY: Cornell University Press.
A very useful introduction to the theory and practice of human rights.

Dunne, T. and **Wheeler**, N. J. (eds) (1999). *Human Rights in Global Politics*. Cambridge: Cambridge University Press.
A wide-ranging collection of writings on human rights and international relations.

Forsythe, D. P. (ed.) (2000). *Human Rights and Comparative Foreign Policy*. Tokyo: United Nations University Press.
Examines the role of human rights in the practice of various foreign policy approaches.

Forsythe, D. P. (2006). *Human Rights and International Relations* (2nd edn). Cambridge: Cambridge University Press.
A comprehensive examination of the place of human rights in international politics.

Freeman, M. (2002). *Human Rights: A Multidisciplinary Approach*. Cambridge: Polity Press.
A useful account of the various approaches to human rights.

Vincent, R. J. (1986). *Human Rights and International Relations*. Cambridge: Cambridge University Press.
A classic account of human rights, linking these to the theoretical approach of 'international society'.

Weiss, T. G. (2007). *Humanitarian Intervention: Ideas in Action*. Cambridge: Polity Press.
Charts the evolution of ideas about humanitarian intervention.

Wheeler, N. J. (2001). *Saving Strangers: Humanitarian Intervention in International Society*. Oxford: Oxford University Press.
An early analysis of the conceptual and practical challenges of interventions, especially those of the 1990s.

WEB LINKS

http://www.amnesty.org/ Homepage of Amnesty International. Amnesty International is best known for its practices of campaigning and its international solidarity with the victims of human rights abuses. It works by mobilizing public pressure and lobbying directly to influence governments, companies, and international organizations worldwide. Established in 1961, by 2007 it had 2.2 million members in 150 countries.

http://www.hrw.org/ Homepage of Human Rights Watch. Human Rights Watch arose directly out of the Helsinki process and the Helsinki Watch human rights monitoring groups. Formed in 1978, it is the largest human rights organization based in the United States.

http://www.un.org/rights/ United Nations Human Rights bodies. This website is a doorway to the many inter-related United Nations human rights treaties and subsidiary organizations.

http://www.crisisgroup.org/home/index.cfm Homepage of the International Crisis Group. The ICG was formed in 1995 as a response to the human rights tragedies of Somalia, Rwanda, and Bosnia to provide early warning of conflicts, field-based analysis, and policy prescriptions to governments and other NGOs involved in conflict analysis, prevention, and resolution. Unlike many other similar NGOs, its senior management team comprises former government members and prominent statesmen and stateswomen.

http://www.osce.org/odihr/ Homepage of the Office for Democratic Institutions and Human Rights (Organization for Security and Cooperation in Europe). ODIHR is the subsidiary body within the OSCE (the successor to the Helsinki process) that seeks to protect human rights and fundamental freedoms in the fifty-six member states of the OSCE, whose geographical scope extends from Vancouver to Vladivostock. Based in Warsaw, ODIHR is committed to the protection of minorities, upholding the rule of law and the transition to democracy in the region.

http://www.cidh.org/DefaultE.htm Homepage of the Inter-American Commission on Human Rights (IACHR). The IACHR is an autonomous organ of the Organization of American States (OAS). It was established in 1959, following the American Declaration on the Rights and Duties of Man adopted in Colombia in 1948. In 1969, the IACHR adopted the American Convention on Human Rights. Although of relatively limited effectiveness during the early decades of its existence, the IACHR is reputed to have strengthened its capacities substantially since the late 1990s, as demonstrated, for instance, in its robust prosecution of former Peruvian leader Alberto Fujimori in 2008.

http://www.achpr.org/ Homepage of the African Commission on Human and Peoples' Rights (ACHPR). The ACHPR was established under the authority of the African Charter of Human and Peoples' Rights, itself entering into force in 1986 under the aegis of the Organization of African Unity (now the African Union). Based in Banjul, Gambia, the ACHPR's members are elected by the OAU's Heads of State and Government.

NOTE

1. We note here that IR theories also include 'critical international theory' and that this approach commands increasing attention from IR scholars focused on normative change in the international system. We do not, however, examine critical theory here because of space restraints, but also because we believe there is considerable congruence—although the extent of this might be debated—between critical theory and constructivism. Scholars examining these issues include Linklater (1998, 2007) and Reus-Smit and Price (1998).

ONLINE RESOURCE CENTRE

Visit the Online Resource Centre that accompanies this book for updates and a range of other resources:

http://www.oxfordtextbooks.co.uk/orc/goodhart/

Human Rights in Comparative Politics

Sonia Cardenas

Chapter Contents

Reader's Guide

Comparative politics—the study of political life within countries—has contributed significantly to our understanding of human rights. On the one hand, this subfield of political science has advanced our knowledge of why states sometimes engage in repression, arbitrarily killing people or practicing torture. Domestic incentives and exclusionary ideologies, for example, are said to increase the likelihood of rights violations. On the other hand, comparative politics has attempted to explain human rights protection, showing how domestic structures (both societal groups and state institutions) can influence reform efforts. This chapter begins by considering alternative logics of comparison, including the merits of comparing a small versus a large number of cases and human rights within or across regions. The leading domestic-level explanations for why human rights are violated and protected are then reviewed, followed by a discussion of how domestic–international linkages can be indispensable for explaining otherwise perplexing human rights outcomes. The chapter concludes with an overview of the various ways in which, in the context of globalization, comparative politics shapes human rights practices.

Introduction

Human rights and domestic politics go hand in hand. Despite the importance of international relations (Chapter 4), domestic politics is vitally important to understanding contemporary human rights. Most human rights abuses occur within the borders of a single country, even if their effects spill over into neighbouring states and elicit global pressure. Human rights norms, moreover, are fundamentally about how states should treat those under their authority. When rights are violated, the domestic context helps to reveal the sources of abuse, the strength of resistance, and the prospects for change. Could we understand the killing fields of Cambodia, apartheid in South Africa, femicide in Latin America, past civil rights struggles in the United States, the persistence of torture and child soldiers, or the proliferation of human rights treaties without examining domestic politics? Put simply, domestic factors (political, economic, and social) are inextricably linked to human rights practices.

Comparative politics—the systematic study of domestic political life, or politics within countries—is an essential tool for grappling with human rights complexities. Its focus is on how domestic interests, identities, and institutions shape political outcomes.

Both the state and society are important domestic actors, influencing human rights practice. Methodologically, comparativists highlight similarities and differences between countries and over time, seeking to isolate significant causes and offer compelling explanations. They compare, not only countries as wholes, but the many discrete and varied political phenomena within countries to achieve a better understanding of the rich diversity of political life in the world. These methods and explanations are the hallmark of comparative human rights research.

Indeed, human rights practices lend themselves particularly well to comparative research because they vary so widely. For example, it is not altogether self-evident why states violate (and protect) human rights to such differing degrees. Why do human rights violations occur? And what are the sources of human rights reform? This chapter is structured around these central questions. The chapter also discusses how comparative politics and international relations are closely interconnected. To put these issues in context, we open with an overview of alternative strategies for comparing human rights practices in an increasingly interdependent world.

The Logic of Comparison

Comparing human rights practices is an essential tool for understanding the sources of abuse and reform. Comparisons allow us to isolate similarities and differences meaningfully, in an attempt to understand underlying causal mechanisms. Take the example of truth commissions (see Chapter 20). If the goal is to understand the conditions under which truth commissions are effective, studying only one commission may be of limited value. Guatemala, for example, had a very well-known truth commission in the 1990s, but focusing on it alone could be misleading: the findings could be unique to Guatemala, given the country's long and bloody civil war and its large rural-Indigenous population. A more useful approach would

be to compare Guatemala's commission with its counterparts elsewhere (Hayner, 2002). In general, then, drawing broader conclusions about human rights practices requires comparing cases across space or over time.

Scholars have applied various logics of comparison to better understand human rights outcomes, and these strategies are available to any student of human rights. Three sets of approaches, in particular, depict the state of comparative human rights research: single case studies; multiple cases using quantitative methods; and a small number of cases, compared within a region or cross-regionally. Each approach has its strengths and weaknesses.

First, one can examine human rights in a single case, with an eye to determining changes over time. The advantage of focusing on only one case such as South Africa is that, given limited time and resources for conducting research, it affords greater depth and detail of coverage. The disadvantage is that evaluating human rights in a single episode can be of limited generalizability, that is, hard to extend to other cases.

Second, human rights practices can be compared across multiple cases, relying on either a large or small number of cases. A very large number of cases can be examined using statistical methods; this quantitative approach requires careful measurement of human rights conditions and other factors (see Chapter 3). The advantage of this approach is that numerous factors can be considered simultaneously and the findings can be relatively reliable. Large-scale comparisons are routinely used in studies seeking to explain why states engage in repression. A typical study might examine more than 100 countries around the world over a ten-year period or longer, measuring different types of repression (e.g. torture and arbitrary killings) and a range of potentially relevant variables. The difficulty is that the analysis may not be as rich in historical or other detail. And while large-scale quantitative studies can tell us how different factors are related to one another, i.e. correlated in a statistically significant manner, these studies are not always capable of tracing causal mechanisms. For example, establishing that democracy and human rights protection are correlated

is not the same as showing *why* democracy enhances human rights. Yet the logic underlying this claim may have important policy implications for those deciding whether force should be used to promote democracy abroad.

Third, fewer cases may be compared without having to rely on statistical methods. Such comparisons can either be restricted to a single region of the world or span more than one region. Even comparing two cases can be very productive, as long as the comparison is structured carefully so that the same questions are addressed across cases. A recent study (Hertel, 2006) comparing why transnational human rights campaigns vary in their effectiveness illustrates this. That study compared transnational campaigns surrounding economic and social rights in Bangladesh and Mexico: while the two countries were very similar in many ways, the campaigns succeeded to varying degrees, revealing how domestic politics mediates transnational influence.

As for comparing human rights practices within a single region—Africa, Asia, Europe, or Latin America—there may be compelling reasons for doing so. The evidence suggests that countries within a single region are more likely to have similar human rights practices, including treaty ratification and levels of repression (see Table 5.1). Comparative politics itself, moreover, has until recently been organized largely in terms of 'area studies', on the assumption that regions are somewhat unique. Likewise, elaborate regional systems of

TABLE 5.1 Human rights practices by region, post-2000.

Human rights practice	Africa	Asia	Europe and North America	Latin America and the Caribbean
Disappearances	Low	Low	Low	Low
Extra-judicial killing	Medium	Medium	Low	Medium
Political imprisonment	Medium	Medium	Low	Low
Torture	High	Medium	Medium	Medium
Freedom of association	Medium	Medium	High	High
Freedom of movement and speech	Medium	Medium	Medium	Medium
Electoral self-determination	Medium	Medium	High	High
Religious freedom	Medium	Low	Medium	Medium
Workers' rights	Medium	Medium	Medium	Medium
Women's economic and social rights	Medium	Medium	High	Medium

Note: Adapted from CIRI Human Rights Data Project (http://ciri.binghamton.edu/index.asp). Data covers the years 2000–2007.

human rights protection—comprised of treaties and other institutions—exist in Europe, the Americas, and Africa, reinforcing the view that regions are unique: rights protections are fairly similar within a region but rather different across regions.

Cross-regional human rights comparisons are nonetheless on the rise, as the previous example of Bangladesh and Mexico indicates. The area-studies approach has come under critical scrutiny, as observers question the value of treating regions as unique entities in the context of globalization. The tendency today is to treat regions less as natural, discrete, and unchanging blocs—cultural stereotypes—and more as historically constructed and thus dynamic entities. Cross-regional comparisons provide an emerging and potentially productive tool for understanding human rights practices around the world.

KEY POINTS

Comparing human rights practices is an essential strategy for revealing significant factors and processes. Human rights practices can be compared across countries, over time, and between issues or campaigns.

Comparisons can vary depending on whether they focus on a few or many cases and on whether they examine human rights in a single world region or cross-regionally. Single cases provide richness and depth; multiple cases offer greater opportunity for generalization.

Statistical methods can be used to compare a large number of cases, simultaneously evaluating the role of numerous factors in explaining outcomes such as state repression.

Cross-regional comparisons of human rights practices are becoming increasingly common.

The Sources of State Repression

Understanding why human rights violations occur is essential. Only by comprehending the root causes of abuse can effective human rights policies be devised to prevent future violations. It is no surprise that scholars have invested a great deal of energy in explaining the vexing question of why human rights violations occur. What moves people to commit atrocities against others, even their neighbours? The conventional wisdom often points to evil or sadistic individuals as the source of human rights violence. A comparative perspective tells us, however, that most human rights violations are fundamentally political: deliberate acts of non-legalized violence or exclusion, most often by the state, targeting those it considers a threat.

Of all human rights abuses, physical integrity violations have perhaps attracted the most attention. More commonly known as repression, coercion, or state terror, physical integrity violations entail the use or threat of violence by the government or its agents. These violations can take various forms, including torture, extra-judicial killings, political imprisonment, and disappearances. While physical integrity violations are not the only, or even necessarily the most

important, human rights abuses, they are particularly common and egregious.

Most accounts of state repression begin with the premise that human rights violations are choices made by rational decision makers. Accordingly, decision makers calculate the costs and benefits of alternative courses of action and choose to engage in repression. Proceeding from this assumption, scholars have attempted to understand which factors are most likely to shape the decision to repress. Under what conditions, that is, will decision makers think it is beneficial to engage in repression, or too costly not to engage in it?

Incentives to Repress

States engage in repression for numerous, mutually reinforcing reasons. Table 5.2 identifies some of the most prominent sources of state repression (see Carey and Poe, 2004). These factors vary in their significance, with only some conditions increasing substantially the likelihood of state repression, including past repression, low levels of democracy, weak economic development,

TABLE 5.2 Sources of state repression: hypotheses and evidence.

Source	Hypothesis	Evidence
Past repression	Repression in the recent past makes future repression more likely	Strong
Democracy	Lower levels of democracy result in higher levels of repression	Strong
Economic development	Repression is greater in poorer countries	Strong
International and civil war	Repression is more likely in the context of war	Strong
Threats and dissent	Repression is greater where states face armed threats and social dissent	Strong
Population size	Repression is greater in countries with large populations	Strong
Military regimes	Countries with military regimes are more repressive	Strong
Economic growth	Rapid economic growth leads to greater state repression	Mixed
Population growth	Repression is greater in countries with high population growth	Mixed
British cultural influence	Repression is greater in countries that were *not* British colonies	Mixed
Leftist regime	Countries with a leftist political regime are more repressive	Mixed
International trade	Countries with low levels of international trade engage in greater repression	Mixed
Ethnic or cultural diversity	Ethnically divided countries are more likely to engage in repression	Mixed

war, as well as the existence of domestic political threats and dissent. The effects of past repression are straightforward. Once a state engages in repression it can be difficult to break the cycle. Repression, after all, depends on an institutional apparatus that may be costly to dismantle. Rules and regulations lay the foundations for repression, stipulating the permissible limits of state action; organizational structures arrange state agents into specialized units (e.g. death squads), while prisons and clandestine detention facilities allocate physical 'spaces' for repression to occur.

The evidence is also overwhelming that state repression relates closely to the level of democracy and, to a somewhat lesser extent, economic development (Chapters 8 and 10). While it may not seem too surprising that weaker democracies and poorer countries are generally more repressive, it is the logic underlying these claims that is most significant. Leaders of non-democracies who engage in repression do not tend in the short term to risk losing power, as elections are either non-existent or rigged. Democracies, in contrast, tend to resolve domestic conflicts peacefully, even if they also engage in repression. Thus, European democracies respect a broad range of human rights, while often mistreating immigrant communities whose members are not citizens and therefore cannot vote. Poverty is another factor that exacerbates repression.

Poorer countries tend to have higher levels of unmet social demands; governments cannot provide basic needs and services, so they are more likely to resort to repression to maintain social control. Of course, not all poor countries have high levels of repression, but poverty is one structural factor that pushes states in that direction.

Another powerful incentive for states to engage in repression is war, whether civil or international. This too may seem unsurprising, given that human rights atrocities so often accompany war. Despite the existence of international humanitarian law, designed to constrain human rights abuses such as the targeting of civilians during armed conflict, wars create a climate of extremism where repression is often seen as a legitimate tool. And, given the perceived high stakes associated with war, leaders may calculate that violating human rights norms is a necessary and relatively low-risk strategy. Even when repression is not deliberate state policy, the breakdown of chains of command and legal systems during armed conflict may permit local state agents to act autonomously and violate human rights (this is one factor contributing to the incidence of rape in wartime).

More broadly, states often respond to armed threats, social dissent or protest, and other challenges to their authority with repression, what one scholar calls the law of coercive response (see Davenport, 2000, 2007b; Davenport *et al.*, 2005). As the actor with a monopoly on the legitimate use of force, states tend to guard zealously their prerogative to rule: governments are often willing to resort to violence to retain a hold on power. Even democracies lash out when faced with concerted threats to their rule, as indicated by the post-9/11 response of the United States. Yet democracies are more likely to have a higher threshold of tolerance for dissent than non-democracies (e.g. they may accept non-violent social protests), just as their response to perceived threats may not be as extensive (e.g. targeting a relatively small group of people or subverting due process but not shooting indiscriminately into a crowd). Despite their differences, all regimes tend to respond to armed challenges with coercion, albeit to varying degrees.

Other factors play a more ambiguous role in state repression. For example, the evidence is mixed regarding the role of economic growth and trade. On the one hand, proponents of globalization (including international financial institutions such as the World Bank) contend that economic growth and trade are good for human rights, trickling down to benefit society as a whole. Sceptics, on the other hand, emphasize how rapid economic growth and intensive globalization—i.e. interpenetration of global economic forces and local markets—can produce social dislocation, as the rewards of economic liberalization are often distributed unequally throughout a population, while exacerbating social inequality and discontent (see Chapter 11).

Likewise, contrary to much conventional wisdom, it is ambiguous whether countries with greater ethnic or cultural diversity are more repressive. Despite the fact that minority groups are often the targets of concerted abuse, it does not appear that a large presence of minority groups *causes* repression. This challenges the view that diverse groups 'can't get along' or that long-standing cultural clashes underlie human rights atrocities, including the dismal picture of abuse often portrayed in Africa. Rather, when ethnic diversity is associated with repression, it may be more useful to examine the following: how political institutions such as statehood (in turn influenced by historical processes such as colonialism) shape group interactions; how powerful actors inside and outside states construct, and capitalize on, social animosities; or how the media perpetuates myths about the sources of ethnic violence.

Exclusionary Ideologies

Rather than directly shaping decision makers' calculations about the utility of engaging in repression, exclusionary ideologies define the conditions under which it seems *appropriate* to repress certain categories of people. Indeed, ideologies and identities can be powerful **non-materialist** sources of state repression (Cardenas, 2007). Whereas international law stipulates that human rights be applied universally to all people, national ideologies and identities often exclude groups of people from human rights protection in practice.

Among the most powerful exclusionary ideologies is **national security doctrine**, which legitimates the state's use of coercion to contain social instability and guarantee national security. This ideology was very influential during the **Cold War**, especially in Latin America, and it has seen something of a resurgence in the context of the war on terror after 9/11. National security doctrine and similar ideologies provide a rationale for why it is acceptable and even necessary to respond to societal challenges with repression. Opponents are labelled 'enemies', 'subversives', and 'terrorists', regardless of the more complex political reality. Without understanding the role of such ideologies, it is not self-evident why states would respond to armed threats so often with violence. States tend to be far more powerful than extremist groups, capable of marshalling substantial bureaucratic resources (including law enforcement agencies and legal systems) to contain perceived threats. Repression is rarely *necessary*, but it is quite often deemed acceptable.

Exclusionary ideologies can also deny some people human rights protections on the basis of their identity. Those whose identity is perceived as somehow threatening to mainstream identities can become the targets of systemic discrimination. Such ideologies often underlie the discrimination and physical repression of people on the basis of gender, sexual preference, race, religion, or ethnicity. For instance, in many parts of the world, gay, lesbian, bisexual, and trans-gendered persons are targets of violence. Even in cases where the state does not actively persecute people on the basis of their identity, it often fails to investigate cases of abuse and punish perpetrators. In Mexico, for example, *femicide*—the systematic and targeted killing of women—continues unabated, with little intervention from state authorities.

Similar stories can be told of the persecution of ethnic and religious minorities around the world.

Exclusionary ideologies are most influential when they are institutionalized. For instance, when exclusionary ideologies become embedded in national laws, they help structure the routines and procedures followed by state agencies. Remarkably, most states bother to justify state repression in terms of national laws, including resorting to 'emergency' (i.e. exceptional) rule or legislation to legitimize actions that are illegal internationally. Exclusionary ideologies also become part of professional training, part and parcel of how ordinary people can be transformed into torturers (Chapter 17). When agents of the state are indoctrinated about the threats that certain groups pose to national well-being and survival, and then given the tools to repress, they are primed to commit unfathomable atrocities in the name of national security. In other cases, exclusionary ideologies can be transmitted by the media, as they were by powerful elites who used Rwanda's airwaves in the days preceding the 1994 genocide to fan the flames of Hutu animosity toward the Tutsi population. Exclusionary ideologies may not be as readily measured or tested as other factors that feed into state repression, but they are no less fundamental, underlying virtually all acts of repression.

Can Repression Be Prevented?

The sources of state repression are no doubt complex, reflecting a combination of factors. Non-democracy, armed conflict, poverty, and exclusionary ideologies are especially significant. Together, these factors create incentives for state leaders to repress opponents. Accordingly, repression can be deemed both an effective way to solve national security problems and a legitimate response to perceived challenges to national identity. The policy implications of this analysis are substantial.

If repression is a political choice, and the evidence strongly suggests that it is, then political reform is at least possible. This flies in the face of many popular explanations, which trace physical integrity violations to static views of human nature and group conflict. Indeed, conventional accounts often assume that human rights atrocities occur because people (or at least some people) are essentially evil or some groups are simply too different to live peacefully alongside one another. This essentialist perspective is deeply sceptical about the human capacity to overcome natural propensities or deeply engrained patterns of interaction. In contrast, insights from comparative politics suggest that repression can be combated with concrete strategies.

Preventing repression requires a comprehensive policy of promoting democracy, demilitarization, and development, while challenging exclusionary ideologies. Unfortunately, there is no shortcut to a world without repression. Long before international human rights norms began to take hold in the twentieth century, sovereign states coerced those within their borders as a way of retaining and extending their control. These dynamics will not disappear in contemporary politics just because repression is now internationally outlawed and labelled a human rights violation. Since repression remains a fundamentally political act, it can be prevented only by targeting its root causes. The alternative of simply promoting compliance with international norms or the virtues of human rights is, sadly, insufficient.

Despite extensive research into the sources of state repression, students of human rights still have their work cut out for them. One crucial question concerns the role of international trade and globalization (see Hafner-Burton, to appear). Ongoing debates in this area have enormous policy consequences, since economic leverage remains a key foreign policy tool in the human rights arena (Chapters 10 and 11). Should countries continue to trade with egregious rights violators such as China? In other words, is economic engagement ultimately better for human rights because it creates openness to new ideas as much as new markets? More broadly, scholars have paid great attention to explaining physical integrity violations while largely neglecting other forms of abuse, including violations of economic and social rights. Recent attempts to conceptualize as well as measure economic and social rights are a step in the right direction (see Hertel and Minkler, 2007). If labour or subsistence rights, for example, are to be protected, it is important to understand why they are violated. Preventing human rights abuses of all kinds requires grappling first with why they occur.

KEY POINTS	
Physical integrity violations, also known as state repression, are among the most notorious human rights abuses. They are the product of both rational incentives and exclusionary ideologies.	Exclusionary ideologies define the conditions under which it is deemed appropriate and even necessary to violate human rights norms. National security doctrines, which are used to justify suspending rights to maintain national stability, are one important type of exclusionary ideology; broader ideologies of discrimination like racism or sexism are another.
Among the most significant incentives that state leaders face to engage in repression are past repression, low levels of democracy, poverty, war, and social threats or dissent. The law of coercive response predicts that states will respond to armed threats and dissent with repression. The role of other factors (including economic growth, trade, or ethnic and cultural diversity) is far more uncertain.	Preventing state repression requires targeting the roots of abuse—weak democracy, militarization, poor development, and exclusionary ideologies—not just promoting human rights standards.

Internalizing Human Rights

If violations are one side of human rights practice, protection is the other. Comparative politics is crucial for understanding both dimensions, including the processes by which a system of abuses is reformed. Even if international actors exert pressure on non-compliant states to initiate human rights reform, the domestic context can be essential. Societal groups and state institutions must embrace international norms if human rights protection is to take root. Where social support for human rights protection is absent, human rights reform is difficult to imagine, let alone realize. Where human rights norms are weakly embedded in state institutions—including the political regime, legal system, and governmental human rights agencies—human rights reforms are likely to remain superficial and weak. Just as preventing repression requires targeting the roots of abuse, it also necessitates that human rights norms be incorporated into domestic structures. The Vienna World Conference on Human Rights (Vienna Conference)—a path-breaking global conference in 1993 that charted the course of post-Cold War human rights policy—recognized this. In its final document, the Conference highlighted the role of domestic legal systems, human rights education, national human rights institutions, non-governmental organizations (NGOs), and the media (Box 5.1).

The 'Spiral Model'

In most cases, human rights change entails a long-term process, usually imperfect and contradictory, wherein state–society relations gradually evolve to accommodate human rights norms. This depiction is consistent with what some scholars have called the spiral model of human rights change (Risse *et al.*, 1999). According to this model, human rights change tends to occur in stages, as states confront pressures both from 'above' (internationally) and 'below' (domestically). In response to these pressures, states initially deny abuses, then they begin making small concessions, move to more concrete if still sometimes cosmetic reforms, and eventually—in some cases—alter their behaviour so that it is consistent with internationally recognized human rights norms.

Whether or not human rights reform occurs is of course highly contingent. It depends on numerous factors, including whether human rights pressure is applied consistently and how domestic conditions evolve. For example, some states may begin making nominal human rights reforms, including releasing political prisoners and undertaking legal reform, but fall short of full compliance. As long as armed conflict persists, or civil society remains weak and divided, human rights progress will be limited and incomplete.

Box 5.1 **Domestic Structures of Protection: Excerpts from the 1993 Vienna World Conference on Human Rights**

The World Conference on Human Rights urges Governments to incorporate standards as contained in international human rights instruments in domestic legislation and to strengthen national structures, institutions and organs of society which play a role in promoting and safeguarding human rights. (Paragraph 83)

Domestic Legal Systems

Every State should provide an effective framework of remedies to redress human rights grievances or violations. The administration of justice, including law enforcement and prosecutorial agencies and, especially, an independent judiciary and legal profession in full conformity with applicable standards contained in international human rights instruments, are essential to the full and non-discriminatory realization of human rights. . . . (Paragraph 27)

The World Conference on Human Rights appeals to Governments, competent agencies and institutions to increase considerably the resources devoted to building well-functioning legal systems able to protect human rights. . . . (Paragraph 74)

Human Rights Education

The World Conference on Human Rights emphasizes the importance of incorporating the subject of human rights education programmes and calls upon States to do so. . . . [E]ducation on human rights and the dissemination of proper information, both theoretical and practical, play an important role in the promotion and respect of human rights . . . and this should be integrated in the education policies at the national as well as international levels. (Paragraph 33)

National Human Rights Institutions

The World Conference on Human Rights reaffirms the important and constructive role played by national institutions for the promotion and protection of human rights, in particular in their advisory capacity to the competent authorities, their role in remedying human rights violations, in the dissemination of human rights information, and education in human rights. . . . The World Conference on Human Rights encourages the establishment and strengthening of national institutions. . . . (Paragraph 36)

Non-Governmental Organizations

The World Conference on Human Rights recognizes the important role of non-governmental organizations in the promotion of all human rights. . . . The World Conference on Human Rights appreciates their contribution to increasing public awareness of human rights issues, to the conduct of education, training and research in this field, and to the promotion and protection of all human rights and fundamental freedoms. Non-governmental organizations and their members genuinely involved in the field of human rights should enjoy . . . the protection of the national law. (Paragraph 38)

The Media

Underlining the importance of objective, responsible and impartial information about human rights and humanitarian issues, the World Conference on Human Rights encourages the increased involvement of the media, for whom freedom and protection should be guaranteed. . . . (Paragraph 39)

Source: Vienna Declaration and Programme of Action (1993).

The spiral model is most helpful in suggesting that human rights change occurs incrementally. Even government responses that seem purely cosmetic can lead over time to consequential reforms. The model also emphasizes the dual importance of state and non-state actors, domestically and internationally, who in the to-and-fro of communicating with each other contribute to human rights change. It is an innovative example of relying on a small number of case studies to elucidate complex human rights outcomes, even if critics sometimes question the model's more general applicability (see Shor, 2008).

Overall, the spiral model and broader comparative research emphasize the role of both societal groups and state institutions in shaping human rights protection. While social pressure is necessary, especially against highly repressive regimes, reform is most fully successful only when a state has 'internalized' human rights. For a state that has internalized human rights norms, national commitments stem from a sense of obligation rather than from external pressures or incentives. In short, human rights reforms succeed best when they reflect domestic commitments.

Societal Groups

From the Mothers of the Plaza de Mayo in Argentina, who marched weekly in the central government square to protest about the disappearance of their children, to national Helsinki committees formed secretly within East European countries during the Cold War to oppose Soviet rule, to student activists who defiantly blocked Chinese tanks in Tiananmen Square, the world has vivid images of human rights groups confronting repressive regimes. And yet it remains difficult to understand why and how people bravely mobilize on behalf of human rights, often at great risk to their lives; nor is it self-evident why such groups can ever be effective against highly repressive regimes. Comparative politics provides valuable insights into the origins and successes of domestic human rights movements.

Human rights groups and movements (see Chapter 9) can organize and mobilize for various reasons, reflecting both their own strength and the opportunities that the broader political environment provides them. Part of the reason why some groups mobilize relates to the power of individual leaders who inspire and energize others, such as Martin Luther King Jr, who was integral to the civil rights struggle in the United States, or Václav Havel, who bravely championed the cause of human rights in the former Czechoslovakia. Some groups also have long-standing experience and extensive resources, including moral authority, to take a firm stand against an oppressive regime: thus religious organizations or lawyers' unions, for example, have played powerful roles in many parts of the world.

Furthermore, when oppressive states make concessions, even if they are symbolic or hypocritical, such gestures create a political opportunity for human rights groups to mobilize. For example, if a state begins to 'talk the talk' of human rights—such as introducing human rights laws, releasing political prisoners, or ratifying a treaty—domestic groups may gain some breathing room to mobilize. As states set a new standard for themselves, domestic groups can in turn demand consistency in practice. This partly explains why human rights groups can mobilize even at the height of repression, as they take advantage of even minute political openings to stake their claims. Over time, moreover, domestic pressures can intensify, as local human rights groups enter into broader alliances with other groups in civil society. As pressure mounts, a government may become unwittingly entrapped in a process of increasing concessions. If these dynamics are sustained over time, they can even contribute to a government's downfall.

Human rights groups tend to vary in terms of their identity, falling into several (sometimes overlapping) categories. Some form broad advocacy groups, committed to human rights protections generally or the promotion of specific rights (e.g. housing, employment, health, etc.). Others focus on the rights of certain groups of people, such as women, children, migrant workers, prisoners, or other vulnerable populations. Still others are primarily professional organizations, including lawyers and health workers, committed to using their specialized skills and expertise to improve human rights conditions. Finally, religious groups often promote social justice and human rights concerns closely overlapping with their broader convictions.

Despite their diversity, domestic human rights groups rely on a wide range of mutually reinforcing strategies. They directly assist human rights victims, from providing them with legal or medical assistance to assuring that they receive other essential social services. They also lobby governments directly, pressuring them to protect human rights, whether by halting abuses, securing economic justice in the face of global markets, implementing legal reform, or holding perpetrators accountable for their wrongdoings. In all of these efforts, domestic human rights groups rely extensively on naming and shaming. This entails first collecting information about abuses; such documentation can be critical for exposing the truth and mobilizing support on behalf of human rights. Activists then disseminate evidence of violations, drawing attention to the gap between human rights standards and state behaviour. The goal is to embarrass, or shame, governments into complying. Very often, moreover, domestic groups engage in socialization, targeted at both civil society and state actors, as they aim to spread awareness of internationally recognized human rights norms. Socialization efforts can range from distributing pamphlets, outlining basic human rights, to training state officials about their obligations under international law.

Given these numerous strategies, local human rights groups can wield far-ranging influence. At a minimum, they can help place human rights issues on a state's agenda. Even if states continue committing violations, pressure from NGOs can be significant in eliciting concessions. Internationally, the information generated by domestic groups can be crucial in mobilizing transnational alliances. Once formed, the success of transnational networks depends in turn on domestic groups, who may be perceived as having greater legitimacy than foreign actors. Finally, when human rights groups join forces with broader currents in civil society, they can play a key role in democratization. Time and again, human rights demands have played a defining role in the fall of oppressive regimes around the world. While pressure from domestic activists is rarely sufficient for bringing about significant human rights change, it is almost always necessary.

State Institutions

If human rights standards are to be protected, they have to be incorporated into state institutions. The state, after all, is the basic guarantor of human rights. It is obligated both to desist from violating human rights and, in a positive sense, to assure that non-state actors within its borders do not violate them. When violations do occur, the state is further obligated to assure that victims have due recourse to legal protection, that violations are investigated, and abusers are punished. These are the touchstones of respect for human rights.

Four kinds of state institution are particularly important for assuring the protection of human rights domestically: democratic structures of governance, domestic laws and rules, national and local courts, and governmental human rights institutions or agencies. In cases where human rights standards are weakly embedded in any of these institutions, human rights protection is likely to suffer. Consequently, human rights reform often requires strengthening these state institutions.

Democratic governance

Human rights standards are most likely to be protected under democratic forms of governance (Chapter 8). Just as non-democratic regimes tend to engage in higher levels of repression, democratic governance facilitates human rights protection. This is true procedurally and substantively. In democracies, individuals whose rights have been violated typically have access to the state, where they can file complaints, demand investigation, and expect accountability. More fundamentally, representative democracies tend to embrace human rights

standards, including notions of human freedom and equality (Goodhart, 2005). Democratic governments are therefore much less inclined than their autocratic counterparts to violate human rights, at least civil and political rights.

Democracy in and of itself, however, does not assure full respect for human rights. The *extent* of human rights protection depends on the quality of democratic governance. For example, in weak democracies human rights protections are more likely to be compromised. This explains why human rights violations can persist even under democratization.

Domestic laws and rules

Human rights protection also reflects domestic laws and rules, which define human rights standards and regulate relevant state–society interactions. In many countries, for example, international treaty obligations are not legally binding unless national implementing legislation is passed. Where domestic laws and rules do not conform to international human rights standards, a process of harmonization is required, wherein domestic standards are aligned with international ones. Domestic laws and rules can be enshrined in the constitution and in bills of rights, as well as in special regulations, guidelines, and procedures.

Beyond constitutions and bills of rights, a wide range of rules can specify human rights standards, define the state's precise duties, and describe the procedures to be followed when rights are violated. Administrative state agencies, moreover, have their own internal rules of relevance for human rights. For example, the rules of conduct for police officials define humane treatments and detail the consequences of non-compliance. Unless human rights standards are incorporated into domestic laws and rules, they are unlikely to have day-to-day impact.

Court systems

National and local courts are essential for guaranteeing human rights protection. Courts vary in the extent to which they provide victims with access, refer to international standards, and abide by the rule of law (i.e. apply legal standards fairly across cases, rather than arbitrarily in response to political calculations). Where human rights victims have no effective recourse to courts or the rule of law is weak, violators are not held accountable for their crimes and a climate of impunity reigns. Weak legal systems often reflect a broader problem of political corruption, as public officials do the bidding of powerful actors rather than protect the rights of individual citizens. Court systems enhance the predictability of justice, and they are a basic prerequisite for any rights-protective society.

As international human rights law (Chapter 2) evolves, moreover, the stock of national courts actually rises. While this may seem counter-intuitive, complaints and cases cannot generally be taken before international or regional bodies until all domestic remedies have been exhausted. The nascent International Criminal Court (ICC) differs somewhat. It can initiate proceedings only when domestic courts fail to prosecute or where domestic proceedings are not credible. Likewise, notions of universal jurisdiction mean that, in principle, egregious human rights cases can be tried in any national court: thus, European countries have attempted to try notorious dictators like Chile's Augusto Pinochet or Chad's Hissène Habré. Domestic courts increasingly complement international legal bodies.

National human rights institutions

National human rights institutions (NHRIs) are relatively new governmental bodies, designed to promote and protect human rights domestically (Cardenas, to appear). Most of these institutions have been created since the 1990s, often with active support from the United Nations. Present in over 100 countries, NHRIs are supposed to be both independent of the executive and representative of society. These are among the key criteria identified in the 1993 Paris Principles, a defining document that stipulates the internationally recognized duties of NHRIs (see Chapter 2). National institutions that do not meet these criteria are not accredited, or recognized, internationally.

These state agencies are charged with a broad range of tasks. On the protective side, they collect petitions from individuals who allege that their human rights have been violated, investigate complaints, and make recommendations to state bodies, though their decisions are not usually legally binding. They often produce an annual report, providing statistics about complaints. In a sense, they are the domestic version of international governmental human rights bodies such as the UN Human Rights Council. On the promotional side, NHRIs—often in cooperation with NGOs—promote human rights education. They may help to insert human rights into school curricula (e.g. holding essay and poster contests), engage in professional training (e.g. of law enforcement officers and health professionals), or launch public education campaigns (e.g. disseminating the Universal Declaration of Human Rights or running radio advertisements). Despite the scepticism of some observers, and the real limitations of many of these institutions, NHRIs can potentially serve as useful intermediaries between the state and society.

Just as understanding the sources of state repression is essential to devising effective human rights policies, sustainable human rights reforms require the commitment of both societal groups and state institutions. This suggests that domestic human rights groups should be empowered, and states must be supported in building effective democratic institutions, laws and rules, court systems, and governmental human rights bodies. Where existing institutions are weak, states should be challenged to incorporate human rights standards into their domestic structures. Human rights reforms can succeed only when they enjoy domestic support: societal groups promote human rights norms, assist victims, and keep governments in check; state institutions define standards and regulate human rights practices. Both sets of actors are necessary for a strong system of human rights protection to thrive.

KEY POINTS

Human rights reform requires embedding international human rights norms in domestic structures. Both societal groups and state institutions must accept human rights standards.

The process by which human rights change occurs is gradual and contingent. Responding to domestic and international pressures, states build on their prior commitments: moving from denial of abuse, to cosmetic changes, to increasingly substantial changes in some cases.

Domestic human rights groups mobilize according to their resources and the opportunities provided to them by the political environment. Human rights groups follow numerous strategies, from naming and shaming to assisting victims and lobbying governments.

State institutions are essential for guaranteeing the protection of human rights. Democratic structures of governance, laws and rules (including national constitutions), court systems, and governmental human rights institutions are especially significant.

Domestic–International Linkages

As important as comparative politics is for understanding human rights issues, it would be a mistake to overlook the significance of international factors, especially in light of increasing global interdependence (Chapter 4). In particular, domestic–international linkages often shed light on otherwise puzzling human rights outcomes. These dynamics are evident in the South African case, where societal pressure and state institutions joined with a broad spectrum of international pressures to achieve meaningful human rights change (Box 5.2). On the one hand, domestic politics can mediate the effects of international human rights treaties and pressures. On the other hand, international actors often shape human rights practices in ways that cannot be reduced to domestic politics.

One recurring puzzle is why international human rights pressure varies in its effectiveness, both cross-nationally and over time. Why was human rights pressure so successful in Eastern Europe, South Africa, and the Southern Cone of Latin America? Why has it proven relatively ineffective when applied against countries as different as China and Cuba? Recent studies (e.g. Cardenas, 2007) show that for states to alter their human rights practices dramatically in response to human rights pressure certain domestic conditions have to be met: the incentives to violate human rights have to be very low while support for human rights has to be relatively strong.

A related puzzle concerns the reasons why states commit to human rights treaties. Treaties, in principle, can challenge traditional notions of state sovereignty and constrain the state's room to manoeuvre. There is widespread agreement that domestic interests and institutions help to explain why states join human

---

Box 5.2 **Human Rights from the Inside Out: The South African Case**

South Africa was subject to human rights pressure longer than any other country last century. For decades, an abhorrent system of apartheid stripped the black majority of its most basic human rights. And then in the early 1990s, apartheid ended and the country democratized: Nelson Mandela was released in 1990 after decades in prison; apartheid was formally dismantled under President F. W. de Klerk, beginning in 1991; and universal-suffrage elections were held in 1994. What explains the timing of these dramatic changes?

Above all, domestic groups such as the African National Congress engaged in active resistance, without which change would have been highly unlikely. By persisting in their armed struggle against the apartheid regime, societal groups made it clear that the state could no longer provide national security. Unlike in other countries where the state was able to crush the opposition, the minority white government in South Africa proved incapable of containing the armed threat. The strength and resilience of domestic groups was therefore crucial.

International actors played a valuable and complementary role. In particular, they provided domestic groups with arms to oppose the state and funding to strengthen their capacities, as well as entering into transnational networks of solidarity that empowered domestic groups in their ongoing struggle. Concurrently, long-standing sanctions and boycotts targeted military and

cultural relations (including sports), and made it more costly for the state to continue its abuses. The apartheid regime responded with numerous concessions, even while it continued to violate human rights. In the longer term, however, human rights change became an increasingly legitimate alternative. Once the incentives to repress were gone, with the state no longer capable of controlling the armed insurrection and the economy on the verge of collapse, the time was ripe for change. The fall of apartheid in the early 1990s was the result of domestic *and* international factors.

Democratization alone, however, was insufficient to assure a high level of human rights protection. When Mandela became president in 1994, he immediately set out to embed human rights norms domestically. For example, in 1994 he signed the Human Rights Commission Act, which created the South African Human Rights Commission—a national human rights institution envisioned in both the country's constitution and bill of rights. In practice, the institution has promoted human rights extensively, both in South African society and within state agencies. But it also has not been sufficiently critical of and independent from the state. If human rights protection is to be fully internalized in post-apartheid South Africa, state institutions must commit more completely to implementing human rights standards.

rights treaties. For instance, among democracies, newer democracies are more likely than long-standing ones to accept human rights treaties. This counter-intuitive outcome can be traced to the domestic interests of leaders in newer democracies, who face higher uncertainty and therefore use treaties as a way of binding a country to long-term human rights compliance (Moravscik, 2000). Among dictatorships, scholars have recently emphasized the importance of 'open' dictatorships, which permit multiple political parties. Such dictatorships provide greater access to political interest groups, who can demand treaty ratification. This explains why open dictatorships are more likely to ratify the Convention against Torture, for example, even though they practise torture extensively (Vreeland, 2008).

Other human rights practices can also be difficult to explain when international factors are overlooked. Two types of international influence are especially important in shaping human rights outcomes. First, international actors contribute to state repression when they send contradictory messages: publicly promoting human rights, while privately accepting ongoing violations; or applying human rights pressure but continuing to sell military equipment, for instance (Sikkink, 2004). A classic example of this is US Secretary of State Henry Kissinger's suggestion to the Argentine junta in 1976 that they finish their dirty work as soon as possible, famously giving them a 'green light' to eliminate opponents.

International factors also help to clarify why states sometimes fail to live up to their human rights commitments, despite their good intentions. For instance, states (often developing countries) can lack the capacity to implement their treaty obligations. In the human rights arena, even foregoing torture may entail enacting new laws, training members of the coercive apparatus, and strengthening legal accountability. In such situations, international actors can be part of the problem if they fail to do their part in building domestic capacities. Domestic–international linkages therefore shed light on why repression sometimes persists even when states face human rights pressures and why human rights reform can be relatively weak despite states' best intentions.

KEY POINTS

In an increasingly interdependent world, understanding human rights practices requires examining international factors alongside domestic ones.

Domestic factors help to explain otherwise puzzling human rights outcomes, including the conditions under which international human rights pressure matters and why states commit to human rights treaties.

Domestic interests and institutions account for why states ratify human rights treaties. For example, emerging democracies and 'open' dictatorships (i.e. those permitting multiple political parties) are most likely to accept a human rights treaty.

International actors can contribute to state repression, accounting for why human rights violations sometimes persist. They also can affect states' capacities to implement human rights obligations.

Conclusion

Human rights practices cannot be understood without some appreciation for the insights provided by the study of comparative politics. By drawing attention to the role of domestic factors, including state–society relations, comparative politics sheds valuable light on why human rights violations occur and the conditions under which reform is possible. A systematic understanding of violations and reform, in turn, is a prerequisite for devising effective human rights policies.

Comparative politics highlights the role of a wide range of factors that can influence human rights outcomes. For example, comparative politics traces physical integrity violations (or state repression) to several structural conditions: weak democratic institutions, poverty, war, armed threats, and exclusionary ideologies. These factors push states to abuse human rights, even when confronted with countervailing human rights pressures. Comparative studies also suggest that human rights reform is possible only when human rights norms enjoy domestic support, both from societal groups and state institutions. While it is tempting to focus on the role of either the state or society, comparative politics emphasizes that both actors are crucial for generating human rights change.

Insights from comparative politics, however, do not produce easy answers; rather, they confirm that human rights practices are highly complex and contested. In particular, the role of international factors cannot be overlooked. In a globalizing world, domestic–international linkages are crucial determinants of human rights practice. Domestic politics, for example, help to explain why similar types of regime commit differently to human rights treaties or why states respond in widely divergent ways, even to similar international human rights pressures. Likewise, international actors can aid and prolong state repression; on the positive side, they can empower societal groups while building the state's

institutional capacity to implement human rights. Methodologically, comparative politics reminds students of the value of comparing human rights practices, whether relying on a few or many cases or focusing on a single region or multiple regions.

The twentieth century saw the 'internationalization' of human rights, as new global standards and institutions were created to regulate state action. Despite enormous progress, human rights abuses persist and reforms are often limited. Comparative politics suggests that a deeper understanding of the domestic dynamics underlying human rights practices is needed. If human rights are fundamental standards about the way the state should treat society, greater attention must be paid to the domestic roots of abuse and the role of societal groups and state institutions in producing sustainable change. The twenty-first century raises the challenge of how to internalize human rights standards, translating principled norms into state practice.

QUESTIONS

INDIVIDUAL STUDY QUESTIONS

1. What is comparative politics, and why is it important for understanding human rights practices?
2. What are some of the major strategies for comparing human rights practices?
3. What are physical integrity violations, and why do they occur? How do exclusionary ideologies contribute to state repression?
4. Can human rights violations be prevented, and if so, how?
5. Why do domestic human rights groups mobilize; and what strategies do they employ?
6. Why are state institutions essential for understanding human rights reform?
7. How do domestic and international politics interact to shape human rights outcomes?

GROUP DISCUSSION QUESTIONS

1. Which explanations for state repression do you find most compelling, and why? Which surprise you most?
2. Drawing on the contributions of comparative politics, what advice would you give human rights organizations targeting a repressive regime?
3. What lessons, if any, does the South African case provide for contemporary human rights campaigns?
4. In your view, what are the potential strengths and weaknesses of national (governmental) human rights institutions?
5. How well do comparative political insights help us understand human rights violations in the United States?

FURTHER READING

Brysk, A. and **Shafir**, G. (eds) (2007). *National Insecurity and Human Rights: Democracies Debate Counterterrorism*. Berkeley, CA: University of California Press.
An exploration of how democracies respond to perceived terrorist threats, this volume examines the relationship between national security and human rights protection.

Cardenas, S. (2007). *Conflict and Compliance: State Responses to International Human Rights Pressure*. Philadelphia, PA: University of Pennsylvania Press.
This book examines how and why states around the world respond to international human rights pressure, emphasizing the domestic sources of repression.

Carey, C. and **Poe**, S. (eds) (2004). *Understanding Human Rights Violations: New Systematic Studies*. Aldershot: Ashgate.
This important volume surveys the research on human rights violations, especially physical integrity violations and the findings from statistical studies.

Davenport, C. (2007). *State Repression and the Domestic Democratic Peace*. Cambridge: Cambridge University Press.
This book uses quantitative methods to reveal which aspects of democracy lead to state repression and which favour human rights protection.

Davenport, C., **Johnston**, H., and **Mueller**, C. (eds) (2005). *Repression and Mobilization*. Minneapolis, MA: University of Minnesota Press.
This volume provides a useful interdisciplinary look at how social mobilization and state repression interact.

Landman, T. (2002). Comparative politics and human rights. *Human Rights Quarterly*, **24**/4, 890–923.
This article provides a valuable overview of how comparative politics contributes to the study of human rights.

Landman, T. (2005). *Protecting Human Rights: A Comparative Study*. Washington, DC: Georgetown University Press.
Drawing on a broad range of social science perspectives, this accessible book offers a framework for studying human rights problems comparatively.

Risse, T., **Ropp**, S., and **Sikkink**, K. (eds) (1999). *The Power of Human Rights: International Norms and Domestic Change*. Cambridge: Cambridge University Press.
This path-breaking book discusses how international and domestic factors interact to produce human rights change.

WEB LINKS

http://www.hrcr.org/ Human and Constitutional Rights is a searchable database of bills of rights and human rights in national constitutions.

http://www.cidcm.umd.edu/mar/ The Minorities at Risk Project provides comparative data on politically active ethnic groups around the world.

http://www.nhri.net/ National Human Rights Institutions forum is a comprehensive website devoted to national human rights institutions around the world.

http://www.statewatch.org/ Statewatch is a non-governmental organization that monitors the state and civil liberties in European democracies.

http://www1.umn.edu/humanrts/research/ Part of the University of Minnesota Human Rights Library, this invaluable site provides hundreds of resources for researching country conditions.

ONLINE RESOURCE CENTRE

 Visit the Online Resource Centre that accompanies this book for updates and a range of other resources:

http://www.oxfordtextbooks.co.uk/orc/goodhart/

Sociological and Anthropological Approaches

6

Damien Short

Chapter Contents

Reader's Guide

Anthropologists and sociologists have typically been either positivists or relativists and consequently they have been slow to develop an analysis of justice and rights, and have therefore lagged behind other disciplines in examining the most significant institutional revolution of the twentieth century—the growth of universal human rights. This chapter will discuss how sociology and anthropology eventually broke free from the shackles of a disciplinary focus on cultural relativism and legal positivism and finally engaged with the concept of universal human rights. We will examine the key contributions to this endeavour from sociologists and anthropologists. We will see how sociology expanded its analysis of citizenship rights to that of human rights, developing a broad, yet nuanced, social constructionist interpretation and how anthropology turned its ethnographic methodology toward an examination of the 'social life of rights', thereby side-stepping the long-standing debate of 'universalism versus relativism'. The concluding sections identify 'social constructionism' as a common bond between the disciplines and emphasize the importance of sociological and anthropological perspectives to the study of human rights.

Introduction

Until relatively recently the discipline of sociology has largely confined its examination of rights to the realm of citizenship (Morris, 2006, p. 1). The concept of citizenship, however, is closely linked with the modern nation state, a political form that has been infected with the problems of imperialism, globalization, migrant workers, refugees, and Indigenous peoples (Turner and Rojek, 2001, p. 109). In a seminal essay for the journal *Sociology*, Bryan Turner (1993) suggested that globalization has created problems that are not wholly internal to nation states and that consequently we should extend sociological inquiry to the concept of *human* rights. While few sociologists have attempted, like Turner (1993), to develop a foundational social theory of human rights, there is now a growing body of research, stimulated by recent anthropological contributions in particular, which analyses the 'social life of rights' (Wilson, 1997, 2001, 2006). Moving beyond legal positivism and investigating 'beneath the surface', such studies have shown that 'rights' are not simply givens, or necessarily beneficial to the rights holders; rather, they are the products of social and political creation and manipulation and should be viewed accordingly. In addition, unlike philosophical debates, which attempt to foreclose the ontological status of rights, recent social research has analysed rights as socially constructed phenomena and attempted to explore their meaning and use. In 1997 Richard Wilson suggested a distinct need for more detailed studies of human rights according to 'the actions and intentions of social actors, within wider historical constraints of institutionalized power' (Wilson, 1997: pp. 3–4). Since then there has been a growth in such work from both sociologists and anthropologists. In the next section we will trace the development of sociological approaches to the study of human rights, from an initial position of non-engagement, due to an emphasis on positivistic social science, to an eventual social constructionist engagement. We will then turn to anthropological approaches and trace their development from the now infamous American Anthropological Association's relativistic 'Statement on Human Rights' through to the years of explicit engagement with human rights and what has been identified as the 'emancipatory cultural politics' turn and the now dominant ethnographic strand of anthropological engagement.

Sociology of Human Rights

Despite the ubiquity of human rights after the Second World War, sociology has had remarkably little to say about this 'age of rights' (Bobbio, 1999). Bryan Turner (1993) was perhaps the first sociologist to confront this disciplinary problem. 'It was prescient of Turner to identify this gap, at a time when few other sociologists had recognised the area of rights as central to social structures, processes and identities, and his writing on the topic is a necessary starting point for all others wishing to focus on these issues' (Morris, 2006).

Classical Sociology

Turner (1993, p. 492) began by suggesting that sociology as a discipline has no obvious foundation for a contemporary theory of rights, the blame for which he lay firmly at the door of classical social theory and its scepticism toward normative analysis of legal institutions. Consequently, he argued that classical sociology, as outlined by the 'founding fathers'— Marx, Durkheim, and Weber—failed to provide an ontological grounding for a theory of rights. For example, Emile Durkheim's desire to distinguish sociology from philosophy, and his injunction to treat 'social facts' as 'things', precluded normative considerations and treated moral and legal norms merely as external restrictions on the behaviour of individuals. Durkheimian sociology suffered from a severely limited positivistic focus that failed to offer adequate causal explanations for issues such as social inequality and injustice (see Turner, 1993).

Similar problems arise if we consider Weber's emphasis on 'value-free' social science and his rejection of any normative foundation for law. In his classic text *Economy and Society* Weber (1978) focused on certain social developments that he showed 'relativized' the law. The axioms of natural law are discredited by the conflict between formal and substantive law, the relativization of legal norms as a consequence, juridical rationalism, the decline of religious tradition, and the spread of legal rationalism. Weber (1978, p. 875) emphasized the increasing 'rationality' of law and the decline of its 'metaphysical dignity'. Thus, Weber rejected the possibility of a universalistic normative foundation for law and hence for rights (Turner, 1993, p. 494).

Turning to Karl Marx, the basis of his views on rights were documented in the essay 'On "The Jewish Question"' (Marx, 1987), his reply to his friend Bruno Bauer's views on Jewish emancipation. The essay reflected his great interest in the revolutionary activity so prevalent in Europe at that time and, in particular, the French revolution and the ensuing Declaration of the Rights of Man and of the Citizen, and its various updated versions. Marx considered the rights to liberty, property, security, and equality as little more than individualistic rights that serve only to divorce the individual from society (see Box 6.1).

The essence of the charge was that the primary rights in the declaration are *individualistic* in nature, and only serve to secure the property interests of the rapacious individual. Such talk of rights blinds us to the gross inequalities inherent in the world between the workers and the owners of the means of production. Thus, the implication in Marx's work is that rights *only* have a place in a society with a capitalist industry and economy, with 'a private individual pursuing material

gain in a context where all his relations with others are mediated by the market and commodity exchange.' For Marx, within political society people were seen as cooperative, while in the economic roles they were competitive, individualistic, and egoistic; the theory of rights merely expressing the division and alienation of human beings (Turner, 1993, p. 492). In short, within Marx's account of capitalist civil society, law is an instrument of class domination and human rights are no more than a tool to obscure fundamental social and economic inequalities.

Thus, the legacy of this sceptical heritage was an absence of a normative basis for the study of rights, which left sociologists with no means of responding to a relativist position on rights and values (Turner, 1993). Consequently, the only substantive disciplinary engagement with 'rights' came through the concept of citizenship, that is the bundle of rights granted by the nation state to the individual citizen, and which was perceived by sceptical sociologists as less problematic since it did not appear to raise problems about universal ontology (Turner, 1993, p. 496). Thus, a sociology of citizenship functioned as a somewhat inadequate substitute for a sociology of rights.

From Citizenship to Human Rights

The concept of citizenship is closely linked with the modern nation state, but this political form has been infected with numerous problems, such as imperialism, globalization, migrant workers, refugees, and Indigenous peoples, which has raised questions about the nation state as the framework for an adequate analysis of citizenship and rights (see Turner, 1993; Turner and Rojek, 2001). As globalization has created problems that are not wholly internal to nation states, so the concept of citizenship rights must be extended to that of human rights. The major problem with sociology's reluctance to engage with human rights is that human rights have now become a powerful institution and play a significant role in political mediation of social conflict (Turner and Rojek, 2001, p. 119).

Turner has argued that the concept of human rights can be understood sociologically by the need to protect vulnerable human beings with social institutions, which in turn can pose threats to those human beings (Turner, 1993, p. 502). The social and legal institutionalization of human rights is the predominant modern attempt

---

Box 6.1 **Marx on the 'Rights of Man'**

The so-called rights of man . . . are nothing but the rights of the member of civil society, i.e. egoistic man, separated from other men and from the community. . . . They merely guaranteed the 'right of self interest' of a monadic and 'restricted individual, withdrawn into himself and separated from the community'.

From Karl Marx's essay 'On "The Jewish Question"' (Marx, 1987).

to resolve this dilemma that is inherent in modern societies. Yet Turner's analysis goes further than mere explanation. He argues that, without some universal moral grounds, it is impossible to talk about justice: 'There has to be some foundation of a universalistic character in order for such discussions about justice to take place. Otherwise we are left with a mere talking shop of difference' (Turner and Rojek, 2001, p. 112). He persuasively deploys sociological theory to explore the moral basis of a universalist doctrine of human rights and proposes that a shared experience of 'human frailty' and the 'vulnerability of the human body' provides a common ground: 'Human frailty is a universal experience of human existence' (Turner, 1993, p. 505; Turner and Rojek, 2001, p. 110). Additionally he argues that we need universal human rights due to the 'precariousness' of 'social institutions', which 'stand in a fateful relationship to human purposes, because they contradict their origins'.

> The institutions that are designed to protect human beings—the state, the law and the church in particular, are often precisely those institutions which threaten human life by the fact that they enjoy a monopoly of power. (Turner, 1993, pp. 501–502)

Finally, Turner (1993, p. 506, my emphasis) invokes the notion of collective sympathy: 'Ultimately my argument has to assume that sympathy is also a consequence of, or a supplement to, human frailty. Human beings will want their rights to be recognised *because they see in the plight of others their own (possible) misery*.'

Social Constructionism

A few years after Turner's initial contribution, Malcolm Waters (1996) took issue with Turner's foundationalist approach, and advocated a social constructionist interpretation of universal human rights. He writes:

> Turner attributes the failure of sociology to adequately theorise human rights partly to its social constructionist orientation, its normal claim that social institutions are not universal but historically contingent and culturally relativised. I want to argue that an adequate sociological theory of human rights must, indeed, take a social constructionist point of view, that human rights is an institution that is specific to cultural and historical context just like any other and that its very universality is itself a human construction. (Waters, 1996, p. 593)

Waters approaches human rights through a social constructionist lens, which emphasizes the socially created nature of social life, and accordingly views the construction of universal human rights as the product of the balance of power between political interests at a particular point in history. The rise of human rights cannot be explained simply through notions of human vulnerability, institutional threats, and collective sympathy, but rather by the assertion of powerful class interests. The original design of the Universal Declaration of Human Rights (UDHR) and the subsequent expansion and enforcement of the human rights principles can be explained by reference to four sets of interests (see Box 6.2).

Yet, Turner (1997, p. 566) pointed out that, 'it is perfectly consistent to argue . . . that human rights can have a foundationalist ontology in the notion that human beings are frail and accept the argument that human rights will be constructed in a contingent and variable way according to the specific characteristics of the societies in which they are developed and as a particular outcome of political struggles over interests. The point of a foundationalist ontology . . . is to provide a universal basis for normative evaluation of human rights abuses.'

Whether or not sociology can provide a normative foundational justification for human rights is debatable, but we can say that Turner's arguments are persuasive and have been influential. The discipline is on far safer ground, however, when it focuses on the social construction of rights and their indeterminacy and when it provides us with the theoretical and conceptual tools to answer the questions of 'how rights came into social being', how they 'operate in social practice', 'whose pur-

---

Box 6.2 **Interests Responsible for Growth of Human Rights Principles?**

The interests of the allied victors of the Second World War in stigmatizing and penalizing their defeated enemies.

The interests of Cold Warriors in seeking to undermine each other's legitimacy.

The interests of superpowers in legitimizing intervention in the affairs of other states.

The interests of disadvantaged groups in claiming rights against the actions of the state.

Adapted from Waters (1996, p. 597).

poses' rights serve and whose 'interests they protect', and finally, how far they are 'guaranteed or constrained by the letter and practice of the law' (Morris, 2006, p. 11). Social constructionist sociology can show that 'few rights are absolutes and most are in some way limited or conditional' (Morris, 2006, p. 11). Thus, sociology should declare an interest in the *indeterminacy* of rights (Morris, 2006, p. 25).

From a social constructionist perspective *universal* human rights should be seen as 'historically and socially contingent, the product of a particular time, place, and set of circumstances, and a work in permanent progress' (Morris, 2006, p. 26). A sociological approach to rights discourses, practices, and struggles is necessary to identify the mechanisms that translate social phenomena into rights disputes. A social constructionist perspective views rights as an artefact produced through social processes of framing and construction, and in this sense, as Ken Plummer (2006) states, 'sociologists view rights as inventions'. Yet, viewing rights this way suggests that we must pay due attention to the social actors involved in their invention/construction if we are to fully understand rights regimes.

Indeed, Stammers suggests that we cannot ignore the link between social movements—networks of people who organize efforts to bring or resist change—and claims for human rights (see Chapter 9). It may be better to use a 'triadic relationship between human rights, social movements and power as an organizing focus for analysis' (Stammers, 1999, p. 981). This would provide a different understanding of rights than the prevailing dominant discourses, which focus on political power, the origins and development of human rights, and potentials and limits of human rights (Stammers, 1999, p. 982). Like Turner, however, Stammers emphasizes the context of globalization, the changing role of nation states and the misplaced view of the nation state as the 'principle duty bearer' of all human rights (Stammers, 1999, p. 1003). Indeed, given abuse of economic and social rights by private economic institutions, we should not look for a solution from the nation state. Alternatively, 'it might prove rather more useful to consider how *social movements* could renew and re-invigorate the challenge to economic power' (Stammers, 1999, p. 1003). Social movements' construction and the use of rights discourses have played a vital positive role in challenging relations and structures of power in respect of concentrated 'sites' of power and in terms of the way that power is embedded in everyday social relations (Stammers, 1999, pp. 987–988).

Power

Within this broad social constructionist sociology we can see an important dimension of sociological enquiry begin to emerge, i.e. the role of *power* in the domain of human rights. Human rights scholar Michael Freeman, in a major interdisciplinary contribution to the area (Freeman, 2002), identifies rights *institutionalization* as a social process and he also displays an acute awareness of the role of power in that process, which he sees as perhaps the major sociological contribution. He writes:

> The institutionalisation of human rights may . . . lead, not to their more secure protection but to their protection in a form that is less threatening to the existing system of power. The *sociological* point is not that human rights should never be institutionalised, but, rather, that institutionalisation is a social process, involving power, and that it should be analysed and not assumed to be beneficial. (Freeman 2002, p. 85)

Freeman further argues that the social sciences have been 'excessively legalistic' and overemphasized the UN system whilst neglecting to look deeper into the role of powerful global institutions and global power politics, most notably the G7, the Bretton Woods institutions, and the foreign policy of the US, in both the violation and construction of human rights (Freeman, 2002, p. 177). The discipline of sociology is well placed to investigate the role of *power* in this regard.

Indeed, the role of power is also a concern of Anthony Woodiwiss (2005) who advocates a sociological understanding of human rights that utilizes Foucauldian notions of discourse and power, suggesting that rights and the law should be viewed primarily as instruments of governments, but instruments that take on their own autonomy and become channels of power in their own right. Contrary to Lockean political philosophy, 'rights' and 'freedom' were *not* in existence before 'power', but rather are the products of the 'new mode of social life' that is modern capitalism (Woodiwiss, 2005, p. 32). Rights have a paradoxical nature in that they contribute to the production of social divisions, while at the same time they provide the language to 'discuss and contest such inequalities' (Woodiwiss, 2005, p. 32). In short, rights and the law in general should be viewed as 'products of discursive formations', but with the emancipatory potential to generate power in order to 'serve the global majority' (Woodiwiss, 2005, pp. 32, 136).

Social structure

Up to this point we have seen that sociology views rights as a socially constructed phenomena and we have discussed the importance of social actors—such as social movements—and power relations in the construction of these rights. One aspect of sociological enquiry that we have not discussed so far is the role of social structure—that is the ordered interrelationships between elements of society such as the different kinships, religious, economic, political, legal, and other institutions of a society—in the *violation* of rights. In the final section of this chapter we will discuss the role of *colonial structures* in the violation of Indigenous peoples' rights, and see how, following indigenous political mobilization, these same structures also restricted the institutionalization of indigenous land rights so as not to include de-colonizing political rights such as the right to self-determination and recognition of indigenous sovereignty. At this point, however, it is worth noting that one of the few sociologists to engage with the role of social structures in a study of human rights violations was Rhoda Howard back in 1988.

Perhaps the main reason for Howard's focus more on the role of social structure was her injunction to view human rights as a normative concept, as 'entitlements' and not 'privileges' or benefits obtained through social struggle. Thus she was not exploring the uses of human rights talk or the socially constructed nature of legal rights. She based her structural analysis on Western and Central Africa, claiming that such societies have gone through significant social change at a structural level such that their cultural 'uniqueness' has all but ceased to exist, whilst the 'modern individual' has flourished (Howard, 1986, pp. 16, 33). Accordingly, she contended that '"culture" must not be used as a defence of human rights abuses' (Howard, 1986, pp. 16, 33), but it could be used 'as a check to radical universalism in carefully defined circumstances'. She was very wary of most claims for cultural relativity, which she viewed as an 'ideological tool to serve the interests of powerful and emergent groups in Commonwealth African society' (Howard, 1986, p. 17), and thus commonly result in withholding human rights from 'other' members of the same society (Howard, 1986, p. 34). For Howard, then, human rights are a truly universal normative concept

that should be applicable to all peoples, regardless of the material and cultural conditions they exist within.

From the above discussion we can identify key sociological questions (see Box 6.3).

Sociological research

So how have these sociological insights informed social research into rights issues? Some researchers have focused sociological enquiry on the question of *how access to rights is operationalized*. Since rights are related to the circumstances in which they emerge, it is the task of the sociologists to understand those circumstances, and to show that claims for the universality of given rights should be replaced by a thorough analysis of the 'variability in why, when, how, and under what circumstances' rights are likely or not to emerge as a demand (Glucksmann, 2006). Others have focused on the conditions that trigger a turn toward universalistic human rights claims by, for example, women's rights campaigners. Elson (2006) has shown how the adoption of human rights talk, as what social movement theorists term a mobilizing master frame, can be explained in the light of the opportunities generated by existing institutional arrangements at an international level. Indeed, sociological research has also drawn attention to how rights claims and rights talk has instrumental use value for many actors.

Social research has shown how rights should be viewed as instrumentally useful strategic resources invoked by social actors in competition for power in

> ### Box 6.3 **Key Sociological Questions**
>
> How have rights come into social being?
>
> How are rights socially constructed—by whom, for whom, and in what social context?
>
> How and why do particular social actors and groups claim and access rights?
>
> How are rights affected by the social, political, and economic context in which they emerge and operate?
>
> What role is played by social structures—are they enabling, constraining, or both?
>
> To what extent are rights guaranteed or limited by the law?
>
> Have power relations affected the construction and functionality of rights?
>
> Whose interests do rights actually function to protect?

domestic and international arenas (Ruzza, 2006). Rights can be constructed through the interplay of domestic and international forces and will be reinforced so long as otherwise powerless social actors find no other alternative but to engage in rights talk. Sociology may be the discipline best equipped to discuss the social forces that underline the genesis of such rights and the social struggles from which they materialize (Plummer, 2006). A primary 'task for sociologists is to become intimately familiar with the crusaders, their claims, and the social processes through which rights emerge' (Plummer, 2006), while being careful to balance claims for universality with the reality of societal and cultural diversity. Sociological researchers are also well placed to examine the 'considerable gap between the recognition of the need for protection and its achievements in practice' (Morris, 2006, p. 3). In summary, the discipline of sociology is well equipped to expose, discuss, and possibly amend obvious limitations in existing conceptions of rights, especially the formal legalistic dimensions, the limitations of which, as we shall see later, are something that social anthropologist Richard Wilson is also concerned to 'move beyond'.

The issue of cultural relativism has of course influenced both sociological and anthropological perspectives on human rights. It was a major factor that led sociology to take such a long time to engage with the phenomena at all; while anthropology, on the other hand, was an influential voice at the outset of the international codification of human rights norms. In the next section we will trace the development of anthropological perspectives on human rights from an initial 'relativistic' position

of deep scepticism to an eventual, rigorously critical yet nuanced, engagement with the 'social life of rights' (Wilson, 2001, 2006). We shall see a significant degree of commonality within the disciplinary approaches to the extent that the two may arguably be considered complementary when it comes to the study of human rights. I will emphasize the main point of convergence in the final section of this chapter through a brief outline of research on indigenous rights in Australia.

KEY POINTS

Until relatively recently the discipline of sociology has largely confined its examination of rights to the realm of citizenship.

Classical sociology suffered from a positivistic focus and an emphasis on 'value-free' social science.

Sociological enquiry needed to expand beyond citizenship to investigate phenomena such as imperialism, globalization, migrant workers, refugees, and Indigenous peoples.

Turner (1993) sought to develop a foundational social theory of human rights.

Subsequent contributions, however, have taken a social constructionist approach, which views rights as an artefact produced through social processes of framing and construction.

Sociologists view rights as inventions, the products of social and political creation and manipulation.

Anthropology of Human Rights

The discipline of anthropology has evolved to be concerned with the study of the entire range of cultures and societies in the world. Given such scope, there are significant points of convergence between anthropology and sociology. Yet in the early stages of its development the discipline tended to focus on non-Western 'primitive' societies, which led to important differences between the disciplines. Indeed, sociology historically tended to focus on Western societies, which consequently generated methodological and

theoretical differences between the two disciplines. For example, when Western sociologists studied their own society they could take much context for granted before hypothesizing about their data, while anthropologists studying other cultures could make few safe assumptions and consequently developed a holistic methodology that emphasized that each social entity or group has its own identity that is *distinct* and not reducible to individual constituent parts. Thus, anthropology would not assume that all cultures shared the same values, which is the fundamental ontological position that guided the discipline's early attitude toward the notion of universal human rights.

The discipline of anthropology's first, most notable, engagement with human rights can be traced back to December 1947 and Melville Herskovits's (AAA, 1947) 'Statement on Human Rights' published in the *American Anthropologist* (*AA*) journal. During what sociologists would call the social construction of the UDHR, formal representations were sought from academics, public intellectuals, and non-government actors on the proposed text in order to make it as fair and unbiased, and hence legitimate, as possible. Herskovits's statement was quickly adopted by the American Anthropological Association Executive Board and consequently published as the lead article in the ultimate *AA* issue of that year (see Box 6.4).

The bad news for the UN was that the statement refused to endorse the proposed Universal Declaration. The rejection was based on the following three arguments.

1. Anthropology, as the social 'science of mankind', had shown that moral systems varied considerably in form and content and thus any assertion of universality that had a moral flavour would always be prescriptive and certainly not descriptive of a social reality.

Box 6.4 American Anthropological Association: Statement on Human Rights (Extract)

Because of the great numbers of societies that are in intimate contact in the modern world, and because of the diversities of their ways of life, the primary task confronting those who would draw up a Declaration of the Rights of Man is thus, in essence, to resolve the following problem: how can the proposed Declaration be applicable to all human beings, and not be a statement of rights conceived only in terms of the values prevalent in the countries of Western Europe and America? . . . Standards and values are relative to the culture from which they derive so that any attempt to formulate postulates that grow out of the beliefs or moral codes of one culture must to that extent detract from the applicability of any Declaration of Human Rights to mankind as a whole. (*American Anthropologist*, October 1947)

---

2. Given the scientific, empirical ethnographic methodology of the discipline, which seeks to describe and then explain social phenomena, it could not contribute to a normative endeavour that implicitly makes moral judgments, based on a set of universal rights, about cultural practices. Quite simply, the point being made was that anthropology as a discipline was fundamentally inimical to the nature of the proposed project.

3. If the proposed Universal Declaration is being designed as an aspirational text for the international community, in an attempt to universally operationalize this particular set of moral values, then the likely consequences of this would surely include the *denial* of freedom to those people whose view of the 'good life' may differ considerably with the prescribed priorities of a Universal Declaration. For example, some cultures may exhibit more collective value systems that emphasize things like collective ownership of land rather than the individual private property rights.[1]

For anthropology, these objections stood as a metaphorical disciplinary wall, blocking engagement with human rights for a very long time. Indeed, following a short-lived exchange of views on the subject of human rights after the publication of the American Anthropological Association (AAA) Statement (Barnett, 1948; Steward, 1948), there was virtually no anthropological interest in the phenomena of human rights *as a specific subject of inquiry* until the mid-1980s (see Goodale, 2006a, p. 2). However, in the years following the publication of the 1947 Statement anthropologists nonetheless continued to practice 'public anthropology', reflecting the discipline's long-standing concern with creating linkages between anthropological research and projects for social justice (see Goodale, 2006a, p. 2). Moreover, anthropologists obviously encountered human rights issues and concerns in their work.[2] The same was true of sociologists during their period of non-engagement, but they did not study this intersection, or the specific human rights dimensions, *in their own right*. When anthropologists did finally seek to specifically investigate and analyse human rights they did so against the backdrop of such previous indirect engagement. Yet the relativistic thrust of the Statement reflected the prevailing attitude of anthropology to human rights for quite some time despite this indirect engagement.

Emancipatory Cultural Politics

Anthropology's relativistic perspective was borne out of a detached scientific methodology that frequently observed a plethora of value systems in its research 'subjects'. This 'detached' approach, however, did not last as the dominant perspective. While many anthropologists were able to maintain an 'objective' detachment from their research subjects, increasingly this approach gave way to immersion and empathy, which in turn led to political activism on behalf of the subjects. It was this political engagement, with its implicit moral dimension, that eventually led to a reorientation of anthropological perspectives on human rights. Perhaps the pivotal moment in this new normative turn came from Clifford Geertz and his 1983 AAA Distinguished Lecture 'Anti Anti-Relativism', which confronted head-on the most commonly cited anthropological objection to the notion of universal human rights. In 1990 a Special Commission was created by the AAA to investigate human rights violations against the Yanomami by the Brazilian state—a quite remarkable turn around when one considers the AAA's prior disciplinary detachment and relativistic stance. This engagement was taken even further in 1992 with the establishment of an AAA Commission for Human Rights. In 1994 the AAA solidified its commitment to engagement with human rights issues by making anthropology and human rights a thematic priority in its annual meetings, while in 1995 it converted the Commission for Human Rights into a permanent Committee for Human Rights. Finally, in 1999 that same Committee wrote a 'Declaration on Anthropology and Human Rights' that confirmed a significant disciplinary realignment since the AAA adopted Herskovits's 1947 Statement.

In 1997 a special issue of the *Journal of Anthropological Research* (*JAR*) sought to develop a distinct vision for a disciplinary engagement with human rights. The arguments contained therein suggested that anthropological understandings of specific cultural processes, which are embedded in wider (what sociologists would term 'structural') social power relationships, should be used to bolster specific endeavours for social change and/or to assist specific marginalized peoples, populations, or groups in resisting threats to their survival. This approach views human rights as a useful tool for serving an ethical commitment toward threatened peoples and cultures. The effectiveness of human rights as a tool in this sense can be greatly improved through more expansive and inclusive definition.[3] Thus, there is a normative suggestion within this approach that anthropologists *should* work to expand the definitions of *human rights* so as to increase their effectiveness for marginalized groups and cultures—an approach termed 'emancipatory cultural politics' (Turner, 1997). This approach, which encourages anthropological engagement with human rights discourse as a political strategy for the protection of threatened populations, was perhaps the first major disciplinary current to emerge in the anthropology of human rights.[4] Perhaps the most notable recent research within this broad approach is that of Shannon Speed, which she has termed 'critically engaged activist research' (Speed, 2006). This approach is concerned to embrace the issues raised by the social actors, not shy away from engagement and commentary, and in fact warns against an *overly detached* anthropology of human rights (Speed, 2006). The focus of the research is not just about *research on* human rights in the particular site—Chiapas, Mexico—but also *advocacy for* human rights there. Consequently, it could be suggested that such research does not fall into the trap of forgetting the 'human' in human rights. For the social actors suffering injustice, human rights are much more than an academic curiosity.

Box 6.5 highlights the three core elements of the *emancipatory cultural politics* strand of the anthropology of human rights.

The Ethnographic Turn

Thus, as with the discipline of sociology, the 1990s was the decade when anthropologists from around the globe

---

Box 6.5 'Emancipatory Cultural Politics': Core Elements

Anthropological understandings should be used to reinforce specific endeavours to assist threatened peoples, populations, or groups.

Human rights are a useful tool for serving an ethical commitment toward this endeavour.

BUT, anthropologists should work toward *more expansive and inclusive definitions* of human rights so as to increase their effectiveness for marginalized groups and cultures.

truly began taking the issue of human rights seriously enough to conduct significant research. From about the mid-1990s, mirroring the reorientation in the AAA, anthropologists from outside the USA began to see merit in the 'social practice of rights' as a worthy *object* of anthropological investigation. The perspectives that emerged from this endeavour were collected in several important edited volumes (Wilson 1997; Cowan *et al.*, 2001; Wilson and Mitchell, 2003) and through several monographs (e.g. Riles, 2000; Wilson, 2001; Merry, 2005; Slyomovics, 2005). These contributions evolved into a second major current in the contemporary anthropology of rights, which can be identified as the 'ethnographic' approach (Goodale, 2006a, p. 3). This second disciplinary thread in the anthropology of human rights seeks to use the discipline's ethnographic methodology to explore and investigate the 'social practice of human rights' or, as Richard Wilson puts it; 'the social life of rights'. Wilson, a social anthropologist, agrees with the main thrust of the sociological approaches that we discussed earlier, arguing that social scientists should be primarily concerned with analysing rights as socially constructed phenomena. He writes:

> The intellectual efforts of those seeking to develop a framework for understanding the social life of rights would be better directed not towards foreclosing their ontological status, but instead by exploring their meaning and use. What is needed are more detailed studies of human rights according to the actions and intentions of social actors, within wider historical constraints of institutionalized power. (Wilson, 1997, pp. 3–4)

Taking up this call, researchers began to focus on an increase in negotiations and claims made by various social groups *in a language of 'rights'*. A trend began to emerge in which long-established theoretical debates about concepts such as rights, justice, and citizenship began to engage with empirical 'data' that contextualizes rights-claiming processes (Cowan *et al.*, 2001). Anthropologists started to advocate the need to explore how exactly universal concepts were being used in local struggles. In essence, the relationship between culture and rights was seen as an issue to be studied *empirically*. The thrust of this approach is thus descriptive and makes no claim to endorse the universality of human rights. It is an effort to uncover how human rights actually function in an empirical sense, to uncover what they mean to different social actors in different social contexts. More attention was gradually being paid to

empirical, contextual analyses of specific rights struggles. This intellectual strategy sought to record how individuals, groups, communities, and states use rights discourse in the pursuit of particular ends, and how they become enmeshed in its logic (Cowan *et al.*, 2001, p. 21). Thus, in contrast to the first disciplinary thread to engage with human rights, that of 'emancipatory cultural politics' (see Goodale, 2006a) that is inherently normative, the ethnographic approach is more *a study of normativity*.

One of the main issues investigated by this approach is the relationship between culture and rights (see Cowan *et al.*, 2001). Anthropologists interested in this relationship have sought answers to questions such as: How do transnational ideas such as human rights approaches to violence against women become meaningful in local social settings? How do they move across the gap between a cosmopolitan awareness of human rights and local sociocultural understandings of gender and family? (Merry, 2006, pp. 38–51.) In exploring these questions anthropologists have sought to construct theoretical frameworks that seek to explain the different ways in which human rights are viewed instrumentally and also experienced by transnational social actors. While theorizing processes of translation, anthropological analysis of translators helps to explain how 'human rights ideas and interventions circulate around the world and transform social life' (Merry, 2006, p. 38).

Anthropological studies in this area often highlight the inherent risks to culture of a hegemonic human rights regime and accordingly advocate an approach to human rights that firmly scrutinizes how rights regimes actually function and in particular their functional impact on culture. Such an approach will not anchor political projects or movements for cultural autonomy based on claims for cultural rights; rather it is an anthropology of interrogation that is pluralist, sceptical, and penetrating (Goodale, 2006a). This sceptical approach to rights, as we shall see in the later section of this chapter, can be evidenced by recent, more sociological, writings on indigenous rights.

A sceptical pluralist view of rights is now a dominant feature of the ethnographic current. It is a view that recognizes the 'plural and fragmentary nature of the international rights regime and the ideological promiscuity of rights talk' (Wilson, 2006, p. 77). Its focus is on the performative dimensions of human rights, social mobilization dynamics, and the attitudinal changes of elite and non-elite social actors toward the formulations of 'rights' and 'justice' inside and outside legal processes (see Wilson, 2006, p. 77). By ethnographically studying the '*social life of rights*' we can move beyond the tired universalism versus relativism debate to examine what actors 'actually do with human rights in specific fields of political contestation' (Wilson, 2006, p. 78).

Thus the essence of the ethnographic approach is the careful documentation of the social life of rights (see Box 6.6). This may involve examining phenomena such as 'the dynamics of social mobilisations in rights-based social movements, or the performative dimensions of rights movements including marches, vigils, funerals, and so forth' (see Wilson, 2006) or, as we shall see in the next section, examining how power politics impacts upon rights construction—often to the detriment of the ultimate rights holders (see Short, 2007). In following this approach we can locate the foundations of human rights in 'everyday human sociality', rather than through complex philosophizing or the 'rational actor and positive law' (Wilson, 2006).

Ecumenical anthropology?

Recently, Mark Goodale (2006b, 2008) has advanced an influential argument that critiques both the ethnographic and emancipatory cultural politics strands and argues for an expanded object of inquiry *beyond human rights* to a slightly larger set of normative processes in which human rights are nonetheless embedded (Goodale, 2006b). This study of 'ethical theory as social practice' would involve anthropologists engaging ethnographically with social actors and processes through which human rights encounter *other normative phenomena*. Within this approach anthropologists would also participate in 'co-theorizing' with social actors as they attempt to make sense of human rights through interpretation and reinterpretation (Goodale, 2006b). Such an engagement with interlocutors distinguishes Goodale's approach somewhat from a straight 'ethnographic' methodology. It is a distinction he sees as necessary 'because of both the conceptual demands that human rights processes place on social actors (including anthropologists) and the fact that human rights discourse links social actors to transnational regimes whose scope and meanings can only partially be captured ethnographically' (Goodale, 2006a, p. 5).

Thus, recent anthropological research sought to newly frame anthropological approaches to human rights beyond the basic distinction between 'emancipatory cultural politics' and an 'ethnography of rights' that we have discussed so far. Researchers have sought to re-engage with a broader range of debates within anthropology and wider problems that lie at the foundation of contemporary human rights. These approaches have been described as representing, broadly speaking, an '*ecumenical anthropology of human rights*' (Goodale, 2006a). It is an anthropology that tolerates and encourages research that is *fundamentally critical of contemporary human rights regimes but also research that is politically or ethically committed to these same regimes*. As Goodale (2006a) suggests, 'an ecumenical anthropology of human rights is one that draws from an internal epistemological pluralism to better understand the pluralism—whether irreducible or not—that characterizes contemporary human rights practice.' This approach aimed to take the anthropology of human rights *beyond what had come before*; nevertheless, much of this recent research could still, broadly speaking, fit within the twofold classification of anthropological approaches to human rights—the 'emancipatory cultural politics' and the 'ethnographic' strands.

The next section highlights a common thread between sociology and anthropology in the study of human rights and shows, through a brief summary of research on Indigenous peoples' rights, how such a perspective goes beyond rhetorical and formal legalistic dimensions and truly sheds light on 'the social life of rights'.

> ### Box 6.6 **The Ethnographic Approach: Core Elements**
>
> The relationship between culture and rights is an issue to be studied *empirically*.
>
> The approach is descriptive and does not implicitly endorse the universality of human rights.
>
> It seeks to uncover how human rights *actually function* and what they mean to different social actors in different social contexts.
>
> It seeks to document and record how social actors use 'rights talk' in the pursuit of particular ends.
>
> Its overarching concern is to ethnographically explore the 'social life of rights'.
>
> The foundation of human rights is *human social activity*, not a universal morality.

KEY POINTS	
1948 *AAA* Statement set out objections, based on the scientific, empirical methodology of the discipline, which blocked engagement with human rights for a very long time.	This was followed by the 'ethnographic' turn, which sought to understand 'the social life of rights', the meaning and use of rights according to the actions and intentions of social actors working within constraints of institutionalized power.
Over time 'objective' detachment gave way to immersion and empathy, which in turn led to political activism on behalf of the subjects.	In 2006 an important argument emerged that attempted to newly frame the anthropology of human rights with an 'ecumenical anthropology of human rights'—an anthropology that tolerates and encourages approaches that are both fundamentally critical of contemporary human rights regimes and approaches that are politically or ethically committed to these same regimes.
An 'emancipatory cultural politics' thread emerged—that saw human rights as a useful tool for serving an ethical commitment toward threatened peoples and cultures.	

A Common Thread: The Social Construction of Rights

As we have seen, despite the initial scepticism toward human rights and the resultant reluctance to engage with the concept, there is now a growing body of research emerging from both sociology and anthropology that analyses the 'social life of rights'. However, from the discussions above we can see that the sociological engagement tended to begin with broad structural observations about human ontology, the capitalist mode of production, or the role of international power politics in the construction of the UDHR and the like. Anthropology, by contrast, usually began with a more microethnographic methodology, only subsequently invoking contextualizing social structural insights that would draw attention to broader, more sociological, issues such as the role of 'institutionalized power' (see Wilson, 1997). While the disciplines display somewhat different points of origin in their study of human rights, they share one common and very important perspective, which can be called a 'social constructionist' view of human rights. It is a view of human rights (see Box 6.7) that shows that such 'rights' are not simply givens, but products of human social interaction, with all its imbalances and imperfections. Thus a common disciplinary lesson is that we should not assume that the rights that emerge from such interaction are necessarily beneficial to the rights holders. A particularly striking

illustration of this key observation is highlighted by recent research into Indigenous peoples' land rights in Australia (see Short, 2007, 2008), to which we shall turn later in this section. Indeed, the study of indigenous rights in general is an excellent example of how these two disciplines can offer complementary insights: the anthropological interest in non-Western cultures and a rigorous ethnographic methodology, coupled with sociological structural appreciation, can combine to help us more fully understand the social life of these particular rights.

Box 6.7 **Common Thread: Social Constructionist View of Human Rights**

The disciplines display different points of origin in their study of human rights, but share a 'social constructionist' view of human rights.

The approach shows that such 'rights' are not simply givens, but products of human social interaction with all its imbalances and imperfections.

A common disciplinary lesson is that we should not assume rights to be beneficial to the rights holders.

Both the construction *and practical functionality* of rights should be carefully examined.

These key observations are highlighted by research into Indigenous peoples' land rights in Australia.

As we have seen, the discipline of sociology was slow to engage with human rights, yet it has been even slower to engage with the specific case of indigenous rights. Historians, anthropologists (not surprising given the discipline's interest in non-Western cultures), and political and legal theorists have all made commentaries and undertaken significant research on Indigenous peoples and their rights (see Chapter 15), yet only a few sociologists have taken an interest in a subject that is now truly global in its ramifications (Samson and Short, 2006). In the face of the homogenizing forces of economic globalization and strong nation states, it is becoming increasingly clear that the affluence produced by international capitalism comes at the expense of both the ecosystem (see Chapter 18) and the cultural vitality of small peoples whose ways of life depend on local environments (Samson and Short, 2006). Global activism of hitherto separate groups of Indigenous peoples has developed in response to these destructive homogenizing forces. Indigenous groups such as the Wirajuri, Ngunnawall, Nahuatl, Ogiek, Blackfoot, Tuareg, and Innu are now intimately involved in the construction of their rights through the United Nations system (Samson and Short, 2006). This quest through the UN system is borne out of frustration at the extreme social and political disadvantage suffered by many Indigenous peoples worldwide and frequently out of disillusionment with the rights conferred on them by the settler states in which they live.

One such domestic rights regime is the so-called 'native title' land rights that have emerged in Australia. Recent research (see Short, 2007, 2008) has shown that in the Australian context the domestic institutionalization of international human rights standards[5] as they pertain to Indigenous peoples is best understood as a product of the balance of power between political interests. In 1992 the High Court of Australia in the *Mabo* case finally acknowledged that to deny indigenous rights to land would be unjust and contrary to contemporary international human rights standards, especially the principle of racial equality. The court was aware of, in sociologist Bryan Turner's (2006, p. 25) terms, the 'vulnerability' of dispossessed Indigenous people and did not seek to worsen their plight by flouting the international moral code that prohibits racial discrimination. Yet, when the Government responded to the landmark case, the interests of vulnerable Indigenous groups were ignored in favour of powerful commercial

interests. The net result was legalization that sought to *limit* indigenous rights behind a veneer of agrarian reform. Thus, as Freeman (2002, p. 85) warned, 'the institutionalisation of human rights may . . . lead, not to their more secure protection but to their protection in a form that is less threatening to the existing system of power.' The research examined the trajectory of indigenous rights to land in a manner that went beyond the formal, legalistic dimensions of such rights, where, as Wilson (2001, p. xvii) pointed out, they will always be a 'good thing'. In contrast to such perspectives, this research's social constructionist approach showed how the institutionalization of 'native title' land rights was a social process bound by colonial structures and ultimately intertwined with power, elites, privilege, and the actions, intentions, and interests of the social actors involved. The research placed the institutionalization of native title rights in the context of political battles for control of resources that pitted Indigenous peoples against powerful commercial lobby groups. It showed how, through the social construction of a discourse of crisis, industry 'uncertainty', and the deliberate generation of unfounded public fear, commercial lobby groups and their political and media supporters successfully pressured the government to severely limit indigenous land rights (see Short, 2007, 2008).

In short, this research showed that seemingly beneficial indigenous land rights were in fact constructed in such a way as to actually *maintain* existing social, political, and economic inequalities and perpetuate the colonial status quo. In this sense the work highlighted a gulf between settler state granted indigenous rights and their normative benchmark: the United Nations *Declaration on the Rights of Indigenous Peoples* (the Declaration).[6] Indeed, the indigenous land rights debate in Australia is an example of, in Turner and Rojek's (2001, p. 127) terms, 'the frequent tension between national systems of rights and international human rights'. Yet, of course, it must also be stated that the 'normative benchmark' of indigenous rights, the UDHR, is itself a social construction. The significant difference between the Declaration and settler state granted indigenous rights, however, is that, despite the inequalities in bargaining power between states and Indigenous representatives in the UN, Indigenous peoples were nonetheless a major force in the construction of the Declaration (see Niezen, 2003, Morgan, 2004). Thus, the international Indigenous peoples' movement has accepted the 2007 United Nations Declaration on the Rights of Indigenous Peoples as a more just articulation of their rights than those imposed on them by 'settler' states. This position is based on the Declaration's inclusion of self-determination, which is seen as a remedial *political right* of distinct dispossessed 'peoples' and 'nations' in contrast to the individual citizenship rights, or limited rights to land occupation, conferred on them by colonial nation states. The broad interpretation of self-determination in this context refers to the right to political autonomy, the freedom to determine political status, and the right to freely pursue economic, social, and cultural development. Consequently, the right is viewed as central to a 'just' response to colonial dispossession and the resultant political and social subordination of Indigenous peoples. Indigenous calls for self-determination derive from the fact that they were self-governing political entities or 'sovereign nations', and in spite of colonization many Indigenous groups still claim such status (see Short, 2008).

> **KEY POINTS**
>
> Despite the initial scepticism toward human rights of both disciplines, there is now a growing body of research that analyses the 'social life of rights'.
>
> In approaching human rights, however, the two disciplines begin from different positions—sociology with broad structural observations, anthropology with a microethnographic methodology.
>
> The disciplines, however, share one common and very important perspective that can be labelled 'social constructionist'.
>
> Rights are seen as products of human social interaction, and most significantly power relations. Consequently, we should not assume them to be beneficial.
>
> The case of indigenous land rights in Australia is a prime example of the importance of a social constructionist perspective.

Conclusion

We have seen how anthropologists and sociologists were historically sceptical of human rights due to the dominant positivistic and relativistic disciplinary biases, and how each discipline eventually moved away from this position toward an engagement with human rights that sought to explore rigorously the nuances, contingencies, contestations, and meanings that are part and parcel of the 'social life of rights'. Indeed, we have seen that there is now a growing body of research emerging from both sociology and anthropology that seeks to go beyond legal positivism and abstract political philosophy, the hitherto dominant avenues of enquiry into human rights, in order to explore the meaning and use of rights. While both disciplines share a social constructionist view of rights, which is acutely aware of contingencies, contestations, and differing meanings, and also of political power and social structures, they differ in their methodological 'point of origin' and consequently on the relative emphasis placed on these factors. We have seen that sociology sought to emphasize the effect that broad structural factors, such as the capitalist mode of production, international political structures, or the colonial nation state, had on the construction of specific

rights, whilst anthropologists usually began with a more microethnographic exploration of the lived experience of rights before seeking to contextualize more broadly with structural insights such as the role of institutionalized power in rights struggles. Yet, despite the different methodological 'points of origin' the disciplines share a common 'social constructionist' view of human rights. As Plummer suggested earlier, 'the task for sociologists is to become intimately familiar with the crusaders, their claims and the social processes through which rights emerge', which is strikingly similar to social anthropologist Richard Wilson's desire for more research into the 'social life of rights'. Such a social constructionist approach to human rights will delve deeper than legal perspectives where, as Wilson warns, rights will always be seen as a 'good thing'.

Through a brief summary of recent 'social constructionist' research into indigenous land rights, we have seen that this is certainly not the case with the seemingly beneficial 'native title' rights in Australia. Such 'rights' have actually functioned to further dispossess Indigenous peoples, which has compounded the tragedy of colonial dispossession and its legacy of extreme social, political, and economic disadvantage (see Short, 2008). Thus, in addition to the knowledge gleaned from legal, philosophical, and political approaches to the study of human rights, we should embrace anthropological and sociological studies, that explore the 'social life of rights', since it is only through such studies that we can hope to fully understand the *practice* of human rights in the modern world.

QUESTIONS

INDIVIDUAL STUDY QUESTIONS

1. Why did it take the discipline of sociology so long to engage with human rights?
2. On what grounds did Turner defend the universality of human rights? Is this compatible with a social constructionist view?
3. Are the insights of the classical sociological theorists relevant to the study of human rights?
4. What broad insights can we attribute to the sociology of human rights?
5. What were the main objections of the discipline of anthropology to the idea of universal human rights and were they overcome?
6. What are the two main currents of the anthropology of human rights and how do they differ?
7. What are the similarities and differences in sociological and anthropological approaches to human rights?
8. How do such approaches aid our understanding of human rights?

GROUP DISCUSSION QUESTIONS

1. Do we need a 'foundational ontology' to study and research human rights?
2. Are the interests that Waters identifies as responsible for the growth of human rights convincing (see Box 6.2)?
3. What precisely is meant by the 'social life of rights'?
4. If you were to choose an anthropological methodology to research a rights issue, which of the two main anthropological approaches would you choose to use, and why?

FURTHER READING

American Anthropologist (2006). 'In focus: Anthropology and human rights in a new key'. **108**/1.
    An excellent collection of anthropological theorizing and research on the topic of human rights by leading scholars in the field.
Goodale, M. (2008). *Human Rights: An Anthropological Reader*. Blackwell Readers in Anthropology.
    A useful guide for students wishing to further their understanding of the broad range of anthropological work on human rights.
Goodale, M. and **Merry**, S.-E. (2007). *The Practice of Human Rights: Tracking Law Between the Global and the Local*. Cambridge Studies in Law & Society. Cambridge: Cambridge University Press.
    Building from their contributions to the *AA* 'In focus' (above), the authors focus on the 'practice' of human rights, which fills a significant gap in theoretical and empirical understanding.
Morris, L. (ed.) (2006). *Rights: Sociological Perspectives*. Abingdon: Routledge.
    To date, the only collection of essays specifically geared toward exploring rights issues sociologically. Students

should pay special attention to the Introduction for a fuller examination of the relevance of classical sociology to the study of contemporary human rights, and to Chapter 9 for a fuller discussion of what sociology can offer the study of Indigenous peoples' rights.

Short, D. (2008). *Reconciliation and Colonial Power: Indigenous Rights in Australia*. Aldershot: Ashgate. Students should pay special attention to Chapters 3 and 4 of this text for an example of a social constructionist approach to understanding indigenous land rights.

Turner, B. S. (2006). *Vulnerability and Human Rights*. University Park, PA: The Pennsylvania State University Press. This book is Turner's definitive work on human rights, which encapsulates and builds on the main arguments of his breakthrough work in the early 1990s. Turner's work is still perhaps the most plausible foundationalist account of human rights to have emerged from the discipline of sociology.

WEB LINKS

http://www.asanet.org/cs/root/leftnav/governance/issue_statements/statement_on_human_rights As evidence of the discipline of sociology's significant reorientation toward human rights see the link above. The American Sociological Association (ASA) took the celebration of its centenary (1905–2005) as an opportunity to reiterate its strongest support for the basic civil and political freedoms of peoples of all nations as articulated by the Universal Declaration of Human Rights (UDHR).

http://www.sfgate.com/cgi-bin/article.cgi?file=/chronicle/archive/2004/08/13/EDGFT87CT01.DTL Mary Robinson's important address on sociology and human rights at 99th annual meeting of the American Sociological Association.

http://www.sociologistswithoutborders.com/

http://ssfinternacional.blogspot.com/2008/02/sociology-and-human-rights.html An initiative that began in Madrid in 2001, *Sociologists without Borders*/Sociólogos Sin Fronteras (SSF) is a non-governmental organization that advances a cosmopolitan sociology with a specific commitment to human rights. The group advances human rights by working with, and in, communities, societies, workplaces, and other social institutions. The second web link explains their specific human rights approach.

http://www.aaanet.org/stmts/humanrts.htm June 1999 Declaration on Anthropology and Human Rights defines the basis for the involvement of the American Anthropological Association, and, more generally, of the profession of Anthropology in human rights.

NOTES

1. See Goodale (2006a) for an excellent detailed discussion of these objections.

2. Goodale (2006a, p. 2) cites some obvious examples, including the work of 'forensic anthropologists in collating evidence for international human rights investigations, linguistic and political anthropologists studying the problem of linguistic minorities' attempts to find protection through a discourse of marginalization that is supported by international human rights instruments.

3. At this point we can see how such an ethical commitment can act as a more idealist counterpoint to the 'social constructionist' approach of sociologist Malcolm Waters—discussed above. Indeed, viewing human rights as a socially constructed phenomena, subject to power politics, does not preclude their construction by marginalized groups—it just makes it more difficult.

4. See Goodale (2006a, p. 4) on this.

5. I am using the term 'standards' here as indigenous rights to land are not fully entrenched in international law as yet. They are, however, an intrinsic part of the United Nations Draft Declaration on the Rights of Indigenous Peoples (UNDD)—see indigenous rights to land (Articles 26 and 27 of the UNDD)—and consequently they have, what in legal terms is known as, strong 'persuasive authority'. Furthermore, freedom from racial discrimination is included in Article 2 of the UNDD but is also an established international norm (for a discussion of such points see Anaya, 2004). In deciding the Mabo case the High Court, especially Brennan J, felt the weight of the international moral code, in particular the rule against racial discrimination.

6. The Declaration represents the human rights of Indigenous peoples and includes the right to self-determination (see Anaya, 2004).

ONLINE RESOURCE CENTRE

 Visit the Online Resource Centre that accompanies this book for updates and a range of other resources:

http://www.oxfordtextbooks.co.uk/orc/goodhart/

Ideological (Mis)use of Human Rights

David Chandler

Chapter Contents

Reader's Guide

This chapter seeks to explain why human rights claims, which assert the need to empower the poor and excluded, often appear to enforce the power of dominant Western states and international institutions. It will demonstrate that there is a paradox at the heart of the human rights discourse, which enables claims made on behalf of the victims, marginalized, and excluded to become a mechanism for the creation of new frameworks for the exercise of power. It will suggest that, rather than understanding human rights frameworks in the international sphere as a challenge to power relations, it would be more accurate to describe them in terms of a challenge to the existing formal international legal order. It will clarify that there is nothing progressive or empowering about human rights claims in themselves and that, if the enforcement and protection of these claims relies on external and unaccountable actors, then existing informal hierarchies of power will become increasingly formalized, while formal protections of the rights of self-determination and self-government will be undermined.

Introduction

Many commentators have observed the fact that human rights frameworks have become an integral part of a new, more hierarchical, international order, undermining UN Charter restrictions on the use of military force and justifying new, more coercive forms of international regulation and intervention in the post-colonial world. To view these consequences of human rights claims and discourses as the ideological 'misuse' or 'abuse' of human rights would already be to approach the question of understanding human rights with a certain set of assumptions. These assumptions would be based upon an idea that human rights claims necessarily challenge entrenched power relations and are an important mechanism of advocacy on behalf of the victims of abuses or those excluded from traditional frameworks of representation. This chapter will suggest that these prior assumptions, of the 'purity' of human rights claims and of their 'abuse' by powerful actors, are themselves problematic.

Human rights claims can not in themselves be accurately seen as either enforcing or challenging the existing relations of power. The one thing that can be asserted with confidence is that human rights claims conflate an ethical or moral claim with a legal and political one. The discourse of the 'human' belongs to the sphere of abstract universal ethics, while that of 'rights' belongs to the framework of a concretely constituted legal and political sphere. In conflating the two spheres, human rights claims pose a challenge to rights as they are legally constituted. The content of this challenge, whether it has any consequences, and, if it does have consequences what these consequences are, are matters for concrete analysis. To suggest that any challenge to the framework of legally constituted rights is necessarily an effective one, or necessarily a good or progressive one, would clearly be naive.

In fact, it was the challenge of naivety that was famously articulated by Jeremy Bentham, the utilitarian philosopher, when he denounced the idea of human rights as 'nonsense on stilts' (see Chapter 1). He had nothing but contempt for the new-fangled universal 'rights of man' proclaimed at the end of the eighteenth century. For Bentham, rights meant nothing unless they were enforceable with clear contractual obligations and backed by law. Declarations of the 'rights of man' were no more than rhetorical fancies and collections of pious wishes that were not worth the paper they were written on. The idea that we were born with universal equal rights simply because we were human made no sense to Bentham. Firstly, we are born into a relationship of dependency rather than equality, and are not considered as moral or legal equals until we reach maturity (children are not born with criminal liability as they are not responsible for their actions). Secondly, it was clear that there could be no universal human equality: the opportunities we have depend fundamentally on the societies we live in and our position within those societies.

However, few people would have the confidence to argue in Bentham's dismissive terms today. It would appear to be undeniable that our understandings of and respect for human rights are central to the way we and our governments make policy and act in international affairs. Yet, despite today's consensus on the fact that 'human rights are a good thing', there is still the nagging sense that Bentham may have a point, that human rights may sound very nice on paper but be much more ephemeral when it comes to giving these aspirations meaning and content, and that, nice as these claims sound, they may be open to abuse.

Claims to anything can be abused and all claims to rights can be misused. However, it is vital to appreciate that it is inherent within human rights claims that they are more open to abuse or misuse than other claims, those of democratic and civil rights for example. The reason for this, in the words of Norman Lewis, is quite simply because human rights are not derived from 'socially constituted legal subjects' (Lewis, 1998, p. 85). Where Bentham saw abstract rights claims as merely childish or superstitious thinking, much as the 'belief in witches or unicorns'; their abstract nature—the fact that they can reflect radical and progressive aspirations rather than merely legally enshrined rights—is held to be a major factor in their use and support across the globe.

This chapter is tasked with focusing on the downside of human rights claims—what is commonly understood by advocates of human rights to be the 'misuse' or 'abuse' of human rights. It will be demonstrated that the ambiguous and abstract nature of human rights claims is at the same time their point of attraction but equally makes the opportunity for 'abuse' a constant one. Unfor-tunately, for the advocates of human rights frameworks, their openness to abuse is not incidental but is intrinsic to the concept of human rights themselves.

Human Rights and the Legal Subject

The discourse of human rights has a pre-history in terms of the claims of **natural rights** from the **Enlightenment** onwards where claims of a universal human nature were an essentialist grounding for ideas of individual equality and self-determination, which challenged the aristocratic and feudal social and political hierarchies (see Box 7.1). Natural rights claims are therefore seen at the centre of the revolutionary movements of liberal modernity: the Declaration of the Rights of Man and of the Citizen of the French Revolution and the Dec-laration of Independence and the Bill of Rights of the American Revolution.

With the development of more social and histor-ical frameworks of thinking, expounded by theorists such as Emile Durkheim, Max Weber, and Karl Marx, the idea of natural rights was discredited (see Chapter 6). In its place was a consensus of understanding that rights were social and political products, dependent on the state and society in which the individual lived. Concrete rights of citizenship replaced the abstract conception of natural rights.

Twentieth-Century Critiques

For the leading political theorists of the twentieth century, the idea of human rights as universal claims made no more sense than it did to Jeremy Bentham. Writing in 1950, in the aftermath of the Second World War, Hannah Arendt remarked that the Holocaust demonstrated the abstract and meaningless nature of the concept of human rights (see Box 7.2). Where Jews were denied the rights of citizenship—their political status—they were forced to fall back on the abstract claims of human rights. In doing so, their status was transformed from active decision-making political sub-jects to objects of the charity or benevolence of others. For Arendt, what makes us human and rights-bearing subjects is not our bare humanity but our capacity to create rights-bearing and rights-giving political com-munities. The lesson of the Holocaust, for the Jews, was not the need to give more attention to human rights, but the need to ensure the political rights of citizenship, achieved through the struggle to establish and safe-guard the state of Israel.

Arendt makes the point here that human rights are 'fictional' rights: they are rights that are not dependent on the collective agency of their subject (Chandler, 2003). Individuals 'freed' from the political process of collective decision making no longer have an active say in what their rights are or should be; at most they are lobbying or begging others for favours and place them-selves in a situation of dependency. For Arendt, the rights of the 'human' are much less than the rights of the 'citizen'. The bearer of merely 'human' rights is sub-ordinate, dependent, and in a position of supplicant to others. The response to these rights claims is therefore

---

Box 7.1 **Sophocles' Antigone: Ethics vs Law**

The conception of human rights can be dated back to ancient Greece and the work of the famous playwright Sophocles. To quote the US State Department pamphlet, 'Human Rights and US Foreign Policy', published in 1978:

> The idea of human rights is almost as old as its ancient enemy, despotism. . . . When Sophocles' heroine Antigone cries out to the autocratic King Creus: 'all your strength is weakness itself against [t]he immortal unrecorded laws of God' she makes a deeply revolutionary assertion. There are laws, she claims, higher than the laws made by any King; as an individual she has certain rights under those higher laws; and kings and armies—while they may violate her rights by force—can never cancel them or take them away. (Cited in Sellars, 2002, p. vii)

This is an excellent example of the essence of human rights claims: legal rights are equated with power and oppression and challenged in the name of a non-legally constituted rights subject.

Box 7.2 **Hannah Arendt and Carl Schmitt on Human Rights**

Hannah Arendt on Human Rights

> . . . the public sphere is as consistently based on the law of equality as the private sphere is based on the law of universal difference and differentiation. Equality, in contrast to all that is involved in mere existence, is not given us, but is the result of human organization insofar as it is guided by the principle of justice. We are not born equal; we become equal as members of a group on the strength of our decision to guarantee ourselves mutually equal rights. (Arendt, 1973, p. 301)

Carl Schmitt on Human Rights

> Humanity as such cannot wage war because it has no enemy, at least not on this planet. . . . When a state fights its political enemy in the name of humanity, it is not a war for the sake of humanity, but a war wherein a particular state seeks to usurp a universal concept against a military opponent. . . . The concept of humanity is an especially useful ideological instrument of imperialist expansion, and in its ethical-humanitarian form it is a specific vehicle of economic imperialism. Here one is reminded of a somewhat modified expression of Proudhon's: whoever invokes humanity wants to cheat. To confiscate the word humanity, to invoke and monopolize such a term probably has certain incalculable effects, such as denying the enemy the quality of being human and declaring him to be an outlaw of humanity; and a war can thereby be driven to the most extreme inhumanity. (Schmitt, 1996, p. 54)

an arbitrary one. Arendt argues that it may result in 'privileges in some cases, injustices in most' because 'blessings and doom are meted out to them [bearers of human rights] according to accident and without any relation whatsoever to what they do, did, or may do' (Arendt, 1973, p. 296).

For Arendt, human rights frameworks, in separating the rights bearer from the agent capable of enacting these rights, legitimize a framework that is in fact worse than that suggested by Bentham's view of pious wishes and utopian dreaming. Arendt suggests that a field of fictitious 'rights' is opened up that is inherently open to abuse and arbitrary interpretation and enforcement.

Carl Schmitt, a German legal and political theorist, writing at the same time as Arendt, was also critical of the idea of universal human rights. Schmitt approached the subject from the opposite end of the spectrum (not from the viewpoint of the human rights subject—the individual claiming human rights—but that of the external actor deemed to be responsible for enforcing human

rights). He argued that claiming to intervene militarily on behalf of universal human rights was an act of power rather than principle, stating famously that 'whoever invokes humanity wants to cheat' (see Box 7.2).

Schmitt makes similar points to Arendt in arguing that the concepts of 'humanity' and of 'human rights' are empty abstractions, i.e. that they do not correspond to any political reality of constituted rights and duties. Schmitt argues that the concept of human rights may well have had a useful polemical appeal at the end of the eighteenth century as a rallying cry against the then existing aristocratic feudal system and the inequalities and privileges associated with it. However, this did not mean that the era of universal human rights had arrived. The fact that the world is divided into different and distinct political societies or states means that universal rights-bearing individuals do not exist. If they did exist then we would have a universal government, giving political and legal form to those universal rights (Schmitt, 1996, p. 55).

For Schmitt, in the absence of a unified world government that could constitute the universal human being as a rights-bearing subject in reality, human rights claims will have no clear court of adjudication or mechanism of enforcement. Schmitt argued that humanitarian action could be unproblematic if it was based on inter-state agreement and administered through a non-political body, such as the International Committee of the Red Cross (ICRC). His point was that if abstract human rights claims were set against the agreed constituted rights framework then they threatened conflict and instability. This was because the subject of these claims was separate from the agency enforcing them. The enforcement of claims of non-socially constituted legal subjects is necessarily an arbitrary one, decided by questions of power rather than principle. Schmitt feared that universal claims to judge the needs or interests of 'humanity' were not just illegitimate acts of power rather than law per se, but that they were also dangerous and destabilizing in a politically divided world (Schmitt, 1996, pp. 53–58).

The Paradox of Human Rights

The points made by Hannah Arendt and Carl Schmitt get to the heart of the paradox of human rights. Their capacity for challenging power as well as for being mechanisms of the exercise of power (unrestrained by law) stem from the fact that human rights claims are made on behalf of non-legally constituted subjects. Human rights claims may reflect the imminent revolutionary overthrow of the established order or they may reflect the oppressive use of governing power to rule beyond the limits of the law. Human rights claims, by separating the holder of rights from the agency of enforcement of these claims, reflect merely the challenge to the legal order. Without a consideration of the context in which a discourse of human rights arises, it is impossible to make a normative judgement as to whether this challenge to the legal order of constituted rights is something to be supported or opposed.

KEY POINTS
Human rights claims conflate ethical and legal claims because the subject of rights is not a socially constituted legal subject.
For this reason, human rights claims challenge the existing legal framework (whether it is authoritarian or democratic).
Human rights claims express a **capacity gap**—where the rights holder is held to lack the capability of acting on their own behalf—therefore an external agent is held to be required to enforce these rights. The dependency on an unaccountable external actor therefore makes enforcement indeterminate and contingent upon the relations (and interests) of power.

The Rise of Human Rights

Natural rights, in terms of human rights, were revived in the sphere of international politics only during the Second World War. The modern government-led human rights movement could be seen to have been born during the War, with US President Franklin D. Roosevelt's famous 'Four Freedoms' speech of 1941 or H. G. Wells's publication *The Rights of Man, or, What Are We Fighting For?* of 1940. The defence of 'essential liberties and freedoms' helped to cohere the Allied War effort against Germany and Japan, but it is important not to confuse the declaration of abstract universal values with the intention (or capability) of enforcing a framework of universal rights in the international sphere.

The gap between human rights as abstract rhetoric and as legally constituted and enforceable rights is illustrated well by the Universal Declaration of Human Rights (UDHR) agreed by the *United Nations General Assembly* (UNGA) in December 1948. There was agreement on thirty human rights expressed as a set of abstract moral claims or aspirations; these rights were abstracted from political questions of concrete societies' priorities and concerns and therefore could be signed up to by states with market- or state-regulated economic systems. There could be common agreement precisely because the UN did not claim to be describing rights that were universally recognized in every state, nor did it attempt to enact or enforce these rights in a legal form.

The Post-War Order

Human rights frameworks can therefore be read back into the formative legal and political moments of the post-War international order. However, if we were to read this focus on universal human rights as either a challenge to sovereignty or a challenge to the dominant framework of international order, we would be reading history backwards from the vantage point of today. It is important to appreciate that the Nuremberg tribunal, the UDHR, and even the 1949 Genocide Convention were seen as enforcing the framework of equal sovereign rights and the principle of non-intervention.

The post-War order was constituted by the establishment of sovereign states as the only rights-bearing subjects of international law (see Chapter 2). This was made explicitly clear in the great power deliberations and international conferences in preparation of the UN Charter. There was no contradiction between state sovereignty and human rights (between the rights of states and the rights of individuals) because the international order did not recognize individuals as legal subjects. Therefore, as US Secretary of State Edward R. Stettinius stated, the legal situation was clear: 'The provisions proposed in the Charter will not, of course, ensure by themselves the realization of human rights and fundamental freedoms for all the people. The provisions are not made enforceable by any international machinery.

The responsibility rests with the member governments to carry them out.' (Cited in Lewis, 1998, p. 88.)

Secondly, natural rights were brought into international relations through the Nuremberg Tribunal. Many human rights advocates argue today that the trial marked a fundamental legal break in the undermining of the rights of sovereign state authorities. This claim makes little sense as, with Germany's unconditional surrender in 1945, the Allied states who organized the military tribunal at Nuremberg did this explicitly as occupying powers with sovereign authority rather than as a supranational authority (see Laughland, 2007, pp. 53–68). Where the tribunal broke new legal ground was in using natural law to overrule *positivist* law, to argue that the laws in force at the time in Germany were no defence against the retrospective crime of 'waging an aggressive war'. This was justified on the grounds that certain acts were held to be such heinous crimes that they were banned by universal principles of humanity (Douzinas, 2007, pp. 21–22). Human rights frameworks were used to undermine positivist law, to cast the winners of the War as moral, not merely military, victors.

Human rights frameworks emerged during and at the close of the Second World War in an attempt to give moral legitimacy both to the Allies' actions during the War and to the post-War international order. While today the UDHR and the Nuremberg Tribunal are understood to have raised a challenge to the rights of state sovereignty, this was not the case at the time. The preparatory discussions for the UN Declaration and the deliberations of the Nuremberg judges both made it absolutely clear that the sovereign state was the subject of international law and that sovereignty was not challenged by any transnational legal authority. States were held to be the upholders and enforcers of both the moral and political order.

Human Rights and the Cold War

The habit of reading the rise of human rights consciousness back to 1945 as a story of the teleological march of universal ethics and values is one that unfortunately underplays the radical shift in the importance of human rights after the end of the Cold War. The strong consensus today that universal human rights are a guide to international policy making is, in fact, a relatively recent development. For the first twenty years after the Second World War, one of the major journals on international relations, *Foreign Affairs*, did not carry one article on human rights (Korey, 1999, p. 151). During the bulk of the Cold War era there was little concern with the implications of the UDHR on state policy or practice. Until the 1980s, the majority of academic commentators and policy makers were not convinced that human rights concerns or ethical considerations were an appropriate subject of study when assessing a state's foreign policy.

This is not surprising as human rights claims were understood to be particular rather than universal. In the West, human rights claims were interpreted as largely synonymous with democracy and the free market. The US Government and the human rights organizations that it funded consistently played down the economic and social aspirations of the UDHR. As a propaganda weapon against the Soviet states, Western governments focused on political and civil freedoms, such as freedom of movement and information and the right to leave and return to one's country. Human rights aspirations were part of the international agenda, but they were a constituent part of the Cold War framework and understood as subordinate to the rights of sovereignty.

Their subordination to the geo-political division of the Cold War was highlighted by the lack of consensus on moving forward the aspirations of the 1948 Universal Declaration. In the 1950s, two separate UN committees were established. These produced two separate international covenants in 1966, one dealing with civil and political rights and the other with economic, social, and cultural rights. The opposition of leading Western states to rights in the economic and social sphere was highlighted in 1986 when the UNGA adopted the *Declaration on the Right to Development*, and the USA, UK, Germany, and Japan either voted against or abstained (Mutua, 1996, pp. 606–607).

It was through attempts to overcome divisions within the US establishment and the need to address the decline of US credibility abroad, following defeat in Vietnam and the US-backed overthrow of Salvador Allende's government in Chile in 1973, that human rights concerns were put back on the international agenda (Sellars, 2002). Human rights became the mechanism by which America's reputation was to be redeemed. In 1974 the Congressional report 'Human Rights in the World Community: A Call for US Leadership' set the tone for Gerald Ford's inclusion of human rights provisions into the East–West Helsinki Agreement of 1975—signed by the United States, Canada, the Soviet Union, and most European states including Turkey—and for President Carter's declaration in his 1977 inaugural speech that 'our commitment to human rights must be absolute' (Sellars, 2002, p. 118). Human rights were on the agenda, but there was still little understanding of these as universal norms, rather than as a weapon in Cold War geo-politics.

From 1975 onwards, human rights were institutionalized as part of Cold War political exchanges through the establishment of the Organization for Security and Cooperation in Europe (OSCE). The Helsinki process of East–West negotiations gradually institutionalized mechanisms of human rights monitoring and information provision under the Human Dimension Mechanism—which allowed OSCE member states to raise issues of human rights concern with other member states. This process was used on over a hundred occasions but, on all but one (Hungary's use against Romania over disturbances in Transylvania), the raising of human rights concerns was directly linked to geo-political divisions (Bloed, 1993; Brett, 1993). As long as the Cold War persisted and human rights issues were used as weapons in the geo-political divide, it was clear that there would be no support for the idea that human

rights concerns could undermine sovereignty. Only in the 1990s did human rights appear to be a subject of concern in their own right, so important as to challenge the rights of states and existing frameworks of diplomatic relations and of policy-making priorities.

KEY POINTS

Universal human rights claims could help provide moral legitimacy to international institutions, but did not undermine or challenge the state-based international order.

Because human rights claims had no socially constituted legal subject they empowered nation states as their agents, deciding on the content of these rights and the means of their enforcement.

During the Cold War, human rights claims were heavily politicized and subordinate to the interests of power, used by both the US and the Soviet Union to achieve instrumental ends.

Human rights were equated for ideological reasons with civil and political rights in the West and with social and economic rights by Soviet states.

Human Rights and International Intervention

With the end of the Cold War, human rights concerns shifted from the margins to the mainstream of international concerns as universal humanitarianism appeared to be a feasible possibility. Western states and international institutions had a much greater freedom to act in the international sphere with the attenuation of Cold War rivalries freeing policy from narrow geo-strategic concerns. The new possibilities for intervention and aspirations for a more universal framework of policy making were increasingly expressed through the expanding discourse of human rights. There were relatively few critical voices until the 1999 Kosovo war—waged unilaterally (without UN Security Council support) by NATO states against Serbia—brought to a head concerns about the potential misuse or abuse of concerns of humanitarianism

and human rights. In particular, there was concern about the idea of 'humanitarian war' tying human rights advocacy with the preponderant use of US military power. In the following sections, the relationship between human rights claims, humanitarian advocacy, international law, and military intervention will be examined with a particular focus on the ethical, legal, and political questions raised by the Kosovo war.

Human Rights and Humanitarianism

It was in the humanitarian sphere that the shift from formal views of rights, based on rational autonomous subjects, to ethical views of rights, based on a lack of capacity and the need for external advocacy and intervention, became a major factor in international relations. The introduction of the human rights-based approach into traditional humanitarian practices reflected two trends: firstly, the increased penetration of external actors and agencies into post-colonial states and societies; and secondly, the transformation of the content of traditional humanitarian principles.

As Western humanitarian non-governmental organizations (NGOs) acquired greater powers and authority within post-colonial states, they redefined the central concepts guiding their work. Universality and neutrality came to be redefined, not on the basis of a universal view of humanity as being equally moral and autonomous, but on the basis of end goals or aspirations. This expansion of external power, through redefining the 'human' as lacking autonomy, effectively set up a hierarchy of the 'helper' and the 'helpless'. Through the ethic of responsibility to assist the 'helpless'—those without autonomy—this discourse reframed political choices as ethical questions. In this way, external NGO actors maintained a 'non-political' stance of neutrality at the same time as claiming extended rights to intervene in domestic political processes. From the late 1960s onwards, international humanitarian NGOs used the discourse of human rights to rewrite the boundaries of their authority through expanding the sphere of ethics into the sphere of political decision making.

The debate within the NGO community, from the late 1960s, over differing approaches to universal humanitarian ethics, counter-posed two views of universality. The former, 'rights equality', view espoused by the ICRC was based on the Enlightenment understanding that the recipients of aid were autonomous capable moral beings and therefore made no judgement regarding the actions or political choices of recipients (see Ignatieff, 1998, pp. 109–163). The human rights-based approach saw the recipients of aid in more judgemental terms: this universality was based on ends-based outcomes of peace, development, justice, etc. The importance of the shift from a universal 'rights equality' approach to that of a 'human rights-based' approach is rarely clarified; one exception is Michael Ignatieff's discussion of ICRC 'impartiality' in his book *Warrior's Honor* (Ignatieff, 1998) (see Box 7.3).

The human rights-based discourse of humanitarianism enabled NGOs to blur the distinction between politics and ethics. Central to this conflation of politics and ethics was the development of new codes of

---

Box 7.3 **The Distinction Between the ICRC and MSF (*Médecins Sans Frontières/ Doctors Without Borders*)**

Michael Ignatieff on Humanitarianism

[The ICRC's] doctrine of neutrality is called into question by organizations like Médecines sans Frontières [Doctors Without Borders], which maintains that humanitarian intervention cannot be impartial between the Serb militiaman and the Muslim civilian, or the machete-wielding Hutu and the Tutsi victim. . . . [T]his leaves the ICRC wondering whether [its] insistence that all victims are equal, whatever the justice of their cause, makes sense in the bitter conflicts where one ethnic group is now seeking to obliterate the other. (Ignatieff, 1998, p. 124)

James Orbinski (MSF) on Humanitarianism

The moral intention of the humanitarian act must be confronted with its actual result. And it is here where any form of moral neutrality about what is good must be rejected. The result can be the use of the humanitarian in 1985 to support forced migration in Ethiopia, or the use in 1996 of the humanitarian to support a genocidal regime in the refugee camps of Goma. Abstention is sometimes necessary so that the humanitarian is not used against a population in crisis. (Orbinski, 1999)

---

practice based around redefining neutrality. Neutrality no longer meant the equal respect for parties to conflict or for locally-instituted authorities, but was redefined as neutrality with respect to human rights frameworks and outcomes. In this way, NGOs claimed decision-making powers over who deserved aid and which practices of development were more appropriate. NGOs accrued more authority through the human rights discourse because they were held to be acting on behalf of rights subjects unable or incapable of acting on their own behalf.

The extension of the power and authority of humanitarian non-state actors took place in relation to changes in approaches to both conflict and to development. First, through the extension of assistance to victims of war, there was a shift from the ICRC approach of aid to casualties and assistance to prisoners regardless of political affiliation, to a more engaged, 'solidarity' approach, advocated by agencies such as Doctors without Borders who argued that there was a need to discriminate between abusers and victims and to intervene in conflict with a view to rights-based outcomes (see Box 7.3). Second, there was a shift in NGO approaches to emergency relief, and an increased understanding that famines and natural disasters could be better addressed by long-term developmental approaches rather than short-term palliative ones (see further Chandler, 2001).

It now appeared that humanitarian NGOs were duty-bound to intervene in much more direct and lasting ways. However, this approach of solidarity and education and training meant that the relationship between NGOs and their beneficiaries changed from one of charity between ostensible equals to one of dependency and empowerment. The humanitarian NGOs shifted from a traditional liberal rights-based approach of equality to an ethico-political approach of human rights that facilitated the inequality of treatment. This has resulted in humanitarian NGOs opposing the provision of aid in cases where it was felt human rights outcomes could be undermined (Leader, 1998; Fox, 2001).

By the end of the Cold War, the discourse of humanitarian universalism had become a highly interventionist one, transformed through the modern discourse of human rights values and assumptions. Once the barriers to state actors intervening were diminished, this discourse was increasingly taken over by leading states and international institutions and NGOs boomed in numbers and authority as new frameworks of intervention were instituted. According to Mark Duffield, the 'petty sovereignty' of NGOs—their increasing assumption of political, decision-making powers in regions intervened in—was 'governmentalized' in the 1990s: integrated within a growing web of interventionist institutions and practices associated with external intervention and regulation (Duffield, 2007).

Human Rights and International Law

Human rights claims, the ethico-juridical claims of a non-constituted legal subject—the human—tend to conflict with formal international legal frameworks, which necessarily operate on the basis of constituted legal subjects—sovereign states. Over the course of the 1990s and the early 2000s the understanding of this conflict has changed. Key to the changing nature of the discussion of human rights and international law have been debates on the redefinition of the meaning and relevance of the legal subject in international law, i.e. the meaning of sovereignty.

The discussion of the meaning of sovereignty reflects the discussions of neutrality and universality,

highlighted in the previous subsection. The universal essence of sovereign equality was not the power or capacity of states, which clearly varied tremendously. The quality of equality was that of moral and political autonomy, the equality of the right of self-government. Since the end of the Cold War, this framework of sovereign equality has been challenged through the framework of human rights, which asserts that formal juridical frameworks are inadequate to address the needs of people living in many states where governments are held to be 'unable or unwilling' to protect their rights (ICISS, 2001).

At the most basic level, sovereign autonomy or self-government is seen as increasingly problematic on its own terms. The possession of formal democracy is no longer seen as adequate to safeguard the rights and interests of individuals. Many commentators follow Fareed Zakaria in his view of the post-Cold War rise of 'illiberal democracies' (Zakaria, 2003). Democracy without liberal cultures and frameworks of rights protections is held to be as likely to be a licence for tyranny as for freedom. In order to prevent the 'tyranny of the majority' or the arbitrariness of democratic mandates (Mill, 1972, p. 73; Guinier, 1994), international human rights enforcements have been increasingly demanded as part of the agenda of 'good governance' and the 'rule of law'.

There is also a second approach of human rights advocacy that undermines the rights of sovereignty, not on the basis of the problems of the formal political framework of citizenship rights, but on the basis of economic and social provisions. This is the discourse of the 'failed' or 'failing' state, where it is asserted that problems with social welfare provision or with economic development indicate that many post-colonial states need external assistance to enhance their 'functional' sovereignty (see Ghani *et al.*, 2005). Here the ethico-juridical framework of human rights redefines sovereignty on the basis of social and economic capacities, creating a sliding scale of sovereignty and marginalizing the importance of a juridical framework based on autonomy and sovereign equality.

Critical commentators are increasingly suggesting that human rights approaches have succeeded in redefining sovereignty so that it lacks any distinct legal meaning and that, in this way, external intervention is no longer seen as conflicting with or as undermining of sovereignty. Mark Duffield suggests that sovereignty has been redefined in terms of the biopolitical—based on the needs of the population rather than the needs of the ruler or government—to justify intervention in the cause of enhancing the standards of human development or human security (Duffield, 2007). Graham Harrison's work on the 'governance state' has highlighted how sovereign institutions of government have become transmission belts for external governance (Harrison, 2004; see also Chandler, 2006). On the basis of human rights frameworks, the claims of sovereign states to legal equality have been weakened, as they have been judged to often be less capable of ensuring that human rights are protected than alternative human rights-based frameworks of international regulation and intervention.

On the basis of the undermining of claims of sovereignty, it is increasingly argued that international law is becoming 'domesticated', i.e. that it is becoming more like domestic law, enshrining the individual as its legal subject. It is often suggested that the prioritizing of individual human rights above the rights of state sovereignty can be understood as the creation of a new international moral legal order, highlighted in the conviction of state leaders for war crimes through the establishment of *ad hoc* international tribunals for former Yugoslavia and Rwanda, the prosecution of Chilean dictator Augustus Pinochet, the establishment of the **International Criminal Court (ICC)**, and the development of ideas of **universal jurisdiction**. For human rights advocates, this new international order is one that is capable of institutionalizing the legal and political equality of individuals in place of the UN Charter framework of the equality of sovereign states.

It is in the area of international law, therefore, that the problematic fact that the individual subject of human rights is not a legally constituted subject becomes clearly highlighted. Rather than extending international law on the basis of reconstituting the formal nature of the international sphere, international law is being transformed into a 'moral–legal order', where the spheres of ethics and of law are becoming blurred (Douzinas, 2007, p. 148). The sphere of law is formally one of equality, where under equal circumstances the punishment is the same. However, the rise of human rights frameworks has introduced an ethical component into international law that, according to Costas Douzinas, 'reconstitutes the structure, subjects and core values of the international system' (Douzinas, 2007, p. 183).

This change reflects and institutionalizes the shifting nature of power relations in the international sphere in the aftermath of the end of the Cold War. During the Cold War, there was a balance of power between the US and the Soviet Union. Although the sides may not have been exactly equal, the key point is that minor disputes or conflicts risked escalating into a nuclear superpower confrontation. For this reason, smaller states found that their sovereignty and independence were safeguarded, not so much because of the letter of international law, but because the maintenance of the status quo and restriction on the use of force to challenge sovereign borders was seen to be vital for world peace and international order. Weak states maintained their sovereignty against more powerful external rivals because of the constitution of the international order (see Jackson, 1990). With the end of this *balance of power*, a new more hegemonic and 'unipolar' world order came into existence, which has been reflected in the renegotiation and overcoming of Cold War formal and informal limits to external intervention.

The human rights framework has facilitated and smoothed the transition away from the formally constituted international order of the Cold War. The ethical challenge of human rights has helped to legitimize the downgrading of the formal legal subjects of the previous order, equal sovereign states, and in their place sets up the more flexible framework based upon the claims of non-constituted legal subjects. In the 1990s the contradictions between the two approaches to framing international order seemed transparent in the debate between the formal 'right of sovereignty' and the emerging 'right of intervention' on behalf of universal human rights claims. This polarization was highlighted in relation to the NATO war over Kosovo in 1999, where human rights were held to trump sovereignty. The problem was that, for many, it was clear that the agency empowered by human rights claims was not Kosovo victims as much as NATO powers who claimed the right of intervention without UN Security Council permission.

Following Kosovo, the UN established an independent commission, the International Commission on Intervention and State Sovereignty, which, with some success, attempted to overcome the problem of clashing rights. In its report 'The Responsibility to Protect' (ICISS, 2001), the Commission suggested reframing the meaning of sovereignty to include the respect for human rights, enabling external intervention to be presented as supporting or enhancing sovereignty, rather than undermining it. At the same time, the report advocated the revival of Just War justifications for military intervention if the UN Security Council was not able to agree to interventions to protect human rights. The Commission's report smoothed the transition away from the formal framework of the UN Charter toward a more flexible moral–legal framework, which inevitably gave more rights to power (Simpson, 2004).

Critical commentators suggest that rights-based approaches shift sovereignty toward a new global centre, but one which is not formally or legally constituted. For many critics, the work of Carl Schmitt (1996) and the more recent work of Giorgio Agamben (2005) highlight that sovereignty, understood as the decision-making power over the exception, has shifted to give Western states, specifically the USA, greater sovereign decision-making power, at the expense of the loss of sovereignty of post-colonial states.

For these critics, the key examples of the shift away from formal equality of sovereignty can be found in the overturning of the principle of non-intervention in Kosovo and Iraq. They highlight the inequalities created by this process: while the USA refuses to be bound by international treaties that are held to limit its powers of sovereign decision making—for example, being the only state (apart from Somalia) not to sign up to the *International Convention on the Rights of the Child*, its refusal to submit to the ICC, etc.—other states have been forced to admit external intervention into their affairs.

For Douzinas, human rights discourses constitute a challenge to the UN Charter legal order, but one that seeks to constitute a hierarchy of unequal rights rather than a more universal order based on the equality of rights (see Box 7.4). The rights of sovereignty and self-determination for smaller or more peripheral states have been removed: 'Lost sovereignty has not disappeared. It has been absorbed and condensed into a super-sovereign centre' (Douzinas, 2007, p. 271; see also Jabri, 2007). For Douzinas, the collapse of traditional restrictions on military intervention and the projection of Western power undermine plural relations of equal sovereignty and reveal that, 'In a historical reversal, an emperor is emerging but the empire is still under construction' (Douzinas, 2007, p. 257).

Human Rights and Military Intervention

The privileging of human rights as individual rights above the sovereign rights of states has altered traditional international practices, especially with regard to international law and the use of force. The human rights-based justification for military intervention is often posed in terms of the revival of pre-modern Just War thinking, which is concerned with the moral and ethical basis of war rather than with its legal grounding. Here the clash between the universal ethics of human rights and the legal framework of international society as it is currently situated comes into stark clarity.

The Kosovo war is often seen as marking the high-point for human rights internationalism. Jürgen

---

Box 7.4 **Cosmopolitanism: A New Hierarchy or a New Universalism?**

Costas Douzinas on Cosmopolitanism

The alleged cosmopolitan character of contemporary politics does not derive from their global subjection to universal rules. The reverse is true: universal rules are created as ideal accompaniments of global phenomena by those who can exercise world policy. Domestic considerations have always played an important role in the calculation of the great powers and determine the ways in which foreign relations are exercised. This leads to a crucial distinction between globalisation and universalisation, which has been almost totally elided in the debate on human rights. (Douzinas, 2007, pp. 180–181)

Vivienne Jabri on Cosmopolitanism

The consequences of what may be referred to as cosmopolitan war are profound, for they suggest . . . a wholesale transformation of social and political relations both domestically and internationally . . . [and] in Foucaultian terms . . . relations of power that seek to discipline conflict and dissent emerging from other societies. . . . What emerges from discourses that seek to modernise, civilise, or democratise, is a conception of a world rendered in hierarchical terms, those that can claim the right of judgement and others who cannot, those within the law and those located beyond the law, those worthy of protection and others not so deserving; all suggesting a hierarchy of worthiness the remit of which is hegemonic domination. (Jabri, 2007, pp. 96–97)

Habermas supported the Kosovo war, despite the fact that it was illegal under UN Charter rules, on the basis that in going to war for human rights NATO was pushing the boundaries of international law into a cosmopolitan, universal direction (Habermas, 1999). The war, alleged to be in the 'grey area' between legality and morality, illustrated the essence of human rights claims as an ethical challenge to law (IICK, 2000). To some commentators, using ethical arguments of human rights to undermine UN Charter law against war was dangerous or an 'abuse' of ethics; for others, as outlined with respect of Habermas, this, on the contrary, was a valuable 'use' of ethics.

However, the rights of the 'human' (of 'human security' or of human rights) that are enforced are not the rights of legally constituted subjects, they are not the rights of states, the subjects of international law. As the rights being enforced are not those of legal subjects, the content and enforcement of human rights is dependent on the *ad hoc* agency of states willing to shoulder the burden of paying for and participating in intervention. The *ad hoc* nature of human rights enforcement means that the ethico-juridical undermining of UN Charter law cannot take a universal form, but is inevitably dependent on a case-by-case approach, with the decision making dictated more by the interests and concerns of the powerful than the needs of the powerless.[1] For some critics, such as Danilo Zolo (2002), it is the global hegemon, the United States, that is empowered by more informal and *ad hoc* decision making, but for others, such as Michael Hardt and Antonio Negri, it is global neoliberal capitalism itself, taking the post-national form of *Empire* (Hardt and Negri, 2001).

Whether the case of Kosovo, where human rights were held to trump sovereignty and international law (HRW, 1999), is understood as a positive step toward a more universal order or as a reactionary step toward a more hierarchical order may be a matter of normative choice. What is beyond dispute is that the existing legal order was challenged and undermined by states powerful enough to take the decision to wage war against the Serbian state. The US and most of the European powers, which backed the war, unilaterally decided to wage war outside the legal restrictions of the UN Charter order. In doing this they claimed that they were waging war on behalf of the rights of the Kosovo Albanians. But the nature of human rights claims is that, while Kosovo Albanians were the subjects of these rights, the active agents in enforcing them were the NATO powers, who in doing so accrued or claimed the right to wage war independently of the UN.

Today, human rights, the rule of law, and good governance provide the key framework of international institutional policy practices. However, when it comes to the international sphere, the lack of mechanisms to generate global consensus, the increased power inequalities, and the limited safeguards make any attempts to institutionalize human rights regimes outside the mutual agreement of sovereign states much more problematic. The problem with constituting frameworks of sanction, intervention, and war on the basis of non-socially constituted legal subjects is that it leaves wide open the problem, raised by Schmitt, of 'who decides?' (Schmitt, 1996, 2003). Whether the intention is to (mis)use human rights ideologically or to genuinely do good in the world, the outcome is the same: ultimately, greater decision-making power and authority accrue to the states (or some would argue the USA as the sole remaining great power) that have the capacity to take on the responsibilities of deciding and enforcing.

KEY POINTS

The human rights-based approach has facilitated humanitarian aid being denied in some circumstances and in support for more militarized humanitarianism—for example, the NATO war over Kosovo.

Human rights approaches appeared to directly challenge sovereignty in the 1990s, but in the 2000s have sought to redefine sovereignty as being compatible with international human rights protections. Central to this shift has been the ICISS report 'The Responsibility to Protect' (ICISS, 2001).

Human rights approaches tend to redefine war fought in the post-colonial world as a matter of human rights crimes and human rights victims; they also tend to redefine war fought by Western powers, seeing intervention in the cause of human rights as more akin to police action than war making.

Human rights approaches have facilitated a more flexible and positive framework for military intervention, shifting away from UN Charter approaches that saw war as the 'scourge of humanity'.

Human Rights and the Search for Meaning

Michael Ignatieff has emphasized that the universalism of human rights and humanitarianism represents a very different type of universalism than that traditionally associated with human rights as a progressive demand based upon human rationality, autonomy, and self-determination. Rather than expressing human aspirations for a better future, the modern universal ethic of human rights tends to view humanity itself as problematic. Here, what draws humanity together as a universal is our capacity to commit crime and to suffer it. He argues that, 'Modern moral universalism is built upon the experience of a new kind of crime: the crime against humanity' (Ignatieff, 1998, p. 19). The universal human subject is the victim: 'genocide and famine create a new human subject—the pure victim stripped of social identity' (Ignatieff, 1998, p. 20).

Human Rights and Political Disillusionment

Rather than universal discourses of human rights expressing a new progressive political era, Ignatieff highlights that the focus on human rights expresses disillusionment with political engagement and social change: the concern that 'there are no good causes left—only victims of bad causes' (Ignatieff, 1998, p. 23). He notes (Ignatieff, 1998, p. 250) the danger of this modern moral universalism, which 'has taken the form of an anti-ideological and anti-political ethic of siding with the victim; the moral risk entailed by this ethic is misanthropy.'

There is a danger that our modern anti-political sentiments and disillusionment with progress and collective aspirations may take the form of a misanthropic view of humanity rather than a critique of economic and social relations in which our political lives are constructed and constrained. This misanthropic view is universalist, but also extremely divisive and self-comforting. Ignatieff (1998, p. 95) suggests that in seeking to rationalize the problems of the world, a depoliticized human rights perspective finds it easy to blame non-Western societies and governments and, in so doing, portray better off Western society as blameless and morally superior.

In fact, it is often difficult to separate our concern for others and the construction of our own self-image or identity. As people and politicians in the West lack a sense of mission and purpose and strong shared or collective self-image, there is a danger that we seek personal and collective affirmation in our relationship to the non-Western world: '. . . when policy was driven by moral motives, it was often driven by narcissism. We intervened not only to save others, but to save ourselves, or rather an image of ourselves as defenders of universal decencies. We wanted to show that the West "meant" something.'

The view that the shift toward framing international politics through the lens of human rights reflects the fact that major Western states and societies lack positive political goals or a strong sense of their own social cohesion, gives a different angle to the (mis)use of human rights than that discussed above. Rather than an assertion of Western (or neo-imperial) interests and power and global aspirations of domination, the human rights discourse expresses a post-Cold War loss of confidence and lack of clear aims among leading Western and international policy actors.

Alain Badiou (2001, p. 31) suggests that citizen rights and the domestic political process no longer provide individuals or societies with a sense of meaning or purpose: 'Parliamentary politics as practiced today does not in any way consist of setting objectives inspired by principles and of inventing the means to attain them.' Rather than representing a new social collectivity, for Badiou, the focus on consensual ethics reflects the 'end of ideology' and political contestation and the lack of instrumental aims or social goals of state leaders (see Box 7.5).

Human Rights and the Lack of a Political Project

The work of Zaki Laïdi (1998) provides some valuable insights into how to tie together the themes of loss of instrumental goals and collective meaning with the search for social cohesion and legitimating 'mission' through the international discourse of human rights activism. Ethics and moral values can be seen to have

Box 7.5 **The Pessimism of Human Rights**

Michael Ignatieff on Universal Humanitarianism

In the twentieth century, the idea of human universality rests less on hope than on fear, less on optimism about the human capacity for good than on dread of human capacity for evil, less on a vision of man as maker of his history than of man the wolf toward his own kind. (Ignatieff, 1998, p. 18)

Alain Badiou on Ethics

Whether we think of it as the consensual representation of Evil or as concern for the other, ethics designates above all the incapacity, so typical of the contemporary world, to name and strive for a Good. . . . For from the beginning it confirms the absence of any project, of any emancipatory politics, or any genuinely collective cause . . . 'concern for the other' signifies that it is not a matter—that it is never a matter—of prescribing hitherto unexplored possibilities for our situation, and ultimately for ourselves. (Badiou, 2001, pp. 30, 33)

displaced instrumental national interests because governments have little sense of themselves as representatives of a collective social project. Human rights claims, because of their ungrounded and abstract nature, fill the vacuum by providing an ethical purpose or set of 'values' that no longer need to be strategically acted upon. The lack of clear instrumental or strategic political goals becomes repackaged as an asset rather than a problem. Human rights abuses (like the threat of terrorism) are held to be issues of urgency, crisis, or emergency, where strategic thinking and long-term planning are no longer called for (see Chandler, 2007b).

The shift from national or collective political interests to global or ethical values indicates a fundamental shift in both the meaning and practice of politics. The importance of this shift is indicated in Max Weber's essay on 'Politics as a Vocation'. Here he argued that there were 'two fundamentally different, irredeemably incompatible maxims', the 'ethics of conviction' and the 'ethics of responsibility' (Weber, 2004, p. 83). The former is about being judged on intention, the expression of values as a statement about oneself; the latter is about being judged on outcomes, the expression of political action as a strategic and instrumental engagement in the world. It would appear that, in the framework discussed in this section, the shift from strategic interests to ethical values is not primarily

about the recasting of interests in an ideological form, but more a rejection of the responsibilities of power. In the new world order of human rights and universal humanity it would seem, states Laïdi, that 'there is no longer any distance between what one does and what one aspires to', with human rights acting as the discursive framework through which political programmes and long-term projects can be side-stepped.

Ironically, the search for values and meaning in the discursive frameworks of human rights and humanitarianism exposes the lack of strategic interests behind military interventions and other forms of human rights conditionality and regulation. Acting on behalf of the 'ethics of conviction' exposes the lack of genuine conviction or strategic concern behind international interventions under the banner of 'human rights', and, for that matter, the 'war on terror'. Interventions and the use of the international arena to find a sense of mission and shared values exposes Western intervention as merely an act of power without meaning (Laïdi, 1998, p. 109). For Laïdi, attempts by Western states and, through them, international institutions, to project their power in order to generate meaning are doomed to failure. This can be understood as a failure in a double sense. Firstly, because the intervention itself is not primarily concerned with the object of intervention there is, therefore, little strategic or instrumental concern with regard to final outcomes. Secondly, there is failure with regard to the attempt to use intervention, or the international sphere more broadly, to generate meaning and purpose. This is because the problem of meaning is an internal one, based on the lack of connection between governing elites and their societies (see Chandler, 2007a, 2007b).

KEY POINTS

Human rights discourses and practices of intervention do not necessarily have to be understood as the narrow projection of traditional great power or imperial interests.

The asymmetries of power, of Western domination, allow the international sphere to be used as an arena for the creation of meaning or purpose, for both governments and individuals.

The use of the international sphere to generate a sense of 'mission' leads to the projection of Western power with little strategic or instrumental consideration. This can be highly destabilizing.

Conclusion

There can be no clear line of demarcation between the ideological use and (mis)use of human rights frameworks in international politics. Because human rights involve a separation between the agent of protection and the rights subject, there is no formal legal and political framework to judge whether claims of human rights at an international level are abused. The question is a normative one. Where there can be a greater level of consensus is at the empirical level: the rise of human rights approaches reflects the declining importance of the UN Charter order of international law, and the development of more *ad hoc* and informal mechanisms of international regulation and intervention.

It has been argued above that the demand to forward claims in the terminology of human rights reflects a world in which the international legal order orientated around the constitutive rights of sovereign states is under challenge. This challenge takes the form of a shift from rights taking a purely legal form, the 'black and white' wording of the UN Charter, to an ethico-juridical form. This shift away from formal legal rights to more informal expressions of rights and duties could be described as a shift toward the dominance of human rights above the rights of states, or as emerging cosmo-politan legal norms. The shift away from legal rights, framed in terms of autonomy, self-determination, and non-intervention, to ethico-juridical rights reflects a more hierarchical and interventionist order, in which issues that were considered to be the domestic affairs of states have become internationalized—from peace processes to issues of internal governance.

Human rights provide the framework for this internationalization. As considered above, the dynamic behind intervention and internationalization is not straightforward, whether this is seen as a matter of reasserting imperialist power or as a reflection of domestic concerns of self-identity, mission, and purpose—or positively as a confluence of self-interest and altruism, or even an act of selfless altruism—the fact remains that human rights frameworks reflect a world in which the enforcement of rights is an unequal and contingent one and where international relations are more open to *ad hoc* and arbitrary policy responses. However we choose to understand the drive behind growing human rights regimes of regulation and intervention, it would be wrong to see the abuse or misuse of power as being an exception rather than the rule.

QUESTIONS

INDIVIDUAL STUDY QUESTIONS

1. What is the difference between the subject of human rights and the subject of democratic and civil rights? Does it make a difference whether we claim rights as 'humans' or as 'citizens'?

2. How do human rights claims challenge the framework of law? Does this make these claims progressive? If not, why not?

3. How did the framework of human rights help to legitimize the post-Second World War order based on state sovereignty? Did human rights clash with sovereignty during the Cold War? If not, why not?

4. Why do human rights approaches challenge the legitimacy of state sovereignty and of international law?

5. How has the debate on the relation between human rights and sovereignty changed between the 1990s and the 2000s?

6. What happens when state sovereignty is undermined? Does sovereignty go elsewhere? If so, where?

7. In what ways do human rights approaches challenge traditional understandings of war? Is war more or less permissible under human rights frameworks?

8. Are human rights interventions subject to the same strategic and instrumental processes of guidance as more interest-based or traditional policy interventions?

GROUP DISCUSSION QUESTIONS

1. How can we explain the rise of human rights frameworks and understandings? Is this purely the exercise of power interests? Does it reflect the congruence of interests and ethical outlooks?

2. Will human rights approaches result in a more ethical or a more peaceful or a more equal world?

3. Do human rights constrain power or facilitate power?

FURTHER READING

Chandler, D. (2006). *From Kosovo to Kabul: Human Rights and International Intervention* (2nd edn). London: Pluto.
A study of human rights approaches as a challenge to universal frameworks of formal rights protection.

Douzinas, C. (2007). *Human Rights and Empire: The Political Philosophy of Cosmopolitanism*. London: Routledge Cavendish.
An analysis of the double-edged nature of human rights as a tool both to challenge power and to enforce it.

Duffield, M. (2007). *Development, Security and Unending War: Governing the World of Peoples*. Cambridge: Polity.
An analysis of human rights frameworks in relation to the use of development interventions as mechanisms of international domination.

Ignatieff, M. (1998). *The Warrior's Honor: Ethnic War and the Modern Conscience*. New York: Chatto & Windus.
A study of the challenge that human rights approaches pose for the traditional humanitarianism of the ICRC.

Laïdi, Z. (1998). *A World without Meaning: The Crisis of Meaning in International Relations*. London: Routledge.
An analysis of the problems that Western governments have in developing clear foreign policy goals and the shift from interests to ethics.

Sellars, K. (2002). *The Rise and Rise of Human Rights*. Stroud: Sutton.
A history of the development of human rights approaches during the Second World War and the US-led revival of human rights concerns in the 1970s.

Zolo, D. (2002). *Invoking Humanity: War, Law and Global Order*. London: Continuum.
An analysis of the challenge that human rights approaches pose to international law and the restrictions on war.

WEB LINKS

http://www.counterpunch.org *CounterPunch*. An online newsletter of critical journalism and comment.

http://www.dissentmagazine.org *Dissent*. A quarterly magazine of politics and culture.

http://www.newleftreview.org *New Left Review*. A bi-monthly independent journal.

http://www.spiked-online.com *Spiked*. An independent website with journalistic commentary and analysis.

http://www.zmag.org/zmag *Z Magazine*. An independent monthly magazine with critical analysis.

NOTE

1. Note the defence of case-by-case approaches in the work of normative theorists, such as Chris Brown (2007) and Richard Devetak (2007); for a critique, see Chandler (2008).

ONLINE RESOURCE CENTRE

Visit the Online Resource Centre that accompanies this book for updates and a range of other resources:

http://www.oxfordtextbooks.co.uk/orc/goodhart/

PART II

Human Rights in Practice

Political Democracy and State Repression

Christian Davenport

Chapter Contents

Reader's Guide

This chapter discusses the relationship between political democracy and state repression. Specifically, it evaluates what research has been conducted on the topic but also what has been ignored. Exploration of the United States and its treatment of African Americans is used as an example of how existing research in this field should change. This case emphasizes the importance of disaggregation (of institutions, actors, and actions). The chapter concludes with specific suggestions for further development.

Introduction

For hundreds of years, activists, policy makers, and ordinary citizens have been interested in reducing the amount and severity of state coercive behaviour directed against those subject to this power (e.g. restrictions on speech, association, assembly, and religion, as well as torture, disappearances, and mass killing). It was not until about thirty years ago, however, that this issue was examined systematically within dozens of articles and books. What do we now know about what diminishes state repression?

Research has revealed that only two variables diminish human rights violations: (1) political democracy—political institutions that involve the governed in the process of governing as well as subject leaders to some degree of oversight/accountability, and (2) economic development—i.e. societies that produce greater amounts of wealth (e.g. Hibbs, 1973; Mitchell and McCormick 1988; Henderson, 1991, 1993; Poe and Tate, 1994; Davenport, 1995, 1996, 1999, 2007a,b; Poe *et al.*, 1999; King, 2000; Zanger, 2000; Camp Keith, 2002; Bueno de Mesquita *et al.*, 2005). Although similar in causal impact, there are some important differences between these explanatory factors. First, the impact of democracy has been far greater in magnitude than that of economic development: democracy is simply a more powerful determinant of state repression than the economy. Second, since the Second World War, it appears that the external 'imposability' and internal development of democracy around the world have been far more successful than efforts to economically develop (Diamond, 2008): it is easier to create and sustain democracy than economic development.[1]

Third, most activists, policy makers, and ordinary citizens see democracy as the solution for repression, and they call for and mobilize to achieve democracy in part for this reason. This follows a relatively long tradition in political science where democracy is viewed as a resolution to a wide variety of problems, but it also follows a relatively long tradition within policy making and non-governmental organization (NGO) communities as well. Indeed, it is only recently that such thinking has been challenged (e.g. Carothers, 2002; Diamond, 2002; Levitsky and Way, 2002).

Despite the sheer wealth of empirical and popular support for the pacifying influence of democracy on state repression, there are, however, some important limitations with existing work. For example, while correlations are consistently statistically significant, the scholarly community is only just beginning to understand what causal mechanisms are involved, in what manner they function, and within what contexts they are most effective (Davenport, 2007a). As a consequence, there is a great need for further examination. This chapter provides an overview of existing research on the democracy–repression nexus, highlighting its strengths. It also outlines a more nuanced way of examining the topic, shedding light on the problems with existing work (disaggregating democracy and repression across space and actors) as well as what could be done to address these limitations. These issues are illustrated through a brief discussion of the relationship between democracy and repression within the United States during the 1940s–1980s. The final section suggests several areas of investigation that might prove to be lucrative.

Understanding the Democracy–Repression Nexus

To understand why governments ban, beat, torture, disappear, and kill their citizens takes some care. Adopting a version of rationalism, most researchers who study the topic highlight the centrality of government leadership (i.e. the executive) and they employ a simple decision calculus to understand when repressive behaviour will be undertaken (e.g. Dahl, 1966; Walter,

1969; Dallin and Breslauer, 1970; Gurr, 1986; Duvall and Stohl, 1988; Karklins and Peterson, 1993; Simon, 1994; Lichbach, 1995; Gartner and Regan, 1996; Bueno de Mesquita *et al.*, 2005; Davenport, 2007a).[2] In this work, coercive activity is expected when (1) the perceived benefits of repressing exceed the costs, (2) there are no viable alternatives for socio-political control, and

(3) the probability of success from repressive action is high. Repression is not anticipated when benefits are low, costs are high, there are alternatives, and the probability of success is minimal.

Given this framework, exactly why does democracy matter? What is it about democratic institutions that reduces state coercion? There are several reasons for a link between democracy and pacification, all directly connected to what is meant by democracy and repressive behaviour—where I will begin.

Democracy and Repression

As conceived within relevant literature, 'democratic' political institutions generally refer to the minimalist conception of the phrase advocated by scholars such as Schumpeter: competition among elites for electoral support. Here, a mechanism of governance is discussed and not the end to which such a mechanism is directed.[3] Of course, there is some variation with regard to the means highlighted. For example, some focus on the constraints placed on political leaders, highlighting veto 'points'/'players' and executive constraints (Tsebelis, 2002). Others focus on the participation of the citizenry in popular elections (Davenport, 1997; Richards, 1999a). Others focus on the representative and/or competitiveness of political parties (Richards, 1999b). Still others focus on combinations of these various elements. In all variations, however, the basic point is the same: there are ways of governing that are more 'democratic' than others. For example, a democracy is more likely to have greater constraints placed on its political leaders so that they will be less able to do what they wish and will feel a greater degree of oversight/constraint. A democracy is more likely to involve more of its citizenry in the selection of its leadership so that those subject to rule can have a greater degree of control over who is guiding the political unit. Finally, a democracy is more likely to have diverse political parties as well as highly competitive electoral contests between them so that a wide variety of perspectives can find their way into the political system.

Similarly narrowed is the conception of repression. As conceived, this phenomenon involves the actual or threatened use of physical sanctions against an individual or organization, within the territorial jurisdiction of the state, for the purpose of imposing a cost on the target as well as deterring specific activities and beliefs perceived as challenges to government personnel, practices, or institutions. Like other forms of coercion, repressive behaviour relies on threats and intimidation to compel targets, but it does not concern itself with all coercive applications (e.g. deterrence of violent crime and theft). Rather, it deals with applications of state power that violate rights concerning expression, due process in the enforcement and adjudication of law, and personal integrity or security (Davenport 2007b, p. 2).[4]

Given these definitions, there are several influences that democracy is expected to have on state repression (Davenport 2007b, pp. 10–11). These are adopted by scholars, activists, advocates, and policy makers the world over:

(1) Democratic institutions are believed to increase the costs of using repressive behaviour because authorities can be voted out of office if their actions are deemed inappropriate.

(2) Individuals in democracies generally accept specific values regarding toleration, communication, and deliberation—values that are challenged and undermined by the use of repression.

(3) Democracies provide an alternative mechanism of control through participation and contestation. They also weaken the justification for coercive activity by reducing the likelihood for human conflict and facilitating the conveyance of grievances.

In the first situation, democracy decreases repression because it frightens policy makers, making them aware that there are likely repercussions for engaging in activity that deleteriously impacts citizens' lives. In the second situation, democracy decreases repression because it socializes societal members against certain types of activities. In the third situation, democracy decreases repression because it provides different ways/means for influencing citizens. Through channelling individuals into pre-existing institutions and regulated behaviour, democratic political systems are able to keep citizens within the system—avoiding more dangerous forms of activity.

It is with these relationships in mind that individuals engage in systematic efforts to analyse causal relationships between relatively 'open' political institutions and coercive state behaviour. Not all of these analyses are comparable, however. Rather, they appear in waves of sophistication.

First Wave Democracy–Repression Scholarship

The earliest examinations of the democracy–repression nexus adopted a large-*N* approach, where they attempted to identify how democracy in the recent past or present influenced repression in the present across as many *nation-years* as they could obtain data for (e.g. Hibbs, 1973; Ziegenhagen, 1986). The underlying assumption of this work was that country-level values on some democracy score correlated with country-level values on some repression measure. As conceived, movement up the first scale, toward more democracy, led to movement down the second, toward less repression.

This first wave of scholarship employed a wide variety of democracy measures, generally composite indices of diverse components such as the **polity index** (Gurr, 1974; Marshall and Jaggers, 2000). Yet the findings of this body of work were clear and consistent.

> Subjecting the relationship between democracy and repression to extensive analysis (across time, space, measurements, and methodological techniques), almost all studies find that democratic political institutions and activities decrease state repressive behavior. Consequently, there is support for what is commonly referred to as a 'domestic democratic peace', mirroring the finding of international relations scholars. (Davenport, 2007b, p. 11)

Although consistently supported within existing scholarship, this work was not without its critics. Indeed, several pieces began to emerge that directly challenged the empirical findings and basic proposition underlying the relationship. The nature of the criticism varied.

Second Wave Democracy–Repression Scholarship

Over time, a few researchers began to speculate about the functional form of the relationship discussed above (Muller, 1985; Fein, 1995; Regan and Henderson, 2002; Davenport and Armstrong, 2004). Adopting the same large-*N* approach as that employed within earlier work, these scholars argued that democratic institutions did not influence repression in a linear fashion, with every increase in democracy leading to a decrease in repression. Indeed, scholars began to suggest that the

relationship and theoretical argument functioned in a very different manner.

For example, some maintained that it was not the degree of democratization that diminished repression but rather the clarity/certainty with which political leaders governed. A distinctive lack of clarity and certainty characterized political systems in the middle of a democratic continuum, and these so-called 'hybrid' or 'anocratic' regimes prove to be the most repressive. This is commonly referred to as the 'more murder in the middle' (MMM) hypothesis (e.g. Fein, 1995), indicating that these regimes in the middle of the spectrum engage in the most repression (an inverted U-shaped relationship). Researchers examined this proposition by introducing democracy and its square into estimated models, consistently finding support for the argument.

Others maintained that it was not clarity/certainty but democraticness that was crucial to understand. On this view, not all movements to democracy are comparable, and it is only when a certain threshold is passed that we should expect an influence (Davenport and Armstrong 2004; Bueno de Mesquita *et al.*, 2005). In order to examine these relationships and also to consider alternative specifications such as the inverted-U relationship of the MMM, the models adopted in this work were more sophisticated than any attempted earlier. For example, Davenport and Armstrong (2004) employed a variety of sophisticated statistical techniques (e.g. LOESS graphs, the binary decomposition model, and time-series cross-sectional analyses) to estimate relationships. The findings of this work have provided the most definitive results regarding functional form: the threshold model (where there is no impact until the highest values of democracy are reached) is far superior to any other.

The form of the relationship was not the only part of earlier scholarship questioned. Researchers also began to speculate about exactly what aspect of political democracy wielded an influence on state repression. This question is extremely important, for it focuses discussion on determining which element of the political system needs to be modified to achieve reductions in repressive behaviour. On this point opinions differ, with researchers advocating/exploring diverse components of democratic regimes, including constitutional structure (Davenport, 1996; Camp Keith, 2002), elections (Davenport, 1997; Richards, 1999a), political party diversity (Richards, 1999b; Bueno de Mesquita *et al.*, 2005), veto points (Davenport, 2007a), executive constraints (Davenport, 2004; Bueno de Mesquita *et al.*, 2005), executive constraints weighted by participation (Davenport and Armstrong, 2004), and, more recently, freedom of the press (Davenport *et al.*, 2008).

To examine the relevant relationships, the basic approach used by first wave scholars was modified. In this case, researchers had to disaggregate measures of democracy and use indicators that *operationalized* the particular mechanisms of interest. This effort was made easier in part because these distinct components were always available; they were just ignored because earlier applications lumped them together into indices. The findings of this research have been mixed. Most of these studies find statistically significant relationships, and thus support is generated for the proposition that there are specific aspects of democracy that influence repression. Unfortunately, there has not yet been an effort to systematically and competitively examine all components against one another. The best of this work has only compared a handful of rival explanations (Bueno de Mesquita, 2005; Davenport, 2007a). Additionally, there has not yet been an attempt to explore nonlinear relationships within these disaggregated efforts.

The Future of the Democracy–Repression Nexus

This section identifies some important elements of what should be the next wave of quantitative research on the relationship between democracy and repression. Specifically, these address three limitations with previous work.

First, existing research has ignored the fact that the nation-year might not be the most appropriate unit of analysis. Research on political culture (Elazar, 1972; Putnam, 1994) as well as political conflict (Ball *et al.*, 1999; Davenport and Stam, 2003; Boudreau, 2004; Wilkinson, 2004; Kalyvas, 2006) has clearly established that important differences exist within countries with regard to their respective areas of interest. Indeed, the research has largely problematized all efforts to examine nation-years, showing that factors within countries are more important predictors of repression and that it is inappropriate to argue that whole territorial units are influenced in the same ways. More directly relevant to the subject at hand, work by Hill (1994) has revealed that

the degree of democracy within a nation state (in this case the United States) varies significantly across space. Additionally, work by Donner (1990) reveals significant variation in political repression across the USA.

Second, related to the last point, existing research has ignored the fact that different aspects of political democracy may exhibit distinct influences on different repressive agents (i.e. the military, the police, the court system, politicians, and non-state militias at local, state, and national levels). This acknowledges that not all actors engaged in coercive activity are similarly or equally influenced by the same factors.

Third, existing research has largely ignored the fact that repression might influence democracy. This influence is commonly addressed within literature on 'liberalization'—which refers to a 'relaxation' of political repression (Wood, 2000). Here, it is expected that relaxing/reducing repression provides an opening within which diverse societal and political actors can take advantage of this opening to advance democratic institutions and behaviour by putting into place diverse mechanisms (i.e. elections and constraints on policy making) that further reduce the likelihood of repression.

Why have these issues been ignored? There are several reasons. One of the most important is that the data used for analyses of the democracy–repression nexus are generally aggregated to the nation-year, and there was nothing that could be analysed below this level. This is beginning to change. Over the last few years, researchers have been disaggregating political and conflict processes with greater frequency. Another important factor is that democracy scholars have not been particularly interested in repression and have been more interested in economic development (e.g. Lipset, 1959; Burkhart and Lewis-Beck, 1994; Przeworski, 2000). Indeed, democracy scholars rarely use the word repression, focusing instead on 'liberalization'. In contrast, repression scholars have long been interested in political democracy.

To redirect scholarship and improve our understanding of what is taking place when repression is applied, therefore, it is imperative that researchers focus within states—paying close attention to who is engaging in relevant behaviour, where they are in the state, how they are connected to those in power, and what connection (if any) they have to relevant democratic institutions. To provide an example of how researchers might begin to think about these issues, a discussion is given in the next section of perhaps the most famous case of how varied quality in democracy within a country influ- enced the application of repressive action within the same country: the coercion of African Americans in the South between the 1940s and 1980s.

KEY POINTS	
Theoretically, scholars have treated the relationship between democracy and repression through a rationalist framework, focusing on the costs/benefits of repression, alternatives for social-political control, and the probability of success.	Different aspects of democracy matter—and matter differently— with respect to their influence on levels of repression. Elections, political party diversity, veto points, executive constraints, competition weighted by participation, and freedom of the press are factors shown empirically to influence repression.
First wave scholarship on democracy and repression found a linear relationship: the more democracy, the less repression.	The nation-year is a problematic unit of analysis. More comprehensive evaluation of the influence of repression in democracy should be considered. These issues have so far been ignored because of a lack of data and because democracy scholars have typically been more interested in economic considerations and uninterested in repression.
Second wave scholarship agrees that democracy has a significant influence on repression, but challenges the linear nature of this relationship. Scholars have identified an inverted U-shaped relationship, with 'more murder in the middle' of the democratic spectrum, and a threshold level of democraticness beyond which repression decreases. The evidence supports the threshold argument.	

Case Study: Democracy and Repression in the United States: A Peculiar Story of African American Persecution and Freedom

When most think of the USA, they think of it as a democracy—perhaps *the* democracy. This is consistent with the views of some of the most prominent scholars of democracy (e.g. Dahl, 1966, 1971; Huntington, 1991; Held, 1996). It is also consistent with some of the most prominent measures of the concept. For example, considering 'the presence of institutions and procedures through which citizens can express effective preferences about alternative policies and leaders' and 'the existence of institutionalized constraints on the exercise of power by the executive' (Marshall and Jaggers, 2000, p. 22) between 1800 to 2004,[5] the polity index indicates that, except for the earliest part of the 1800s, the United States has been in the highest categories of democracy for about two hundred years (see Fig. 8.1 and Box 8.1). During the early 1800s there were significant restrictions on the regulation of parties, but these were changed in 1809 during James Madison's inaugural year—a point

after which the USA would never return to a level below the highest two categories on the measure.

Disaggregating Nation States

Now, immediately someone will note that the quality of this democracy was limited for much of this history. For instance, women had not obtained the right to vote until 1920 (with the Nineteenth Amendment to the Constitution) and African Americans, the focus of this chapter, were effectively disenfranchised until 1965, when the Voting Rights Act was passed.[6] The neglect of this point can be directly attributed to the measure being used. Polity does not include information on suffrage, and thus this issue would not (and has not) come up in most of the research relying upon this indicator (which is commonly viewed as the

FIGURE 8.1 Democracy in the United States: The Polity Index, 1800–2004.

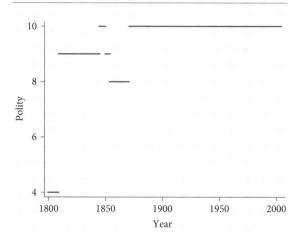

most popular indicator for democracy in the social sciences). This issue of neglect should not be levied against only Polity. Given the similarities between this measure and others it is likely that this would be the same for them as well (e.g. Munck and Verkuilen, 2002).

When one considers suffrage in the African American case, however, it is clear that variability in democracy exists, especially in the southern part of the country. Indeed, it is generally understood that, from the period of slavery up through the late 1960s and early 1970s, extensive voting rights restrictions and other aspects of authoritarianism existed in the Deep South: Alabama, Arkansas, Florida, Georgia, Louisiana, Mississippi,

Box 8.1 **Understanding the Polity Measure**

Polity is conceived on a 10-point scale—with 10 as the highest value of 'democracy' and 'autocracy' that one could achieve. Different points are provided for distinct aspects of political democracy. Source: Gurr, T., Marshall, M., Davenport, C., and Jaggers, K. (2002). Polity IV, 1800–1999: A reply to Munck and Verkuilen. *Comparative Political Studies*, **35**/1, 40–45. Additional source for polity project: http://www.systemicpeace.org/polity/polity4.htm.

North Carolina, South Carolina, Tennessee, Texas, and Virginia.[7] These restrictions were almost exclusively based on ethnicity. Historically, there is thus significant spatial variation within the United States regarding the quality of political democracy as gauged by one of its core components—the right to participate in the political process.[8]

Even after accepting this point, we should be careful not to simply view all of these states as comparable. Although uniformly less democratic (more authoritarian) in nature toward blacks, there was significant variation even among these southern states. For example, the percentage of voting age African Americans registered to vote was less than 0.5 in Alabama (where blacks make up 35 per cent of the total population), Louisiana (36%), Mississippi (49%), and South Carolina (43%); the percentage of voting age African Americans registered to vote was between 2 and 9 per cent in Arkansas (25%), Florida (27%), Georgia (35%), Texas (14%), and Virginia (25%); and the percentage of voting age African Americans registered to vote was between 10 and 16 per cent in North Carolina and Tennessee—where, respectively, blacks made up 27% and 17% of the total population (Hill, 1994, p. 29).

Looking at party competition reveals similar patterns (Hill, 1994, p. 60). Here, we find that Georgia, Louisiana, Mississippi, South Carolina, Texas, Alabama, Arkansas, Florida, North Carolina, Virginia, and Tennessee were one-party, and thus less competitive, democratic states in the 1940s. South Dakota, Vermont, and North Dakota were one-party republican states. In contrast, Rhode Island, Missouri, Utah, Nevada, Washington, Massachusetts, Minnesota, Delaware, Montana, Nebraska, Colorado, Connecticut, and Illinois were two-party, competitive states.

While one could obviously extend a discussion of repressive activity directed against African Americans back to slavery and the slave codes (1619–1865) or the legal restrictions and activities of the black codes (1800–1866), I focus on the period associated with *Jim Crow* (1876–1965; see Box 8.2). Although neglecting the worst horrors of the earlier periods (floggings, whippings, and lynchings), this period is of interest because it immediately precedes the efforts to desegregate (begun with *Brown* v. *Board of Education of Topeka, Kansas*), the civil rights movement (1955–1968), and democratic revolution within the South (in the Civil and Voting Rights Acts). This period therefore establishes the context within which three of the most important events in US democratic history occur. It is also the period that has some of the most extensive documentation on relevant government activities, and it immediately follows the initial period of data collection undertaken by Hill (discussed above).

By far the most extensive effort to identify state authorized/required restrictions on African Americans during the Jim Crow era was undertaken by Pauli Murray (1951). This voluminous work identifies all of the legislative controls that were imposed to enforce racial segregation across a wide variety of categories: amusements, public halls, education, employment, hospitals, penal institutions, welfare institutions, transportation, and miscellaneous. The work was intended to be as comprehensive as possible:

> [t]he compilation includes segregation and anti-miscegenation statutes, laws relating to public accommodations and which are popularly called 'civil rights' laws, fair educational practice acts, fair employment practice acts, statutes directed against lynching and the activities of the Ku Klux Klan, alien land laws, and miscellaneous anti-discrimination measures. (Murray, 1951, p. 5)

This said, Murray was careful not to misrepresent the effort, stating that the compilation, while extensive, is not complete (Murray, 1951, p. 5). Additionally, she notes that her research does not interpret laws but rather presents what they say and draws the direct

implications of this language. The actual implementation of the laws is ignored, creating the possibility that the real world looks different from the one imagined by the statutes.

What type of repressiveness do we see when this work is considered? In the situation of relative authoritarianism, how were African Americans treated? Murray's summary table is replicated in Table 8.1.

What is perhaps most striking from the compiled information is the wide variety of restrictions that were placed on African Americans. Races were segregated in pool rooms, race tracks, circuses, schools, facilities at work, medical care, prison, housing, and even diverse forms of sports such as boxing. Mirroring the discussion above about democracy, we also see significant variation across space. Directly in line with expectations, the least democratic states are the most restrictive on African Americans: Alabama (with 18 different types of restriction out of 51), Arkansas (20), Florida (19), Georgia (16—the low), Louisiana (19), Mississippi (21), North Carolina (26—the high), South Carolina (23), Tennessee (18), Texas (21), and Virginia (23). Within these states one sees pervasive limitations across diverse aspects of life, reflecting a clear effort to keep blacks within their place and to prevent racial mixing.

In contrast, there are no segregation restrictions authorized by law in the states that would traditionally be conceived as being the most democratic in the 1940s: e.g. Connecticut, Illinois, Maine, Massachusetts, Michigan, Pennsylvania, Rhode Island, New Hampshire, New Jersey, New York, and Vermont. Similarly, there are a few or one restriction in states fairly high on a democracy scale: e.g. Washington, Indiana, Kansas, Minnesota, and Colorado.

By far the largest number of restrictions existed in the realm of education. Not only were there extensive attempts made to prevent ordinary young children from coming together in public and private institutions, but there were also attempts made to separate those having trouble in school (juvenile delinquents), those who were challenged in some way (the deaf, blind, and dumb), as well as those seeking to improve themselves by learning a trade or pursuing higher education. The second most pervasive restriction, across states, existed in the realm of prohibiting intermarriage. This particular category is interesting because this prohibition was adopted, not only by all states in the South, but also within almost all other states at the time.

In line with existing literature, therefore, we find some preliminary support for the argument that the lowest levels of democracy at the state level were associated with some of the highest levels of political repression. There is also some support for the general argument in the middle values of the continuum as well. For example, while West Virginia would normally be considered to be on the middle of a democratic continuum (Hill, 1994, p. 96), it is found at the mid-level of repression during the period in question, with 14 restrictions being found. As West Virginia is generally considered to be part of the upper-South/mid-Atlantic (between what is traditionally considered the South and North—thus not subject to all of the cultural and political influences in either), this middle position makes sense. This 'more repression in the middle' argument also accounts for the orientation of Maryland (with 12 restrictions). In line with this, Oklahoma would normally be considered to be on the lower end of a democratic continuum (Hill, 1994, p. 98). This accounts well for its relatively high level of repressiveness (with 21 restrictions).

From an evaluation of democracy (suffrage and party competitiveness) and repression (restrictions on civil liberties) across the states of the USA, it is clear that the basic argument of the domestic democratic peace is sustained at a lower-level aggregation below the nation state: more democratic states (i.e. states where blacks had the right to vote and where party competition was higher) tended to repress African Americans less (i.e. these states tended to have fewer restrictions on what blacks could do within the relevant territorial domain). This work suggests that it is not only possible but crucial to examine relationships within and not just across countries. National-level assessments of political democracy and state repression are simply too coarse to adequately capture the reality on the ground.

Aspects of Democracy and Repression

Within this brief chapter, I do not mean to suggest that all aspects of democracy are relevant for all aspects of repression. Above, I highlighted that two often neglected aspects of US democracy, suffrage and party competition, were crucial for understanding exactly why repression was enacted against part of the American population: African American citizens did not have the ability to select less-repressive leaders, nor did they have the opportunity to legally remove those that engaged in behaviour that they disliked. In this context, those interested in using repressive action were able to do so with impunity.

Another illustration from the American case concerns the existence of vigilantes and popular militias. After the *Brown* decision by the Supreme Court in 1954, which eliminated the legal justification for separate educational facilities, it was left for state authorities to enforce the ruling. This was extremely problematic in two ways. First, because some authorities, as well as diverse citizen organizations such as the Mississippi State Sovereignty Commission and White City Councils, did not support the ruling, those attempting to exercise their newly-won rights were left unprotected. As a result, it was frequently the case that restrictive practices were allowed to continue for some time. Second, enforcement was problematic because African Americans and whites who attempted to adhere to the newly established federal law were hindered by local-level violence and repression enacted by mobs, Klansmen, and other whites—violence and repression abetted by police and political inactivity.

The situation did not continue indefinitely.

> After the beating of a white minister who was trying to help black students enter the school . . . (U.S. Attorney General) Brownell . . . announced the federal government would prosecute persons who forcefully interfered with the integration of Clinton High. U.S. marshals then received orders to round up troublemakers, and on December 5, 1956, the Justice Department for the first time asserted its own authority to halt interference with a desegregation order. (Belknap, 1987, p. 39)

National guardsmen, the US military, and agents of the Justice Department were used in similar situations throughout the South.

This development was important because local instability, caused by a lack of effective policing of a hostile part of the white population, compelled a response from higher-level political authorities as the unrest directly addressed the federal government's ability to enact laws and policies. In short, the violence not only threatened human life but directly challenged the rule of law and maintenance of order that were essential for

TABLE 8.1. Segregation authorized or required by state law (Murray, 1951, Chart III).

	AL	AK	AR	CA	CO	CT	DE	DC	FL	GA	ID	IL	IN	IA	KS	KY	LA	ME	MD	MA	MI	MN	MS	MO	MT	NE	NV	NH	NJ	NM	NY	NC	ND	OH	OK	OR	PA	RI	SC	SD	TN	TX	UT	VT	VA	WA	WV	WI	WY
Amusement																																																	
Billiards										✓																													✓										
Public halls																																																	
Parks																									✓										✓	✓													
Public halls								✓																																	✓								
Racetracks		✓																																															
Circuses																	✓																						✓										
Education																																																	
Constitutional provision	✓						✓		✓	✓						✓	✓						✓	✓								✓			✓				✓		✓	✓			✓		✓		
Statutory provision—public school	✓		✓				✓	✓	✓	✓						✓	✓						✓	✓					✓			✓			✓				✓		✓				✓		✓		✓
Private school									✓							✓																			✓				✓		✓								
Schools for deaf		✓						✓	✓							✓	✓						✓												✓						✓	✓			✓				
Schools for dumb									✓							✓	✓																		✓						✓	✓			✓				
Schools for blind		✓					✓	✓	✓							✓	✓						✓												✓						✓	✓			✓				
Reform schools	✓						✓	✓	✓	✓						✓	✓		✓				✓	✓								✓			✓				✓		✓	✓			✓				
Trade schools	✓						✓	✓	✓							✓	✓						✓									✓			✓				✓		✓	✓			✓				
Higher education	✓						✓		✓	✓						✓	✓		✓				✓									✓			✓				✓		✓	✓			✓		✓		
Teacher's training	✓						✓		✓	✓						✓	✓		✓				✓									✓			✓				✓		✓	✓			✓				
Separate schools—Indians						✓																										✓																	
Separate textbooks—black/white									✓																							✓																	
Separate libraries																																										✓							
Employment																																																	
Separate washrooms in mines		✓																																															
Separate toilets in manufacturing businesses																																			✓						✓	✓							
Segregation in cotton textile factories																																							✓										
Hospitals																																																	
Segregation generally	✓									✓												✓																	✓										
Mental patients	✓									✓						✓	✓		✓			✓	✓	✓								✓		✓	✓				✓		✓				✓		✓		
Tubercular patients	✓					✓										✓	✓																	✓					✓			✓							
Nursing	✓																						✓																✓										

Penal institutions
Segregation generally
Separate chain gangs

Welfare institutions
Homes for ageing/orphans
Paupers

Transportation
Buses
Railroads
Street cars, etc.
Steamboats/ferries
Waiting rooms
Sleeping compartments

Miscellaneous
Mixed marriages
White–Negro/Mulatto
White–Indian
White–Asian
Cohabitation prohibited
Adoption by persons of same race only
Separate army batallions
White–Negro boxing prohibited
White–Negro fraternal organization prohibited
Cannot advocate social equality
Telephone booths
Voting lists, etc.
Voting places
Housing

the functioning of the political system. As an Eisenhower speechwriter recalled after the fact:

> [t]he President, so slow to take firm federal action in support of civil rights, could and would respond with dispatch to a public challenge to presidential and constitutional authority. (Belknap, 1987, p. 49)

As the President stated, '[f]ailure to act . . . would be tantamount to acquiescence in anarchy and the dissolution of the union' (in Belknap, 1987, p. 49). In this context, it was revealed that democratic processes within certain aspects of government do not directly resonate with all aspects of the repressive apparatus. Indeed, they might be completely disconnected from one another.

Another example is provided by federal responses to the extensive bombing campaign undertaken by supporters of white supremacy in the mid-to-late 1950s and into the 1960s. By this time, African Americans were less likely to be targeted with the lynch rope. Rather, given the higher degree of mobilization, extremist whites used explosives to undermine black organizations and to intimidate those seeking an extension of democracy. Toward this end, the homes of religious leaders (such as Martin Luther King Jr) were targeted. In addition to this, meeting places (churches and education facilities) were also targeted.

Unlike the high degree of political complicity identified above, in this case the efforts of local officials moved against white extremism. As stated by Belknap (1987, p. 55), 'most public officials in the South do seem to have made a sincere effort to stamp out the epidemic of dynamiting that was plaguing their region.' The evidence was clear.

> In South Carolina the attorney general, the governor, and the chairman of the judiciary committees in both houses of the legislature all pressed for tougher laws against bombing and bomb threats. Tennessee Governor Frank Clement and Alabama Governor James Folsom both offered rewards for information leading to the arrest of bombers. So did Montgomery's mayor and city commissioners. Perhaps the best evidence of how serious southern officials were about halting the terroristic use of explosives was their creation of the Southern Conference on Bombing (SCB). Initiated by Jacksonville Mayor Haydon Burns after dynamite ripped a black high school and a Jewish community center in his city, the SCB began with a meeting of seventy delegates in May 1958. The founders included ten mayors and law enforcement officers from twenty-one southern communities. (Belknap, 1987, p. 55)

The reason for repression was thus not completely local in nature—i.e. attributable to an acute awareness of state authorities that lethal violence was unacceptable and to popular fears of growing conflict. Rather, similar to the situation discussed above, the reason for repression was also federal. Southern authorities knew that if they could not control overt activity directed against African Americans attempting to exercise rights granted by higher political institutions, others at the federal level would do so. Although initially federal authorities under President Eisenhower were hesitant about becoming involved, over time, however, a variety of new laws or newly interpreted laws facilitated and enhanced federal involvement. For example, the intrastate nature of the violence was used to invoke federal authority in connection with the transportation of explosives and incitement to violence. The implications of these developments were significant but not too far-reaching—at least not in the short term. The **Civil Rights Act** of 1964 created new federal offences with significant punishments, but it represented simply another step along a continuum of increasing federal intrusion into the southern states. It would not be until the violence associated with the **Freedom Riders** and vicious attacks on non-violent demonstrations associated with the Southern Christian Leadership Conference a few years later that even greater strides would be made in this direction.

This element of the story is better known and thus I will not go into it here. What is important is that southern political actors eventually decided to enforce federal law and subdue those within their communities who were engaged in violent behaviour. This represented a sea change in the attitude and behaviour of local government authorities. It also paved the way for the development of democracy within the South.

Repression as a Determinant of Political Democracy

What is interesting about the case under discussion here is that different actors engaged in different repressive acts, having important implications for the overall outcome. For example, within the South legal and political restrictions as well as violence were enacted against African Americans. Some of these activities were undertaken by agents of the state (e.g. politicians, judges, and police officers) but some were not (e.g. White City Councils and Klansmen). In some cases, these were the same people. Whatever the case, those who were not favourably disposed toward African Americans were outmatched and outnumbered. Additionally, there was little possibility of any punishment being levied against the perpetrators of repressive activities. After changes at the federal level—in the realm of law as well as political sensibility—this situation changed. In this context, those who were against black persecution (particularly the more violent form, which was not popularly supported) had greater leverage for challenging the repressors. Additionally, there was a growing (albeit slow) possibility that the actions undertaken would be investigated and potentially prosecuted.

What becomes interesting is that repression that was once enacted or supported by local authorities became criminalized as political officials and diverse citizens attempted to distance themselves from what was taking place. At the same time, the federal government began to increasingly engage in repressive activity against the subset of the southern population that had been marginalized by their adoption of and commitment to racial violence—something which was viewed as disruptive and threatening to law and order as well as unconstitutional.

> [b]etween roughly 1960 and 1980, a literal revolution in political rights occurred, giving millions of previously disenfranchised citizens the right to vote and otherwise participate in the governmental process. That change was largely the product of federal government intervention in voting rights policy, with the express purpose of making our political process more democratic. Doubtless, too, that intervention has made this a more democratic nation. (Hill, 1994, p. 18)

Not all things had improved to the same degree, however. While the number of 'democratic' states improved dramatically over time (none would now be considered autocratic), the Deep South still falls at the bottom of any summary measure: i.e. Georgia, South Carolina, Mississippi, Texas, Alabama, Louisiana, and North Carolina (Hill, 1994, pp. 96–98).

The US case is somewhat at odds with existing democracy scholarship in numerous ways. First, it is an increase in repression and not its relaxation that appears to explain the movement to democracy within the American South. Or, perhaps a certain degree of targeted repression precedes the relaxation that other scholars highlight, thus pushing the relevant time period under investigation backward. This would seem to be similar to the South African case, as the African National Congress was subject to a significant amount of repression prior to its de-radicalization of its political programme and negotiation with the Apartheid government. Second, the same acts are interpreted quite differently under different contexts. For example, what was earlier tolerated, supported, and/or enacted by government officials later became intolerable, unsupported, criminalized, and prosecuted. This leads us to focus on not only what is done but by whom, acknowledging that clear associations with political authorities may not always be possible.

KEY POINTS

Generally, researchers consider country-level assessments of democracy and repression but this is problematic. For example, in the case of the United States as it related to the treatment of African Americans there was incredible variation in the quality of democracy and repression across states. Some states were quite democratic and treated African Americans quite well. Other states were quite autocratic in nature and treated blacks poorly. All of these states were found within the same country however.

Perhaps the most important aspect of democracy regarding African Americans was the right to participate. For most of their existence in the US, blacks were not able to vote. Consequently, they were not able to hold authorities responsible for how they were treated coercively. In those states where blacks were able to vote, they tended to be treated better.

Repression can also facilitate political democracy. By eliminating those within the society who were coercively engaging with other citizens (e.g. local elites suppressing the freedom of African Americans), federal governments were able to facilitate the extension of democracy at local levels.

The Path to Peace: Directions for Future Research

This chapter has attempted to provide an overview of the existing literature regarding the relationship between democracy and repression as expressed within the quantitative research community—work extending back over approximately forty years. This review involved identifying the general approach and findings of this work, noting both strengths (rigour and consistency in results) and weaknesses (a failure to examine causal mechanisms in greater detail as well as a failure to disaggregate units of analysis). The historical case of the United States, with specific reference to the treatment of African Americans, was used as an example of exactly what is being missed within existing research. This section seeks to outline more precisely what subsequent examinations of the democracy–repression nexus must address in order for our understanding of the topic to improve.

Different Questions

The first shift in scholarship that I would recommend concerns a transformation in the type of questions that are asked. It is no longer necessary to ask if democracy influences state repression and human rights violations or even to ask about the nature of the specific relationship. This issue has already been addressed. It is now important for researchers to pinpoint the causal mechanisms at work—i.e. identifying exactly which aspect of democracy is relevant and for what type of repression, as well as for which repressive agents. The latter issue is much less developed than the others. In following from this, it would also be valuable to explore how and why variation in democracy within a nation state leads to variation in repression within the same territorial jurisdiction. It is no longer appropriate to talk about democracy influencing human rights violations without acknowledging that the quality of democracy varies across relevant territorial units.

A different line of inquiry, but one that is clearly emerging in the pages of newspapers around the world, is the issue of subcontracting. It has recently been discovered that many governments (including some democracies) send those who they wish to be

tortured or otherwise coerced to other countries to be dealt with (see Chapter 17).[9] This is important, for it reveals that political leaders have a concern with the costs involved with relevant behaviour (e.g. they fear being discovered as it could cause them to lose legitimacy and/or office). At the same time, it reveals that political leaders are not deterred from repressive action as much as they are deterred from repressing in an obvious fashion. These issues need to be explored in greater detail. Related to this is the issue of non-lethal mechanisms of torture. It has recently been discovered (e.g. Rejali, 2007) that democracies have pioneered the use of repressive techniques that are less likely to leave trace evidence (i.e. marks on their victims). This is important for it again reveals that, while the costs of repression influence democracies, they may simply lead to shifts in tactics away from the most obvious/egregious forms of repression. Similar arguments could be made about the use of political surveillance.

Disaggregating Data

In order to explore the issues raised above, there would need to be a fundamental change in how researchers conceptualize the relevant unit of analysis. While most literature in comparative politics and international relations examines nation-years, it is imperative that future analyses of the topic consider lower-level aggregations. It is becoming less reasonable to assume that one summary score captures well the degree of democracy within a country. There is significant variation within nation states regarding the role and influence of the mass population, as well as the type and magnitude of restraints on political authorities. In addition to this, the role and use of diverse repressive tactics in their efforts to establish and maintain socio-political order varies significantly within nation states. If researchers, policy makers, activists, and ordinary citizens are interested in understanding how repressive power is wielded by political authorities, then it is incumbent upon them to explore the nuances of exactly how coercion is wielded.

Relevance

A third and final direction for future research concerns the connection between human rights scholarship, policy, and activism. For too long these areas have been held apart from one another—to the detriment of all. This is unfortunate because discussions and debates about the 'war on terror', counter-insurgency, and protest policing have taken place without being informed by an important branch of social science devoted to studying these precise topics. This is also unfortunate because round tables, journal articles, and academic books on these subjects have been developed without any concern for their immediate and practical implications in the current context. For example, one topic area that would be improved by explicitly considering the democracy–repression nexus is the issue of democratic development and the effectiveness of counter-insurgency. Within my recent book examining 137 countries from 1976 to 1996, I find that, while certain aspects of democracy (measures of competition/participation and executive constraints) influence repression in the expected manner, some do not (suffrage and the number of veto players). Additionally, I find that the pacifying influence of democracy on repressive behaviour is increased in the context of inter-state war, decreased in the context of violent dissent, and mixed in the context of civil war. As Iraq has revealed all three contexts, it thus provides an interesting opportunity for the generalizability of this argument to be

further explored. Unfortunately, the insights garnered from a human rights/repression approach have not yet been applied to this case; most individuals engaged in research on this topic have adopted approaches developed within the areas of inter-state and civil war (as well as the somewhat less rigorous work on counter-insurgency and counter-terrorism). Applying the democracy–repression nexus to this case and competitively evaluating it against arguments emerging within other disciplines and subfields of political science might prove to be useful as we attempt to understand how political violence is used and could be lessened in the world.

KEY POINTS

Researchers need to improve the way in which they think about the relationship between democracy and repression. For example, they need to ask different questions, moving to understand exactly how democracy influences repression and why.

Researchers need to modify how they gather information about democracy and repression, collecting information on a highly disaggregated level. This would allow examinations to be as accurate and as realistic as possible.

Researchers as well as policy makers and activists should attempt to overcome their differences and work together on the problems that concern all of them: the elimination or reduction of state repression.

Conclusion

This chapter discussed the relationship between political democracy and state repression—the democracy–repression nexus. It began with an evaluation of the diverse ways in which researchers have investigated the relationship, discussing dominant conceptualizations, consistent findings, and diverse puzzles that have emerged from this work: (1) disaggregating nation states and exploring within-country variation, (2) considering how different aspects of democracy influence different types of repression, and (3) considering how repressive behaviour influences political democracy. The chapter then explored these different puzzles

within the context of the United States and its treatment of African Americans. The chapter ended with several suggestions for future research. These included: shifting the questions that are being asked from the general issue of whether and if democracy influences repression to how and where; improving the way that data is collected to facilitate an examination of relationships in a more disaggregated and nuanced fashion; and, finally, making a better connection between academic research and political activism and policy making that allows the discussions taking place in each venue to be receptive to and influenced by the other.

QUESTIONS

INDIVIDUAL STUDY QUESTIONS

1. What is democracy?

2. What is repression?

3. Why and how does democracy influence repression?

4. What are the common errors in existing scholarship?

5. What should be examined in the future?

GROUP DISCUSSION QUESTIONS

1. Can democracy and repression be separated from one another conceptually?

2. Do you believe that democracy influences repression, that repression influences democracy, or both?

3. Do you believe that democracy or economic development is more important for reducing state repression?

FURTHER READING

Della Porta, D. and **Reiter**, H. (1998). *Policing Protest: The Control of Mass Demonstrations in Western Democracies.* Minneapolis, MA: University of Minnesota Press.
This book discusses general approaches to how dissent is repressed within political democracies.

Gibson, J. L. (1988). Political intolerance and political repression during the McCarthy Red Scare. *American Political Science Review*, **82**/2, 511–529.
This article provides an insightful analysis of the causal mechanisms involved with democratic applications of state repression.

Powell, G. B. (2000). *Elections as Instruments of Democracy: Majoritarian and Proportional Visions*. New Haven, CT: Yale University Press.
This book explores how and to what degree democracy can function as a mechanism of popular will.

Reiter, D. and **Stam**, A. C. (2002). *Democracies at War*. Princeton, NJ: Princeton University Press.
This book explores exactly how and why democracies do what they do when conflict is underway—specifically when they enter and how they fight wars.

Rosato, S. (2003). The flawed logic of democratic peace theory. *American Political Science Review*, **97**/4, 585–602.
This article attempts to identify the limitations with democratic peace theory and provide some insights into how it could be better formulated as well as examined.

Stohl, M. (1976). *War and Domestic Political Violence: The American Capacity for Repression and Reaction*. Beverly Hills, CA: Sage.
This book explores the dynamics of how democracies use repression within situations of inter-state war.

WEB LINKS

http://web.mac.com/christiandavenport/iWeb/Christian%20Davenport/Human%20Rights%20and %20Repression%20Data.html *Human rights and repression data.* This link provides information on all known human rights/repression databases.

http://www.state.gov/g/drl/ *US Bureau of Democracy, Human Rights and Labor*. This site provides information on human rights conditions in the United States and throughout the world. There are also links to US evaluations of their efforts to establish democracies around the world.

http://coginta.com/ *The World Database on Policing*. This site has information about policing institutions from around the world.

http://www.pbs.org/wnet/jimcrow/themap/map.html *The Rise and Fall of Jim Crow*. This site provides an interactive mapping program that allows the viewer to explore diverse aspects of the Jim Crow system (e.g. the laws, population movements associated with the relevant period, and violent activity directed against African Americans).

http://www.jimcrowhistory.org/resources/gateway.htm *The History of Jim Crow*. This site provides a variety of easily accessible resources on the topic.

http://www.inmotionaame.org/home.cfm?bhcp=1 *In Motion—The African American Migration Experience*. This site links to a variety of maps across US history that capture the physical movement of African Americans throughout the states.

NOTES

1. Since the invasion and occupation of Iraq, the opinions about imposing democracy have shifted, but that these political systems have been created with greater frequency is undeniable.

2. As discussed by Goldstein (1978, p. 558):

   [t]he most important, and the *only* variable which *must* change for levels of political repression to change, is the attitude of policy-making authorities with regard to political dissidents. In order for political repression to increase, political authorities must decide to take actions that will increase it; in order for political repression to decrease, political authorities must decide to take actions that will decrease it. These actions manifest a shift in attitude on the part of political authorities, and this shift is the only variable which, by itself, can change the level of political repression.

3. This is problematic for those who advocate a liberal–democratic perspective (e.g. Dahl, 1971; Beetham, 1994; Diamond, 2008) because there is a conscientious effort made to separate means/ processes and ends/objectives.

4. Clearly the conception adopted here is a bit more encompassing than that applied by others, which tends to focus on only one aspect of coercive governance. As a result, there is a wide variety of activities that would be included: e.g. mass killing, torture, disappearances, imprisonment, political banning, wiretapping, and the use of *agents provocateurs*. Regardless of the increased scope of behaviour believed to be relevant, however, it is readily understood what is at issue: coercive behaviour directed against citizens for the explicit purpose of controlling what they think and do.

5. This is broken into four components: the competitiveness of executive recruitment, the openness of executive recruitment, constraints on the chief executive, and the competitiveness of political participation.

6. Although the Fifteenth Amendment made restrictions based on race illegal in 1870, there was still a wide variety of strategies employed to prevent African Americans from participating.

7. Many scholars also note that southern politics was not only about how whites would control blacks but also which whites would exercise this control (Woodward, 1951, p. 328).

8. There were various restrictions on voting rights outside of the South, but these were less obvious and less pervasive in nature.

9. For interesting discussion see the following link: http://www.pbs.org/frontlineworld/stories/rendition701/map/.

ONLINE RESOURCE CENTRE

 Visit the Online Resource Centre that accompanies this book for updates and a range of other resources:

http://www.oxfordtextbooks.co.uk/orc/goodhart/

Global Civil Society and Human Rights

9

Marlies Glasius

Chapter Contents

Reader's Guide

This chapter will explore the relationship between global civil society (GCS), under-stood as 'people organizing to influence their world' and the normative ideal of a 'global rule-bound society'. After an introduction on the concept of GCS, the chapter will survey some of the GCS actors involved in human rights issues and focus on their background, motivations, methods, and influence. The activities of individuals and organizations in civil society in relation to human rights can be divided into three kinds, which can be considered as related to three different phases: shifting norms; making law; and monitoring implementation. The three types of activities will be illus-trated with three brief case studies: norm-shifting activities in relation to economic and social rights; law-making activities in relation to the International Criminal Court, with an emphasis on gender-related crimes; and monitoring through the observation mission to the referendum on self-determination in East Timor.

Introduction

Civil society, let alone global civil society (GCS), is a confusing term. There are as many definitions of civil society, and GCS, as there are authors—in fact, more: Lewis extracts four definitions of civil society from the literature on Africa alone, Howell and Pearce juxtapose two versions, and Kaldor gives no less than five versions of GCS (Howell and Pearce, 2001, pp. 13–37; Lewis, 2002; Kaldor, 2003, pp. 6–12).

Nevertheless, this chapter quite intentionally uses this term, rather than other current ones such as global social movements (Cohen and Rai, 2000), advocacy networks in international politics (Keck and Sikkink, 1998), or global citizen action (Edwards and Gaventa, 2001). Its history is bound up with the notion of rules to protect citizens, i.e. civil rights. The term goes back to ancient Rome (*societas civilis*), but was used particularly in the Enlightenment to express opposition to the idea that a ruler could treat his subjects as he pleased. Civil society referred to a voluntary association, based on a hypothetical social contract that outlined the rights and obligations of citizens (see Seligman, 1992). With the exception of Kant (1991), Enlightenment thinkers conceived this rule-bound society in national terms. However, the post-War notion of universal human rights, coupled with a thickening network of international rules directly affecting citizens, has given birth to the dream of a global rule-bound society. Hence, the idea of GCS is historically connected with the ideas behind humanitarian and human rights law.

This connection is more than a historic accident without contemporary relevance. GCS in the modern sense of the whole of border-crossing, non-profit, non-governmental entities remains intimately connected with human rights law. It may be intuitive that the emergence of a GCS depends on the development and observance of the international rule of law. The opposite connection is less obvious, but the history of humanitarian and human rights law (see Chapter 2), has been much more a product of the activities of people outside government than is commonly accepted. Almost every significant treaty in international humanitarian law originates with the International Committee of the Red Cross (ICRC). The idea for a Universal Declaration came from a small group of lawyers, some of whom had themselves been political refugees; the insertion of human rights provisions in the UN Charter was the work of non-governmental organizations (NGOs); and a post-War treaty like the Convention Against Torture was almost solely the brainchild of human rights NGOs (see Burgers, 1992; Keck and Sikkink, 1998, p. 85; Clark, 2001, pp. 55–67).

It would be quixotic to believe that international law could emerge without the backing of states, or overcome the opposition of a majority of states. This has never happened in the past and, whatever one may believe about the erosion of state power through globalization, it is not possible today. However, those parts of international law that protect the interests of humanity, rather than the interests of states, rely heavily on the involvement of GCS. While the final authorization comes from states, the moral and intellectual impulse to draft such rules inevitably comes from GCS. When the rules exist, states once again have neither the capacity nor the political will to monitor them without the mediation of GCS.

What is GCS?

Some authors prefer terms like 'transnational' or 'international' civil society. They argue that 'global' sounds too grandiose; if it means really uniting people from every part of the globe, it just does not exist, nor is it inevitable (Smith *et al.*, 1997; Keck and Sikkink, 1998; Florini, 2000). Empirically, they have a point: some parts of the world (Europe, North America) are much more linked up than others (rural China, Chad).

However, while 'global' may overstate the situation, 'transnational' understates it. A single border crossing is transnational; in that sense, civil society has been transnational for centuries. 'Transnational' does nothing to capture the revolution in travel and communications and the opening up of many formerly closed societies that have recently made civil society much more global than ever before. Moreover, only 'GCS' can be posed as a complement as well as a counterweight to the process now universally called globalization. Finally, the term GCS has a normative aspiration that 'transnational civil society' does not. Just as the term 'human rights' has a universalistic intent that 'civil rights' lacks, GCS can be seen as an aspiration to reach and include citizens everywhere and to enable them to think and act as global citizens. Some of the literature on globalization stresses the emergence of a global consciousness, an 'imagined community of mankind' (Shaw, 2000). GCS is an expression of that consciousness, even if some participants cannot travel or even use the telephone (Anheier *et al.*, 2001, pp. 16–17)

So what exactly *is* this GCS? In the *Global Civil Society Yearbook*, we adopted the following working definition: 'global civil society is the sphere of ideas, values, institutions, organizations, networks, and individuals located *between* the family, the state, and the market and operating *beyond* the confines of national societies, polities, and economies' (Anheier *et al.*, 2001, p. 17). Here, I adopt a definition that is a little narrower and much simpler: GCS consists of people organizing to influence their world. Hence, it involves some sort of deliberate get-together. It is a political definition, excluding people who organize to play darts or make money. It includes even those who attempt to influence their world in undesirable directions, or by unpalatable means. The subjective 'their world' suggests people concerned with the world they see

themselves living in, their *life-world*, not necessarily that they have planetary ambitions. That life-world is increasingly shaped by the forces of globalization. This definition, finally, suggests that (global) civil society is a contested terrain (Howell and Pearce, 2001, p. 234), populated by value-driven actors who do not necessarily share harmonious value systems: indeed, their values sometimes clash.

This chapter explores the relationship between the empirical 'people organizing to influence their world' and the normative ideal of a 'global rule-bound society'. To avoid confusion, I use the term GCS only in the former sense to refer to 'actually existing civil society'. The next sections will introduce some of the GCS actors involved in human rights issues, focusing on their background, motivations, methods, and influence. As will become clear, many are motivated by the very fact that a 'global consciousness' is part of their life-world. This is where the descriptive concept and the normative ideal reconnect.

KEY POINTS

GCS can be considered as a part and even a driver of globalization, but also as a potential counterweight to aspects of globalization.

GCS is populated by value-driven actors, organizing to influence their world, but they do not all have the same values. GCS is therefore also an arena of contestation.

GCS actors in the area of human rights are often driven by a global consciousness and a belief in global rules and global citizenship.

Case Study: GCS as Paradigm-Shifters: Economic and Social Rights

From Dead Letter to Activist Tool

Economic and social rights, despite being enshrined in international law via the Universal Declaration of Human Rights (UDHR) and the International Covenant on Economic, Social and Cultural Rights (ICESCR), had few civil society champions on either side of the political divide for most of the twentieth

century, caught as they were in the crossfire between liberal and socialist ideologies (Glasius, 2007, p. 63).

This began to change in the early 1980s, when small groups of activists and academics separately but simultaneously began to rediscover the most compelling of all economic and social rights, the right to food. Two seminal texts advanced novel arguments. Amartya Sen's *Poverty and Famines* (Sen, 1981) challenged the consensus among developmental economists that famines were caused by a general decline in the availability of food. Instead, he argued, access to food depends on entitlements that are governed by socio-economic relations (Sen, 1981, pp. 154–155). 'The focus on entitlements', Sen concluded his essay, 'has the effect of emphasizing legal rights' (Sen, 1981, pp. 165–166).

Political philosopher Henry Shue (1980) attacked the distinction between civil and political rights, constructed mainly as *negative rights* requiring only a duty of non-interference, and economic and social rights, constructed as *positive rights* requiring active intervention (see Chapter 1). Instead, Shue distinguished three types of duties governing both types of rights: to avoid depriving people of their rights, to protect them against such deprivation by others, and to aid those whose rights have already been deprived (Shue, 1980, pp. 35–64). This categorization of obligations, later adapted to 'respect/protect/fulfil', has been a tremendous inspiration to subsequent generations of legal scholars.

At the same time, some grassroots membership groups of Amnesty International, frustrated with the organization's limited mandate, started networking with development and solidarity groups focused on the right to food. After three years, the network was transformed into a formal human rights organization, the Food First Information and Action Network (FIAN). Inspired by the Amnesty approach, it focused on blatant violations such as famines related to forced relocation, and undertook urgent actions, writing letters to governments, 'Even though we did not quite know what was a violation of the right to food, we were finding that out as we were doing it.'[1]

Finally, international lawyers began to take notice of economic and social rights, formulating the **Limburg Principles on the Implementation of the International Covenant on Economic, Social and Cultural Rights** as a point of reference for interpreting the sometimes obscure and contradictory legal text of the ICESCR. This sparked innumerable articles and a spate of doctoral dissertations, constituting a new field of expertise within human rights scholarship. The literature began to address objections against economic and social rights as 'too vague', 'too costly', or 'not amenable to judicial review'. More recently, scholars have taken their cue from activist work by transferring their focus from the nature of the obligations to a **violations approach**, working outwards from the most egregious violations.

In the NGO field, the foundation of FIAN was followed in 1987 by Habitat International Coalition, in 1992 by the Centre on Housing Rights and Evictions (COHRE), and in 1993 by the Center for Economic and Social Rights (CESR) in New York. All have grown from kitchen-table initiatives into medium-sized international NGOs, and have since been joined by hundreds of other, mainly domestic organizations working specifically in the area of economic and social rights. Many are now part of ESCR-Net (International Network of Economic, Social, and Cultural Rights), a civil society network founded in 2003.[2]

Between them, the philosophers, the lawyers, and the grassroots activists promoted a new way of thinking that considered issues such as hunger, homelessness, and ill health not just as personal tragedies or social problems, but as violations of human rights. But mainstream organizations, both non-governmental and intergovernmental, took some convincing.

Elevation into International Politics

Mainstream global human rights organizations slowly and gingerly began to take up economic and social rights from the mid-1990s. Some, such as the International Commission of Jurists, have always supported them in principle but devote relatively little attention to them. Amnesty International still considers itself to be in a learning phase in relation to economic and social rights, and is only gradually expanding its focus, starting with 'respect' violations directly connected to earlier campaigns on civil and political rights (Amnesty International, 2005). While the vast majority of human rights organizations now recognize work on economic and social rights as a legitimate part of their mandate, there remains confusion and controversy on what that means in practice. Such differences of opinion were highlighted by a series of exchanges between Ken Roth, Executive Director of Human Rights Watch (see Box 9.1), and Leonard Rubenstein of Physicians for Human Rights (see Box 9.2).

Within the United Nations human rights apparatus, too, economic and social rights remained something of a backwater until the second High Commissioner for Human Rights, the vocal Mary Robinson, committed herself to redressing the imbalance. She famously emphasized that extreme poverty was the worst kind of human rights abuse. This constituted a paradigm shift.

Box 9.1 **Kenneth Roth on How International Human Rights NGOs Should Approach Economic and Social Rights**

Kenneth Roth contends that what international human rights organizations do best is 'investigate, expose, and shame', and that they can only effectively do so when there is relative clarity about violation, violator, and remedy. While progress has been made on documenting violations of economic and social rights, there is much less clarity on who the violator is, and what the remedy should be, than in the case of civil and political rights.

Therefore, international human rights organizations should restrict their work on economic and social rights to cases where governments are guilty of arbitrary or discriminatory conduct: for instance, South Africa's initial ideologically-based denial of anti-retroviral treatment to HIV-infected mothers, or the US exclusion of child farm workers from general child labour regulations. International human rights organizations should stay away from economic and social rights issues that primarily concern allocation of resources. On the contrary, they need to move the public away from seeing economic and social rights purely as a matter of distributive justice.

Some developing countries simply lack the means to meet even the 'minimum core' standards set by the Covenant and its implementing Committee. In such cases, residents of the country in question have the clearest standing on how to allocate resources, and international human rights organizations are poorly placed to comment on government action plans. They cannot legitimately insist on trade-offs between different legitimate government investments.

Even when it comes to pressuring a Northern government or an international financial institution, international human rights organizations are not (yet) in a position to mobilize domestic human rights constituencies in Western states simply to demand more resources. Stigmatization on the basis of arbitrary or discriminatory spending is more likely to be successful. (Roth, 2004a, 2004b)

Box 9.2 **Leonard Rubenstein on How International Human Rights NGOs Should Approach Economic and Social Rights**

Rubenstein argues that human rights organizations must not rely on **naming and shaming** alone. They can collaborate with partner organizations in developing countries in lobbying for service delivery systems that respect economic and social rights, monitoring compliance of all states with the increasingly explicit legal obligations that they have in relation to these rights, and advocating for more resources from wealthy countries to be dedicated to economic and social rights.

International human rights organizations have decades of experience in making policy recommendations, including those with resource implications, in the area of civil and political rights, building up detailed knowledge on, for instance, weapons capabilities or designing an effective court system. If human rights organizations are not yet very good at identifying rights aspects of health or education policies, they will just need to get better at it. 'By the time bad social programs are designed and in place and the naming and shaming occurs, resources will have been misspent and human rights violated in a way that is not easily undone.' It is not necessary to restrict advocacy of economic and social rights to situations where there is a single identifiable villain: dealing with multiple layers of responsibility is the bread and butter of human rights organizations. Moreover, such a frame will have more resonance with the communities affected: HIV/Aids victims who are being denied treatment want to demand anti-retrovirals on the basis of their right to survive, not on the basis of arbitrary government conduct.

The ICESCR stipulates that states must spend on economic and social rights 'to the maximum of its available resources', and that other states have a duty of 'international assistance and cooperation'. It is therefore legitimate for human rights organizations to advocate for more resources. Moreover, advocating for resources is not a zero-sum game. Both at the domestic level, where international human rights organizations may play a support role to local ones, and at the international level, pressure for resources tends to increase the pot. At the domestic level, this is borne out by various cases of advocacy for the provision of anti-retrovirals or medication to combat new strains of tuberculosis, which have finally been provided by the government in question without being at the expense of other health needs.

At the international level, Rubenstein relates the experience of Physicians for Human Rights with mobilizing the medical profession in the US to advocate for greater transfer of resources to combat HIV/Aids in developing countries in a manner consistent with human rights. This campaign showed that it is possible for human rights organizations to mobilize Western publics for resources. (Rubenstein, 2004a, 2004b)

Most human rights experts at that time, and perhaps still, would have identified situations of genocide or ethnic cleansing as the worst form of human rights abuse. Most development experts would have been inclined to think of extreme poverty as an intractable problem, not a human rights violation. Also at the UN, a campaign to create an individual complaints procedure through an 'optional protocol' to the ICESCR has been a priority for human rights advocates since the 1990s. After years of deliberation, the Optional Protocol was approved by the Human Rights Council in 2008.

The international financial and trade organizations remain unconverted to the cause of economic and social rights, however. Despite protests, civil society has not challenged them effectively. Nonetheless, an important concession to the right to health was made, as the result of massive civil society pressure, at the World Trade Organization (WTO) negotiations in Doha: developing countries are allowed 'flexibility' in producing, importing, and exporting generic drugs when they can demonstrate that a national health crisis requires it (WTO, 2003).

National and Regional Successes

Perhaps the greatest (or at least most visible) advances in economic and social rights have been made at the national level. Parliaments have adopted laws and constitutional changes that directly recognize economic and social rights and attendant state obligations. Courts have begun interpreting national and international law in ways that require state redress of violations. Mostly, these new laws, legal judgments, and changes in policy have come about after sustained civil society campaigns.

In South Africa, the landmark 'Grootboom' decision on the right to housing demonstrated that a judicial court could review and enforce even the 'obligation to fulfil' economic and social rights using a standard of 'reasonableness' that is familiar in many legal systems (Pieterse, 2004). But the case also raises questions about how much lawsuits can do: the urgent housing needs of the South African poor have not been substantially alleviated since the judgment.

India's Supreme Court has held that its Constitution requires improvements in the food distribution system,

sparking a nationwide campaign on the right to food. Some participants have since expanded their work to include the right to employment.[3]

In Ecuador, civil society groups concerned over the implications of a Free Trade Agreement with the USA for access to affordable medicine succeeded in convincing their national trade delegation to take into consideration the constitutionally protected right to health (Ecuador, 2004).

Even in the United States, historically one of the staunchest opponents of economic and social rights, and one of a handful of states that has not ratified the ICESCR, economic and social rights are gaining friends and prominence in civil society against relatively little resistance. A new umbrella coalition founded in 2003 and including major human rights and special-interest groups has made advancing economic and social rights one of its core principles (Lobe, 2003). This is further evidence of a profound paradigm shift: rather than being considered mere 'wish lists', economic and social rights are now widely accepted as central to the human rights agenda even in the USA.

New Synergies

Initially, due to ignorance or mutual suspicion, there was little contact or overlap between the anti-capitalist or social justice movement and the much smaller economic and social rights community. Recently, this has begun to change. The 2005 World Social Forum, a global gathering of civil society activists founded in reaction to the World Economic Forum in Davos, made human rights one of its themes. Approximately one-third of the human rights events concerned economic and social rights topics (Forum Social Mundial, 2005).

One of the biggest areas of convergence has been over the right to health. One notable success was the South African Treatment Action Campaign's triumph in persuading the South African Supreme Court that the right to health required national roll-out of a particular anti-retroviral drug, and then, in coalition with international NGOs, in persuading the WTO to allow more flexibility in the manufacture and trade of drugs. Other successes include HIV/AIDS treatment in Thailand, Brazil, and other countries (Seckinelgin,

2002, pp. 123–125). Patients (especially people with AIDS), health professionals, human rights lawyers, development organizations, and anti-privatization activists are all part of this growing movement. Another momentous area of synergy is the right to water. Like food, water is so vital to human life that to claim it as a right has intuitive appeal. This issue appeals to development organizations, anti-dam campaigns, groups focused on political conflicts such as that between Palestine and Israel, and with anti-privatization campaigns (Dicke and Holland, 2007, p. 126). Still, the extent of the convergence remains uncertain, with important discursive differences reflecting differing priorities (Glasius, 2007, p. 81).

The rise of economic and social rights is due to relentless arguing by its advocates. The groups and individuals first advocating for economic and social rights were neither large in number nor particularly well funded or well connected. Through logical, moral,

legal, and linguistic arguments, and through years of repetition, they gradually shifted the opinion of mainstream human rights organizations, development organizations, and United Nations agencies. But there is much convincing left to do, for which the movement needs to continue to create new alliances and explore new methods.

KEY POINTS
The achievements of the economic and social rights movement are based neither on mass mobilization nor on large funds, but on the shifting of mindsets.
The United States Government, the International Monetary Fund (IMF), the WTO, and the private sector remain unconverted.
Lately, the movement has seen the emergence of new synergies with other movements.

Case Study: GCS as Lawmakers: Establishment of the International Criminal Court

The Idea of an International Criminal Court

The idea that there are certain moral standards for the treatment of any human being is a touchstone of international human rights law. International criminal law, and an International Criminal Court (ICC), go a step further, establishing enforceable penalties for rulers or other individuals who commit or condone crimes against a population. These steps embed norms in an international system of enforcement, seeking to end the impunity of war criminals and perpetrators of crimes against humanity.

The idea of such a Court was first mooted by Gustave Moynier, founding member of the ICRC, in 1872, and was widely supported by civil society organizations in the 1920s. It came under consideration immediately after the Second World War, but the Cold War foreclosed this opportunity. A draft code of international crimes

languished in the UN's International Law Commission as ethnic cleansing in Yugoslavia and genocide in Rwanda prompted the Security Council to establish *ad hoc* tribunals (see Glasius, 2006, pp. 6–14). The *ad hoc* tribunals provided proof that international criminal courts could work despite the lack of precedent and conflicting legal systems. They also formed a valuable training ground for those in GCS who were pushing for a permanent international criminal court.

The Campaign

The Coalition for an International Criminal Court (CICC) was founded in 1995. By the time of the final negotiations on the ICC Statute in Rome in 1998, it had grown into a network of over 800 organizations, 236 of which sent one or more representatives to Rome (Glasius, 2006, pp. 35–37).

Drafting the rules of the ICC was a delicate but fascinating task from a strictly legal point of view: different areas of domestic and international law all converged in new ways in the Statute. But human rights groups had particular reasons to take an interest in the ICC. After decades of working to build regional and global human rights mechanisms, human rights experts began to realize that, while the body of human rights law had become substantial, human rights violations in the world were not actually declining. The emphasis therefore shifted toward implementation and the punishment of individual perpetrators as it became increasingly clear that the exclusive focus on states and their responsibility for violations obscured the complexities of power structures and interfered with human rights enforcement. Experience in many Latin American and other countries after transition to democracy showed that it was legally, politically, socially, and psychologically very difficult to prosecute perpetrators of human rights violations, contributing to the embrace of international criminal enforcement. The large international human rights organizations dominated the ICC negotiations, devoting full-time staff and writing key advocacy documents. They also dominated the CICC Steering Committee, with repercussions for the wider campaign.

Other groups working for the ICC included many women's organizations, peace and conflict resolution organizations, groups focused on global governance and strengthening the United Nations, and representatives of churches and religious organizations. The only civil society groups not affiliated with the CICC were the North American anti-abortion or 'pro-family' groups who were largely opposed to creating an ICC (Glasius, 2006, pp. 28–35). Active members of the Coalition engaged in lobbying, produced expert documents, convened conferences, and strengthened state delegations with legal experts and interns. There were remarkably few adversarial or media-oriented actions, such as demonstrations (Glasius, 2006, pp. 27–44) (see Figs 9.1 and 9.2).

Despite the loose formal structure of the CICC and its members' varied interests, it was extremely effective in its coordinating role, particularly at the Rome Conference. In order to be as effective as possible, it split up into three sub-groups—regional caucuses, who lobbied

FIGURE 9.1 Functional representation.

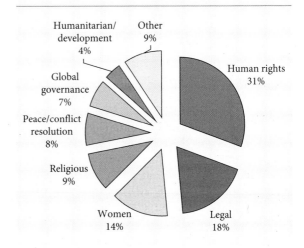

state representatives of their own regions, issue-based caucuses on gender justice, victims, children, peace, and a caucus of faith-based organizations, and twelve working groups, which shadowed the working groups of state representatives and made daily reports available to NGOs and state delegates (Pace and Thieroff, 1999, p. 394).

The level of recognition of the Coalition's role by state representatives and United Nations officials was

FIGURE 9.2 Regional representation.

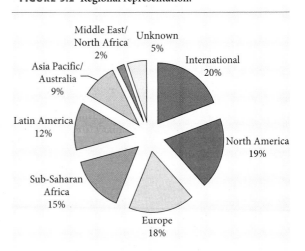

probably unprecedented. Various committee chairs as well as many other official delegates took the participation of NGOs in the proceedings for granted, and the Coalition was their first point of contact (see, for instance, Bos, 1999, pp. 45–46). It was also asked by the United Nations to organize the accreditation of NGOs to the Rome Conference, a unique form of self-regulation (Pace, 1999, p. 209).

The methods of most members of GCS involved in the ICC campaign, and their interaction with state representatives, are characteristic of what Peter Haas and others have termed an *epistemic community*: 'The epistemic community members' professional training, prestige, and reputation for expertise in an area highly valued by society or elite decision makers accord them access to the political system and legitimise or authorize their activities' (Haas, 1992, p. 17). They placed much emphasis on informing and persuading state representatives, and, while they did not hesitate to expose and condemn official views and tactics that they disapproved of, their relations with state delegates were mostly cordial and marked by mutual respect. Seeing the GCS activities with regard to the Court as those of an epistemic community helps us to understand them and their influence.

Achievements of GCS

Many state representatives in the ICC negotiations, including the successive chairs of the negotiations, have remarked on the strong involvement and influence of GCS in negotiating the Statute (Bos, 1999, p. 45; Kirsch and Holmes, 1999, pp. 11, 37). Perhaps the strongest expression of this sentiment came from a diplomat who did not belong to the like-minded group of states in favour of a strong independent Court. Israeli Chief Counsel Alan Baker acknowledged: 'In all my years of international work, I've never seen the NGOs play a more powerful role. . . . They were in on nearly every meeting. They were in on everything' (from the *Wall Street Journal*, quoted in Pace, 1999, p. 201). Taking a broader view, it can be considered the achievement of GCS that there should be a Court at all. The idea was first conceived, kept alive, developed, and advocated in international legal

associations for 125 years. Even a few years before the adoption of the Statute, CICC coordinator Bill Pace was told by a leading expert in international affairs to 'keep working on this, but don't get your hopes up too high for it isn't going to happen in your lifetime, or your children's lifetime, or your grandchildren's lifetime' (Pace, 1999, p. 193).

In terms of the content of the Statute, undoubtedly the most important achievement was the prosecutor's authority to choose his own cases. By the admission of the key diplomats involved, this could not have been achieved without sustained and overwhelming NGO pressure. Beyond NGOs, the active involvement of the prosecutors of the Yugoslavia and Rwanda tribunals was central in legitimizing the idea of an independent prosecutor. Within a few years, GCS succeeded in persuading a majority of states that independent authority of the prosecutor was desirable and achievable (Glasius, 2006, pp. 47–60). While civil society's role in relation to the jurisdiction regime of the ICC is more problematic, that states automatically accept the Court's full jurisdiction for all the crimes in the Statute upon ratification is another success, compared with the 'à la carte' jurisdiction regime originally proposed. Automatic jurisdiction was the consistent and unanimous position of civil society actors, and, like the prosecutor, gradually came to be accepted by states (Glasius, 2006, pp. 63–66).

Largely through the advocacy of a very large, active, and expert Gender Caucus, the Rome Statute greatly advances the gender-sensitiveness of international law (see Bedont and Hall Martinez, 1999; Oosterveld, 1999). On the other hand, partly due to pressure from 'pro-family' groups, the terms *gender* and *forced pregnancy* were defined so as not to pose obstacles to any state's ratification, regardless of its policies on gender.

Intense pressure from civil society ensured the inclusion of war crimes committed in internal conflict situations. A special Victims Rights Group played an important role in forging rules that balance the need for fair and effective prosecutions with protection, sensitive treatment, and rights, of victims and witnesses. The Child Rights Caucus played a role in the criminalization of conscription of children under fifteen, a new element in humanitarian law.

Controversies Within GCS

While the ICC negotiations were largely characterized by mutual respect and camaraderie, they were also the scene of a confrontation between two groupings of civil society with diametrically opposed interests: the women's movement and the pro-family movement. The surfacing of two social movements with contradictory aims at the same venue highlights recurring questions about GCS participation in international forums: Who is legitimate? Who is representative? Who has a right to be there? Women's groups have been confronted with diverse voices from within the movement, but they still tend to collectively consider themselves as the sole representatives of women's concerns. Pro-family groups explicitly question this notion.[4]

The Women's Caucus for Gender Justice was formed in February 1997 and quickly grew to be a coalition within a coalition, with hundreds of member organizations and support from the CICC. The Women's Caucus could accurately claim to represent a global audience, with delegates from all continents. It was highly visible in Rome (see Glasius, 2006, p. 81), with women from conflict areas and experts on the 'hard-core legal stuff' attending.[5] The Women's Caucus had good relations with many of the influential state delegates.

The pro-family groups came to the ICC not just with an anti-abortion agenda, but also with concerns about 'forced social change by feminist, homosexual and other radical groups' (Campaign Life Coalition quoted in *The Interim*, 1998). They did not so much seek a Statute that would reflect their concerns as oppose the establishment of a Court generally, as 'many pro-lifers also see the court as a crucial step in the abandonment of national sovereignty, and the establishment of a tyrannical world government' (*The Interim*, 1998). There were far fewer pro-family groups represented at the negotiations, and they appeared to come from only two countries: Canada and the United States. While tolerated by the Coalition, the pro-family groups were not exactly welcomed. Most NGOs and many state delegates greeted them with irritation and hostility. The Australian delegate who chaired negotiations on gender issues, for instance, called their lobbying an 'unfortunate departure from the generally constructive role played by NGOs

throughout the Conference' (Steains, 1999, p. 368). However, they also had some very strong state allies, particularly in the Vatican and to a lesser extent Catholic and Arab countries (C-FAM, 1998; Bedont and Hall Martinez, 1999).

Relations between representatives of the women's groups and the pro-family group can be described as hostile, even vitriolic. Members of the Women's Caucus have described the involvement of the opposition as an 'intense and sustained attack by an alliance of religious fundamentalists and conservative organisations' (Oosterveld, 1999, p. 39), 'intent on undermining the Court's ability to appropriately address sexual and gender crimes' by making 'misleading linkages' (Bedont and Hall Martinez, 1999, p. 67). Pro-family groups usually referred to the opposition simply as 'radical feminists' and sometimes as the 'anti-life, anti-family movement' (*The Interim*, 1998). Both sides accused the other of having privileged access to certain state delegates (Evans, 1998; *Life Advocate Magazine*, 1998; REAL Women of Canada, 1998) and occasionally of 'dirty tactics' (see note 5).

The clashes between the two movements focused on two issues: the use of the word 'gender' and the crime of 'forced pregnancy'. Pro-family groups objected to gender as potentially providing 'protection for "other genders" including homosexuals, lesbians, bisexuals, transgendered, etc.' (REAL Women of Canada, 1998), whereas women's groups insisted on the relevance of the socially constructed behaviour of men and women. Forced pregnancy was experienced in Bosnia, where Muslim women were not only raped but subsequently forced to carry their babies to full term. However, the Vatican and pro-family groups argued that defining forced pregnancy as a crime would make it illegal for states to prohibit abortion.

In both cases, narrow definitions were finally negotiated that took the sting out of the controversy. In the ICC Statute, 'the term gender refers to the two sexes, male and female, within the context of society. The term gender does not indicate any meaning different from the above' (Steains, 1999, pp. 374–375). Forced pregnancy remained a crime in the Statute, but defined only as 'the unlawful confinement of a woman forcibly made pregnant, with the intent of affecting the ethnic composition of any population or carrying out other grave violations of international law. This definition shall not in any way be interpreted as affecting national laws relating to pregnancy' (Steains, 1999, pp. 366–368). On the basis of these definitions, both groups could interpret the outcome of the negotiations as a qualified victory (Glasius, 2006, pp. 91–92).

These examples show that GCS is not a harmonious entity with a single set of shared values. It is populated by actors with strongly held values, 'organizing to influence their world', but these strongly held values differ; they may diverge or even clash. Plurality and even discord are part and parcel of GCS. But what is most remarkable about this case is that compromises were in fact found, in multilateral negotiation, that satisfied both these diametrically opposed groups to a reasonable extent.

> **KEY POINTS**
>
> The International Criminal Court is a civil society achievement: the idea was first developed in civil society, was kept alive in international legal associations, and would not exist in its current form without the civil society campaign of the 1990s.
>
> The influence of civil society on the Rome Statute was in part based on the close alignment in expertise and values between the civil society activists and a majority of state representatives.
>
> There was a deep antagonism between representatives of the women's movement and representatives of the pro-life or pro-family movement at the ICC negotiations; nevertheless, solutions were reached that satisfied both camps.

Case Study: GCS as Human Rights Monitors: The East Timor Solidarity Movement

East Timor and Indonesia, 1975–1991

The invasion and subsequent subjugation of East Timor by Indonesia in 1975 were accompanied by gross and systematic violations of human rights, generally estimated to have directly or indirectly caused the deaths of approximately 200,000 people, one-third of the population (Dunn, 1983; Budiardjo and Liong, 1984). In the late 1980s, Indonesia changed its policies, trying to win the 'hearts and minds' of the Timorese while also opening up the province to Indonesian migrants and foreign visitors. These changes increased the space for an increasingly active civil opposition movement, led by Indonesian-educated yet disaffected youngsters and tacitly supported by the Catholic Church. It staged demonstrations during visits by the Pope and the US Ambassador in 1989 and 1990. In late 1991, the emotional temperature between the East Timorese and the Indonesian army rose further in anticipation of a visit by a Portuguese parliamentary delegation. When the visit was cancelled, it was with a 'defiance born of despair' that the Timorese resistance engaged in a demonstration, accompanied by foreign journalists, on 12 November 1991. At the cemetery of Santa Cruz, the unarmed demonstration was met by soldiers shooting into the crowd and stabbing and clubbing demonstrators, leaving between 200 and 400 people dead. A British journalist managed to get some film footage, which was subsequently transmitted across the world (Feith, 1992; Schwarz, 1994, pp. 194–229; Glasius, 1999a, pp. 233–307).

Reactions to the Massacre and Emergence of a GCS Network, 1991–1999

Before the Santa Cruz massacre, there were small pockets of GCS activity on East Timor focused around anthropologists, lusophone popular movements, anti-Soeharto activists in exile, or the Catholic Church. They tended to describe the East Timor situations as a 'forgotten war', or a 'forgotten genocide'. After the massacre, such characterizations were no longer appropriate. Footage of the massacre gave a strong impulse to non-governmental solidarity groups in various, mainly Western and lusophone, countries and caused many new groups to spring up (Glasius, 1999a, pp. 261–262).

Box 9.3 **The Role of Charismatic Personalities: Xanana Gusmao**

The rise of GCS in the 1990s has given rise to a new kind of activist/politician: individuals who appear to have internal legitimacy as leaders of their people, but who at the same time appeal to norms and networks beyond the repressive state to seek solutions to their peoples' situation. Nelson Mandela, Vaclav Havel, Ken Saro-Wiwa, and Aung San Suu Kyi all fit this description.

East Timor itself had no shortage of charismatic civil society leaders, the flamboyant diplomat-in-exile Jose Ramos-Horta, the impressive Bishop Belo, and the converted collaborator Manuel Carrascalao among them. But the most important symbol of the Timorese resistance was Xanana Gusmao, who took over the leadership of the armed resistance group Falintil in 1978. He understood early on that his tiny, impoverished, and half-starved guerrilla army stood no chance of winning independence militarily. Falintil launched few attacks, but the fact that the Indonesian army was unable to eradicate it was of symbolic importance to both sides in the conflict. Meanwhile, he devoted much attention to broadening the political base of the resistance from the revolutionary front Fretilin to a much larger coalition of anti-occupation groups and began to foster links with the wider solidarity movement.

The arrest of Xanana Gusmao in November 1992 was celebrated by the Indonesian army as an important victory, but it turned out to be a strategic mistake. Due to the international attention drawn to East Timor by the Santa Cruz massacre a year earlier, Gusmao could not simply be executed as his predecessor had been. His trial attracted press and diplomatic attention for months, and, after an initial show of cooperation, he used the end of the trial to make an impassioned speech for independence before being silenced and led away.

He was then detained in Jakarta's Cipinang prison, from where he constantly sent messages to the outside world, calling attention not only to the situation in East Timor, but also to other Indonesian human rights abuses and even made passing reference to similar injustices in Burma and Tibet. He received a visit from Nelson Mandela and had great influence on a new generation of Indonesian political prisoners. His concern with injustice in Indonesia and beyond made him rise above the national struggle alone.

Xanana Gusmao played a crucial role when militia violence engulfed East Timor after the referendum in September 1999. Falintil troops came under great pressure to take up arms in order to protect the population, but Xanana convinced the commanders to remain inactive: he realized that a humanitarian intervention would be much less likely if the situation came to resemble a civil war rather than one-sided violence.

Despite expressing reluctance to enter politics after independence, Xanana Gusmao stood for president and was elected in 2002 with 82 per cent of the vote. He declined another term but has since become prime minister of a coalition cabinet in opposition to the Fretilin party from which he once emerged.

The USA-based East Timor Action Network, founded immediately after the massacre, quickly grew to encompass dozens of local chapters. The capture of guerrilla leader Xanana Gusmao (see Box 9.3) a year later gave a further boost to the movement.

The East Timor solidarity network emerged at exactly the right time in two respects: it profited from the spreading use of e-mail to maintain contacts between different groups and with the Timorese resistance in exile; and it connected with the increasingly strong internal opposition to the Soeharto regime in Indonesia, although primarily with student leaders and labour activists, not the senior leadership. In 1996, East Timor received renewed attention when Timorese Bishop Carlos Filipe Ximenes Belo and Timorese leader in exile Jose Ramos-Horta were jointly awarded the Nobel Prize for Peace.

The emerging movement had a wide base, including activists who saw themselves primarily as opposed to US imperialism as well as more religiously or anthropologically motivated members, but it framed its demands in human rights terms. It had two main demands. First, it sought an end to and accountability for human rights violations in East Timor. This demand was wholly uncontroversial and lip service was paid to it by Western politicians and even some Indonesian officials. The second demand, made by dedicated groups but not by mainstream human rights organizations such as Amnesty International and Human Rights Watch, was that the East Timorese right to self-determination be realized through a free vote on independence. Despite its strong basis in international law, this demand was politically much more sensitive.

Referendum; Violence; Intervention

In January 1999, after President Soeharto had stepped down, his temporary successor Habibie suddenly announced that if those ungrateful Timorese really wanted independence, they could have it. This was seen as a 'window of opportunity' in a volatile time in Indonesian politics that could quickly close again. Negotiations took place between the former colonial power, Portugal, the occupying power, Indonesia, and the United Nations. The East Timorese themselves were left out: the agreement decided about them, purportedly for their sake, but was reached without them. Various influential East Timorese leaders, including Bishop Belo, the pro-independence coalition National Congress for the Reconstruction of East Timor (CNRT), and others, had developed plans for the implementation of a referendum well before President Habibie made his announcement. Their proposals all shared two important elements. They all stipulated that a 'cooling-off' period of many years should precede the referendum to allow healing, debate, and a free and rational choice. They also insisted that, during this time, the Indonesian armed forces should withdraw, making way for a United Nations police or peace-keeping force (Glasius, 1999b). The cooling-off period was not attractive to the United Nations, which was eager to get the issue off the agenda with a minimum of fuss. Experiences with the Western Sahara, where negotiations about a referendum on independence had been stalled for more than seven years, compounded the haste of the United Nations (Glasius, 1999b). A United Nations force policing the island was declared unacceptable by Indonesia. Hence, the tripartite agreement concluded on 5 May 1999 authorized a referendum on independence organized by the United Nations, but gave responsibility for maintaining peace and security during the referendum to the Indonesian army, even though for twenty-four years the Indonesian army had committed serious human rights abuses in preventing any moves toward self-determination. Still, this was the only deal on offer, and the East Timorese independence movement decided to seize the historic opportunity despite grave misgivings about security.

The international network of solidarity groups focused on East Timor also feared violence but hoped to play a role in mitigating it. Under the umbrella of the International Federation for East Timor (IFET), it organized an all-volunteer referendum observation mission to monitor the registration and voting and the human rights situation. It began to observe and publicize minor incidents of intimidation and violence as soon as the first teams arrived.[6]

The vote, held on 30 August 1999, proceeded relatively peacefully, with the Timorese population voting overwhelmingly for independence. This widely expected result seemed to surprise Indonesian authorities (Martin, 2001; Chesterman, 2002). In the following days a campaign of intimidation by Indonesian military and allied Timorese militias ensued. Instead of providing protection, the IFET teams actually became targets. It became increasingly clear that the perpetrators of violence intended to scare away all foreigners—journalists, observers, and UN personnel—from East Timor. The IFET teams were first withdrawn to the capital Dili, and then evacuated along with most UN personnel (see note 6).

Two weeks after the vote, President Habibie bowed to pressure and accepted an Australian-led intervention force to protect the Timorese. Overwhelmingly backed by public opinion, the Australian government, previously often reviled by civil society groups for its excessive caution in dealing with human rights issues in Indonesia, did not hesitate to send its soldiers on a potentially dangerous mission. After a controversial two-year tenure by the United Nations, the very small, very poor East Timorese nation achieved full independence.

Strengths and Weaknesses of the GCS Network

Analysis of the East Timor observer mission exposes several paradoxes that go beyond the particular case study. First, devoted as it was to a free choice for the East Timorese people, the solidarity movement committed itself to the UN referendum whilst knowing that freedom of choice would be compromised by the Indonesian military presence. Although the military's plan to wreak revenge if the vote favoured independence was widely known, there was no space (or time) for a debate either within Timorese civil society or in the solidarity network on whether the referendum should be supported at all without UN peace-keeping troops. While the overwhelming turnout seemed to validate the decision to go ahead, the experiences of the IFET mission raise a more general question about who gets to take strategic decisions in a situation where the local civil society cannot freely deliberate the options.

Secondly, the fate of the observer project highlights the fragility of unarmed civil society missions. Some have argued that military missions are necessarily polluted by non-humanitarian state interests, and that civil society interventions are therefore preferable (Marcon and Pianta, 2001). Arguably, 'accompaniment' missions such as those by Peace Brigades International have sometimes helped to protect local civil society figures by relying on the political ramifications of harming someone of a Western nationality. On the other hand, the International Solidarity Movement with Palestine has lost several members to Israeli military violence, and in the East Timorese case the observers were simply intimidated into leaving. Such experiences bring to mind Hannah Arendt's (1969) dictum that Gandhi's non-violent resistance tactics would not have stood a chance if his opponent had been Hitler or Stalin.

Yet some things have changed. First, scrutinizing the human rights record of other states has become a normal part of international politics, and politicians come under pressure from GCS at least to speak, and sometimes to act, in response to massive violations. Second, as the USA found in relation to the Abu Ghraib scandal, it has become much more difficult for any government to hide instances of human rights violations. While the film footage of the East Timor massacre had to be smuggled out of the country, nowadays it could be relayed instantly through mobile phones. The civil society observation mission to the referendum initially failed to protect the Timorese, but, without the publicity it gave to what was happening, there might have been no intervention and no independence.

KEY POINTS

The consequences of the 1991 Santa Cruz massacre in East Timor are illustrative of the increased effect of global media on global civil society mobilization, and in turn on subsequent political decision making.

In crisis situations, international civil society actors come to translate the aspirations of oppressed people without thorough prior consultation.

Unarmed civil society missions are 'purer' than military interventions, but also more fragile.

Conclusion

This chapter has attempted through three brief case studies to demonstrate the interdependence between the emergence of GCS and the development of human rights law. The first function of GCS in relation to human rights, that of shifting norms through what Keck and Sikkink (1998, pp. 16–23) have called 'information politics' and 'symbolic politics', is the least controversial. At the global and domestic levels, civil society's right to inform, debate, and persuade on the basis of particular ethical convictions is not generally questioned. In the latter half of the twentieth century, the project of increasing the popularity of human rights has been incredibly successful. Not only politicians, but also corporate and religious leaders, now routinely invoke human rights values, and outright rejection of human rights by any kind of public figure has become almost unthinkable.

But human rights are not the only ethical frame prevalent in GCS. In the early twenty-first century, at least two other significant ideological master frames can be discerned: the social justice frame, more overtly concerned with power relations and redistribution than with human rights, and religiously-informed frames, above all the frame of the 'Umma', the Islamic brotherhood of mankind. Adherents to all three of these frames have in common a global project and a belief that their frame alone represents solutions for the marginalized and downtrodden of the Earth. Yet all three have been open to abuse by power holders. A fourth frame, of renewed importance with the advance of climate change, may be that of environmentalism (see Chapter 18). None of these frames is necessarily entirely incompatible with any of the others. Historic separation and suspicion tend to accentuate the areas of conflict, but the search for common ground is urgent if there is to be one (pluralist) GCS instead of several separated and opposing strands.

The second function outlined above, participation in law making, is much less an obvious right of GCS. A remarkable feature of the negotiations on the ICC was that leading state delegates appeared to take this participation for granted. As Adriaan Bos noted, GCS involvement 'fills in gaps arising from a democratic deficit in the international decision-making process' (Bos, 1999, pp. 44–45). That there is such a deficit is generally acknowledged, but can GCS really fill the democratic gap?

It can be argued on the basis of the ICC case that GCS can greatly strengthen certain features of democratic procedure, in particular transparency, equality, and deliberation (Glasius, 2006, pp. 114–127). But GCS cannot be seen as offering a form of representation of the global *demos*, or at least not representation in its traditional form. It could be conceptualized as a form of participation ('a voice not a vote', Edwards, 2003), but in practice this participation is so limited and so uneven that GCS cannot entirely be considered to be an adequate 'functional equivalent' (Rosenau, 1998) or 'alternative mechanism' (Scholte, 2001) to parliamentary democracy, operating at the global level. However, another contribution is made by GCS: that of moral values.

If it is accepted that GCS moves states toward appreciating, or at least appearing to appreciate, 'ethical' or 'common good' arguments over national interest arguments, then the question remains which ethical projects make it to those forums and get taken up. In the ICC negotiations, while there was some open (on gender) and some muted (around weapons of mass destruction) contestation, there was clearly a dominant civil society project: to prise away from states the power to punish perpetrators of genocide, war crimes, and crimes against humanity. But if multilateral institutions like the United Nations are serious and sincere about being 'open to civil society', they should be open to all civil society representation, not just representation that reflects their own values. If human rights groups have a right to be active at forums such as the ICC negotiations—and they have fought hard for that right—then so do other groups. It is only on the basis of such ethical pluralism that GCS participation in international law making can be defended.

The third form of GCS activism in the field of human rights, monitoring, raises yet another democratic question. Civil society activists take personal risks in order to bear witness to violations of human rights of which we might not otherwise be aware. But what typically characterizes these efforts, whether in East Timor, Zimbabwe, or Darfur is that the population cannot speak freely about its own political aspirations. Therefore, human rights activists end up making recommendations for these populations without any mandate save their own consciences. This is a necessary function of GCS in an imperfect world, but it should at the same time be recognized as a problem.

GCS cannot be artificially insulated from money, violence, or existing power structures, but what sets GCS apart from other international actors is that it operates on a different logic: the logic of persuasion. Human rights activism has been characterized by courage and determination, but this must be combined with humility and openness to other civil society perspectives for the human rights paradigm to remain persuasive.

QUESTIONS

INDIVIDUAL STUDY QUESTIONS

1. In what ways are GCS and the international rule of law interdependent?

2. What is an epistemic community? Can you think of examples other than the ICC negotiations?

3. Why were the civil society actors engaged in negotiations on the ICC relatively successful?

4. Is there a danger of civil society actors being co-opted when they are so close to power holders? Where would you see yourself as a human rights activist, outside protesting or inside negotiating?

5. Does participation of GCS in international negotiations, such as on the ICC, on a complaints procedure for economic and social rights, or on climate change, make such negotiations more democratic? In what ways?

6. Was it irresponsible for the International Federation for East Timor to launch a civil society observation mission when it was aware of the risk of severe violence associated with the referendum on independence?

GROUP DISCUSSION QUESTIONS

1. What is GCS according to you? Is it really global?

2. If you were a human rights activist, would you campaign on economic and social rights? If so, how would you make the case for them?

3. Should civil society groups be given a role in the deliberations of an intergovernmental body such as the Human Rights Council? If so, on what basis?

4. East Timorese leader Xanana Gusmao, who was undoubtedly responsible for the death of Indonesian soldiers when he was a guerrilla commander, is portrayed here as a GCS figure. Do you agree with that characterization?

5. Who bears responsibility for taking decisions in a 'solidarity network' such as that related to East Timor, Burma, or Darfur?

FURTHER READING

Bell, D. and **Coicaud**, J.-M. (eds) (2007). *Ethics in Action: The Ethical Challenges of International Human Rights Nongovernmental Organizations*. New York: Cambridge University Press.
This edited volume is the result of a project bringing together leaders of human rights NGOs and political theorists to discuss ethical dilemmas.

Glasius, M. (2005). *The International Criminal Court: A GCS Achievement*. London: Routledge.
A detailed account of the role of GCS in the establishment of the ICC, with some wider considerations about the role of GCS in global governance.

GCS Yearbook Series (2001–). For 2001–2003 published by Oxford University Press, Oxford; 2004 onward by Sage, London.
Most exhaustive resource on all aspects of GCS. Each book contains a section on concepts, on issues, on infrastructure, and a data programme. From 2007/8, the books are themed.

Ishay, M. (2004). *The History of Human Rights: From Ancient Times to the Globalization Era*. Berkeley, CA: University of California Press.
This history of human rights is at the same time an accessible history of the human rights movement.

Kaldor, M. (2003). *GCS: An Answer to War*. Cambridge: Polity Press.
A readable yet insightful introduction to the concept of GCS.

Keck, M. and **Sikkink**, K. (1998). *Activists Beyond Borders: Advocacy Networks in International Politics*. Ithaca, NY: Cornell University Press.
Groundbreaking work on the emergence of transnational advocacy networks, with an emphasis on human rights networks.

Yamin, A. (2005). The future in the mirror: Incorporating strategies for the defense and promotion of economic, social and cultural rights into the mainstream human rights agenda. *Human Rights Quarterly*, **27**, 1200–1244.
Practical yet profound article on what the human rights community needs to do to get better at defending and promoting economic and social rights.

WEB LINKS

http://www.oneworld.net A civil society media network covering human rights and sustainable development news beyond what the mainstream media offer.

http://www.civicus.org CIVICUS is a large general alliance of civil society organizations dedicated to strengthening citizen action and civil society throughout the world.

http://www.opendemocracy.net Independent website on global current affairs, promoting dialogue and debate on issues of global importance.

http://www.lse.ac.uk/Depts/global/researchgcspub.htm Free downloads of chapters from older editions of the *GCS Yearbook*, see above.

NOTES

1. From a telephone interview with Rolf Kuennemann, founding Director of FIAN, 15 December 2005.

2. See the ESCR-Net website: http://www.escr-net.org/.

3. Interview with Biraj Patnaik, Adviser to the Commissioner of the Supreme Court of India: Right to Food, 21 November 2005. See also the Right to Food Campaign website: http://www. righttofoodindia.org/.

4. See the REAL Women of Canada website: http://www.realwomenca.com/about.htm.

5. Interview with Katherine Hall Martinez, Deputy Director, International Program, Center for Reproductive Law and Policy, 4 December 2001.

6. See IFET's 1999 East Timor Observer Project on the IFET website: http://www.etan.org/ifet/.

ONLINE RESOURCE CENTRE

 Visit the Online Resource Centre that accompanies this book for updates and a range of other resources:

http://www.oxfordtextbooks.co.uk/orc/goodhart/

Human Rights and Politics in Development

Sakiko Fukuda-Parr

Chapter Contents

Reader's Guide

This chapter addresses the importance of politics to the relationship between human rights and development. It presents the two major ways in which human rights struggles have focused on development processes in the last two decades: the right to development, the struggles of poor countries for a better deal in the global economic system; and the human rights-based approach to development, the struggles of poor people for development to realize their rights. The chapter begins by exploring the conceptual nexus of human rights politics and development. It then presents the basic concepts and debates surrounding the right to development and the human rights-based approach to development. A case study analyses the Millennium Development Goals, which reflect the current international consensus on development, and presents a human rights critique of the Goals to illustrate some of the key conceptual points.

Introduction

This chapter is about human rights and development—how human rights are part of development and development is part of human rights as challenges, concepts, and practice. These two fields, which evolved separately, have come to interact with each other as human rights activists began to address poverty as a human rights challenge and development practitioners began to adopt human rights principles in their work. Theorists in both fields began to develop concepts, measures, and analyses. Because this is a new area of theory and practice, it is still 'in the making' and basic ideas are evolving.

Politics are central to the relationship between human rights and development because development can be a process to realize human rights, but often poor people—both individually and collectively as communities and states—have to struggle to claim their rights.

The chapter presents the two major ways in which human rights struggles have focused on development processes in the last two decades: the right to development (RTD), the struggles of poor countries for a better deal in the global economic system; and, the human rights-based approach to development (HRBA), the struggles of poor people for development to realize their rights.

The chapter is in four parts. The first part explains the nexus of human rights and development in terms of concepts, and how development can promote the fulfilment of human rights. It explains why politics are an important aspect of this nexus. The second and third sections review RTD and HRBA, respectively. These sections include the basic concepts and some of the current issues being debated, the context in which they emerged, and how they evolved in practice with attention to the political factors that shaped the evolution. The section on RTD is short since it has had less reach in implementation than HRBA. The fourth section looks at the case of the Millennium Development Goals (MDGs), the current consensus development priorities of the international community, and presents a human rights critique to illustrate the conceptual points made in the chapter. Because this is an emerging area of study and practice, there are many controversies, which makes it an exciting new way that human rights is engaging with contemporary challenges that people face in their lives.

Development and the Struggles for Human Rights

Politics and Human Rights

Human rights is an idea that 'empowers' the weak and vulnerable, protecting them from abuse of their rights to a life of dignity and freedom. Education, for example, may be a developmental goal for a Planning Ministry economist, or an aid agency programme officer. But it is an entitlement for a girl that she claims when denied schooling because there is no school provided by the state, or because the teacher does not turn up to teach, or because the parents do not value schooling for girls. In such a situation, social institutions have failed to ensure that she can enjoy her right to education. The language of rights is important in this case as the girl struggles to claim her right to education, the right to non-discrimination, and the right to equality. Her cause is helped if she can build alliances with others struggling for the same rights.

These struggles are part of claims being reaffirmed as human rights.[1] In explaining the emergence of human rights, philosopher and economist Amartya Sen (2006) explains that human rights are ethical norms that are a product of 'social ethics and public reasoning', while political scientist Jack Donnelly (2006) refers to their development through a history of 'social learning'. Human rights norms develop because people claim that certain conditions of life are entitlements and demand that they become recognized as human rights. These norms also emerge because people confront various threats to their survival as human beings and claim security against such threats (Shue, 1996).

People-Centred Approaches to Development

Struggles for human rights are also part of the process of development. Development expands material resources and restructures the economy, social institutions, and norms that help to achieve the realization of human rights. Economists have dominated the development field and focus their analysis on economic activities and material production. But this is not the only perspective or discourse on development. Running alongside for decades have been more people-centred approaches to development, such as ideas about community development in the 1960s, the world employment programme of the 1970s, the basic needs approach of the 1970s and early 1980s, and, since the 1990s, the human development and capability approach (HD/CA) advocated by Sen and the UNDP Human Development Reports. These approaches point out that the ultimate end of development is to improve human well-being. Sen (1988, 1989, 1999) has argued in many of his writings, starting in the 1980s, that development is essentially about expanding human capabilities that enable people to be and do the things that they value, an idea most widely known under the title of his 1999 book *Development as Freedom*, and among scholars as the capabilities approach. Mahbub ul Haq, the architect of the concept of *human development* (HD), expresses the same idea in a different way with different words: that development is a process that creates an enabling environment that expands opportunities for people, and that expands the capabilities that people have to lead lives that they value (UNDP 1990; Haq 1995).

Development is not only about economic growth but also about how the benefits of economic growth are distributed among people—income groups, ethnic groups, racial groups, women or men, young or old, regional populations, rural or urban populations, workers in different occupations, and so on. It is also about how the resources generated by economic growth are put to use by government. How budgets are allocated among different sectors and uses has important consequences. Some uses are more likely to contribute directly to the fulfilment of human rights as supporting primary education, primary health care, social security, the judicial system and legal aid for people who cannot afford private legal services, or rural roads, while uses such as mining or military spending are less likely to contribute to the realization of human rights and may even have negative consequences.

The struggles of poor people for their rights are at least in part about those government policies and legal institutions that would advance the realization of their human rights—economic, social, cultural, political, and civil. Human rights are interdependent and indivisible; human dignity and freedom depends on the realization of all of these five rights, and these rights are reinforcing. The plight of poor people illustrates this point: poor people are often denied their human rights in all of these five areas, and the denial of one right can reinforce denial of another. For example, a woman who is a victim of human trafficking for prostitution is denied her rights to bodily integrity, to security, and to freedom of movement; she is likely to have been vulnerable because she came from a low-income family, had no access to protection from the courts and the police, and was perhaps illiterate and unable to access information. These multiple denials of civil, political, economic, and social rights combine to leave her vulnerable. Moreover, the discrimination she may suffer on account of her gender, ethnicity, religion, or race may compound her vulnerability and explain why she was exploited by traffickers. Poor people from politically marginalized communities are vulnerable because their human rights are not guaranteed.

In these ways, development and human rights are inherently intertwined. Development is a process that can help to fulfil human rights, but not all types of development can do so. The struggle for human rights must therefore include a struggle for a process of development that can be positive for the promotion of human rights and not one that takes human rights backwards. This is the central point in linking human rights and development.

Linking Human Rights and Development: Right to Development and Human Rights-Based Approach to Development

It is only recently that theories and practices of human rights and development have interacted and been brought together. This started in the 1980s with the emergence of the RTD. Developing countries promoted this concept as a claim to a global environment that would be conducive to their development, including such issues as resource transfers, financial markets, and trade. This was followed by another move in the 1990s with the emergence of the HRBA, advocated by civil society groups and development practitioners for development policies and programmes based on human rights principles.

RTD and HRBA are often conflated, but they are two quite distinct concepts promoted by two different sets of actors. RTD is a discourse in the human rights field. The key actors are governments of developing countries, supported by some human rights scholars, seeking recognition of right to development as a category of human rights in international human rights law. The terrain of contestation is in international negotiations on human rights treaties. RTD arose in the Cold War context when the Third World pursued an agenda of a New International Economic Order (NIEO) from the East and West. These negotiations have advanced little in the last decade.

HRBA is a discourse in the development field. The key actors are civil society groups and development practitioners, supported by some scholars. It defines the objective of development as the realization of human rights, and uses the principles of human rights in the process of development, such as participation, empowerment, equality, and the tools of human rights such as the international human rights law. HRBA emerged as a reaction against structural adjustment policies and globalization (Darrow and Tomas, 2005), and as a challenge to the neoliberal approach that focuses on economic growth and market integration as the core priority in development (Nelson and Dorsey, 2003). HRBA has become a significant discourse on devel-

opment, along with others such as economic growth, environmental sustainability, and capabilities/human development.

Both RTD and HRBA are driven by the concern with global poverty as an affront to human freedom and dignity, and as a matter of injustice. Unlike the economic analysis of poverty, which looks to poor economic performance, inadequate resources, or inadequate policies as the causes of poverty, human rights is concerned with unequal distribution of power and wealth within and between countries as poverty's root cause. While RTD is a challenge to the unequal distribution of political and economic power among countries, HRBA is also concerned with inequalities within countries.

> **KEY POINTS**
>
> Human rights is an idea that empowers people because it asserts that individuals have an entitlement, a claim on society, by virtue of the fact that they are human.
>
> Just because people have rights, it does not mean that society confers them; people have had to and continue to have to struggle for their rights.
>
> Development is a term that is often used synonymously with economic growth. Currently there are several discourses on development and there is a large literature on these different concepts and their policy implications. One of the significant discourses is the human development and capabilities approach.
>
> Human rights and development evolved as separate fields, interacting little. The human rights community addressed issues of development in the context of RTD. The development community did not address human rights until the emergence of HRBA in the 1990s. Whereas RTD is a human rights concept, HRBA is a development approach.

The Right to Development (RTD)

Emergence of RTD and its Context

The right to development emerged in the context of the politicized human rights debates of the Cold War and the development discourse of the NIEO. Just as

the Eastern bloc championed social and economic rights, and the West civil and political rights, the Third World championed the right to development. It was formulated as a claim by less-developed countries to an international economic system that would create a more favourable—or enabling—environment for development. It emphasized issues in the global economic systems, many of which were legacies of colonialism, such as full control of natural resources, self-determination, and international obligations of states to formulate appropriate policies and to provide international cooperation (Beetham, 2006). These ideas resonate with the *dependency theory* of development that emerged in the 1960s, which traced the origins of underdevelopment to the persistence of colonial economic systems. Dependency theorists such as Frank, Sunkel, and Cardoso argued that developing countries would remain underdeveloped even when colonization ended because they continued to be periphery countries in an economic system supplying primary commodities to the metropolis.

Conceptual Issues

There are substantial debates about the content of the right to development (Andreasson and Marks, 2006). There are questions about how the right of a nation's economic development can be linked to the individual's fulfilment of human rights for a life of dignity and freedom. The right to development implies a collective right, a right belonging to a group rather than an individual, which is much contested. Beetham (2006) argues that individuals can only enjoy human rights through a guarantee of the collective right to development. Both he and Sengupta (2006) argue that the right to development is therefore a right to a particular kind of development that would contribute to the fulfilment of human rights—for example, one where the benefits of development are widely shared. The right to development cannot be consistent with development where the state does not respect, protect, and fulfil human rights in the process. For example, investing in mineral exploration and exploitation by giving contracts to foreign multinationals that would primarily benefit the investors and political elites, while dislocating people from their homes, polluting the rivers, and clearing forests that provide an essential livelihood for the local population is hardly a kind of development consistent with human rights. Another issue is the difficulty of identifying the obligations of

duty bearers and what constitutes an infringement of the rights.

In practice, RTD debates focus on the obligations of rich countries to provide international assistance, especially development aid, but also global economic systems in trade, finance, technology, and debt relief that are conducive to development. There is also an important debate about the obligations of corporations.

Implementation

Political and conceptual controversies have mired the implementation of RTD. Of the many different rights that have been recognized in international law since the adoption of the Universal Declaration of Human Rights (UDHR) in 1948, RTD has been one that has been particularly slow to be agreed and defined. It was debated for many years before it was finally proclaimed in 1986 through the *Declaration on the Right to Development*. The 1986 Declaration was almost unanimously adopted and was reaffirmed in the Vienna Declaration of the 1993 World Conference on Human Rights, but attempts to develop a treaty that would bind states legally have not advanced. There is little support for this initiative, especially among the developed countries. Moreover, the concept of RTD is rarely used in policy debates about international development.

KEY POINTS

RTD has been advocated by developing countries and resisted by developed ones.

The 1986 Declaration on RTD has not moved forward into a legally binding covenant or a convention.

The content of RTD is ambiguous.

RTD is an entitlement to a particular kind of development that would fulfil human rights of individuals.

RTD imposes obligations on rich countries to provide development assistance and to put in place policies conducive to Third World development.

Human Rights-Based Approach to Development (HRBA)

Emergence of HRBA and its Context

The emergence of HRBA as a development discourse can be traced back to the 1995 publication by the Human Rights Council of Australia, 'The Right Way to Development: Human Rights Approach to Development Assistance' (HRCA, 1995). HRBA aims to reorient the theory and practice of development. It sees development and human rights as pursuing the same objectives—defined as the realization of human rights and the respect of human rights principles in the process of development. HRBA often refers to programme approaches adopted by development cooperation agencies that have introduced new priorities and activities. But these approaches are embedded in a broader 'discourse', and the term HRBA is also used broadly to refer to the discourse, synonymously with 'human rights in development' and 'rights-based development'. HRBA builds on the alliance formed between the human rights and development communities in the 1980s to campaign for the *Convention to Eliminate All Forms of Discrimination against Women* (CEDAW), and the *Convention on the Rights of the Child* (CRC).

HRBA emerged in the context of globalization and the economic and political trends of the 1980s and 1990s in reaction to neoliberal economic policies that led to the neglect of many social and equity priorities (Nelson and Dorsey, 2003; Darrow and Tomas, 2005).

Cold War politics had driven a divide between civil and political rights, on the one hand, and economic and social rights on the other. Separate covenants developed, and civil and political rights became a tool of the West against the Eastern bloc countries and their Third World allies. Western human rights communities neglected, and many scholars and activists rejected, economic and social rights. Leading activists such as Aryeh Neier (2003) argued that they were excessive claims that could not be held up in a court of law; Kenneth Roth (2004a), President of Human Rights Watch, recognized economic and social rights but argued that international human rights organizations were ill equipped to advocate for them. On the other side, some Third World

leaders argued that social and economic rights had to be established before political and civil rights could be promoted. For example, this was a major part of Lee Kwan Yew's 'Asian Values' argument that social and economic development had to precede democracy. Since the 1990s, powerful challenges to these views have been launched. Theorists such as Sen (2004, 2005, 2006) argue that justiciability is not a criterion for human rights and that law is the 'child of human rights', not the other way round. Others, such as Pogge (2007), argue that global poverty is a massive human rights violation.

The end of the Cold War cleared the political obstacles for the development community to engage with human rights and for the human rights community to give attention to economic and social rights and the challenges of poverty. It opened the way for new political dynamics in international agendas for both human rights and for development. Leading advocates starting with Mary Robinson, as UN High Commissioner for Human Rights, began to champion economic, social, and cultural rights, and the indivisibility and interdependence of all human rights. She also put global poverty on the human rights agenda, and human rights on the development agenda (UNDP, 2003; Robinson, 2005). Her successor, Louise Arbour (2007, p. iii), continues to take this position, stating that 'Poverty and inequities between and within countries are now the gravest human rights concerns that we face.' The human rights community began to embrace global poverty and development as human rights challenges. The decision by Amnesty International, which had historically focused exclusively on civil and political rights, to devote its 2010 campaign to global poverty is an important milestone in this shift.

The spread of HRBA was also facilitated by the rise of civil society movements who championed HRBA in developing countries and international networks. These movements were facilitated by democratization across the world and by the growth of global civil society (see Chapter 9). Throughout Latin America, Africa, and Asia, authoritarian regimes gave way to multi-party democracies in what is called the 'third wave' of democratization. Non-governmental organizations (NGOs) concerned with human rights and development began to proliferate in countries where authoritarian regimes had suppressed them, often taking up the cause of poverty. These organizations formed global advocacy networks. Just as globalization integrated markets and intensified the exchange of goods, it integrated social movements and intensified the flow of ideas and advocacy (UNDP, 1999, 2002).

HRBA was also facilitated by changes in the development field. When a people-centred discourse on development emerged as a strong intellectual counter-current to the growth-centred discourse, development and human rights could be conceptualized as mutually supporting and compatible. In the early 1990s, HD/CA emerged, arguing that the ultimate end of development was improvement in human lives, in particular the expansion of capabilities—or choices to be and do what an individual values—rather than expansion of material output or economic growth. Economic growth is important, but only as a means, not the end (Sen, 1989, 1999; UNDP, 1990). Such concerns were long-standing, but it was in the 1990s that they became prominent in international development debates. Defined in this way, development was no longer seen as antagonistic to human rights, but rather as a process supporting their fulfilment.

In 2000 the UNDP Human Development Report argued that these two concepts shared a common motivation: the pursuit of a life of freedom and dignity as the central concern. The two concepts also share policy priorities that emphasize equality, participation, and agency. The tools of analysis and implementation approaches differ but are complementary and reinforcing. These arguments (UNDP, 2000; Sen, 2004, 2005) contributed to the conceptual framework of HRBA.

The HRBA Concept—Key Elements and Comparison with Human Development/Capabilities and Neoliberal Approaches

HRBA applies human rights norms and principles to development policy and programmes on two fronts: the enjoyment of human rights by people, the rights bearers; and the obligations of duty bearers. From the rights bearers' perspective, the principles include: (i) equality and non-discrimination; (ii) true participation; and (iii) indivisibility and interdependence of all human rights. From the perspective of the duty bearer (principally the state but extending to other actors such as international corporations), the principles include the obligations: (i) to respect, protect, and fulfil; (ii) to achieve progressive realization subject to maximum available resources, non-retrogression, and immediate realization of core minimum standards; and (iii) to implement international human rights norms and standards.

How does HRBA differ from other approaches to development, particularly the neoliberal market approach and the HD/CA approach that is also widely endorsed by many practitioners?[2] As explained above, HRBA emerged in part as a reaction against the neoliberal discourse on development. So there are important contrasts with that approach, but similarities with HD/CA (see Table 10.1).

The similarities between HRBA and HD/CA are grounded in a common motivation to enhance human dignity and freedoms. HRBA conceptualizes this in terms of human rights, HD/CA in terms of capabilities, but these are complementary if not overlapping concepts (Nussbaum, 1997; UNDP, 2000; Sen, 2004, 2005). Both contrast with the neoliberal approach, which seeks to maximize economic welfare, not the full range of human welfare, and which conceptualizes human well-being in terms of utility (Jolly, 1999). Sen (1981) has long critiqued the utility approach to welfare because it focuses on material means and consumption rather than on what people can be and do (their capabilities and functioning). Thus HD/CA and HRBA have compatible and consistent philosophical foundations at odds with the neoliberal approach.

The similarities and contrasts among these approaches are more complex in the operational context. HRBA and HD/CA share common policy priorities but build on different tools. HD/CA and neoliberal approaches use the same tools but argue for different policy priorities.

Equality and participation are the two human rights principles that lead to the most striking policy contrasts. While mainstream international debates emphasize development and poverty reduction, the human rights approach is explicitly concerned with inequality. All three approaches share a commitment to policies to expand education, health, and nutrition, address gender

TABLE 10.1 Comparing key features of three approaches to development: human rights, human development, and neoliberalism.[3]

Approach	Human rights	Human development	Neoliberalism
Conceptual framework			
Objectives of development	Realization of human rights	Expansion of choices, capabilities, and freedom	Maximization of economic welfare
Concept of human well-being	Dignity and freedom	Capabilities as freedom	Utility
Focus of concern	Individual as rights bearer and state conduct as duty bearer	Individuals and people	Markets
Guiding principle	International human rights law norms and standards	Equity, justice, and expansion of choice	Economic efficiency
Operational approaches			
Evaluation of progress:			
Main criteria for evaluating development progress	Right holder perspective: enjoyment of all rights; equality; non-discrimination	Human capabilities; equality of outcomes, fairness, and justice in institutional arrangements	Economic impacts
	Duty bearer perspective: accountability for legal obligations to respect, protect, and fulfil; subject to progressive realization; non-retrogression	Assessment of human impact of development policies	Assessment of policy choice on grounds of efficiency and effectiveness
Measurement and evidence base	Cases of rights denials documenting individuals rights violated and duty bearer failure to comply with obligations	Progress in human outcomes (e.g. literacy, child mortality)	Economic activity and condition
		Average, deprivational, and distributional measures; disaggregated measures	Averages and aggregate measures
Key indicators	No indicator sets in widespread use	Social and economic indicators: Human Development Index (HDI), Gender-related Development Index (GDI), Gender Empowerment Measure (GEM), and Human Poverty Index (HPI)	GNP per capita; GNP growth; headcount measure of income poverty incidence
Human agency in development:			
People as ends and/or means	Ends: beneficiaries with focus on the poorest and excluded	Ends: beneficiaries	Ends: not explicit
	Means: agents of change—claiming rights	Means: agents of change—taking charge to make their lives better	Means: human resources for economic activity
Mobilizing agency	Individual action through the courts; collective social action	Individual action and collective action	Individual action as entrepreneurs
Locus of action	Civil society and legal institutions	Civil society	Markets

TABLE 10.1 continued

Policy priorities			
Education, health, and nutrition	Ends in themselves as human rights. High priority for education and health of the least well off and excluded	Ends in themselves as expansion of capabilities	Important means—human resources—for improving productivity essential to economic growth
Ending gender, ethnic, and other discrimination, and reducing inequality	Central policy goal across all sectors and themes	A human right, an important priority across all sectors and themes. Concern with reconciling possible tensions with efficiency	A social or ethical issue. Concern with trade-off with efficiency
Economic growth	No position—little research on economic growth and human rights. Widespread perception that fast growth often undermines human rights	Essential means to enhancing human capabilities and choices	Central policy objective of development policies
Governance	Strengthening state capacity to meet human rights obligations in economic, social, cultural, civil, and political domains. Emphasis on access to justice for the poor and marginalized	Democratic and inclusive governance to democracy. Enhance voice of people and accountability of the state. Emphasis on state functions	Role of institutions necessary for efficient operation of the market. Emphasis on rule of law, contracts, and eliminating corruption

and other inequalities, promote economic growth, and improve governance. The differences lie in the relative priorities and choices made about trade-offs among them. For example, in education and health policies, the neoliberal approach would justify education and health policies that would strengthen growth prospects, while the HRBA would emphasize education as an end in itself and stress the obligation to ensure equal access to all, with priority attention to the least well off and the marginalized. In the area of governance, HRBA would focus attention on those institutional arrangements that would enhance voice and participation of the poorest people in claiming their rights, while the neoliberal policy focus would be on those arrangements that facilitate investment and innovation. Such differences are apparent in the human rights critique of the MDGs as the case study in this chapter will illustrate.

The Adoption of HRBA by Key Stakeholders

HRBA has been gaining momentum among development practitioners, particularly local and international NGOs, civil society groups, bilateral and multilateral donors, and think tanks. Many leading national and international networks such as Oxfam, Care International, and Action Aid now work with HRBA principles. For example, Oxfam International[4] states: 'Our mission is a just world without poverty and our goal is to enable people to exercise their rights and manage their own lives.' Similarly, Action Aid states, 'We work with local partners to fight poverty and injustice worldwide, reaching over 13 million of the poorest and most vulnerable people over the last year alone, helping them fight for and gain their rights to food, shelter, work, education, healthcare and a voice in the decisions that affect their lives.' The United Nations has adopted a common policy—a 'common understanding'—across all agencies to base all of its development work on human rights principles (UNDG, 2003).

The United Nations Children's Fund (UNICEF) has been a pioneer in this approach, building on its commitment to children's human rights and its involvement in the 1980s with the formulation and passage of the CRC. It has developed many important programmes using the HRBA, such as budget analysis and monitoring in Ecuador (Box 10.1). Among bilateral development agencies adoption has varied: the UK, Sweden, and Norway have prepared elaborate policies and guidelines, while others such as the USA have engaged little. But all have endorsed the principle of the importance of human rights under the Organization for Economic Cooperation and Development's Development Assistance Committee policy of 1994. The most recent restatement of this policy recognizes human rights norms as 'an accepted normative framework reflecting global moral and political values'. It notes, 'there is growing consensus on the value of human rights principles—such as participation, non-discrimination and accountability—for good and sustainable development practice. The application of these principles builds on and strengthens good and sustainable development practice, with equal attention to process and outcomes' (OECD/DAC, 2007).

The human rights community has also increasingly engaged with poverty and development as priority concerns. Issues of poverty and development have long been a concern for human rights organizations in the South, though they have only recently become a priority for Northern NGOs, as discussed earlier. As for the UN machinery, a wealth of important new initiatives have been undertaken since the 1990s, such as the appointment of special rapporteurs on extreme poverty, on the right to development, health, food, and other relevant issues. The Office of the High Commissioner for Human Rights (OHCHR) has also begun important substantive work to build up a battery of conceptual and analytical tools in this new area.

Implementation of HRBA—from Rhetoric to Action

Implementation of a particular development approach can range from: (i) adoption of the language and 'rhetoric' as important ends; (ii) policy agenda reflecting HRBA priorities; and (iii) use of human rights-specific tools and methods (Uvin, 2004). According to recent reviews of development agencies (Uvin, 2004; OECD/DAC, 2007; Piron, 2005), the adoption of the language of rights is widespread and many have also shifted programme priorities, particularly in the governance areas, to strengthen civil and political rights such as access to justice. HRBA has contributed to shifting international policy priorities, especially in raising issues of state–citizen linkages by use of the duty bearer–right holder and accountability perspectives, the structural roots of poverty, and

focus on exclusion as an obstacle (OECD/DAC, 2007). In the areas of women's rights and children's rights, international human rights instruments (CEDAW and CRC) have had an important impact in many countries around the world.

These are important innovations and show significant spread of HRBA as development practice. But they remain limited and have remained at the margins of both human rights and development practice. HRBA has been embraced by the UN system, many major international NGOs, and some bilateral agencies, but has had little impact on some of the major actors in international development, most notably the World Bank and the International Monetary Fund (IMF). Some studies (Uvin, 2004; Darrow and Tomas, 2005; ODI, 2006; OECD/DAC, 2007) also observe that some agencies claim to use HRBA when all they are doing is 'rhetorical repackaging' of the same programmes with the same methods and agendas. This is one way of looking at the position that the World Bank took over many years: stating that their programmes were in fact promoting human rights without using those terms. HRBA's reach has not extended to most national governments of the Global South, with some notable exceptions such as Brazil and South Africa.

HRBA has had little impact on the mainstream priority-setting tools of governments supported by the international community, such as the Poverty Reduction Strategy Papers (PRSPs), which are policy frameworks for poverty reduction prepared by governments of low-income countries for mobilizing donor support, thus reflecting the policy priorities of national governments that are supported by official donors. Recent analyses of PRSPs find that human rights are very superficially considered, if mentioned at all, in most of these strategies (Fukuda-Parr, 2008b). The predominant approach to development in the PRSPs follows the neoliberal approach and does not reflect human rights priorities, including reducing inequality and democratic governance (Fukuda-Parr, 2008b). HRBA agendas are missing in countries where human rights are clearly serious issues. Only a handful of countries have prepared PRSPs that go beyond the rhetorical use of the term 'human rights' and associated principles of equality, participation, and accountability. But these exceptional cases are especially interesting documents that incorporate some elements of the human rights perspective on poverty and development.

Box 10.1 **UNICEF HRBA Experience in Ecuador: The Principles of Universality and Participation—a Budget for Implementing Social Rights in Ecuador**

The following text is adapted from Elizabeth Gibbons (2006).

Ecuador experienced a serious macroeconomic crisis during the late 1990s, which resulted in sharply decreased spending on social programs, thus undermining the rights of children, as well as adults, to health care, education and adequate nutrition. Concerned about these cuts, UNICEF began a dialogue with the Congress over the government's proposed budget. This led to an agreement with the Ministry of Finance under which UNICEF was authorized to have access to the Ministry's financial data to analyze the national budget, monitor its execution, and communicate its findings. Helping legislators and the public to understand how the budget functions and what priorities it reflects were the objectives of this exercise, whose goal was to encourage the creation of more equitable public policies based on a shared consensus regarding society's obligation to fulfill the human rights of all of its members.

Analyzing, monitoring, communicating budget revenues and expenditures

Analysis of the budget and spending patterns revealed that spending on social programs was plummeting. For example, investment in education dropped from US$611 million in 1996 to US$331 million in 1999; and health spending fell from US$198 million to US$96 million. The budget analysis also revealed that spending for social sectors was disproportionately low (15% for 2000) compared to allocations for debt repayment (60%) and other non-social sectors. In addition, certain regions (the rural sector, Andean Highlands and the Amazon)—particularly those with a majority Indigenous population—were not getting a fair share of social benefits.

Ecuadorian President Jamil Mahuad and UNICEF then agreed UNICEF should track social expenditures and the key indicators of the national crisis. UNICEF created a series of visual tools—tables, bar graphs, pie charts, etc.—to make budget data accessible and comprehensible to ordinary Ecuadorians. Over time, this data became available online. UNICEF then undertook an ambitious outreach effort, sharing the information with a wide variety of partners, including legislators, business leaders, academics, media representatives, and Indigenous, religious and trade union groups. The central issue during these meetings was how to make public spending more equitable. The key message of this advocacy effort was the universality of human rights translated into three goals: health and education for all and hunger for no one. It was a values-based message, offered in the spirit of overcoming a crisis felt by all, but seriously threatening the survival of the country's poor and Indigenous people.

UNICEF and government officials worked together to draft programs consistent with the overriding goals of universality and equity, including: expanding existing school nutrition and income-support programs; nutritional support for children under two and pregnant and lactating mothers; and subsidies for poor families to send their children to school. All programs were targeted to reach the most marginalized and impoverished segments of the population. In the following years, UNICEF's role expanded to include monitoring revenue as the government was preparing a proposal for tax reform. This information on tax reform was also shared widely; the tax issue received press coverage and was the topic of a national conference sponsored by the Ecuadorian Congress.

Impacts

In 2001, the percentage of total government spending devoted to social programs rose to 22.1% and then again to 23.2% in 2002, exceeding the 1996 figure of 19.1%. By 2002, *per capita* social spending had surpassed pre-crisis levels, although due to population growth, the poorest Ecuadorians were still receiving considerably less than in the past.

In addition, the need to reform the national tax structure and generate additional revenues resulted in important institutional changes. The capacity of the Internal Revenue Service was strengthened so that an additional four to five percentage points were collected in taxes, and a new Customs Service was created, which added a further two percentage points. Consequently, between 1999 and 2002, government revenue from taxes increased from 6.4% to 13.7% of GDP, although the underlying tax structure still relies mainly on indirect taxes, and efforts to modify the structure are ongoing.

Lessons for building a human rights-based society

From the perspective of building a human rights-based society in Ecuador, the results were also impressive. A broad social consensus around the need for more just and equitable public-spending policies clearly emerged during the first few years of UNICEF's public budget work. The leader of one of the country's largest Indigenous groups noted that the work had 'democratized budget information.' Previously, few Ecuadorians were aware of, or able to understand, the national budget.

In facilitating this process, Ecuador's political leaders made tremendous strides towards accountable and transparent governance. By increasing and targeting social sector investment in light of the discovery of critical inequities, the government took a human rights-based

(Cont.)

stance that placed priority on fulfilling the rights of the country's most vulnerable citizens.

Perhaps the most important lesson learned from the Ecuadorian experience on implementing economic, social and cultural rights is that a human rights-based message can resonate and provoke change if it is based on widespread consensus and perceived as a positive contribution to the society. Even in an historically-inequitable society, most people share an underlying belief in human rights and social justice that, once tapped, can influence public policymaking. Although Ecuador had ratified the CRC on March 23, 1990 and approved a Code for Children and Adolescents in 2002, it was less these legal instruments than the principles of universality and

participation sustaining them that propelled the process forward. At no time, whether analyzing the budget or sharing its findings with wide sectors of society, did UNICEF encounter resistance to the underlying premise that rights must be universal. This experience, rooted in democratic institutions and processes, challenges contemporary assessments of exclusionary public policy in Latin America and offers a positive model of building solidarity for social inclusion, even in a context of extreme resource scarcity.

Reproduced with the permission of Canada's International Development Research Centre (http://www.idrc.ca) and of the author.

KEY POINTS

HRBA is a development discourse that defines development as the fulfilment of the human rights of all individuals. It emerged in the 1990s, after the Cold War's end, in response to the human consequences of neoliberal economic policy reforms. It has spread rapidly, adopted by many development organizations, including bilateral agencies and large international NGOs.	HRBA and human development approaches contrast with neoliberal approaches in critical ways, including the way development and human well-being are defined, the priorities for economic and social policy, and the role of people in the development process.
HRBA shares much in common with other people-centred discourses on development, notably the HD/CA approach; both are motivated by the concern for human freedom, dignity, and equality.	The influence of HRBA on mainstream government policy and international development policy has been limited. There are concerns that its adoption has been 'rhetorical repackaging', yielding no real change in policies and programme priorities. But there is an important debate and HRBA is a significant challenge to the mainstream policy agendas.
HRBA is defined by the application of basic human rights principles, including participation, equality and non-discrimination, empowerment of people, and accountability of duty bearers for their obligations to respect, protect, and fulfil human rights. HRBA also explicitly makes use of international human rights norms.	

Case Study: The Millennium Development Goals (MDGs) and Human Rights

The MDGs define the consensus agenda of the international development community. In many respects, MDGs set an agenda for promoting human rights, yet closer scrutiny also shows contradictions between

them. HRBA analysis of the MDGs helps to illustrate why the human rights community is concerned that the current international development agenda does not reflect human rights priorities.

MDGs—the Concept, Emergence, and their Importance

In September 2000, heads of state and government of nearly all of the world's 200 countries met at the Millennium Summit to commit their nations to 'doing their utmost' for global development. They vowed to overcome poverty and achieve peace, human rights, democracy, and environmental sustainability while respecting the principles of equality and solidarity. The resulting Millennium Declaration (MD) contained some specific goals and timeframes for development, giving concrete meaning to these lofty objectives.[5] These were reconfigured into a more coherent set of eight goals, eighteen associated targets, and forty-eight progress indicators—the Millennium Development Goals.

Human Rights Principles as the Purpose and Motivation of the MDGs

We recognize that, in addition to our separate responsibilities to our individual societies, we have a collective responsibility to uphold the principles of *human dignity, equality and equity* at the global level. As leaders we have a *duty therefore to all the world's people*, especially the most vulnerable and, in particular, the children of the world, to whom the future belongs. (Millennium Declaration, UN General Assembly, September 2000)

The MDGs are the key objectives that world leaders agreed to as their common vision for ending poverty and promoting development in the twenty-first century. They address seven key dimensions of poverty, hunger, primary education, gender equality and empowerment of women, maternal mortality, child mortality, HIV/AIDS and other major diseases, and environmental sustainability. The eighth goal is to strengthen global partnerships for development through the actions of the rich countries in development aid, trade, debt relief, and technology transfer (see Box 10.2).

The MDGs are unprecedented in the high level of policy commitment that they have mobilized and in forging a consensus on defining a common purpose for development. They express in simple terms, without theory, what development means and why it is important.

MDGs and human rights—overlaps and reinforcing agendas

There are many overlaps between MDGs and human rights. *First, there is a substantial overlap between*

MDGs and core economic and social rights. Several of the MDGs directly address human rights and none are inconsistent with human rights. Moreover, human rights values frame the MD and its vision: freedom, dignity, solidarity, tolerance, and equity among people and nations. It is important to remember the origins of the MDGs in the MD and their strong human rights elements. MDGs are not ends in themselves nor a comprehensive development strategy, but merely tools intended to help implement and monitor the MD commitments made by world leaders.

Second, the MDGs focus on human well-being, not on economic growth, and thus highlight some of the key human rights priorities as important development priorities. This is a significant shift away from the neoliberal development agenda of the 1980s and 1990s. The consensus on MDGs reflects an important endorsement of poverty and human well-being as the central objectives of development (Fukuda-Parr, 2005), and broadens the development agenda by including social sectors as priorities.

Third, the MDGs constitute a compact among rich and poor countries of the world to eliminate global poverty (UNDP, 2003). For the first time, rich countries' inputs are considered alongside the objectives of poor countries. Of the eight MDGs, the eighth is the most significant departure from the past. It commits rich countries to do more in the areas of access to trade, aid, debt relief, and technology transfer. This goal's inclusion was central to the endorsement of the MDGs by developing countries.

Fourth, the MDGs can be used as a framework of accountability for the political commitments made by world leaders. Unlike with typical UN declarations, governments and political leaders can be held to account for their commitments to the MD because implementation can be monitored by the MDGs. People can hold governments and the international community accountable for their achievement. Governments can hold the international community accountable, and vice versa.

Human Rights Critique of MDGs

Despite the overlaps with human rights, there has been a vigorous critique of the MDGs from the human rights perspective, leading to a growing number of publications and debates, including the comprehensive review by OHCHR (2007).[6] As this and other publications (e.g. Saith, 2006) point out, there are several important contradictions between MDGs and human rights.

Box 10.2 **Human Rights in the MDGs**

Each of the MDGs reflects a core human right, but not fully—as indicated in the note following each goal in brackets. There is no mention of the principles of equality, non-discrimination, or participation.

Goal 1. Eradicate extreme poverty and hunger [Right to adequate standard of living—*for all*]

- Target 1A: halve, between 1990 and 2015, the proportion of people whose income is less than $1 a day.
- Target 1B: achieve full and productive employment and decent work for all, including women and young people [Right to work].
- Target 1C: halve, between 1990 and 2015, the proportion of people who suffer from hunger [Right to food].

Goal 2. Achieve universal primary education [Right to free primary education]

- Target 2: ensure that, by 2015, children everywhere, boys and girls alike, will be able to complete a full course of primary schooling.

Goal 3. Promote gender equality and empower women [Women's right to equality—*in many more areas than education*]

- Target 3: eliminate gender disparity in primary and secondary education, preferably by 2005, and in all levels of education no later than 2015.

Goal 4. Reduce child mortality [Right to life—*for all*]

- Target 4: reduce by two-thirds, between 1990 and 2015, the under-five mortality rate.

Goal 5. Improve maternal health [Women's right to life and health—*for all*]

- Target 5A: reduce by three-quarters, between 1990 and 2015, the maternal mortality ratio.
- Target 5B: achieve, by 2015, universal access to reproductive health.

Goal 6. Combat HIV/AIDS, malaria, and other diseases [Right to health]

- Target 6A: have halted by 2015 and begun to reverse the spread of HIV/AIDS.

- Target 6B: achieve, by 2010, universal access to treatment for HIV/AIDS for all those who need it.
- Target 6C: have halted by 2015 and begun to reverse the incidence of malaria and other major diseases.

Goal 7. Ensure environmental sustainability [Right to environmental health, Right to water and sanitation, Right to adequate housing—*for all*]

- Target 7A: integrate the principles of sustainable development into country policies and programmes and reverse the loss of environmental resources.
- Target 7B: reduce biodiversity loss, achieving, by 2010, a significant reduction in the rate of loss.
- Target 7C: halve, by 2015, the proportion of people without sustainable access to safe drinking water.
- Target 7D: have achieved by 2020 a significant improvement in the lives of at least 100 million slum dwellers.

Goal 8. Develop a global partnership for development [Right to development, Obligations of assistance]

- Target 12: develop further an open, rule-based, predictable, non-discriminatory trading and financial system (includes a commitment to good governance, development, and poverty reduction—both nationally and internationally).
- Target 13: address the special needs of the least-developed countries.
- Target 14: address the special needs of landlocked countries and small island developing states.
- Target 15: deal comprehensively with the debt problem of developing countries through national and international measures in order to make debt sustainable in the long term.
- Target 16: in cooperation with developing countries, develop and implement strategies for decent and productive work for youth.
- Target 17: in cooperation with pharmaceutical companies, provide access to affordable essential drugs in developing countries.
- Target 18: in cooperation with the private sector, make available the benefits of new technologies, especially information and communications technologies.

First, the contents of the MDGs do overlap with human rights but there are also important omissions. For example, core human rights principles of participation and equality are not reflected in the MDGs, even though they frame the MD. Important rights such as reproductive health were initially left out and were only added after much pressure; gender equality and empowerment targets are very weak. MDGs aim at primary schooling for all, but human rights norms also require that it be free.

Second, MDGs do not go far enough to realize human rights: for example, to fulfil human rights requires eliminating, not just halving, poverty. Moreover, the goals do not give adequate priority to the most deprived; halving the proportion of people living in extreme poverty and hunger can be achieved by improving the well-being of the best off amongst them. Pogge (2007) argues that MDG-1 is a betrayal of human rights.

Third, partnership goals are weak, without any quantitative targets or agenda for institutional reform (Fukuda-Parr, 2006). The formulation of MDG-8 is even weaker than the wording of the MD, which states a commitment 'to an open, equitable, rule-based, predictable and non-discriminatory multilateral trading and financial system'; MDG-8 omits the term 'equitable' (OHCHR, 2008). Issues such as the decision-making processes of the World Trade Organization (WTO), the governance of multilateral institutions, and the restructuring of the global financial architecture are excluded.

Fourth, the MDGs are overly technocratic. They could lead to top-down planning and implementation, thereby promoting a donor-led agenda that is inconsistent with a participatory approach in which communities set their own priorities. They could also lead to a preoccupation with quantitative achievement, such as placing *x* number of children enrolled in schools while neglecting the quality of the education. Experience from other UN initiatives suggests an excessive focus on the mobilization of financial resources and technical solutions rather than on transforming power relations (OHCHR, 2008).

Fifth, MDGs could disempower the people and their authorities because they are set globally. Even if the MDGs were set by a participatory process, each country has its specific set of challenges and obstacles, and it is up to the people and government authorities to decide on priorities. A single set of goals can also distort priorities: for example, certain diseases are singled out (e.g. malaria, HIV/AIDS, and other communicable diseases) while other emerging issues (e.g. tobacco) are ignored.

MDGs could help build a framework of accountability for human rights, but are not sufficient. More indicators, especially ones revealing discrimination and inequality, would be required.

Since the launch of the MDGs in 2001, the human rights community has been slow to embrace them or to make use of them in pursuing their own agendas. Many of the international NGOs have been some of the most vigorous critics of the MDGs. One important reason why the MDGs are not embraced by the human rights community is the perception that the rich countries dominated their formulation and will use them to hold poor countries to account for development failures. Both NGOs and human rights machinery tend to defend developing country interests and are suspicious that the World Bank and the donor countries had the dominant role in formulating the MDGs.

Alston (2005) found that MDGs are not mentioned even in Human Rights Commission resolutions dealing with issues such as housing, right to food, and education, and are not included in the work of special rapporteurs—with the notable exception of the work on health and the working group on the right to development. He concludes that the human rights community and the MDGs are like 'ships passing in the night' (Alston, 2005, p. 755), ignoring each other while moving toward the same destination.

KEY POINTS	
The eight MDGs address key dimensions of poverty and include a goal for strengthening global partnership on development through aid, trade, debt relief, and technology transfer.	MDGs and human rights overlap significantly, but there are also important gaps, including equality and empowerment. The MDG agenda can potentially be a significant aspect of the HRBA, but not unless care is taken to address these gaps.
MDGs define the common agenda of the international community for development. They are important for the high level of political commitment and the consensus that has been achieved.	The human rights critique of the MDGs illustrates how human rights concerns have influenced development agendas and how they remain controversial.

Conclusion

As most writers on the subject observe, the 'integration' of development and human rights has proven partial and difficult (Sano, 2000; Uvin, 2004; Robinson, 2005). HRBA is still at the margins of both the fields of development and human rights, and the two communities do not communicate well. Many development practitioners remain highly sceptical of the idea that human rights are the ends and means of development (Ingram and Freestone, 2006). They continually ask, 'What is the value added' of human rights to development (Kanbur, 2007)? To which the reply from the human rights community is that there is a need for 'value change' in development agendas (Eide, 2006). Both communities face difficulty in integrating rights and development, as illustrated in the discontinuities between human rights and MDGs.

The difficulties of such integration can be explained by many factors, such as different traditions, analytical concepts, and implementation methods (Fukuda-Parr 2008a). Among them is the role of politics. Human rights promotion has been a political process, of people demanding their entitlements and making alliances with supporters in a political process of challenging states to deliver on their human rights commitments. This adversarial process is directly contradictory to the development process of working with government, to support their efforts to invest in development and to implement policies.

QUESTIONS

INDIVIDUAL STUDY QUESTIONS

1. How did the Cold War influence the evolution of international human rights law and movements?

2. What are the different ways in which development is defined and what are the main discourses on development today?

3. What is the difference between RTD and HRBA?

4. What are the key arguments for and against the RTD?

5. How does HRBA differ from the mainstream neoclassical approach and from the human development approach?

6. What was the historical context in which HRBA emerged?

7. What are the key human rights principles in HRBA?

8. What are MDGs?

GROUP DISCUSSION QUESTIONS

1. Do you think that the MDGs promote human rights?

2. If you were the head of an NGO for women's rights, what position would you take on the MDGs and what would be your organization's strategy—ignore them, criticize them, change them, or use them in your advocacy and action?

3. If you were revising the MDGs, how would you change them to make them better reflect the HRBA agenda? What targets and indicators would you add?

FURTHER READING

Andreassen, B. A. and **Marks**, S. P. (eds) (2006). *Development as a Human Right: Legal, Political and Economic Dimensions*. Cambridge, MA: Harvard School of Public Health. Distributed by Harvard University Press.
This volume collects some of the cutting-edge work on the theories of development as a human right and includes conceptual underpinnings, defining obligations, specific national challenges, and global processes. The contributors are leading thinkers on the issue and address some of the controversial issues on the right to development and on the human rights approach to development.

Alston, P. and **Robinson**, M. (eds) (2003). *Human Rights and Development: Towards Mutual Reinforcement*. New York: Oxford University Press.
This edited volume addresses the challenges of implementing a human rights-based agenda in development. It includes chapters by leading scholars and practitioners in both development and human rights fields. While the Andreassen/Marks volume is more theoretical, this is more practice oriented, and focuses on HRBA rather than RTD.

Donnelly, J. (2003). *Universal Human Rights in Theory and Practice* (2nd edn). Ithaca, NY: Cornell University Press.
This volume is an important theoretical work for exploring the relationship between human rights and development from political and other perspectives. It addresses the issue of universalism and the charge that human rights are a Western construct that may not apply to other parts of the world, especially the Third World.

OHCHR (2004). *Human Rights and Poverty Reduction: A Conceptual Framework*. New York: United Nations. http://www2.ohchr.org/english/issues/poverty/guidelines.htm.
This short publication presents a useful conceptual framework for the links between human rights and poverty that is simple and up to date. It is useful for practitioners as a document on concept that complements more specific operational guidelines.

OHCHR (2006). *Frequently Asked Questions on Human Rights-Based Approach to Development Cooperation*. New York: United Nations. http://www.unhchr.org.
This short publication is an excellent document that clarifies basic concepts and definitions about the HRBA.

Shue, H. (1980). *Basic Rights: Subsistence, Affluence and U.S. Foreign Policy*. Princeton, NJ: Princeton University Press.
This classic in the theory of human rights is an important foundation for exploring the relationship between human rights and development. It presents a theoretical defence of basic subsistence and survival rights, including economic rights that have been contested in the literature.

UNDP (2000). *Human Development Report 2000: Human Development and Human Rights*. New York: Oxford University Press.
Written from the human development perspective, this is a comprehensive text that clarifies the overlaps and complementarities between the HRBA and HD/CA. It includes chapters on concepts (written by Amartya Sen), history, democracy, the use of indicators, poverty, and a policy agenda.

Uvin, P. (2004). *Human Rights and Development*. Bloomfield, CT: Kumarian Press.
This book reviews the challenges of HRBA as a development practice. It provides a systematic analytical framework for this review, and sets the analysis in the context of divergent development discourses. It reflects on the obstacles and critiques of the HRBA approach without rejecting it.

WEB LINKS

http://www2.ohchr.org/ The official website of the OHCHR is a must-visit site for the study of human rights and development—in particular, the web pages on development, poverty, and MDGs.

http://www2.ohchr.org/english/issues/development/ This page contains basic documents and information on current debates and activities of the working group on the right to development.

http://www2.ohchr.org/english/issues/poverty/ This page contains basic documents on poverty as a human rights issue. It provides information on current activities, reports of the independent expert on extreme poverty, and links to documents.

http://www2.ohchr.org/english/issues/millenium-development/index.htm This page on MDGs contains UN OHCHR perspectives on why MDGs are relevant to human rights, and documents on the subject.

http://www.chrgj.org/ The website of the Center for Human Rights and Global Justice of the New York University School of Law, a premier research centre on human rights and the consequences of globalization on poor people and poor countries. It contains a wealth of information and working papers on the latest research in this area.

http://www.cdhr.org.in/about.htm This website of the Centre on Development and Human Rights located in New Delhi, India contains information on reflections on the right to development.

http://www.iidh.ed.cr/default_eng.htm This website of the Inter-American Institute of Human Rights, a premier research and training institution in Latin America, provides a wealth of information on the human rights situation and analysis. The site provides information on specific rights and on current activities of the Institute.

NOTES

1. This is a common characterization of human rights made particularly in the practice of human rights by advocates and defenders. See Chapter 2, which documents the history of human rights as global struggles. See particularly 'The Ongoing Global Struggle for Human Rights' (UNDP, 2000, pp. 27–29) which documents milestones and progress in the evolution of human rights in international legislation.

2. There are many others, notably the sustainability approach, the 'local first' approach, or the post-development approach. These approaches are not all mutually exclusive. A full discussion of these approaches is beyond the scope of this paper. Greig *et al.* (2007) provides a good summary review of these approaches.

3. Some of the elements are drawn from Jolly (2004), which compares the differences and overlaps between the human development approach with neoliberalism.

4. See the Oxfam International website http://www.oxfam.org/en/about.

5. The MDGs were not formulated overnight by the United Nations. They build on a global consensus reached in the 1990s among governments—a dialogue to which many civil society groups actively contributed (Emmerij *et al.*, 2001). All but two of the eight MDGs are, in fact, commitments outlined in the agendas negotiated and adopted at the UN development conferences of the 1990s, conferences which all involved a protracted preparatory process of country, regional, and global consultations. MDGs also build on the consensus of the rich countries of the world; the Development Assistance Committee of the Organization for Economic Co-operation and Development (OECD) had earlier drawn up its own set of development goals (OECD, 1996).

6. John Foster (2002); Howard White and Richard Black (2002); Roberto Bissio (2003); Jolly (2004).

ONLINE RESOURCE CENTRE

Visit the Online Resource Centre that accompanies this book for updates and a range of other resources:

http://www.oxfordtextbooks.co.uk/orc/goodhart/

Economic Globalization and Human Rights

David L. Richards and Ronald D. Gelleny

Reader's Guide

This chapter uses statistical methods to examine the relationship between economic globalization and government respect for two subcategories of international human rights known as physical integrity rights and empowerment rights. First, an overview of different theoretical approaches regarding the relationship between economic globalization and government respect for human rights is provided. Then, research findings from the quantitative literature examining this relationship are discussed. Finally, an original study using quantitative methods is conducted to examine whether a developing country's ability to attract foreign investment is affected by its level of governmental respect for human rights. We find that governments that respect their citizen's physical integrity and empowerment rights will be better able to attract foreign economic capital.

Introduction

In this chapter, we examine the relationship between economic globalization and government respect for human rights. First, we provide an overview of different theoretical approaches regarding the relationship between economic globalization and government respect for human rights. Second, we provide an assessment of the quantitative literature examining this relationship. Finally, we engage in a case study, including statistical tests, to examine whether a less developed country's (LDC) ability to attract foreign investment is affected by its level of governmental respect for human rights.

We define economic globalization as both the implementation of neoliberal economic policy reforms (e.g. deregulation and privatization policies) by governments and an increase in the worldwide flow of goods, services, labour, and capital (Richards and Gelleny, 2002, 2007). Increasingly, globalization has been viewed as the latest and, perhaps, final stage of the inevitable march of capitalism throughout the world. Countries that have been excluded from the process, owing perhaps to ideological policies, national policies of protectionism, or even self-imposed isolation from the world economy, are becoming entrenched in the international economic system. Governments view economic globalization as the principal means to develop economically and politically. In recent years, there have been surges of participation by Central and Eastern European countries in the world market and international organizations designed to promote and maintain the capitalist system, such as the International Monetary Fund (IMF), the World Bank, and the World Trade Organization (WTO). China and India, seeking to expand economic growth, likewise have become more integrated into the world market. Moreover, many countries in Africa—including Ghana, Kenya, Mauritania, and Tanzania—have begun to initiate free market policy reforms in an effort to attract more international investment (UNCTAD, 2007).

At the same time, the global community has become more focused on the relationship between globalization and human rights, questioning whether the process of globalization has enhanced or undercut government respect for human rights. Globalization is often imposed on a country's population from above, and those most adversely affected often have little or no input in its implementation. Indeed, much of the anti-globalization backlash hinges on the accusation that globalization permits multinational corporations (MNCs) to reap economic rewards at the expense of human rights. The media has spotlighted some of the notorious human rights violations associated with MNCs to our attention. The oil conglomerate Unocal, for example, was accused of involvement in forced labour, rape, and a murder allegedly carried out by soldiers along a natural gas pipeline route in Myanmar.[1] Shell and Chevron have also been accused of abusing human rights in Nigeria. Wal-Mart suppliers in China and Honduras have been found in violation of numerous human rights. Furthermore, it was revealed that former talk show host Kathie Lee Gifford's clothing line, sold by Wal-Mart stores, was produced by sweatshop workers in Honduras. Because of globalization's potential for harming human dignity, scholars must provide as transparent an understanding as possible of the consequences of the globalization process.

Economic Globalization and Government Respect for Human Rights: Two Opposing Views

The Optimistic View: Globalization and the Road to Development

Economic globalization can enter developing countries' economies in several ways. That is, MNCs and financial investors ensure their presence in economies worldwide through foreign direct investment (FDI) and portfolio investments. FDI consists of building plants in another country or acquiring a controlling interest (more than 10 per cent of outstanding stock) in an existing overseas company. Owing to the direct investment in buildings, machinery, and equipment, FDI is generally thought of as a long-term investment. Portfolio investment consists of the purchase of stocks and bonds of less than 10 per cent of the outstanding stock in foreign firms. Since portfolio investors have no controlling stake in the investment, these investments are of a much more fluid nature than FDI (see Kenen, 1994; Walther, 1997).

Countries that embrace globalization will raise their economic wealth, while countries that fail to join the movement will find themselves languishing in underdevelopment: studies have found a correlation between increased investment flows and a country's rate of economic growth and overall socio-economic welfare (see Box 11.1, Example A).

Many view MNC investment as the engine behind economic globalization. Developing countries that open their markets to FDI experience greater access to advanced technology, exposure to the most sophisticated management and marketing skills, stronger economic growth, and an expansion in the employment market. Moreover, MNC-generated jobs in developing countries tend to pay more than equivalent local employers (Harrison and Scorse, 2003; Bhagwati, 2004; Gray *et al.*, 2006).

MNCs can also be seen as a driving force of change, diminishing the power of local elites, as well as altering traditional value systems and social attitudes in devel-

oping countries (Diebold, 1974; Biersteker, 1978). To attract and maintain MNC investment, governments may have to reshape traditional policies that benefit local interest groups at the expense of less affluent groups. Governments may be encouraged to establish and respect property rights, create a non-discriminatory hiring/employment environment, and invest in social services and infrastructure. Often, the MNCs export labour and hiring practices to their overseas operations that surpass local hiring requirements and working-safety conditions (Mears, 1995; Harrison and Scorse, 2003). Additionally, MNCs may exceed their corporate mandate and finance programmes supporting local infrastructure projects or invest in efforts to combat local social problems (see Box 11.1, Example B). Consequently, MNCs can directly break down insular interests and stabilize internal relations within developing countries.

In addition to FDI, scholars point to portfolio investment as playing a critical role in promoting economic growth in LDCs. The liberalization of portfolio investment allows surplus assets (beyond the home market) to be funnelled to cash-impoverished borrowers in developing countries. A significant problem hindering economic growth in developing countries has been the lack of funds available to finance the expansion of domestic enterprises. Small and medium enterprises, typically shut out of the financial market, are now presented with opportunities to finance expansion and technological improvements from international sources, thereby creating new local jobs and raising wages. Governments of developing countries are also less likely to carry out infrastructure projects. Instead, contracts are increasingly awarded to private companies that finance the infrastructure projects through international capital markets to garner a profit (Likosky, 2003). Proponents of this shift argue that infrastructure projects are completed more efficiently and at a lower cost to the taxpayer.

Another aspect of economic globalization is the liberalization of trade. The reduction and/or elimination of tariffs and non-tariff barriers have been a driving force behind globalization. Trade exposes domestic enterprises to international competition. To maintain high levels of national employment and income, local enterprises must be able to compete efficiently against foreign firms. With the decline of US trade dominance in the wake of globalization, many developing countries have marshalled their (limited) resources

---

Box 11.1 Examples of the 'Optimistic View'

(A) Access to global finance and export markets has enabled parts of China, such as the region of Zhejiang, to experience a boom in the expansion of many small and medium-sized enterprises, thereby raising the living standard for a large number of ordinary citizens (Eckholm, 2003). Since cutting barriers to trade and capital, India has begun to rival Chinese economic growth rates. India's economy surged 9.2 per cent in 2006 and between 2002–2006 grew at a yearly rate of about 9 per cent (*The Economist*, 1 February 2007).

(B) British Petroleum has provided refrigerators in Zambia for the storage of anti-malaria vaccines and invested in computer technology in Vietnam for flood-related damage control while Chevron has invested in Nigeria's water infrastructure to develop a more reliable water supply system for its citizens (Monshipouri *et al.*, 2003; Nwankwo *et al.*, 2007).

to create competitive advantage, thereby raising their citizens' standard of living. Frankel and Romer (1999) found that an increase of about one percentage point in the ratio of trade to *gross domestic product* (GDP) increases income by at least one-half per cent. For example, Morocco experienced a decline of the poverty rate from 26 per cent to 13 per cent of the population in just five years after trade was liberalized (Keller-Herzog, 1996).

A final aspect to consider is **structural adjustment policies** (SAPs). SAPs are lending policies of the IMF and the World Bank designed to promote economic efficiency and growth in developing countries by minimizing the role of the state in the economy. Essentially, the IMF and World Bank provide loans to cash-strapped countries in exchange for the implementation of free market policies. These policies include slashing barriers to the flow of goods and capital, privatizing government enterprises, taming inflation, cutting government spending, and shrinking the government bureaucracy.

According to the pro-globalization school, economic growth owing to unfettered participation in the global trade and financial markets will translate into greater democracy and respect for human rights in LDCs. Specifically, as the economy grows and modernizes, the middle class will expand in size. The middle class generally represents a segment of society that will be more tolerant of others, challenge the status quo of the political elites, demand a greater voice in the political process for not only their own class, but also of those who are less fortunate, and progressively oppose political violence and repression (Lerner, 1958; Lipset, 1959; Nelson, 1987). The demand for government respect for political and human rights will grow and strengthen as long as the middle class continues to flourish. Thus, the globalization process generates economic growth that in turn creates a stable and tolerant political environment.

The Pessimistic View: Economic Globalization and the Race to the Bottom

The pessimistic, or anti-globalization model, sees economic globalization as a threat to the well-being of developing countries. Critics of globalization assert that the implementation of neoliberal market ideology makes states less capable or willing to carry out traditional societal tasks such as providing social safety nets and enforcing worker safety standards. That is, as a government decreases its role in the economy in order to promote global competitiveness and attract international investment, the state relinquishes its responsibilities regarding the provision of education, health, water, and other social services to its citizens. Consequently, the economic globalization process exploits workers and citizens of developing countries.

MNCs, in contrast to the neoliberal view, are not seen as agents of beneficial change. Instead, they are seen as profit-seeking conglomerates that fail to consider the social welfare implications of their actions. MNCs extract more money from developing countries than they invest, displace local capital, and add to unemployment by promoting capital-intensive production rather than labour-intensive activities, and they use the threat of exit to extract other 'business-friendly' policies (see Burgoon, 2001; Burkhart, 2002; Frenkel and Kuruvilla, 2002; Arnold and Hartman, 2006). Hence, developing governments are progressively held captive to market principles if they wish to sustain high levels of MNC investment. The ensuing competitive environment created by the mobility of MNCs and financial firms encourages a *race to the bottom* between LDCs, in which different countries compete to lower tax, wage, labour, unionization, and social welfare standards.

Sceptics of economic globalization also argue that MNCs and foreign investment firms tend to invest in LDCs that exhibit political stability. Simply put, regime change increases the financial risk of these investors. Portfolio investment is particularly susceptible to internal political and economic shocks, thereby causing a swift and massive exit of financial capital. Domestic elites, often profiting from the prevailing economic situation, are usually willing to do what is necessary to maintain the political climate required to preserve foreign capital (Maxfield, 1998; McCorquodale and Fairbrother, 1999; Darrow and Thomas, 2005).

Critics of globalization also point out that the pay-offs from trade liberalization are not equally dispersed. Instead, the benefits of trade are skewed toward companies that can move swiftly and effortlessly across international borders. Thus, countries that embrace liberal trade policies are not guaranteed to experience greater economic growth (Rodrik, 1997; Aaronson and Zimmerman, 2006). Furthermore, workers for MNCs often find themselves working long hours in unsafe working conditions in order to minimize production costs (Rodriguez, 2004; Arnold and Hartman, 2006). Domestic firms that face intense international competition are often forced to cut jobs and lower work and safety standards to maintain their presence in the world economy. Those displaced from their jobs owing to international competition are individuals with little education, who find it difficult to find a replacement job quickly (Moghadam, 1993; Cheng, 1999).

Finally, opponents of economic globalization see the imposition of SAPs by the IMF and the World Bank as detrimental to the economic and political development of LDCs. Some studies suggest that these policies fail to provide the promised economic conditions and can even impair economic growth (Przeworski and Vreeland, 2000; Vreeland, 2003). If economic growth declines, governments cut social programmes and eliminate public sector jobs due to an inability to raise necessary funds (see Box 11.2, Example A).

The result of maintaining a 'business-friendly' climate and the imposition of austerity policies upon developed countries has the effect of heightening societal tension. Governments must suppress threats to political and economic stability and move to aggressively suppress political opponents, union leaders, and other political activists who may challenge current policies. Similarly, opposing political party members, union members, and other political activists often respond to the imposition of SAPs with food riots, demonstrations, and violent protests. Ruling authorities respond by restricting citizens' political and civil liberties (Howard-Hassmann, 2005; see Box 11.2, Example B).

> ### Box 11.2 **Examples of the 'Pessimistic View'**
>
> (A) Zimbabwe was forced to eliminate educational funding owing to an IMF-imposed structural adjustment policy (SAP) (McCorquodale and Fairbrother, 1999). For the first time since independence, tuition was charged for primary-level schooling and, while decentralizing education helped the government move toward meeting some SAP goals, it exacerbated the education gap between rich and poor (Kanyongo, 2005, p. 71).
>
> (B) On 30 July 2006 over 100,000 individuals in Ordu, Turkey protested the low prices of hazelnuts. Farmers were upset that the government refused to assist in the purchase of surplus hazelnuts from a bankrupt cooperative, thereby further depressing the price of the commodity. IMF austerity measures, imposed in 2003, required the Turkish government to suspend its policy of subsidizing hazelnut farmers by purchasing surplus supplies. Ensuing clashes with the police in Ordu resulted in about 35 arrests and 51 injuries. Interestingly, the chief of police was relieved of his position for being too lenient with the demonstrators (Akinci, 2006).

> ### KEY POINTS
>
> Financial and investment globalization enter developing countries primarily in two ways: foreign direct investment (FDI) and portfolio investments.
>
> According to the pro-globalization school, economic growth owing to unfettered participation in the global trade and financial markets will translate into greater democracy and respect for human rights in LDCs.
>
> Critics of globalization assert that the implementation of neoliberal market ideology makes states less capable or willing to carry out traditional societal tasks such as providing social safety nets and enforcing worker safety standards.

Globalization and Human Rights: Examining the Empirical Results

Scholars examine the relationship between globalization and human rights in several ways. Quantitative studies use statistical techniques to examine a number of countries together over a period of time in the search for generalizations that can be made from these countries' collective experiences. Qualitative studies tend to focus on an in-depth case analysis of a particular country or reference group such as women, or a particular ethnic group.[2] Qualitative studies have provided some of the most thoughtful theoretical critiques of globalization.

The results of quantitative studies examining the relationship between economic globalization have been mixed, but lean toward implying that in many places and times economic globalization is associated with better respect for human rights. Below, we provide a short illustrative outline of this literature, incorporating findings from some major studies.

Meyer (1996) found US-based FDI to be associated with better respect for human rights in recipient countries. However, Smith *et al.* (1999), using alternative globalization and human rights indicators, failed to replicate Meyer's findings. This is one peril of quantitative studies—that findings may be an artefact of the way the study is conducted. Other research supports Meyer's finding, however. There is evidence that trade liberalization, a mainstay of the globalization process, leads to greater government respect for human rights. For example, it has been found that governments of countries that traded more were less likely to violate a category of internationally-recognized human rights known as physical integrity rights (summary execution, torture, disappearance, and political imprisonment) (Apodaca, 2001) and that trade liberalization is associated with lower infant mortality rates in developing countries (Apodaca, 2002). A number of studies have also shown that trade liberalization is associated with greater *women's status*, defined as the extent to which women are able, both in an absolute and relative sense, to exercise precise rights codified in a large body of international human rights law and to enjoy the objectives of those rights (Richards and Gelleny, 2007). Trade liberalization has also been associated with improving female life expectancy and literacy rates (Gray *et al.*, 2006).

The effect of FDI on government respect for human rights also seems to be generally helpful, judging from the quantitative literature on this relationship. Increases in MNC investment has been found to be reliably related to greater political rights and civil liberties, including the freedom from censorship and freedom of religion, political participation, travel, and unionization (Meyer, 1996, 1998; Richards *et al.*, 2001). Apodaca (2001, 2002) found evidence that FDI improved government respect for physical integrity rights and reduced infant mortality rates in developing countries. That said, Tuman and Emmert (2004) found FDI to flow to Latin American and Caribbean countries with poorer human rights records. Results are also mixed in the area of women's status. While Richards and Gelleny (2007) found FDI to be generally related to higher scores on both the United Nations' Gender Empowerment Measure and Gender-related Development Index, Gray *et al.* (2006) found FDI to have a corrosive influence on female life expectancy and literacy.

The findings regarding the influence of portfolio investment on government respect for human rights have been less conclusive. Several studies have shown that developing countries that opened their markets to this type of investment have experienced greater respect for physical integrity rights and lower infant mortality rates (Richards *et al.*, 2001; Apodaca, 2002). However, other findings suggest that portfolio investment has a corrosive influence on women's status (Richards and Gelleny, 2007). SAPs have not been shown to have a helpful influence on government respect for human rights. Abouharb and Cingranelli (2006) refute the neo-liberal assertion that SAPs should improve economic performance, thereby creating better human rights practices. Instead, they find that World Bank adjustment policies have the effect of worsening government respect for physical integrity rights.

While physical integrity rights and women's rights are likely the most-studied categories of rights in the quantitative globalization literature, there are studies of other types of rights and human rights environments. Burgoon (2001) found mixed results when examining the results of trade openness on welfare policies. Colonomos and Santiso (2005) found globalization to carve an issue space in France allowing for the adoption of human rights-based corporate social responsibility codes. Contrary to the race to the bottom logic, Kucera (2001) found foreign investors to favour countries with higher labour standards rather than lower standards.

KEY POINTS	
Scholars examine the relationship between globalization and human rights in several ways. Quantitative studies use statistical techniques to examine a number of countries together over a period of time in the search for generalizations that can be made from these countries' collective experiences. Qualitative studies tend to focus on an in-depth case analysis of a particular country or reference group such as women, or a particular ethnic group.	The results of quantitative studies examining the relationship between economic globalization have been mixed, but lean toward implying that in many places and times economic globalization is associated with better respect for human rights.
Qualitative studies have provided some of the most thoughtful theoretical critiques of globalization.	

Case Study: Do MNCs Invest in Human Rights?

Traditionally, respect for human rights has not been considered a responsibility of multinational corporations. Instead, human rights have been considered a domestic government issue (Skogly, 1993; Kinley and Joseph, 2002). In recent years, however, there has been an upsurge in the judgement that MNCs should also be held accountable for human rights violations. Clearly, MNCs are powerful international entities, and corporate decisions have a vast impact that stretches far beyond the boardroom. Yahoo! executives found themselves under scrutiny after handing over data to Chinese authorities that led to the arrest of two dissidents. In November 2007, Yahoo!'s chief executive and chief lawyer were denounced by US Congressman Tom Lantos as 'technology giants but moral pygmies' (*The Economist*, 17 January 2008). Such instances, combined with the growth in the number of MNCs that have created codes of corporate social responsibility, hint strongly that investing in countries that violate human rights is becoming an important matter for MNC executives. This raises the following question: Are MNCs more likely to make future investments in countries where governments respect human rights than countries that abuse them?

Human Rights Determinants of FDI

As we will see, MNCs and other international investors have varying incentives or disincentives to consider human rights when making investment decisions. Below, we survey these factors and conduct a statistical analysis to ascertain which factors are generally stronger.

Property rights

Any MNC investment is a risk since firms can never be certain of the eventual success of the project owing to both political and economic factors. However, property rights appear to be one of the most important factors in attracting FDI. Guaranteeing political and civil rights, such as independent judiciaries and a democratically functioning electoral system, further strengthens property rights.[3] Consequently, MNCs that invest where regimes respect the rule of law hope to find their investments protected from nationalization by predatory dictators.

Mozambique provides an example of an LDC reaping positive economic benefits as a consequence of establishing a political environment that is more respectful of human rights. Mozambique was plagued by internal strife for much of the 1980s and 1990s. Yet, by the mid-1990s, with the help of the United Nations, Mozambique had held successful elections and largely ended its abuse of physical integrity rights. The result was a growing economy spurred forward by an influx of foreign investment. About six billion dollars worth of foreign investment was committed to Mozambique in projects ranging from mining to farming and tourism, twice the amount invested in the rest of sub-Saharan Africa (excluding South Africa; *The Economist*, 15 May 1997).

Zimbabwe provides an example where a government's lack of respect for political and civil rights hinders foreign investment. Compared to other African countries, Zimbabwe had experienced strong levels of FDI, education, and economic growth into the 1990s. However, the imposition of a messy political land reform policy, combined with increased political violence, chaotic economic policies, and soaring inflation rates, reduced foreign investment flows to a trickle. The passage of Zimbabwe's September 2007 Indigenisation and Empowerment Bill, giving the state controlling interest in foreign-owned businesses (including banks and mines), only added to an already hostile investment environment. Business leaders warned that the legislation would prompt a further 30 per cent decline in foreign investment (*Financial Times*, 12 November 2007).

Concerns about stability may cause MNC disinvestment even for those companies whose foreign footprint is constrained by geology. Industrial firms, such as mining companies, must generally locate near sites where their raw materials exist. In 2001, Lukas Lundin of Lundin Petroleum AB noted, 'We go where the big resources are', and when asked about investing in war-torn Sudan (where Lundin has a history of investment) he added, 'There's 250 million barrels there' (Hasselback, 2001, C08). A year later, Lundin President Ian Lundin announced that his company was suspending operations in Sudan 'until there is a "sustainable" period of peace' and that, 'We need some type of sustainable and peaceful environment for us to look at long-term investment.'[4] It is instructive to note, however, that as Sudan's conflict morphed into genocide (see Chapter 16), Lundin Petroleum was again operating in Sudan, earning a place on the Sudan Divestment Task Force's 'Highest Offenders' list of companies found to be 'unresponsive to engagement by shareholders or unwilling to alter problematic practices in Sudan' (Sudan Divestment Task Force, 2007, p. 7).

Labour policies

Before expanding production facilities to LDCs, MNCs evaluate labour and wage policies. Policies of concern include the right of workers to organize, safety standards, social welfare policies, and wage rates. Firms that produce goods that do not require skilled labour or intense investments of capital are often attracted to countries that have a large number of low-waged, non-unionized labourers. Additionally, MNCs seek to increase profits by locating in countries where taxes, such as employer social security and unemployment contributions, are relatively low. Furthermore, as competition among countries increases for FDI, countries compete with each other to provide MNCs with a 'business-friendly' environment regarding the above policies.

Reputation

Companies may seek to improve their reputations by associating their product with improving human rights (Spar, 1998; Colonomos and Santiso, 2005). Otherwise, MNCs may run the risk of being exposed to an embarrassing media campaign highlighting their connections to regimes with human rights abuses. For example, in 2007 the British engine producer Rolls-Royce announced that it planned to withdraw from Sudan. The company cited its concerns about the worsening humanitarian condition in Darfur as the principal reason that it had chosen to leave (*Financial Times*, 19 April 2007).

One study of Fortune 500 companies showed that '36 percent of respondents "decided not to proceed with a proposed investment project because of concerns over human rights abuses" while 19 percent "have disinvested from a particular country because of human rights concerns"' (Cowell, 2000, C4). The same study found that 44 per cent of companies that have written codes of ethics mention human rights in those codes.[5] Major companies employing such codes include Shell, Reebok, and Levi Strauss.

Nevertheless, others maintain the traditional view that corporate policies based on human rights concerns, including image campaigns, are wrong-headed and dangerous; corporations should not be in the business of ethics and should only be concerned with generating profits for their shareholders. Milton Friedman (1962, p. 133) aptly summed up this view by stating, 'there is one and only one social responsibility of business—to use its resources and engage in activities designed to increase its profits.'

Multinational corporations consider a number of other factors when deciding whether to invest capital overseas. Below, we outline these additional factors.

Market conditions

Corporations are likely to invest in countries that have large populations and stable and growing economies where sales potential is greater (Crenshaw, 1991; Asiedu, 2002; Bandelj, 2002; Tuman and Emmert, 2004). China, for example, has a large and growing market in which many MNCs are eager to establish a presence. India is another large market where MNCs have sought to increase their market share. Seeking to expand economic growth, Indian politicians reversed their long-standing opposition to foreign investment in the 1990s. Consequently, MNCs have reacted to these new policies enthusiastically and have significantly increased FDI investment in India.

Inflation rates have also been used as an indicator of LDC domestic macro-economic stability. High inflation is a disincentive for MNCs to invest in LDCs because it makes it difficult for multinational firms to accurately evaluate production costs and profits, thereby increasing the risk of foreign investment projects.

Tariff and capital barriers

Government economic policies directly targeted at attracting multinational foreign investment—including lower capital barriers, financial subsidies, and tariff rates—must also be considered by MNCs (Edwards, 1990; Gastanaga and Nugent, 1998; Asiedu, 2002). Governments may entice companies to relocate production facilities by implementing high tariff rates. Companies may find it cheaper to relocate to foreign markets to avoid the cost imposed on their products by high tariff rates. However, firms are more likely to search for regions to which they can profitably shift their subsidiary labour-intensive assembly and then export finished products back to the parent firm. Therefore, MNC subsidiaries must be able to import inputs and capital goods from the home market of the parent firm with a minimum of costs. As such, MNCs often prefer to invest where trade barriers are negligible and few restrictions limit the flow of capital. Consequently, the majority of FDI and other investment flows are likely to be a function of openness to foreign capital (Gilpin, 2001; Asiedu, 2002; Tuman and Emmert, 2004). Decreased market regulation also provides MNCs with access to a variety of capital opportunities and, perhaps, greater advantage over local domestic competition.

Political risk and stability

All investors are concerned with political risk and may consider withdrawing their assets to less risky countries. Indeed, MNC executives report that political instability is one of the most critical factors influencing foreign investment assessments (Bandelj 2002). Governments that are experiencing internal or external conflict may be more likely to implement repressive business policies than politically stable countries. In order to appease political allies or raise required resources quickly, fearful governments may implement policies that include restricting the movement of goods and capital, increasing corporate taxes, and the forced sale or seizure of foreign enterprises. Furthermore, constant civil strife increases the probability of governmental change, thereby heightening MNC anxiety regarding the stability of business policies. The possibility of continual regime instability increases the risk of changing business regulations, thus increasing the uncertainty of production costs and profits. Thus, countries with stable regimes and respect for the rule of law are rewarded by increased flows of foreign investment.

Although we expect countries experiencing high amounts of internal and external conflict to attract lower amounts of FDI, studies have revealed mixed results regarding the relationship between political stability and FDI. Indeed, empirical research has reported findings about political stability and FDI ranging from no effect to both helpful and harmful effects (Asiedu, 2002; Bandelj, 2002).

Market infrastructure and skill level

Others argue that foreign investors are attracted to countries that comprise a reasonably well-educated workforce and modern infrastructure (Gelleny and McCoy, 2001; Tuman and Emmert, 2004). That is, the combination of a low wage and educated workforce is a very attractive feature to a foreign investor. Furthermore, LDCs that are modernizing in the transport and communication sectors provide an environment that is appealing to multinational corporations. An educated workforce and a growing modern infrastructure are expected to increase productivity and profitability.

KEY POINTS	
Protection of property rights through rule of law appears to be one of the most important factors in attracting FDI. MNCs that invest in regimes that respect property rights find their investment protected from nationalization by predatory dictators.	Multinational corporations often prefer business environments with negligible trade barriers and few restrictions managing the flow of capital.
Multinational corporations seek to increase profits by locating in countries where taxes, such as employer social security and unemployment contributions, are relatively low, as are wages. Furthermore, as competition among countries increases for FDI, countries compete with each other to provide MNCs with a 'business-friendly' environment regarding the above policies.	All investors are concerned with political risk and may consider withdrawing their assets to less risky countries in favour of countries that are perceived to be stable, as regime instability increases the risk of changing business regulations, thus increasing the uncertainty of production costs and profits.
Companies may seek to improve their reputation by associating their product with improving human rights; otherwise, MNCs may run the risk of being exposed to an embarrassing media campaign highlighting their connections to regimes with human rights abuses.	Some argue that foreign investors are attracted to countries that comprise a reasonably well-educated workforce and modern infrastructure. An educated workforce and a growing modern infrastructure are expected to increase productivity and profitability.

Data and Research Design

Sample

Our study examines LDCs for the years 1981 to 1999. Because of source bias in human rights reports, information about government respect for human rights is unreliable before 1981, thus dictating our lower temporal boundary. Our sample of LDCs encompasses all developing regions including Africa, Asia, the Caribbean, East Europe, and Latin America. Since economic and political data for many LDCs is not systematically recorded across time and space, the actual number of cases is depressed somewhat because of missing data.

Model and Estimation Technique

Our general model is illustrated in Table 11.1. The plus and minus signs indicate our hypotheses about the relationship between each of the independent variables (those to the right of the equal sign) in the model and our dependent variable (FDI).[6] A plus sign indicates that we expect a *positive* relationship: as the independent variable increases, FDI is expected to increase.

A minus sign indicates that we expect a *negative* relationship: as the independent variable increases, FDI is expected to decrease. Where there is a '+ / –', we are unsure what to expect.

Although in this section of the chapter we are chiefly interested in the effect that government respect for human rights has on FDI inflows, it has been shown (e.g. Meyer 1998; Richards *et al.*, 2001; Richards and Gelleny, 2002) that foreign economic investment can influence government respect for human rights. Thus, our model must account for any influence FDI may have on government respect for human rights, while at the same time investigating the effect of government respect for human rights on FDI. To accomplish this task we estimate two models simultaneously, thereby allowing us to test for reciprocal effects (i.e. where human rights and FDI influence one another at the same time). The bracketed variables in Table 11.1 show a second model, nested inside our general model that examines the relationship between FDI and government respect for human rights. This nested model, where respect for human rights is the dependent variable and the variables in the brackets are the

TABLE 11.1 General model for statistical analyses.

Foreign direct investment =	+/– Constant
	+/– Level of respect for human rights
	[= Foreign direct investment
	– Domestic conflict
	– Inter-state conflict
	+ Regime type
	+ Level of economic development
	– Population size]
	– Domestic conflict
	– Inter-state conflict
	– Capital controls
	+ Market wealth
	+ Trade openness
	+ Urbanization
	+ Infrastructure
	+ Literacy
	– Inflation

independent variables, is estimated simultaneously with the general model.

Dependent Variable

Foreign direct investment

While we discussed many ways in which the global economy can enter an LDC, for the purposes of this illustrative chapter we focus on one foreign direct investment (FDI). Specifically, our dependent variable is a measure of FDI as a percentage of GDP, which is the total amount of services and goods produced in a country in a given year. This measure of FDI is regularly used in the literature (Asiedu, 2002; Bandelj, 2002; Alderson, 2004; Truman and Emmert, 2004) and was drawn from the World Bank's *World Development Indicators on CD-ROM* (2005).

Independent Variables

We use a number of independent variables to help explain a country's level of FDI. Below, we list and explain these variables.

Government respect for human rights

To measure the level of government respect for human rights, we use two additive ordinal indices from the CIRI Human Rights Dataset (Cingranelli and Richards, 2008).[7] These two indices represent the level of government respect for physical integrity rights and empowerment rights, respectively, in a given year. Physical integrity rights include the rights to freedom from torture, disappearance, extrajudicial killing, and political imprisonment. The CIRI physical integrity rights index is a nine-point scale ranging from zero (*no respect* for any of the four physical integrity rights) to eight (*full respect* for all four physical integrity rights). The CIRI empowerment rights index is an eleven-point scale constructed from five indicators of government respect for political rights and civil liberties: open and free political participation, workers rights, freedom of domestic travel, freedom of religion, and free media. This measure ranges from zero (*no respect* for any of these five empowerment rights) to ten (*full respect* for all five of these rights).

Trade and capital restrictions

Government policies regarding both trade and capital (investment) play an important role in a country's ability to attract and maintain foreign investment. Regarding trade policies, multinational corporations that engage in export-oriented ventures will prefer to invest in open (less-regulated) economies. To measure policies relating to trade, we use what has become a standard measure of trade openness: the ratio of a country's trade exports and imports to its GDP. We obtained these data from the World Bank's *World Development Indicators on CD-ROM* (2005).

A country can similarly be described as open and closed based on its capital control policies. We expect to see a negative relationship between the institution of capital controls and foreign investment in LDCs. In the early 1990s, countries became more open to foreign investment by attempting to attract foreign firms to invest directly in their markets (Spero and Hart, 1997; Gilpin, 2001; Cohn, 2003). To measure capital restrictions we use a variable from the International Monetary Fund's 'Annual Reports on Exchange Arrangements and Exchange Controls' (IMF, various years). The variable is an index of state restrictions on foreign exchange and both current and capital accounts, ranging from zero to four and indicating which (if any) of the following existed in a given country and year: multiple exchange rates, current account restrictions, capital account restrictions, and export proceeds surrender requirements.[8] For example, a score of zero designates no capital restrictions and a score of four indicates complete capital restrictions.

Domestic economic conditions

A country's macro-economic condition also needs to be considered in any model examining FDI. Thus, we include three measures accounting for LDC economic growth and market stability. First, we use GDP per capita (using its logarithmic value so as to reduce the effect of extreme values) to measure a country's level of economic development or its market wealth. Some assert that foreign investors are attracted to growing and dynamic regions (Crenshaw, 1991; Bandelj, 2002; Cohn, 2003). To measure potential market size we turn to a country's degree of urbanization—the share of the total population living in areas defined as urban. Finally, we also include a country's inflation rate as a measure of its macro-economic stability. All three variables were obtained from the World Bank's *World Development Indicators on CD-ROM* (2005).

Political risk and stability

Our indicators of domestic and inter-state conflict are ordinal variables from version three of the PRIO Armed Conflict Dataset (Gleditsch *et al.*, 2002). The domestic conflict measure indicates the highest level of conflict between a state and organized groups in that country in a given year. It ranges from 0 (no conflict) to 3 (internal war). The inter-state conflict measure indicates the highest level of conflict in a given year

between two or more states, and ranges from 0 (no conflict) to 3 (inter-state war).

Infrastructure and skill levels

Multinational companies are more likely to invest in LDCs that have skilled workers and a modernizing infrastructure. To measure the state of infrastructure, we include in our models a measure of the number of telephones per 1000 people in a country. Although this measure only considers one aspect of a country's infrastructure, it does have the advantage of being available for most LDCs (Asiedu, 2002). To measure the skill of the domestic labour force we turn to adult literacy rates. That is, we utilize the percentage of people aged 15 and above who can, with understanding, read and write a simple account on their everyday life. Both variables were obtained from the World Bank's *World Development Indicators on CD-ROM* (2005).

KEY POINTS

Our study examines LDCs for the years 1981 to 1999. Our sample of LDCs encompasses all developing regions including Africa, Asia, the Caribbean, East Europe, and Latin America.

Our dependent variable is a measure of FDI as a percentage of gross domestic product (GDP), which is the total amount of services and goods produced in a country in a given year.

We use a number of independent variables to help explain a country's level of FDI: government respect for human rights, domestic economic conditions, political risk and stability, and infrastructure, and skill levels.

Findings

To statistically *estimate* (test) our models examining the relationship between government respect for two types of human rights and FDI, we used what is known as fixed effects two-stage-least-squares regression. This technique allows us to account for the possibility that respect for human rights may be affecting FDI at the same time that FDI may be affecting respect for human rights. It also allows us to produce results that are not

biased by the way we assembled our data (we did so in what is known as a 'pooled' form, where a single spreadsheet contains many years worth of data for a large number of different countries).

Table 11.2 shows the result of models examining the relationship between government respect for physical integrity rights and FDI (Model 1), and for empowerment rights and FDI (Model 2). At the bottom of

TABLE 11.2 Two-stage least squares fixed-effects estimation of the relationship between foreign direct investment and government respect for human rights.

	Model 1	Model 2
Lagged FDI (t − 1)	P	P
Physical integrity rights	P	–
Empowerment rights	–	P
Domestic conflict	P	p
Inter-state conflict	p	p
Capital controls	N	N
Market wealth	n	P
Trade openness	p	P
Urbanization	n	p
Infrastructure	P	P
Literacy	P	P
Inflation	N	N
Constant	N	N
N	1204	1205
F-test	0.00	0.00

$P < 0.10$

P = Statistically reliable positive relationship.

p = Statistically unreliable positive relationship.

N = Statistically reliable negative relationship.

n = Statistically unreliable negative relationship.

Table 11.2, 'N' stands for the number of cases of data that are used to estimate each model. Each individual case, called a country-year, is data for a single country in a single year (e.g. France 1997 or Brazil 1993). Next, the F-test values tell us about the usefulness of a particular model. For both models in Table 11.2, the values of 0.00 tell us that, given the data we have collected, both of these models are better than ones without these particular sets of independent variables.

One basic purpose of estimating these models is to discover whether each of these independent variables is reliably or unreliably associated with a country's FDI (expressed as a percentage of GDP). By 'reliable', we mean that we are confident to some degree that the relationship between an independent variable and FDI is not likely to have merely occurred due to chance, or luck. The '$P > 0.10$' at the bottom of Table 11.2 says that we need to be 90 per cent sure that a relationship is not due to chance to report it as being 'reliable'. We label any

independent variable that we cannot be 90 per cent sure of as 'unreliable'. Note the letters P, p, N, and n at the bottom of Table 11.2. We use these to note whether a particular independent variable is reliably or unreliably associated with a country's FDI, and what direction, positive or negative, that relationship takes.[9] For example, an independent variable receiving a P means that particular variable has a relationship with FDI such that higher levels of that variable are associated with higher levels of FDI, and we can be at least 90% sure that that association is not due to chance alone.

Model 1: Physical Integrity Rights

Looking at Model 1 in Table 11.2, we see that a government's level of respect for physical integrity rights is reliably and positively associated with a country's FDI intake. Because of the statistical technique we used, this is true, even controlling for any influence that FDI may simultaneously have on respect for human rights. At the very least, this tells us that those countries with better respect for physical integrity rights receive more FDI than do countries with less respect. Further, we might expect FDI to increase in countries with greater respect for human rights. Were we to look at the actual numerical coefficients from the statistical analysis, they would show that, for each one-unit increase in government respect for physical integrity rights on the CIRI scale, we can expect a corresponding increase of about one per cent in FDI (as a percentage of GDP).

Model 1 also tells some other stories. First, FDI seemingly continues to go to places with respectable levels of domestic conflict. This may be driven by places such as Senegal, which saw corresponding increases in both FDI and domestic conflict in the late 1990s. Likewise, countries such as Jamaica, which in the early-to-mid 1980s lost FDI despite having no significant domestic conflict, would also drive the same result. Second, as expected, Model 1 shows that better infrastructure and greater literacy levels attract FDI, while more capital controls and higher inflation levels tend to reduce FDI. Also, as expected, past levels of FDI are strongly predictive of current levels.

Statistical analysis allows us to go beyond assessing merely whether the relationship between two variables is reliable. We can also determine the strength of these relationships. Figure 11.1 shows the relative strengths of

FIGURE 11.1 Relative impacts of statistically reliable variables from Model 1 on FDI.

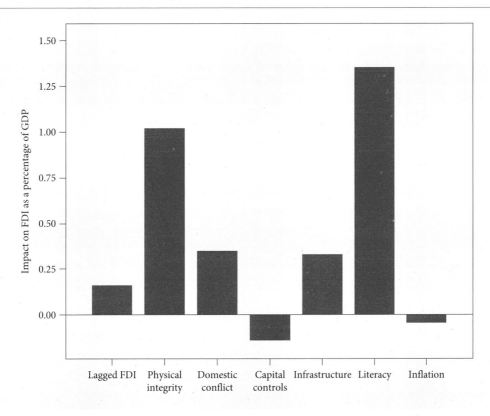

the reliable relationships shown in Model 1 in Table 11.2. The higher the bar is above the 0.00 horizontal line, the greater the return (in terms of FDI) on increases in a particular variable. If a bar drops below the 0.00 line, then this means that higher levels of that variable are associated with losses in FDI (a negative relationship). We see that only a country's literacy rate has a greater impact on FDI than does government respect for physical integrity rights. A one-standard-deviation increase in respect for physical integrity rights leads to a one-standard-deviation increase in FDI as a percentage of GDP. The greatest negative impact is that of capital controls.

Model 2: Empowerment Rights

Model 2 in Table 11.2 examines the relationship between government respect for empowerment rights and FDI.

We see that a government's level of respect for empowerment rights is a statistically significant predictor of the level of FDI for that country. Again, this is true, even controlling for any influence that FDI may simultaneously have on respect for human rights. As we saw with physical integrity rights, this tells us that those countries with better respect for empowerment rights receive more FDI than do countries with less respect. Further, we might well expect FDI to increase in countries with increased respect for human rights. The actual numerical coefficient from the statistical analysis would tell us that for each one-unit increase in government respect for empowerment rights on the CIRI scale, there is a corresponding increase of about 0.63 per cent in FDI (as a percent of GDP).

However, Model 2 shows several things that are in contrast to the results from Model 1. First, there is no reliable relationship between either type of conflict and FDI. Second, market wealth and trade openness are found to be reliably associated with increased FDI. Finally, literacy was not found to be reliably associated with FDI in Model 2.

There were several factors (aside from the significance of the human rights variables) that proved to be consistent across Models 1 and 2. Capital controls and inflation were both reliably associated with decreases in FDI. Also, neither urbanization nor inter-state conflict were found in either model to be a reliable associate of FDI. Finally, past levels of FDI were strong predictors of current levels.

Figure 11.2 can be read in exactly the same manner as Figure 11.1, and shows the relative strengths of the statistically reliable coefficients on FDI. Unlike in Figure 11.1, we see that government respect for human rights (empowerment rights here) has the greatest impact upon FDI. A one-standard-deviation increase in respect for empowerment rights leads to a 0.80

standard-deviation increase in FDI as a percentage of GDP. Only market wealth comes close to matching this impact. As in Figure 11.1, the greatest negative impact on FDI comes from capital controls.

KEY POINTS

A government's level of respect for physical integrity rights is reliably and positively associated with a country's FDI intake. Further, FDI seemingly continues to go to places with respectable levels of domestic conflict.

A government's level of respect for empowerment rights is a statistically significant and positive predictor of the level of FDI for that country. However, there is no reliable relationship between either type of conflict and FDI regarding respect for empowerment rights.

FIGURE 11.2 Relative impacts of statistically reliable variables from Model 2 on FDI.

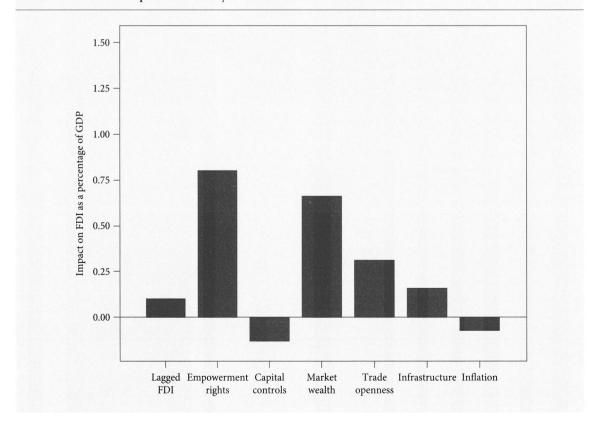

Conclusion

This case study has yielded some interesting findings relating to the relationship between government respect for human rights and foreign direct investment. First, we found that countries with greater levels of respect for the rights to freedom from torture, disappearance, extrajudicial killings, and political imprisonment seem better able to attract capital from foreign sources. A couple of things may account for this finding. Any foreign investment poses a considerable risk for private investors and companies doing business in countries where human rights are grievously abused, as they themselves may ultimately be exposed to charges of putting profits ahead of human dignity. For example, human rights groups may launch prominent media campaigns designed to damage the reputation of brand-name products. Continued abuse of physical integrity rights can heighten citizen resentment and can result in domestic conflict—possibly damaging or capturing private foreign-owned property and/or destabilizing an economy. Investors are often hesitant to expose their capital in such an environment, unless the possible pay-off is considerable.

Second, we found respect for empowerment rights to be strongly associated with greater levels of FDI. Countries where government respect exists for open political participation, an open media, the right to form unions, religious freedom, and the freedom to travel, experience higher levels of FDI. Or, MNCs appear willing to invest in countries where political and civil rights are better respected. Countries with such an environment are more likely to follow the rule of law, thereby establishing a stable business environment for MNCs via reducing the risk of costly policy changes.

Together, these findings imply that governments that respect their citizens' physical integrity and empowerment rights will be better able to attract foreign economic capital. Thus, such governments should be better placed to compete for and attract much-needed foreign investment. This is significant, as FDI is generally thought to be of critical importance for LDC economic development. Foreign investment not only provides new jobs, but it also introduces new technology and managerial skills that can be applied to other sectors of the host economy. Consequently, a growing economy can provide a government with additional economic resources that can be used to implement policies that enhance and maintain an attractive environment for FDI. Additional resources can be used to improve education and infrastructure, thereby increasing the probability of solidifying economic and political stability. At the very least, should a country not choose to make further human rights and infrastructure improvements in light of FDI-driven economic growth, it can no longer claim poverty as a reason and the naming and shaming of the international human rights regime can commence to exert pressure toward reform.

QUESTIONS

INDIVIDUAL STUDY QUESTIONS

1. Describe two ways in which women, as a group, may be affected by economic globalization.

2. What is the consensus finding from the quantitative literature investigating economic globalization's effect on respect for human rights? What questions about economic globalization and human rights remain that can be addressed by quantitative study?

3. This chapter examines respect for physical integrity rights and empowerment rights in light of economic globalization. How might other types of rights, such as economic, social, and cultural rights, be affected?

4. What are the advantages and/or disadvantages of choosing to study the relationship between economic globalization and human rights using quantitative methods as opposed to qualitative methods?

5. How connected to the global economy does a country's own economy have to be in order to be considered 'globalized'?

6. Should one expect foreign investment originating in a developing country to affect human rights in a different way than would investment from a developed country?

7. As developing countries become more industrialized and more integrated into the world economy, should we expect the relationship between FDI and human rights to change or stay the same? Why?

GROUP DISCUSSION QUESTIONS

1. Divide your group or class into two, with one representing the 'optimistic' view of globalization and the other representing the 'pessimistic' view of globalization. Choose a group or class member or the instructor as moderator and take turns arguing your side's take on how economic globalization will affect respect for human rights. Have the moderator choose as winner the group who best makes their case.

2. Divide your group or class into two, with one representing 'developed' countries and one representing 'developing' countries. Work together to create a treaty on foreign investment and human rights standards that each side feels addresses its needs.

3. Can the 'race to the bottom' hit bottom? That is, can wages and other labour standards become so low, worldwide, that there is nowhere cheaper for MNCs to relocate? If so, what will happen to economic globalization? Divide your group or class into two, representing the 'optimistic' and 'pessimistic' views and answer from those perspectives.

4. Divide your group or class into two, with one representing the quantitative research tradition and one representing the qualitative research tradition. In these groups, have members discuss the strengths and weaknesses of their approach as relates to studying government respect for human rights. Then, have the class assemble as a whole and discuss as a group whether and/or how one might integrate aspects of both these research traditions in order to improve human rights research.

FURTHER READING

Brysk, A. (ed.) (2002). *Globalization and Human Rights*. Berkeley, CA: University of California Press.
A number of prominent scholars offer essays about globalization's effect on a variety of human rights.

Friedman, T. L. (2004). *The Lexus and the Olive Tree*. New York: Random House.
New York Times columnist (and proponent of globalization) examines globalization as a framework in which to understand the post-Cold War world in essays examining the reach and types of globalization, and how globalization affects tensions between the modern and the traditional elements both in and across societies around the world.

Lechner, F. J. and **Boli**, J. (eds) (2004). *The Globalization Reader*. Malden, MA: Blackwell.
This book provides a wide variety of contrasting points of view on what is globalization and how it affects societies.

Stiglitz, J. (2002). *Globalization and Its Discontents*. New York: W. W. Norton & Company.
Nobel Prize-winning economist Joseph Stiglitz examines how the policies of large intergovernmental economic institutions such as the IMF and the World Bank affect individual countries' economies and the global economy, and what are the societal effects of these policies.

Wallerstein, I. (2006). *World-Systems Analysis*. Durham, NC: Duke University Press.
This is an introduction to world-systems analysis, which provides a theoretical challenge to the neoliberal goal of the 'endless accumulation of capital'.

Yergin, D. and **Stanislaw**, J. (2002). *The Commanding Heights: The Battle for the World Economy*. New York: Touchstone.
This book examines the modern global economy's early-twentieth-century roots, and weaves a story tracing the world economy's growth through the recent era of globalization.

WEB LINKS

http://www.amnesty.org/en/business-and-human-rights Amnesty International's 'Business and Human Rights' website offers country-specific information about how globalization affects human rights and what activists are doing to affect this relationship.

http://www.humanrightsdata.org The *Cingranelli–Richards (CIRI) Human Rights Data Project* provides standards-based quantitative information on government respect for fifteen internationally recognized human rights for 195 countries, annually from 1981 to the present.

http://www.pbs.org/wgbh/commandingheights/ *'The Commanding Heights: Battle for the World Economy'* website is designed to promote better understanding of globalization, world trade, and economic development, including the forces, values, events, and ideas that have shaped the present global economic system.

http://www.hrw.org/doc/?t=corporations Human Rights Watch's 'Business & Human Rights' website offers in-depth reports and news updates about how the global economy affects respect for human rights.

http://www2.ohchr.org/english/issues/globalization/business/index.htm The *Office of the United Nations High Commissioner for Human Rights'* website, 'Globalization—Business and Human Rights', offers information, original documents, and learning tools about how multinational companies interface with states regarding human rights.

NOTES

1. In 2005 the company settled a lawsuit based on these charges.
2. Examples of large quantitative macro-analyses studies include Apodaca (2001), Richards *et al.* (2001), Hafner-Burton (2005), Hafner-Burton and Tsutsui (2005), Abouharb and Cingranelli (2006), and Gray *et al.* (2006). Smaller quantitative studies have been conducted by Meyer (1996), Smith *et al.* (1999), Apodaca (2002), Burkhart (2002), and Tuman and Emmert (2004). For qualitative studies see Pollis and Schwab (2000), Monshipouri *et al.* (2003), Rodriguez (2004), Colonomos and Santiso (2005), Howard-Hassman (2005), and Arnold and Hartman (2006).
3. See North (1990) and Olson (1993).
4. See http://www.gasandoil.com/goc/company/cna21657.htm.
5. The University of Minnesota's online Human Rights Library provides access to business codes of conduct as well as industry initiatives and multilateral instruments at http://www1.umn.edu/humanrts/links/allcodes.html.
6. The dependent variable is the one whose variation is being explained (here, FDI) and the independent variables are the ones explaining variation in the dependent variable.
7. Measurement schemes, coding details, and estimates of the interrater reliability for all of the human rights data used in this paper are available online at http://www.humanrightsdata.org.

8. Many scholars apply similar scales (see Garrett, 1995, 1998; Li and Resnick, 2003).

9. In actuality, all coefficients listed as either P or N in Table 11.2 are reliable with 95 per cent confidence, except inflation in Model 1, which is reliable at 90 per cent confidence. We report only $P > 0.10$ to avoid confusion.

ONLINE RESOURCE CENTRE

Visit the Online Resource Centre that accompanies this book for updates and a range of other resources:

http://www.oxfordtextbooks.co.uk/orc/goodhart/

Trafficking for Sexual Exploitation

12

Andrea M. Bertone

Chapter Contents

Reader's Guide

Human trafficking is undoubtedly one of the major human rights concerns of our time, as it affects men, women, and children in nearly every country. Persons of any race, age, or socio-economic status can be trafficked, and a country may be a destination, transit, and/or origin for trafficking victims. Human trafficking, simultaneously defined as a process (recruitment and transportation) and a severely exploitive work situation (psychological and physical control), is not a new phenomenon. In fact, sexual and labour exploitation in their many forms have always been a part of the human condition. However, political leaders, activists, advocates, academics, and other concerned individuals have recently taken an intense interest in the issue of trafficking due in part to the greater global awareness of human rights issues in general and the development of anti-trafficking advocacy networks across countries in particular.

Introduction

In 2004, Thai police and other Thai officials raided a makeshift garment factory producing jeans in Bangkok where eighteen girls—aged 11 to 14 years—from Lao People's Democratic Republic (PDR) were rescued. Police found the girls hidden in a space measuring 10 by 13 feet under the floor of a room that was padlocked. Several weeks earlier, two girls had escaped from the factory and told police that the girls had been dropped off at the factory by a Laotian recruiter who promised them paid work. After six months they had not been paid at all; they were forced to work from 6 a.m. to midnight, were poorly fed, and were beaten. The Thai husband and wife running the factory were arrested and charged with human trafficking, unlawful detention and illegally hiring migrant workers (Pearson, 2005).

Having been abandoned by her parents and sexually abused by the son of distant relatives, 15 year old Noi ran away to Bangkok to work as a prostitute. She then accepted an offer of a job as a waitress in Japan where she was told that she would not have to take clients if she did not wish to. In Japan, she was hired by a bar where she was told that she had to pay off a debt of one million yen (approximately US $9,500), and her food, rent, and other expenses would be added to this amount. Clients paid the mama san (a woman in charge of overseeing the girls and women in a sex establishment) directly for taking the women out during the debt repayment period, and Noi realized that the only way for her to pay off the debt was to go out with as many clients as possible. She lived with thirty other girls between the ages of 14 and 30. Sometimes the police would come in to check if there were overstayers of visas. A Japanese nun helped Noi get back to Thailand, but she had savings of only 30,000 Thai baht (approximately US $900) after five years of struggle (adapted from Raymond *et. al.*, 2002).

In 2005, a recruiter came to rural Thailand and convinced thirty Thai men to accept farming jobs in the United States. They were offered three years of work in North Carolina, in the south-eastern part of the country, to be paid US $8 an hour. However, they would have to pay $11,000 in recruiters' fees to get there. When they arrived, the labour contractor confiscated their passports and return plane tickets. The Thai men said that the owners stole their money, failed to pay them for their work, and held them captive with threats of violence. They got only two or three days of work a week on farms. They lived in a small storage building behind the home of the president of their recruiting company, a native from Lao PDR, and they were not provided with adequate food or allowed to leave the property. When the work in North Carolina ran out, the workers were taken to New Orleans where they spent a few weeks in a condemned hotel, damaged by Hurricane Katrina, without electricity or clean water. During the day they demolished parts of the hotel in which they lived. They were never paid for their work in New Orleans, so they trapped and ate pigeons. Finally, they escaped and were provided assistance by social service organizations in the United States (Collins, 2007).

These stories capture the economic, social, and political complexities of what it means for men, women, and children to be trafficked across international borders for labour and sexual exploitation. The story of the Lao PDR girls in a Bangkok sweatshop reflects the problems of many Laotians who migrate to Thailand with incomplete information about working conditions. For Noi, her experience of sexual violence was a cumulative one that began at childhood and persisted through her adulthood. The characteristics that make this a trafficking case are not necessarily that she was taken to another country to be a prostitute *per se*, but that she was duped by the Thai broker that she would be a waitress, and was stuck in a debt bondage situation in Japan. For the Thai men in the United States, it is yet another story of being duped and then finding themselves in an untenable debt bondage situation.

This chapter is concerned with two main issues: first, the ways that the international community has defined and framed the issue of human trafficking over the last century; second, the ways that the international community, and particularly the United States, has responded politically to the problem of human trafficking. Contemporary movements against international social issues can be traced to ideologically-motivated precursor movements. There are striking similarities in the tactics, rhetoric, and framing strategies between earlier movements and the contemporary anti-trafficking movement. In fact, it is necessary to go back more than a century to understand current debates on trafficking. This chapter provides a critical examination of the strategies of the contemporary anti-trafficking movement by explaining the competing interpretations of trafficking and how they led to the development, acceptance, and implementation of anti-trafficking norms.

Definitions of Human Trafficking

Trafficking is a term that has been used to describe a broad spectrum of criminal acts encompassing sexual and labour exploitation. Most generally, it can be viewed as a process with multiple phases: the recruitment or transport of persons using some form of force, fraud, or coercion for an exploitive purpose (Chuang, 2006, p. 443). Other issues that are often subsumed under the umbrella term human trafficking include: sex tourism; child sex tourism; commercial sexual exploitation of children (CSEC); exploitation in domestic, restaurant, agricultural, factory, and sweatshop work; debt bondage; forced prostitution; forced begging; and servile marriage through the mail order bride industry. The word trafficking connotes movement of people, either across international borders or within a country, to circumstances of exploitation, and has often been confused with people smuggling.

International law requires coerced or forced movement in order to constitute a trafficking situation. Trafficking is also associated with the exploitive situation of the person's destination; for example, in the American legal context, movement is not required in order to constitute a situation of trafficking. Some have sought to simplify the terminological ocean by calling trafficking a 'modern-day form of slavery' (US Department of Justice, 2007, p. 1). However, some argue that the term trafficking has been so overused that it should be jettisoned (Kempadoo, 2005b, p. ix).

In the three cases cited above, the individuals made it out of the trafficking situations. However, since there are few reliable statistics about how many people are being trafficked around the world, it is also unknown how many make it out and how many are forced to endure horrible conditions. The statistics provided in Table 12.1 show the range of estimates of the scope of human trafficking, although none of these numbers has been verified.

Trafficking was codified in international law several times in the first half of the twentieth century. However, the traffic in women and children for exploitation in prostitution was the primary focus; forced labour as a form of trafficking and men as trafficking victims were excluded from these definitions. In 2000, trafficking was codified in the **Protocol to Prevent, Suppress,**

TABLE 12.1 Estimates of human trafficking victims worldwide.

Estimate	Source
• 27,000,000 'slaves' globally	http://www.FreetheSlaves.net
• 14,500–17,500 enter the United States annually and become exploited	US Department of State
• 800,000 trafficked across international borders. Approximately 80 per cent of transnational victims are women and girls, and up to 50 per cent are minors. The majority of transnational victims are females trafficked into commercial sexual exploitation	2008 US Department of State Trafficking in Persons Report
• 1.2 million persons are trafficked annually	International Labour Organization
• 12.3 million people in forced labour, bonded labour, forced child labour, and sexual servitude at any given time	
More than 300,000 children under 18 are being exploited in more than 30 armed conflicts globally. The majority of child soldiers are between the ages of 15 and 18 and some are as young as 7 years old	UNICEF

and Punish Trafficking in Persons, especially Women and Children (Palermo Protocol), supplementing the United Nations (UN) Convention against Transnational Organized Crime. Although the Palermo Protocol negotiations in Vienna, Austria, known as the Vienna Process, were extremely contentious, they marked the first time that the international community agreed upon a comprehensive definition of human trafficking. The Palermo Protocol redefined the international norms on trafficking, in the sense that it acknowledged that people may be trafficked for purposes other than exploitation in prostitution.

The internationally accepted definition of trafficking (see Box 12.1) does not describe a single act leading to one specific outcome, but rather refers to a process (recruitment, transportation, and control) that can be organized in many ways and involve a variety of actors and outcomes. The elements identified in the Palermo

---

Box 12.1 **Definitions of Human Trafficking**

Trafficking in persons is defined as:

Recruitment, transportation, transfer, harbouring or receipt of persons, by means of the threat or use of force or other forms of coercion, of abduction, of fraud, of deception, of the abuse of power or of a position of vulnerability or of the giving or receiving of payments or benefits to achieve the consent of a person having control over another person, for the purpose of exploitation. Exploitation shall include, at a minimum, the exploitation of the prostitution of others or other forms of sexual exploitation, forced labour or services, slavery or practices similar to slavery, servitude or the removal of organs. (Protocol to Prevent, Suppress, and Punish Trafficking in Persons, especially Women and Children)

'Severe forms' of trafficking are defined as:

(a) sex trafficking in which a commercial sex act is induced by force, fraud, or coercion, or in which the person induced to perform such act has not attained 18 years of age; or

(b) the recruitment, harboring, transportation, provision, or obtaining of a person for labor or services, through the use of force, fraud, or coercion for the purpose of subjection to involuntary servitude, peonage, debt bondage, or slavery;

(c) if the person is under 18 years of age, any commercial sex act, whether or not force, fraud or coercion is involved.
(Trafficking Victims Protection Act)

Protocol definition of trafficking themselves present definitional problems, however. For example, there is no international consensus regarding the definition of sexual exploitation—or even of exploitation—and abuses that come under the umbrella of trafficking can vary in severity, generating a spectrum of experiences (Anderson and O'Connell Davidson, 2002, p. 12).

Significantly, the same year that the Protocol was signed in Palermo, Italy, the United States developed and passed its own Trafficking Victims Protection Act (TVPA). The TVPA is significant because it was at the time (and remains) the most progressive domestic anti-trafficking statute in the world, and also because the law was written in such a way that it can be used (and has been used) as a foreign policy tool for the United States to export its own anti-trafficking norms to other countries (Chuang, 2006).

The most significant source of tension among those governments and organizations negotiating the Protocol in Vienna and among the US Congress and the organizations involved with formulating the TVPA in Washington was the extent to which prostitution was considered a form of trafficking or exploitation. Many feminist and conservative groups joined together to negotiate during the Vienna Process in hopes of resolving a century-old debate about whether trafficking comprised all forms of adult prostitution or only involuntary prostitution. Feminists split into two sub-groups: those who advocated for the abolition of prostitution in all of its forms (abolitionist feminists) and those who advocated for a focus on forced prostitution only (human rights feminists).

The distinction between sex trafficking and severe forms of sex trafficking is significant in the American legal context. The TVPA includes a definition for sex trafficking: 'the recruitment, harboring, transportation, provision, or obtaining of a person for the purpose of a commercial sex act' (United States Code, 2000), and a separate definition of severe forms of sex trafficking (see Box 12.1). The sex trafficking definition excludes the requirement of coercion contained in the Palermo Protocol definition of trafficking and thus encompasses consensual migrant prostitution. However, the TVPA limits the operational application to severe forms of trafficking in persons—i.e. trafficking involving force, fraud, or coercion for the purpose of the inducement of a commercial sex act (Chuang, 2006, p. 450).

KEY POINTS	
Trafficking was most recently codified in the Protocol to Prevent, Suppress, and Punish Trafficking in Persons, especially Women and Children, supplementing the United Nations Convention against Transnational Organized Crime.	The same year that the UN agreed upon the Protocol, the US government passed its own Trafficking Victims Protection Act.
The internationally accepted definition of trafficking does not describe a single act leading to one specific outcome, but rather refers to a process (recruitment, transportation, and control) that can be organized in many ways and involve a range of actors and outcomes.	The Vienna Process revived a long-running debate about whether all forms of prostitution should be considered instances of trafficking or exploitation.

The Anti-White Slavery Movement and the Rise in International Consciousness about the Traffic in Women

Contemporary concerns about trafficking can be traced back to a late-nineteenth-century movement in the United States and Western Europe against a phenomenon known as white slavery. White slavery, or the white slave trade, is a term that was used to describe the kidnapping and transport of white girls and women for the purposes of prostitution inside or outside of the United States and Europe (Doezema, 2002, p. 22). It was also used to describe the movement of young, white women from rural areas of the United States into houses of prostitution in large American cities at the turn of the twentieth century (Bell, 1910).

Many people in the United States and Europe fervently believed, on the basis of cases spotlighted by the print media, that large numbers of white girls and women were being abducted or lured into prostitution. However, contemporary historians question the extent of this trade, and most scholars now agree that the number of victims of white slavery were, compared to the sensationalistic accounts in the media, actually very small. More congruous to actual events, there was an increase in migration from Southern and Eastern Europe to the United States and Latin America, and some of those migrants may initially have been prostitutes (Doezema, 2002, Footnote 4) or simply women travelling alone from countries in Europe with high levels of poverty and unemployment. It is believed that stories and narratives about white slaves were triggered by this migration.

International and Domestic Responses to a Perceived Problem

The term white slavery had different meanings for different social actors, depending on their geographic location. The discourse on white slavery was neither monolithic nor consistent. For some, white slavery meant prostitution in general; others saw white slavery and prostitution as distinct but related phenomena. Many made the distinction between domestic prostitution and international migration of women for prostitution (Doezema, 2002).

The demographic and social issues at the turn of the twentieth century, combined with Victorian values, led to fears about declining moral standards and racial purity, and the extent of the discourse about white slavery has been extensively documented by academics in the late twentieth century.[1] David (1999, p. 4) argues that these fears fuelled the creation of myths of innocent girls being forced into sexual slavery on a large scale, myths intended to discourage inter-racial relations, extra-marital sex, and travel by single women. In this way, the white slavery metaphor represented anxieties of the American and European middle classes instead of factual accounts of women's experiences (Doezema, 2002, p. 26). In fact, the fears surrounding the white slave trade escalated to a panic, which was fuelled by sensational reports in the media, and by generally moralistic and racist middle class attitudes and beliefs in Europe and the United States (Irwin, 1996).

Intense international activism in Europe and the United States developed against white slavery. There were several international agreements made decrying the trade. This activism was primarily motivated by unsubstantiated reports of women from Europe and the United States being kidnapped and taken to the Middle East and Africa. The fact that black slaves had been traded for centuries was diminished by white slave rhetoricians. Alfred Dyer wrote in 1880 that the coercion into prostitution of white, English girls was 'infinitely more cruel and revolting than negro servitude' because white slavery was 'not for labour but for lust; and more cowardly than Negro slavery' (Dyer, 1880, p. 6). Irwin (1996) argues that Dyer's assessment devalued the humanity of blacks and ignored the fact that black women experienced high levels of sexual exploitation in their situation of slavery. Thus the use of white women as sexual slaves was afforded a form of moral disapprobation that the sexual exploitation of black women did not have.

The international and domestic movements against the white slave trade became quite extensive at the turn of the twentieth century. However, international campaigns against white slavery need to be analysed in the context of the European and American nineteenth-century discourses and narratives on prostitution. For example, Edwin A. Sims, the US District Attorney in Chicago at the beginning of the twentieth century, was concerned about the trafficking of white slaves, who he depicted as innocent white girls from rural areas who were being exploited by Parisians and dark-skinned Mediterranean men (Bell, 1910, p. 261). E. A. Bell, Secretary of the Illinois Vigilance Association and a legislator, wrote that, while not all traffickers were French, Paris was an epicentre for systematizing commercial sex (Bell, 1910, p. 261). Sims and Bell never mention the 'upstanding' Chicago businessmen who may have been just as involved in prostituting young girls as the dark-skinned Mediterranean men (Kraut, 1996).

In Britain, the issues of white slavery and child prostitution were linked in W. T. Stead's series of articles,

---

> **Box 12.2 The white slavery hysteria**
>
> I admit that the vast majority of those who are on the streets in London have not come there by the road of organized rape. Most women fall either by the seduction of individuals or by the temptation which . . . vice can offer to the poor. . . . Some are simply snared, trapped and outraged either when under the influence of drugs or after a prolonged struggle in a locked room, in which the weaker succumbs to . . . downright force. Others are regularly procured; bought at so much per head in some cases, or enticed under various promises into the fatal chamber from which they are never allowed to emerge until they have lost what woman ought to value more than life. (W. T. Stead (1885), The Maiden Tribute to Modern Babylon, *The Pall Mall Gazette*)

'The Maiden Tribute to Modern Babylon', which was published in the *Pall Mall Gazette* in 1885 (see Box 12.2). In this sensational series, Stead claimed to have evidence of hundreds of English girls deceived, coerced, and sometimes drugged into prostitution, and he accused poor parents of selling their daughters to procurers (Doezema, 2002, p. 28). This sensational series helped to spark a fury among the middle classes in Europe. Stead recognized that some women voluntarily migrated for prostitution. For example, after having worked in prostitution in their home countries, women may have accepted offers to work in prostitution in other countries because they were promised a more lucrative situation.

Early International Conventions

In 1895, the first international conference on traffic in women was held in Paris, followed by two other conferences in London and Budapest (Long, 2004, p. 20). In 1904, the first International Agreement for the Suppression of the White Slave Traffic was passed in Paris with representatives from sixteen countries. Since some countries, such as France, regulated prostitution, the International Agreement did not make white slavery synonymous with prostitution. Instead, it addressed international recruitment for prostitution (Doezema, 2002, p. 23).

In 1910, the International Convention for Suppression of White Slave Traffic was expanded to include the recruitment for prostitution within national boundaries. In 1921, the International Convention for the Suppression of Traffic in Women and Children included trafficking in boys. These early agreements focused on recruitment and neglected the aspect of enslavement or conditions in prostitution. They distinguished between prostitution as a personal choice and slavery-like prostitution due to coercion or traffic in persons. They banned the international traffic in persons but regarded prostitution as a human rights violation only when it involved overt coercion or exploitation. However, the drafters were faulted for failing to acknowledge less visible forms of coercion such as economic, social, and psychological forms, which critics claimed pushed girls and women into prostitution (Doezema, 2002).

The 1933 International Convention on the Suppression of Traffic in Women of Full Age made an explicit link between traffic in women and voluntary or involuntary prostitution, thus reflecting an abolitionist perspective in an international legal document (Doezema, 2002, p. 23). States were required to punish anyone who procured or enticed a woman, regardless of whether she has consented to work in prostitution in another country.

The 1949 Convention for the Suppression of the Traffic in Persons and of the Exploitation of the Prostitution of Others further solidified the connection between traffic in women and all forms of prostitution. There was a move away from gender and race specific language (Uçarer, 1999). Like the 1933 Convention, the 1949 Convention made sexual trafficking punishable even with the woman's consent. It neglected the critical element of force, violence, or coercion when defining the crimes around prostitution and trafficking, and for the first time in an international instrument declared prostitution and trafficking to be 'incompatible with the dignity and worth of the human person and [to] endanger the welfare of the individual, family and the community.' The convention made no distinction between forced and voluntary prostitution; it viewed prostitutes as victims and did not recognize the individuals' right to choose to work as a prostitute (Lim, 1998, p. 15).

KEY POINTS
The contemporary anti-trafficking movement has its roots in a precursor movement against the white slave trade at the turn of the twentieth century.
White slavery and the white slave trade are terms that were used to describe the abduction and transport of white women for prostitution out of, or within, the United States and Europe.
It is believed that stories and narratives about white slaves were triggered by the migration of young women from Europe.
A series of international conventions and agreements from 1905 to 1949 attempted to define and refine the international community's ideological position on prostitution.

Origins of the Contemporary Anti-Trafficking Movement

Decades of Silence: 1950–1979

After the 1949 Convention, the problem of trafficking in women did not disappear, but the political commitment to confront it nearly vanished. During the 1950s, 1960s, and early 1970s, the international community remained strangely silent on the issues of trafficking into prostitution, save for a few anti-slavery activists and feminists carrying the torch through the later mid-century. Very little discourse was written during or has been written about this time period, perhaps because the international political tensions of the Cold War eclipsed other international social issues. The only international instrument that was negotiated in the 1950s that related to trafficking was the 1956 Supplementary Convention on the Abolition of Slavery, which addresses 'selling women' and 'turning children over for exploitation and debt bondage schemes' (Farrior, 1997, p. 213).

Domestic and international women's movements emerged in the 1970s and 1980s, and forums for discussions opened. At a global level, the UN International Decade for Women (1976–1985) catalysed both activism and research on a range of issues affecting women around the world. For those interested in bringing the issues of international sexual slavery and forced prostitution back to the international agenda, there was hope in the 1970s when the United Nations Commission on the Status of Women was created, as well as the 1975 International Women's Year Conference in Mexico City (Barry, 1979, p. 64). The 1979 *Convention on the Elimination of All Forms of Discrimination Against Women* (CEDAW) directed states' parties to take measures to prevent all forms of traffic in women, and prostitution of women (United Nations, 1979). However, the major thrust of CEDAW was to address problems of political discrimination, an emphasis reflecting the concerns of Western women more than those of women in non-Western countries.

In 1979, Kathleen Barry re-introduced the issue of sexual slavery to an academic audience in a book entitled *Female Sexual Slavery*. She argued that trafficking for prostitution was very much alive during the 1960s and 1970s and provided evidence suggesting that high-level officials in certain countries were directly involved with trafficking women from developing countries for purposes of commercial sexual exploitation. Barry shows that INTERPOL knew of these problems from reports that the group made in the 1960s and 1970s. When the Anti-Slavery Society requested of INTERPOL to release a particularly damning report to the public, INTERPOL refused. In fact, Barry argues that there was a concerted effort to suppress the evidence even in the UN, as countries did not want to implicate or embarrass other countries (Barry, 1979, pp. 58–62).

Women's Rights as Human Rights: 1980–1995

The contemporary movement to combat trafficking benefited from precursor movements and the development of certain norms to push the notion that women's rights are human rights. Beginning in 1980, the United Nations held a number of international women's conferences, out of which came several key developments. First, the state's attention was redirected to the women's legal status and family practices that reinforced structures of gender inequality. Second, women's inequality was recognized to be global in nature. Third, several important women's human rights non-governmental

organizations (NGOs) were formed (Brown Thompson, 2002, pp. 99–100). Beginning in the late 1980s, many women's rights organizations identified an important way to frame women's rights as an inseparable aspect of human rights (Brown Thompson, 2002, p. 102). Women's networks were formed by women who came together in unprecedented numbers in the context of the UN conferences where they legitimized these issues (Keck and Sikkink, 1998, p. 169).

The discussions during the 1993 Vienna World Conference on Human Rights solidified the idea that women's rights are human rights (Brown Thompson, 2002, p. 107). At the Vienna conference, *violence against women* became a key issue among activists from all over the world. The issue of violence against women 'arrived late and dramatically in the international women's movement' (Keck and Sikkink, 1998, p. 166). The matter differed from the more classic problems of suffrage, equality, and discrimination around which Western women had long mobilized. These problems of Western women did not resonate with women from developing countries, who suffered from corrupt governments and Western economic policies that increased poverty, underdevelopment, and the commoditization of women (Keck and Sikkink, 1998, p. 166).

Violence against women emerged as a common advocacy position around which women's organizations could agree and collaborate (Keck and Sikkink, 1998, p. 166). Keck and Sikkink argue that violence against women was a category that

> … served some key strategic purpose for activists trying to build a transnational campaign because it allowed them to attract allies and bridge cultural differences. This strategic focus forced transnational activists to search for a basic common denominator—the belief in the importance of the protection of bodily integrity of women and girls. (Keck and Sikkink, 1998, p. 172)

The networks built around violence against women could draw upon pre-existing communication networks. The emergence of violence against women as a topic around which groups could advocate shows how separate transnational networks—human rights and women's rights—began to find common language and transform one another (Keck and Sikkink, 1998, p. 166). Women's groups in developing countries pressed the issue of violence against women most forcefully, and, fortuitously, they found support among groups working on similar women's issues in the West (Brown Thompson, 2002).

Women's groups refocused the human rights activism from campaigning around state-perpetrated violence in the public sphere to male-perpetrated violence against women in the private sphere. This was an advance in the global women's movement and it allowed separate campaigns to develop on specific practices of violence against women in a domestic context. For example, rape and domestic violence was an issue in the United States and Europe, female genital mutilation was relevant in Africa, commercial sexual exploitation was of concern in Europe and Asia, dowry deaths were in the media in India, and torture and rape of political prisoners was a grave problem in Latin America (Keck and Sikkink, 1998, pp. 171–173).

The issue of trafficking for sexual exploitation remained in the background until the campaign on violence against women solidified, and then rode the wave of the international women's movement into the mid-1990s. The 1995 Fourth World Conference on Women in Beijing solidified the movement working to combat violence against women (see Box 12.3). A broader view of trafficking that included forced marriage and forced labour emerged from this conference, along with the idea that governments bear responsibility for the rights of women in the 'private' sphere.

Box 12.3 **Combating trafficking for sexual exploitation**

The effective suppression of trafficking in women and girls for the sex trade is a matter of pressing international concern. Implementation of the 1949 Convention for the Suppression of the Traffic in Persons and of the Exploitation of the Prostitution of Others, as well as other relevant instruments, needs to be reviewed and strengthened. The use of women in international prostitution and trafficking networks has become a major focus of international organized crime. The Special Rapporteur of the Commission on Human Rights on violence against women ... is invited to address, within her mandate and as a matter of urgency, the issue of international trafficking for the purposes of the sex trade, as well as the issues of forced prostitution, rape, sexual abuse and sex tourism. (*Platform for Action* (1995), Fourth World Conference on Women, Beijing, China)

Contemporary Politics of Addressing Human Trafficking

Deep-seated disagreements in the women's human rights movement became evident during the international negotiations for a new international instrument on human trafficking, which culminated in the Palermo Protocol. Unresolved issues about the relationship between trafficking and prostitution that had been percolating since the late 1970s finally came to a head in Vienna. The Palermo Protocol reflects only a weak international consensus on this transnational problem (Chuang, 2006, p. 438). During the Vienna Process, one group of states, adopting the abolitionist perspective, viewed any distinction between forced and voluntary prostitution as morally unacceptable. It opposed any definition of trafficking that would include a coercion requirement and argued that the definition should encompass all migration for sex work. Another group of states took the position that including non-coerced migration for sex work would make the trafficking definition over-broad and divert scarce resources away from the real problem (see Table 12.2).

These debates underlined the complexity and divisiveness of the issue. Moreover, ongoing controversy over these questions still hampers collaborative efforts among anti-trafficking advocates, NGOs, and governments to bring about a coordinated legal response (Chuang, 2006, p. 443).

The Palermo Protocol departed from its sister conventions earlier in the twentieth century by making elements of force or coercion essential parts of the definition of trafficking. This is a significant departure from the abolitionist stance of the 1949 Convention, and it left states free to recognize voluntary prostitution as labour and to regulate it. But while the Protocol makes an important distinction between coerced and non-coerced migration for prostitution, it does not offer many concrete human rights protections for trafficking victims (Chuang, 2006, p. 447).

Although the Protocol does recognize the need to respect the human rights of trafficked persons, it is conspicuously not a human rights document. States insisted that they be permitted to enact measures to protect themselves against transnational organized

TABLE 12.2 Ideological camps addressing human trafficking.

Abolitionist feminists	Human rights feminists
Ideology:	*Ideology*:
Abolitionist feminists believe that prostitution, whether voluntary or involuntary, is exploitive. Trafficking is, by definition, the act of forcing or coercing an individual into a situation of sexual or labour exploitation. Therefore, those involved in prostitution are always in a trafficking situation.	Human rights feminists de-link prostitution and trafficking by arguing that some adult women and men are in prostitution voluntarily and should not be considered victims; only those who are forced or coerced to be prostitutes should be considered trafficking victims.
Organizations:	*Organizations*:
• Coalition Against Traffic in Women	• Global Alliance Against Traffic in Women
• Equality Now	• Global Rights
• The Polaris Project	
• International Justice Mission	

crime, specifically the elements of organized crime that smuggle people across borders and/or exploit their labour after the movement across the border. The implicit purpose of the Protocol was to provide a mechanism for states to criminalize trafficking and, as a result, prosecute traffickers. Thus the Protocol has often been described as a protector of *states* rather than a protector of victims of human trafficking.

KEY POINTS	
The international community became relatively silent on the issue of trafficking between 1950 and 1979 largely due to the international political pressures of the Cold War.	Violence against women emerged as a common advocacy position around which women's organizations could agree and collaborate. The Vienna Process was a significant step in crystallizing international norms on combating human trafficking.
Discussions began to open up in the 1970s, spearheaded by the UN, about issues affecting women all over the world and by the appearance, in 1979, of Kathleen Barry's seminal book *Female Sexual Slavery*.	Two ideological camps coalesced around the Protocol negotiations; they were focused nearly exclusively on the nature of prostitution.
The contemporary movement to combat trafficking benefited from precursor movements and the development of certain norms to push the notion that women's rights are human rights.	

The Ascendancy of Trafficking as an Issue in the 1990s

Few of the issues raised in contemporary forums to discuss human trafficking are unique to this time period. In fact, the reasons why this issue has gained ascendancy at the turn of the twenty-first century parallel those explaining its rise at the turn of the twentieth century. Doezema (2000, p. 24) aptly compares the trafficking victim from one century to another:

Recent research indicates that today's stereotypical 'trafficking victim' bears as little resemblance to women migrating for work in the sex industry as did her historical counterpart, the 'white slave.' The majority of trafficking victims are aware that the jobs offered them are in the sex industry, but are lied to about the conditions they will work under. Yet policies to eradicate 'trafficking' continue to be based on the notion of the 'innocent' unwilling victim, and often combine efforts designed to protect 'innocent' women with those designed to punish 'bad' women: i.e., prostitutes.

As this assessment suggests, the contemporary anti-trafficking movement has its roots firmly entrenched in debates going back as far as the late 1880s. The rhetoric has changed slightly in over a century; however, the abolitionist feminist/human rights feminist split with regard to the issue of trafficking as prostitution is still very much alive. The inability of these two camps to find common ground has contributed to the particular character of the current global anti-trafficking movement. There are several reasons why the contemporary, global anti-trafficking movement has been able to sustain itself: a proliferation of domestic and international NGOs; hundreds of millions of dollars spent globally to combat trafficking since 2001; US unilateralism; sensational media coverage; and the facility with which organizations and people communicate across international borders in order to undertake transnational advocacy activities.

In 1991, the Soviet Union collapsed, destabilizing Central and Eastern Europe. The end of the Cold War precipitated an intense interest in the issue of trafficking in persons in Western countries, primarily because of the fear and concern of mass migration out of the former Soviet Union and Eastern Europe to Western Europe. Whereas a large number of people did make their way to Western Europe, an exodus did not materialize. Trafficking in women and children for sexual exploitation into the European Community came to the attention of a growing number of non-governmental organizations in Western Europe. Interestingly, some of these European NGOs had been working on related issues, with Asian activists, since the 1980s and were aware of Southeast Asian women involved in forced and voluntary prostitution, as well as of abusive marriages between European men and Asian women.

However, Asian and African women in European brothels in the 1980s did not raise the same flags that the appearance of foreign, white women in the French, British, and German sex industries in the 1990s did. In much the same way that the white slavery panic of the early twentieth century was sparked by the migration of women out of Eastern Europe coupled with revulsion at the thought that white women were being enslaved sexually, an intense interest in the issue resurfaced with the end of the Cold War and the migration of women and men out of former Soviet countries and the belief that many of these (white) women were being enslaved sexually in Western European and American brothels. Jahic and Finckenauer (2005, p. 26) ask poignant questions about why there was a rise in interest in this issue in the 1990s:

> Was the rise in concern for victims simply the result of a sudden increase in trafficking? Why did special interest groups, governments, and organizations suddenly become interested in a problem that had actually been present for decades? Was there something unusual about the new wave of trafficking from Eastern Europe and the former Soviet Union?

The answer they provide, which is in line with other findings, is that, unlike the women from Asia and Africa who were women of colour, the new trafficking victims were more recognizable to politicians and other middle class do-gooders. The image of white slaves was unconsciously invoked, and this image resonated with activists and advocates in the West (Jahic and Finckenauer, 2005, p. 26).

Jahic and Finckenauer (2005, p. 27) also make a powerful argument about why trafficking has become such an important issue since the 1990s. The trafficking victims have been portrayed in the media as young, naive victims in need of protection. This portrait of a trafficking victim has made it easier to form anti-trafficking task forces. This is a particularly important point to make because, although transnational advocacy networks are the main facilitators of maintaining this issue on the international political agenda, Jahic and Finckenauer provide an explanation for the fuel for the advocacy networks. In addition to portraying prostitutes as victims to make anti-trafficking activities more palatable for public discourse, the issue that has also fuelled the activities of advocacy networks is the fact that those working on this issue do not have a clear sense of the scope of the problem. This has not stopped people from claiming that the problem is growing in magnitude. Most organizations and governments collect different kinds of data, which makes it difficult to reach meaningful conclusions about the scope of the trafficking (Jahic and Finckenauer, 2005, p. 27).

The accounts of women trafficked into exploitive prostitution have often been portrayed to justify a particular political, moral, and economic regime by governments and faith-based organizations. These accounts position women as victims who need the protection of powerful interests. By focusing only on the women's labour, sexuality, or mobility, these institutions fail to address the root causes of trafficking in the countries of origin, such as high rates of unemployment, abuse in families, and limited opportunities for legal migration. Media accounts capitalize on the combination of sexuality and exploitation to provoke a public voyeurism by transforming the stories to be about the dehumanizing experience; the women are treated in the media as objects instead of subjects of their own histories. Long (2004, p. 7) argues that, 'Contemporary sexual trafficking experiences remain largely invisible, reflecting in large part the particular interests and agenda of those defining trafficking for sexual exploitation rather than the lived experiences and perceptions of those who are trafficked.'

KEY POINTS

Rhetoric on slavery and prostitution has many similarities throughout the twentieth century. Just as the white slave provoked hysterical discourse about young, white women at the turn of the twentieth century, feminist abolitionists were similarly motivated by the increased presence of Eastern European women in Western European and US brothels after the Cold War's end.

Prostitute as victim has been a powerful way to invoke increased interest in the issue of human trafficking.

Case Study: Human Trafficking in the United States

Brief Background of Trafficking Problems in the United States

The United States is a destination country for men, women, and children trafficked for the purposes of forced prostitution and forced labour. The most recent US Department of State estimates claim that 14,500 to 17,500 people are trafficked into the United States every year (US Department of State, 2006). Individuals are trafficked to and exploited in nearly every state of the United States; no community is immune, though the majority of trafficking cases have occurred in larger metropolitan areas and traditional ports of entry: New York, Miami/Florida, Texas, Los Angeles, San Francisco, Chicago, and Atlanta (US Department of Justice, 2007). People have been found trafficked in traditional and non-traditional sex industry establishments—brothels, bars, massage parlours—as well as in factories, sweatshops, farms, restaurants, private homes, even begging on the street. Young women are trafficked from the former Soviet Union, Latin America, and Asia into sexual servitude. Latin American and African women are also trafficked into domestic servitude. Latin American and Asian men are trafficked into forced labour or extremely exploitive labour situations in factories, farming, construction, agriculture, and landscaping.

It is unknown if there are more situations of individuals in trafficking for forced prostitution than in labour trafficking. The US government maintains that 80 per cent of trafficking in the world is for sex trafficking—a figure that reflects its expansive view of sex trafficking—and that over 50 per cent of those trafficked are minors (US Department of State, 2008). The majority of prosecutions that the US Department of Justice has handled have been for forced prostitution (US Department of Justice, 2007). These figures contribute to a general assumption in the United States and elsewhere that sexual servitude is more prevalent than labour trafficking (US Department of State, 2006). However, research is providing evidence to the contrary (Webber and Shirk, 2005).

It is not surprising that the United States is a magnet for migrants from all over the world. It is also not at all surprising that many of these migrants are duped by recruiters in their home communities. Recruiters paint rosy pictures of what it is like to live and work in the United States. In addition, because the routes for legal migration into the United States are limited, individuals seeking to get into the country increasingly turn to unscrupulous smugglers and traffickers.

Research has also shown that it is not the poorest of the poor who are trafficked or become trafficked in the

United States, nor is it the least educated—though low levels of education do affect the likelihood of someone becoming exploited (Bales and Lize, 2005). In 2006, the *San Francisco Chronicle* ran a four-part story in which the reporter extensively interviewed one South Korean woman who came to the US from a lower middle class family in Korea. This young woman, in order to fit in with her friends in South Korea, had obtained a credit card and bought tens of thousands of dollars worth of clothing and jewellery. When she was unable to pay off the credit card with her job as a waitress, she became desperate and agreed to pay money to a smuggler to bring her to the United States to work—she thought—as a waitress in California. She was unaware of the immigration and visa rules and allowed her smuggler to arrange the paperwork. Little did she know that she would first be flown to Mexico, smuggled illegally across the border into the United States, and then forced to work as a prostitute to pay off, not only her credit card debts, but also the money she owed to her smuggler. After several months of working as a prostitute against her will, she had paid off enough of her smuggling debt that if she wanted to leave prostitution, she could. However, she chose to stay working as a prostitute for many more months to reduce her credit card debt in South Korea; besides, she did not know what her options were because she was an illegal alien. Eventually, after leaving the prostitution industry, her experiences came to the attention of an NGO. It was determined, by the group as well as by the US government, that she was a victim of trafficking, making her eligible for certain compensations under the TVPA (May, 2006). The details of this case illustrate the complexities of trafficking in the United States: not only can a person be smuggled then trafficked, but this woman chose to stay working in the sex industry after she could have exited because of her financial obligations in South Korea.

The situation of trafficking in the United States is distinctive because the majority of traffickers traffic people of their own ethnic/national groups. For example, Bales and Lize (2005, p. 27), in a report on human trafficking in the United States, found that in eight of the twelve cases that they studied the victims were recruited by a person from their community of origin, meaning that someone from their neighbourhood, family, or ethnic group lured them to the United States. Forced labour is a phenomenon found within ethnic/national communities populated by a steady flow of migrants from the same geographic areas (Bales and Lize, 2005, p. 143). The fact that victims of trafficking are very often exploited within ethnic community enclaves in the United States is one of the factors that prevents local and federal law enforcement and non-governmental organizations from finding or discovering victims of trafficking throughout the United States. The psychological and physical coercion victims experience in exploitive situations is much more powerful when a trafficker knows the victim's family in her or his home country and can threaten to hurt those family members, especially children left behind.

Development of US Norms to Combat Human Trafficking

In 1995, President Bill Clinton established the President's Inter-Agency Council on Women (PICW) within the Department of State in order to create a mechanism to carry out commitments that the United States made in connection with the Beijing women's conference. The Chairperson of this Council was First Lady Hillary Rodham Clinton, who had been present at the Beijing conference and had given a stirring speech about women's rights as human rights. By early 1998, the ideological camps on the issue of prostitution's relationship with trafficking had already re-formed in the US. Abolitionist feminists sided with conservative social groups and a growing Christian conservative presence in the US Congress.

In January 1998, a round table entitled 'The Meaning of "Trafficking in Persons": A Human Rights Perspective' was sponsored by the International Human Rights Law Group (now Global Rights) in Washington, DC. The purpose of the round table was to define trafficking in persons as well as to formulate a conceptual framework for appropriately responding to the problem of trafficking in the contexts of international human rights and US law and policy (Miller and Stewart, 1998, p. 11). This round table was significant because it framed trafficking in a more complex way. First, trafficking was connected, not only to prostitution, but also to a variety of exploitive or abusive labour situations, such as forced prostitution, sweatshop labour, and domestic service (Miller and Stewart, 1998, p. 16). Second, the organizers of the round table advocated for an approach that included a variety of activities including crime prevention, social welfare, protection of rights, and prevention through international development (Miller and Stewart, 1998, p. 12). The majority of the participants at this round table were human rights feminists; the organizers of the round table did not invite abolitionist feminists to participate. This was the first of many meetings and round tables in which competing interpretations and understandings were discussed.

On 8 March 1998—International Women's Day— President Clinton issued an Executive Order on Trafficking in Women and Children that set out a comprehensive and integrated policy framework of domestic and foreign anti-trafficking initiatives. This Executive Order became the blueprint for US legislation on human trafficking. The Clinton Administration established bilateral working relationships with several countries and spearheaded the drafting of the Palermo Protocol (Chuang, 2006, p. 449). The Executive Order also outlined an implicit normative framework for how the US Government and international organizations should address trafficking for the next decade, prescribing three important ways to combat trafficking: prevention of trafficking, protection of trafficking victims, and prosecution of traffickers (often referred to as the 3Ps). Congressional leaders introduced legislation in 1999 on sex trafficking that was later broadened to include all forms of human trafficking, and in late 2000 President Clinton signed the Trafficking Victims Protection Act into law.

The motives underlying this legislation are interesting and important to understand. Several cases of human trafficking were brought before the US courts in the mid-1990s. In 1995, approximately 100 deaf Mexicans were found being forced to peddle trinkets in New York City. In 1997, approximately seventy Thais were found locked up in a sweatshop in El Monte, California, where they had been held for 17 years. Unfortunately, prosecutors did not have at their disposal statutes that addressed the specific problem of people being *psychologically coerced* and enslaved for work. Before the TVPA, US law recognized only physical, not psychological, coercion as part of slavery cases. These cases revealed that special attention was needed for people who might have agreed to be taken across the border but nonetheless ended up in situations of deception, coercion, and violence.

Chuang (2006) argues that these two cases prompted members of Congress to propose comprehensive anti-trafficking legislation. However, these cases were discovered in 1995 and 1997, and legislation was not introduced in Congress until 1999. While they most certainly played a role in raising attention to the issue of worker exploitation, they were not the primary catalyst for Congress to pass anti-trafficking legislation. The years 1999 and 2000 were turning point years in the consolidation of US congressional and NGO support for action on the issue of trafficking. In addition to the several congressional hearings held about human trafficking— specifically trafficking for sexual exploitation—members of Congress introduced various bills on trafficking and sex trafficking (Hyland, 2001, pp. 60–61).

The Congressional co-sponsors of a developing policy on trafficking were greatly motivated by evidence presented by the NGO Global Survival Network (GSN) showing that a steady stream of girls and women from the former Soviet Union were being trafficked into prostitution in the US and Western Europe. On 28 June 1999, Congressman Chris Smith (R-NJ) held a hearing entitled 'The Sex Trade: Trafficking in Women and Children in Europe and the United States'. At that testimony, Congressman Smith stated (emphasis added):

> Although trafficking has been a problem for many years in Asian countries, it was not until the end of communism in East-Central Europe and the break up of the Soviet Union that a sex trade in the OSCE region began to develop. This appalling trade has grown exponentially over the ensuing decade. Trafficking is induced by poverty, lack of economic opportunities for women, the low status of women in many cultures, and the rapid growth of sophisticated and ruthless international organized crime syndicates. Trafficking rings exploit vulnerable women and children; and amidst the devastated economies of Eastern Europe and the newly independent states where women are unable to find jobs, traffickers have no shortage of potential victims.

Evidence provided by GSN sparked sentiments and compassion similar to those of the early abolitionists at the turn of the twentieth century of white slavery. US policy makers responded to advocacy about problems of forced prostitution of East European and former Soviet women; they did not pay as much attention to the domestic problem of human trafficking, or human trafficking taking place in other areas of the world.

Moral Authority and Exporting US Norms Abroad

For well over a century, trafficking has been a problem that has evoked some moral obligation upon which to act—it concerns situations in which girls and women are being raped for the profit of others, men's labour is being severely exploited, or children are being abused. Unique political alliances and debates between liberals, represented by human rights advocates and feminists, and conservatives, represented by abolitionist feminists and the conservative, religious right in the US, have elevated human trafficking to a high place on the political agenda. The religious conservatives' and the abolitionist feminists' cooperation on the linkages between prostitution and trafficking was sufficient to maintain Congressional interest in the issue of human trafficking, especially among the Republicans, years after the passage of the TVPA.

Early academic literature on the formation of transnational advocacy networks signifies an acceptance of the fact that people and organizations network because they perceive a moral obligation or urgency to act on issues such as human rights, environmental destruction, or women's human rights. However, others have challenged this view, arguing that activism is as much about politics and posturing as it is about morals. Clifford Bob (2005) asks why some issues get put on the global agenda while others are ignored. He comes up with several answers. First, local groups seek to transform their grievances into rights claims. Second, international human rights NGOs act as 'gatekeepers', screening such claims and deciding which to bring to the international level. Third, states and international organizations translate claims into rights by codifying and institutionalizing them (Hertel, 2006, p. 15).

After the UN adopted the Palermo Protocol and the United States passed the TVPA, international campaigns such as the Global Alliance Against Traffic in Women (GAATW) and the Coalition Against Traffic in Women (CATW) set out to advocate their respective positions on trafficking and prostitution with regards to them. The human rights camp was perceived to have won the debate, which empowered GAATW to organize its entire agenda around advocating governments' ratification of the Palermo Protocol. However, in 2001, almost immediately after the TVPA was passed, the US

administration changed from Democratic to Republican. Even though it had been signed by a liberal president, the TVPA was implemented under a conservative administration.

Chuang (2006) argues that the TVPA has forced US norms into the international arena, risking 'undermining the fragile international cooperation framework created' by the Palermo Protocol. The US took advantage of the fact that it would be unlikely that the Protocol would be rigorously enforced due to insufficient funding and the lack of a central and powerful office at the UN tasked with responsibility for its implementation. In fact, the international cooperation framework collapsed, creating a global leadership vacuum on the issue of trafficking. Therefore, the US slowly replaced the UN as the 'global sheriff' combating human trafficking (Chuang, 2006).

US confidence in this new enforcement role grew once it gauged the reaction of the international community to its tier designations in the Trafficking in Persons Report (published by the US Department of State in 2001 and each subsequent year). Because the TVPA includes a sanctions regime, which is used as a foreign policy tool, it reaches beyond US borders to influence anti-trafficking policy abroad. This threat of sanctions elevated US norms above international norms by 'giving the former teeth that the latter so often lack' (Chuang, 2006, p. 439). The sanctions regime and regular US Government engagement with other governments influenced many countries to develop laws and policies to combat human trafficking. What is interesting is that the US encouraged other governments to adopt and employ selective and sometimes ambiguous references to the norms of the Palermo Protocol (Chuang, 2006, pp. 439–440). The US supported nearly all of the norms delineated in the Palermo Protocol, with one crucial exception. Here the US employed a 'bait and switch' tactic through its distinction between sex trafficking and severe forms of sex trafficking as defined in the TVPA (Chuang, 2006).

The contemporary anti-trafficking movement spearheaded by the international community in the late 1990s has become a platform to keep the debate alive on the nature of prostitution in the 2000s. The site of the global debate on prostitution and its relationship to trafficking shifted to Washington, DC, where some US-based organizations, whose abolitionist ideology on prostitution has afforded them the political and financial support of the US Government, are located. US foreign policies on human trafficking have been viewed as both progressive and aggressive, and US-based organizations also took advantage of the global leadership vacuum mentioned above. With a sense of both empowerment and moral authority, they decided to travel to other countries to combat trafficking. For example, the NGO International Justice Mission (IJM), flush with US Government funding, tried in the early 2000s to put an end to prostitution in northern Thailand by breaking down brothel doors and removing girls and women from the brothel. They came to Thailand with 'arrogant perceptions' (Gunning, 1992) that child prostitution was some aberration of the Thai culture that could be fixed by better-knowing Western, white males and females. IJM's activities backfired, and many domestic and international organizations rejected them as an illegitimate actor in the anti-trafficking community. As this example shows, US enforcement of its own norms has been simultaneously successful and problematic.

KEY POINTS

Victims of trafficking are found in every corner of the United States.

There is an assumption that trafficking for sexual exploitation is more prevalent, but evidence has shown that labour trafficking may be a larger problem.

Under the Clinton Administration, the US Government developed norms to combat trafficking: prevention, protection, and prosecution.

Despite prominent labour trafficking cases in the mid-1990s, US Congressional leaders were motivated to address human trafficking when it came to their attention that women from the former Soviet Union were being forced into prostitution.

The US has assumed the responsibility of global sheriff on enforcing anti-trafficking norms internationally.

Conclusion

In the exploration of a historical perspective, patterns of political behaviour across an entire century are evident. Without better research, it is difficult for many organizations, activists, and advocates to transcend the emotive language that maintains stereotypes and influences narrowly-conceived policies and projects around the world. Theoretically, it is important to examine the history of the anti-trafficking movement so that we understand the motivations of organizations and map their interaction with one another. Rhetoric and framing are important components in the development of alliances and networks. The ideological camps are still firmly entrenched, and we can anticipate a trajectory of continued debate.

QUESTIONS

INDIVIDUAL STUDY QUESTIONS

1. What were some of the precursor international instruments to the Protocol to Prevent, Suppress, and Punish Trafficking in Persons, especially Women and Children (Palermo Protocol)?

2. What are the strengths and weaknesses of the Palermo Protocol?

3. What are the differences between the definition of trafficking in the Palermo Protocol and the United States Trafficking Victims Protection Act?

4. What was the most significant source of tension for those organizations and individuals negotiating the Protocol in Vienna?

5. How was the interest in trafficking rekindled for the international community in the 1990s?

6. What is the nature of the problem of human trafficking experienced by the United States?

GROUP DISCUSSION QUESTIONS

1. What are the differences and similarities between the way that trafficking was framed at the turn of the twentieth century and then at the twenty-first century?

2. How were contemporary norms to combat human trafficking developed?

3. How was the women's human rights movement connected to the movement to combat human trafficking?

4. What role do the United States Government and organizations play in enforcing contemporary norms to combat human trafficking?

5. How has the rhetoric of slavery played a role in mobilizing activism against trafficking?

6. What were the motivations of US Congressional leaders to address human trafficking in the United States?

FURTHER READING

Anderson, B. and **O'Connell Davidson**, J. (2002). *Trafficking—A Demand Led Problem?* Washington, DC: Save the Children.
The authors review current debates and research on the demand side of trafficking, arguing that the demand aspect of trafficking is problematized by the various definitional and political challenges that surround the issue and that questions about supply and demand cannot be separated in the analysis of any given market.

Bales, K. and **Lize**, S. (2005). *Trafficking in Persons in the United States*. Washington, DC: National Institute of Justice.
Commissioned by the National Institute of Justice, the research by Bales and Lize opens a window on how people are trafficked into the United States and how the US Government is using the available legal tools to address this problem.

Barry, K. (1979). *Female Sexual Slavery*. New York: New York University Press.
Barry, considered to be an abolitionist feminist, argues that men are responsible for constructing social institutions that allow the exploitation and objectification of women to occur.

Chuang, J. (2006). The United States as global sheriff: Using unilateral sanctions to combat trafficking. *Michigan Journal of International Law*, **27**, 437–494.
Chuang argues that the United States Government has undermined and replaced the United Nations as the global enforcer of anti-trafficking norms. She questions the usefulness of the sanctions that the US Government can impose on other governments that do not comply with the norms defined by the Trafficking Victims Protection Act of 2000.

Doezema, J. (2002). Who gets to choose? Coercion, consent and the UN trafficking protocol. *Gender and Development*, **10**/1, 20–27.
Doezema argues that the vague way in which trafficking in persons is defined by the Palermo Protocol will serve to undermine future efforts to combat human trafficking at national levels. She is particularly concerned with the global norms to address prostitution as a form of trafficking and believes strongly that voluntary prostitution is not exploitive.

Keck, M. and **Sikkink**, K. (1998). *Activists Beyond Borders*. Ithaca, NY: Cornell University Press.
Keck and Sikkink examine networks of activists that form and operate transnationally. They focus on the impact that transnational activism has had on human rights, environmental politics, and the campaign around violence against women.

Kempadoo, K. (ed.) (2005a). *Trafficking and Prostitution Reconsidered*. Boulder, CO: Paradigm Publishers.
Kempadoo and her colleagues argue against sensationalizing the issue of human trafficking. They provide alternative understandings of transnational migration, forced labour, sex work, and livelihood strategies within the context of globalization.

Lim, L. L. (ed.) (1998). *The Sex Sector*. Geneva: International Labour Office.
Lim and her colleagues show that the prostitution industry reflects other economic sectors because of its diversified structures. They also argue that prostitution is a social phenomenon related to unequal relations between men and women, and between children and parents.

WEB LINKS

http://HumanTrafficking.org An Internet resource on human trafficking in Southeast and East Asia, and the United States.

http://ChildTrafficking.com A comprehensive library on articles related to human trafficking.

http://no-trafficking.org A website of the United Nations Inter-Agency Project on Trafficking in the Mekong Greater Sub-region.

http://www.ungift.org/ Website of the United Nations Global Initiative to Fight Human Trafficking.

http://www.state.gov/g/tip Website of the United States Department of State Office to Monitor and Combat Trafficking in Persons.

http://www.childtrafficking.org/ Website of the UNICEF Innocenti Research Centre.

NOTE

1. See Bristow, 1977; Connelly, 1980; Walkowitz, 1980; Gibson, 1986; Corbin, 1990; Grittner, 1990; Irwin, 1996; Fisher, 1997.

ONLINE RESOURCE CENTRE

Visit the Online Resource Centre that accompanies this book for updates and a range of other resources:

http://www.oxfordtextbooks.co.uk/orc/goodhart/

Children's Human Rights Advocacy

Vanessa Pupavac

Chapter Contents

Reader's Guide

This chapter explores some theoretical and practical problems in global children's rights advocacy. First, the chapter discusses the novelty of children's rights and the problem of identifying the moral agent of children's rights. Who determines what children's rights and interests are, and how they are interpreted, is not straightforward. Second, the chapter explores tensions between the universalism of human rights advocacy and the relativism of development advocacy. Children's rights research is influenced by social constructivist theories, which highlight the history of childhood and childhood norms. Early social constructivist approaches identified the concept of childhood underpinning the Convention on the Rights of the Child as a Western construction based on Western experiences and its exclusion of the experience of childhood in developing countries. Children's rights advocacy globalizes norms on childhood which arose during the industrial development of specific countries, without this economic development being universally shared or envisaged. More recent social constructivist approaches emphasize how childhood norms are constructed and therefore can be reconstructed. Third, the chapter highlights the attempt to eradicate corporal punishment of children globally as a case study of global children's rights advocacy. The chapter indicates problems with attempting to globalize childhood norms without globalizing material development.

Introduction

It is now eighteen years since the UN *Convention on the Rights of the Child* (CRC) came into force (United Nations General Assembly, 1989). Children born in the year of its creation have formally entered adulthood according to its definitions. The Convention's coming of age is encouraging children's rights advocates to take stock of its impact. The CRC is seen as creating a global geo-political social contract for children and overcoming children's previous lack of international rights. Virtually all states have ratified the document. Only two states—the United States and Somalia—have yet to do so. Advocates want to move beyond law and address deep structural obstacles to children's rights and embed the CRC's provisions into cultures globally. To what extent might children globally be empowered by children's rights? What are children's interests and who should interpret them? How do legal norms become embedded as cultural norms in different social conditions globally? This chapter is concerned first with global children's rights advocacy and the problem of children's empowerment, and second with the tensions between global norms mobilized under the Convention and international development models. Analysis of children's rights raises problems relevant to global human rights advocacy more broadly.

International Children's Rights Come of Age

The CRC was codified at the end of the Cold War, which witnessed the rising status of international human rights standards. In the three decades preceding the ratification of the two Covenants, the Universal Declaration of Human Rights (UDHR) was treated as merely aspirational in the international system (Henkin, 1981). There has only been significant international political will to consider human rights obligations binding under international law in the last two decades, although human rights advocates have argued that they were always binding. Forgotten in today's consensus on children's rights is how United Nations Children's Fund (UNICEF), as the key international children's organization, had been hostile to a children's rights convention and did not become involved in the drafting process until the mid-1980s (Black, 1996, p. 13). As UNICEF's commentary on the Convention explains, human rights agreements were 'not originally intended to have binding force' (UNICEF, undated). Yet, within a short period, UNICEF reversed its hostility to human rights approaches and now believes that they have 'gained binding character as customary law' (UNICEF, undated). Its commentary further considers that the term 'convention' as 'a formal agreement between States' is 'synonymous with the generic term treaty', although earlier international legal opinion saw them as distinct (see Chapter 2). Symbolically, the Secretary General's end-of-decade review, entitled 'We the Children' (UN Secretary General, 2001), invited comparisons to the UN Charter's opening declaration 'We the Peoples' (United Nations General Assembly, 2001), illustrating international policy makers' greater will to recognize children's rights in international politics.

The CRC outlines a framework of responsibilities that go far beyond the earlier League of Nations' 1924 and the UN 1959 Declarations of the Rights of the Child. Moreover, the Convention has been accompanied by burgeoning supplementary international and regional norm-setting documents, taking up the cause of children: the International Labour Organization's (ILO) Convention Concerning the Prohibition and Immediate Action for the Elimination of the Worst Forms of Child Labour, the Organisation of African Unity's 'African Charter on the Rights and Welfare of the Child' (OAU, 1990), and the National Plans of Action arising from the 1990 World Summit for Children—to name just the most prominent documents. The reporting mechanisms of the Convention have been complemented by UNICEF's annual publication 'State of the World's Children' or its various 'Progress of Nations' reports that expect countries to adopt global child rights policy approaches. Perhaps, more significantly,

UNICEF's concerns are being incorporated into the internationally guided national Poverty Reduction Strategy frameworks and integrated into global governance strategies although advocates want stronger laws on children's rights (Pender, 2002, 2007; Duffield, 2007). In addition, the CRC has been invoked by the Security Council as part of the revised international security strategies. Through the Security Council's use of the Convention, children's rights have significance beyond child welfare related to international peace and security. Thus the potential scope of international children's rights in international politics is far-reaching.

KEY POINTS
The CRC came into being in 1989 at the end of the Cold War.
Virtually all states have ratified the document.
The CRC outlines a framework of responsibilities and reporting mechanisms.
Children's rights concerns are being incorporated into international development strategies.
The CRC has been invoked by the Security Council.

Constructing the Children's Rights Movement

The evolving international human rights framework emphasizes the interdependence and indivisibility of rights (Donnelly, 2003, pp. 27–33). Children's rights advocates also affirm the interdependence and indivisibility of rights under the CRC. At the same time many children's rights advocates, especially the more sophisticated, would identify themselves as social constructivists. Social constructivist approaches toward human rights have become more influential in the last couple of decades and have long informed children's rights thinking. Social constructivist approaches, pioneered by Ariès (1962), have sought to explore the historically or culturally contingent character of social norms and social organization. Ariès's own account documents French society's changing historical understanding of children in the early modern period down to the very portraiture of children. Other studies have pursued both cross-country cultural and historical differences (Boyden, 1994; Burman, 1994; James and Prout, 1997). These build on earlier anthropological studies demonstrating the diverse forms of human ways of life and childhood (Mead and Wolfenstein, 1955).

Constructivist histories have also analysed the character of national and international advocacy movements for children (Platt, 1977; Parton, 1985; Cunningham, 1995). These histories identify a 'child-saving movement', which seeks to protect children, and a 'children's rights movement', which seeks to empower them. The latter needs to be distinguished from the more marginal idea of a child liberation programme, which was mooted in the early 1970s and argues for children's rights to

self-determination and freedoms similar to adults. The child-saving approach dominated international organizations until the 1980s; since then, a rights-based approach has become more common. Nevertheless, the child-saving approach persists within the framework of rights and empowerment, as will be discussed below. Tensions between child-saving and enabling approaches are revealed in debates on prohibiting the recruitment of child soldiers or child labour (Hart, 2006).

Protective Rights to Enabling Rights

Traditionally children's rights were conceived as rights of protection and welfare. This model of rights is evident in the earlier 1924 and 1959 international children's rights documents.

Constructivist thinking sees this traditional approach as paternalistic. Constructivist theories see human rights as helping constitute individuals as political subjects (Donnelly, 2003, p. 61). Moreover, as Jack Donnelly (2003, p. 16) outlines, 'human rights constitute individuals as a particular kind of political subject: free and equal rights-bearing citizens.' On this view, law is seen as an active engine of social change, rather than as simply following changes.

The human rights approach contrasts with the classical understanding of rights that premised recognition on capacity. This approach is condemned by critics as exclusionary, however, because it effectively excludes vulnerable groups most in need of being able to appeal to their rights (Federle, 1994; Freeman, 1997). Children's incapacity bars them from acquiring rights at the same time that their vulnerability renders them in need of rights to defend their interests.

Opposing the classic conception of rights as exclusionary for making capacity a prerequisite, advocates seek to reconceptualize rights as 'not premised upon capacity but . . . powerlessness' (Federle, 1994, p. 366). They emphasize the socially-constructed nature of childhood and the potential to empower children. They see the granting of rights as challenging the exclusion and powerlessness of children in which 'powerful elites decide which, if any, of the claims made by children they will recognize' (Federle, 1994, p. 344). Children's immaturity and need for special protection is not disputed. Nevertheless, recognition of children as distinct rights holders is regarded as transforming attitudes toward children as well as children's views of themselves and their participation in society (Minow, 1990; McGillivray, 1994; Franklin, 1995). The legal philosopher Martha Minow (1990, pp. 297–298) argues that, 'Including children as participants alters their stance in the community from things or outsiders to members . . . by signalling deserved attention, rights enable a challenge to unstated norms, to exclusion, and the exclusive perspectives.' CRC is distinct from earlier international children's rights approaches in codifying participatory rights, not just protective rights. Aspiring to treat children as rights holders and to promote their voices, Article 12 (1) of the CRC gives children the right to express their views in matters affecting them and for their views to be taken into account according to their age and maturity (see Box 13.1).

Capacity Gap in Children's Rights

Yet do children's rights transcend a paternalistic model? Although the child is transformed into a rights holder in children's rights discourse, the issue of powerful elites deciding 'which, if any, of the claims made by children they will recognize' (Federle, 1994, p. 344) is still pertinent. Childhood dependency may be artificially prolonged but it cannot be dismissed as a social construct (O'Neill, 1992, p. 38). The dependence of children on adults is biologically inevitable in their early years. For a period 'Children have interests to protect before they have wills to assert,' as the children's rights theorist Michael Freeman acknowledges (Freeman, 1997, p. 27). Since children lack the ability to assert their will, inherent to the notion of children's rights is the necessity of advocates acting on their behalf.

Children's enabling rights are therefore not the same as classic civil liberties in which the rights holder and the moral agent of rights are one and the same person. The concept of children's rights leaves open the identity of the moral agent to act on the child's behalf, whereas the traditional approach regarded parents (or guardians) as representing the child's interests. As the children's rights theorist Michael Freeman (1997, p. 27) has insightfully noted, 'Questions of "by whom" and "how" have not been satisfactorily answered.'

Box 13.1 Extracts from International Children's Rights Documents

League of Nations Declaration of the Rights of the Child 1924

(2) The child that is hungry must be fed; the child that is sick must be nursed; the child that is backward must be helped; the delinquent child must be reclaimed; and the orphan and the waif must be sheltered and succored;

UN Declaration of the Rights of the Child 1959

Principle 2: The child shall enjoy special protection, and shall be given opportunities and facilities, by law and by other means, to enable him to develop physically, mentally, morally, spiritually and socially in a healthy and normal manner and in conditions of freedom and dignity. In the enactment of laws for this purpose the best interests of the child shall be the paramount consideration.

CRC 1989

Article 3 (1): In all actions concerning children, whether undertaken by public or private social welfare institutions, courts of law, administrative authorities or legislative bodies, the best interests of the child shall be a primary consideration.

Article 12 (1): States Parties shall assure to the child who is capable of forming his or her own views the right to express those views freely in all matters affecting the child, the views of the child being given due weight in accordance with the age and maturity of the child.

The dependent nature of children's rights is evident under the CRC, which makes 'the best interests of the child' under Article 3a 'primary consideration', not children's views themselves (discussed in Lewis, 1998). Authorized advocates determine decisions affecting children and what they consider is in children's best interests, including how mature they consider children to be and what weight to give to their views under Article 12. In short, children's rights are interpreted and enforced by external advocates.

Who Should Represent the Child?

Who is to represent the child and define the child's best interests? How are potential conflicts of views and interests between professionals, or between the child and the child's appointed representative(s), resolved? Despite the inherent need for third party advocacy, the agent's accountability to the child is not addressed by children's rights advocates. Insofar as the question is addressed, it is in questioning the moral agency of parents. Indeed, the ultimate rationale for children's rights lies in the problematizing of parental moral agency. As Geraldine Van Bueren (1995, p. 46) observes, 'The Convention challenges the concept that family life is always in the best interests of the children and that parents are always capable of deciding what is the best interests of children.' Children's rights effectively empower officials in relation to parents, rather than empowering children. As such, children's rights advocacy, while often characterized as comparable to earlier civil rights movements, departs from the beliefs of these struggles. While classic civil liberties essentially embody freedoms from state interference, the expanding children's rights framework represents a trend toward external governance of interpersonal relations (Pupavac, 2002). Accordingly, children's rights advocacy is sceptical about the autonomy of the private sphere associated with classic civil liberties and about the ideal of the free and equal moral citizen (Arendt, 1959, p. 54; Rawls, 1973, pp. 161, 565; Mill, 1985; Habermas, 1996, p. 455). Critics warn children's rights advocacy is empowering the state to discipline ordinary people for departing from preferred professional parenting norms and risks giving a licence to repressive state powers and undermining human rights (Lewis, 1998; Pavlovic, 2007).

KEY POINTS

CRC is distinct from earlier international children's rights approaches in codifying participatory rights, not just protective rights.

Children's participatory rights in the CRC permit children a voice, but are subject to 'the best interests of the child' determined by authorized agents.

Children's rights as empowerment rights tend to challenge parental representation of children's interests, but the question of who is authorized to represent children's interests is not clear.

Children's rights express a capacity gap—children as rights holders do not have the capacity to determine their best interests and enforce their rights. Therefore, children's rights depend upon an externally authorized agent to do so. Their dependency means that children cannot hold the externally authorized agent accountable, so power relations remain.

Constructing and Reconstructing Childhood

The preamble of the CRC sets out a universal model of childhood embodying a space in which the child develops his or her personality 'in an atmosphere of happiness, love, understanding', protected from adult responsibilities and orientated toward 'an individual life in society'.

Constructivist approaches show that a particular history underlies the norms of childhood and children's rights globalized through the CRC—namely, the industrialization of European and North American societies (see Box 13.2). Industrialization culminated in removing children from the workforce and incrementally extending childhood as a period of education and play, free from employment and other adult responsibilities (Berger *et al.*, 1974, pp. 171–174; Boyden, 1990; Cunningham, 1995; Cox, 1996).

Donnelly (2003, p. 71) has questioned the *genetic fallacy* or the belief that because the concepts of human

> ### Box 13.2 **Construction of Childhood**
>
> Medieval art until about the 12th century did not know childhood or did not attempt to portray it. It is hard to believe that this neglect was due to incompetence or incapacity; it seems more probable that there was no place for childhood in the medieval world. An Ottonian miniature of the 12th century provides us with a striking example of the deformation which an artist at that time would inflict on children's bodies. The subject is the scene in the Gospels in which Jesus asks that little children be allowed to come to Him. The Latin text is clear: parvuli (children). Yet the miniaturist has grouped around Jesus what are obviously eight men, without any of the characteristics of childhood; they have simply been depicted on a smaller scale. (Ariès, 1962, p. 33)

rights historically developed in Western societies that they are therefore only relevant to Western societies. He and others rightly argue that the historical origins of a concept or product do not rule out its applicability for other societies, whether Arabic mathematics or Chinese fireworks (Donnelly, 2003, p. 71). But what happens when historical experiences are not shared?

CRC Excluding Childhood of Developing Countries

Initially constructivists criticized the CRC for embodying a Western model of childhood and excluding the experience of children in developing countries who take on adult responsibilities much earlier than the age of 18 (Boyden, 1990, 1994; James and Prout, 1990; Burman, 1994, 1995; Franklin, 1995; Bar-On, 1996; Lewis, 1998). However, constructivist theories of children's rights are increasingly invoked by advocates to draw attention to how cultures are not fixed, as a prelude to discussing how the CRC can be mobilized to change cultural behaviour towards children.

Logically, particular historical experiences encourage particular childhood norms, and shared historical experiences encourage norms to converge. This points to a problem in global children's rights advocacy if the historical conditions that fostered the childhood norms embodied in the CRC are not universally enjoyed. The ambition to universalize these conditions was abandoned prior to the creation of the Convention, as will be explored below. Contemporary international development policy imagines a very different destiny for developing countries, involving substantial retention of traditional ways of rural survival (Pupavac, 2005; Duffield, 2007). Codifying a model of childhood derived from the social conditions of only part of the world delegitimizes other childhood experiences in different societies (Boyden, 1990, 1994; James and Prout, 1990; Burman, 1994, 1995; Franklin, 1995; Bar-On, 1996; Lewis, 1998; Hart, 2006).

Linking Material Improvement and Social Progress

Since the Enlightenment moral improvement and social progress have been linked to material improvement. The importance of material improvement for other goods has been axiomatic to secular progressive thinking. 'All human progress, political, moral, or intellectual, is inseparable from material progression', wrote the sociologist Auguste Comte (1896, p. 222). Sociology's founding writers gave weight to the relationship between material progress and cultural progress. Max Weber (1954) saw an 'elective affinity' between the rise of universal, impartial legal norms, the ideals of individual rights and equality before the law, and an impersonal public sphere and the modernizing institutions of the modern industrial economy and the state. Karl Marx (1990) specifically located the rise of universal legal norms in capitalist market relations. Notwithstanding the important distinctions between classic sociology and Marxist approaches, both emphasized the importance of advances in technological production (Berger et al., 1974, pp. 29–43, 90–105).

Conversely, a society based around household production fosters particular communal obligations, kinship duties, and a personalized public sphere. The personalized character of social relations and obligations in traditional non-industrial societies circumscribe the operation of universal impartial legal norms and autonomous rights. A weak productive capacity limits the welfare resources available for societal redistribution, while a weak national infrastructure limits the ability to redistribute resources equitably and effectively. The traditional (non-industrial), semi-industrial, industrial, or post-industrial character of society fundamentally conditions childhood norms as well as the scope of law and its ability to influence childhood norms.

Limits of Law to Improve Society

Previously, international policy saw legislation as only having a limited role in addressing the problems of children in poorer countries. As UNICEF argued in a 1963 report:

> In the richer countries, much can be done to meet the needs of children through legislation, and substantial resources can be mobilized for aid through community or voluntary channels. Since the number of children with serious unfulfilled needs is relatively small, it is possible to mount very effective programmes of action to deal with these needs. In the least developed countries, on the other hand, where the needs of children are most extensive, it is difficult to improve the condition of children without raising the living standards of the population as a whole. (UNICEF, 1963, p. 23)

This view clearly follows the classic sociological tradition.

An alternative strand of sociology views society as the sum of interpersonal relations and social change as the culmination of interpersonal change. Contemporary children's rights advocacy is closer to the idealist strand of sociology, which emphasizes the role of professional interventions and de-emphasizes the economic and social conditions (Boyden, 1994, 1997; King, 1997, pp. 7–8). Historically, Western social reform movements, including advocacy on behalf of children, as compared to mass political movements, have tended to emphasize moral/behavioural reform more than material goods (Williams, 1963; Parton, 1985).

Social constructivist studies were previously closer to the classic strand of sociology in emphasizing the inter-relationship between norms and material conditions. However, in recent years social constructivist approaches have become increasingly non-materialist and closer to the idealist strand of sociology in how they regard society as constructed through inter-subjectivity. Idealist and non-materialist interpretations are especially marked among professional children's rights advocates. Idealist interpretations present childhood norms as constructed and therefore open to being reconstructed. Yet they effectively end up disregarding the complex integral relationship of norms to the material conditions of a society highlighted in earlier constructivist studies as they divorce normative transformation from material transformation. Contemporary approaches may acknowledge the earlier social constructivist studies, which trace distinct conceptions of childhood to the historical development from traditional to industrial to post-industrial society. But they overlook the implications of these studies for today's global children's rights advocacy when they divorce normative transformation from material transformation. Impediments to enforcing rights are commonly presented as problems of political will, even when references are made to the political economy (for example, Donnelly, 2003, p. 29).

Global advocacy believes in the universal applicability of human rights norms and wants to universalize the childhood norms arising in the post-industrial societies and embodied in the CRC, albeit with cultural modification. Conversely, international development thinking does not believe that developing countries should follow the same industrial development as the developed countries and has evolved relativist models. Global advocacy emphasizes the interdependence and indivisibility of political, social, and economic rights, but paradoxically not the interdependence and indivisibility of political, social, and economic conditions. Global policy invites the question of how childhood norms can be globalized if developing countries are envisaged as following distinct non-industrial development paths. In their decoupling of normative transformation from material transformation, global advocates echo classic philosopher–legislators, whose model of the good life focuses on spiritual goods and disparages material wants. The rest of this chapter explores tensions between the universalism of human rights advocacy and the relativism of economic development.

KEY POINTS

Social constructivist studies show how childhoods have been constructed differently historically and cross-culturally.

CRC embodies a model of childhood to the age of 18 as a period of happiness, free from adult responsibilities, which is informed by the historical experiences of the advanced Western industrial countries.

The CRC attempts to globalize childhood norms without globalizing the historical conditions that fostered those norms, i.e. normative transformation is divorced from material transformation.

Previously, studies believed that legislation could only play a limited role in improving child welfare, especially in developing countries.

Global children's rights advocacy embodies an idealist non-materialist approach to improving the condition of children.

From Universal Development to Relative Development Models

From Industrial Modernization to Non-Industrial Sustainable Development

International development was established after 1945 to address the aspirations of the newly independent states (see Chapter 10). In a political climate of heightened post-colonial expectation and Cold War competition, the aspirations of international development were nothing less than for the developing world to catch up with the industrialized world and to realize universal prosperity and well-being. The Western and Soviet blocs offered rival visions of national development to win the hearts and minds of the newly independent states (see Box 13.3). In this vein, US President Truman's 1949 Four Point Programme for Humanity outlined the need to pass on the benefits of scientific advances and industrial progress to developing countries. Thus the early decades of international development policy sought a green revolution, which would transform the hardships of rural life through the use of modern machinery and the application of scientific knowledge to improve crop yields.

International policy makers hoped modernization through industrialization would lead to the convergence of values through the convergence of living standards (Rostow, 1960). Modernization models of develop-

ment were essentially economic models of development focused on growth. Nevertheless, their approach was endorsed, not just by international economic organizations, but also by international welfare organizations such as UNICEF. In the 1950s and 1960s UNICEF viewed economic development as a prerequisite for advancing the welfare of children and argued that prioritizing national economic growth was consistent with promoting the position of children (UNICEF, 1963, 1964).

In practice, developing countries had difficulty securing capital investment unless they were of strategic interest. Western policy makers remained ambivalent about the industrialization of the Third World. They were concerned about the political and social culture of developing countries (Pye and Verba, 1965; Weiner, 1966). Did developing countries have a culture and personality conducive to fostering development? How would populations cope with change? How might parents help foster an appropriate personality in their children for development? Parents were considered to play a core role in mediating social change and preparing their children to be able to meet change in their future lives (Inkeles, 1963, p. 365). Anthropological studies commissioned by international organizations analysed modernity's destabilizing impact on traditional societies and asked how social stability could be maintained and alienation prevented in societies

---

Box 13.3 **Modernization Approaches**

Development of the 'have-not' countries will bring them closer to the 'have' countries, not only in economic terms, but also in their social, cultural, and political structure, since economic development both requires and effects modernization in all these spheres. Thus differences of interest and viewpoint among countries will be reduced, and a major barrier to international consensus formation will be removed. (Etzioni, A. (1962). *The Hard Way to Peace: A New Strategy*, p. 203. New York: Crowell-Collier)

During the early part of the development era, organizations concerned with poverty in the developing world as it affected people rather than as it affected nations concentrated their efforts in the countryside. Convention

held it that poverty in its most grinding forms was to be found in the lined face and prematurely ageing bodies of the peasant farmer and his wife, working in the fields from sun-up to sundown in everlasting backwardness and ignorance. Rural life was regarded as invariably harder than town life since all work demanded unremitting toil, prospects were severely limited, services were fewer and disease rates and illiteracy noticeably higher. . . . it was received wisdom that children born into poverty-stricken rural families were automatically worse off in terms of exposure to disease and malnutrition, as well as educationally, than their counterparts in town. (Black, 1996, p. 119) undergoing rapid change (Mead, 1953). The anthropologist Margaret Mead, who pioneered childhood studies in non-industrial societies, advised various UN agencies on their child and health policies (Mead and Wolfenstein, 1955; Mead, 1966).

The rise of development studies as a distinct subject paralleled the inauguration of international development and the need to train development professionals. It also attracted individuals who felt solidarity with post-colonial developing countries. Underdevelopment and dependency critiques of modernization policies, inspired by Marxist ideas, argued that they advanced the interests of Western countries rather than developing countries. They drew attention to international economic inequalities and how these fostered uneven development and held back developing countries (Frank, 1971; Amin, 1976). Critiques were not originally against industrialization, but rather opposed particular modernization models that they regarded as furthering Western interests. Instead they encouraged economic development independent of foreign exploitation, focusing on approaches that favoured development of non-industrial sectors, which were less dependent on external capital investment and were less tied into the relations of the world economy dominated by the Western states.

In rejecting capitalist development, critical development theorists increasingly became disenchanted with the very idea of economic development. They rejected Marx's theory that social industrial production would transcend capitalist economic relations. At the same time, they embraced environmental thinking. As a consequence, underdevelopment theories ironically adopted conservative *Malthusian* models on the limits to growth—models that Marx had refuted in his writings. Underdevelopment theories themselves and their materialist critiques were displaced by the convergence of official and radical theories around sustainable development, which are sceptical of economic growth approaches.

Alarm over Urban Alienation and Street Children

From the late 1960s a universal model of international development was questioned more profoundly both in official and radical international development thinking.

Western policy makers feared the existing economic strategies were not securing developing countries politically to the Western bloc and could jeopardize Western access to their raw materials. Alarm grew that modernization strategies were politically destabilizing societies and exacerbating social problems rather than alleviating them (Huntington, 1968). Rapid urbanization, it was feared, was creating millions of displaced people and 'rising frustrations' (Lerner, 1967, p. 28).

International development policy originally regarded urban poverty as a step up from rural poverty, as urban life provided the poor more employment opportunities and access to services, however inadequate, and viewed rural poverty as the most urgent problem (Black, 1996, p. 119). Studies continued to suggest that urban migration offered poor families the chance of upward mobility that was not available in rural areas (Nelson, 1969). Gradually, however, urban poverty came to be seen as worse, particularly in its impact on the young (Black, 1996, p. 129). Early optimism that many urban problems were transitional eroded, and fears grew that urban life eroded family ties and left the young without appropriate parental guidance. The phenomenon of street children (see Box 13.4) symbolized for many international policy makers how modernization strategies were threatening social cohesion and welfare (Black, 1996, pp. 128–130).

Social psychological approaches suggested that growing shanty towns and urban slums fostered social pathologies, producing maladjusted young people at risk of delinquency: 'social disorganization leads to the family's failure to ensure that the personality of young people develops satisfactorily, since, lacking the requisite norms, they are apt to indulge in all kinds of anti-social behaviour' (Hauser, 1961, p. 54).

Both official and radical critiques came to reject industrialization for the developing world, albeit from very different perspectives. Western policy makers feared urbanization was promoting political radicalism, while radical circles had the opposite concern that modern states created conformist individuals and that political opposition could only emerge from those outside the processes of the modern industrial state (Marcuse, 1964; Illich, 1997).

Developing countries maintained a belief in industrialization and that states should play a primary role in development, in keeping with the idea of national independence struggles. Government critics who wanted

Box 13.4 **Alarm over Urban Poverty**

The unskilled poor are streaming away from subsistence agriculture to exchange the squalor or rural poverty for the even deeper miseries of the shantytowns, favelas, and bidonvilles that, year by year, grow inexorably on the fringes of the developing cities. They . . . are the core of local despair and disaffection—filling the Jeunesse movements of the Congo, swelling the urban mobs of Rio, voting Communist in the ghastly alleys of Calcutta, everywhere undermining the all too frail structure of public order and thus retarding the economic development that alone can help their plight. (Barbara Ward (1964). The uses of prosperity. *Saturday Review*, 29 August, pp. 191–192. Cited in Nelson (1969, p. 6))

The growth of cities in the developing world and the increasing hardship experienced by many of their inhabitants were altering the terms of family life. In the traditional rural setting, children participated in the daily working round on the land or in the household as an integral part of their upbringing. . . . Few occupations in the modern city lent themselves to a parallel process of learning and working under family tutelage. But the need for all members of the family to contribute to the household economy was as severe, if not more so, because cash was needed for all basic necessities: food, shelter, water, fuel. . . .

Even if the youngster's working life began at a parent's side, it rarely stayed that way. In most cities a hierarchy of informal occupations developed, some of which were dominated by the young . . . Many such occupations exposed youngsters to hazardous influences, especially accidents. As the children became caught up in the street world, their peers often began to exert more affective influence than parents. As the bonds of family life weakened, children might gravitate to a lifestyle centred on the street . . . Some became separated from their families altogether, taking up an open-air or doorway abode, sleeping rough, living rough and sometimes descending into drugs, alcohol and crime. . . .

Until a relatively advanced stage of the urbanization and industrialization process in the developing world, the presence of children on the street and in the marketplace was so familiar a feature of the urban landscape that it had barely attracted notice. But as their numbers rose, and as in some cities their presence began to feel not only ubiquitous but threatening, the late 20th century rediscovered these child victims of poverty-stricken urban sprawl as 'street children'. This label principally described the venue in which they were noticed and their dirty and unkempt appearance; it implied a mix of abandonment, vagrancy and youthful criminality. (Black, 1996, pp. 128–129)

more resources devoted to people's basic needs also saw the state playing a primary welfare role. But development studies were linking the nation state (and national development by association) with violence—primarily through superpower military interventions and support for sympathetic military regimes in the developing world. The decline of mass political movements and Third World nationalism and the end of the Cold War together allowed international development policies to abandon the idea of developing countries catching up with the advanced industrial countries.

Rise of Sustainable Development and Anti-Materialist Development Thinking

Official and radical thinking converged around the concept of sustainable development (see Chapter 18) and basic needs. Sustainable development thinking is informed by anthropological, anti-materialist, and environmental critiques of modernity. From Schumacher's *Small is Beautiful* (1973) to the *Brandt Report* (Brandt Commission, 1980), international development thinking proposed that different non-industrial development paths were appropriate for developing countries. The sustainable development model legitimizes different material expectations for developing countries than for industrialized countries. Adopting a culturally relative and idealist perspective, it challenges earlier assumptions that developing countries should aspire to become like the advanced industrial societies. Sustainable development advocates often consciously reverse the previous stages of development models by positively contrasting the materially simpler lifestyle of populations in developing countries to the ethically inferior consumerism of Western societies.[1] Gandhi's 'Quest for Simplicity' is commonly quoted as being against Nehru's modernization vision for India (Gandhi, 1997, pp. 306–307). The influential writer Ivan Illich (1997) saw underdevelopment as 'a state of mind' and proposed a more spiritual anti-materialist model of development (Illich, 1997, p. 97). The anthropologist Marshal Sahlins suggested that a hunter-gatherer society was 'the original affluent society' and superior to modern society (Sahlins, 1997).

In this reversal, sustainable development thinking follows earlier Western romantic and cultural anthropological thinking. Modernity's incursions are commonly blamed for the worst cruelties in the developing world. In this idealized view negative aspects of traditional agricultural societies—such as the typical gender divisions of labour, conservative cultural norms, and suspicion of difference—are glossed over. The disturbing features of traditional societies are regarded as peculiar to particular groups, not as intrinsic to traditional ways of life, and therefore open to reform.

Critiques of economic growth strategies have been absorbed into international policy circles. Even the World Bank has come under the influence of anti-materialist thinking; its report *The Voices of the Poor* (Narayan *et al.*, 2000) emphasizes the spiritual and psychological aspects of poverty over the material and does not envisage substantial material transformation (Pender, 2002, 2007; Pupavac, 2005; Duffield, 2007). However, turning from modernization to sustainable development has

not addressed the problem of international development policy reproducing 'endlessly the separation between reformers and those to be reformed' (Escobar, 1997, p. 93). International relativist development and rights-based approaches are just as susceptible to criticisms of reproducing unequal relationships as the earlier modernization strategies, since they also revolve around normative programmes to reform individuals and communities.

KEY POINTS
International development policy originally promoted economic industrialization models, which saw economic modernization as encouraging the convergence of global cultural, political, and social norms.
International policy makers feared that modernization was causing political and social instability.
They feared urbanization was creating social problems such as street children, who were represented both as victims and social threats.
International development policy shifted to non-industrial sustainable development approaches.

Crisis of Economic Development and the Rise of Children's Rights

Ironically, while universal development was abandoned in the 1970s, that decade witnessed a renewed movement to universalize human rights and expand normative reform programmes. There is not the space here to consider the international political context that fostered renewed international attention to human rights (Evans, 1996, 1998; Sellars, 2002). A catalyst for UNICEF adopting a children's rights approach was its growing alarm at the impact of urbanization, economic crisis, and structural adjustment programmes on families (Black, 1996). It hoped that a children's rights approach might help prioritize the needs of children and mitigate effects of the 1980s' world recession on children.

During the debt crisis of the 1980s, UNICEF pioneered crisis management strategies under the banner

of 'adjustment with a human face' (Cornia *et al.*, 1987), selecting low-cost interventions that would have the greatest overall impact on child survival (Black, 1996, pp. 18–21). Similarly, UNICEF's Children in Extremely Difficult Circumstances programme targeted interventions at groups of children deemed particularly vulnerable. The selective interventions pioneered by UNICEF improved child survival rates but did not contribute to substantial material development. Moreover, the international retreat to selective welfare interventions designed to impact on the general survival rates of a population (Duffield, 2007) contradicts the CRC, which purports to address the rights of every individual child globally. This contradiction reflects a deeper tension in global children's rights advocacy.

Idealist Reconstructions of Childhood

There is a fundamental paradox in global children's rights advocacy, which seeks to globalize the childhood norms of post-industrial societies without globalizing the material conditions of childhood that fostered those norms. Consider how the 1990 African Charter on the Rights and Welfare of the Child proclaims that children are to be protected from 'economic exploitation' and 'performing any work that is likely to be hazardous or to interfere with the child's physical, mental, spiritual, moral, or social development' (Article 15). Even international child poverty models consciously seeing themselves as holistic and highlighting the allocation of resources overlook how the resources and means of allocation in societies organized around basic technological household production, as opposed to advanced industrial production, are qualitatively different. Yet sustainable development envisages small-scale family farming based on low or medium technology to be the backbone of the economies of developing countries. The focus on redistribution tellingly overlooks how the mode of production of predominantly agrarian societies requires child labour. Whatever romantic pastoral images sustainable development conjures up, family farming without modern machinery involves intensive labour, including child labour. Some insightful research has been conducted on the impact of the global political economy on children and problems with global advocacy for children (Lewis, 1998; Nieuwenhuys, 2000, 2001; Watson, 2006). But the implications of the sustainable development model for children have been under-explored.

Debates on universalism or relativism in human rights have focused on contention over Asian values, but have not seriously asked if universal human rights promotion is compatible with relativist models of development. Donnelly suggests 'the sharp break with traditional ways implicit in the idea and practice of equal and inalienable rights' (Donnelly, 2003, p. 76). He is rare in asking whether a rights approach requires particular social conditions to flourish, but his analysis does not satisfactorily answer the problem of grounding rights that he raises. He treats the uneven development caused by modernity as making human rights imperative rather than unrealizable. Thus Donnelly writes of how 'the conditions created by modernization render the individual too vulnerable in the absence of human rights' (Donnelly, 2003, p. 85). The prevailing idealist philosophy of human rights does not follow through the contradictions of the international political economy that undermine individuals' rights highlighted by the earlier underdevelopment theories (Frank, 1970, 1971; Amin, 1976).

> **KEY POINTS**
>
> Global advocacy is underpinned by universalist human rights models but by relativist development models.
>
> The CRC addresses the individual child, but international policies targeting selective basic needs address problems at the level of populations.
>
> Non-industrial, low-technological household economies rely on child labour, with consequences for childhood norms.

Idealist Reconstruction of Cultural Norms

How does global children's rights advocacy understand culture and changing cultural norms? Children's rights advocacy follows the idea that human rights are universally relevant with cultural modifications (Donnelly, 2003). Advocates sympathize with relativist understandings of culture and tend to eschew universalist definitions of culture as the highest achievements of humanity. The term culture is loosely used in global

advocacy, but nevertheless remains a core concept underpinning interventions. Culture is sometimes synonymous with a way of life or a people's identity, or sometimes refers more narrowly to symbolic communication. In key respects children's rights advocacy echoes anthropological and *behaviouralist* approaches toward culture, whereby each people has a culture or patterns of behaviour and recognizes cultural identity as important for a functional personality (Benedict, 1961). Thus the CRC's preamble states how the Convention takes 'due account of the importance of the traditions and cultural values of each people for the protection and harmonious development of the child.' In the same vein, it is commonly observed by advocates that the African Charter on the Rights and Welfare of the Child recognizes the responsibilities that children have toward their families as an example of how human rights advocacy does take into account regional differences (Article 31). Within the text of the CRC, Articles, 8, 29, and 30 recognize as rights the preservation of identity and enjoyment of culture. They deny a hierarchy of cultures, although they identify certain cultural practices as illegitimate. At the same time, cultural norms are regarded as learned behaviour, and as learned behaviour may be unlearnt and reformed.

Here global children's rights advocacy diverges from the functionalist approach to culture, which had a strong influence on twentieth-century anthropology. Functionalism treats cultures as having an overall coherence and proposes that the integral function of cultural norms and behaviour: customs or practices, which may seem bizarre, irrational, or harmful to outsiders, will, with more cultural insight and understanding, be recognized as functional. Human rights advocacy chimes more with an influential idealist strand of anthropology, which treats culture as distinct from social organization (Kuper, 1999). In this vein, human rights advocates refer to culture as a site of contestation (Donnelly, 2003, p. 102), made up of 'fluid complexes of intersubjective meanings and practices' (Donnelly, 2003, p. 86). The model of indeterminate cultural flux over cultural coherence loses the social analytical understanding of the interdependence of cultural norms, ways of life, and material social conditions.

Paradox of International Cultural Reform Programmes

To what extent can the norms of behaviour toward children in traditional societies be changed while retaining their traditional economic organization around family labour? If childhood norms are to transform substantially then the underlying material social conditions also need to transform substantially. Global advocates want to respect traditional ways of life without sustaining their negative features, such as female genital mutilation or harsh corporal punishment. Thus the African Charter on the Rights and Welfare of the Child stresses 'the preservation and strengthening of positive African morals, traditional values and cultures' as part of children's education (Article 11), while stipulating that states discourage harmful practices (Article 3). Advocates want to use culture as a flexible resource, picking up those aspects of it that they like while rejecting its disturbing aspects. But how convincing is an *à la carte* approach to culture?

Global children's rights advocacy does not explain why people would or should make significant changes in their personal relationships and behaviour in the absence of broader social change. People's security in household subsistence farming is inherently precarious and subject to the forces of nature. Unable to rely on welfare support, they have to bear its hardships stoically and have little scope for error or experimentation. Why, if they are expected to continue their traditional way of life in its essentials, would they venture to adopt new family norms of behaviour (see Box 13.5)? Embracing such an experiment only makes sense if their horizons are expanded, their social expectations are raised, and they see the younger generation preparing for a radically different way of life.

The problems of culture and development were familiar concerns to the early international development

---

> ### Box 13.5 **Challenges for Cultural Reform Programmes**
>
> Social structure and social relationships change more slowly than do other aspects of culture, such as agricultural practices, economic forms of exchange, fashions in clothing and housebuilding, and so on. The health worker whose programme is aimed at changing people's cultural habits in child care, diet, or sanitation may be brought up sharply against a refusal to alter a cultural habit because it will offend deep-rooted social relationship or a tenaciously held religious conviction. These aspects of cultural change, illustrating the problems inherent when modern practices are superimposed on traditional culture patterns, call for intensive study both before and during the adoption of new health programmes. (Mead, 1966, p. 54)

thinkers of half a century ago, who sought to fire populations' enthusiasm for modernization. However, prior development research showing the limited impact of public programmes that did not address social expectations seems to be neglected in today's global rights advocacy. The conservative anti-experimental character of traditional agricultural communities has long been observed by economists, anthropologists, and writers alike (Mead, 1953, pp. 185–186; Galbraith, 1964, 1977). To expect traditional communities to adopt radically different interpersonal norms is to expect them to undertake a huge social experiment. The very undertaking would involve them changing from an internally-orientated, tradition-based society to an externally-orientated, risk-taking society with wider expectations. Yet the rights-based sustainable development approach wants people to undertake this great social experiment of interpersonal norms while keeping them traditional in other respects.

Why would people expected to experiment radically with their primary intimate relationships want to adhere to the precautionary principle economically and limit themselves to low-technological sustainable development? People are invited to compare their family behaviour against global human rights standards, norms of adult–child relations derived from post-industrial societies. But why would their comparisons end there? The invitation to live up to global norms invites people in developing countries to live in real time with people in developed countries (Laïdi, 1998), even though sustainable development rules out the national development of developing countries to the standards of post-industrial states. So, while global advocates verbally sanctify modest locally-based sustainable development, their very appearance communicates non-verbal messages of cosmopolitan mobility and affluence. Anthropologists in the past observed the 'wide-spread repercussions' of even a small change (Mead, 1953, p. 192). This observation is not to imply that people cannot cope with change. Margaret Mead's study of the Manuan community showed how a 'stone age' community could adapt to modern industrial society in a generation—contrary to the cautious assumptions of anthropologists including Mead herself (Mead, 1956).

External intervention in family relationships involves serious responsibilities, especially if global policy essentially expects families to look after their own material welfare. Past anthropological studies observed how even well-intentioned welfare interventions could disturb existing family relations and thereby unwittingly undermine family bonds, with overall negative consequences for the welfare of its members. From Mead's research, 'Even when we only introduce new techniques we make a break with the sustaining tradition which gives security' (Mead, 1953, p. 181), 'where security lies in the very continuity of the individual with the social unit' (Mead, 1953, pp. 214–215). The disturbance of existing patterns of interdependencies and responsibilities risks making people's lives more insecure unless new sources of security are being created. International development thinking of fifty years ago aspired to build new national support systems and comprehensive universal public welfare services. Yet global children's rights advocacy involves trying to change adult–child relations fundamentally while expecting people to find material security in traditional relations.

Children's rights advocacy is sensitive to the anthropological concerns over changing practices 'without upsetting the basic meaning of life' (Mead, 1953, p. 204) and 'educating the people to find a place for these changes in their systems of values and beliefs' (Mead, 1953, p. 213). Global advocates consciously want their programmes to accommodate existing cultures. However, their cultural sensitivity suddenly displays a more narrow view of culture as symbolic rituals, folklore, or craftwork distinct from social practices. Revealingly, the use of the word 'practices', instead of cultural customs, is applied to those cultural features deemed by advocates as undesirable and dispensable. Thus cultural self-determination is formally affirmed on a narrow basis, and external intervention legitimized against broader cultural practices treated as arbitrary and superfluous to cultural identity. Global advocacy can end up displaying a rather superficial view of cultural change and culture as a way of life, isolating particular features of culture considered undesirable from the totality of relations.

Anthropological studies seem to be raided to find evidence of groups whose behaviour can be invoked by children's rights advocates as role models. Thus we have a pick 'n' mix social constructivism, against an earlier anthropological functionalism, which ends up treating cultural norms as rather arbitrary phenomenon that can be reformed and adopted at will. But past studies on the interdependence between development and culture could help inform substantial analysis into the continued reproduction of cultural norms, contrary to the CRC and the social barriers to realizing more humane childhood norms.

The next section examines the current campaign for the universal prohibition of the physical punishment of children as a case study of the idealist character of global children's rights advocacy.

KEY POINTS
Global children's rights advocacy raises the question of whether cultural norms can be changed without substantial material change to a way of life.
Anthropological studies understand culture as patterns of learned behaviour.
Earlier anthropological studies understood culture in functionalist terms, i.e. cultural norms and practices were coherent within a particular community's way of life, although outsiders may find them abhorrent.
Earlier studies concluded that it was difficult to change the cultural norms of communities in the absence of social change.
Global children's rights advocacy follows idealist constructivist approaches that understand culture in terms of inter-subjective relations.

Case Study: Punishing Childhoods

Campaign for the Universal Prohibition of the Physical Punishment of Children

The current campaign for the universal prohibition of the physical punishment of children is useful to discuss as a case study of the idealist character of global children's rights advocacy.

Physical punishment has long been viewed as violent assault by children's rights advocates and is currently a major theme of global advocacy. However, earlier children's rights documents do not contain specific clauses prohibiting physical punishment. For example, under Article 20 on Parental Responsibilities of the African Charter on the Rights and Welfare of the Child, parents have the duty 'to ensure that the best interests of the child are their basic concern at all times', 'to secure, within their abilities and financial capacities, conditions of living necessary to the child's development', and 'to ensure that domestic discipline is administered with humanity and in a manner consistent with the inherent dignity of the child'.

International children's rights advocates are seeking to extend both international and national provisions to outlaw corporal punishment globally. Various campaigning organizations globally came together in 2001 under the Global Initiative to End All Corporal Punishment of Children (http://www.endcorporalpunishment. org/), which calls for a universal legal prohibition against all forms of corporal punishment, including smacking in the home. A number of individuals and organizations associated with the Global Initiative helped inform the UN Secretary General's study on violence against children (UN Secretary General, 2006), which supports universally outlawing corporal punishment, including in the home.

Global campaigns are beginning to influence national laws on corporal punishment of children, as the Global Initiative's 'Countdown to universal prohibition' indicates (http://www.endcorporalpunishment.org/pages/frame.html), but professionals speak of difficulties in changing attitudes among ordinary people. The physical punishment of children has progressively softened in Western countries over the last century, although what is deemed acceptable punishment among ordinary people may still clash with the views of children's rights advocates. For example, the Scottish Children's Commissioner has repeatedly attempted to introduce a law in the Scottish Parliament banning parents from smacking their children (MacMahon, 2007), although smacking remains culturally acceptable among much of the population (Schofield, 2007).

The gulf between the norms on discipline espoused by global children's rights advocates and ordinary people is much wider in developing countries. Earlier studies were aware of how discipline norms, like childhood norms in general, have a social history. Discipline gradually softened in Western industrial countries as children were freed from work and their childhood became a period of education and play. Discipline over children has relaxed in post-industrial societies, only imposing minimal social responsibilities on children and lacking strong beliefs to instil in children. Children's rights advocacy's suspicion of adult discipline over children reflects these developments.

Earlier studies on modernization in developing countries emphasized that softened cultural norms of discipline followed a shift from a traditional way of life to a modern way of life. The loosening of discipline was linked toward the growth of individualism under modernity, and this tendency was expected to be strongest amongst the middle classes who are most integrated into modern society.

> The parents characterized by modern child-rearing goals and practices are not distributed randomly within and among nations. Being products and agents of educational and economic development, they are concentrated where these processes have reached their peaks, i.e. more among educated white-collar and professional people than among the manual workers; more in the cities than in the country; more in the industrialized than the non-industrialized nations. (LeVine *et al.*, 1967, p. 223)

It was argued that, 'Movement from the traditional end of the continuum to the modern end can be accomplished in one generation, but may often take two generations of change' (LeVine *et al.*, 1967, p. 253). In short, earlier studies saw cultural change as premised on a break with traditional ways of life. Yet the historical experiences, which fostered the gentler norms that advocates wish to enforce, are not shared globally. Effectively, global children's rights advocacy aims to globalize post-industrial professional norms of childhood discipline onto non-industrial conditions.

Punishing Experience of Child Labour

Forms of discipline need to be seen in the totality of social relations. Where children are allocated social responsibilities in the household division of labour, then their community will have norms of discipline sufficient to ensure children fulfil their social roles. The persistence of rural household subsistence farming without advanced technology under international sustainable development models necessitates child labour and children disciplined to labour. The household security of all its members may be jeopardized if children do not carry out their allotted responsibilities properly. How do adults make their children consistently labour in tough conditions, irrespective of tiredness or boredom? The relentlessly demanding conditions of subsistence farming themselves are a hard physical discipline over both adults and children, leaving little leeway for error. If children are careless, then animals may be lost or crops damaged. Harsh conditions and high stakes make for tough discipline.

There is something disingenuous about condemning people to a hard way of life and condemning their rough norms of behaviour. Tough discipline is treated as superfluous to the physically onerous tasks demanded of children. However, global children's rights advocates, predominantly urban and middle class, appear to have a rather hazy romantic view of rural subsistence life, as compared to the critical attention paid to the hazards of urban life for children. Today's idealizing of traditional rural subsistence and simple technology contrasts with the original international development concerns, which sought a green revolution introducing modern machinery and high-yield crops to alleviate back-breaking rural labour and transform rural lives. In summary, past studies assumed that easing social conditions softened norms of behaviour, but present campaigns to prohibit physical punishment break the link between social conditions and cultural norms.

Delegitimizing the Developing World

Furthermore, international advocacy over punishing childhoods in the developing world has implications for the international legitimacy of developing states if the problems they face are constructed in normative terms divorced from the prevailing material conditions. There is a danger that global children's rights campaigns claim moral legitimacy against developing societies by isolating physical punishment from the harsh physical conditions of the developing world. The prevailing conditions in developing societies dictate that children take on difficult, hazardous adult responsibilities at a young age, which means that their childhood deviates from the model of safe childhood universalized as a right under the CRC. Contemporary children's rights advocacy tends to moralize the gap between the ideal of childhood under the CRC and the reality of many children's lives globally, rendering their societies in violation of their rights. As a consequence, developing countries are morally delegitimized as representatives of their children's best interests and become sites of extensive intervention under evolving relationships of global governance between the North and the South (Lewis, 1998; Pupavac, 2001).

Global children's rights advocacy, just as it mistrusts the private sphere domestically, regards the principles of sovereignty and non-interference in the internal affairs of states as cloaks for abuse. But democratic freedoms, whether of individual or national self-determination, risk being inverted in the name of children (Lewis, 1998; Pavlovic, 2007) (see Box 13.6).

KEY POINTS

Global children's rights advocates are campaigning to eradicate physical punishment of children globally.

Historically, punishment of children in the post-industrial societies softened as children were withdrawn from labour responsibilities.

The campaign to eradicate physical punishment of children abstracts the problem from the harsh social conditions of many communities globally and their need to use child labour.

Global children's rights advocacy isolates cultural norms from the material social conditions of children's lives globally.

Global children's rights advocacy risks reinforcing international inequalities, without substantially improving the welfare of children globally.

Box 13.6 **Children's Rights and Neo-Imperialism**

In effect, the Convention openly condemns southern societies for their failure to give an equal share of resources and rights to children in general, and the girl child, in particular. The demand for children's rights, although presented as a positive intervention, in actual fact, represents a fundamental intrusion into the domestic affairs of these states, effectively destroying their sovereign status, because the call carries an agenda which insists that these societies have to alter their social structures and to allocate their limited resources according to an externally constructed set of priorities. This standard—a so-called 'universal' one which is externally determined—now represents the measure of the ability of these states to fulfil the criteria of legitimate state behaviour.

Remarkably, very few advocates of this new interventionalism feel it necessary to dwell upon some of the glaring inconsistencies embedded in the discourse. It seems that the insistence on the paramountcy of the child suffices to justify a level of intrusion into southern societies of which most Victorian colonialists could only have dreamt. While it might sound good, the principle of paramountcy is as fallacious as is the notion of children's rights and global childhood. Indeed it does more than set an interventionist agenda. It globalizes a double standard which in effect condemns the South, while hiding the failures of the West itself. What is never spelled out is how children's interests are not allowed in western societies to determine how our society is organized. . . . This is hidden from view by locating the problem at the level of individual parent responsibility. But when it comes to the South, the formula is reversed: the position of children is analysed at the level of individual values, but in this case, southern *society* is held responsible.

Once this framework is in place, the positive exercise of rights is inextricably linked to outside agency and thus, outside intervention. . . .

In all essentials, what advocating children's rights means in this context is giving up the right to national self-determination. The UN Convention, from this point of view, represents the codification of a new moral division in world affairs—between the South as failure and source of problems and the West as provider and solution. Today, it suffices merely to invoke the principle of child paramountcy to demand armed international intervention into southern societies where children are threatened by armed conflicts . . . In short, what we see evolving before our eyes, is a new interventionist framework which legalizes international inequality in the guise of a new moral universalism. (Lewis, 1998, pp. 96–97)

Conclusion

The aspiration to improve children's lives globally is important. However, there are questions over whether children's rights are capable of empowering children and the extent to which legal approaches may address the problems faced by children globally. Moreover, children's rights advocacy risks inverting civil rights and democratic freedoms. There are further contradictions in contemporary global children's rights advocacy located in its normative universalism and material relativism that legitimize the perpetuation of social conditions that necessitate insecure childhoods. Selective moral campaigns based on a weak historical understanding risk distracting the development of analysis and action essential to realize a more humane world. Norms of a secure childhood cannot be globalized without universally transforming the material conditions of childhood. Post-industrial norms of childhood cannot be realized in non-industrial conditions. The fundamental interdependence between material advancement and social advancement needs to be re-established as a starting point for progressive thinking and practice that will substantially address the problems of children enduring punishing childhoods around the world.

QUESTIONS

INDIVIDUAL STUDY QUESTIONS

1. How does the CRC differ from the earlier international children's rights documents?

2. How does the global children's rights advocacy movement compare to earlier political and civil rights movements?

3. Why was UNICEF initially opposed to the creation of a convention on the rights of the child? What concerns led UNICEF to adopt a children's rights approach?

4. What is the model of childhood that underpins the CRC? How have social constructivist approaches influenced children's rights thinking? What criticisms have been made about the model of childhood in the CRC?

5. To what extent does the CRC empower children? What conceptual and practical problems exist? Consider the implications of Article 3 and Article 12.

6. Who is responsible for children's rights and against whom may the rights under the CRC be claimed? Who should have the authority to speak on behalf of children domestically or globally? What actors does the CRC empower in international relations?

7. How has international development policy changed over the decades? How does the CRC reflect changing international development policy?

8. To what extent are the social concerns of developing countries incorporated into the CRC? To what extent does the CRC recognize cultural differences? To what extent is it possible to realize the CRC norms in developing countries? What is the relationship between cultural norms and social conditions? What are the implications of the CRC for developing countries?

GROUP DISCUSSION QUESTIONS

1. What is novel about the CRC's concept of children's rights?

2. Why do critics speak of the 'fallacy' of children's rights?

3. What are the implications of the CRC for international relations? Will enforcing the CRC lead to a more just and equal world?

FURTHER READING

Black, M. (1996). *Children First: The Story of UNICEF*. Oxford: Oxford University Press.
An informative account of UNICEF changing child policies. Black explains why UNICEF was initially opposed to children's rights and why UNICEF came to adopt a children's rights approach.

Burman, E. (1994). Innocents abroad: Western fantasies of childhood and the iconography of emergencies. *Disasters*, **18**/3, 238–253.
One of various insightful articles by Burman, which discusses how Western disaster aid responses construct recipient countries as children and a form of 'disaster pornography'.

Detrick, S. (ed.) (1992). *The United Nations Convention on the Rights of the Child: A Guide to the 'Travaux Preparatoires'*. Dordrecht: Martinus Nijhoff.
Provides very useful insights into the drafting process of the CRC and the concerns of developing countries with the CRC provisions.

Freeman, M. (1997). *The Moral Status of Children: Essays on the Rights of the Child*. The Hague: Martinus Nijhoff.
One of the most sophisticated accounts of children's rights by an advocate of children's rights.

Hart, J. (2006). Saving children: What role for anthropology? *Anthropology Today*, **22**/1, 5–8.
An article usefully highlighting problems that arise for children whose lives deviate from children's rights or humanitarian models, such as child soldiers.

James, A. and **Prout**, A. (eds) (1997). *Constructing and Reconstructing Childhood: Contemporary Issues in the Sociological Study of Childhood* (2nd edn). London: Routledge.
Constructivist accounts highlighting children's different childhood globally and how they depart from the ideal of childhood embodied in the CRC.

King, M. (1997*). A Better World for Children? Explorations in Morality and Authority*. London: Routledge.
Critically analyses deficits of a legal approach to children's welfare.

Lewis, N. (1998). Human rights, law and democracy in an unfree world. *Human Rights Fifty Years On: A Reappraisal* (ed. T. Evans). Manchester: Manchester University Press.
An international relations critique of international children's rights. Critically analyses international children's rights as an anti-democratic development, which undermines the legitimacy of developing countries and legitimizes the rights of the most powerful states over weaker states.

Nieuwenhuys, O. (2001). By the sweat of their brow? Street children, NGOs and children's rights in Addis Ababa. *Africa*, **71**/4, 539–557.
One of various insightful articles by Nieuwenhuys analysing problems with children's rights programmes in practice.

Pupavac, V. (2005). Human security and the rise of global therapeutic governance. *Conflict, Security and Development*, **5**/2, 161–181.
Critically outlines how international development policies have changed over the decades from models linking material improvement and social progress to idealist models that have abandoned substantial material improvement.

WEB LINKS

http://www.ILo.org/ipec/lang--en/index.htm ILO International Programme on the Elimination of Child Labour (IPEC). The IPEC gives insights into current international approaches to the problem of child labour. IPEC has useful papers and links.

Http://www2.ohchr.org/english/bodies/crc/index.htm UN Committee on the Rights of the Child. The Committee reviews national implementation of the CRC and its website includes national reports submitted to the Committee and the Committee's evaluations and recommendations.

http://www.unicef.org UNICEF, as the leading international children's organization, is a Core source of international children's rights policies and programmes.

http://www.unicef-irc.org/ The UNICEF Innocenti Research Centre collates research on children globally related to UNICEF's mandate and implementation of the CRC. The centre has useful databases and research papers highlighting the challenges to effective implementation of the CRC.

http://www1.umn.edu/humanrts/crc/crc-page.html University of Minnesota Human Rights Library, Committee on the Rights of the Child. A usefully organized set of core children's rights documents.

NOTE

1. *The Post-Development Reader* (Rahnema with Bawtree, 1997) has a useful selection of some of the key texts of relativist development thinking.

ONLINE RESOURCE CENTRE

Visit the Online Resource Centre that accompanies this book for updates and a range of other resources:

http://www.oxfordtextbooks.co.uk/orc/goodhart/

Human Rights and
Forced Migration

Gil Loescher

Chapter Contents

Reader's Guide

This chapter[1] outlines how the international community has prioritized the human rights protection needs of forced migrants and the difficulties that international organizations have in persuading states to observe their responsibilities to this group. It begins by identifying the human rights problems confronting forced migrants both during their flight and during their time in exile. It then outlines the differing definitions accorded refugees today and the difficulty in achieving a widely accepted definition. The chapter goes on to explain the roles and functions of the Office of the UN High Commissioner for Refugees and the international refugee regime. In particular, it explores the tensions between the regime's normative agenda of promoting refugee protection and achieving solutions to refugee problems and the constraints and challenges of states' power and interests. It explains how the regime has institutionally adapted over time in order to respond to an ever-expanding and growing crisis of forced displacement. The case study of Myanmar/Burma illustrates many of the human rights features of a protracted refugee and internal displacement crisis. Finally, the chapter concludes by examining how the international community might respond in the future to meet new and emerging challenges in forced migration and world politics and better adapt to address the ongoing tension between the power and interests of states and upholding refugees' rights.

Introduction

Human rights violations and refugee flows go hand in hand. Refugees are prima facie evidence of human rights abuses and vulnerability because people who are persecuted and deprived of their homes and communities and means of livelihood are frequently forced to flee across the borders of their home countries and seek safety abroad.

Over fifty million people are victims of forced displacement caused by wars, violence, human rights abuse, and ethnic and political tensions. This figure means that about one out of every 130 persons on Earth has been forced from his or her home. Many of them cross borders to seek safety and protection in the territory of another state and to become refugees. In some cases, they find the protection they need in a country of asylum, but they can suffer further human rights violations while in exile. Many enter refugee camps or live on the margins of overcrowded cities in the developing world. Many will remain in these conditions for years—even decades—trapped in protracted refugee situations. About two-thirds of the world's refugees today are in protracted refugee situations. The average length of major refugee situations, protracted or not, has increased from 9 years in 1993 to over 17 years today.

Forced migration is a human rights concern, but it also raises serious political and security issues. States have increasingly come to see the mass arrival and prolonged presence of refugees as a security concern and a burden on local and national economies. Refugees and migrants have been blamed for increased pressures on social cohesion and national identities, and are the focus of popular hostility in many countries. A solution to the problems of forced migration requires not only humanitarian measures, but also coordinated political and strategic responses.

Assessing the Problem

No continent is immune from mass displacement. While the refugee crisis is global, some regions of the world are more affected than others. For example, most of the world's refugees are located in the poorest developing countries, while less than 5 per cent of refugees seek asylum in the Global North. The great majority of forcibly displaced people remain within the borders of their own countries and are known as internally displaced persons (IDPs). IDPs are defined as 'persons in a refugee-like situation who have not crossed the borders of their country'.

Causes of Refugee Flows

Forced migration is often closely related to the phenomenon of failed and fragile states. The majority of refugee movements and internal displacements are caused by war, persecution, ethnic strife, weak institutions, and sharp socio-economic inequalities, or a combination of these factors. The difficulty in building durable state structures in the context of deep ethnic divisions and economic underdevelopment has resulted in much of the domestic conflict and political instability that developing states have experienced. In addition, forced migrations are generated by actions on the parts of both governments and non-state actors, ranging from decrees and overt use of force to more covert persecution, intimidation, discrimination, and inducement of an unwanted group to leave. Governments and non-state actors alike take steps to effect ethnic cleansing in their areas of control, forcing out perceived enemy social classes and ethnic groups in order to consolidate political control.

Forced migrants also frequently face a number of severe human rights problems in the countries to which they flee. By seeking asylum in another country, refugees no longer enjoy the legal protection of their home country. Refugees frequently face a precarious existence, especially in host countries that forbid refugees from living in urban areas. Urban refugees lack documentation and formal legal status, and are forced to live on the margins of society. They often work for wages far below the local level, are subjected to widespread discrimination, and can be evicted from their homes and even expelled from their host country without recourse. Urban refugees without legal status typically do not have access to the education or health systems of the host country, and seldom receive assistance from international or national agencies. In most instances, urban refugees and undocumented migrants do not benefit from international protection or assistance.

Encampment and Protracted Refugee Situations

Many host governments now require the vast majority of refugees to live in designated camps, and place significant restrictions on refugees seeking to leave the camps, either for employment or educational purposes. This trend, recently termed the *warehousing* of refugees, has significant human rights and economic implications. The prolonged encampment of refugee populations leads to the violation of a number of rights contained in the *1951 UN Refugee Convention*, including freedom of movement and the right to seek wage-earning employment. Restrictions on employment and on the right to move beyond the confines of the camps deprive long-staying refugees of the freedom to pursue normal lives and to become productive members of their new societies. Faced with these restrictions, refugees become dependent on subsistence-level assistance, or less, and lead lives of poverty, frustration, and unrealized potential.

Prolonged exile, especially in confined camps, further compounds the vulnerability of certain categories of refugees, in particular refugee women and children. Significant increases in levels of domestic and sexual violence occur in situations where employment opportunities are restricted, freedom of movement curtailed, and where refugees are fully dependent on international assistance to survive over long periods of time. Likewise, prolonged exile and encampment can often lead to a breakdown of family structures, placing additional burdens on refugee women. Refugee children also face particular challenges. Opportunities for secondary or post-secondary education are often denied them. Many camps have strict control mechanisms administered by host government forces or by the refugees themselves to make certain that security is maintained. Armed groups among the exiled communities often exert firm control over refugee populations and this leads to frequent instances of the forced recruitment of child soldiers from the camps. Finally, in situations where refugee youths lack opportunities and see no prospect for the future, they frequently turn to delinquency and petty crime. Prolonged exile also places disproportionate burdens on disabled and medically vulnerable refugees, including the elderly. Programmes for social support, counselling, and rehabilitation are often among the first to go if there are funding cuts.

Asylum Flows to Industrialized Countries

Those refugees who do not find protection and safety in nearby host countries travel across continents to seek asylum in the industrialized countries. In response to increasing numbers of asylum seekers trying to gain access to their territories, Western governments have installed a number of restrictive measures impeding and deterring entry. Human rights organizations such as Amnesty International and Human Rights Watch have documented numerous cases of asylum seekers, including vulnerable women and unaccompanied children, being routinely detained, maltreated, or sexually abused. Some governments deny asylum seekers work permits or meaningful social assistance while they await their claims being heard. At times, asylum seekers are forcibly returned to their home countries, despite the risk to their safety. In order to circumvent the border controls put in place by Northern governments, asylum seekers are turning to illegal people traffickers to gain access to Western countries. Thus the travel arrangements of these trans-continental asylum seekers have become increasingly precarious and dangerous. International criminal syndicates get involved, making huge profits on the stealing and forging of travel documents, passports, and work and residence permits. The asylum seekers using these traffickers are in danger of physical abuse and financial exploitation, and in the worse circumstances even death. In June 2000, British customs officers at the port of Dover discovered fifty-four dead Chinese men and women who had suffocated in a sealed container truck in their failed attempt to secretly enter the United Kingdom. In recent years, thousands of desperate Africans, in search of protection or a new beginning in Europe, have drowned in the Atlantic and Mediterranean as their flimsy boats have capsized and sunk. Many Haitians fleeing poverty and strife have faced a similar fate crossing the Caribbean. Those more fortunate migrants who manage to safely reach their destinations often find that they have to turn to crime to pay off their debts to traffickers. Increasingly, illegal migrants and asylum seekers are forced to transport or sell drugs for criminal organizations, or engage in prostitution or other criminal activities.

Internally Displaced Persons

In addition to refugees and asylum seekers, the human rights plight of internally displaced persons or IDPs has risen on the international agenda. Internal displacement can be caused by conflict, environmental disaster, economic change, or large-scale development projects. Like refugees, IDPs have been displaced from their homes, suffer many of the same deprivations and human rights violations as refugees do, and are in need of protection. However, they do not receive the same rights and opportunities as refugees. While there has been a relatively clear legal and institutional framework regulating refugee protection, the IDP issue was rarely recognized or debated until the end of the 1980s. The international regime governing IDP protection and assistance has only recently begun to take shape. Since the early 1990s, a Special Representative of the Secretary General for IDPs has been appointed, a set of guiding principles on internal displacement has been compiled

and widely endorsed by states, and a new institutional framework has begun to emerge.

The global crisis of forced migration confronts the international community with a range of urgent human rights and political challenges for which there are no easy answers. This chapter attempts to address the following questions: What defines a refugee and what factors account for the recent large and sudden movements of displaced people? What international organizations exist to protect refugees? How can the Office of the United Nations High Commissioner for Refugees (UNHCR) reconcile its normative agenda of protecting refugees with the realpolitik interests of states? And how can the international refugee regime respond more effectively to forced displacement? How can the international community formulate a more comprehensive approach to the problem of refugees and other forced migrants?

KEY POINTS

Individuals fleeing persecution who cross borders to seek safety and protection in the territory of another state are considered to be refugees. IDPs are persons in a refugee-like situation who have not crossed the borders of their country.

The majority of refugee and IDP movements are caused by war, persecution and ethnic strife, weak institutions, and sharp socio-economic inequalities, or a combination of these factors.

Refugees can suffer further human rights violations while in exile through enforced encampment, discrimination, extortion and exploitation, and a number of other human rights violations.

The Problem of Defining Refugees

The growth of an international refugee regime based on the idea that refugees should have international protection has been striking, and has been a prime example of the increasing importance of human rights in global affairs over the last sixty years. International concern for refugees is centred around the concept of the protection of human rights and had its origins in the immediate aftermath of the Second World War. The experience of persecution during the 1930s and 1940s—particularly

the Holocaust, which resulted in the murder of millions of Jews, Gypsies, Slavs, and others in German-occupied Europe—had a significant impact on the response of states to victims of persecution. Consequently, human rights and justice emerged as central themes of post-War agreements and institutions. For example, Article 14 of the 1948 Universal Declaration of Human Rights (UDHR) provided that 'everyone has the right to seek and enjoy in other countries asylum from persecution.'

While this so-called 'right to asylum' was not enshrined in future agreements, significant new steps were taken to improve refugee protection. The Office of the United Nations High Commissioner for Refugees was created in 1950 in order to protect refugees and to ensure their eventual integration within either their country of origin or another country. The following year the international community formulated the Convention Relating to the Status of Refugees, which defined a refugee as:

> Any person who, owing to a well-founded fear of being persecuted for reasons of race, religion, nationality, membership of a particular social group or political opinion, is outside the country of his nationality and is unable or owing to such fear, is unwilling to avail himself of the protection of that country . . .

According to international legal norms, a refugee is a person who has fled across the physical borders of his homeland to seek refuge in another place and who, upon being granted refugee status, receives certain rights not available to other international migrants. These rights include the right of resettlement and legal protection from deportation or forcible return to his country of origin (the so-called *non-refoulement* protection). People requesting refugee status and seeking permanent settlement in a country of first asylum to which they have already fled are referred to as asylum seekers.

Regional Widening of the Definition of Refugee

Since the early 1950s, however, the question of precisely who is, and who is not, a refugee, has been one of considerable controversy. The term 'refugee' has been widened in practice beyond the 1951 legal definition to cover a variety of people in diverse situations who need assistance and protection. The most notable of these expansions is found in the OAU Convention Governing Specific Aspects of Refugee Problems in Africa, a regional instrument adopted by the Organization of African Unity in 1969, which includes as refugees people fleeing 'external aggression, internal civil strife, or events seriously disturbing public order' in African countries. The Cartagena Declaration of 1984 covering Central American refugees also goes further than the 1951 UN Convention by including 'persons who have fled their country because their lives, safety or freedom have been threatened by generalized violence, foreign aggression, internal conflicts, massive violation of human rights or other circumstances which have seriously disturbed public order' (see Box 14.1).

These regional legal norms, particularly in Africa and Central America, are in fact much more inclusive and in keeping with the actual causes of flight throughout the Global South than are those of the

---

Box 14.1 **UN and Regional Refugee Definitions**

1951 UN Convention Relating to the Status of Refugees

Geneva, 28 July 1951

Article 1 defines a refugee as a person who 'owing to well-founded fear of being persecuted for reasons of race, religion, nationality, membership of a particular social group or political opinion, is outside the country of his nationality and is unable or, owing to such fear, is unwilling to avail himself of the protection of that country; or who, not having a nationality and being outside the country of his former habitual residence as a result of such events, is unable, or owing to such fear, is unwilling to return to it.'

The 1969 Organization of African Unity Convention Governing the Specific Aspects of Refugee Problems in Africa

Addis Ababa, 10 September 1969

In addition to the definition outlined in the 1951 UN Convention Relating to the Status of Refugees, the OAU

Convention states: 'The term "refugee" shall also apply to every person who, owing to external aggression, occupation, foreign domination or event seriously disturbing public order in either part or the whole of his country of origin or nationality, is compelled to leave his place of habitual residence in order to seek refuge in another place outside his country of origin or nationality.'

Cartagena Declaration of Refugees of 1984

The declaration, like the 1969 OAU Convention, broadens the definition of the term *refugee* found in the 1951 UN Convention. Conclusion 3 includes in the refugee definition: 'those persons who have fled their country because their lives, safety, or freedom have been threatened by generalized violence, foreign aggression, internal conflicts, massive violation of human rights, or other circumstances that have seriously disturbed public order.'

UN. They respond to the reality that many refugees are in fact fleeing generalized violence and severe human rights violations in which it is often impossible for asylum seekers to generate the documented evidence of individual persecution required by the 1951 Refugee Convention. While causes of specific refugee movements may differ in terms of how they affect the direction, duration, and size of population displacements, most contemporary mass exoduses occur when political violence is of a generalized nature, such as intrastate conflicts or severe repression rather than a direct individual threat.

Recognizing these realities, the UNHCR has (in practice) broadened its protective umbrella beyond those categories of the persecuted listed in the 1951 Convention to include those who have been forcibly displaced from their countries because of internal ethnic or religious upheavals or armed conflicts (see Box 14.2). However, in recent years there has been great resistance in the West to this pragmatic expansion of the refugee definition and of the UNHCR's mandate. In the Global North, the 1951 definition, with its focus on individuals and on persecution, is used for resettlement and asylum purposes, although groups of people at risk of death or

---

Box 14.2 Comprehensive Plan of Action for Indochinese Refugees

The international response to Indochinese refugees brought to an end one of the most protracted refugee problems confronting the international community. The consolidation of power within the Socialist Republic of Vietnam after 1975 resulted in an estimated three million people fleeing Vietnam and neighbouring Cambodia and Laos in the following two decades. Most Vietnamese fled their country in small boats, and many died in shipwrecks or were targeted by pirates in their attempt to reach neighbouring countries in Southeast Asia. Humanitarianism, coupled with the geo-political interests of the United States, motivated Western states to resettle many of the 'boat people'. However, more than 550,000 Indochinese sought asylum in Southeast Asia between 1975 and 1979, far more than the 200,000 who were resettled to Western countries.

Southeast Asian governments declared in June 1979 that the scale of the crisis exceeded their ability to respond, and that they were no longer willing to accept new arrivals of boat people. This reluctance, and reports of regional states pushing boats carrying asylum seekers away from their shores, led to an International Conference on Indochinese Refugees in July 1979. This led to a *quid pro quo* agreement between Western and Southeast Asian governments. Western states agreed to resettle refugees in exchange for assurances of first asylum by Southeast Asian governments.

The agreement resulted in over one million Indochinese refugees being given temporary asylum in Southeast Asia and then resettled in the West between 1979 and 1988. However, by the end of 1988 the number of people fleeing Vietnam was increasing and the outflows included both refugees and economic migrants. The willingness of both host states in the region to offer protection to new arrivals and of Western countries to offer resettlement dramatically declined.

The Indochinese Comprehensive Plan of Action (CPA), adopted in Geneva in 1989, relied upon a three-way commitment by countries of first asylum in Southeast Asia, the main country of origin, Vietnam, and resettlement countries. Countries of first asylum in the region recommitted themselves to the principle of temporary asylum, pending a solution elsewhere. Vietnam, as the main country of origin, agreed not only to facilitate the return of those found not to be eligible for refugee status, but also to manage an 'orderly departure programme' for those fleeing the country. For their part, resettlement states agreed to resettle all those who arrived in countries of first asylum up to a certain date, and to resettle all those who arrived after the cut-off date and were determined to be refugees by individual status determination.

By 1996, the camps and detention centres in the region had been cleared in accordance with the CPA and the issue of the Vietnamese 'boat people' was finally resolved. The CPA has often been criticized by human rights advocates, especially given concerns relating to the forcible return of those determined not to be refugees and the conditions of detention in countries of first asylum. Despite these criticisms, the CPA is seen to have generally achieved its objectives of reducing the number of clandestine departures and finding extra-regional durable solutions for recognized refugees. In 1989, roughly 70,000 Vietnamese sought asylum in Southeast Asia. By 1992, this number had fallen to 41. At the same time, over 1,950,000 refugees had been resettled by the end of the CPA in 1995; 1,250,000 were resettled to the United States alone. On this basis, the CPA is seen by many as a success, and an unprecedented example of the UNHCR successfully facilitating an inter-state political agreement in order to overcome a long-standing mass exodus.

grave harm from violence if returned home are often given temporary protection.

Other Categories of Refugees and Forced Migrants

In addition to the variety of legal definitions of refugees, there are several other categories of uprooted people (see Box 14.3). For example, almost 4 million Palestinians are registered with and assisted by the UN Relief and Works Agency for Palestine Refugees in the Near East whose mandate is limited to Syria, Lebanon, Jordan, and the Israeli-occupied territories. There are also an estimated 9 to 11 million stateless persons in the world today who have lost or are denied their nationality and are without citizenship or other documentation. Those who are disenfranchised and with few rights include the Biharis in Bangladesh, the Muslim populations of Burma/Myanmar, in particular those residing in or originating from northern Rakhine state, the Bedouins throughout much of the Middle East, some Kurds in Syria, and in many populations across Southeast Asia.

There are also large numbers of IDPs, namely, people who are uprooted within their own countries because of armed conflict, ethnic strife, and natural disaster, or because of forcible relocation by their governments or opposition movements, and who do not or cannot seek refuge across borders. Many IDPs are victims of the same civil wars or ethnic strife that produce refugees from countries in conflict.

The distinction between refugees and IDPs has been based on the principle of state sovereignty. As the central tenet of international law, sovereignty has been taken to imply the territorial integrity of states and the acceptance of the principle of non-intervention in the internal affairs of states. Consequently, border crossing has been a central distinguishing feature of the refugee definition for two main reasons. Unlike refugees who have lost the protection of their home government, with IDPs, the bond between citizen and state is never entirely severed. Consequently, the primary responsibility for protecting its own population continues to rest with the home state. Also, IDPs are not necessarily within reach of international assistance. Consequently,

there has been a practical obstacle to protection that does not exist where border crossing, such as in the case of refugees, takes place.

As the number of IDPs grew from some 2 million in the early 1980s to about 25 million worldwide in the 1990s, the issue took on growing international significance (see Box 14.4). During the late 1990s and early twenty-first century, the discussion about new international norms surrounding the Responsibility to Protect, coupled with renewed efforts at UN reform to co-ordinate international responses to IDP situations, led to calls for the UNHCR to take a greater role in responding to the protection and assistance needs of IDPs. During this time, extraordinary natural disasters, such as the Indian Ocean tsunami of December 2004 and the Pakistan earthquake of October 2005, also generated massive numbers of displaced people, attracting widespread media attention. These developments led the UNHCR to become increasingly involved, not only in IDP operations, but also in international responses to those displaced by natural disasters. The UNHCR's expanded new role was finally formalized in September 2005 when the Office was assigned the lead role for protection, shelter, and camp management in IDP situations. At the end of 2007, the UNHCR was conducting a wide range of protection and assistance activities for some 18 million IDPs in twenty-four countries.

In the future, IDPs are likely to comprise an increasingly significant part of the international refugee regime. Large parts of the world are likely to suffer outbreaks of war and social disruption as climate change erodes lands, destroys farmlands, raises seas, melts glaciers, and increases storms and other natural disasters. Under such conditions, people will flee their homes and seek shelter and protection in other communities or across borders. Climate-linked migrations triggered by severe cyclones and flooding in coastal areas in Bangladesh have already caused mass migrations within the country and across the border to India. There remain serious gaps in international law regarding the protection and assistance of victims of natural disasters and climate change.

Another group in need of protection and assistance are those who have been refugees and who have repatriated to their countries of origin. Sometimes returnees go home under the auspices of the UNHCR, from

Box 14.3 **Protracted Refugee Situations**

The UNHCR defines refugee situations as protracted when the number of refugees of a certain origin within a particular country of asylum has totalled 25,000 or more for at least five consecutive years. Table 14.1 identifies thirty-three protracted refugee situations, totalling more than 5.5 million at the beginning of 2005. Industrialized countries are not included in this table. Most significantly, the data also does not include the more than 4 million Palestinian refugees under the mandate of the UN Relief and Works Agency for Palestine refugees in the Near East (UNRWA).

TABLE 14.1 Major protracted refugee situations, 1 January 2005.

Country of asylum	Origin	End 2004
Algeria	Western Sahara	165,000
Armenia	Azerbaijan	235,000
Burundi	Dem. Rep. of Congo	48,000
Cameroon	Chad	39,000
China	Viet Nam	299,000
Congo	Dem. Rep. of Congo	59,000
Côte d'Ivoire	Liberia	70,000
Dem. Rep. of Congo	Angola	98,000
Dem. Rep. of Congo	Sudan	45,000
Egypt	Occupied Palestinian Territory	70,000
Ethiopia	Sudan	90,000
Guinea	Liberia	127,000
India	China	94,000
India	Sri Lanka	57,000
Islamic Rep. of Iran	Afghanistan	953,000
Islamic Rep. of Iran	Iraq	93,000
Kenya	Somalia	154,000
Kenya	Sudan	68,000
Nepal	Bhutan	105,000
Pakistan	Afghanistan (UNHCR estimate)	960,000
Rwanda	Dem. Rep. of Congo	45,000
Saudi Arabia	Occupied Palestinian Territory	240,000
Serbia and Montenegro	Bosnia and Herzegovina	95,000
Serbia and Montenegro	Croatia	180,000
Sudan	Eritrea	111,000
Thailand	Myanmar	121,000
Uganda	Sudan	215,000
United Rep. of Tanzania	Burundi	444,000
United Rep. of Tanzania	Dem. Rep. of Congo	153,000
Uzbekistan	Tajikistan	39,000
Yemen	Somalia	64,000
Zambia	Angola	89,000
Zambia	Dem. Rep. of Congo	66,000

Note: Adapted from Loescher and Milner (2006, p. 107).

Box 14.4 **Global IDP estimates (1990–2007)**

Figure 14.1 traces the growth of both internally displaced persons and refugees (including both UNHCR mandate refugees and Palestinians under the care of UNRWA) over the past seventeen years. At the end of 2007, the global IDP population stood at an estimated 26 million, an increase of 1.5 million, or six per cent, on the previous year. This was the highest year-end estimate since the first half of the 1990s, when the global IDP population peaked as a result of the conflicts erupting in the wake of the break-up of the former Yugoslavia and the Soviet Union. With variations, the global IDP figure has been oscillating around the 25 million mark since the beginning of this decade, while the number of refugees has been declining. The yearly global IDP estimates from 1990 to 2007 are shown in Fig. 14.1.

FIGURE 14.1 The number of internationally displaced persons and refugees from 1990 to 2007.

Internal Displacement Monitoring Centre, http://www.internaldisplacement.org/8025708F004CE90B/(httpPages)/10C43F54DA2C34A7C12573A1004EF9FF?OpenDocument&count=1000

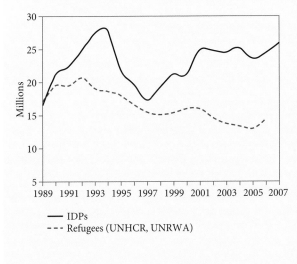

Year	Global IDP figure	Source
1989	16,500,000	USCR
1990	21,300,000	USCR
1991	22,500,000	USCR
1992	25,000,000	USCR
1993	27,500,000	USCR
1994	28,000,000	USCR
1995	22,000,000	USCR
1996	19,700,000	USCR
1997	17,400,000	USCR
1998	19,300,000	USCR
1999	21,300,000	USCR
2000	21,200,000	USCR
2001	25,000,000	IDMC
2002	25,000,000	IDMC
2003	24,600,000	IDMC
2004	25,300,000	IDMC
2005	23,700,000	IDMC
2006	24,400,000	IDMC
2007	26,000,000	IDMC

which they receive temporary assistance. But usually such people go back without international sponsorship because they do not want to be publicly known as former refugees for fear of placing themselves in danger. Moreover, there are many constraints on providing protection and assistance to returnees, especially when the conditions in the countries of refugee origin that generated the exodus continue to exist.

Economic Migrants and the Asylum–Migration Nexus

There are also those who leave their countries because of economic factors and who are thus considered to be economic migrants. These people do not qualify for UNHCR protection or assistance. However, in many developing countries that have few resources and weak government structures, economic hardships are generally exacerbated by political violence. In many poor countries, economic hardship is the proximate cause of flight, but the root causes are political. Therefore, it has become increasingly difficult to distinguish between refugees and economic migrants.

Further, the nature of displacement is fundamentally changing at the start of the twenty-first century. Globalization has created new opportunities and incentives for international migration. It has brought with it the development of improved transportation and telecommunications, new diaspora networks (comprising overseas immigrant communities with close links to their homelands), the dramatic growth of human trafficking and smuggling, and the aspirations created by an increasingly global media. These trends have contributed to ever-increasing South to North migration since the 1980s. As access to legal migration has become limited across much of the Global North, increasing numbers of both asylum seekers and illegal migrants have turned to the same trafficking channels to evade controls at border crossings and claim asylum in Western countries.

It is increasingly difficult to distinguish between those in need of international protection and those moving in search of better economic opportunities. The distinction between refugees, asylum seekers, and other migrants has become blurred, leading governments to impose stricter limits on immigration, to employ additional tactics to curb asylum claims, and to apply increased scrutiny to such claims. Western governments have adopted a series of migration control measures to deter new arrivals, by increasing pre-arrival screening, routinely detaining asylum seekers, and deporting refugees to so-called safe third countries.

The expansion of forcibly displaced persons in need of protection and assistance and the mixing of forced and voluntary migration flows today raise questions about the applicability of conventional concepts to current realities. For the purposes of this chapter, however, the term refugees refers to people who have been forcibly uprooted because of persecution or violence, regardless of whether they have left their country of origin or whether they are recognized as refugees by the governments of their host countries or by the UNHCR.

> **KEY POINTS**
>
> The UN Refugee Convention defines a refugee as: 'Any person who, owing to a well-founded fear of being persecuted for reasons of race, religion, nationality, membership of a particular social group or political opinion, is outside the country of his nationality and is unable or owing to such fear, is unwilling to avail himself of the protection of that country . . .'
>
> Despite this legal definition, the question of precisely who is, and who is not, a refugee, has been one of considerable controversy among states.
>
> Over the past six decades, the term 'refugee' has been widened in practice beyond this legal definition to cover a variety of people in diverse situations who need assistance and protection, such as victims of armed conflict and internally displaced persons.
>
> For the purposes of this chapter, the term refugees refers to people who have been forcibly uprooted because of persecution or violence, regardless of whether they have left their country of origin or whether they are recognized as refugees by the governments of their host countries or by the UNHCR.

The UNHCR, Human Rights, and the International Refugee Regime

Today, the UNHCR is widely recognized as the UN's refugee agency. The Office's 1950 Statute set out a clear mandate focusing on two principal areas: ensuring refugees' access to protection and to a solution to their plight, usually involving their return to and reintegration within their home country or their integration within a new country.

In addition, the Refugee Convention defines a list of rights for refugees. Because refugees are individuals who have fled their home country and no longer enjoy the legal protections afforded to citizens of a state, the Convention stipulated that refugees should have access to national courts, the right to employment and education, and a host of other social, economic, and civil rights on a par with nationals of the host country. However, states decided not to grant refugees a right to asylum, notwithstanding the provisions of the UDHR.

Perhaps the most significant right granted to refugees by the 1951 Convention is *non-refoulement*: the right of refugees not to be returned to a country where they risk persecution. *Non-refoulement* remains the cornerstone of international refugee protection. It would also become central to the later principle of voluntary repatriation, as states were prohibited from repatriating refugees until the dangers that confronted them in their home country had disappeared. Moreover, refugees themselves had the choice of deciding either to voluntarily return to their home countries or remain in exile.

The UNHCR and the International Refugee Regime

Since its inception, the UNHCR has been the central organization within the global refugee regime. **Regimes** comprise the norms, rules, principles, and decision-making procedures that regulate the behaviour of states. They are generally created by states in order to facilitate international cooperation in a particular issue area, such as trade or the environment. The centrepiece of the global refugee regime remains the 1951 Convention that defines states' obligations toward refugees. The Convention also explicitly identifies the UNHCR as having supervisory responsibility for its implementation. The Office, therefore, has responsibility for monitoring and supporting states' compliance with its norms, rules, and decision-making procedures.

The UNHCR and the global refugee regime were established in the immediate aftermath of the Second World War, which was a time when principles of human rights and justice played a significant role in the establishment and shaping of global institutions. During the past six decades, however, the international refugee protection regime has faced the difficult challenge of persuading states to meet their obligations toward refugees within a changing international society. Power and interests are now the dominant influences in world politics. Consequently, the international refugee protection regime has been less successful in upholding its normative agenda than in previous decades.

In response to this changing international political context, the UNHCR faces the challenge of upholding the regime while adapting its work to meet the opportunities and constraints posed by the changing context of world politics. The UNHCR's core mandate has undergone a number of changes, and the scope of its work has been expanded over time. In the 1960s and 1970s, for example, the UNHCR shifted its focus from refugees in Europe and became increasingly involved in refugee situations in the Global South. During the 1960s, violent decolonization and post-independence strife generated vast numbers of refugees in Africa. Refugee emergencies during the next decade emerged on all continents. Mass exoduses from East Pakistan, Uganda, and Indochina highly politicized refugee crises in Chile and Argentina, and the repatriation of refugees and IDPs in southern Sudan expanded the UNHCR's mission around the globe. The 1980s saw the Office shift away from its traditional focus on legal protection and assume a growing role in providing assistance to millions of refugees in camps in Southeast Asia, Central America and Mexico, South Asia, the Horn of Africa, and Southern Africa. The 1990s saw it assume a wider role in providing massive humanitarian relief and engaging in repatriation operations across the Balkans, Africa, Asia, and Central America. The late 1990s and early twenty-first century have seen the UNHCR take on ever greater responsibility for the protection of IDPs. The expansion of the Office's work to include these new areas has often been controversial, and there have been concerns that the UNHCR has been used by states in ways that may contradict or undermine its refugee protection mandate.

Constraints on UNHCR Action

Within this process of adaptation and expansion, the UNHCR has had little political power of its own. Since its inception, the Office has faced the constraints of being dependent upon the voluntary contributions of key donor states and reliant upon host governments for permission to initiate operations on their territory. About 98 per cent of the Office's funding comes from voluntary contributions from governments, and most of this comes from a small number of the major industrialized states, particularly the United States, Japan, and the European Union (EU), who exercise a disproportionate amount of influence on the organization. Governments exert leverage on the Office by earmarking about 80 per cent of their funds for programmes that are of political or strategic interest to them, such as foreign policy, security, migration, and trade relations. States also influence the UNHCR through their membership on the Office's Executive Committee, which oversees the agency's budget and advises it on policy issues.

The scope and extent of the authority of the High Commissioner are further limited by the importance that states attach to the international norms of sovereignty and non-intervention in the domestic affairs of states. The UNHCR's Statute restricts the authority of the High Commissioner to assist refugees who have crossed international borders and expressly forbids the High Commissioner from involving himself in political activities. Because the causes of refugee flows are considered to fall outside the organization's humanitarian and non-political mandate, the UNHCR is reluctant to become involved in human rights monitoring in countries of asylum.

In addition to raising money from donor governments to support its programmes, the UNHCR must secure permission from countries of asylum to operate within their territories. As a result, the world's principal refugee protection agency is reluctant to publicly criticize either host or donor governments' policies toward refugees. UNHCR officials are inclined to avoid raising delicate political questions when dealing with humanitarian issues for fear of overstepping their mandate or damaging relations with sensitive governments, most of whom would consider such intrusions to be interference in their internal affairs. The UNHCR must navigate carefully between these states' interests and the norms that it seeks to uphold.

Human Rights and the Refugee Regime

Resolving refugee problems depends on a range of human rights activities. Establishing civil societies and pluralistic political systems, reinforcing legal and government structures, and empowering local grass-roots organizations remain central to establishing conditions for refugees to return to their home countries. However, neither ensuring good governance nor respect for human rights falls within the UNHCR's domain.

The system of international refugee protection differs from the UN human rights mechanisms. No supranational authority exists to enforce the rules of the international refugee regime. There is no formal mechanism in international refugee law to receive individual or inter-state petitions or complaints. States that are parties to the 1951 Refugee Convention have not given full effect to the requirement that they provide the UNHCR with information and statistical data on the implementation of the Convention. There is no system of review of country practices through the examination of state party reports or other such information that can be used to formulate recommendations for government authorities. There are few, if any, safeguards built into the law itself to prevent abuse by states. Many governments have in recent years circumvented several of the major provisions and have exploited areas left unregulated.

In the realm of asylum, states remain the final arbiters of refugees' fates. They retain the power to grant or to deny asylum. The international refugee instruments leave it up to governments to tailor refugee determination procedures to their administrative, judicial, and constitutional provisions. States regard these procedures as part of their national sovereignty and have been unwilling to transfer this authority to the UNHCR or any other intergovernmental body.

In recent decades, this trend has been evident in the EU, where member states have greatly increased their cooperation on asylum matters and have drawn up a number of treaties and agreements regulating European refugee and asylum policies. Most of these intergovernmental discussions have been closed to outside observers, including the UNHCR, reflecting the close link between sovereignty and control of borders in Europe and the growing trend toward restrictionism in the region. In the United States, apart from the possibility of contacting government authorities to express its views, the UNHCR has no role at all in the refugee determination process.

There is an urgent need to develop a coherent and integrated approach to the defence of human rights, the protection of the forcibly displaced, and the resolution of the global refugee problem. This will continue to be an uphill struggle as long as states continue to guard their sovereignty and remain fundamentally opposed to international human rights monitoring and intervention.

Refugees as a Political, Development, and Security Concern

In addition to being a human rights concern, refugee issues also play a central role in national, regional, and world politics. With increased political and economic volatility, continuing local and regional conflicts, and new environmental pressures, states are increasingly concerned about movements of people within and across national borders. In some unstable regions, host governments fear that refugee camps on their territory will serve as bases and sanctuaries for armed groups that are sources of insurgency, resistance, and terrorist movements. Refugee crises can also have an impact on local economies and societies. The presence of refugees can sometimes exacerbate previously existing inter-communal tensions in the host country, shift the balance of power between communities, or cause grievances among local populations. Many host governments, in both the North and South, now justify restrictive policies that would not otherwise be permissible by presenting refugee populations as threats to national security and national identity.

The international refugee regime's ability to protect refugees is related in complex ways to the contemporary nature of conflict. Since the end of the Cold War, the majority of the world's wars have been intrastate conflicts, often with a complex regional dimension. Instead of engaging with the underlying causes of these conflicts, states have often left humanitarian agencies to address the most visible symptoms of those conflicts. Yet the UNHCR's ability or inability to fulfil its mandate is inextricably related to the resolution of those conflicts. If the UNHCR is to fulfil its objective of protecting and assisting refugees, states need to do a better job at conflict resolution, post-conflict reconstruction and development, and sustainable peace-building.

Too little financial and political support has been invested in rebuilding countries emerging from years of conflict, despite a virtually universal consensus that peace agreements must be consolidated by investments that improve the security and economic well-being,

not only of former adversaries and victims of conflict, but also of returning refugees. International funding invariably declines soon after ceasefires are put in place and elections are held. Assistance given to countries emerging from wars is conditioned in ways that emergency relief funds are not, with major impacts on humanitarian and social initiatives. Greater resources must be devoted over longer periods of time to catalyse sustainable forms of development and to create conditions that will prevent refugee movements from reoccurring.

Although there have been greater efforts at co-ordination between the UNHCR and development and financial institutions such as the UN Development Programme (UNDP) and the World Bank, far more effective inter-agency planning, consultation, and implementation are required. There is a widespread perception within the UN system that refugees are the UNHCR's 'problem'. Solutions to refugee situations have been more successful when they include the sustained engagement of a wide range of actors within the UN system, especially development actors, such as the UNDP. However, the roles and responsibilities of refugee and development agencies in many refugee situations continue to be determined on an *ad hoc* situation-by-situation basis. In most countries, emergency relief aid is administratively and programmatically divorced from development concerns. Unlike refugee and relief-oriented organizations, development agencies usually work on the basis of long-term plans and programmes, which makes it difficult for them to respond to unexpected events such as refugee movements or repatriation programmes. So a *development gap* exists between short-term humanitarian relief assistance and long-term development programmes. The UNHCR is not a development agency, and the task of the overall rehabilitation after an emergency or conflict has to be carried out by the UNDP, the World Bank, or by other agencies in the UN system that can more appropriately deal with reconstruction and development. This requires a full transfer of responsibility from the UNHCR to the development agencies after the immediate emergency relief phase is over. But this is something that the UNDP consistently resists because it views such programmes as being emergency responses and therefore outside its mandate, which is long-term development. Inter-agency co-ordination is especially important in the large-scale repatriations after protracted conflicts.

Political instability and new displacements are likely to occur without improved economic prospects for returnees and foreign aid and investment for rebuilding the physical infrastructure in these countries.

In countries where central government itself is weak or non-existent and therefore unable to protect its citizens, the key issues include not only how to bring together contending groups, but also how to build institutions of governance. In such situations, economic development and social stability are inseparable. Rehabilitative relief and development activities must be accompanied by support for civil society in order to be effective. Sustainable progress can only be achieved if built on a strong civil foundation that allows the gains made to be consolidated throughout society. Without this foundation, relief and development activities will constitute a one-time consumption of resources that will result in little long-term change.

In an effort to make the UN system more coherent and collaborative, the UN Peace-Building Commission was created in 2005. This new institution offers an opportunity for more collective action by a broader range of UN actors to respond to the various consequences of conflict and to find solutions for refugees. With its focus on post-conflict recovery, the Commission could play an important role in drawing together the various UN actors to address both the underlying causes of displacement and the preconditions for sustainable repatriation of refugees from neighbouring countries. At the same time, the UNHCR should ensure that the Commission does not overlook the links between refugees and the regional dynamics of peace-building, especially given the potential positive and negative roles that refugees can play in post-conflict reconstruction.

The UNHCR's current work is also taking place in a changing international security environment. The global 'war on terror' that emerged after the terrorist attacks in the USA on 11 September 2001 has reinforced states' concerns with security. This has led to increasingly restrictionist asylum policies as states have attempted to assert ever greater control over the entry of foreign nationals into their territory. Consequently, in Northern states, there has been a reassertion of the use of policies such as detention, interdiction, limitations on asylum seekers' right of appeal, and proposals for offshore processing centres. Many Southern states, meanwhile, have used the same rhetoric as do North-

ern states to further justify restrictions of refugees' rights, leading to forcible repatriation and encampment as measures to control and restrict refugee movements on their own territories.

While the UNHCR has tried to uphold its responsibilities, it has had little power other than moral authority and persuasion to fulfil this task. It has faced the challenge of working within an international political environment where power and interests dominate and define outcomes. The Office has therefore faced the question of how to reconcile its normative agenda with the self-interests of states in a rapidly changing world.

KEY POINTS

In addition to being the UN refugee agency, the UNHCR is the central organization within the global refugee regime. For sixty years, within a changing international society, the UNHCR has faced the fundamental challenge of persuading states to meet their human rights obligations toward refugees.

The international refugee regime is limited by a number of constraints. Reconciling the need to have an independent influence on states with being responsive to donor and host state interests has been a precarious balancing act for the Office. In addition to raising money from donor governments to support its programmes, the UNHCR must secure permission from countries of asylum to operate within their territories.

While resolving refugee problems depends on a range of human rights activities, there does not yet exist a coherent and integrated approach to the defence of the human rights of the forcibly displaced and the resolution of the global refugee problem.

Solutions to refugee situations have been more successful when they include the sustained engagement of a wide range of actors within the UN system, especially development actors such as the UNDP. However, the roles and responsibilities of refugee and development agencies in many refugee situations continue to be determined on an *ad hoc* situation-by-situation basis.

Refugee issues play a central role in national, regional, and world politics. The global 'war on terror' has reinforced states' concerns with security and has led to increasingly restrictive asylum policies in both the Global North and Global South as well as to policies that aim to contain the refugee problem to the regions of refugee origin.

Case Study: Forced Displacement in Myanmar

The poor human rights and political situation in Myanmar (Burma) is one of the most intractable in the world today. Prolonged conflict in that country has also caused one of the most protracted refugee situations in Asia. For over half a century, the Burmese military regime has remained in power through a dual campaign of preventing democratic change and waging war against the country's numerous ethnic nationality parties and minority groups. After decades of political repression, conflict, poor governance, corruption, and the underdevelopment of remote ethnic nationality populated border areas, Myanmar today is one of several failed and fragile states in the developing world.

The refugee rights group, Refugees International, estimates that three million people have been forcibly displaced in recent decades by these crises. The protracted conflict in Myanmar has produced huge numbers of internally displaced persons and created at least four separate but related protracted refugee situations. There are also large and protracted Burmese refugee populations in neighbouring Thailand, Bangladesh, India, and Malaysia. Tens of thousands of Burmese are physically confined in camps in Thailand and Bangladesh, where they have no freedom of movement and are without access to employment in the local community. Several generations of refugee children have now grown up in these camps and have little prospect for a decent future. In addition, over two million other Burmese eke out a meagre living in neighbouring countries as migrant workers or illegal aliens. Many of these migrants have fled Myanmar for some of the same reasons as refugees and face similar human rights problems.

There have been two principal causes of forced displacement. The first, and the cause that attracts the greatest amount of international attention, is the suppression of the Burmese pro-democracy movement, led by the Nobel laureate Aung San Suu Kyi. Her party, the National League for Democracy (NLD), was overwhelmingly elected to power in 1990. The Burmese army refused to honour the outcome and forcibly and illegitimately held on to power. In the wake of these events, the Burmese military launched an intense nationwide campaign to crush civil protest and to exterminate support for Aung San Suu Kyi and the NLD. In fear for their lives, thousands of Burmese students and political activists fled to neighbouring countries. In 2007, more widespread demonstrations against the military's political repression and economic mismanagement broke out throughout Myanmar. The army responded again with brutal force, imprisoning and torturing large numbers of political activists, including Buddhist clergy who had led some of the demonstrations.

The second cause of refugee movements from Myanmar is a result of conflict between the military regime and ethnic minority groups, such as the Karen, Karenni, Mon, and Shan, among others, who live in the eastern borderlands of Myanmar. The military has attempted to unify the country under a single territorial sovereignty and a strong central government. This has resulted in armed conflict against minority groups who are fighting for political autonomy in previously semi-autonomous border regions along the eastern border with Thailand. This struggle has produced by far the largest number of refugees.

Most displacement has occurred as a consequence of these protracted conflicts and counter-insurgency operations. The military strategy employed in the border areas seeks to undermine ethnic minority political and military organizations by targeting their civilian support base. Continuous armed conflict has directly undermined human and food security throughout Myanmar and has impoverished large parts of the civilian population. Thus huge numbers of people have been displaced as a consequence of military occupation, social control, and/or state-sponsored development activities. The Burmese army forcibly confiscates villagers' land and relocates civilians to new government-controlled villages as part of their counter-insurgency strategies and in an effort to obtain free labour and other resources. Large infrastructure projects such as the construction of dams, roads, bridges, and airports and the extraction of natural resources such as timber and minerals have required the massive forced recruitment of labour. The International Labour Organization has repeatedly criticized the Burmese Army for using large numbers of ethnic minority people as forced labour for military and development purposes.

In the wake of military repression and government economic policies in the eastern borderlands, at least half a million Burmese are currently internally displaced and without significant international assistance. Liable to various taxes and extensive forced labour, many civilians are unable to support themselves. Food insecurity, lack of education and basic health services, and the outbreak of major health crises (malaria, cholera, HIV-AIDS) have resulted in a major humanitarian and health crisis in Myanmar and left the civilian population extremely vulnerable to natural disasters such as the cyclone that devastated the Irrawaddy delta region in southern Burma in May 2008.

For the past several decades the Burmese military has clashed with ethnic minority populations all along the 2,400 kilometre Thai–Burmese border, causing large refugee outflows to Thailand. There are now approximately 150,000 Karen, Karenni, and other national minority peoples who live in nine refugee camps strung along the border. In addition, there are probably at least 300,000 refugees outside camps in Thailand, including 250,000 Shan refugees, plus at least 1.5 million Burmese migrants in Thai provincial towns and cities. For Thailand, Burmese refugees have not only posed a humanitarian problem, but have also presented a security problem for the Thai military. In the past, the Burmese military made several cross-border incursions and launched attacks on refugee camps and settlements inside Thailand.

In northern Rakhine state near the border with Bangladesh, the Burmese army has pursued a policy of discrimination against the Muslim Rohingya populations during the past several decades. Government policy has not only rendered the Muslim Rohingyas stateless, but in many instances has systematically crushed the cultural, religious, and ethnic aspirations of the Rohingya and other minority peoples, such as the Chin who live in Chin state near the border of northeast India. Such policies have led to the destruction of community life, religious environments, and local cultures. These repressive measures have contributed to the repeated waves of refugee flows to neighbouring states during the past several decades. In two separate refugee exoduses in 1978 and in 1991, over 250,000 Rohingyas fled their homes in northern Rakhine state to Bangladesh on each occasion. Some

27,000 Rohingyas remain in refugee camps, while an estimated 200,000 Rohingyas live outside the camps in Bangladesh today. Another 80,000 Chin refugees have fled similar military repression and have taken refuge in India. Tens of thousands of Burmese refugees of all ethnic groups have also sought asylum in Malaysia during the past two decades. In their desperate attempt to reach Malaysia, thousands of Rohingya have set sail in unsafe wooden trawlers from both Bangladesh and northern Rakhine state. Some of these journeys end in tragedy, with its passengers dying from starvation and dehydration.

In May 2008, a major cyclone struck southern Myanmar, killing over 100,000 people. About a million civilians were immediately made homeless. Without shelter, fresh water, and food, even more deaths from disease and starvation in the period after the cyclone seem inevitable. Despite being forewarned about this disaster, the military regime failed to prepare its population for the approaching danger. In the immediate aftermath of the crisis, the government demonstrated its incompetence and callous disregard for its citizens by refusing the entry of international aid workers and by deliberately impeding life-saving international shipments of aid that were sent by the international community. Fearing that the influx of foreign aid workers might undermine its absolute control over the population, the Burmese military preferred to ensure its own survival over the welfare of its own people. The crisis illustrates both the difficulty of helping those in extreme need without the permission of the home government and the difficulty of getting international agreement about how to protect and assist endangered people in the face of such intransigence.

The plight of IDPs in Myanmar and the presence of Burmese refugees throughout South and Southeast Asia constitute one of the most difficult and complex refugee situations in the world today. The Burmese military views the United Nations and the international aid community with great distrust, and has consistently restricted their access to displaced civilian populations. Even in the neighbouring countries hosting Burmese refugees, the UN has a limited presence. Most states in the region view refugees primarily as a security rather than a humanitarian concern. The majority of host states have not signed the UN Refugee Convention and place restrictions on the protection and assistance roles that the UN and NGOs can play in their countries. The United States and a score of other countries have resettled thousands of Burmese refugees in recent years, but a resolution to the crisis of forced displacement of the Burmese depends ultimately on achieving a political solution to the causes of the crisis. The conflict between the military regime and ethnic minorities, the denial of citizenship rights to the Rohingyas and other minorities, and the suppression of the pro-democracy movement all need to be more fully addressed before the Burmese protracted refugee situation can be fully resolved.

> **KEY POINTS**
>
> The protracted exile of Burmese refugees is a consequence of political repression, armed conflict, and military occupation in the border regions of Myanmar, and economic mismanagement.
>
> In addition to the huge numbers of exiled populations in countries neighbouring Myanmar (Thailand, Bangladesh, Malaysia, India, and China), there are hundreds of thousands of internally displaced people in Myanmar itself.
>
> Until a political solution is found for the crisis in Myanmar, there will be no end in sight for Burmese forced migrants.

The Way Forward: The Need for New Alliances and New Actors

In the current international political and economic environment, there is increasing recognition that solutions to forced migration cannot proceed solely within the mandate of international humanitarian organizations and the international refugee regime. In short, the UNHCR cannot resolve the problems of refugees, IDPs, and other forced migrants single-handedly. The solutions to forced migrations cannot be separated from other areas of international concern such as human rights, international development, peace-building, and security. Because refugee problems are multi-dimensional in nature, the UNHCR needs to build bridges between itself and organizations dealing with these other issues. This new approach to refugee problems involves an increase in the range of actors in the search for solutions, an increase in the range of issues that the refugee regime seeks to address, and an increase in the range of people it is designed to benefit.

The UNHCR as a Catalyst in the UN System

By engaging more proactively with other organizations, the UNHCR must guard against infinitely expanding its mandate and becoming a migration organization or a development organization. Rather, the UNHCR should play a facilitative and catalytic role in mobilizing other international actors to fulfil their responsibilities with respect to refugees. In order to fulfil its core mandate, the UNHCR may need to 'do more by doing less' and become more focused and strategic in the advocacy, coordination, and facilitation role that it plays.

Ensuring effective protection and access to solutions for refugees relies upon a UN system-wide approach. Although the UNHCR is the principal international organization with responsibility for refugees, the refugee regime itself goes beyond the UNHCR. Refugees should not be seen as exclusively the UNHCR's responsibility. Rather, development actors, other humanitarian actors, the UN Peace-Building Commission, and a possible UN migration organization all need to recognize their role in refugee issues. The UNHCR needs to develop clearly defined partnerships with these actors and draw upon their expertise. In order for such collaborative agreements to be effective, the Office of the Secretary General and the UN General Assembly must make other agencies aware of their responsibilities toward refugees and of the need to work cooperatively with the UNHCR. Within this overall framework, the UNHCR would have the crucial role of coordinating and facilitating the response of the UN system.

The UNHCR also needs to become a more politically engaged actor and more aware of the highly politicized environment within which it works. This environment is largely determined by the interests and capacities of states. The enduring challenge for the UNHCR when working with states is to facilitate and encourage international cooperation and burden sharing that is appropriate in scale, scope, and duration in responding to the global refugee problem.

In the future, states should ensure that they engage fully in two forms of burden sharing. States may engage in financial burden sharing by providing the resources required by the UNHCR and by host states to ensure effective protection and to find solutions. In the past, states' contributions to burden sharing have been limited and highly selective. Where such contributions have been made, they have rarely been for purely altruistic reasons. Rather, states have historically contributed to the UNHCR's annual budget or provided resettlement because they have had a perceived interest in a specific population or situation. Such interests are usually not related to refugee protection *per se*, but rather emerge from linked issue-areas. In the Cold War context, for example, contributions were often motivated by strategic or foreign policy interests. In the post-Cold War era, they are often motivated by concerns with security, migration, or development.

It is clear that the refugee regime cannot withdraw from recognizing and responding to world politics. Historically, the UNHCR has been at its most effective when it has played a politically engaged role and has been willing to recognize and engage with states' wider interests. In contrast, the UNHCR has been at its least effective when it has attempted to take on a passive and technocratic role. The challenge is to appeal to interests and engage with politics without being involuntarily shaped and moulded by political circumstances or inadvertently legitimizing the restrictionist policies of states.

KEY POINTS

The UNHCR cannot resolve the problems of refugees, IDPs, and other forced migrants single-handedly. The solutions to forced migration cannot be separated from other areas of international concern such as human rights, international development, and security. The UNHCR needs to build bridges between itself and organizations dealing with issues such as human rights, sustainable development, and peace-building.

The UNHCR should take on a facilitative and catalytic role in mobilizing other international actors to fulfil their responsibilities with respect to refugees.

The UNHCR needs to become a more politically engaged actor and work with states to facilitate and encourage international cooperation and burden sharing.

States may engage in financial burden sharing by providing the resources required by the UNHCR and host states to ensure effective protection and to find solutions. States may also engage in physical burden sharing by hosting refugees as a country of asylum, by allowing refugees to locally integrate, or by providing a solution to refugees through resettlement.

Conclusion

As the twenty-first century progresses, forced migration is likely to become one of the most significant human rights concerns. The UNHCR now works not only with refugees, but also with IDPs, returnees, stateless people, and other forced migrants. The increase in the number of persons displaced by natural disasters and a dramatic rise in the number of economic migrants around the world, along with predictions that these numbers will rise further with global warming and globalization, means that the challenge of forced migration is likely to increase in scale and complexity in the future. In practice, the definition of forced migrants incorporates many different kinds of displacement. However, there remain serious gaps in international law and inadequate institutional frameworks to deal with the range of forced migrants described in this chapter.

The UNHCR's position highlights the challenges faced by an international organization vested with responsibility for upholding the human rights of refugees in the context of a changing international society. The scope and extent of the authority of the UNHCR and the international refugee regime are limited by the continued importance attached by states to the pre-eminence of order over justice in international affairs and to international norms of state sovereignty and non-intervention in the domestic affairs of states. Perhaps, most importantly, in the wake of globalization and the 'war on terror', states' perceptions of refugees have hardened in recent years. The future protection of forced migrants is endangered by the overriding concern of states with the threats of terrorism, organized crime, and illegal migration. Whereas refugees were once viewed as victims of persecution who had good cause to seek protection, today refugees are frequently seen as illegitimate or even criminal, and are the object of active measures of exclusion. With these changing circumstances, therefore, states seem unwilling to give international action in support of refugee protection a high priority.

The protection and assistance of forced migrants go far beyond the scope of the UNHCR and the contemporary international refugee regime. Addressing this problem in the future relies upon the creation of a UN-wide collaborative institutional framework that would incorporate a more intensive role for the Office of the Secretary General, development agencies such as the World Bank and the UNDP, peace and security actors such as the UN Security Council and the UN Peace-Building Commission, and the Office of the High Commissioner for Human Rights.

QUESTIONS

INDIVIDUAL STUDY QUESTIONS

1. How are forced migrants a human rights issue?

2. What is a refugee? Does the 1951 Refugee Convention adequately define a refugee? How has the term refugee been widened over the past sixty years beyond its narrow legal definition?

3. What are the differences between the ways that refugees and internally displaced persons are treated by the international community? What special problems do IDPs present?

4. What are the major constraints facing the UNHCR in fulfilling its role of protecting and assisting refugees? What does this tell us about the problems of governance in a world in which the interests of states dominate the global agenda?

5. How have the attitudes and policies of states in the Global North and the Global South toward forced migrants changed in recent years?

6. How is the problem of refugees related to the prevalence of failed and fragile states?

7. Why is the issue of refugees beyond the scope of any single UN agency? What range of actors need to become involved in the search for solutions to the problems of forced migrants?

GROUP DISCUSSION QUESTIONS

1. From a human rights perspective, should economic migrants be entitled to the same protections as refugees?

2. How is the problem of finding solutions to refugees related to other global issues such as human rights, development, and peace-building?

3. Should the systematic repression of a population that causes a massive refugee exodus to a neighbouring country be considered 'a threat to international security' and grounds for intervention by the international community?

FURTHER READING

Feller, E., **Türk**, V., and **Nicholson**, F. (eds) (2003). *Refugee Protection in International Law: UNHCR's Global Consultations on International Protection*. Cambridge: Cambridge University Press.
Provides the documents and papers that the UNHCR, governments, NGOs, and experts used as the basis of discussions for the global consultations on refugee protection.

Goodwin-Gill, G. and **McAdam**, J. (2007). *The Refugee in International Law*. Oxford: Oxford University Press.
The standard work on international refugee law.

Helton, A. (2002). *The Price of Indifference: Refugees and Humanitarian Action in the New Century*. Oxford: Oxford University Press.
Discusses the major policy issues confronting the international community regarding humanitarian action in the early twenty-first century.

Loescher, G. (2001). *The UNHCR and World Politics: A Perilous Path*. Oxford: Oxford University Press.
Provides a comprehensive political history of the UNHCR and the refugee issue in international politics.

Loescher, G. (2003). Refugees as grounds for international intervention. *Refugees and Forced Displacement: International Security, Human Vulnerability, and the State* (ed. E. Newman and J. van Selm). Tokyo: United Nations University Press.
Argues the case for considering mass refugee outflows as a threat to international security, warranting intervention by the international community.

Loescher, G., **Betts**, A., and **Milner**, J. (2008). *UNHCR: The Politics and Practice of Refugee Protection into the 21st Century*. London: Routledge.
Provides an up-to-date analysis of the major issues concerning refugee protection and the role of the UNHCR.

Loescher, G., **Milner**, J., **Newman**, E., and **Troeller**, G. (eds) (2008). *Protracted Refugee Situations: Political, Security and Human Rights Implications*. Tokyo: United Nations University Press.
Provides a comprehensive analysis of the political, security, and human rights implications of protracted exile.

Phuong, C. (2005). *The International Protection of Internally Displaced Persons*. Cambridge: Cambridge University Press.
Provides an analysis of the legal and political implications of protecting internally displaced persons.

Steiner, N., **Gibney**, M., and **Loescher**, G. (eds) (2003). *Problems of Protection: The UNHCR, Refugees and Human Rights in the 21st Century*. London: Routledge.
A number of experts discuss the ethical, legal, and political implications of refugee protection.

UNHCR (2006). *Human Displacement in the New Millennium*. Oxford: Oxford University Press.
Examines the changing dynamics of forced displacement and the challenges to the international community, and discusses possible solutions to protracted refugee situations and IDPs.

Zolberg, A., **Suhrke**, A., and **Aguayo**, S. (1989). *Escape from Violence: Conflict and the Refugee Crisis in the Developing World*. New York: Oxford University Press.
Offers an historical account of the causes and consequences of refugee flows in the Global South.

WEB LINKS

http://www.forcedmigration.org/ Forced Migration Online is the most comprehensive website listing research sources on forced migration issues around the world.

http://www.internal-displacement.org/ The website of the Internal Displacement Monitoring Centre provides comprehensive information and analysis of the problem of internally displaced persons.

http://www.prsproject.org The website of The PRS Project details the work of this policy research project based at Oxford University and related policy initiatives and research on the issue of protracted refugee situations.

http://www.refugeesinternational.org/ The website of Refugees International, a leading NGO that provides up-to-date news, research, and advocacy on refugee situations across the globe.

http://www.unhcr.org The website of the UNHCR contains up-to-date information about the organization and the refugee populations it protects and assists globally.

NOTE

1. This chapter draws upon some of my earlier writings, including Loescher (1999, 2001) and Loescher *et al.* (2008).

ONLINE RESOURCE CENTRE

Visit the Online Resource Centre that accompanies this book for updates and a range of other resources:

http://www.oxfordtextbooks.co.uk/orc/goodhart/

Indigenous Peoples[1] Human Rights

Paul Havemann

Chapter Contents

Reader's Guide

Indigenous peoples are among the most vulnerable people on Earth, yet states are ambivalent about recognizing their rights. Several factors explain this. First, Indigenous peoples have been denied legal personality since the fifteenth century because of cultural, political, and economic differences between Indigenous peoples and Europeans and because recognition was not compatible with colonization. Second, the liberal individualism of the contemporary human rights regime fails to protect and promote the group rights of Indigenous peoples to existence and self-determination. While Indigenous peoples see these rights as inextricably linked, states regard self-determination for Indigenous peoples as an unacceptable challenge to external sovereignty and internal stability.

Introduction

Those with power to determine who does and does not have rights have for centuries simultaneously acknowledged and denied the individual and group rights of Indigenous peoples. This ambivalence has dire consequences.

The chapter begins by defining who Indigenous peoples are. Some historical context provides the background as to how indigenous rights have evolved since the 1970s and the negative consequences of ambivalence toward them. A case study examines climate change and Indigenous peoples, and the limited character of twenty-first-century human rights discourse for Indigenous peoples. The chapter concludes with a brief explanation of ambivalence toward accommodating the group rights of Indigenous peoples and some principles that could inform stronger recognition.

Three Types of Rights

Three broad, interrelated and interdependent types of human rights critical to Indigenous peoples inform the conceptual framework for this chapter: the right to existence, the right to self-determination, and individual human rights.

The right to existence is a group right inferred from the 1951 UN Genocide Convention (Thornberry, 1991) that established the right not to suffer genocide. The right to self-determination is a group right expressed in the 2007 UN Declaration on the Rights of Indigenous Peoples, which emphasizes self-government, participatory development, and free, prior, and informed consent.

Individual human rights, developed in international law within the UN framework since 1945, are expressed through a host of conventions and declarations emanating from the UN and its specialized agencies. These rights comprise: civil and political rights; social, cultural, and economic rights; and, more recently, rights to development and to a healthy and sustainable environment, among others. In the 1993 Vienna Declaration the UN declared these rights to be 'universal, indivisible, interdependent and interrelated'.

Who are Indigenous Peoples According to International Law?

Modern law and policy constantly categorize and classify people to determine eligibility for certain rights or services. For this reason, definitions of the categories 'Indigenous people', 'minority', 'peoples', and 'tribal peoples' are hotly contested (Capotorti, 1977; Daes and Eide, 2000). Moreover, the categories overlap with respect to several salient characteristics. Gudmundar Alfredsson (2005, pp. 163, 165) estimates that altogether there are 12,000 to 14,000 Indigenous and minority groups in the world who number 1.5 billion individuals and amount to about 25% of the world population.

The UN Permanent Forum for Indigenous Issues (PFII) estimates that there are 350 to 370 million Indigenous people spread across ninety states (UNPFII, 2006, 2008). Estimates suggest that there are at least 5,000 distinct Indigenous groups (IFAD fact sheet, undated). No country, not even Japan, which now grudgingly acknowledges the Ainu of Hokkaido (Hirano, 2007), is without an ethnic or national minority or Indigenous group(s).

Surprisingly, international law defines neither 'minorities' nor 'peoples'. José R. Martinez-Cobo, Special Rapporteur of the UN Sub-Commission on Prevention of Discrimination and Protection of Minorities, offered the most widely recognized definition of Indigenous peoples (see Box 15.1). Martin Scheinin (2005, p. 3) identifies three key characteristics of Indigenous people. First, they are distinctive from the dominant society and they self-identify as, and desire to be, different from that society. Second, Indigenous people are uniquely connected to their lands, which form the central element in their history, culture, economy, and spirituality. Third, Indigenous peoples assert that they are 'first in time': that they have occupied their land

Box 15.1 Martinez-Cobo's (1986) Definition of Indigenous Communities, Peoples, and Nations

Indigenous communities, peoples and nations are those which, having a historical continuity with pre-invasion and pre-colonial societies that developed on their territories, consider themselves distinct from other sectors of the societies now prevailing on those territories, or parts of them. They form at present non-dominant sectors of society and are determined to preserve, develop and transmit to future generations their ancestral territories, and their ethnic identity, as the basis of their continued existence as peoples, in accordance with their own cultural patterns, social institutions and legal system.

This historical continuity may consist of the continuation, for an extended period reaching into the present of one or more of the following factors:

(a) Occupation of ancestral lands, or at least of part of them;

(b) Common ancestry with the original occupants of these lands;

(c) Culture in general, or in specific manifestations (such as religion, living under a tribal system, membership of an indigenous community, dress, means of livelihood, lifestyle, etc.);

(d) Language (whether used as the only language, as mother-tongue, as the habitual means of communication at home or in the family, or as the main, preferred, habitual, general or normal language);

(e) Residence on certain parts of the country, or in certain regions of the world;

(f) Other relevant factors.

On an individual basis, an indigenous person is one who belongs to these indigenous populations through self-identification as indigenous (group consciousness) and is recognised and accepted by these populations as one of its members (acceptance by the group). This preserves for these communities the sovereign right and power to decide who belongs to them, without external interference.

and territories since 'time immemorial'. Now-dominant populations colonized them, dispossessing them of their land and usurping their sovereignty. Finally, Indigenous peoples experience political, economic, social, and cultural subordination to the dominant population.

Two UN special rapporteurs found the following differences between Indigenous peoples and minorities (Daes and Eide, 2000): international human rights norms accord Indigenous people a degree of autonomous development, whereas minorities are assumed to have a duty to participate actively in the larger society; the 1992 UN Minorities Declaration, unlike the draft Indigenous Declaration, did not address right to lands and natural resources; and the Minorities Declaration referred to the rights of a 'person belonging to a minority', whereas the Indigenous Declaration refers to 'peoples'.

KEY POINTS

Every state has groups of people who for linguistic, religious, or cultural reasons are not dominant.

International human rights law distinguishes among Indigenous peoples, tribal peoples, and minorities. Indigenous peoples differ in that their occupation of territory pre-dated that of the majority of the state's present population.

Indigenous peoples human rights need to be considered in terms of group rights to existence and self-determination, as well as individual rights.

Centuries of Ambivalence about the Recognition of Indigenous Peoples

From first contact, explorers, colonists, and states displayed deep ambivalence toward recognizing Indigenous people as human beings with rights to life, liberty, and ownership of property. Denial of Indigenous people's rights made it so much easier to appropriate their land and resources.

Denial of Individual and International Legal Personality

A basic organizing concept of law is that of *legal personality*. This concept allows legal orders to determine who has standing within each system to sue and be sued, own property, and enjoy the protection of the state. Those persons with standing are deemed to have the capacity to exercise rights, perform duties, bear liabilities, and exercise powers, coupled with the competence to use their capacities rationally with an understanding of the consequences of their choices. Slaves, women, and Indigenous persons (overlapping categories) were deemed to lack standing or personality on the grounds of their lack of capacity. The Euro-American legal order privileged the patriarchal authority of the individual and his right to property ownership among the bundle of individual rights accorded subjects and citizens. Citizens are eligible to participate fully in the state political–legal order. In many states citizenship was denied to Indigenous people until the late twentieth century. Initially, questions about their capacity turned on whether they were Christians and had souls and consciences to guide them. Later, states used eugenicist concepts derived from Darwinian evolutionary theory to label Indigenous peoples as not evolved or civilized enough to have sufficient capacity to be legal persons.

The concept of international legal personality evolved to identify which nations have standing as sovereign states. The Law of Nations that regulated the Westphalian model of inter-state relations from 1648 (Held, 1995) limited membership of the 'family of nations' to Christian sovereign states. Each had the right to make and enforce its own laws without interference from other states. Indigenous peoples did not qualify for international legal personality.

Much of the Westphalian model survived the creation of the UN in 1945. Only states have standing as members of the UN. International law sourced from UN activities reflects a compromise of state interests. Indigenous peoples, as peoples, have no standing due to the very limited enforceability of the self-determination right to assert their international legal personality (Meijknecht, 2001). Instead, their entitlements are expressed as duties imposed on states. In 2002 the PFII was set up to enhance indigenous participation in the UN—but half its membership is determined by states.

Territorial acquisition by European states through war, trade, and settlement profoundly affected Indigenous peoples and ecosystems all over the world. Acquisition gave the state sovereignty over the territory acquired, allowing for the establishment of extractive colonies to access raw materials and cheap labour, as well as for settler colonies where European states could send their surplus population. The Law of Nations authorized the following five modes of acquisition: prescription, the acquisition of territory based on its effective possession over a period of time; cession, the acquisition of the territory of another state through a treaty; accession or accretion, the acquisition of territory that has emerged through natural processes; conquest, the acquisition of territory by the victor in a war; and finally occupation, the acquisition of territory not under the power of another sovereign. Such territories were sometimes described as *terra nullius* (Latin for 'land of no one', i.e. uninhabited).

Colonizing states often conflated the absence of an occupying sovereign with the absence of inhabitants with legal personality recognized by civilized nations. The fact that people were already inhabiting territory acquired by occupation was highly problematic, morally and legally, for the assertion of internal sovereignty over the land and, sometimes, external sovereignty against other states. Moral or legal niceties did not, however, inhibit the acquisition of the territories of Indigenous peoples by conquest and genocide, as well as by legal sleight of hand concerning the validity of treaties of cession or peace made with Indigenous peoples.

Centuries of Debate about Indigenous Rights

Continuity, rather than any doctrinal rupture, marks the debates over Indigenous peoples rights over the centuries (see Box 15.2).

In 1492 Christopher Columbus found the periphery of the Americas but claimed that he had discovered a new route to India. Upon this 'discovery' the Catholic Church debated the status of Indigenous peoples in territories conquered by Christian kingdoms such as Spain and Portugal. European colonizers understood the acquisition of sovereignty, and hence territory, as a matter of divine law. A moral–legal question

Box 15.2 **Ambivalence Toward Indigenous Legal Personality 1492–1945**

1492 Pope Alexander VI promulgates a Papal Bull denying the legal personality of Indigenous peoples in newly discovered territories unless they are converted to Christianity.

1514 Dominican priest Bartholemé de Las Casas advocates for the rights of the 'Indians' of the Spanish Indies.

1539 Theologian Franciscus de Victoria advocates the recognition of Indigenous peoples' rights to life and property.

1550 In a formal debate with Las Casas convened by the King of Spain, scholar Juan Gines de Sepulveda describes 'Indians' as 'natural slaves' without rights.

1552 In *The Devastation of the Indies: A Brief Account* Las Casas (1992) documents genocide and enslavement of Indians in the Spanish Indies (Cuba) and advocates the recognition of their legal personality.

1604, 1625 Dutch legal scholar Hugo Grotius advocates recognizing Indigenous peoples legal personality and international legal personality, and restricting territorial acquisition under the doctrine of occupation to places that are truly *terra nullius*.

1690 English philosopher and public servant John Locke in *Two Treatises of Government* (Locke, 1960) denies the individual and international legal personality of Indian people of North America because they live in a primitive 'state of nature', lack a recognizable political system, and do not cultivate the land as Europeans do.

1743 German legal scholar J. G. Heineccus equates international legal personality with the power to resist domination and exclude other states from territory.

1763 The King of England issues a *Royal Proclamation* to regulate settler behaviour in British North America and stabilize relations with Indian nations or tribes. It reserves lands west of the Appalachians for Indians and recognizes their rights as property owners and as tribes, implying a collective legal personality.

1765 English legal scholar William Blackstone states in his *Commentaries on the Laws of England* (Blackstone, 1765–1769) that Indigenous peoples live in 'primeval simplicity' and therefore lack individual or international legal personality.

1776 Captain James Cook of the British Royal Navy sets out on a voyage of discovery with orders to acquire 'with the consent of the natives' any territory found. Landing on the southeast coast of Australia he finds ample evidence of Indigenous people but claims to have discovered an empty continent (*terra nullius*).

1787 The *Constitution of the United States* seemingly recognizes the international legal personality of Indian Tribes. The Commerce Clause (Article 1, section 8) states: 'The Congress shall have Power . . . to regulate Commerce with foreign Nations, and among the several States, and with the . . . Indian Tribes.'

1787 The *Northwest Ordinance* Article III concerning the government of territories northwest of the Ohio River recognizes the legal personality of Indians. It states:

> The utmost good faith shall always be observed towards the Indians; their lands and property shall never be taken from them without their consent; and in their property, rights, and liberty they never shall be invaded or disturbed unless in just and lawful war authorized by Congress; but laws founded in justice and humanity shall, from time to time, be made, for preventing wrongs being done to them, and for preserving peace and friendship with them.

1823 The US Supreme Court in *Johnson v. McIntosh* rejects the power of Indian Chiefs to deal in land on behalf of the Tribes, thereby denying their individual and international legal personality.

1831 The US Supreme Court in *Cherokee v. State of Georgia* recognizes the standing of Indian Tribes to have group rights in the form of limited self-government as 'dependent domestic nations', thus endowing them with partial legal personality as a group.

1837 The British Parliament accepts a report from the *Select Committee on Aborigines* containing widespread evidence of massacres of Indigenous people in Australian colonies and resolves that Indigenous peoples as British subjects shall be respected, protected, and assimilated, thereby endowing them with partial legal personality.

1895 English legal scholar John Westlake asserts that treaties made with Indigenous peoples need not be honoured, as Indigenous peoples are uncivilized and therefore do not have legal personality.

1919 In *Re Southern Rhodesia* (AC 211) the Privy Council, highest court of appeal in the British Empire, rejects the legal personality of certain Indigenous peoples who 'are so low on the scale of social organization that their usages and concepts of rights and duties are not to be reconciled with the institutions and legal ideas of civilized society.'

1921 In *Amodu Tijani v. Secretary, Southern Nigeria* the Privy Council holds that the legal personality of peoples in conquered or ceded territory ought to be recognized.

1928 In the *Island of Palmas* case the Permanent Court of International Arbitration dismisses Indigenous peoples' standing, characterizing them as 'savage', semi-civilized peoples with no international legal personality.

1933 In the *Legal Status of Eastern Greenland* case the Permanent Court of International Justice deems Greenland to be a *terra nullius*; Indigenous Inuit peoples—the majority of the population—are not considered to have legal personality relevant to the case.

1930s Various ILO conventions aim to overcome the virtual slavery of Indigenous workers by suppressing their forced recruitment and forced labour, and abolishing penal and corporal sanctions for breach of employment contracts.

was: Do Indigenous people have standing as human beings whose rights to life and property merit recognition by the conqueror? Some theologians thought not; others, asserting that ignorance of God's law ought not excuse the denial of rights to people such as the 'Indians' of the Americas, recognized the sometimes-conditional legal personality of Indigenous people. This implied their rights to life and possibly property, but not sovereignty.

In the seventeenth and eighteenth centuries other European states embarked upon imperial ventures, including the establishment of settler colonies in the New World. These states too debated the standing of Indigenous persons and peoples. Secular scholars rejected the notion that divine law conferred sovereignty, but they remained ambivalent about the standing of Indigenous people. Colonization was becoming an increasingly significant feature of imperialism, and recognizing Indigenous inhabitants as landowners would have impaired its progress. Nonetheless, one school of thought was inclined to recognize Indigenous peoples legal and indeed international legal personality.

Throughout the nineteenth and early twentieth centuries, settlers' rhetorical claims to liberal civilization clashed with their need to dispossess Indigenous peoples. The Law of Nations drew heavily on liberal legal ideology from the English-speaking world. This was exemplified by respect for sovereignty, property rights, and principles such as the rule of law to fetter the power of the state over individuals. The state was supposed to protect the rights of individual citizens to life, liberty, and property. However, the development of new political economies in the colonies was obstructed by the presence and rights claims of Indigenous peoples. The need to dispossess, disperse, or assimilate them led to coercion and unofficial genocidal practices rationalized by eugenics (distorted Darwinian evolutionary theory), infantilization, and the denial of the legal personality of Indigenous people and nations on the basis of cultural differences. Despite instances of humanitarianism and fidelity to liberal principles, in this period the overwhelming practice of states, rationalized by the

official jurisprudence, was to deny Indigenous people both legal personality as individuals and international legal personality as peoples.

After the First World War (1918), the League of Nations and the International Labour Organization (ILO) were established as state-based intergovernmental organizations (IGOs). The League principally focused on protecting national minorities as groups, but 'native' inhabitants were of concern too. It mandated some victorious states to ensure good government, including the supervision of the well-being of Indigenous peoples in the colonial territories of defeated European powers.[2]

The ILO was created, and still operates, as a tripartite organization representing states, employers, and employees in the setting and monitoring of labour standards. It became the first and most prominent IGO to focus on Indigenous people. ILO conventions impose duties on states rather than recognize indigenous rights.

Similarly, national and international courts and international law jurists also denied the international legal personality of Indigenous peoples, and so ruled them out of participating in determining their own destiny. A. H. Snow's report on the 'Question of Aborigines and the Practice of Nations' (1918) for the US State Department exemplified the dominant line of reasoning between 1918 and 1945. He constructed the relationship between 'backwards races' and 'civilized nations' as that of ward and guardian. Thus, agreements with Indigenous peoples could not be described as 'treaties' because backwards peoples had insufficient capacity as legal persons to enter into such binding international transactions.

Lack of international legal personality as peoples, tribes, or nations meant that Indigenous peoples' occupation of territory was acknowledged as merely factual occupation, not recognizable by law, until the International Court of Justice in the *Western Sahara* case repudiated the *terra nullius* doctrine in 1975. Not until 1992 in *Mabo* v. *Queensland* did the High Court of Australia repudiate the occupation of *terra nullius* as the basis of Australia's title to its territory.

The United Nations and Indigenous Group Rights

The global character of the Second World War, the failure of the League of Nations, and the experience of the Holocaust precipitated a radical rethinking of the architecture of international governance. The ILO survived. In place of the League of Nations, the UN was created to address international peace, security, and well-being.

The Triumph of Individual Human Rights Discourse 1945–1975

A new world order centred on the UN and its specialized agencies took shape. The Charter states that the 'peoples' (strangely, not the 'nations') of the UN reaffirm 'faith in fundamental human rights, in the dignity and worth of the human person, in the equal rights of men and women and of nations large and small.' The basic innovation of the UN-centred world order was the adoption of a platform of human rights for all human beings. The assumption was that the individual human rights regime would deliver equality and make group rights largely irrelevant, except in extreme circumstances. Group rights to freedom from genocide (right to existence) and to self-determination have major symbolic significance,

yet yield little practical benefit to Indigenous peoples and minority groups (Thornberry, 2002).

Ignoring the Link Between Existence and Self-Determination

Indigenous peoples see their right to existence and their right to self-determination as being inextricably linked, while states regard their own sovereignty and territorial integrity as non-negotiable.

The right to existence

The 1951 Genocide Convention implies the right to existence as a group and the recognition of group rights under certain circumstances. Under Article 2, genocide involves specified acts 'committed with intent to destroy, in whole or in part, a national, ethnical, racial or religious group. . . .' This right is limited in three important ways. First, the Convention requires proof of intent. Intention has been hard to establish. Further, the Convention omits linguistic groups. Language is often the nexus that binds the group into its culture and distinguishes Indigenous and minority groups from the dominant population. Finally, the Convention eschews the broader concept of cultural genocide or ethnocide. It took until 1998 for the first individuals to be prosecuted for offences under the Convention. These prosecutions arose from the Rwanda genocide (see Chapter 16). Only in 2007 were states first found liable, in a case against Serbia and Montenegro brought by Bosnia and Herzegovina concerning genocidal actions. The Convention has never been invoked to protect Indigenous peoples.

In 1957 the ILO Convention on the Protection and Integration of Indigenous, Tribal, Semi-Tribal Peoples (No. 107) articulated standards in terms of individual as well as, for the first time, group rights. The Convention attempted to reconcile integrationist and cultural preservationist discourses surrounding Indigenous people. Only twenty-seven state parties ratified it. Indigenous peoples repudiated it on the grounds of its paternalism and perceived assimilationist objectives, which they regarded as undermining their right to existence as peoples, tribes, and nations.

The right to self-determination

Self-determination was intended as the path to decolonization for peoples in the overseas colonies of European powers (the saltwater or blue water thesis), not for minority or Indigenous peoples within these colonies or within other established states. The group right to self-determination was first articulated in the 1960 UN Declaration on the Granting of Independence to Colonial Countries and Peoples. Paragraphs 1 and 2 champion Indigenous peoples' rights; yet paragraphs 6 and 7 severely qualify the circumstances in which the right to self-determination may be invoked, illustrating the tension between preserving the 'national unity and the territorial integrity of a country' while at the same time urging 'respect for the sovereign rights of all peoples and their territorial integrity'.

Similar ambivalence is clear in the 1965 UN Convention on the Elimination of All Forms of Racial Discrimination (CERD). This Convention reflects the international condemnation of apartheid in South Africa. It reiterates the right to equality and freedom from discrimination on the grounds of the race of individuals. Where CERD does acknowledge group rights through provision of special measures, such measures can only be temporary (Article 4). This implies that, once individual equality is achieved through the recognition of separate rights for the group, these special measures (for instance, self-government or the ownership of communal lands) would cease.

The International Covenant on Civil and Political Rights (ICCPR) and the International Covenant on Economic, Social and Cultural Rights (ICESCR) both recognize the right to self-determination in their first articles. Despite the plain meaning of the text, there is broad legal and diplomatic consensus that the right to self-determination does not apply to Indigenous peoples and minorities in the sense of secession from a state (Castellino, 2005), though it may imply self-government and limited autonomy within a state—i.e. internal self-government. Since 1977 the UN *Human Rights Committee*[3] has construed Article 27 of the ICESCR, which concerns the rights of persons 'in community with the other members of their group', as implicitly protecting group as well as individual rights (Orlin *et al.*, 2000).

After 1975: Beginning to Link Existence with Self-Determination?

By the end of the 1970s, Indigenous people and supportive non-governmental organizations (NGOs) had become an effective lobby group in the UN system as well as within some states. Canada, New Zealand, the Nordic states, and some Latin American states gave some constitutional recognition to indigenous rights to self-government. Incrementally the UN has created mechanisms to allow Indigenous peoples to campaign for greater recognition of their rights in the international arenas.

For instance, in 1977 Indigenous participants at the UN NGO Committee on Human Rights and the Indigenous NGO Conference on Discrimination against Indigenous Populations framed a draft declaration that signalled the emergence of indigenous activism that would ultimately lead to the 2007 UN Declaration on the Rights of Indigenous Peoples.

Throughout the 1980s the World Bank adopted new policies on involuntary resettlement in response to evidence of massive displacement of Indigenous people by Bank-financed projects such as dam building in Latin America. In 1982 the World Bank published 'Tribal Peoples and Economic Development: Human Ecologic Considerations'. This report stressed the link between

Indigenous people and the environment, and the risks that developments funded by the World Bank pose to them. However, rather than promoting self-determination, the report promoted the concept of reserves for some Indigenous people, as well as their 'acculturation' into the mainstream political economy. Such official policy statements operate as soft law. They illustrate the power of international financial institutions (IFIs) such as the World Bank to radically impact on the life chances of millions of people in the developing world (Spiliopoulo Akermark, 2005).

The *UN Economic, Social, and Cultural Organization* (UNESCO) hosted a committee of experts who passed the San José Declaration Against Ethnocide in 1981. This defined ethnocide to mean that 'an ethnic group is denied the right to enjoy, develop and transmit its own culture and its own language, whether collectively or individually' and declared it to be equivalent to genocide.

In 1982 the UN set up an expert Working Group on Indigenous Populations (WGIP). Until 2002 this was the sole mechanism available to Indigenous peoples in the UN context. The word 'populations' in its title carefully avoids recognizing Indigenous *peoples* as potentially self-determining peoples who could be the subjects of international law (i.e. like states, persons with standing in the international legal system). In 1986 UN Special Rapporteur Juan Martinez-Cobo delivered his major report, 'Study of the Problem of Discrimination Against Indigenous Populations', which highlighted the plight of Indigenous peoples as being among the least advantaged groups on Earth.

By the mid 1980s indigenous claims were world news, and Indigenous leaders used the politics of embarrassment to highlight injustices perpetrated by host states. In 1984 Atlantic coast Indigenous people complained to the Inter-American Commission on Human Rights about their forced integration in Nicaragua by the Sandinista Government. As a result of the Commission's findings, Nicaragua granted significant self-government to Indigenous people in the region under the 'Autonomy Statute of the Atlantic Regions of Nicaragua' (1987). This was the first recognition of indigenous self-government rights in Central America (Hannum, 1990).

The ILO continued its work with a new Convention concerning Indigenous and Tribal Peoples in Independent Countries, intended to replace the unpopular one of 1957. The new Convention (No. 169) made a modest shift in the direction of self-government for Indigenous peoples, but ambivalence about self-determination was expressed by the proviso in Article 1(3): 'The use of the term "peoples" in this Convention shall not be construed as having any implications as regards the rights which may attach to the term under international law.' The Convention nonetheless articulated the governance principle of free, prior, and informed consent as well as the right to free participation in all levels of decision making that impact upon Indigenous and tribal peoples. Further, the Convention imposed on states a duty of consultation concerning any measures affecting Indigenous peoples (Articles 6 and 7). This right to participate was subsequently affirmed in new World Bank policies requiring the participation of Indigenous peoples as well as assurances from beneficiaries of loans that Indigenous people are likely to benefit from Bank projects. The new policy also stresses the sustainability of cultural distinctiveness rather than economic growth.

Indigenous peoples' rights achieved unprecedented recognition in 1992 at the UN Conference on Environment and Development in Rio de Janeiro, also known as the Earth Summit. Participation by states (172) and NGOs (2,400) was on a scale never seen before. Even an alternative summit attracted 17,000 people. Rio Earth Summit instruments identified the duty of states to respect the traditional environmental knowledge (TEK), closeness to nature, and stewardship duties of Indigenous peoples. Four instruments—Agenda 21, the Rio Declaration on Environment and Development, the Statement of Forest Principles, and the United Nations Convention on Biological Diversity—explicitly recognized Indigenous peoples' rights, connectedness to the environment, and role in environmental conservation. One instrument, however, did not: the United Nations Framework Convention on Climate Change (UNFCCC). Only after a decade of protest were formal steps taken to increase indigenous participation.

In 1993—the UN International Year of Indigenous People—the UN World Conference on Human Rights issued the Vienna Declaration, which, on the one hand, stressed the importance of the 'effective realization of this right' (of self-determination), but on the other stressed 'the territorial integrity or political unity of sovereign and independent States . . . possessed of a Government representing the whole people belonging to the territory without distinction of any kind.' The latter concern appears to be directed at discouraging outside interference from other states in the affairs of 'States conducting themselves in compliance with the principle of equal rights and self-determination of peoples'. Principle 20 of the Declaration exhorts states to honour their obligations to Indigenous peoples in 'recognizing the value and diversity of their distinct identities, cultures and social organization', but simultaneously assumes the absolute value of 'political and social stability', which seems to preclude rights of self-determination for Indigenous peoples.

Recognition that the right to existence is inextricably bound up with the right to self-determination—the viewpoint of Indigenous peoples' organizations—was not much evident in the UN-sponsored human rights discourse of the 1990s. The exception was the expert WGIP, which presented a draft Declaration on the Rights of Indigenous Peoples to the UN Sub-Commission on the Prevention of Discrimination and the Protection of Minorities in 1993. State parties, the WGIP, and Indigenous peoples' organizations worked continuously on successive drafts, but states remained adamant that the right to self-determination was not to be explicitly stated. In 2001 this unresolved tension led the UN to appoint a Special Rapporteur on the Situation of Human Rights and Freedoms of Indigenous Peoples, with a role complementary to that of the WGIP. A year later the UN created the PFII to supersede the WGIP.

The PFII may reflect a shift from a state-centred world governance structure toward a somewhat more multi-actor, multi-centric, and multi-layered, networked form of global governance (Held, 2004; Slaughter, 2004) as no other non-state group as yet has permanent representation within the UN. The Permanent Forum serves as an advisory body to Economic and Social Council of the UN (ECSOC) concerning indigenous issues such as economic and social development, culture, the environment, education, health, and human rights. Its mandate is: to provide expert advice and recommendations on indigenous issues to the Council and, through the Council, to funds, agencies, and programmes of the United Nations; to raise awareness and promote the integration and coordination of activities related to indigenous issues within the UN system; and to prepare and disseminate information on indigenous issues.

Still, the very name given to this Permanent Forum, referring to 'Indigenous *Issues*' rather than '*Peoples*',

signifies the continued wariness of state parties about self-determination claims. The state-centric model also remains explicit in the form and process of PFII membership. ECSOC elects eight of the sixteen members from the nominees of states; the other eight are nominated by indigenous organizations, but ultimately appointed by the President of ECSOC. Members serve as individual experts and are not representatives of peoples. Membership reflects vast regions designated by the UN: Africa; Asia; Central and South America and the Caribbean; the Arctic; Central and Eastern Europe, Russian Federation, Central Asia and Transcaucasia; North America; and the Pacific.

In 2007 the Declaration of the Rights of Indigenous Peoples was finally adopted. Notable among the opposing states were initially the African states as well as Canada, Australia, New Zealand, and the US. The compromise formulation in the Declaration attempted to address flaws in preceding rights regimes from the differing perspectives of both states and Indigenous peoples. Individual rights are reconciled with collective rights in Article 1. The right to existence as a group and as individuals is articulated in Article 7. This Article, incidentally, subsumes the forcible removal of children under 'any act of genocide or any other act of violence', thus neatly skirting the issue of whether forcibly removing children (as in Australia's stolen generations) constitutes genocide. Article 3 leaves open the question of external self-determination; Articles 4 and 5 favour internal self-determination. Other articles concern: participatory development and other economic and social rights; the principle of free, prior, and informed consent; the right to consultation about activities on their lands; and the right to determine membership of and to maintain indigenous institutions, as well as relations between and within states that affect Indigenous peoples.

Consequences of Denial of Rights

Indigenous peoples are among the most discriminated-against groups, regardless of recognition, in nearly all states. The Special Rapporteur for the UNPFII (Stavenhagen, 2007), the UN High Commissioner for Refugees (UNHCR, 2006), and NGOs, such as US-based Survival International and Denmark-based International Work Group on Indigenous Affairs, report evidence of the denial of group and individual rights.

Genocide, persecution, and discrimination continue; social exclusion and pauperization are the common experience of Indigenous and tribal peoples. Large-scale infrastructure developments frequently force their displacement within the state or cause them to become economic, environmental, or political refugees elsewhere. Extractive industries pollute their lands and resources (Forest Peoples Programme & Tebtebba Foundation, 2006).

States frequently facilitate the dispossession of Indigenous people from their traditional lands and territories and their exclusion from access to natural resources fundamental to their way of life and survival. Coercive assimilation through education, child welfare, and market economics leads to the loss of language, culture, and skills. Paternalist and non-inclusive governance and service delivery models perpetuate the denial of culture and the denial of the right to existence as self-determining groups, and exacerbate the participation deficit. Worldwide, dependency and disempowerment make the preservation of cultural, political, social, and economic integrity and social and economic development virtually impossible. Life expectancy, health, and well-being are markedly lower for Indigenous and tribal peoples than for the dominant population almost everywhere (CSDH, 2007; Oxfam, 2007).

Mental health suffers, too. After enduring centuries of colonization accompanied by a denial of rights by the dominant population, many Indigenous people suffer from 'historical trauma' or intergenerational post-traumatic stress disorder (Kirmayer *et al.*, 2001; Maviglia, 2002).

Figure 15.1 links colonialism, globalization, and ethnocide to global warming and ecocide (the killing of ecosystems, including planet Earth), illustrating the multiple jeopardy suffered by Indigenous peoples.

KEY POINTS

After the Second World War the UN established an individual human rights regime anchored in the Universal Declaration of Human Rights, namely, the ICCPR and the ICESCR. The group right of self-determination is referred to in both covenants but applied only to the beneficiaries of decolonization by European powers.

A corresponding group right to existence is inferred from the prohibition and punishment of the crime of genocide, but the Genocide Convention has seldom been invoked against individuals or states and never in the protection of Indigenous peoples.

Indigenous peoples became an effective lobby group in the 1970s. Agitation for a UN declaration on the rights of Indigenous peoples started in 1977 but the meaning and implications of the rights to self-determination in drafts of the declaration were to be a major stumbling block for states for thirty years.

In the 1980s, rights of consultation, participation, and prior informed consent emerged in various quarters, including the Earth Summit, the WGIP, and the ILO.

Set up in 2002, the PFII is the first UN body to give standing to peoples who are not states in the context of the UN's state-based system. The UN and states, however, control its membership. The 2007 Declaration on the Rights of Indigenous Peoples conferred the right of internal self-determination on Indigenous peoples but failed to establish a framework for relations involving Indigenous peoples, states, and the UN.

Genocide, dispossession of their territories, and the denial of their rights as legal persons and nations through colonization and globalization have placed Indigenous people amongst the most vulnerable groups in the world.

Case Study: Indigenous Peoples and Climate Change

Climate change-precipitated disasters underline the importance of basic human rights for millions of poor people, many of them Indigenous (Tauli-Corpuz and Lynge, 2008). Indigenous peoples are among those already experiencing negative impacts of climate change that include loss of food security, sea level rise and coastal erosion, desertification, deforestation, intensification and frequency of 'natural' disasters, unprecedented species extinction, and the spread of vector-borne diseases. Further, climate change has already displaced twenty-five million people worldwide (Institute for the Study of International Migration

FIGURE 15.1 Colonization, globalization, ethnocide, and ecocide.

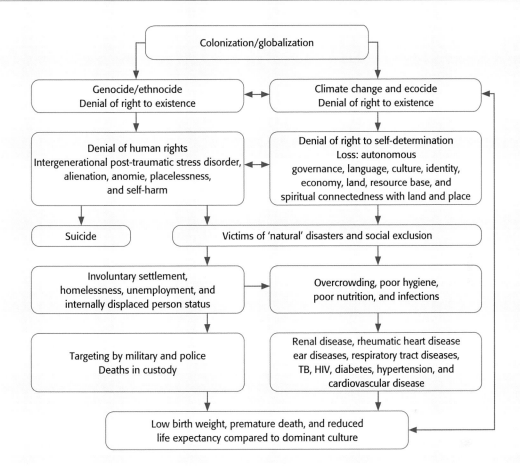

and Brookings-Bern Project, 2008). These people are among the most vulnerable to the abrogation of (failure to honour) all types of human rights.

By the end of 2007 most states had unequivocally accepted a direct link between human activity and global climate change. The UN Intergovernmental Panel on Climate Change (IPCC) presents compelling evidence for this link in its fourth report (IPCC, 2007). The UN Environment Program and the World Meteorological Organization set up the IPCC in 1988 to assess relevant scientific, technical, and socio-economic information. Consensus in favour of urgent global human intervention to stop the growth of greenhouse gas emissions was reflected first in the 1992 UNFCCC and then in the 2005 Kyoto Protocol to the UNFCCC. The Framework Convention obliges states to reduce emissions and to take measures to mitigate and adapt to the profound ecological, economic (Stern, 2006), political, social, and cultural effects of climate change.

Unabated, climate change seems likely to derail the attainment of the UN's eight Millennium Development Goals and thus cause the poorest of the poor, of whom Indigenous peoples constitute a high proportion, to suffer profound adverse impacts. UN Secretary General Ban Ki-moon (Ban, 2007) recognized that those least responsible and least able to cope bear the greatest burden, yet the rights of Indigenous peoples to participate in discussions about climate change mitigation and adaptation are still limited.

In every region of the Earth, Indigenous people are on the front line of climate change—frequently in parts of the developing world where the state is least equipped or willing to respond. In the Arctic region, very rapid climate change is fundamentally threatening the health and food security of Indigenous Inuit people at a speed and on a scale that makes mitigation and adaptation very difficult. In Southern Africa, drought and temperature rise leading to desertification are rendering 2.5 million hectares of the Kalahari area unusable for grazing or as a source of food for the Indigenous San people. In Asia, rising temperatures and decreased rainfall are leading to forest system collapse, crop failures, and mass fires. Coastal zones of Bangladesh and China are experiencing erosion, salt water dilution of fresh water supplies, and population dislocation. In the Himalayas, glaciers are melting and high altitude ecosystems collapsing while, downstream, flooding causes people to move from low-lying areas, increasing population pressures on Indigenous populations. In Central and South America and the Caribbean, deforestation is widespread from the Amazon basin to the alpine forests of the Andes. Altered weather patterns are disrupting traditional agriculture and threatening food security. Coastal erosion is making areas of many small island developing states uninhabitable, forcing population movement onto scarce land. In the Pacific regions, coastal erosion, high tides, and stormy seas are threatening Tuvalu, the Cook Islands, and Kiribati and leading to migrations in the Marshall Islands and Papua New Guinea that force traditional owners into conflict with newcomers.

The predicament of Indigenous peoples also stems from adverse factors attributable to the lingering ideology of colonization (Macchi et al., 2008), which denies rights to existence and self-determination. Climate change exacerbates vulnerability to continuing poverty and poor health. Absence of political and economic power limits the ability to defend and assert rights to land, natural resources, and diversified traditional livelihoods in an increasingly cut-throat competitive environment. Restricted access to information communication technologies further limits the ability to adapt to or mitigate the effects of climate change.

The Right to Participate in Mitigation and Adaptation?

State parties to the UNFCCC have been intransigent toward repeated requests from the International Forum of Indigenous Peoples on Climate Change (IFIPCC) to participate. This intransigence effectively abrogates rights to participation, to prior informed consent, and to consultation, supposedly enshrined in international human rights law. While the UNFCCC and Kyoto Protocol oblige developed states to assist developing countries, they acknowledge neither the situation of Indigenous peoples nor the contribution that TEK can make to successful adaptation. Indigenous peoples at present have no formal place in the work of expert bodies that advise the UNFCCC. Conferences of the parties to UNFCCC have repeatedly declined Indigenous peoples' request to create an Expert Group on Indigenous People, though they have been allowed to attend and make statements, along with NGOs and industry lobbyists.

The IPCC has neglected Indigenous people in its analysis of the data or presented them as 'helpless victims of changes beyond their control' (Salick and Byg, 2007)—though it does acknowledge the importance of TEK in assisting scientists and policy makers, as well as Indigenous and traditional communities in adapting to climate change (Parry et al., 2007).

In May 2008 the UNPFII held its seventh session on 'Climate change, bio-cultural diversity and livelihoods: the stewardship role of Indigenous peoples and new challenges'. This session repeated the call for better recognition by the UNFCCC, inclusion of Indigenous peoples' issues in the work of the IPCC, and acceptance by states that the Declaration on the Rights of Indigenous Peoples should be the framework for further interaction between states and Indigenous peoples nationally as well as internationally.

Including Indigenous peoples in the work of entities such as the UN and the World Bank is critically important as these bodies are designing and implementing global measures for climate change mitigation and adaptation that will affect Indigenous people profoundly. For instance, under the Kyoto Protocol three market-based mechanisms for reducing emissions have been introduced. These include 'clean development mechanisms', such as hydropower and dam building, and emissions trading. Dams often cause involuntary resettlement that is likely to infringe rights. Emissions trading encourages the development of plantation crops such as oil palms for bio-fuels. In Asia, planting single crops for bio-fuels contributes to the deforestation of vast areas of tropical rainforest and to declines in food security and biodiversity, again infringing Indigenous peoples rights. In Uganda, reforestation for voluntary carbon offset businesses in Europe has infringed indigenous rights through the forced eviction of peoples from their lands (Tauli-Corpuz and Tamang, 2007).

Signatories to the UNFCCC are committed to formulate and implement regional mitigation and adaptation programmes. These include irrigation and rain water catchment, disaster planning, measures to address coastal erosion, and forest management schemes that are likely to intrude upon Indigenous peoples' existing way of life. Participation, prior informed consent, and consultation rights, as well as recognition of TEK and respect for land and natural resources rights, are all likely to be areas of struggle between states and Indigenous peoples.

The World Bank's Forest Carbon Partnership Facility contributes millions of dollars to the UNFCCC programme of action for reducing emissions from forest degradation and deforestation. NGOs suggest that the approach is seriously flawed: it neglects the Bank's own policies and obligations regarding respect for the participation, consultation, and informed consent rights of Indigenous peoples.

Unfortunately, the reluctance of parties to the UNFCCC and the World Bank to recognize the standing of Indigenous peoples and to allow their active participation and consultation not only robs Indigenous peoples of their rights and increases their vulnerability, but also robs humanity as a whole of the contribution Indigenous people stand ready to make.

rights are 'universal, indivisible, interdependent and interrelated'.

Basic to existence are rights to life, adequate food, water, health, shelter, and freedom from torture, found in the UDHR and many other UN human rights instruments (Von Doussa *et al.*, 2008). International law is weak in articulating an individual right to a healthy planetary ecosystem as a basic right of existence. The Rio Declaration's Principles suggest that rights derive from states' duties, for example: to consider environmental needs of future generations (Principle 3); to conserve, protect, and restore the health of the Earth's ecosystems (Principle 7—echoed in Article 29 of the Indigenous Peoples Rights Declaration); and to take a precautionary approach despite the absence of full scientific certainty where irreversible damage is threatened (Principle 15).

Self-determination is a fundamental dimension of disaster management. The bundle of rights associated with self-determination include self-government, participation in mitigation planning, and access to information, found in the ILO Convention (No. 169), the UN Declaration on the Rights of Indigenous Peoples, Agenda 21, the Dublin Declaration on Access to Environmental Information, and the Aarhus Convention on Public Participation in Environmental Matters.

Linking rights to existence, self-determination, and individual human rights in an active rights-based approach to climate change will demand unprecedented and hitherto unachieved whole-of-system involvement in recognizing, respecting, and protecting all types of human rights.

Climate Change and the Human Rights of Persons Affected by Disasters

Because they are among the estimated 200 million people per year affected by so-called 'natural' disasters (many of them related to climate change) (Brookings-Bern Project on Internal Displacement, 2007), Indigenous peoples are among those most in need of the human rights-based approach to disaster relief that the UN Inter-Agency Standing Committee advocates (Brookings-Bern Project on Internal Displacement, 2008). A human rights-based approach to reducing, mitigating, and adapting to climate change requires putting into practice the principle that all human

KEY POINTS

Science shows that Indigenous peoples are among those being hit hardest by climate change.

IPCC research supports the contention of Indigenous peoples that TEK can contribute to mitigation and adaptation measures.

The IFIPCC repeatedly but unsuccessfully requested, between 2000 and 2008, that the IPCC and UNFCCC recognize Indigenous peoples rights to participate in deliberations about mitigation and adaptation.

The UN advocates a human rights-based approach to climate change measures.

Reconciling Indigenous Self-Determination with State Sovereignty?

Indigenous peoples conceive their right to existence as indivisible from, interconnected with, and interdependent upon their right to self-determination. Consequently, indigenous movements since the last quarter of the twentieth century have pursued self-determination.

Jorge Valadez (2000, pp. 185–234) categorizes three strands within these movements: *accommodationists* will settle for a degree of self-determination within the structures of the state; *autonomists* seek self-determination through autonomous institutional arrangements within the state; *secessionists* seek to form independent states. Secessionists are not a majority. Even so, states have persistently interpreted Indigenous peoples' assertion of rights to self-determination as claims to external self-determination—tantamount to rights of secession. Most states perceive aspirations to self-determination as threats to their territorial integrity and sovereignty.

Many Indigenous leaders accept that the greatest gains are likely if self-government is delimited as internal—ideally, along lines that 'autonomists' would accept. Thus Indigenous peoples have pursued rights to their own political–legal institutions, to participate in and be consulted about decisions concerning them, and to give prior informed consent to the implementation of decisions concerning or impacting upon them. States are unused to having to respect these rights, even in the context of IGOs such as the UNFCCC that make decisions of direct and mortal relevance to Indigenous people.

Recognizing a right to internal quasi-autonomous self-government appears to conflict with traditional liberal models of democracy, separation of powers, and the rule of law. Citizenship is universal, equal, and individual. Democracy is majoritarian. There is one law, and one set of rights, for everyone. Clearly, introducing separate forms of autonomous self-government for Indigenous peoples would challenge this model. Most states have therefore pursued the assimilation of Indigenous peoples as individual citizens, denying their claims to group rights and autonomy.

However, some liberal theorists and some democratic states recognize that imposing one model on everyone regardless of culture or history may violate liberal values of tolerance and recognition of difference (Taylor, 1994). Furthermore, they accept that principles of good governance such as inclusiveness, subsidiarity, and equivalence require the authentic involvement of those whose life expectancy—let alone life choices and life chances (Held, 2005, pp. 258–259)—are most affected.

Liberal theorist Will Kymlicka (1995, pp. 6–8, 30–41) suggests a compromise between assimilation and separation, universalism and relativism. He suggests that liberalism requires three kinds of rights to accommodate Indigenous peoples and help them realize equal citizenship through recognition of differences. He proposes rights of self-government over internal affairs based on traditional mechanisms and institutions, such as in the Territory of Nunavut in Canada; polyethnic rights to protecting traditional religious practice, hunting and fishing, and stewardship of land and natural resources, such as some native title rights in Australia; and representation rights that would give groups a voice in state institutions when these deliberate matters directly affecting the groups, such as the Saami Parliaments in the Nordic states. Differentiated citizenship can be justified in various contexts and on several grounds: in treaty obligations that oblige the state to honour its historical undertakings; in special measures to assist those whose right to existence has been jeopardized by state practices; or as a means of empowering Indigenous peoples to perform duties to the environment for the benefit of humankind.

In addition, international human rights relating to Indigenous peoples, tribal peoples, and minorities since the 1989 ILO Convention are premised on the idea that preserving a distinct human culture—its laws and institutions, language, religion, and way of life—is a good in itself and that states have a duty to take measures to ensure this preservation.

The sticking point for liberal democratic states in recognizing differentiated citizenship arises when apparently universal, individual citizenship rights appear to be abrogated by the exercise of indigenous self-government powers, for example through rules discriminating against women. For a state to condone a denial of the rights of a citizen would be to fail in the duty to protect and promote the human rights of all citizens equally. This would imply that citizenship rights are not universal but depend on one's identity or status—totally contradicting the idea of citizenship and the principle that human rights are interconnected, interrelated, and indivisible.

Seyla Benhabib (2002, pp. 18–19, 147–148) suggests that a resolution to the universalist v. relativist conundrum posed by differentiated citizenship could be guided by principles that protect the individual's rights from being sacrificed for the sake of the group without denying the right of the group to exist and govern itself within these limits. These principles recognize that state power should be shared by all, that minorities should not have fewer rights than the majority, that group membership must be voluntary and not imposed, and that group members should have a meaningful right of exit from the group.

Another challenge—apparent in connection with issues such as climate change—is that the world increasingly has to be understood as a single place for governance purposes (Rosenau, 1997). Yet intensified globalization processes correlate with intensified secessionist pressures upon states (Hechter, 2000) by peoples without states (Guibernau, 1999), such as Indigenous peoples.

KEY POINTS

Indigenous peoples conceive the right to existence as indivisible from, interconnected with, and interdependent upon their right to self-determination.

States ascribe secessionist motives to Indigenous peoples' claims to self-determination.

The accommodation of Indigenous peoples' self-determination with state sovereignty is possible when states recognize that internal self-determination is compatible with as well as necessary for good governance.

Good governance requires the adoption of basic principles such as inclusiveness, subsidiarity, and equivalence to accommodate the rights and needs of distinct communities to differentiated citizenship within the state.

Conclusion

Much of the explanation for ambivalence about the rights of Indigenous peoples lies in the politics and economics of colonialism. Profit in the context of international competition depends upon access to territory, raw materials, cheap labour at the lowest compliance, and monetary costs. Even partial recognition of Indigenous peoples' rights would have raised the cost and stalled the pace of growth. The neoliberal ideology driving much of globalization today perceives the same problem and overcomes it in much the same way.

The Law of Nations, constituted from the coalescence of Euro-American, Judaeo–Christian, liberal legal, and capitalist ideologies, has rationalized, justified, and regulated territorial acquisition. Differences between Indigenous peoples and settlers (such as not being Christian or farmers or gardeners, and not having a European-style political society or economy or concept of individual private property) were used to justify the denial of recognition of legal personality to Indigenous peoples. This denial prevented Indigenous peoples from exercising or enjoying sovereignty and self-determination, as well as many other individual and group human rights associated with the right to existence. Despite the rhetoric of today's international law, for Indigenous peoples, deep ambivalence concerning the recognition of these rights remains evident at both national and international levels.

States and IGOs must work toward models of governance that provide both for Indigenous peoples' rights to participation in the global arena and for the right to self-determination within the state. State recognition of Indigenous peoples' rights in these ways is an expression of state sovereignty and not a restriction upon it, and ensures that local as well as global governance is inclusive, not exclusive, of those whose life choices and life chances are most affected by decisions.

QUESTIONS

INDIVIDUAL STUDY QUESTIONS

1. Distinguish group rights from individual rights. As a group debate whether individual rights are a necessary and sufficient type of right for the protection of Indigenous peoples human rights.

2. According to UN experts and international conventions, how are Indigenous peoples distinguishable from other peoples?

3. The ILO was created in 1919 and became a UN specialist agency after 1945. What has been its contribution to identifying the rights of Indigenous and tribal peoples?

4. In international law, how is the crime of genocide defined? Why is it linked to the right to existence?

5. What is meant by legal personality for individuals and for peoples or nations? Why has refusal to recognize their legal personality contributed to the vulnerable economic, political, cultural, and ecological position of Indigenous peoples and minorities?

6. What are the political and economic drivers of colonization? Why is the recognition of Indigenous peoples' rights seemingly incompatible with governance principles of liberal states and capitalist economies?

7. Contrast internal and external self-determination. Do you think that the states that drafted and adopted the ILO Convention (No. 169) in 1989 or the UN Declaration on the Rights of Indigenous Peoples in 2007 intended to endow Indigenous peoples with the right to internal or external self-determination?

8. Which international environmental law instruments were adopted by states at the 1992 Rio Earth Summit? Which Indigenous peoples' rights and duties were singled out by most of these?

9. Why are Indigenous peoples particularly vulnerable to climate change? How, and with respect to what aspect of responding to climate change, do Indigenous peoples seek greater voice at the conferences of the parties (COPs) of the UNFCCC and in the work of the IPCC?

GROUP DISCUSSION QUESTIONS

1. As a group, debate the indigenous case for, and the state case against, self-determination for Indigenous peoples.

2. As a group debate whether the requirement of an intent ought to be retained in the definition of genocide.

FURTHER READING

Anaya, S. J.[4] (1996). *Indigenous Peoples in International Law*. Oxford: Oxford University Press.
This is the classic exposition of the development of Indigenous peoples' rights in International law. It offers a thorough and detailed historical overview of the emergence of Indigenous peoples' rights, as well as a very rigorous analysis of the right to self-determination and its changing meaning and attributes in the late twentieth century.

Ghanea, N. and **Xanthaki**, A. (eds) (2005). *Minorities, Peoples and Self-Determination—Essays in honour of Patrick Thornberry*. Leiden: Martinus Nijhoff.

This is an edited collection of essays on Indigenous peoples and minorities. Many of the essays are by scholars who have served as UN special rapporteurs concerning indigenous and minority issues. Differences between the rights of each group are explained and the meanings of the right to self-determination critiqued.

Kymlicka, W. (1995). *Multicultural Citizenship: A Liberal Theory of Minority Rights*. Oxford: Oxford University Press.
This evaluates how the rights and status of minority cultures, such as Indigenous peoples, can be accommodated within liberal democracies. It argues that certain collective rights of minority cultures are consistent with liberal democratic principles, and that standard liberal objections to such rights can be answered.

Salick, J. and **Byg**, A. (eds) (2007). Indigenous peoples and climate change. Oxford: Tyndall Centre for Climate Change Research. http://www.tyndall.ac.uk/publications/Indigenouspeoples.pdf.
This edited report provides an interdisciplinary analysis of the impact of climate change on Indigenous peoples. The region-by-region, issue-by-issue analysis contrasts with the light treatment given to this set of issues by the IPCC.

Valadez, J. (2000). *Deliberative Democracy, Political Legitimacy, and Self-Determination in Multi-Cultural Societies*. Boulder, CO: Westview.
This examines some of the fundamental issues in political theory concerning democratic deliberation in multicultural societies, the nature of self-determination, the justification of distinct human rights such as cultural rights, as well as the rationale for regional self-governance and secession.

Xanthaki, A. (2007). *Human Rights and United Nations Standards: Self-Determination, Culture and Land*. Cambridge: Cambridge University Press.
This evaluates in detail the extent to which the human rights claims of Indigenous peoples are accommodated by contemporary international law and the UN system. The book argues that Indigenous peoples' persistent assertion of their rights has altered international law and the processes of the UN.

WEB LINKS

http://www.un.org/esa/socdev/unpfii/ Website of the UN Permanent Forum on indigenous Issues.

http://www.tebtebba.org Website of Tebtebba (Indigenous Peoples' International Centre for Policy Research and Education): a Philippines-based Indigenous peoples' NGO advocating that the rights of Indigenous peoples are recognized, respected, and protected worldwide.

http://www.survival-international.org Website of Survival, a US-based NGO supporting Indigenous and tribal peoples worldwide.

http://www.iwgia.org Website of a Denmark-based NGO supporting Indigenous peoples' struggle for human rights and self-determination.

http://www.forestpeoples.org The FPP is a UK-based NGO whose mission is to bridge the gap between policy makers and forest peoples through advocacy, practical projects, and capacity building.

NOTES

1. For brevity, the phrase 'Indigenous peoples rights' (with no apostrophe) refers to both Indigenous people's rights as individuals and Indigenous peoples' rights as groups—though most of this chapter concerns their group rights.

2. For instance, the Dominion of South Africa's mandate in German Southwest Africa.

3. *Chief Bernard Ominayak and the Lubicon Lake Band* v. *Canada* (Communication No. 167/1984). Views adopted 26 March 1990. Report of the Human Rights Committee, GAOR, 38th Session. Suppl. No. 40(A/38/40), 1–30.

4. The UNPFII appointed Professor Anaya as a Special Rapporteur in 2008.

ONLINE RESOURCE CENTRE

 Visit the Online Resource Centre that accompanies this book for updates and a range of other resources:

http://www.oxfordtextbooks.co.uk/orc/goodhart/

Genocide and Human Rights

Scott Straus

16

Chapter Contents

Reader's Guide

Genocide is one of the most extreme forms of human rights violations and the subject of an early human rights treaty. However, the definition of genocide is contested, and the treaty's promise of prevention oversells the actual international mechanisms put in place to stop genocide. The chapter examines different definitions of genocide as well as some of the treaty's weak points. Also explored in the chapter are theories of why genocide occurs. Over the years, social scientists have put forward a number of different explanations of genocide, focusing variously on inter-group divisions, authoritarianism, deprivation, ideology, wartime strategy, and political development. The chapter ends with case studies of Rwanda and Darfur. The case studies describe the background to the mass violence in both locations, as well as the international responses; the case studies also illustrate the conceptual and theoretical points raised earlier in the chapter.

Introduction

The problem of genocide has been and remains one of the most acute in the realm of international human rights. Frequently recognized as the 'crime of crimes' and one of the most extreme forms of human rights violation, genocide is the subject of an early and theoretically powerful treaty, the 1948 United Nations Convention on the Punishment and Prevention of the Crime of Genocide (Genocide Convention). The treaty obligates state parties to 'punish' and to 'prevent' genocide where it occurs. In recent years, international actors have intensified efforts to punish genocide perpetrators through international criminal justice mechanisms. Nonetheless, despite widespread ratification, the overall record on genocide prevention during the past sixty years has been dismal.

This chapter presents an overview of major topics in the scholarship on genocide. The first section focuses on the origins of the concept of genocide. The section introduces Raphael Lemkin, who coined the term in 1944, and subsequently became a leading advocate for an international treaty on the punishment and prevention of genocide. The section in turn discusses the resulting treaty, the Genocide Convention. Finally, the section presents some controversies and disagreements on how genocide is defined. In the second section, the chapter focuses on social scientific theories of why genocide occurs. The section discusses both classic theories of genocide, as well as more recent scholarship. The third section focuses on two contemporary cases, Rwanda and Darfur. The section presents empirical overviews of the cases, historical background, and summaries of the international response. The section also links the case studies to the conceptual and theoretical material introduced in the first two sections.

The Origins of the Concept of 'Genocide'

Raphael Lemkin and the Origins of Genocide

Few major human rights concepts have as clear a point of origin as the concept of genocide does (Courthoys and Docker, 2008). Although the Holocaust during the Second World War prodded the international community to recognize and pledge to prevent genocide, the term itself was coined by Raphael Lemkin, a Polish international lawyer (see Box 16.1). It combines the Greek 'genos' (meaning race, nation, or tribe) and the Latin 'cide' for 'killing'.

In his 1944 book and subsequent writings, Lemkin argued that the main idea of genocide was the destruction of human groups, specifically nations and ethnic groups (Lemkin, 1944, p. 79; 1947, p. 147). More specifically, Lemkin (1944, p. 79) defined genocide as, 'a coordinated plan of different actions aiming at the destruction of the essential foundations of the life of national groups, with the aim of annihilating the groups completely.' These statements form the core of the common notion of genocide as group annihilation. The contemporary Oxford English Dictionary, for example, defines genocide as, 'The deliberate and systematic extermination of a national or ethnic group.'

Substantively, a key dimension of genocide is that the intent of violence is to destroy groups. What distinguishes genocide from other crimes is the focus on group destruction; even though individuals suffer violence, genocide is defined by this special intent or purpose of annihilating groups. In Lemkin's words, 'The acts are directed against groups, as such, and individuals are selected for destruction only because they belong to these groups' (Lemkin, 1947, p. 147)

For Lemkin, genocide entailed not only killing, but also a range of different activities that prevented or substantially endangered the life of groups. That is, genocide included not just murder, but acts that destroyed the social, economic, cultural, religious, and moral foundations of a group. In his original formulation, Lemkin listed acts of genocide ranging from forced sterilization, abortion, artificial infection, deliberate separation

Prior to the Second World War, Raphael Lemkin, a Polish Jew and jurist, had been attracted to legal constructs as a way of protecting civilian social groups against mass violence. As a young legal scholar, Lemkin proposed the term 'barbarity' to outlaw the premeditated destruction of specific population categories. However, his proposal never gained much traction and effectively died prior to the outbreak of war. During the Holocaust, Lemkin's family was decimated, but he managed to survive by fleeing Poland in 1940. Lemkin eventually landed in the United States where he first worked as a law professor at Duke and later as an adviser to the U.S. War Department. During the war, Lemkin amassed a collection of information about policy in Nazi-occupied territory and subsequently published a book on the topic. That book, *Axis Rule in Occupied Europe*, not only catalogued Nazi practices, but also coined the term 'genocide' to refer to the atrocities. Having given the crime a name, Lemkin did all he could to use the law to prevent and punish genocide. (Power, 2002)

of families, as well as replacing one nation's institutions with those of another nation (Lemkin, 1944). Genocide, Lemkin wrote, consisted of two phases: destroying a group and imposing the 'national pattern of the oppressor' (Lemkin, 1944, p. 79).

Genocide in International Law

Having coined the term, Lemkin worked tirelessly to promote it. The first official use of the term came in the indictments of twenty-four Nazi officials by the International Military Tribunal (IMT) at Nuremberg (the Nuremberg Tribunal). The IMT charged the Nazi defendants with crimes against peace, crimes against humanity, and war crimes; under the latter, the tribunal alleged that the defendants had 'conducted deliberate and systematic genocide, viz. the extermination of racial and national groups, against the civilian populations of certain occupied territories' (International Military Tribunal at Nuremberg, 1946, Section VIII A). However, the ultimate judgment from the IMT did not make reference to genocide.

The next major development was a 1946 Resolution from the United Nations General Assembly—a resolution that was indebted to Lemkin's lobbying effort. The

resolution formally recognized genocide as a crime under international law and called for a draft convention on the prevention and punishment of genocide. The drafting process began about a year later, and, in a series of sessions, different state representatives debated exactly how genocide would be defined and incorporated into treaty form. The net result was the Genocide Convention, which the General Assembly adopted on 9 December 1948—a day before endorsing the Universal Declaration of Human Rights.

The topics of debate in the drafting process are instructive. Most famously, the Soviet Union objected to 'political groups' being included as a protected category. The Soviets worried that Communist policies could fall under the Convention were political groups protected (Kuper, 1981). Lemkin similarly argued that political groups did not have the same permanency as racial, national, and ethnic groups (Schabas, 2000). For its part, the USA opposed a statement on 'cultural genocide' in the Convention—a position Lemkin opposed. Other debates focused on the place of intentionality, whether a group could suffer 'partial' destruction, how genocide related to crimes against humanity, how parties to the Convention should respond to genocide where it occurred, and how genocide should be prosecuted (Schabas, 2000). The debates were prescient: each of these issues in the sixty years since the Convention was drafted have proven complex and at times confusing.

In the end, the drafters defined genocide as the 'intent to destroy, in whole or in part, a national, ethnical, racial or religious group, as such' (see Box 16.2). The definition's key dimensions are as follows:

1. there must be *intent* to destroy a group as such; in other words, to demonstrate genocide a deliberate, usually planned campaign of violence with the express purpose of destroying a protected group must be in evidence;
2. only national, ethnical, racial, or religious groups are protected—political, disabled, regional, gender, and other conceivable groups are not explicitly protected;
3. genocide may be constituted by 'partial' destruction of a group, which courts have subsequently interpreted to mean that a 'substantial' part of the group must be destroyed.

No genocide ever succeeds in total extermination; at the same time, the standard for determining when 'substantial' group destruction indicates intent to destroy a group is murky.

In Article III, the treaty lists a number of different methods of genocide. These include killing, causing serious physical or mental harm, inflicting 'conditions of life calculated to bring about its physical destruction in whole or in part', preventing birth, and transferring children (see Box 16.2). Several ideas resonate with Lemkin's notion that genocide may take the form of preventing the reproduction of a group; however, the methods are indirect, making proof of the special intent to destroy groups difficult.

On the question of prevention, Article I of the Genocide Convention holds that contracting parties 'undertake to prevent' genocide. However, what 'undertaking to prevent' means is unclear, and the matter received comparatively little attention in the drafting process (Schabas, 2000). Article VIII holds that parties 'may call upon competent organs' of the United Nations to take action under the Charter to prevent and suppress acts of genocide (see Box 16.2). In short, the treaty language implies that states may intervene, perhaps against the wishes of a sovereign state, to stop genocide. Many have interpreted the Convention this way. However, in reality the treaty language is fairly vague and weak as to specific mechanisms, policies, and procedures that states must take to prevent genocide. The example of Darfur is a case in point, as discussed below.

By contrast, the Convention has considerably more on punishment. The treaty lists five specific charges and conditions for extradition. The law additionally states: that individuals may be punished whether or not they are public officials; that contracting parties must enact legislation outlawing genocide; and that persons charged with genocide must be tried by a domestic or international court. In recent years—more specifically, with regard to the crises in the former Yugoslavia, Rwanda, and Sudan—the Genocide Convention's

---

Box 16.2 **The United Nations Genocide Convention (Selected Articles)**

The Contracting Parties,
Having considered the declaration made by the General Assembly of the United Nations in its resolution 96 (I) dated 11 December 1946 that genocide is a crime under international law, contrary to the spirit and aims of the United Nations and condemned by the civilized world, Recognizing that at all periods of history genocide has inflicted great losses on humanity, and Being convinced that, in order to liberate mankind from such an odious scourge, international co-operation is required,

Hereby agree as hereinafter provided:

Article 1
The Contracting Parties confirm that genocide, whether committed in time of peace or in time of war, is a crime under international law which they undertake to prevent and to punish.

Article 2
In the present Convention, genocide means any of the following acts committed with intent to destroy, in whole or in part, a national, ethnical, racial or religious group, as such:

(a) Killing members of the group;

(b) Causing serious bodily or mental harm to members of the group;

(c) Deliberately inflicting on the group conditions of life calculated to bring about its physical destruction in whole or in part;

(d) Imposing measures intended to prevent births within the group;

(e) Forcibly transferring children of the group to another group.

Article 3
The following acts shall be punishable:

(a) Genocide;

(b) Conspiracy to commit genocide;

(c) Direct and public incitement to commit genocide;

(d) Attempt to commit genocide;

(e) Complicity in genocide.

Article 4
Persons committing genocide or any of the other acts enumerated in article III shall be punished, whether they are constitutionally responsible rulers, public officials or private individuals.

Article 8
Any Contracting Party may call upon the competent organs of the United Nations to take such action under the Charter of the United Nations as they consider appropriate for the prevention and suppression of acts of genocide or any of the other acts enumerated in article III.

punishment provisions have proven more effective than those on prevention. That reality is consistent with a general strengthening of international judicial mechanisms for the criminal punishment of mass violations of human rights. Today there are international or hybrid domestic–international courts for crimes committed in the former Yugoslavia, Rwanda, Cambodia, and Sierra Leone. The International Criminal Court has also come into existence in the past decade. Nonetheless, embedded in the language of the 1948 Genocide Convention is clearly more specific language on punishment than on prevention.

The Genocide Convention came into force in January 1951. Today the treaty has 140 state parties and wide regional endorsement. Among the first states to ratify were Australia, Bulgaria, Cambodia, Costa Rica, Ecuador, El Salvador, Ethiopia, France, Guatemala, Iceland, Israel, Jordan, Laos, Liberia, Monaco, Panama, the Philippines, Korea, Saudi Arabia, Sri Lanka, and Turkey. The United States was one of the first to sign the treaty—President Truman's administration did so only two days after the General Assembly adopted the Convention. However, the treaty ran into a phalanx of opposition when the Senate considered ratification. The American Bar Association took aim at the ambiguities in the Convention: in particular, the potentially low threshold of 'causing mental harm' and the notion of group destruction 'in part'. Southern Senators, in particular, opposed ratification, worrying that discriminatory laws against African Americans could constitute genocide under the Convention. The treaty died in the Senate until William Proxmire (Wisconsin, D) took it up as a personal cause, making thousands of speeches on the Convention. Eventually, a controversy during Ronald Reagan's second term, in which the president visited a German cemetery where SS officials had been buried, triggered a process that ultimately led to US ratification in 1988 (Power, 2002).

Enduring controversies in the definition of genocide

The Genocide Convention is the first binding international human rights treaty to emerge from the post-War United Nations system. The law is theoretically one of the most powerful in its obligation to punish and prevent genocide where it occurs, and the treaty itself is testament to a rhetorical commitment to end one of the worst forms of human rights violation. Nonetheless,

embedded in the concept of genocide and the Convention are issues that limit the power of the innovation. In particular, genocide is a contested concept with important ambiguities around the types of groups protected, the extent and means of violence that would constitute genocide, and the difficulty in demonstrating intent. Since the Convention, there have been numerous attempts to redefine genocide (Straus, 2001).

To account for the ambiguities, scholars have proposed other terms, such as *politicide* (the systematic destruction of political groups; Harff, 2003), *democide* (mass killings by governments; Rummel, 1994), and *mass killing* (the intentional killing of more than 50,000 civilians in a five year period; Valentino, 2004). The net impact is that within the literature there is neither a set definition of genocide nor a settled list of cases. The literature veers between narrower definitions of genocide (as the extermination of racial, ethnic, or religious groups) and broader definitions (intentional mass killing on the basis of group membership). The differences in definitions have important consequences for what gets counted as 'genocide' or a related term (see Table 16.1).

Moreover, despite the rhetorical international commitment to prevention and to 'never again' allow genocide to occur, the key international treaty lacks clear and specific enforcement mechanisms that could trigger collective action to stop genocide. The conceptual openness and the status of genocide as the crime of crimes ironically make the genocide label one that is attractive to diverse actors, who use the term to grab attention to their case. At the same time, the conceptual ambiguities and weak enforcement provisions make debates about whether acts constitute 'genocide' frequently irresolvable and often without dramatic practical consequences.

KEY POINTS
Genocide was first defined in 1944 by Raphael Lemkin during the Holocaust.
The 1948 Genocide Convention obligates state parties to punish and prevent genocide.
The Convention has wide international acceptance. The punishment provisions have been more influential than the prevention ones.
The meaning of the term 'genocide' is subject to significant disagreement.

TABLE 16.1 Genocide cases in the twentieth century.

Manus Midlarsky	Barbara Harff
The Killing Trap: Genocide in the Twentieth Century (2005, p. 23)	'No Lessons Learned from the Holocaust? Assessing Risks of Genocide and Political Mass Murder Since 1955' (2003, p. 60)
Narrow definition of genocide	Broad definition of genocide and politicide
Three genocide cases in twentieth century:	1955–1999 cases include:
Armenian Genocide, 1915–1916	Sudan, 1956–1972
The Holocaust, 1941–1945	China, 1959
The Rwandan Genocide, 1994	Algeria, 1962
	Iraq, 1963–1975
	Rwanda, 1963–1964
	Congo–Kinshasa, 1964–1965
	Burundi, 1965–1973
	Indonesia, 1965–1966
	South Vietnam, 1965–1975
	China, 1966–1975
	Pakistan, 1971
	Philippines, 1972–1976
	Uganda, 1972–1979
	Chile, 1973–1976
	Pakistan, 1973–1977
	Angola, 1975–2001
	Cambodia, 1975–1979
	Indonesia, 1975–1992
	Argentina, 1976–1980
	Ethiopia, 1976–1979
	Congo–Kinshasa, 1977–1979
	Afghanistan, 1978–1992
	Burma, 1978
	Guatemala, 1978–1996
	El Salvador, 1980–1989
	Uganda, 1980–1986
	Iran, 1981–1992
	Syria, 1981–1982
	Sudan, 1983–2001
	Burundi, 1988
	Iraq, 1988–1991
	Somalia, 1988–1991
	Sri Lanka, 1989–1990
	Bosnia, 1992–1995
	Burundi, 1993–1994
	Rwanda, 1994
	Serbia, 1998–1999

Theories of Genocide

If one major question concerns the definition of genocide in and outside law, a separate major area of focus is explaining why genocide occurs. For many years, that question was marginal to the social sciences—for at least three reasons. First, some objected to the notion that genocide could be explained. To some, genocide is unimaginable violence; moreover, explaining genocide risks rationalizing it. Second, until the 1990s, the principal reference point for discussing genocide was the Holocaust, and to some that case was unique in the extent and method of violence. Comparison was thus discouraged. Third, genocide was not a matter for considerable discussion in the public domain. The key turning point was the mid-1990s: in particular, with the mass violence in the former Yugoslavia and Rwanda. Genocide became a matter of pressing concern as well as a political phenomenon that could and should be explained like other social outcomes. As a result, after a period of slow development, there has been a surge of research on genocide since the early 1990s.

Genocide is a big outcome and a quite complex phenomenon. Genocide involves multiple social dimensions and sometimes lasts many years. Different aspects of state and government frequently play a part, including—in different cases—the political elite, the military, a state-backed militia, the police, and administrative institutions. Private actors in the media and business are also often part of how genocide is perpetrated. On the victim side, genocide usually entails the loss of hundreds of thousands, if not millions, of lives, and how groups are targeted and how they survive are complicated stories. The literature on particular cases or genocide in general reflects the macro-nature of genocide, as well as the diversity of topics that can be examined.

In this section, the focus is on studies that seek to explain the root causes of genocide. Broadly speaking, such studies emphasize either the macro-level conditions that shape why genocide occurs or micro-level dynamics that prompt individuals at the local level to perpetrate atrocity. Social scientists in various disciplines—anthropology, history, psychology, political science, and sociology—have addressed both sets of questions. For brevity's sake, the concentration here is on macro-level explanations.

Classic Theories of Genocide

The early scholarship on macro-level causes of genocide reflects three main lines of analysis, each importantly influenced by understandings of the Holocaust. One set of arguments focuses on inter-group antipathy. At the most general level, the insight is that genocide is more likely to occur in societies that exhibit deep misgivings between ethnic, racial, or religious groups. In one of the first formulations, Leo Kuper argued that the root of genocide is a divided society, one in which there are 'persistent and pervasive cleavages' between different groups often created by colonial rule (Kuper, 1981, p. 57). In the extreme, deep divisions take the form of stratified, unequal groups where one group dominates another. Kuper argued that different genocides had different processes—some were more, some less organized—though all involved the state. Another constant was the dehumanization of the other (Kuper, 1981).

Kuper, a political scientist, is recognized as a pioneer of genocide studies. Another pioneer is sociologist Helen Fein. In a 1979 book, as well as in subsequent publications, Fein contends that a precondition for genocide is a form of prejudice and dehumanization—namely, that a perpetrator group defines a victim group 'outside the universe of obligation' (Fein, 1979, p. 9). The 1979 book is based on an innovative study of Jewish victimization rates in different countries during the Second World War; in the book, she proposes a four-part hypothesis. In addition to dehumanization, a state must suffer decline through war or internal conflict, a ruling elite must adopt a nationalist ideology to justify group domination, and, finally, wartime changes the calculus of genocide, she argues (Fein, 1979).

A second stream of argumentation pivots less on inter-group antipathy and more on state power and authoritarianism. Two theorists stand out here. The first is Irving Louis Horowitz, who in 1976 published *Genocide: State Power and Mass Murder*. Horowitz argued that genocide is connected to the absolute concentration of power. Genocide, Horowitz claims, is the 'operational handmaiden of a particular social system, the totalitarian system' (Horowitz, 1997, p. 36). The second author of note is Rudolph Rummel who claims that 'absolute power kills absolutely' (Rummel, 1994, p. 19). For both Horowitz and Rummel, the institutionalization of democracy is the best bulwark against genocide. In Rummel's language, limits and restraints on power diminish the likelihood of democide.

A third stream of argumentation focuses on hardship and crisis. The causal logic here is that in the context of widespread social deprivation and deep social crisis—economic depression, starvation, war, even rapid social change and revolution—groups blame other groups for their suffering: they scapegoat. The argument is especially well articulated in the work of psychologist Ervin Staub. Staub claims that, in the context of 'difficult life conditions', human beings feel threatened and frustrated, which in turn gives rise to a feeling of hostility and a desire to blame others for their troubles. That desire to find an outlet for the anger is channelled through existing cultures: in particular, where certain groups are denigrated or where there exists a culture of obedience. The result can be genocide (Staub, 1989).

In many respects, these three streams of analysis—on inter-group antipathy, regime type, and widespread hardship—formed the core of a 'first generation' of macro-level analysis of the causes of genocide. To be sure, other influential research was conducted (e.g. Melson, 1992), but the three identified approaches were especially prominent.

Recent Theories of Genocide

In recent years, there has been a new surge of comparative research on genocide. The impetus was primarily the high-profile cases of the 1990s: in particular, the former Yugoslavia and Rwanda. As these cases captured scholars' attention, comparative social scientists began to ask what the cases had in common with historical cases of genocide. The result is a newly-energized field of inquiry (Straus, 2007). The new research on genocide is diverse. Some is quantitative (Harff, 2003; Valentino et al., 2004). The majority, however, is qualitative, country-case comparisons of different episodes of genocide in different regions of the world. The new work is exciting, broad, and rapidly expanding. To summarize

the emerging scholarship, the section focuses on three emerging lines of argument.

The first argues that *ideology* in some way is the root of genocide. To be sure, the importance of ideas was present in the earlier studies of genocide, but in the new wave of literature ideology receives a new primacy and articulation. Historian Eric Weitz, for example, claims that genocide emerges from quests to achieve utopia. When leaders seek transcendence for their societies based on racial or nationalist ideals, Weitz argues, the idea of eliminating categories of people becomes thinkable (Weitz, 2003). In a similar vein, French political scientist Jacques Sémelin argues that quests to achieve purity in the context of acute crisis constitute the main origins of genocide (Sémelin, 2007). In a sweeping study of genocide through time, historian Ben Kiernan argues that there are several ideological pathways to genocide, including ideologies based on race or religion, agrarian romanticism, cults of past glory, and fears of biological contamination (Kiernan, 2007).

The second line of argument focuses on the strategic aims of leaders and state interests. The claim is most clearly articulated in the work of political scientist Benjamin Valentino (2004). He argues that leaders engage in mass killing and genocide when they believe that doing so is the best available means to achieve their most cherished political and military goals. Valentino identifies several principal scenarios in which elites will engage in mass killing and genocide: in particular, in the contexts of guerrilla war, Communist revolution, and ethnic conflict. A key insight for Valentino is that leaders who commit mass killing and genocide make calculated decisions; genocide is not the product of totalitarianism *per se*, deep social hatred, or even widespread deprivation. Fellow political scientist Manus Midlarsky similarly claims that leaders choose genocide from a decision-making calculus. But Midlarsky argues that the decision is less rational, more a product of 'imprudent' thinking after a state has lost territory in a war. Midlarsky also points to the importance of international allies who create a permissive environment for genocide to happen (Midlarsky, 2005).

The third major recent approach is to situate the genocide in the context of long-term political development. Two exemplars of the approach are sociologist Michael Mann and historian Mark Levene. Mann directly challenges the claim that genocide is the product of authoritarianism; rather, he argues that genocide is a perversion of democratic ideals. The key for Mann is organic nationalism—namely, the idea that a state belongs to a core ethnic group. Mann contends that this idea is rooted in a democratic quest to establish a state in the name of the people. Organic nationalism arises when 'the people' is conceptualized as an ethnic group (Mann, 2005). Levene focuses more on the development of the modern nation state. Genocide, Levene argues, is rooted in the ways in which a modern state monopolizes violence, homogenizes populations, and aggregates power (Levene, 2005).

The above discussion of the determinants of genocide is not meant to be comprehensive, but rather indicative of some major ways of approaching the subject from a social scientific perspective. Two points should be especially clear. First, the literature is rich with different ideas about the causes of genocide. If micro-level theories and other theories were added to the mix, the literature on causes would appear even more diverse. Second, there is relatively little consensus on the determinants of genocide. Different scholars emphasize inter-group animosity, authoritarianism, deprivation,

ideology, strategic objectives, and the historical development of nationalism and nation states. Theoretical consensus about the determinants of large-scale political and social phenomena eludes many topics. The field of genocide studies may have specific reasons for the lack of theoretical convergence (Straus, 2007). Nonetheless, given the importance of the outcome, the topic of what causes genocide is likely to remain a lively field of inquiry in years to come.

KEY POINTS
Since the 1990s, there has been a surge of scholarship on genocide.
Classic theories of genocide emphasize inter-group antipathy, authoritarianism, and hardship.
More recent theories emphasize ideology, strategic calculations and state interest, and political development.
The literature lacks consensus on the primary causes of genocide.

Case Studies: Rwanda and Darfur

Having addressed the history of the concept of genocide and macro-level theories of genocide, the chapter now turns to two cases to illustrate some of the points. In particular, the chapter focuses on the mass violence in Rwanda in 1994 and in Darfur from 2003 to 2008. Genocide occurs in all regions—indeed, the most famous case (the Holocaust) was in Europe, as was Bosnia in the mid-1990s, which some argue was a case of

genocide. In Asia, genocide arguably occurred in Cambodia under Pol Pot during the late 1970s, and in Latin America some scholars argue that genocide occurred in Guatemala in the 1970s and 1980s (Sanford, 2008). The Africa focus here is partly because Rwanda and Darfur have received considerable attention in the past decade; they are also critically important human rights cases not covered extensively in other parts of the volume.

Rwanda

The mass violence that occurred in Rwanda in Central Africa in 1994 is widely acknowledged today as an unambiguous case of genocide and one of the worst mass atrocities of the second half of the twentieth century. In approximately three months, Hutu hardliners in the government and military orchestrated

a systematic campaign of violence against the Tutsi minority in that country. In a country of roughly seven million persons, Hutus constituted a majority of between 85–90%, and Tutsis a minority of 10–14%; Rwanda had a third major group, the Twa, who comprised 1% of the population. Estimates differ as to the total number killed during the genocide, but the most careful calculations put the toll at around 500,000 Tutsi civilians murdered by government forces (Des Forges, 1999). That number constitutes roughly three-quarters of the resident Tutsi population in Rwanda at the time of the genocide. In addition, rebel forces killed primarily Hutu civilians as the soldiers advanced. While the extent is not known, the rebel violence was on a smaller scale in 1994 than the genocidal violence committed by government forces.

Historical Background

The immediate context in which the genocide occurred was twofold. On the one hand, Rwanda was undergoing a democratic transition from one-party rule to multi-party elections. Rwanda's transition was part of a broader post-Cold War trend in Africa in which sub-Saharan states were pressured to end single-party dictatorships in favour of competitive, multi-party politics. In Rwanda, the ruling regime was headed by Juvénal Habyarimana, a Hutu military general who had been president since he took power in a *coup* in 1973. The main domestic opposition was composed of Hutu politicians, who drew support from people and regions of the country that were not well represented under Habyarimana.

On the other hand, the Habyarimana regime was in the middle of a civil war. The armed opponents were primarily Tutsi exiles who lived in neighbouring countries or who had joined the rebellion once it had started. The name of the rebel organization was the Rwandan Patriotic Front (RPF). The RPF had invaded northern Rwanda from Uganda in October 1990. Backed by the governments of France and Zaire, Rwandan government forces initially repelled the rebels, though later the rebels gained and held territory. In 1993, government forces, opposition politicians, and the rebels agreed to a ceasefire and power-sharing agreement known as the Arusha Accords (so-named after the city in Tanzania where they had been signed). The agreement was largely favourable to the rebels, apportioning them significant representation in a proposed new military and transitional government (Jones, 2001). As part of the agreement, the United Nations would deploy a peacekeeping force to monitor the ceasefire agreement. That peacekeeping force would ultimately be headed by Canadian General Roméo Dallaire.

In short, on the eve of the genocide the elites in or with access to power faced two major challenges to their power: on the one hand, a domestic largely Hutu political opposition and, on the other, a predominantly Tutsi rebel fighting force. In addition, a formal peace agreement that President Habyarimana had signed substantially eroded the power of the ruling party and the entrenched interests in the state. The genocide began on 6 April 1994, immediately after President Habyarimana was assassinated. The political and military officials who orchestrated the violence were largely those who had been threatened by the democratization and civil war processes.

In addition to the immediate context, Rwanda also has a deeper history of politicized and polarized ethnicity. To be brief, in the centuries immediately prior to colonial rule, a dynastic kingship governed Rwanda. Recognized as one of the most sophisticated monarchies in Eastern Africa, the Rwandan kingdom was predicated on a status distinction between animal raisers and agriculturalists. By and large, animal raisers were of higher status and were often identified as 'Tutsi'. By contrast, agriculturalists were of a lower status and were often identified as 'Hutu'. The kingship was additionally dominated by Tutsis from particular clans. The social categories 'Tutsi' and 'Hutu' were thus largely based on status and economic activity in pre-colonial Rwanda. Social relations were nonetheless complex. Hutus and Tutsis were in the same clans; they spoke the same language; with enough cattle and status, a Hutu could become Tutsi and vice versa. The hierarchy was also codified through labour and land: some Hutus would exchange labour in exchange for access to land to grow crops (Chrétien, 2003). Pre-colonial Rwanda was neither harmonious nor simple; a strict hierarchy existed, but the main point is that the social categories Hutu and Tutsi were more complex than 'tribes' or 'races', which is how they would come to be interpreted.

European travellers first began exploring the region in the second half of the nineteenth century, and Rwanda (together with the neighbouring kingdom of Burundi) was eventually apportioned to Germany during the great colonial partitioning of Africa. Germany controlled Rwanda until just after World War I, when Rwanda (and Burundi) was awarded to Belgium as part of a colonial trusteeship programme. The European intervention had many impacts, but one consistent theme is the way

in which Europeans interpreted Rwanda's social categories and the effects of those interpretations.

Upon finding Rwanda's sophisticated governing
system and social hierarchy, European travellers, and
later colonialists, concluded that they were in the presence of two distinct races. The Tutsi, they concluded,
were a superior race of 'Hamites' who had descended
from Northern Africa to subjugate the agricultural
Hutu, who were seen as more typically negro 'Bantus'.
Europeans referred to Tutsis as smarter, more elegant,
and natural-born rulers. This interpretation of Rwanda's
social categories was in step with then-current theories of race and especially a theory called the 'Hamitic
hypothesis'. That theory held that all civilization in black
Africa was the product of Hamites who had descended
from Northern Africa or the Middle East (Mamdani,
2001; Chrétien, 2003).

As the Germans, but especially the Belgians, established their colonial authority, the racial interpretation
had important implications. For one, the colonial
powers backed not only the existing monarchy, but
Tutsis more generally. Through a series of reforms,
Tutsis came to occupy positions in the colonial administrative apparatus; Tutsis were sent to receive Western
education; literacy allowed them to participate in the
new colonial governing system. In summary, under
colonial rule Tutsis were systematically elevated to positions of authority and power. In addition, the colonial
authorities entrenched and further racialized the social
categories. National identity cards were introduced in
the 1930s, and a person's 'race' was entered. During the
colonial period, anthropologists and others sought to
identify scientifically racial differences by measuring
height, cranium, and noses of Hutus and Tutsis. The
colonial intervention thus not only widened the power
differential between Hutus and Tutsis, but also institutionalized and racialized the social categories (Newbury,
1988; Mamdani 2001). All of these changes would have
an effect as Rwanda's political history unfolded.

The Tutsi favouritism of the colonial period stayed
in place until the heady period after the Second World
War. For a mix of reasons in that period, the Belgian
administration and clergy took steps to increase Hutus'
power. Tutsi elites who had benefited under colonial
rule resisted the change, leading the Belgians to lend
further support to Hutu counter-elites. For their part,
young Hutu intellectuals began espousing an ethnic
nationalist position—namely, that since Hutus were

the majority and since democracy meant majority
rule, Hutus should govern. All that set the stage for a
rapid cascade of sometimes violent events known as the
'Hutu Revolution', during which the Belgians abolished
the Rwandan monarchy, appointed a Hutu head of state,
and oversaw the purging of Tutsis from positions in the
administration. By the time independence was granted
in 1962, there had been a near complete reversal of representation, with Hutus dominating the state and Tutsis
largely out of power. The period also saw massacres of
Tutsi civilians and the exile of many Tutsis, who sought
refuge in neighbouring countries (Lemarchand, 1970).
It would be the descendants of the early Tutsi exiles
from the late 1950s and 1960s who formed the core of
the RPF rebel movement that invaded in the 1990s.

Rwanda and Theories of Genocide

What does this brief history of the Rwandan case tell us
about theories of genocide? When the violence started
and the images and stories of massacres circulated,
much of the initial commentary focused on antipathy.
Many claimed that the genocide was the product of
'ancient tribal hatred' between Hutus and Tutsis. That
idea remains somewhat popular but, as the brief history
shows, the reality is considerably more complex. First,
Hutus and Tutsis are not 'tribes'; they speak the same
language, come from the same regions, intermarry,
and the like. Moreover, the differences between the
categories were originally based on status, and then the
European encounter racialized the identities. Second,
the European intervention had a decisive impact, so
the notion of tribes who have hated each other for centuries is wrong. Third, in Rwanda there exists an ethnic
nationalist ideology that is predicated upon European
racial categories and that is similar to nationalist ideologies in other cases of genocide. Fourth, the notion
of tribal fighting severely underplays the state-level,
top-down orchestration of the violence.

Evidence from the Rwandan case in truth supports
multiple theories. Even if 'ancient tribal hatreds' is a
misleading cue, Rwanda had elements of a divided
society that Kuper described. Even if Rwanda was
undergoing a democratic transition at the time of the
genocide, Rwanda had been an authoritarian state, and
the country has a firmly entrenched hierarchical system
of government. For those who emphasize deprivation

(e.g. Uvin, 1998), Rwanda had widespread poverty and the country was at war. For those who emphasize ideology or ethnic nationalism, the Hutu hardliners who unleashed the genocide embraced a specific racial ideal that held that Hutus were the majority and should rule. For those who emphasize the strategic interests of leaders or statist calculations in the context of wartime territorial loss, the Rwandan case again provides support for the theory. And finally, the case may be interpreted to show the importance of a modern state and the ways in which modern ideas of race play a role. To be sure, different scholars emphasize different aspects of the Rwandan case to make their argument; nonetheless, to say that many theories fit the case also shows how difficult it is to evaluate theories of a relatively rare and complex macro-social event like genocide.

The International Response

This section turns to a more traditional human rights concern, the international response. As noted, the United Nations had deployed a small peacekeeping force to Rwanda as part of the peace agreement. Several months before the genocide, General Dallaire had received information about militia training to kill Tutsi civilians. However, when he sought authorization to use his troops to raid militia weapons caches, the UN Department of Peacekeeping Operations refused. The story was much the same once the genocide started. Quickly realizing that a major atrocity was unfolding, Dallaire requested reinforcements to protect Rwandan civilians. However, the response from his superiors in New York, as well as from all of the most powerful international actors, was to avoid direct confrontation. Indeed, the international response from European states and the USA in the first weeks of the genocide was, firstly, to evacuate their nationals and, secondly, to neuter the UN peacekeeping force on the ground (Dallaire with Beardsley, 2003). In effect then, the international response was to allow the genocide to unfold in Rwanda, despite widespread ratification of the Genocide Convention.

Several explanations of the international response are put forward in the literature. First, the Rwandan genocide unfolded less than a year after the debacle in Somalia in which eighteen American soldiers died. The Somalia violence was a foreign policy blow to the Clinton Administration, as well as to UN peacekeeping operations, and neither the USA nor the UN had the appetite for a risky intervention in another African state (Barnett, 2002; Power, 2002). Second, Rwanda is a small, landlocked, francophone, coffee-and-tea exporting state in Central Africa. Rwanda had little name recognition in the Anglophone world and little strategic value to Northern powers. The European country with some of the strongest interests in Rwanda, Belgium, advocated for the withdrawal of UN forces shortly after Belgian peacekeepers were killed on the first day of the genocide. Third, the language of 'ancient tribal hatreds' that saturated the public coverage created little incentive to intervene. If Rwanda was composed of tribes that hated each other for centuries, the international community would have poor odds in staunching the killing. Fourth, interviewed after the fact, Clinton Administration officials acknowledged that there had been little public outcry for action (Power, 2002). Finally, the genocide happened quite quickly. Many commentators refer to Rwanda as the 'preventable genocide' given early warnings of escalation, the already existing presence of a peacekeeping force, the rudimentary means of violence used in the country, and finally the lack of ambiguity about genocide (OAU, 2000). Nonetheless, the sheer speed of the violence was a major obstacle to mobilizing an effective response (Kuperman, 2001).

If the international response was to avoid intervention, a corollary was to refuse to label unequivocally the events in Rwanda as 'genocide'. Within the Clinton Administration, the concern was that if officials called the violence 'genocide' then they would be obligated to act to prevent the massacres under the Genocide Convention. Initially, US spokespeople were instructed to avoid the term; US officials also thwarted attempts at the United Nations to declare the violence 'genocide'. Eventually, the policy allowed US officials to speak of 'acts of genocide'. Nonetheless, the idea was to sidestep obligations under the terms of the Convention by refusing to label events in Rwanda definitively as 'genocide' (Power, 2002).

More than a dozen years after the Rwandan genocide happened, the case is frequently recognized as one of the most significant foreign policy and human rights failures of the late twentieth century. In many respects, lessons from this case shaped the international response to Darfur (as discussed below). At the same time, despite the failure on the prevention side, the aftermath of the genocide has seen a flurry of activity on the punishment side. In late 1994, the United Nations established the International Criminal Tribunal for Rwanda to prosecute the major architects and planners of the genocide. Inside Rwanda, the victorious RPF initially established domestic courts to prosecute perpetrators. They later followed with a large experiment in 'community justice' called *gacaca*, in which ordinary Rwandans would judge perpetrators in open-air sessions. Each of the three justice mechanisms has its problems (ICG, 2001; Waldorf, 2006; Peskin, 2008). These issues in transitional justice are beyond the purview of this chapter (see Chapter 20), but the level of activity around justice and punishment is consistent with other cases: the punishment provisions of the Genocide Convention have proven more influential than the prevention ones.

KEY POINTS

The Rwandan genocide is one of the worst mass human rights atrocities of the late twentieth century.

In three months, at least 500,000 civilians were killed, mostly of the minority Tutsi group. The violence was systematic and government led.

The proximate context was a transition to multi-party politics, civil war, and the assassination of President Juvénal Habyarimana.

Rwanda also has a history of racialized and politicized ethnicity in which European colonial intervention played a major role.

The international community failed to respond to early warnings of genocide and largely abandoned Rwanda as the genocide started.

Darfur

The second major case discussed in this chapter concerns Darfur in western Sudan. Darfur is composed of three separate provinces, comprising an area roughly the size of France and home to some six million people prior to the latest conflict. The violence and mass human rights abuses that put the region on the international map began in mid-2003 and continue as of this writing in mid-2008. Estimates of the number killed vary, with the high-end estimate being around 450,000 and a more conservative estimate of about 200,000. In addition to those who have perished as a direct consequence of the fighting, some 2.5 million Darfurian civilians have been displaced during the conflict (see Chapter 14). Given the relative recentness of the conflict, less is known about the proximate and deep origins of the violence, in comparison to Rwanda. But from an international human rights perspective, the case is again instructive with regard to the difficulty of prevention.

Historical Background

Darfur is enormously complex demographically, with dozens of tribes and clans operating in the region.

However, the contours of the conflict largely revolve around a cross-cutting cleavage between, on the one hand, farmers and herders, and, on the other hand, 'Arabs' and 'non-Arabs'. In Sudan, one of the enduring cleavages is between those who identify their origins as 'Arab' and who have a North African and Middle East orientation versus those who identify as 'non-Arab', with a more sub-Saharan African orientation (Deng, 1995; Lesch, 1998). In most of Sudan, the ethnic identity cleavage is overlaid with a religious and regional one: most Northerners are Muslim and many identify as 'Arab', while most Southerners are Christian or Animist and identify as 'non-Arabs'. The North–South, Muslim–Christian, Arab–African cleavage was the source of two long civil wars in Sudan, one from 1955 to 1972 and one from 1983 to 2005. Darfur is exceptional in at least two respects, *vis-à-vis* the rest of Sudan. First, Darfurians are uniformly Muslim. Second, the Arabs and non-Arabs are integrated within the region. Nonetheless, in Darfur, as in the rest of Sudan, there exists a cleavage between those claiming Arab identity and whose main economic activity is pastoralist herding, and those who identity as non-Arab and whose main economic activity is sedentary agriculture.

In most periods of time, differences between Arabs and non-Arabs were not a source of violence in Darfur. Indeed, there is evidence of much intermarriage in the region, and visitors to the region cannot tell apart physically an Arab from a non-Arab. Nonetheless, starting in the mid-1980s and proceeding to the early twenty-first century, relations between some Arab and some non-Arab tribes began to deteriorate in the region. This was the case for three main reasons. First, increased drought and desertification meant that competition for the most important resources in the region—water and arable land—increased. As a consequence, some herders encroached on farmers' lands, sometimes violently. In response, farmers formed self-protection units to protect their lands. Second, there was an influx of weaponry and Arab supremacist ideology. Both largely had to do with a spill-over war from neighbouring Chad. In the late 1980s, Chadian rebels used Darfur as a staging ground, receiving weapons from Libya. Third, when Arabs clashed with non-Arabs, successive Arab-dominated governments in the Sudanese capital Khartoum backed the local Arabs and often appointed them to positions of local authority. All three changes upset pre-existing relations and increased tension and violence between groups in Darfur (Prunier, 2005; Daly, 2007; Flint and de Waal, 2008).

The conflict came to a head in 2002 and 2003 when two separate Darfur rebel groups formed and began attacking government positions in the region. The two groups, the Sudan Liberation Army and the Justice and Equality Movement, drew their support primarily from among Darfur's non-Arab populations: in particular, the Fur, Massaleit, and Zaghawa tribes. Initially, the government did not pay terrific attention to the rebel forces. The government had been focused on the twenty-year civil war between Northern and Southern forces. But in early 2003 the rebels scored a series of victories, including one spectacular attack on an air base in El Fasher. With that attack in particular, the Darfur emergency began.

Responding to the rebel attacks, the government's strategy was to target the rebels' purported civilian supporters and to fight the insurgency using a proxy militia force. The latter was recruited primarily from Darfur's Arab populations, including those who had come into conflict with non-Arabs during earlier land clashes. The government-backed militia in the latest crisis is widely referred to as the *janjawid*, which roughly translates into mean-spirited men on horseback. Most research conducted on the patterns of violence indicates that government forces and militias have routinely been involved in joint attacks on non-Arab civilian populations. A common pattern is for government aircraft to bomb villages, followed by militias riding into the villages, killing stragglers, looting, setting buildings and homes on fire, and poisoning wells. Sexual violence has been widespread (Askin, 2006). Many deaths are due to direct killing; many Darfurians have also died as a consequence of forced displacement from their homes.

Darfur and Theories of Genocide

What does Darfur say about theories of genocide? It should be noted that much of the in-depth research that has shaped an understanding of the Rwandan case is still in process for Darfur. The latter is quite recent. Nonetheless, the evidence from the case lends itself to numerous theories. If one were to stress deep, etched visions, the Arab/non-Arab cleavage at the local and national levels is an important dimension. As for regime type, during the Darfur conflict Sudan is going through a political opening: in particular, through the integration of Southerners as part of a peace deal from the North–South war. Nonetheless, the government in Sudan is largely authoritarian. At the national level, the deprivation argument is harder to make—though the North–South peace deal amounts to a significant change in society. Nonetheless, in Darfur the water and land shortages exacerbated by environmental factors are critical factors in the conflict. For those who point to ideology, the key points are the influx of Arab supremacist thinking in Darfur as well as a broader commitment to Arab nationalism among Northerners in Sudan. Like Rwanda, Darfur is occurring in the midst of a civil war—and those who stress the wartime, strategic dimensions of genocide have a clear argument. Finally, with regard to political development, more research should be done, but an argument pointing to the ethnic purging and killing as part of a consolidation of power and identity would have a case to make. In short, different theories highlight different contributing dimensions of the violence, and more research and careful hypothesis testing will be in order to weigh the merits of the possible theoretical claims.

The International Response

On the international side, the Darfur crisis received relatively limited attention during the first year of violence. However, 2004 was the tenth anniversary of the Rwandan genocide, and as Rwanda was commemorated Darfur received a surge of new attention, especially in the USA. Much of the subsequent response to Darfur was driven by lessons from Rwanda. In particular, activists in the USA formed a diverse civil society coalition to put pressure on the Bush Administration. Moreover, the initial focus was to have the Administration label the violence 'genocide' under the theory that doing so would trigger action under the Genocide Convention. To make a long story short, in historic moves both Congress and the Administration ultimately called Darfur 'genocide', the latter doing so after an innovative study (Straus, 2005; Totten and Markusen, 2006). However, the Administration interpreted the Convention's terms to indicate that the obligation meant taking the issue to the United Nations.

At the United Nations, the primary obstacles to intervention lay with the Security Council. China and Russia opposed non-consensual coercive action that would effectively 'prevent' genocide. Both countries generally oppose policies in which human rights issues are a pretext for armed intervention. Moreover, China has large oil interests in Sudan, and Russia sells military hardware to the Sudanese government. As Permanent Five members of the Security Council with veto power, China and Russia formed an initially insurmountable obstacle to forcible intervention. Moreover, given commitments in Iraq and Afghanistan, the United States was not in a position to lead a mission.

Facing such realities, Secretary General Kofi Annan appointed a commission to study whether the violence in Darfur was genocide. In a 2005 report, the commissioners detailed the violence but concluded that they lacked evidence to indicate genocide. In particular, the commissioners did not find sufficient indicators of top-level intent to destroy the non-Arab population of Darfur (COI, 2005). The report recommended the matter be referred to the International Criminal Court (ICC), a recommendation that the Security Council ultimately endorsed. In 2007, the ICC indicted two Sudanese; as of this writing, neither had been arrested, and the ICC is continuing its investigation.

On the prevention side, the question of whether the United Nations would use military force to protect civilians simmered until mid-2006. In May, under significant international pressure, the government and one rebel faction signed a ceasefire agreement, which included a provision on accepting a UN peacekeeping mission. The Security Council subsequently agreed to send a large peacekeeping mission to Darfur with a robust mandate to protect civilians. However, the government of Sudan opposed different dimensions of the plan, especially the composition of the forces—Sudan wanted more African representation. There followed a new negotiation leading to a new Security Council resolution authorizing a hybrid United Nations/African Union force of about 26,000 peacekeepers. Even so, the mission has been very slow to deploy. Meanwhile, the situation in Darfur grew even more complicated, with rebel groups splintering into multiple factions and some fighting amongst themselves (ICG, 2007).

In short, more than five years after the violence started, the international community as represented by the United Nations had yet to put into place an effective civilian protection force. Despite the recognition that Rwanda was an international failure, a decade after Rwanda another case has shown how difficult prevention is and how limited the international commitments to prevent genocide are.

KEY POINTS

During 2003–2008, between 200,000 and 450,000 civilians have died, and 2.5 million have been displaced from Darfur in western Sudan.

The violence is perpetrated primarily by government forces and state-backed Arab militias known as the *'janjawid'*. The victims primarily come from the non-Arab populations of Darfur.

The proximate context is a civil war and clashes over land and water.

The deeper context is a country with politicized ethnicity and cleavage between Arabs and non-Arabs.

The US has called Darfur 'genocide'; a UN Commission of Inquiry has not.

After years of negotiations, a 26,000 hybrid United Nations/African Union force was approved to deploy to Darfur to protect civilians.

Conclusion

Since the Holocaust, international actors have regularly pledged 'never again' to allow genocide to happen. The landmark treaty on genocide, the United Nations Genocide Convention, is the law that embodies that promise. Measured against the pledge to prevent genocide, the rhetorical commitments and the Convention have proven weak and ineffective. Nonetheless, the problem of genocide is receiving greater and greater attention. Scholarship on the topic is rapidly expanding, and the hope of 'punishing' genocide is an increasing reality. As a major human rights violation—the 'crime of crimes' in one common formulation (Schabas, 2000)—genocide has a special place in the firmament of international human rights treaties. The question for the future is how and whether the promise to rid this 'odious scourge' (to cite the Convention's language) will come to pass.

QUESTIONS

INDIVIDUAL STUDY QUESTIONS

1. In what ways do the discussions in the drafting of the Convention prefigure debates on what constitutes genocide?

2. What are the strengths and weaknesses of the United Nations Genocide Convention?

3. What are the most important points of difference about the definition of genocide and why do they matter?

4. Using both the definitions in the United Nations Genocide Convention and Raphael Lemkin's original definition of genocide, what are the elements of the Darfur and Rwanda cases that do or do not indicate genocide?

5. What theories of genocide apply most clearly to the Rwanda case and what theories apply most clearly to the Darfur case?

6. What are the important similarities and differences between the causal factors in Rwanda and Darfur?

7. In what ways did the international failures in Rwanda shape the international response to Darfur?

8. What does Darfur show the international community that Rwanda does not?

GROUP DISCUSSION QUESTIONS

1. In what way is the history of the United Nations Genocide Convention similar and different to the story of other major international human rights documents that emerged after the Second World War?

2. What do the Rwanda and Darfur cases reveal about the ambiguities in the definition of genocide and the weaknesses of the Genocide Convention?

3. In the chapter, it is argued that over time the punishment provisions of the Genocide Convention have proven stronger than the prevention ones. What does this say about international human rights more generally?

4. In what ways do the theories of genocide presented in the chapter conform to your own understanding of genocide? In what ways are they different?

5. In what ways is Rwanda similar and different from the Holocaust?

6. What should be the takeaway lessons from Darfur, if any?

FURTHER READING

Dallaire, R. with **Beardsley**, B. (2003). *Shake Hands with the Devil: The Failure of Humanity in Rwanda*. Toronto: Random House Canada.
An excellent memoir by the Canadian head of the peacekeeping mission to Rwanda.

Daly, M. (2007). *Darfur's Sorrow: A History of Destruction and Genocide*. New York: Cambridge University Press.
A comprehensive discussion of the history and politics of Darfur.

Flint, J. and **de Waal**, A. (2008). *Darfur: A New History of a Long War, Revised and Updated*. London: Zed Books.
A rich and thoughtful discussion of the crisis in Darfur and the proximate context.

Hari, D. (2008). *The Translator: A Tribesman's Memoir of Darfur*. New York: Random House.
A powerful first-person account of surviving the violence in Darfur and aiding reporters who covered the story.

Power, S. (2002). *A Problem from Hell: America and the Age of Genocide*. New York: Basic Books.
A Pulitzer-Prize winning account of international, especially US, failures to prevent genocide; also a good discussion of Raphael Lemkin.

Prunier, G. (1995). *The Rwanda Crisis: History of a Genocide*. New York: Columbia University Press.
An overview of Rwandan history and the genocide.

Schabas, W. (2000). *Genocide in International Law: The Crimes of Crimes*. Cambridge: Cambridge University Press.
The definitive text on the drafting of the United Nations Genocide Convention and various legal dimensions of the treaty.

Stone, D. (ed.) (2008). *The Historiography of Genocide*. London: Palgrave Macmillan.
An overview of historical debates of around more than a dozen cases.

Valentino, B. (2004). *Final Solutions: Mass Killing and Genocide in the Twentieth Century*. Ithaca, NY: Cornell University Press.
A well-written accessible political science account of the causes of genocide and mass killing.

WEB LINKS

http://www.ushmm.org/conscience/ The Committee on Conscience website provides analysis and advocacy on contemporary genocides.

http://www.enoughproject.org/ The Enough website provides analysis and advocacy on ending genocide and crimes against humanity.

http://www.crisisgroup.org/home/index.cfm The International Crisis Group website provides analysis of contemporary conflicts, including Darfur.

http://www.ictr.org Website of the International Criminal Tribunal for Rwanda.

http://www.icc-cpi.int/home.html&l=en Website of the International Criminal Court provides information on prosecuting mass atrocities in Darfur and beyond.

http://genocidescholars.org/ Website of the International Associate of Genocide Scholars.

http://www.tandf.co.uk/journals/titles/14623528.asp Website of the *Journal of Genocide Research*.

http://www.utpjournals.com/gsp/gsp.html Genocide Studies and Prevention.

ONLINE RESOURCE CENTRE

Visit the Online Resource Centre that accompanies this book for updates and a range of other resources:

http://www.oxfordtextbooks.co.uk/orc/goodhart/

Torture

William F. Schulz

Chapter Contents

Reader's Guide

Torture is among the most common human rights crimes in the world. It is usually associated with interrogation procedures but is often inflicted to intimidate political opponents, reinforce cultural practices, or spread gratuitous violence. This chapter examines the use of torture in Western history and examines such questions as: Are all torturers sadists or can an average person be trained to be a torturer? Are some societies more prone to practise torture than others? And is torture ever justified? In respect to this last question, the chapter examines in detail the pro and con arguments of the hypothetical case in which a suspect is thought to know the location of a ticking bomb that is about to explode and may injure large numbers of people. It concludes that such a scenario is extremely rare and describes how the far more common forms of torture may most successfully be diminished.

Introduction

Miguel Angel Estrella is one of the world's great pianists. In 1977 he was arrested and thrown into Uruguay's notorious Libertad prison for alleged 'subversive associations'. His case attracted international attention and the Queen of England herself intervened on his behalf, requesting the head of the Uruguayan military junta to allow Estrella, at the very least, access to a piano. The authorities agreed and the Queen sent a piano to be presented to him. What the great performer received, however, was merely the keyboard ripped out of the body of the instrument and therefore inoperable. 'Your playing will disturb the other prisoners', the musician was informed (Weschler, 1990).

When we think of torture, we customarily conjure up images of dark chambers and brutal physical treatment. Indeed, there is plenty of that. When Belgium's King Leopold ruled the Congo in the late nineteenth century, his minions were fond of punishing the Indigenous workers with whips made from raw, sun-dried hippopotamus hide cut into long, sharp-edged corkscrew strips. Twenty-five lashes brought unconsciousness and one hundred brought death (Hochschild, 1998, pp. 120–123). Beatings, electroshock, rape—all of these are common forms of torture. The United States has acknowledged using water-boarding (in which the victim's mouth is covered with cloth and water poured over his face to simulate drowning) to extract information from terror suspects (Schoof, 2008; see Fig. 17.1).

Some torturers are fiendishly creative. I remember reading about the technique used by the *mujahadeen* (religious warriors) in Afghanistan. They would strap their captured enemies to corpses and let the two bodies, one dead, one alive, rot together in the sun. In Brazil during the 1970s prisoners were stripped naked and left in a small concrete cell with only one other occupant—a boa constrictor (Dassin, 1986, pp. 16–17). In the Philippines at the turn of the twentieth century, American prisoners of war were buried up to their

FIGURE 17.1 Water-boarding.
Adapted from Carter (2005).

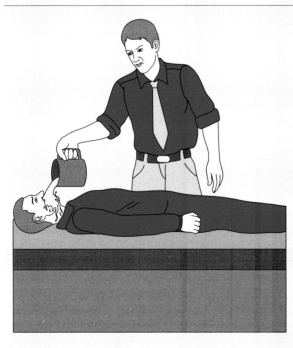

Name: Water-boarding
Description: According to University of Wisconsin history professor Alfred McCoy, this technique was first developed by the French and published in a six-teenth-century interrogation manual. Practitioners of 'water torture', or 'question de l'eau', placed a piece of cloth over the victim's mouth and nose, and then poured water into the mouth to force the cloth down the victim's throat. The effect was to make breathing impossible, thus creating the psychological perception of drowning.
Physical, psychological, or other effects: Severe mental suffering; no physical effects unless the tactic results in suffocation.
Legal opinion: The Geneva Conventions and Protocols surely prohibit this method as torture and as a form of cruel or degrading treatment. The International Covenant on Civil and Political Rights and the CAT also forbid water-boarding because it inflicts severe mental suffering, as does the Uniform Code of Military Justice and federal criminal law.

necks in manure, molasses was then poured over their heads, and fire ants let loose on their scalps (Schulz, 2003, p. 155).

The Americans got their revenge, however, by employing the popular 'water cure' against the Filipinos. One US soldier described it this way:

> Lay them on their backs, a man standing on each hand and each foot, then put a round stick in the mouth and pour a pail of water in the mouth and nose, and if they don't give up pour in another. They swell up like toads. (Kramer, 2008, p. 38)

But psychological torture, such as that employed against Estrella, has also been popular. The Soviets, for example, would frequently deceive a man in custody by informing him that the screams he heard in the next room were from his wife or daughter who were themselves being tortured. It was a sure-fire way to get him to talk (Solzhenitsyn, 1973, pp. 106–107).

It is hard to know how widespread the use of torture is today, but Amnesty International reports that it 'has documented torture in more than 150 countries. . . . In more than 70 countries, it is widespread. People in 80 countries have died as a result . . .' (Amnesty International, 2008a). Among the countries where torture has been documented are some of the most populous, including China, Russia, and the United States.

No matter exactly how many people have been subjected to torture, we know it is one of the most common human rights violations (see Box 17.1). And while no respectable observer would defend wife-beating or ter-

---

Box 17.1 **What Is It Like To Be Tortured?**

With depictions of brutality pervasive in movies, television, video games, and on the Internet, it is easy to imagine other people being beaten up and abused. But it is harder to wrap our minds around what it would truly be like to be tortured ourselves. So try a little experiment. Try standing to attention in the middle of the room without moving a muscle. This is one of the simplest and most popular forms of torture because none of us can hold that position for very long. Imagine if the moment that you moved or twitched you received a powerful electric shock or were beaten on the back of your legs with a club. Now think what it would be like to stand like this under a broiling sun. For an hour. For ten hours. For a day.

---

rorism, there are more than a few who can imagine circumstances in which torture is justified. That is one reason why it is so important to understand the phenomenon.

In this chapter we will look first at the history of torture in the Western world and then consider what it takes to turn someone into a torturer. We will explore whether some social conditions make the use of torture more likely and whether there are cases in which its employment is justified. Finally, we will describe what can be done to diminish, if not end, the instances of torture and how those efforts complement other developments in the field of human rights.

Torture in Western History

Today the use of torture is largely hidden, conducted in secret locations, never advertised to the public. Most governments deny that they would even think of manhandling prisoners. Even those who defend the practice agree that it should be employed only rarely and within strict limits. But, interestingly enough, in ancient times people found the use of torture as natural as can be.

Torture of Slaves: 'I Cannot Tell a Lie'

Perhaps it is not surprising that the ancient Greeks and Romans felt little compunction about torturing slaves.

Marginalized people, people with less power, are often more likely to be subjected to harsh treatment than those who possess political and economic might. But what is intriguing about the practice of torture in early Greek and Roman history is the *rationale* for slaves being subjected to torture. It was because slaves (in contrast to free citizens) lacked the quality of reason (what the Greeks called *logos*) and hence lacked the capacity to lie. Free citizens could tell the difference between truth and falsehood. But not possessing *logos*, a slave could not think through the consequences of telling the truth or prevaricating. If forced, he had no choice but to tell the truth. Therefore, if public officials were trying to determine what *really* happened—who really stole the wine; who really killed the shepherdess—they had merely to torture a slave (DuBois, 1991, pp. 63–66).

Here is an early example of a common characteristic of victims of torture: they are regarded as somehow less than fully human, as missing some quality (in this case reason) that warrants their being treated with the same degree of respect as everyone else. They are therefore regarded as 'outsiders', different from 'us', and hence it is less heinous to abuse them. We will see this dynamic at work again and again.

But at least the Greek and Roman legal systems had an honourable motive for the torture of slaves (which is not to say, of course, that many slaves were not tortured for less than honourable reasons): they were seeking the truth. Eventually, however, the limitations of relying upon slave testimony alone became obvious. There were only so many slaves, among other things, and not every crime was conveniently accompanied by a slave witness. Other means for ascertaining the facts in a criminal matter would have to be discovered. Fault could be decided by the reputation of the parties involved or the credibility of oaths that they were willing to swear. Physical tests (called 'ordeals') could be undertaken. If, for example, the accused could carry a hot piece of metal in his bare hand for nine feet without the hand blistering, he was judged not guilty; in contrast, the appearance of blisters was unimpeachable evidence of guilt. By the twelfth century, however, it was generally agreed that one means of telling truth from falsehood was superior to all others: a confession!

'The Queen of Proofs'

So reliable were confessions considered by the late Middle Ages that they came to be known as '*the Queen of Proofs*'. And what was the most effective way to elicit a confession? Torture, of course. Torture therefore became a routine part of everyday criminal procedure and interrogation. Indeed, the very word *quaestio* (Latin for 'the question falls') came to be synonymous with torture.

The judicial system of the age adopted an elaborate series of 'safeguards' to govern the use of torture. If there were two witnesses to a crime, for example, a confession

(and hence torture) was not necessary. Before someone could be tortured, there either had to be one witness to the offence or profound circumstantial evidence of guilt. Interrogators were forbidden to use suggestive questioning (Langbein, 1977). Despite these and other restrictions, many innocent people were brutalized, often in the most horrendous ways, as tales of medieval torture chambers readily attest.

It was difficult enough to decide likely guilt sufficient to warrant torture in civil cases. But when it came to religious questions like heresy (deviation from official church doctrine) and witchcraft, the matter became even more complicated. These were, after all, in large measure crimes of thought, not deed, and hence hard to prove. But that only reinforced the need to secure confessions. The Church itself undertook inquisitorial tribunals in which torture was commonplace.

From the standpoint of religious officials, of course, heretics and witches were even more dangerous than common thieves and murderers because they were thieves and murderers of the eternal soul. If their pernicious beliefs spread and were adopted by others, thousands of innocents would not just be deprived of earthly property or physical life, as was the case with common crimes, but would be subjected to eternal torment. The torture of a few miscreants was a small price to pay to prevent such a tragedy.

But how could anyone know for certain that the right people were being punished? Under torture, victims confessed to all sorts of things. Most of those accused during the Salem, Massachusetts, witchcraft trials of 1692, for instance, eventually admitted that they were guilty even *before* they were tortured! Like the slaves of ancient times, theological deviants were categorized as less worthy of the legal protections that accrued to the rest of society. The result was that often those who were innocent suffered the same penalties as those who were guilty.

The Cry for Abolition

Gradually a reaction to such injustices set in. Five years after the Salem trials, one of the judges, Samuel Sewall, stood up in church and passed a piece of paper to his minister to read to the congregation: 'Samuel Sewall,' the preacher read while Sewall bowed his head, '. . . being sensible . . . as to the Guilt contracted, upon the opening of the late [court] at Salem . . . Desires to take the Blame & Shame of it, asking pardon of Men, And especially desiring prayers that God . . . would pardon that Sin . . .' (Francis, 2005, p. 181).

In 1734 Sweden became the first country to abolish virtually all forms of torture, and a few years later Prussia did away with the practice altogether. Other countries followed. The French historian Michel Foucault suggested that the rejection of orthodoxy and 'superstition' that characterized the **Enlightenment**, along with the cruelty that accompanied them, accounts for the change. There was a vast repulsion at the public displays of brutality that had typified the Middle Ages. 'It was as if', Foucault (1977, p. 9) wrote, 'the punishment was thought to equal, if not exceed, in savagery the crime itself . . . to make the tortured criminal an object of pity and admiration.'

Anti-abolitionist sentiment, as expressed most popularly by the Italian economist Cesare Beccaria in his 1764 'An Essay on Crimes and Punishment' (Kramnick, 1995, pp. 525–532) and the French *philosophe* Voltaire in his 'On Torture and Capital Punishment' (Kramnick, 1995, pp. 532–535) the same year, was sweeping Europe. Lynn Hunt (2007), an historian, attributes this in large measure to empathy for other people's suffering occasioned by the popularity of eighteenth-century novels depicting the plight of heroines with whom the public identified. Coupled with growing personal modesty—an end to urinating in the street or blowing one's nose in one's hand—that signalled the advent of the self-contained and hence inviolable body, this trend helped to usher in new respect for human rights.

The eminent legal historian John Langbein (1977, pp. 10–12) offers a different theory. He contends that the trigger was not changing views occasioned by the Enlightenment but a shift in the way proof was established by the courts that occurred two centuries before, namely, that judges began evaluating the evidence pro and con based on its merits without the need for confession or torture. Whatever the case, by the turn of the nineteenth century cultural norms in Europe had turned sharply against torture—or at least the torture of fellow Europeans (we have seen that King Leopold had no hesitation about torturing Africans well into the twentieth century). Combined with growing opposition to slavery (the slave trade was abolished in Great Britain in 1833), there was reason to think a more humane form of civilization might be at hand.

The early development of international **humanitarian law** (sometimes called 'the laws of war') reinforced such optimism. In 1863 the International Red Cross was formed and the next year sixteen European countries adopted the first of the **Geneva Conventions and Protocols** that mandated humane treatment of battlefield casualties and protection for the civilians who offered them aid. This in turn was followed by the **Hague Conventions** of 1899 and 1907 that sought to make warfare itself less brutal by banning such things as nerve gas and hollow point bullets and the Third Geneva Convention of 1929 that offered protocols for the treatment of prisoners of war. It was not of course that torture and war crimes ceased altogether, but that no one could any longer claim official sanction for such atrocities.

Until, that is, the coming of the Holocaust. The crimes of the Nazis and their collaborators were not only unprecedented in ferocity and scale—the Second World War has been dubbed a 'total war' because, in addition to the customary attacks on troops, civilians and their property were indiscriminately targeted—but what had been regarded as the most cultured nation in Europe had planned and executed them. In reaction to the catastrophe, both the United Nations and eventually the modern human rights movement were born. The 1948 Universal Declaration of Human Rights (UDHR) declared in Article 5 that 'No one shall be subjected to torture or to cruel, inhuman or degrading treatment or punishment.' Adopted without dissent, the UDHR established norms and expectations not just for Europeans but for the entire world.

Since that time, dozens of other treaties, conventions, codes of conduct, and other international legal instruments have reiterated the prohibition of torture (see Box 17.2) until today it is regarded as **customary international law**, that is, law that is so fundamental and universal as to be beyond dispute and hence is applicable to and the responsibility of all governments; and torturers are considered *hostis humani generis* or enemies of all humankind. The most important of these international instruments is the **Convention Against Torture and Other Cruel, Inhuman, or Degrading Treatment or Punishment (CAT)**, which entered into force in 1987 and has been ratified by more than 140 countries.

And yet, despite all this opprobrium, torture endures.

Box 17.2 **Extracts from the Principal International Instruments Against Torture**

Universal Declaration of Human Rights

'No one shall be subjected to torture or to cruel, inhuman or degrading treatment or punishment.' (Article 5)

Geneva Conventions and Protocols

'. . . the following acts are and shall remain prohibited at any time and in any place whatsoever with respect to the above-mentioned persons:

    (a) violence to life and person, in particular, mutilation, cruel treatment and torture; . . .

    (c) outrages upon personal dignity, in particular humiliating and degrading treatment, . . .'

    (Common Article 3)

International Covenant on Civil and Political Rights

'No one shall be subjected to torture or to cruel, inhuman or degrading treatment or punishment. In particular, no one shall be subjected without his free consent to medical or scientific experimentation.' (Article 7)

European Convention for the Protection of Human Rights and Fundamental Freedoms

'No one shall be subjected to torture or to inhuman or degrading treatment or punishment.' (Article 3)

American Convention on Human Rights

'No one shall be subjected to torture or to cruel, inhuman, or degrading punishment or treatment. All persons deprived of their liberty shall be treated with respect for the inherent dignity of the human person.' (Article 5)

African Charter on Human and Peoples' Rights

'Every individual shall have the right to the respect of the dignity inherent in a human being and to the recognition of his legal status. All forms of exploitation and degradation of man, particularly slavery, slave trade, torture, cruel, inhuman or degrading punishment and treatment, shall be prohibited.' (Article 5)

UN Convention against Torture and Other Cruel, Inhuman or Degrading Treatment or Punishment

'Each State Party shall take effective legislative, administrative, judicial or other measures to prevent acts of torture in any territory under its jurisdiction.' (Article 2)

Inter-American Convention to Prevent and Punish Torture

'The States Parties shall ensure that all acts of torture and attempts to commit torture are offenses under their criminal law and shall make such acts punishable by severe penalties that take into account their serious nature.' (Article 6)

UN Body of Principles for the Protection of All Persons under Any Form of Detention or Imprisonment

'No person under any form of detention or imprisonment shall be subjected to torture or to cruel, inhuman or degrading treatment or punishment.' (Principle 6)

Convention on the Rights of the Child

'No child shall be subjected to torture or other cruel, inhuman or degrading treatment or punishment . . .' (Article 37)

UN Declaration on the Elimination of Violence against Women

'Women are entitled to the equal enjoyment and protection of all human rights and fundamental freedoms in the political, economic, social, cultural, civil or any other field. These rights include, *inter alia*:

    . . . (h) The right not to be subjected to torture, or other cruel, inhuman or degrading treatment or punishment.' (Article 3)

UN Code of Conduct for Law Enforcement Officials

'No law enforcement official may inflict, instigate or tolerate any act of torture or other cruel, inhuman or degrading treatment or punishment . . .' (Article 5)

KEY POINTS

The ancient Greeks and Romans regarded slaves as incapable of telling a lie because they lacked the capacity to reason. It was therefore thought completely appropriate to torture a slave (as opposed to a free citizen) in order to ascertain the truth about a criminal matter.	Gradually, whether because of new cultural norms ushered in by the Enlightenment or changes in the legal system, torture became prohibited throughout most of Europe. Coupled with codification of the laws of war and international humanitarian law, there appeared to be promise of a more civilized approach to international relations.
In the medieval period, legal authorities considered a confession to be the 'queen of proofs', the most reliable way to resolve a question of guilt or innocence. Since torture was an efficient way of eliciting confessions, it was commonly used, albeit in accordance with a set of guidelines. The church had little reticence about using torture to expose heretics and witches.	Such promise was badly set back by the Holocaust, though one of the consequences was the development of the modern human rights movement, including a now universal legal prohibition on the use of torture.

How to Make a Torturer

Are torturers madmen? Deviants? Hardened criminals? Sexual predators? Almost never. In fact, most police and military units weed out the psychological misfits because they know such people have trouble taking orders. The horrible truth is that the vast majority of torturers are average Joes, like Jose Valle Lopez (see Box 17.3) or, on far rarer occasions, Janes.

The Psychology of Transformation

Turning Joe into a torturer is remarkably easy. You put him in a restricted environment, such as a police or military training camp, under the command of a vaunted authority figure. It helps if the recruit is young and impressionable but people of all ages are susceptible

---

Box 17.3 **The Case of Jose**

Jose Valle Lopez did not think of himself as a bad man. He had joined the army of his native Honduras at fifteen; slowly gained more authority within its ranks; married and fathered two children. Over the years Jose, who, because of his weight, was known as *El Gordo*, 'The Fat One', developed a kind of hardened attitude to prove that he could take the teasing, that he had *cojones*—manliness, courage. As a result, when word spread among the military authorities in the 1980s that the Honduran army would not allow the Communists to infiltrate Honduras as they had done in neighbouring Nicaragua and threatened to do in El Salvador, Jose was more than willing to do what he was told to protect his country.

At first he was assigned to surveillance; then to kidnapping. But the hours of the latter were erratic, so Jose was transferred to the torture division in order to have

more regular time with his family. As a journalist who told his tale years later put it, 'he would kiss his wife and children goodbye, pick up his lunch and go off to work in the torture chambers . . .'. There he would submerge his victims in water, suffocate them, and apply electroshock to their genitals.

Eventually he could no longer tolerate the screaming. But when he asked for a transfer, the ridicule began again: 'What's the matter, El Gordo? No *cojones*?' But Jose persisted: he wanted out. And that is when the threats began: 'The day you leave, Jose, we will cut your head off.' So Jose fled with his family to Canada and finally went public with his story. He wanted the world to know that he was not a monster. He wanted to make the case that, under similar circumstances, many others would have done the same thing. (Adapted from Atkinson, 1989)

Box 17.4 **The Milgram and Stanford Prison Experiments**

Two experiments in social psychology have become classics in the field, often cited to illumine the motivations of those 'average citizens' who inflict cruelty on their fellow human beings. Each experiment has been criticized both as to its ethics and its methodology, but both also reflect at least a germ of truth that is worth exploring.

The experiments conducted by Yale psychologist Stanley Milgram beginning in 1961 involved an authority figure (the experimenter) instructing a subject who had been designated the 'teacher' to issue an electric shock to another person (designated 'the learner') every time the learner made an error in a word test. The voltage of the shock supposedly increased at a regular pace and, though the teachers could not see the learners, they could hear them expressing pain, screaming, and eventually begging the teacher to stop shocking them. (In reality, no shocks were being administered.) Despite hearing these pleas, a significant number of teachers, when instructed to do so by the authority figure (the experimenter), continued to issue

the shocks. Milgram concluded that most people had a strong tendency to obey authority and that therefore ordinary people could be transformed into agents of destruction under the right circumstances (Milgram, 1974).

The Stanford prison experiment was led by Stanford University psychologist Philip Zimbardo in 1971. One group of university students were designated 'guards' and another 'prisoners' and then placed in a simulated prison environment in the basement of the Stanford psychology department building. Because the behaviour of many of the guards quickly took on a sadistic character—even though all participants knew the situation was no more than a simulation—Zimbardo stopped the experiment prematurely, concluding, like Milgram, that in certain situations otherwise well-balanced individuals will act in a cruel fashion toward others perceived to be weaker or different, especially when given sanction to do so (Haney *et al.*, 1973).

---

to the demands of authority under the right circumstances—even murderous demands, as the famous Milgram and Stanford prison experiments demonstrated (see Box 17.4).

You then subject your recruit to intense stress, harassment, and brutality. The Greek military police in the time of the Greek generals (1967–1974), for example, were renowned for their torture squads. Each of the recruits to those squads was forced to go weeks without food and undergo severe beatings, sometimes not being permitted to defecate for up to fifteen days at a time (Haritos-Fatouros, 1988). Joan Golston (1993), a psychotherapist who has studied torturers, theorizes that the abuse heaped on trainees casts them in the 'victim' role and, in order to mitigate the shame of that experience and differentiate themselves in their own minds from 'real' victims, they in turn inflict abuse upon others. This is what she calls 'the torturer's bind'.

Be that as it may, once we have created an angry, desensitized, but obedient servant, the next steps are to train that servant in torture techniques—the object is to inflict enormous pain but not to kill—and to provide sanction for employing those techniques against a vulnerable but despised and dehumanized object: 'These are the people who are threatening our country.' 'This is the person who killed your comrade.'

One thing that virtually every victim of torture has in common is that he or she has been defined as alien to the dominant culture; one of 'them', not one of 'us'; in short, a 'barbarian', to use the word the novelist J. M. Coetzee chooses in his famous story, *Waiting for the Barbarians*

Box 17.5 **Waiting for the Barbarians**

In his classic 1982 novel *Waiting for the Barbarians*, the South African novelist J. M. Coetzee captures the phenomenon of dehumanization concisely. He describes a large crowd that is awaiting the appearance of a group of prisoners—'Barbarians!'—who are tied to each other by a rope around their necks. In addition, a metal wire has been looped through a hole in each prisoner's cheek that connects in turn to a hole in his hand. 'It makes them meek as lambs', one soldier says, 'They think of nothing but how to keep very still.'

The prisoners are paraded in front of the crowd so that 'everyone has a chance . . . to prove to his children that the barbarians are real.' Then the Colonel of Police steps forward.

Stooping over each prisoner . . . he rubs a handful of dust into his naked back and writes a word with a stick of charcoal . . . 'ENEMY . . . ENEMY . . . ENEMY . . . ENEMY.' He steps back and folds his hands . . . Then the beating begins. (Coetzee, 1982, pp. 102–105) (see Box 17.5). Those who are labelled outsiders, as having violated our most sacred values, can be thought to have sacrificed their claim to the protection of rights, including their right to be regarded as human.

In many cases the torturers, like Jose Valle Lopez, convince themselves that they are acting in a higher cause, that the questions they ask and the information they procure are essential to other people's welfare or the survival of a way of life. But all too often the motivation for torture is not so 'high-minded'. Often the real goal is intimidation of the prisoner or the members of his or her group or community. Unlike those earlier forms of torture that were prompted by a desire to solve crimes or save souls, modern-day torture often reflects little more than a sadistic character, a desire to display complete sovereignty over the will of another person. This is certainly the case, for example, when rape is used as an instrument of war, as it was in the war in the Balkans (Allen, 1996), or when prisoners are led around in leashes or forced to masturbate for the cameras, as they were at the US prison at Abu Ghraib, Iraq (Danner, 2004).

Whatever the motivation, there is one more characteristic shared by virtually all torturers: they believe they will get away with their crimes. Very few act on their own whim. Torture is rarely the case of 'a few bad apples' acting contrary to the wishes of their superiors. Whether they have received explicit orders or only a 'wink and a nod', most torturers believe that those to whom they are accountable will at least privately approve of what they do. Indeed, torture does not survive long without impunity, that is, the belief that the perpetrator will be exempt from any punishment or penalty.

And yet sometimes—again Jose is an example—the stress of the job itself begins to take its toll. Frantz Fanon (2004, p. 195), a psychiatrist who became a famous philosopher of anti-colonialism, tells of treating a police officer who came to him suffering from depression. 'The thing is they never wanted to confess', the officer said of the people he had tortured.

> Sometimes you feel like telling them that if they had any consideration for us, they'd cough up and not force us to spend hours on end squeezing the information out of them. But you might as well talk to the wall . . . So of course we had to give them the works. But they scream too much. At first it made me laugh. But then it began to unnerve me . . . Now I can hear those screams even

at home. Especially the screams of the ones who died at police headquarters. Doctor, I'm sick of this job. If you can cure me, I'll request a transfer . . . If they refuse [to transfer me], I'll resign.

But getting out is not always easy, both because torturers have been taught psychologically to revere authority and obey it and because they are often threatened by their colleagues and supervisors if they try to leave. Few systematic studies of the mental health of torturers have ever been undertaken—the universe of those willing to admit their guilt and subject themselves to testing is too small!—but it is not hard to believe that those who inflict brutality sustain emotional damage too. In a paradoxical way, then, the phenomenon of torture creates two sets of victims.

The Social Preconditions of Torture

If large numbers of 'average' people can be made into torturers, are all societies equally susceptible to resorting to the practice or are there some social conditions that make torture more likely?

In a broad sense, as we have seen, torture requires there to be a significant differential in power between torturer and victim. Based upon his studies of Turkey during the years of the Armenian genocide (1914–1918), Nazi Germany (1933–1945), Pol Pot's Cambodia (1976–1979), and Argentina in the period of the 'Dirty War' (1976–1983), Erwin Staub (1990, pp. 49–50), one of the few social scientists to have studied the 'social indicators' of genocide and torture, identifies scapegoating of a subgroup as a social condition conducive to the rise of torture. Other characteristics of societies that resort readily to torture are: strong respect for authority and hence little questioning of leadership; a monolithic culture that militates against expression of conflicting views; widespread concepts of cultural superiority that may mask self-doubt or economic anxiety; and the presence of an ideology that rationalizes mistreatment of a minority or out-group.

All this is well and good. But we know that democracies—even robust democracies like the United States that sanction vigorous political debate and proclaim their commitment to equal treatment of all—can also succumb to the temptations of torture. Ronald Crelinsten (2005, pp. 76–77), a criminologist, has expanded upon and reframed Staub's list based on contemporary examples associated with the post-9/11 'war on terror'. He, too, finds the dehumanizing of an out-group—in this case, Muslims—central to the institutionalization of torture. But he cites additional factors that make it more likely: a national emergency or perceived threat to security; the need to process large numbers of suspects; authorization to violate standard social norms (and here he does not limit that authorization to government or military officials but includes members of the media and academia who provide the rationale for brutality); and the presence of a 'sacred mission' in whose name anything is acceptable.

Suffice it to say that societies that feel themselves under threat are more likely to strike out at those whom they fear and leaders of even the most open society can leverage that fear for unfortunate ends. But might there not indeed be circumstances where such fear is justified and the use of 'unusual methods', including torture, legitimate? We turn now to the hypothetical case of the 'ticking bomb'.

KEY POINTS

Many regimes have transformed average people into torturers by exposing them to authority figures who subject them to brutal training, teach them the techniques of torture, and then provide sanction for the mistreatment of some despised individual or group of people who are regarded as less than human.

Torture requires a sense of impunity. Few people will engage in the practice without the encouragement of their superiors.

Torture takes an immense toll on its victims, of course, but may also do damage to the mental health of its perpetrators, who may find it difficult to extract themselves from a torture regimen even if they want to.

Certain social conditions, including concepts of cultural superiority and an exploitation of feelings of fear among a populace, may increase the likelihood of torture being practised, even in largely open, democratic societies.

Case Study: Ticking Bomb Torture

The Arguments for Torture

No respectable commentator has ever tried to defend torture inflicted for the sheer sadistic pleasure of it, but many noteworthy philosophers, including the great Jeremy Bentham (1748–1832), have argued that under a narrow set of circumstances torture is not only defensible but morally obligatory. The hypothetical case is usually put something like this: suppose that the authorities have in custody an individual whom they believe has information that, if they can procure it quickly, will help them prevent the detonation of a bomb that, if allowed to explode, will kill hundreds, if not thousands, of people. Would they not be justified in using whatever coercive means were necessary to force the revelations they seek? Indeed, could they not be accused of dereliction of duty if they allowed moral reservations to prevent them from doing so, thereby sacrificing the lives of many innocent people?

The argument for the use of torture under these circumstances is based upon a pretty straightforward

cost–benefit calculation: torture one suspect; save 1000 (or however many) lives. It is hardly surprising that Bentham should favour torture, having been a thorough-going utilitarian, a system of ethics most simply explained as holding that the moral worth of an action can be determined by the degree to which it brings the greatest amount of happiness or pleasure to the greatest number of people. This is an example of what is called consequentialism, namely, the notion that we ought to judge an act by its consequences (sometimes expressed simply as 'the ends justify the means') in contrast to a deontological approach in which acts are considered intrinsically good or bad, no matter their consequences.

On the face of it, the argument for 'ticking bomb torture' seems unassailable. It is not, however, without its weaknesses and serious scholars who have advanced it have recognized that and tried to respond. One weakness is that it is not always easy to know who has the information we seek and who does not. No one believes that it is justifiable to torture an innocent person. So philosophers such as Michael Levin (1982), who argue for the legitimacy of ticking bomb torture, have agreed that we should 'torture only the obviously guilty', such as would be the case if '40 million people see a group of masked gunmen seize an airplane on the evening news'.

Another potential weakness is the so-called 'slippery slope', the danger that, once we have allowed torture under very limited conditions, authorities will be tempted to expand upon the number of people tortured or the circumstances in which it is allowed. Alan Dershowitz (2002), a well-known law professor, has proposed that if authorities wish to torture someone then they should be required to go to a judge and obtain a torture warrant that would limit the brutal treatment as to target, duration, intensity, etc. and have the additional virtue of placing responsibility squarely on the backs of higher authorities rather than on the low-level police or military officer who has to inflict the punishment directly.

In 1987 the Israeli government faced accusations that its security arm, Shin Bet, had been applying undue physical pressure to Palestinian prisoners and a Commission of Inquiry headed by former Israeli Supreme Court Justice Moshe Landau was asked to investigate. The Landau Commission Report (1989) concluded that, faced with a ticking bomb situation, 'moderate physical pressure' (a detailed description of which was included in a secret annex to the report) could be applied as the lesser of two evils and could be legally defended under the doctrine of necessity, that is, the notion that one harmful act may be justifiable to prevent a second far more harmful act.[1]

The Arguments against Torture

To marshal the arguments against ticking bomb torture is a more complicated task than to argue the affirmative unless one feels comfortable relying upon a strictly deontological stance and proclaiming, perhaps on the basis of religious doctrine or natural law philosophy or simple illegality, that torture is intrinsically wrong under all circumstances. Exploration of such topics is beyond the bounds of this chapter, however, so we will restrict ourselves to arguments of a pragmatic or consequentialist nature.

As we have seen, the ticking bomb scenario looks like a situation in which torture is not only justified,

but may even be morally imperative: we are certain that our suspect knows where the bomb is hidden; we must obtain that information quickly and we know that torture will be an effective means to pry accurate information out of him; we voluntarily limit our brutality to the suspect himself and limit the amount of pain we inflict to the minimal necessary to get him to talk; and more people will live as a result of our action than would otherwise die. This is what we will call the 'pure scenario' and, if this is the hypothesis we are faced with, it is difficult to bring persuasive consequentialist arguments to bear against it.

The problem is that in real life such a scenario is extraordinarily rare—we cannot say it has never arisen, but there are no documented cases of it having done so in exactly this form—and the last and most important calculation, namely, that more people will live than die as a result of our use of torture, is, as we shall see, impossible to prove. So let us take the elements of the scenario one by one.

'We are certain that our suspect knows where the bomb is hidden.' But how certain do we have to be for torture to be justified? Levin appears to say that we must be one hundred per cent certain. But how often are fallible human beings one hundred per cent certain of anything? (And how do we measure degree of certainty anyway?) Even in the example that Levin gives—'40 million people see a group of masked gunmen seize a plane on the evening news'—there is room for doubt. The gunmen are, after all, 'masked'. And we know that television pictures can easily be altered to show just about anything. Moreover, the world in which torture interrogations take place is a world of shadows. Suspects are not paraded before the public or caught on camera; their bad deeds are rarely fully known. (Indeed, if they *were* known, we would have little reason to torture them.) So one hundred per cent certainty seems like a pipe dream. What, then, if we were only ninety-five per cent certain? Should we refrain from torture then, even if we think coercion would save thousands of innocent lives? How about if we were only fifty per cent certain? If we had a fifty-fifty chance of saving people, would that not be worth the gamble? What if we only had a one per cent sense of certainty? Would it not be reasonable, even if we had only vague suspicions, to torture one individual if the consequences of not doing so were the loss of thousands of innocents? And yet, if we were to follow that path, we would certainly end up torturing lots of suspects who had no relevant knowledge to share at all. You can see how quickly the 'limited circumstances' under which torture is justified morph into something much larger.[2]

'We must obtain the information quickly and we know that torture will be an effective means to pry it out of the suspect.' The vast majority of interrogations in which torture is used involve the quest for long-term information, the names of comrades, patterns of behaviour, and the structure of networks. The United States has acknowledged torturing many alleged terrorists in order ostensibly to prevent future 9/11s, but there is no reason to believe that those would-be attacks came within only minutes of being carried out but for the timely use of torture to prevent them. Moreover, there is good reason to believe that torture is an ineffective means of obtaining accurate information. Prisoners in excruciating pain are notorious for telling interrogators anything they want to hear. As a former FBI interrogation instructor put it,

> Interrogation is an art form, not a street fight. It is built on guile, perseverance, and a keen understanding of how people respond to need. People will tell you anything if you present the questions in the proper context. You simply have to find the right way to ask. (Whitcomb, 2002)

'We voluntarily limit our brutality to the suspect himself and limit the amount of pain we inflict to the minimal necessary to get him to talk.' But, under a consequentialist ethic, what possible reason is there for limiting our torture in any way? Why do we need to have any scruples at all about the techniques we employ? Furthermore, we know from reports of torture victims that it is often far more painful to see a loved one brutalized than to be subjected to harm oneself. If our initial acts of torture do not work, therefore, why are we not fully justified in torturing the suspect's spouse or teenage child or two-year old baby to get him to talk? Would not even harm to one baby be morally justified if it saved the lives of hundreds of other people, including, no doubt, dozens of babies? What about torturing two babies to save four babies? Under the ticking bomb scenario, there is no good reason ever to stop. This is exactly why torture that is intended initially to be highly circumscribed so often ends up sliding down that slippery slope. Tens of thousands of people have been subjected to torture over the years. It is hard to believe that they all knew the whereabouts of a ticking time bomb.

'More people will live as a result of our action than would otherwise die.' This is of course the nub of the issue. If we cannot show that torturing a prisoner ultimately does more good for more people than abstaining from torture would, we cannot make a defensible case for the practice, given all the problems we have raised thus far. Under the pure ticking bomb scenario, the cost–benefit calculation is self-evident. But in real life the consequences of torture may be far more complex. Let us assume that, by torturing a suspect, we manage to save 1000 lives. How do we know that, upon learning that their brother or comrade had been brutally tortured, other members of the suspect's community will not want to even the score by killing 2000 people? What happens to our cost–benefit calculation then? We certainly know that many armed groups opposed to governments around the world often motivate their members by citing government atrocities. As the founder of the Israeli chapter of Physicians for Human Rights put it, those Palestinians subjected to torture by Israel 'are broken after their experience . . . Their families . . . want to take revenge' (*Village Voice*, 2001). And this is to say nothing about the damage done to the reputations of those governments that condone torture—damage that may very well make their citizens and property far more vulnerable targets of attack. As the former chief prosecutor for the US military commissions at Guantanamo Bay, Cuba, pointed out, one of the reasons the Iraqi army surrendered readily in the 1991 Persian Gulf war, thereby saving untold American lives, was because they believed that they would not be tortured by the American military (Davis, 2008). 'Would it have been different', he asked in 2008, 'if the perception of [Americans] as purveyors of torture and humiliation existed back then?' Even the strict utilitarian argument for ticking bomb torture may not stand up to scrutiny.

Twelve years after the Landau Commission Report, the Israeli Supreme Court struck down virtually all of the techniques of 'moderate physical pressure' that the Commission had allowed as 'not reasonable', 'not fall[ing] within the sphere of a "fair" interrogation' and 'impinge[ing] upon the suspect's dignity, his bodily integrity and his basic rights . . .' (Supreme Court of Israel, 1999).[3] The Court did not rule out 'necessity' as a means of defence against the use of torture. But it said that necessity could not be cited *before the fact* as a rationale. It could only be called upon after an indictment had been brought against an alleged torturer to explain and excuse his acts.

Law professor Oren Gross (2004, pp. 229–253) has elaborated upon this notion, arguing that torture should always be banned and hence its employment always illegal but that state agents, be they the torturers themselves or the higher authorities who directed them, might well seek *ex post facto* (retrospective) ratification of their acts either in a court of law or the court of public opinion. Such an approach presumably preserves the state's image (not least of all its self-image) as a righteous nation committed to the rule of law while recognizing the political and legal reality that, in the face of a pure ticking bomb scenario, authorities who resort to torture are unlikely to be punished. In contrast to Dershowitz's 'torture warrant' proposal, which codifies torture as a legitimate option before the fact, thereby offering certain impunity to officials and colouring the image of the society as one that tolerates cruelty, Gross's proposal forces authorities to commit civil disobedience and live with the knowledge that they may or may not be exonerated afterwards—knowledge that might discourage the kind of capricious use of torture that has been so common in the twentieth century and beyond.

> **KEY POINTS**
>
> Torture is often justified by its defenders with reference to a hypothetical situation in which a suspect has knowledge of a ticking time bomb that is about to go off and, if it does, will kill many people. Is it not justified to use torturous interrogation techniques against such a suspect under that limited circumstance to procure information necessary to avert an enormous tragedy?
>
> This defence is based upon a straightforward cost–benefit analysis: doing harm to one person in order to avoid harm to many more is a moral act.
>
> Opponents of the use of torture argue that the pure hypothetical situation described in the ticking bomb scenario is not reflected in real life and that the calculations are far more complicated than they at first appear.
>
> Israel has been one of the few countries that have regularly debated this issue in public and its experience may be useful.
>
> A key issue is whether we ought to agree ahead of time that torture may be legitimate under some circumstances or whether we should always regard it as illegal and require those who break the law to justify their actions after the fact.

Putting an End to Torture: New Developments and High Promise

Regardless of one's opinion on the ticking bomb question, the fact is that it represents a tiny fraction of the instances in which torture is used. Far more common is the mistreatment meted out by police or military officials for political or religious reasons, to inflict retaliation, or to foster intimidation.

But what exactly constitutes torture? Where does cruel behaviour end and torture begin? The CAT requires torture to involve '*severe* pain and suffering'. But what is the definition of severe? And is it not true that human pain thresholds vary and that what one person considers 'severe' pain another might consider relatively mild?

The European Court of Human Rights (ECHR) addressed this question in a landmark case, *Ireland* v. *United Kingdom* (1978), in which it ruled that five techniques—wall-standing; hooding; subjection to loud noise; deprivation of sleep; and deprivation of food and

drink—used by British officials against Irish nationalists, while they 'did not occasion suffering of the particular intensity and cruelty implied by the word torture', did amount 'to a practice of inhuman and degrading treatment', and that in itself was a breach of the European Convention on Human Rights, which prohibited such practices. The point is that, while understandings of what constitutes torture may vary, even acts that do not rise to the level of torture are outlawed under most human rights conventions. Recall that the name of the most pertinent convention is the Convention Against Torture *and Other Cruel, Inhuman, and Degrading Treatment or Punishment*.[4]

The CAT defines torture, then, as

. . . any act by which severe pain or suffering, whether physical or mental, is intentionally inflicted on a person for such purposes as obtaining from him or a third person information or a confession, punishing him for an act he or a third person has committed or is suspected of having committed, or intimidating or coercing him or a third person, or for any reason based on discrimination of any kind, when such pain or suffering is inflicted by or at the instigation of or with the consent or acquiescence of a public official or other person acting in an official capacity.

Yet even this definition is incomplete. The ECHR ruled in *Aydin* v. *Turkey* (1997) that rape while in state custody constituted torture, thus expanding the category to include instances of gratuitous violence. Nor does it make sense to limit torture to acts involving public officials. After all, **non-state actors**, such as armed opposition groups, terrorist organizations, private security contractors hired by corporations, and tribal elders enforcing cultural traditions such as *female genital mutilation (FGM)*, engage in practices that look very much like torture, even if they are not covered by the CAT definition. Many observers (Copelon, 1994) would now include severe forms of domestic violence and child abuse within the rubric too.

Once we have established the breadth of the problem, the final and most crucial question becomes: What can we do about it? We know that laws in and of themselves cannot stop criminal acts and that much international law goes unenforced. Over the past decade and a half, however, several important developments carry considerable promise that torture may be successfully combated, even if it is never eliminated.

In the first place the vast majority of the world's nations have incorporated laws against torture into their own constitutions and legal statutes. This includes prohibitions against crimes that are often considered culturally sanctioned, such as burning the faces of brides who displease their husbands, dowry killings (the killing of brides whose dowries are not considered adequate), and female genital mutilation. While such laws are often sporadically enforced, they provide the legal basis for indigenous human rights activists, whose numbers and sophistication have been growing rapidly, to challenge these practices, both legally and socially. Contrary to the old slogan 'You cannot legislate morality', the fact is that one of the ways to shift cultural norms is by declaring certain practices out of bounds legally and hence unacceptable to those who want to understand themselves as abiding by the rule of law. The more that torture is outlawed, the more it

becomes socially deviant to practice or support it. The international community would not countenance today a debate about whether slavery or piracy was an acceptable practice, and that is slowly becoming the case with torture as well.

But we need not rely on political pressure or social shaming alone. Perhaps the most important development of recent years has been the increasing vibrancy of the legal concept of **universal jurisdiction**, the doctrine that certain crimes are so serious that, regardless of where they were committed, any country on earth may claim jurisdiction over them and seek prosecution of those alleged to have committed them. States party to the CAT are obligated either to prosecute those credibly accused of torture whom they find on their territory, even if the torture was committed elsewhere, or extradite them to a country that will.

This doctrine has largely been honoured in the breach, but in 1999 the British Law Lords (the United Kingdom's highest court) ruled that General Augusto Pinochet, the former president of Chile who had come to Great Britain for medical treatment and hence was on British soil, could not claim **sovereign immunity**[5] and could be extradited to Spain to stand trial for the torture and murder of Spanish citizens even though those acts were alleged to have been committed in Chile. Pinochet was eventually judged too ill to stand trial and returned to Chile, where he later died, but the precedent that those accused of torture might legitimately be prosecuted anywhere in the world had been established by a highly respected court. Utilizing the doctrine of universal jurisdiction, Belgium in 2001 successfully prosecuted four Rwandan citizens accused of involvement in the 1994 Rwandan genocide. In principle, then, those who commit crimes against humanity, such as torture, need not only fear prosecution before such tribunals as the International Criminal Court, if it can claim jurisdiction, or various *ad hoc* tribunals, if they exist, but may also face indictment before national courts that are inclined to pursue them. Coupled with the burgeoning use of truth commissions (see Chapter 20) to sort out the facts of past human rights crimes and hold the appropriate people responsible for them, universal jurisdiction provides still one more way to effect a degree of accountability for crimes like torture.

In the United States such accountability is being pursued through the use of the Alien Torts Claims Act

(ATCA) of 1789, which provides jurisdiction in federal courts over lawsuits by aliens (foreign nationals) for torts (wrongs) committed either in violation of international law or of treaties to which the United States is a party. The Act was originally intended as a mechanism to compensate those who had lost property to pirates, but in a historic case, *Filartiga* v. *Pena-Irala* (1980) (see Box 17.6), a US court ruled that torturers resident in the US could be sued for civil damages under the Act by their victims or their victims' families. Since then the Center for Justice and Accountability (CJA), among others, has successfully assisted a myriad of victims of torture and other crimes to bring such suits, many of which have been successful. In December 2005, for instance, a federal jury found a former El Salvador military colonel guilty of crimes against humanity and ordered him to pay $6,000,000 to four people who had been tortured or had relatives killed by his security forces. Plaintiffs do not always collect on these judgments but, even when they do not, they often feel that justice has been served because the guilt of the accused has been established publicly. Moreover, those who are found guilty of such crimes may well be subject to deportation from the United States. Moreover, ATCA may also be a vehicle for holding corporations to account for human rights abuses. In 2004 UNOCAL corporation, without admitting guilt, reached a settlement in a case in which fifteen Burmese villagers alleged that it had commissioned Burmese soldiers to protect its gas pipeline in Yadana, Burma, even though it knew that those soldiers were committing murder, rape, and forced labour. Because the case was settled without judgment, it is an unsettled legal question as to whether ATCA can successfully be used in the future against corporate entities, but the possibility is intriguing.

None of these legal tools by themselves will put an end to torture. They must be supplemented by continuing vigilance on the part of international and indigenous human rights organizations, aided by: new forms of electronic communication, to bring torture out of the shadows; pressure from such bodies as the European Union, which has used Turkey's interest in joining the Union, for example, as a vehicle for encouraging that country to improve its record on torture significantly (Worden, 2005); and the systematic training of police and military officers in appropriate and effective methods of interrogation.

Torture will no doubt continue to claim its victims; fortunately, health professionals are establishing more and more treatment centres for victims of torture to ease the pain of the experience and help survivors rebuild their lives. But torturers can be less certain than in decades past that they will get away with their crimes. As the human rights movement matures and grows, that uncertainty will build and, just as nothing encourages torture to flourish more than impunity, so nothing will hasten its decline more readily than the sure knowledge that the use of such brutality will no longer go unpunished.

Box 17.6 *Filartiga* v. *Pena-Irala*

Joel Filartiga was a Paraguayan physician who ran a clinic for the poor and was suspected by the government of being involved with a guerilla organization. In 1976 his son, Joelito, was kidnapped by a police official named Americo Pena and others, and tortured until he died of cardiac arrest. Though the Filartiga's brought suit against the Paraguayan government, they received no satisfaction in that country's courts.

In 1978 Pena, his mistress, and two relatives took up residence in Brooklyn, NY. When they were discovered, US officials arrested them for overstaying their visa. Pena sought to be deported to Paraguay. But Dolly Filartiga, Joelito's sister, who was living in Washington, DC at the time, along with her father, filed a $10 million civil suit against Pena under the Alien Tort Claims Act (ATCA) for compensation in the death of Joelito. The suit was initially dismissed on the grounds that ATCA precluded consideration of a foreign government's treatment of its own citizens. But in June 1980 that judgment was reversed.

Finding that customary international law forbade torture, the US Circuit Court ruled (630F.2d 876; 1980 U. S. App. LEXIS 16111) that the reach of such law extended everywhere and that therefore US courts *did* have jurisdiction over matters of this nature even though they had occurred in other countries. Since this precedent-setting decision, ATCA has been used frequently to bring civil suits against alleged torturers who have taken up residence in the United States. (Claude, 1983)

KEY POINTS	
The definition of what constitutes torture is not exact, but cruel, inhuman, and degrading treatment is also outlawed by international human rights law and hence we need not quibble overly much about definitions.	In the United States the Alien Torts Claims Act has been used successfully by victims of torture to seek civil damages from their torturers.
Torture is not a phenomenon the use of which is limited to government officials. Non-state actors are guilty of it too.	Ending torture requires a combination of factors but the key is to convince would-be torturers that they will be punished for their crimes.
Fortunately, most countries now outlaw torture in most of its various forms and major developments in international law, including an increasingly robust principle of universal jurisdiction, lend encouragement to the hope that the frequency of torture may be reduced.	

Conclusion

Why human beings so frequently inflict grievous injury in the form of torture upon one another is a complex scientific and perhaps theological question. One neuropsychologist has suggested that the howls of pain that emanate from our fellow human beings are so appealing, especially to males, because they evoke the success of the hunt, hearkening back to the Palaeozoic era, and hence signal personal and social power (Nell, 2006). Other observers would attribute the appeal to the inherent human capacity for sin.

While we have dealt in this chapter with torture as it has occurred in the West, it is a worldwide phenomenon that has been found in virtually every region of the globe. As we have seen, the rationale for torture, dating back to the earliest eras of Western history, is often a perceived need to obtain information, but brutality has often been used for less 'reputable' reasons as well. It is not necessarily difficult to convince individuals to become torturers—a fairly standard process involving authority figures, isolation, brutalization, technical training, and assurances of impunity has been documented to work effectively. When such a process

is introduced into a society that has identified a group of people as threatening outsiders and hence as people possessing fewer claims to rights or even to be considered human, torture is often almost inevitable.

Some have argued that a ticking time bomb scenario may warrant the use of torture, but such instances are extraordinarily rare and the question far more complex than it initially appears to be. The more common uses of torture, e.g. for political or social intimidation, may best be combated by strictly enforced laws against it, cultural norms that forbid it, and assurance that those who engage in it will pay a significant penalty.

It is said that Vladimir Lenin, one of the most brutal and hard-hearted men in the world, could not listen to Beethoven's *Appassionata* because it made him cry. It will take far more than beautiful music to rid the world of torture. Lenin's tears remind us that even the most corrupted soul may retain a spark of humanity to which we may appeal, but the far more important lesson that they teach is that tender thoughts can be misleading and that the only way to truly put an end to cruelty is to be vigilant in pursuit of its cessation.

QUESTIONS

INDIVIDUAL STUDY QUESTIONS

1. Why did the ancient Greeks and Romans think it appropriate to torture slaves to obtain information? Why was that practice ultimately considered inadequate as a way to solve crimes?

2. What is the 'Queen of Proofs'? Why were heretics considered to be even more dangerous than common thieves by the medieval church?

3. Describe two theories as to why European governments gradually came to abandon the use of torture as an official practice. Does one of these theories seem more plausible to you than another?

4. What is 'customary international law' and why does the prohibition of torture fall under its rubric? What are *hostis humani generis*?

5. Describe the general process by which police or military recruits are often transformed into torturers. Do you think that you yourself might be vulnerable to such a transformation?

6. Describe some of the characteristics of societies in which torture tends to be found. Name four or five societies, past or present, that you think meet these criteria.

7. What is 'universal jurisdiction' and why is it such an important tool in the fight against torture?

8. What is the Alien Torts Claims Act and how has it been used against alleged torturers in the United States?

GROUP DISCUSSION QUESTIONS

1. What is the 'ticking bomb scenario'? Describe the arguments in favour of the use of torture in such a situation and those against such use? Do you find one set of arguments more compelling than the other? Ought torture to be outlawed in all cases and those who engage in it forced to defend their use after the fact, or ought it to be possible to grant judicial permission for torture before it is employed?

2. What are the keys to diminishing the use of torture around the world? How do cultural norms change? Is it better to have laws on the books against torture even if they are not always adequately enforced or do such 'sham laws' do damage to the integrity of the rule of law itself?

3. Is some amount of torture inevitable or do you believe it can be significantly reduced? What is your theory as to why brutality such as torture appears to be so frequently and commonly employed by human beings against one another?

FURTHER READING

Conroy, J. (2000). *Unspeakable Acts, Ordinary People: The Dynamics of Torture—An Examination of the Practice of Torture in Three Democracies*. New York: Knopf.
A gripping account based on first-hand interviews with torturers and their victims of the use of the practice in Northern Ireland, the United States, and Israel.

Danner, M. (2005). *Torture and Truth: America, Abu Ghraib, and the War on Terror*. London: Granta.
A comprehensive look at the United States's use of torture at the Abu Ghraib prison camp in Iraq by a prize-winning *New York Times* reporter.

Levinson, S. (ed.) (2004). *Torture: A Collection*. Oxford: Oxford University Press.
An excellent collection of essays on the philosophical and legal dimensions, with special attention to debate over whether torture is ever justified.

Peters, E. (1996). *Torture*. Philadelphia, PA: University of Pennsylvania Press.
Widely considered to be the definitive history of torture in the Greek, Roman, and medieval periods. Superb appendix of documents.

Roth, K. and Worden, M. (eds) (2005). *Torture: Does It Make Us Safer? Is It Ever OK?* New York: New Press.
Largely original essays with special attention to the US's practice of torture.

Scarry, E. (1985). *The Body in Pain: The Making and Unmaking of the World*. Oxford: Oxford University Press.
A complex, highly sophisticated exploration of the experience and psychodynamics of torturing and being tortured.

Schulz, W. (ed.) (2007). *The Phenomenon of Torture: Readings and Commentary*. Philadelphia, PA: University of Pennsylvania Press.
An extensive digest of readings—some hard to find elsewhere—on all aspects of torture from first-hand accounts of the experience to essays on the psychodynamics between torturer and victim, the ethics of its use, and the efforts to combat it.

Weschler, L. (1990). *A Miracle, A Universe: Settling Accounts with Torturers*. New York: Pantheon.
A moving, extraordinarily well-written account of torture in Latin America in the 1970s. Full of astonishing stories. A classic.

WEB LINKS

http://www.amnesty.org The world's oldest and largest international human rights organization, Amnesty International, carries updated information on torture in dozens of countries and what citizens can do about it.

http://www.cvt.org The Center for Victims of Torture is one of the major organizations treating survivors of the experience.

http://www.hrw.org Website of Human Rights Watch, a US-based human rights organization that tracks the use of torture around the world.

http://www.omct.org Created in 1986, the World Organisation Against Torture (OMCT) is today the main coalition of international non-governmental organizations (NGOs) fighting against torture, summary executions, enforced disappearances, and all other cruel, inhuman, or degrading treatment.

http://www.kspope.com/torvic/torture.php This website provides links to all major organizations working against torture.

NOTES

1. A commonly used example of the defence of necessity is the hypothetical situation in which one is asked by a would-be killer of a loved one to reveal the loved one's whereabouts. It is generally agreed that, while under most conditions lying is not morally defensible, under these circumstances the morally dubious act of lying is necessary and justifiable to prevent the far more morally egregious act of murder.

2. Germany, for example, was rocked some years ago by a case in which the police tortured a suspect to get him to reveal the location of a child he had kidnapped (Bernstein, 2003).

3. Justice Landau himself acknowledged publicly many years after the issue of his Report that he felt betrayed by Shin Bet for its having often exceeded the constraints that his Report had recommended (Felner, 2005, p. 39).

4. 'Cruel, inhuman, and degrading treatment' is sometimes referred to by its acronym, CID.

5. The legal principle that a head of government is immune from prosecution for acts committed in his official role as sovereign as opposed to acts committed in pursuit of his/her own private interests. It is generally understood that, while a head of state could be prosecuted for such things as personal corruption or murder of a spouse, he/she could not be prosecuted for the consequences of state policies.

ONLINE RESOURCE CENTRE

 Visit the Online Resource Centre that accompanies this book for updates and a range of other resources:

http://www.oxfordtextbooks.co.uk/orc/goodhart/

The Environment

John Barry and Kerri Woods

18

Chapter Contents

Reader's Guide

The aim of this chapter is to examine the ways in which environmental issues affect human rights, the ways in which human rights are relevant to environmental campaigns, and to consider proposals for extending human rights to cover environmental rights, rights for future generations, and rights for some non-human animals. The structure of the chapter is as follows. We begin by looking at the relationship between human rights and the environment in both academic literature and national and international law and policy. Thereafter, we consider the impact that economic globalization has had on the environment and the ways in which environmental insecurity causes human rights issues. Next, we ask two questions: Is the human rights framework an appropriate one in terms of which to address environmental issues? Are there alternative moral/ethical idioms that might better accommodate environmental issues, e.g. the language of justice? Finally, we look at the plausibility and potential advantages and disadvantages of extending the current human rights framework to include environmental concerns. We consider the view that sustainability, understood to encompass environmental, social, and economic concerns, is central to any proposed extension of the human rights framework to encompass environmental concerns. This, however, means that the appropriate way to think about human rights in this area is to focus on a broader understanding of sustainability rather than environment.

Introduction

In this section our aim is to outline the ways in which the environment and sustainable development/unsustainable development can be understood to be a human rights issue.

At the crux of the relationship between the environment and human rights is the inescapable fact that humans are ecologically embedded beings. That is, humans are utterly dependent upon and vulnerable to changes in their relationships with the non-human world. Yet the ramifications of this fact for our social, political, and economic practices are often neglected. The concept of sustainable development can be seen as an attempt to bring to the fore the ecological embeddedness of all human activity (especially economic activities) and therefore the need to weigh the ecological consequences of our decisions in developing and refining our social, political, and economic thinking, practices, and structures.

The concept of sustainable development has been embraced by a wide variety of actors, including governments, non-governmental organizations (NGOs), environmentalists, Indigenous peoples, trade unionists, women's groups, human rights activists, and also businesses. In the developing countries there has been talk of a right to development, while in the richer Western countries sustainable development has sometimes been seen as a way of 'greening growth' or translated to mean the 'ecological modernization' of the economy (Barry, 2004). Sustainable development as a normative concept has been circulating in green political and development theory since at least 1987, when the report of the World Commission on Environment and Development (WCED) called for a strategy integrating environment and development. Development is necessary in the South to achieve social and economic human rights, which in many countries currently are chronically underfulfilled. The strategy proposed was sustainable development, defined as 'development that meets the needs of the present without compromising the ability of future generations to meet their own needs' (WCED, 1987, p. 24). The report of the WCED was the principal inspiration for the United Nations Conference on the Environment and Development (UNCED), popularly known as the Earth Summit, held in Rio in 1992, which produced Agenda 21 (see Box 18.1), a global plan of local action to realize sustainable development. Ten years later world leaders reconvened, this time in Johannesburg, to discuss the implementation of Agenda 21. The report of this World Summit on Sustainable Development (WSSD) affirmed the need to 'delink economic growth from environmental degradation' and 'promote economic development within the carrying capacity of ecosystems' (WSSD, 2002, p. 21).

Box 18.1 **Agenda 21**

Agenda 21 is a blueprint of action to be taken globally, at global, national, and local levels, to manage human impacts on the environment, agreed at the United Nations Conference on Environment and Development in Rio de Janeiro in 1992 and adopted by over 178 governments. It represents a comprehensive attempt to manage the global economy so as to reduce environmental degradation. It includes agreements on managing all aspects of human–environment relations, including agriculture, biodiversity, energy, forests, health, industry, poverty, technology, waste, and water.

The implementation of Agenda 21, reaffirmed at the World Summit of Sustainable Development in Johannesburg in 2002, is monitored by the Commission on Sustainable Development, a commission of the United Nations Economic and Social Council (Eco-Soc). The Commission reviews implementation policies at a regional level and reports to Eco-Soc on progress.

Agenda 21 is welcomed by many governments and NGOs as a comprehensive and systematic global policy for delivering sustainable development, crucially linking environmental sustainability and human rights. The Argentinian environmentalist and human rights activist Romina Picolotti (2003, p. 49) argues that, '[t]he main concern of Agenda 21 is to meet the basic needs of human beings, such as nutrition, health preservation, decent housing, and education, each of which has a corresponding human right.'

(Cont.)

However, ecocentrists will identify this as an obviously anthropocentric set of concerns, and even those who reject ecocentrism as a basis for environmental ethics are not necessarily persuaded by the idea of sustainable development embodied in Agenda 21. For example, Timothy Doyle (1998) claims that Agenda 21 presents a vision of sustainable development that 'constructs all environmental problems as "efficiency" issues', and thus does not question either the logic of equating human development with economic development, or of prioritizing economic growth over other goals, such as greater democratic participation or socio-economic justice.

The Impact of Economic Globalization on the Environment and Human Rights

The processes of economic globalization are held to have had a positive impact on people's lives for two reasons. First, globalization makes available a greater variety of goods and services, at cheaper prices, to consumers in all corners of the globe, in every season (Stiglitz, 2002). Second, consequent upon the growth in the worldwide economy that follows from the expansion of markets, worldwide prosperity is increased because of the 'trickle-down' effect, which can be explained with reference to Adam Smith's idea that 'a rising tide lifts all boats'. Indeed, former US President George Bush claimed that '[g]rowth is the agent of change and the friend of the environment' (quoted in Doyle, 1998, p. 773). However, both of these arguments can be shown to be misleading. First, while the economic cost of numerous goods has fallen, the ecological costs are often not counted; rather, they are 'externalized' and not included in the final price or economic calculation. However, they nevertheless accrue, with significant repercussions for the health and integrity of our global ecosystems and major impacts on human health and society. Moreover, the ecological costs of globalization generally affect the poorest first, if not most. Second, while total global wealth has been increasing in recent decades, the gap between the rich and poor has also been increasing, both between the North and South, and within countries.

Some researchers have suggested another potential benefit of globalization in the form of an environmental Kuznets curve (EKC), 'whereby environmental damage starts to decrease as a country becomes rich enough' (Andersson and Lindroth, 2001, p. 113). Yet this too is misguided since, as critics have pointed out, the empirical evidence for EKC only holds for a limited range of airborne and locally specific environmental pollutants rather than overall ecological impact (Ekins, 2000; Barry, 2004). Also, an ecological footprint analysis (see Box 18.2) suggests that richer communities displace their environmental costs onto poorer ones, both within and between countries. Environmental damage does not disappear; it simply disappears from the sight of wealthy consumers. This 'out of sight, out of mind' perspective is an example, not of 'problem solution', but rather 'problem displacement' (Dryzek, 1987)—the rich world effectively shipping the ecological costs of globalization to poorer countries. It is for this reason that many environmentalists view North–South relations in terms of the 'ecological debt': the rich, minority world owes the poorer 'Global South' (Simms, 2005). Increasing disparities between rich and poor thus present an ecological problem as well as a social and political one. To explain how this is relevant to human rights, we need to demonstrate two things: first, that economic globalization is a causal factor in the maintenance of unsustainable patterns of production and consumption; second, that these unsustainable patterns of production and consumption lead to human insecurity, and thus threaten human rights.

The Environmental Impact of Economic Globalization

One possible starting place for understanding the environmental impact of economic globalization is the globalizing agenda promoted by the Bretton Woods

Box 18.2 **Ecological Footprint**

Simply put, the ecological footprint is the total ecological impact of a given thing, be it a consumable product, an individual, a family, a community, or a state. It is a particularly appealing concept in environmental politics because it demonstrates, in a way that market values do not, the full ecological cost of whatever is being measured, and, in sophisticated models, can illustrate the distribution of that cost.

The idea was originally put forward by Matthias Wackernagel and William Rees to measure the 'area of ecologically productive land (and water) . . . required on a continuous basis to (a) provide all the energy/material resources consumed, and (b) absorb all the wastes discharged . . . *wherever that land is located*', by a given population (Andersson and Lindroth, 2001, p. 114). The ecological footprint is therefore an accounting tool that enables researchers to identify countries that run an ecological deficit—that is, use up more ecological space than is available within their territory.

Today, humanity's ecological footprint is over 23% larger than what the planet can regenerate (see http://www.footprintnetwork.org/en/index.php/GFN/page/world_footprint/). As a consequence, environmental resources are being consumed and used unsustainably. Two-thirds of Organization for Economic Co-operation and Development (OECD) countries run an ecological deficit, including the UK, the USA, the Netherlands, Belgium, and Germany. Among non-OECD countries, the worst offenders are Singapore, Hong Kong, and Israel. The ecological debt of some countries is explicitly recognized in their sustainable development plans—for example, the latest UK sustainable development strategy says 'one planet living' is a core objective.

For further information see also the Global Footprint Network's website (http://www.footprintnetwork.org/index.php) where you can also find a number of films on ecological footprint and sustainable development.

institutions and, in particular, the International Monetary Fund (IMF) and the World Trade Organization (WTO). This is an appropriate beginning because, while globalization is often (rightly) associated with advances in technology that facilitate communication and transport at faster and cheaper rates than at any other time in history, commentators from the political economist Ngaire Woods (2000) to the anti-globalization campaigner Jerry Mander (2003) note that globalization is also made possible by policy choices. Globalization is neither natural nor inevitable—despite what pro-globalization interests and advocates insist. It is artificial, in the sense of being human-made, and it is driven not (only) by technological developments or inexorable market forces, but by human choices about how to respond to these. The Bretton Woods Institutions were established in the aftermath of the Second World War with the aim of financing the reconstruction of countries devastated by the War and of stabilizing the global economy following the destructive effects of the global depression of the 1930s. Former World Bank economist Joseph Stiglitz (2002) records that the character and remit of the IMF changed somewhat in the 1980s with the adoption of a neoliberal ideological outlook—promoting a global free market, sometimes known

as the 'Washington Consensus' (Nitzan and Bichler, 2000)—which also came to dominate the WTO and, to a lesser extent, the World Bank. Certainly, the IMF and the WTO have been at the centre of debates and public demonstrations expressing concern and anger about the negative effects of globalization since the well-publicized demonstrations at the WTO meetings in Seattle in 1999 and Gothenburg in 2001.

Structural adjustment programmes

Criticism of the IMF centres on the fact that states receiving development loans from the World Bank have, since the 1980s, been required by the IMF to implement structural adjustment programmes (SAPs), designed by IMF economists. SAPs are intended to stimulate economic growth, stabilize the national economy, and reduce government debt. They typically entail significant cuts in public spending (including health, education, and social welfare budgets) and the deregulation of agriculture and industry to facilitate the integration of a particular country into the world economy and attract foreign investment (see Chapter 11). In particular, poor and developing countries have been strongly encouraged by the IMF to welcome foreign direct investment (FDI) and to invest in export-oriented industries where they have a competitive advantage in the global market. Export-led growth has been a key to the success of many 'winners' in the game of globalization, such as South Korea and Singapore.

The environmentalist objection to SAPs is three-fold. First, and most obviously, deregulating has an adverse effect on the environment where it involves reducing environmental standards. Second, cutting public spending has typically meant cutting environmental protection budgets (which is fine if there are no longer any standards to police) as well as those of other public services such as health, education, and welfare. This has an impact on human rights as well as the environment. Third, in agriculture—a key component of the national economy for most poor and developing countries—pursuing a competitive advantage in the global market has often meant abandoning subsistence crops in favour of cash crops, reducing or eliminating crop rotation, increasing pesticide use, and increasing pressure on irrigation sources. Raymond Bryant and Sinéad Bailey (1997, p. 61) sum up the problem thus: SAPs 'often simultaneously reduce the ability of states to respond to environmental problems and increase the seriousness and intensity of those problems.' At the same time, dependence on cash crops leaves countries vulnerable to prices falling for such low 'value added' primary products on the world market, as has happened with coffee, fruit, rubber, and other primary resources.

Trade and the World Trade Organization

The dominance of neoliberal economic ideas is also said to be evident in the activities of the WTO. The WTO is the forum in which global trade rules are agreed. The *raison d'être* of the WTO is to facilitate trade across the globe. Thus, when Shiva (2003) criticizes the WTO for its emphasis on 'barriers to trade' rather than 'barriers to justice', she is criticizing the WTO for doing exactly what it is supposed to do. The WTO's environmental record is, in its own terms, much better than many of its critics suggest. Contrary to the 'regulatory chill' that the WTO is said to inspire, Eric Neumayer finds that 'WTO jurisprudence has become increasingly environmentally friendly' (Neumayer, 2004, p. 1), though others have pointed to evidence of a 'race to the bottom' with poorer countries lowering environmental and labour standards in order to attract FDI (Klein, 2007).

The environmental flaws of the pro-trade WTO position can be seen in its assumption that the gains from trade will outweigh any environmental costs. Critics allege that WTO rules make it too difficult for countries to establish labour and environmental protections. As Cole points out, 'Nations have traditionally been allowed to do as they please within their own borders, *but in an ecologically interdependent world, where production processes in one country can affect the global environment, such a notion may be outdated*' (Cole, 2000, p. 36; emphasis added).

The globalization of the economy not only displaces environmental costs, it also creates new ones. A Danish government study that showed that '1 kilogram of food traded globally generates 10 kilograms of carbon dioxide' (Shiva, 2003, p. 146). Given that countries such as Britain typically export almost as much butter, for example, as is imported, the environmental inefficiency of (at least some) global trade seems obvious. The ecological cost of the economic benefits is too often overlooked. For example, according to a 2006 new economics foundation report, in 2005 the UK imported almost the same amount (in quantity) of potatoes, chocolate covered waffles, milk and cream, boneless chicken, and gingerbread as it exported (new economics foundation, 2006, p. 2).

It should also be noted that, from an environmental point of view, the problem identified here is not just the globalization of the economy, it is first the nature of the economy that has been globalized—a market economy that is neither completely free nor sufficiently regulated in ways that protect the environment (and so is criticized by free market environmentalists as well as by those who would advocate substantive interference in the market to protect the environment). Second, the problem is, most acutely, one of scale. The human population is estimated to have increased four-fold in the past century, and is expected to level out at 10 billion toward the end of the twenty-first century. Correspondingly, '[s]ince 1960, the size of the world economy has doubled and then doubled again' (Speth, 2003, p. 2). In ecological terms, these developments represent a massive and rapid increase in the consumption of resources and the production of wastes. On current trends, the global economy is simply not sustainable, and the impact on human security, and thus human rights, is significant.

The Environment, Human (In)Security, and Human Rights

Almost every state has formally endorsed the Universal Declaration of Human Rights (UDHR). Article 3 of the UDHR asserts that all persons have the right to 'life, liberty and security of person'. Security of person can be threatened by a number of environmental factors. First, environmental degradation and the depletion of resources such as oil and clean water have been a cause of or contributory factor in violent conflict in many parts of the world, from the invasion and occupation of Iraq to the Darfur conflict in Sudan. This is particularly acute in the case of oil as we face the twin threats of 'peak oil' (oil running out and getting more expensive) and climate change. The dominant economic model of development promoted by the neoliberal 'Washington consensus' is—to put it crudely—addicted to and based on the availability of cheap oil. When oil resources are threatened (as in Iraq under Saddam Hussein) 'resource wars' can follow.

Second, access to clean air and water is crucial for human life. Similarly, sustainable access to a sufficient quantity and quality of food is dependent on the environment in important ways and can clearly be regarded as crucial to human security and to the fulfilment of human rights. As Vandana Shiva (1999) argues, the human right to freedom of speech can be undermined by hunger as well as by political repression. Third, human security is threatened when people are removed from their land because of environmental threats, whether these threats are pollution, such as oil spills, other chemical spills, or radioactive contamination, or from flooding and rising sea levels, or landslides and soil erosion. Another relevant consideration here is the removal of people from their lands to make way for development projects, such as mining and dams (see Case Studies section).

There is a vast literature on the ways in which human security has been threatened and compromised in the context of activities associated with globalization and the degradation of the environment. Joan Martinez-Alier's work on 'the environmentalism of the poor' is often cited in this regard. In the face of development strategies to exploit minerals, oil, and timber resources, 'the poor often find themselves fighting for resource conservation and a clean environment even when they do not

claim to be environmentalists' (Martinez-Alier, 2003, p. 201). The environmental justice movement emerged largely in response to localized threats to environmental security arising from corporate externalities, that is, the ecological costs that are not included in the market price of a given commodity (because the producer does not have to pay for the costs). For instance, the effects of oil production in the Niger Delta and the struggle of the Movement for the Survival of the Ogoni People have been much publicized since the execution of environmental activist Ken Saro-Wiwa in 1995 by the Nigerian military junta (see Box 18.3).

These particular examples point toward a general conclusion: that humans cannot be said to enjoy security of person when preponderant patterns of production and consumption, both in local communities and globally, are ecologically unsustainable. Moreover, these local instances indicate a global interconnectedness—the oil companies operating in the Niger Delta, say, supply oil to petrol stations in Europe and North America—such that they may be said to be indicative of a more general problem of ecologically unsustainable patterns of production and consumption, and a generalized responsibility for the perpetuation of environmental threats to human security. Therefore, if we can be said to have a right to security, then it follows that we have a right to certain environmental goods that are crucial to our security: clean water, a

---

Box 18.3 **Ken Saro-Wiwa**

Ken Saro-Wiwa was a human rights activist, environmentalist, and internationally acclaimed author and poet who was hanged by the Nigerian military junta in November 1995, along with eight other members of the Ogoni tribe for their activities in opposing the environmental, economic, and social disruption caused by the oil corporation Shell in Ogoniland in the Niger Delta. It was to fight the destruction of their environment by oil drilling that Ken Saro-Wira formed the Movement for the Survival of the Ogoni People (MOSOP) and began his non-violent campaign to protest the destruction of the Ogoni people and their lands. He, along with other members, was arrested and, despite international pressure from human rights groups, states such as America and the United Kingdom and the Commonwealth, the military junta judicially executed him.

sustainable source of food, and the right, perhaps, not to be removed from our land to make way for development or conservation projects. Yet, as is discussed in the next section, it cannot straightforwardly be assumed that environmental concerns can be subsumed within the rubric of human rights in this way.

KEY POINTS	
The basis of the relationship between the environment and human rights is the inescapable fact that humans are ecologically embedded beings.	Structural adjustment programmes and the World Trade Organization are allied to neoliberal economic globalization and therefore undermine human rights.
Economic globalization can, through negatively impacting on the environment, have a negative effect on human rights.	A growth-orientated global economy, dependent on dwindling resources such as oil, leads to a more competitive and less secure world for the realization of human rights.
The growth imperative and up-scaling of the human economy at the heart of neoliberal economic ideology has led to a globally unsustainable economy.	If we can be said to have a right to security, then it follows that we have a right to certain environmental goods crucial to that security.

Problems of Compatibility

In this section we address the assumed compatibility between human rights and the environment as normative agendas. Human rights and environmental sustainability at a first glance look like natural bedfellows—who among those in favour of human rights would say that they do not agree that the environment should be protected? And who among those campaigning on environmental issues would not recognize both the normative status and the strategic value of human rights? Indeed, dominant understandings of sustainable development place a concern with the protection and promotion of human rights as constitutive elements (UNDP, 1998).

Philosophical Underpinnings

Human rights are about protecting individuals now from harm (usually at the hands of the state), and about protecting and extending freedoms: the freedom to say and print what one thinks, and the freedom to live as one chooses subject to the caveat that one does not impede the lives of our contemporaries. Human rights are individualistic, they are arguably liberal at least in their origins, they are about entitlements rather than duties, and, above all, they affirm the normative status of humans as special beings deserving of dignity and specific types of appropriate treatment and non-interference. They are in many ways at odds with the most dominant concerns in environmental politics.

Environmental politics is often about the citizen as bearer of duties. It is also sometimes about circumscribing the freedom to behave in ecologically unsustainable ways, rather than protecting and extending freedoms. Some early environmental theorists have sometimes argued that even political and civil freedoms should be restricted for the sake of the environment (Hardin, 1977; Ophuls, 1977), though later green thinkers have comprehensively rejected such eco-authoritarian positions (Barry, 1999; Humphrey, 2007). Environmental citizens are required to live in ways that do not inhibit the like freedom of future generations as well as contemporaries. It is also the case that most green politics is about asserting the right of individuals and communities to a decent and healthy environment, so there are both duties and rights at the heart of green politics.

Ecocentric theorists have argued that humans do not necessarily have a special moral place in the universe, and, indeed, hold that much of the current and historical damage to the environment has been predicated on the idea that humans are morally more important than other animals and ecosystems. Therefore, ecocentrists hold that we should recognize the environment, as well as humans, as a source of intrinsic value. Even weak anthropocentrists seek to diminish the extent to which humans are seen as occupying a privileged position in nature, and suggest that what is required is a less 'arrogant' and more reflexive and modest form of 'ecologically enlightened anthropocentrism' that sees humanity as a part of, as well as apart from, the non-human world (Barry, 1999).

Can Human Rights and Environmental Concerns be Reconciled?

How far, if at all, can these positions be reconciled? Key to this is to recognize the ecological embeddedness of all human freedom. Thus, Klaus Bosselmann proposes an 'ecological limitation' to environmental human rights. Such a limitation 'refers to the fact that individual freedom is determined not only by a social context—the social dimension of human rights—but also by an ecological context' (Bosselmann, 2001, p. 119). But this dimension is easy to neglect when many environmental problems, such as climate change and biodiversity loss, build up slowly and incrementally, and human lifespans are short relative to the timescales involved. Indeed, promoting human rights today by, for example, clearing land to grow food for the hungry, may well undermine environmental sustainability over the long term and diminish the environmental resources available to future generations. Such conflicts between the interests and rights of humans now and future generations—as well as interests and rights of human beings in different parts of the world—are at the heart of sustainable development, which undertakes the almost impossible task of rendering competing claims and rights to the use of the environment for human purposes compatible.

KEY POINTS
The relationship between human rights and environmental sustainability is a lot more complex than them being putatively compatible.
Human rights are framed in individualistic terms, whereas 'environmental sustainability' is often collectively framed.
Environmental politics often stresses 'duties' and questions the automatic (and arbitrary) ethical superiority of humans, which may run counter to the stress on rights and the privileged position of humanity in human rights discourse.
Environmental sustainability raises issues about the relative balance between the rights of present and future generations.

Implementing Environmental Human Rights?

In this section we consider the plausibility and the potential advantages and disadvantages from a green perspective of embedding environmental issues in the human rights framework. We also look at the issue of whether we need to shift our thinking and action from an environmental focus to one in which sustainability (understood to contain environmental, social, and economic dimensions and claims) is central.

The Merits of Environmental Human Rights

The concept of environmental human rights has been proposed by a number of theorists and activists working in both environmental politics and in the field of human rights. From an environmental point of view, there are a number of clear strategic advantages in presenting environmental claims in the language of human rights. First, there can be little doubt that human rights discourse has come to be *the* authoritative language in which moral claims are presented in the context of both democratic polities and international political forums. Reflecting this dominance, the legal codification of human rights has developed and multiplied since the 1948 UDHR. Adopting rights language lends legitimacy and intelligibility to complex claims that are often poorly understood by the general public. Institutionalizing these rights in international conventions and/or national constitutions increases the opportunities for the legal protection of the environment.

Greening the rights discourse

The rights discourse has its origins in liberal politics (Eckersley, 1996). For some, this renders it implacably opposed to environmental ends, given, for example, the tendency in liberal politics to value the individual abstracted from his (social and ecological) environment. Yet one attraction of the rights-based approach is that it may afford the opportunity to reshape the terms of human rights. Engaging in an influential discourse presents opportunities to challenge the understandings of the terms in which debate is conducted. Pointing to the advent of the idea of social and economic rights, Neil Stammers (1999) argues that the scope of 'liberal rights' (by which he means political and civil rights) was extended by nineteenth-century social movements adopting the language of rights to further their aims.

Drawing on Stammers' work, Robyn Eckersley (1996) observes the success of the socialist inspired 'immanent critique' of liberal rights and asks whether the green movement could achieve something similar. Thus the notions of autonomy and justice that Eckersley finds central to the mainstream conception of human rights should be understood in broader terms than is currently the case. What is needed to ensure the fulfilment of human rights is more than their legal protection, it is also the capacity to realize them. The task of the human rights advocate is therefore to identify institutions or structures that inhibit or undermine the realization of human rights, as well as those that directly threaten human rights. If a sustainable environment were understood to be as much a material precondition for the exercise of civil and political rights as food and water are thus argued to be, then, such rights may be thought

to be 'indivisible' from environmental rights also, and norms or institutions that threatened or undermined sustainability would also be the target of human rights claims. Environmental human rights thus understood might well be consistent with Thomas Pogge's institutional model of human rights—indeed, Tim Hayward's (2005) understanding of constitutional environmental human rights is explicitly derived from Pogge's model, whereby, in contrast to the contemporary human rights regime, the underfulfilment of human rights is taken as the relevant standard.

The green logic of human rights

A second respect in which environmental human right(s) may be attractive is apparent in the logic of human rights. '[R]ights are a way of marking out a protected area within which the rights-holders are free to pursue their goals' (Merrills, 1996, p. 27). The point of claiming environmental human right(s) is therefore to promote some minimum level of environmental sustainability as being beyond the sphere of political compromise. Thus debates about whether governments should prioritize the environment over development, or vice versa, are easily settled where further development is not essential to the fulfilment of other human rights. In this context, the advantage of a rights-based approach is that 'it serves to "trump" competing claims for utility maximisation' (Eckersley, 1996, p. 216).

Hayward expands upon this line of argument by suggesting that embedding environmental rights in national constitutions serves a broader purpose than simply providing for the protection of the environment by legal action. One effect of environmental human rights would be the mandating of a number of procedural rights, such as rights to be informed of proposed developments in a particular local area, rights to information about environmental impact assessments, rights to freedom of assembly to facilitate protests against unwanted development, and extended rights to self-determination, including rights to participate in decision-making forums. The legal recognition of such rights would have a positive impact on the democratic credentials of environmental decision-making procedures, would help facilitate environmental justice, and would foster an ethic of custodianship—all key aspects of a sustainable society. Another positive effect would be to introduce environmental ethics to a wider and younger audience wherever citizenship training is part of the national curriculum, and to contribute to the environmental education of the general public. Finally, 'Such effects would serve to consolidate the essential aims of environmental protection as being a matter of public interest rather than partisan cause' (Hayward, 2005, p. 126).

Examples of procedural environmental rights include Principle 10 of the 1992 Rio Declaration, which states that:

> Environmental issues are best handled with the participation of all concerned citizens, at the relevant level. At the national level, each individual shall have appropriate access to information concerning the environment that is held by public authorities, including information on hazardous materials and activities in their communities, and the opportunity to participate in decision-making processes. States shall facilitate and encourage public awareness and participation by making information widely available. Effective access to judicial and administrative proceedings, including redress and remedy, shall be provided. (UNEP, 1992)

The Aarhus Convention on Access to Information, Public Participation in Decision-making and Access to Justice in Environmental Matters can be seen as an attempt to implement Principle 10 and is often held up as a good example of the positive linking of human rights and environmental concerns. Article 1 of the Aarhus Convention states that:

> In order to contribute to the protection of the right of every person of present and future generations to live in an environment adequate to his or her health and well-being, each Party shall guarantee the rights of access to information, public participation in decision-making, and access to justice in environmental matters in accordance with the provisions of this Convention. (UNECE, 1998, p. 4)

Thus both Principle 10 of the Rio Declaration and the Aarhus Convention offer examples of how procedural environmental rights can be integrated into justice and democratic dimensions of environmental issues and decision making, specifically in relation to citizen–state relations.

Institutional models of green human rights

Finally, environmental human rights could be interpreted along the lines suggested in Thomas Pogge's (2002) institutional model of human rights, whereby individuals have a negative duty not to uphold institutions that contribute to the underfulfilment of human rights globally. In environmental terms, individuals would have a negative duty not to support institutions that foster unsustainable patterns of production and consumption. This individual duty could be readily assimilated as a practice of environmental citizenship, at the same time as providing citizens with a means of conceptualizing the link between actions and environmental impacts. If, as is often claimed, one of the primary obstacles to active environmental citizenship is a lack of knowledge and understanding of environmental issues, then environmental human rights so understood could prove an important educative tool.

KEY POINTS

From an environmental point of view, there are a number of clear strategic advantages in presenting environmental claims in the language of human rights.

Environmental human rights create increasing opportunities for legal action to protect the environment.

The idea of environmental protection and its importance is arguably strengthened, and is authoritatively embedded in the legal and political fabric, if some form of environmental human rights is recognized.

Claiming environmental human rights may create opportunities to reshape the understandings of key elements of our political vocabulary.

Environmental human rights understood on an institutional model may provide a conceptual tool that would help explicate the link between actions and environmental impacts to putative environmental citizens.

Problems with Environmental Human Rights?

On the other hand, there are also a number of reasons for caution with regard to the attractiveness of the idea of environmental human rights. One respect in which

the logic of human rights is potentially problematic for environmentalists is its inherent anthropocentrism. To claim a human right is to say that there is something morally significant about being human. Human rights discourse recognizes that individual humans have a right to what they need, or a right to pursue their own interests, in a way that individual snails, or giant pandas, or (more complicatedly) forest ecosystems do not. This issue raises the question of whether the current human rights framework could or should be extended to include rights for non-human animals, such as Great Apes, or for ecosystems (see Box 18.4). The fact that in the present human rights framework individuals of other species are not valued in the same way as individual humans are means that, where environmental human rights are accepted and there is a conflict between 'human interests' and 'non-human interests', it then seems highly likely that 'the human interest will prevail' (Hayward, 2005, p. 34).

Indeed, the ecological context that can support human life need not necessarily be as biodiverse as, or be less polluted than, it is today. There is, therefore, reason for concern about the quality of environmental sustainability that a human rights-based approach could offer. If we work to satisfy all humans' rights to adequate food, water, and shelter without regard to increasing population levels, then, over time, we may achieve this at the expense of leaving sufficient ecological resources for many of the non-human animals with whom we share the planet. Environmental human rights protect the habitats of all animals insofar as they protect the Earth, but they protect the Earth for humans first and foremost, an approach that may undermine the already threatened livelihoods of endangered species.

Strategic Considerations

Nevertheless, the question is whether, strategically—that is, with the aim of effecting widespread political change in a democratic manner (if not always in a democratic context)—environmental human rights are useful. De-Shalit (2001) advises that the ecocentric approach is often unpersuasive to the public at large, who may be more concerned with immediate economic security than long-term environmental sustainability. Moreover, there has been a shift in green thinking toward a weak or 'reflexive' anthropocentrism that asserts the need for a strong model of environmental sustainability because of the ecological embeddedness of human life (Barry, 1999). In particular, a weak anthropocentrism concerned with protecting the environment for the sake of future generations can yield a robust and coherent model of sustainability.

However, it is doubtful whether future generations can be said to have rights, rather, environmental human rights may be of use to the present generation in preserving the environment for its successors (see Box 18.5). Environmental human rights are thus tools of use to environmental citizens who take on the role of stewards.

For example, if environmental human rights afford me the right to be informed of proposed developments, or rights to access environmental impact assessments, then, as an environmental citizen, I might find these rights crucial in deciding what action I should take for the sake of future generations. Furthermore, such

---

Box 18.4 **The Great Ape Project**

There have long been campaigns for the recognition of animal rights. The Great Ape Project (GAP), founded by Peter Singer and Paolo Cavalieri, and based in Seattle, USA, argues for humans to extend the 'community of equals' to include humans, chimpanzees, bonobos, gorillas, and orang-utans, such that all have a right to life, a right to the protection of individual liberty, and a right to freedom from torture. The GAP calls for a declaration on the rights of great apes in the manner of existing human rights declarations. In 2006, a Spanish Green MP proposed a parliamentary resolution on the rights of great apes, with the effect of ending ownership rights for great apes and instead requires that great apes be treated as 'legal persons' under Spanish law.

The purpose of extending rights to great apes is neither to frustrate the coherence of human rights, nor to deny

that other animals are deserving of rights, but rather to bring coherence to moral standards with regard to the treatment of creatures that are genetically and behaviourally very close to human beings, as Singer (2006) explains:

> Recognizing the rights of great apes does not mean that they all must be set free, even those born and bred in zoos, who would be unable to survive in the wild. Nor does it rule out euthanasia if that is in the interest of individual apes whose suffering cannot be relieved. Just as some humans are unable to fend for themselves and need others to act as their guardians, so, too, will great apes living in the midst of human communities. What extending basic rights to great apes does mean is that they will cease to be mere things that can be owned and used for our amusement or entertainment.

Box 18.5 **Rights of Future Generations**

The question of whether future generations can be said to have rights is important in environmental ethics and politics because, if future generations have rights, then the present generation may have corresponding duties. Therefore, the present generation would have to ensure that its choices with regard to resource consumption did not threaten to undermine the rights of future generations.

However, philosophically, it is difficult to establish that future generations do have coherent rights. There are a number of reasons for this. Firstly, there is no currently identifiable subject that can be said to be the future generation rights holder (Macklin, 1981, pp. 151–152; Beckerman, 2001, p. 18). Therefore, there is no subject whose rights can be said to have been violated.

In reply to this, Ernest Partridge (1990) offers the example of a campsite, which is said to prove that future generations can have certain types of rights. The campsite example runs as follows. If I stay at a campsite then I am generally recognized as having a duty to leave the campsite in as good a state as I found it for the next potential user. This holds true whether the next person comes along next week or many years after I am dead. Partridge is confident

that this proves that future generations can have what he calls 'designative rights', which are rights correlated to duties that are owed to a collective of people who can be described but not identified.

It is not clear why future people have rights here. The most plausible explanation is that they have an interest in having a clean and viable campsite (or environment). But for a person to have interests, they have to have an interest in existing, and this right therefore has the potential to create unacceptable procreative duties on present generations (de-Shalit, 1995, pp. 114–116).

However, the difficulties with justifying rights for future generations do not preclude present generations having duties with respect to the environmental resources that we bequeath to our successors. Indeed, Partridge's campsite example arguably offers a coherent vision of environmental citizenship duties rather than future generations' rights. And environmental human rights—such as rights to be informed about development projects or rights to participate in decision making about the management of environmental resources—might well assist the environmental citizen in honouring his obligations to future generations.

---

rights would have an impact on some cases within the present generation. Not all environmental problems are gradual and incremental. The decision as to where to site a toxic dump, for instance, can immediately impact on the health and well-being of local people. Similarly, those who have been made environmental refugees by virtue of conservation policies that equated environmental protection with wilderness preservation might well argue that the right to an environment adequate for health and well-being (Hayward, 2005), or the right to ownership of natural resources (Hancock, 2003), would have meant that they ought not to have been removed from their lands. So, although environmental human rights encounter some problems in relation to future generations, this does not render the idea of environmental human rights redundant or incoherent.

Remaining Challenges

What all this suggests is that the idea of environmental human rights is indeed plausible and also has the potential to be useful to environmental citizens. But there are problems with the contemporary international

human rights regime that may yet mean that environmental activists should not be too hasty in framing environmental claims in the language of human rights. Non-Western critics of human rights have at times rejected the universalism they see in the idea of both human rights and sustainable development. Indeed, it is clear from the case of environmental refugees who lost their homes to conservation projects that there are reasons to be sceptical of environmental standards that are applied without the informed consent of the people affected. Human rights are undeniably universalist, and the terms in which human rights are defended by political theorists sometimes do little to assuage the concerns of those who fear that human rights proponents are opposed to cultural difference.

Implicit in much of the preceding argument has been the claim that human rights work as a package deal, and that environmental sustainability, being crucial to human security, ought to be recognized as part of the package. This view of human rights is exemplified in Shiva's point (above), which is that civil and political rights and social and economic rights are interdependent, presumably with environmental rights as well. On this basis, it matters very much to the environmentalist if human rights to freedom from discrimination are not respected. It might be, for instance, that a particular ethnic group is discriminated against in that the land that they live on is polluted by toxic waste and the relevant authority does not prevent or correct this. In this instance, freedom of speech, to be able to speak out about the injustice, is also important. Thus it is easy to see the strength of the package deal approach.

But there are also corresponding weaknesses. The adoption of the human rights framework enjoins environmentalists to argue for a package, some elements of which are not universally respected. It may be that environmental issues are more amenable to having universal appeal as a human rights issue than freedom from discrimination on the grounds of gender, or freedom of religion may have. In this case, environmentalists might feel that their case would be enhanced if they argued that the right to an environment adequate for human well-being (or whatever the chosen formulation) is a more important human right than these other rights with less universal appeal. But if it is permissible to cherry-pick which rights are recognized, then the whole package begins to unravel. An important question for environmental theorists and activists, then, is whether an alternative moral idiom might provide a better framework in terms of which to present environmental claims.

KEY POINTS

Fulfilling humans' rights to adequate food, water, and shelter may be achieved with a less biodiverse world and therefore at the expense of non-human animals with whom we share the planet.

Non-human based arguments for environmental protection, such as ecocentrism, suffer from having little persuasive power in human-centred (anthropocentric) political and legal discourses.

Environmental human rights in terms of intergenerational justice may be said to denote that environmental citizens should take on the role of stewards who have a duty to look after the environment, rather than future people having 'rights' *per se*.

Human rights are universal, and this raises concerns of those who fear that human rights proponents are opposed to cultural difference and particularity.

Case Study: Climate Change and Environmental Refugees

In 2003, Saufatu Sopoanga, Prime Minister of Tuvalu, told the United Nations General Assembly:

> We live in constant fear of the adverse impacts of climate change. For a coral atoll nation, sea level rise and more severe weather events loom as a growing threat to our entire population. The threat is real and serious, and is of no difference to a slow and insidious form of terrorism against us. (http://www.tuvaluislands.com/warming.htm)

Tuvalu is a small island nation in the South Pacific. Its highest point is a few metres above sea level, and it is widely regarded as being under threat from global warming. Rising sea levels cause problems, not only in terms of flooding, but also in terms of increased salt levels, rendering previously fertile land incapable of supporting crops, both of which problems may force people to leave homes on low-lying land. Like other kinds of refugees, environmental refugees typically face a number of problems that can be conceptualized in human rights terms: lack of shelter; lack of livelihood; lack of secure access to food, water, and medical services; and discrimination by host communities that feel threatened by the presence of refugee populations. The Intergovernmental Panel of Climate Change predicts that as many as 150 million people will be displaced from their homes by rising sea levels by 2050 (Black, 2001). According to the latest UN Development report, 'Fighting Climate Change: Human Solidarity in a Divided World',

> Climate change is the defining human development challenge of the 21st Century. Failure to respond to that challenge will stall and then reverse international efforts to reduce poverty. The poorest countries and most vulnerable citizens will suffer the earliest and most damaging setbacks, even though they have contributed least to the problem. Looking to the future, no country—however wealthy or powerful—will be immune to the impact of global warming. (UNDP, 2008)

The impact of climate change has meant that there are now more environmental refugees in the world than refugees from wars. This is a major challenge to the international community in coping with millions of people displaced because of climate and environmental change, and underscores the relationship between policies dealing with climate change and environmental sustainability and human and international security. Creeping environmental deterioration has already displaced up to 10 million people per year and the situation is set to get worse, creating 50 million environmental refugees by the end of this decade. However, this new category of refugee is not currently recognized in international agreements. Campaigners such as Andrew Simms (Conisbee and Simms, 2003) of the new economic foundation call for

governments to recognize the environmental refugee as a specific status for asylum purposes, in order to help protect the human rights of 'climate refugees'.

According to a report by the charity Tearfund in 2006, migration of peoples and the creation of environmental refugees is already occurring and is mostly related to water shortages,

> By exacerbating existing water stresses, climate change impacts many other areas of human development such as health and even industry. Already, there are an estimated 25 million 'environmental refugees'. Experts such as ecologist Norman Myers suggest this figure could soar to 200 million in less than 50 years. Unseen and uncounted, millions are already on the move in search of greater water security. (Tearfund, 2006, p. 6)

Case Study: Development Projects and Environmental Refugees

There are many examples of people being displaced from their lands or facing threats to their livelihoods because of development projects, and thus facing threats to their human rights, again in terms of rights to security of person, shelter, secure access to food and water, and so on. There have also been instances of the violation of civil and political rights on the part of governments and private security contractors confronted with protests against development projects.

One much publicized example is the judicial killing in 1995 of Ken Saro-Wiwa and eight other activists protesting against Shell Oil exploitation in the Niger Delta (see Box 18.3). The Movement for the Survival of the Ogoni People has long campaigned against the polluting practices of Shell, which have resulted in the contamination of freshwater supplies in the region as well as the destruction of natural habitats (Sachs and Peterson, 1995). The Movement for the Survival of the Ogoni People has explicitly phrased its campaigns in terms of human rights, arguing for the right to control of its lands and for the local people (and not the Nigerian state) to decide on *what* sort of development takes place in Ogoniland and, equally importantly, *who* decides on development proposals.

Another development project that has been opposed in explicitly human rights terms is the Narmada Valley

Development Plan in India, a substantial dam-construction project that the Asian Human Rights Commission claims has caused 'large scale abuse of human rights and the displacement of many poor and underprivileged communities' (AHRC, 2003). The Indian Government's plan is to build 30 large, 135 medium, and 3000 small dams to harness the waters of the Narmada and its tributaries to provide the large amounts of water and electricity that are desperately required for the purposes of development. Opponents of the dam view the forced displacement of Indigenous peoples as a human rights violation. Indigenous peoples have often been displaced by development projects with little or no consultation, and insufficient compensation (O'Neill, 2007) (see Chapter 15).

Opponents have pointed out that 'The controversy over large dams on the River Narmada has come to symbolize the struggle for a just and equitable society in India' (Friends of River Narmada, 2008). Opponents of the dam question the basic assumptions of the government and believe that its planning is unjust, and the construction is causing large-scale abuse of human rights and the displacement of many poor and underprivileged communities. At another level, the questions that arise in the Narmada struggle challenge the dominant model of development that holds out the promise of material wealth through modernization but perpetuates an unequal distribution of resources and wreaks social and environmental havoc. In simple terms, the struggle over the river Narmada is a case study in different development futures for India in how development relates to justice, human rights, equality, and democracy.

KEY POINTS

Environmental issues directly impact on the human rights of those who become refugees because of environmental problems, such as those displaced from lands by the threat of climate change and also by development projects.

The plight of environmental refugees illustrates the complex interlinking of environmental issues with issues of human rights, justice, and democracy in contemporary global politics.

Human Rights and Environmental Sustainability

An earlier generation of green theorists took a starkly authoritarian line with respect to the freedoms that citizens could reasonably enjoy if the environment were to be sufficiently protected (Hardin, 1977; Ophuls, 1977). The contemporary green movement, however, sees freedom and rights as necessary features of sustainability. Thus greens welcome, though not uncritically, the values of human rights. This represents a move away from a narrow 'environmentalism' to a comprehensive 'politics of sustainability', in which concern for the environment is nested within objectives related to such concerns as social and environmental justice, democratic participation, good governance, and human rights. That being the case, it makes sense for environmentalists to work to promote human rights, since they are at the heart of an expanded green agenda of sustainability. Equally, this line of argument, which suggests the evolution from a rather narrow 'environmental' focus toward a more expansive politics of sustainability, also offers an answer to the question: 'What sort of society are we sustaining?' To build social and economic 'bottom lines' into green political objectives means that a 'sustainable society' is not simply one that does not undermine ecological conditions, but also one that does not undermine principles of social and environmental justice and democratic values and practices.

Environmental problems are, in the several ways indicated here, human rights issues that require careful thought and concerted action. But human rights do not in themselves represent a solution to environmental problems, nor can human rights be uncritically accepted by the environmental movement. Rather, human rights are a resource that environmentalists might make use of, and a set of norms and values that green theorists and activists can work with others to renew and reshape.

KEY POINTS

While some earlier 'eco-authoritarian' green writers were willing to compromise human rights (and democracy and social justice) for sustainability, modern green advocates see human rights as an essential part of their politics and a constitutive feature of a 'sustainability society'.

'Promethean' or 'techno-fix' approaches to the challenge of environmental sustainability advocate a 'business as usual' view in which achieving environmental sustainability does not require major socio-economic or political changes when such transformation is precisely what greens advocate is needed.

Human rights do not in themselves represent a solution to environmental problems, but they are a necessary part of the solution and are now an embedded feature of green politics.

Conclusion

This chapter has explored some of the ways in which environmental issues affect human rights, and the complex ways in which human rights are relevant to environmental campaigns—especially in relation to 'environment versus development' controversies. A key issue in the relationship between human rights and the environment is the economy—its character and how it is structured. This chapter has shown how the neoliberal model of economic globalization has had profoundly negative impacts on the environment and, by extension, on certain human rights. While there are continuing theoretical/philosophical issues concerning the compatibility of human rights and environmental sustainability—particularly in relation to the rights of non-humanity and future people and ongoing issues of the implementation of environmental human rights— human rights are firmly embedded as constitutive aspects of environmental sustainability in general and green political theory and practice in particular.

QUESTIONS

INDIVIDUAL STUDY QUESTIONS

1. How and in what ways are environmental issues related to human rights?

2. What human rights are related to the environment?

3. How does economic globalization impact on the environment?

4. What human rights are threatened by the dominant neoliberal model of 'development' and economic globalization?

5. Do current patterns of economic globalization result in the underfulfilment of human rights?

6. What are the main areas of tension/incompatibility between green demands for 'sustainable development' and human rights? How can these be reconciled?

7. What are the main features of 'environmental human rights' and how do they differ from other human rights?

8. From a green political perspective, what are the relative advantages and disadvantages of seeking to represent environmental claims in a moral idiom other than human rights?

GROUP DISCUSSION QUESTIONS

1. Does the creation of a sustainable society and one that safeguards human rights require the transcendence of current capitalist forms of economic globalization?

2. Do we need environmental human rights as a 'third generation' of human rights, or can most of the issues raised by greens be dealt with by first and second generation human rights?

3. If you were to define and codify environmental rights within a constitution, what would these be (in order of priority), and how might they clash with other rights enshrined in a constitution of a liberal democratic state?

FURTHER READING

Barry, J. (1999). *Rethinking Green Politics: Nature, Virtue and Progress*. London: Sage.
Barry offers an immanent critique and outline of the main ethical, philosophical, political, and economic dimensions of green political theory and outlines a virtue-based conception of democratic green citizenship as ecological stewardship.

Barry, J. (2007). *Environment and Social Theory* (2nd edn). London: Routledge.
This is an introductory textbook on the relationship between conceptions of nature and environment within Western and non-Western social, political, and economic thinking and explores the complex ways in which thinking about external nature always connects with thinking about internal human nature.

Bosselmann, K. (2001). Human rights and the environment: Redefining fundamental principles? *Governing for the Environment: Global Problems, Ethics and Democracy* (ed. B. Gleeson and N. Low). Basingstoke: Palgrave.
Bosselmann, a legal theorist, proposes here an 'ecological limitation' to the sphere of legitimate human action.

Boyle, A. E. and **Anderson**, M. R. (eds) (1996). *Human Rights Approaches to Environmental Protection.* Oxford: Clarendon Press.
This is a collection of essays on environmental law from a human rights viewpoint, including conceptual discussions as well as studies of the international law dimension and national case studies.

Eckersley, R. (1996). Greening liberal democracy: The rights discourse revisited. *Democracy and Green Political Thought: Sustainability, Rights and Citizenship* (ed. B. Doherty and M. de Geus). London: Routledge.
Eckersley here looks at the idea of adopting an immanent critique of liberal rights theory from a green point of view, as others have done from a socialist point of view.

Hancock, J. (2003). *Environmental Human Rights: Power, Ethics and Law*. London: Ashgate.
Hancock argues for the existence of two environmental human rights: the right to freedom from toxic pollution and the right to ownership of natural resources.

Hayward, T. (2005). *Constitutional Environmental Rights*. Oxford: Oxford University Press.
Hayward explores the implications of embedding environmental rights in national constitutions, and argues that environmental rights ought to be constitutionally guaranteed in any liberal democracy as human rights are now.

Hiskes, R. P. (2006). Environmental human rights and intergenerational justice. *Human Rights Review*, **7**/3, 81–95.
Hiskes here looks at the question of intergenerational justice in relation to environmental human rights.

Woods, K. (2006). What does the language of human rights bring to campaigns for environmental justice? *Environmental Politics*, **15**/4, 572–591.
Woods's essay looks, from a green perspective, at the merits and drawbacks of adopting the rights idiom for environmental claims.

Zarksy, L. (ed.) (2003). *Human Rights and the Environment: Conflicts and Norms in a Globalizing World*. London: Earthscan.
This collection of essays presents discussions of a number of case studies, based on extensive empirical research, of conflicts in which environmental issues and human rights issues come into play.

WEB LINKS

http://www.ehumanrights.org/ Website of Advocates for Environmental Human Rights, with information, resources, and opportunities for online action.

http://www.cedha.org.ar/en/ Centre for Human Rights and Environment homepage, with links to a wide variety of information and resources.

http://www.footprintnetwork.org/index.php Global Footprint Network website, including an individual footprint calculator as well as national footprint information for most countries.

http://www.tuvaluislands.com/warming.htm Government of Tuvalu website, detailing government concerns about the threat to the country posed by global warming.

http://www.greatapeproject.org/ Information on the Great Apes Project, including the Declaration on Great Apes, as well as recent news and links.

http://www.mosop.net Website of the Movement for the Survival of the Ogoni People, with history, news, and other information.

http://www.sierraclub.org/human-rights/ Sierra Club web page devoted to discussion of the links between human rights and the environment.

http://www.unep.org/ The homepage of the UN Environment Programme, with a wealth of data and other information.

ONLINE RESOURCE CENTRE

Visit the Online Resource Centre that accompanies this book for updates and a range of other resources:

http://www.oxfordtextbooks.co.uk/orc/goodhart/

Humanitarian Intervention

Alan J. Kuperman

Reader's Guide

This chapter explores humanitarian intervention and its relation to the promotion of human rights. The first section examines the evolution of humanitarian intervention, especially in the wake of WWII and the Cold War, to include military force and the violation of traditional norms of neutrality and state sovereignty. The chapter then discusses some obstacles to effective intervention—including the speed of violence, delays in accurate information, logistical hurdles to military deployment, and insufficient political will. Next it analyses unintended consequences, including how the 'moral hazard' of humanitarian intervention may inadvertently trigger and perpetuate civil conflict, thereby exacerbating civilian suffering. A detailed case study of humanitarian intervention in Bosnia—from 1992 to 1995 by the United States, European Community, United Nations, and NATO—illustrates many of these concepts. The conclusion offers recommendations to improve humanitarian intervention and to reconcile it with the promotion of human rights.

Introduction

Humanitarian intervention is not identical to the promotion of human rights but is related to it—in ways that sometimes are obvious but also can be quite counterintuitive. Strictly speaking, humanitarian intervention is the use of diplomatic, economic, and military resources by one or more states or international organizations intended primarily to protect civilians who are endangered in another state. These civilians may be at risk either from natural disaster or from political violence (including war) in which they are targeted deliberately or suffer from the resulting social disruption.

Because civil war may be both the cause and consequence of human rights violations, there is an intimate relationship between humanitarian intervention and the promotion of human rights. Persistent violations of a group's human rights may cause members of that group to feel so aggrieved and frustrated that they eventually take up arms and rebel, triggering a civil war. During the course of war, civilians may suffer both humanitarian

deprivation—inadequate food, water, shelter, and medical care—and blatant violation of their human rights, including arbitrary detention, forced displacement, or summary violence. International action that is able to end the war may alleviate both problems, so that humanitarian intervention sometimes also promotes human rights.

But at other times, the two goals are contradictory. Efforts to promote human rights may exacerbate humanitarian suffering. Or humanitarian intervention may exacerbate violations of human rights. In such cases, advocates may have to decide which of these two worthy causes is their higher priority, and temporarily sacrifice the other. Philosophers and social scientists label this the dilemma, or trade-off, between 'peace and justice'.

Many of these dynamics are illustrated in Bosnia, a European country that suffered a bloody civil war from 1992 to 1995 and was subject to many forms of humanitarian intervention. The case of Bosnia will be detailed later in this chapter.

Evolving Concepts

Humanitarian intervention was originally defined narrowly as the provision of vital materials to at-risk civilians, expressly avoiding any action or even commentary related to the possible political causes of civilian suffering. The prototypical humanitarian organization in this tradition is the International Committee of the Red Cross (ICRC), which originated in 1863 at the international conference that also gave rise the following year to the original version of the Geneva Convention and Protocols that assure wartime protection of medical care for civilians and soldiers. The ICRC philosophy is to eschew any political criticism of the states where it intervenes, in order to facilitate its humanitarian mandate. For example, if the ICRC were to criticize a government for intentionally harming its civilians, that government might bar the organization from entering the country to provide humanitarian aid, resulting in greater harm to the civilians. Thus, traditional humanitarian organizations, such as the ICRC, explicitly subordinate concern over human

rights violations in order to facilitate their humanitarian objective. (See Box 19.1.) On several occasions, the ICRC has been harshly criticized for this strictly neutral stance—notably during the Holocaust, when it witnessed but did not report or condemn Nazi crimes.

A broader definition of humanitarian intervention has emerged over the last four decades. A key turning point was Nigeria's 1967–1970 secessionist war in its Biafra region, when some ICRC employees rejected their organization's political neutrality. They believed that the government of Nigeria was intentionally inflicting humanitarian deprivation on the Biafra region in a ruthless attempt to compel the secessionists to abandon their aspirations of self-determination and independence. In their opinion, merely providing humanitarian aid to the victims, as ICRC was doing, did not address the root cause of the suffering. Accordingly, these frustrated humanitarians split from the ICRC and formed their own organization in 1971, namely, *Médecins Sans Frontières* (MSF; Doctors Without Borders), which would not only provide aid but also condemn state policies that they believed created suffering in the first place. MSF abandoned the ICRC's principle of political neutrality on grounds that naming and shaming human rights violations was the best way to reduce humanitarian suffering in the long run, even if it might interfere with their ability to provide aid in the short run.

Impartial and Neutral

Humanitarians often claim to be both impartial and neutral in their interventions, but in practice it may be impossible to attain both goals simultaneously during a civil war. Impartiality denotes that aid is delivered solely on the basis of need, without consideration of

the political or military allegiance of the recipient. Neutrality means that the intervention strives not to affect the balance of power between the contending parties. The incompatibility of impartiality and neutrality stems from two facts: civil wars are usually lopsided rather than symmetric, and humanitarian intervention also conveys strategic benefits. At any point in a civil war, one of the sides is usually winning in the sense of suffering less. Accordingly, when interveners deliver humanitarian aid impartially, they provide it mainly to the weaker party and often require the stronger party to halt hostilities to facilitate delivery. Both of these actions alter the balance of power in the conflict, strengthening the weaker party relative to the stronger, so that the intervention is not neutral. If interveners strive to be neutral, then they must provide equal aid to the side

---

Box 19.1 Selected Humanitarian NGOs

American Jewish Joint Distribution Committee

http://www.jdc.org
Founded in 1914 as the overseas arm of the American Jewish community, it now also provides non-sectarian aid to victims of natural and man-made disaster.

Care

http://www.care.org
Conducts global anti-poverty programmes, in addition to providing emergency relief.

Caritas

http://www.caritas.org
Confederation of 162 Catholic relief, development, and social service organizations.

Catholic Relief Services

http://www.crs.org
Founded in 1943 by the US Catholic Bishops, but provides services impartially.

International Committee of the Red Cross

http://www.icrc.org
Prototypical, strictly neutral humanitarian organization, created in 1863, at the conference that also gave rise to the first Geneva Convention.

International Rescue Committee

http://www.theirc.org
Provides resettlement services and advocacy for refugees, in addition to emergency relief.

Médecins Sans Frontières (Doctors Without Borders)

http://www.msf.org
Provides medical aid impartially, but also willing to name and shame perpetrators of violence.

Mercy Corps

http://www.mercycorps.org
Created in 1979, originally to help refugees from genocide and war in Cambodia.

Oxfam

http://www.oxfam.org
Founded in 1942 as the Oxford (UK) Committee for Famine Relief, now a worldwide confederation of thirteen NGOs.

Save the Children

http://www.savethechildren.org
Created in 1932 to address Depression-era poverty in the USA; now provides health, education, and financial assistance to women and children worldwide.

World Vision

http://www.worldvision.org
Founded in the 1950s to help children orphaned by the Korean War, this Christian organization now provides relief globally.

that is not suffering as much, which would violate the principle of impartiality.

In the 1990s, the concept of humanitarian intervention was expanded again to include the use of military force, not merely to protect delivery of aid, but in some cases to deter or defeat actors perceived as aggressors endangering civilians. The end of the Cold War broke the US–Soviet deadlock in the United Nations Security Council, enabling the authorization, on a case-by-case basis, of intervention using all necessary means, including military force, to protect civilians. Examples are discussed in the next section.

In 2001, following several such interventions, the *ad hoc* International Commission on Intervention and State Sovereignty (ICISS, 2001) concluded that there was a Responsibility to Protect—that is, a generalized obligation of states to intervene through a variety of means to protect civilians on humanitarian grounds. These means included 'all forms of preventive measures, and coercive intervention measures—sanctions and criminal prosecutions', as well as 'military intervention'. In December 2004, a UN panel agreed: 'We endorse the emerging norm that there is a collective international responsibility to protect' (United Nations, 2004, p. 66). Finally, the UN General Assembly, at the 2005 World Summit, codified the 'responsibility to use appropriate

diplomatic, humanitarian, and other peaceful means . . . to help protect populations from genocide, war crimes, ethnic cleansing, and crimes against humanity' and to authorize force 'on a case-by-case basis . . . should peaceful means be inadequate' (United Nations, 2005, p. 30).

KEY POINTS

Humanitarian intervention was traditionally the provision of vital materials to at-risk civilians.

Interveners traditionally avoided entanglement in politics, as when the ICRC refused to criticize even the Nazis.

Modern intervention often confronts the political root causes of civilian suffering: for example, by naming and shaming offenders who target civilians.

Impartiality is the delivery of aid solely on the basis of need. Neutrality is not altering a conflict's balance of power. The two goals are typically not compatible.

Since 1991, military force has been used increasingly in humanitarian intervention, both to protect the delivery of aid and to target perceived aggressors.

The United Nations, in 2005, acknowledged the responsibility to protect civilians through humanitarian intervention, including military force if authorized.

Military Intervention

During most of modern history, the norm of sovereignty prohibited states from intervening in the internal affairs of other recognized states (which typically excluded territories in the New World populated by Indigenous peoples; see Chapter 15). The norm was adopted to reduce the incidence of war and to promote international stability. It arose in response to the horribly bloody 'religious wars' between Catholics and Protestants in Europe during the sixteenth and seventeenth centuries that culminated in the 'Thirty Years War' of 1618–1648. Such wars were fought largely over the internal behaviour of states—specifically, their religion—rather than their external behaviour. Wise statesmen and jurists realized that war could be frequent and particularly savage if it were permitted to be fought over such internal differences, in light of

the inherent diversity of states and the intense passions aroused by disputes over ostensibly universal values.

Accordingly, a norm of sovereignty was established in 1648 by the Treaty of Westphalia, ending the Thirty Years War. Henceforth, war could legally be fought only over the external, not internal, behaviour of states. States would enjoy total sovereignty over their internal affairs, and no other state could intervene with force or otherwise. Although the norm was sometimes violated (Krasner, 1999), it stood as a pillar of international law for over 300 years. The principle was reiterated in the UN Charter of 1945, which in its first chapter (Articles 2.4 and 2.7) prohibits intervention by either the United Nations or its members in the internal affairs of states: 'All Members shall refrain in their international relations from the threat or use of force against the territorial integrity or political independence of any state. . . . Nothing contained in the present Charter shall authorize the United Nations to intervene in matters which are essentially within the domestic jurisdiction of any state or shall require the Members to submit such matters to settlement under the present Charter.' These prohibitions hold unless the Security Council approves a resolution in a specific case under Chapter VII of the Charter, authorizing intervention in response to a threat to *international* peace and security, or unless a state is acting in self-defence against aggression under Article 51 of the Charter.

Eroding the Norm of Sovereignty

The first modern, legal intrusion on the norm of sovereignty was the UN's 1948 Convention on the Prevention and Punishment of the Crime of Genocide, adopted in the wake of the Holocaust. In the convention, signers 'undertake to prevent and to punish' the crime of genocide. Given that genocide may be committed by a state against its own citizens, the convention thus commits signers to intervene in another state based solely on the internal behaviour of that state. The responsibility to protect further erodes the norm of sovereignty, endorsing intervention to prevent not only genocide but other massive violations of human rights that occur within a state, including war crimes, ethnic cleansing, and crimes against humanity. To remain consistent with the UN Charter, advocates maintain that the widespread violation of human rights is no longer 'essentially within the domestic jurisdiction of any state'. In this way, the norm is gradually evolving to privilege some individual human rights over state sovereignty, although the ultimate extent of that evolution is still to be determined.

Even prior to the formal erosion of the sovereignty norm, states occasionally intervened in the internal affairs of other states on humanitarian or human rights grounds. In the late nineteenth century, for example, some European states intervened with diplomatic pressure and threats against the Ottoman Empire over treatment of its Christian peoples, including Armenians, who were seeking greater rights. In the late 1960s, several states intervened in Nigeria on behalf of ethnic Ibos, who were suffering from the government's response to the armed secession of their Biafra region.

Military Force

The widespread advent of humanitarian intervention, especially with military force, emerged after the Cold War. The model was established in 1991, following the Gulf War that expelled Iraqi troops from Kuwait. In March of that year, in northern Iraq, ethnic Kurd separatists launched a rebellion against the Baghdad regime of Saddam Hussein. The Iraqi army responded with brutal suppression, compelling ethnic Kurds to flee northward toward the mountains bordering Turkey, creating a humanitarian emergency. In April 1991, the United States launched Operation Provide Comfort, a military intervention justified on humanitarian grounds. The United Nations (in Security Council Resolution 688) quickly urged its members to contribute to the humanitarian effort, and a coalition of states then helped the United States to protect the Kurds, establish refugee camps, provide humanitarian aid, and assist with resettlement. The United States also spearheaded a no-fly zone over the Kurdish area of Iraq, conducting missions from bases in Turkey to patrol and shoot down any Iraqi aircraft operating in that airspace. The intervention thus provided not merely emergency humanitarian aid, but long-term military assistance that shifted the balance of power within Iraq, effectively rewarding the Kurds with political autonomy that also promoted their human rights.

The use of military force in humanitarian intervention has since become widespread. Such action is sometimes carried out with the consent of the target state, typically authorized under Chapter VI of the UN Charter. In other cases it is non-consensual, authorized either under Chapter VII of the UN Charter or outside the legal bounds of that charter, as in Kosovo where intervention controversially was authorized by NATO rather than the UN. Interveners have deployed troops to protect civilians in at least twenty countries: Afghanistan, Albania, Bosnia, Burundi, Central African Republic, Croatia, Democratic Republic of Congo, East Timor, Georgia, Haiti, Iraq, Ivory Coast, Kosovo, Liberia, Macedonia, Rwanda, Sierra Leone, Somalia, Sudan, and Tajikistan—some on multiple occasions. In addition, interveners have deployed troops or monitors to support peace processes in another sixteen countries: Cambodia, Chad, Comoros, El Salvador, Eritrea, Ethiopia, Guatemala, Guinea Bissau, Kuwait, Libya, Moldova, Mozambique, Papua New Guinea, Peru, Solomon Islands, and Western Sahara. Although the latter missions are not explicitly authorized to protect civilians, they are motivated heavily by the desire to shield civilians from renewed violence. In some cases, such as Sudan's long-standing north–south civil war, the international community has also applied sanctions against states or provided covert aid to rebels in an attempt to coerce a halt to violence.

The increased frequency and extent of humanitarian intervention has spurred rapid growth in both government spending and the number of non-governmental organizations (NGOs) devoted to this mission. Annual spending on official humanitarian assistance, excluding military costs, increased from $3 billion to $9.6 billion during 1990–2005.[1] (These amounts are measured in constant dollars and so represent more than a threefold real increase.) Such increased spending has triggered a proliferation of humanitarian organizations, so the role of NGOs in aid delivery is no longer filled exclusively by major institutions such as the ICRC, MSF, Oxfam, and CARE, but often involves literally hundreds of organizations for a single emergency.

Major Interventions

Over the last two decades, several cases of humanitarian military intervention have been especially prominent (see Box 19.2). In 1992, the United Nations and the United States deployed troops to Somalia to facilitate the delivery of humanitarian aid to civilians who had been cut off, sometimes deliberately, by a long-running civil war. Although impartial, the intervention was not neutral in that it diminished the power of a Somali warlord, Mohammad Farrah Aideed, who retaliated by killing UN troops from Pakistan. The United States responded by targeting the warlord, who again retaliated by killing eighteen US troops in a single battle in October 1993, an engagement immortalized in the film 'Blackhawk Down'. The interveners withdrew during the next eighteen months, after alleviating the immediate humanitarian emergency but failing to address the root causes of instability that still produce civilian suffering in Somalia.

From 1992 to 1995, the United Nations and NATO—a US–European military alliance—conducted a complex humanitarian military intervention in Bosnia, as detailed later in this chapter.

Soon after, in neighbouring Serbia's Kosovo province, ethnic Albanian militants of the Kosovo Liberation Army responded to government oppression by launching a secessionist rebellion. Serbian leader Slobodan Milosevic retaliated with a harsh counter-insurgency that targeted the rebels but also killed several hundred civilians and displaced hundreds of thousands during 1998. The United States first intervened to protect these civilians by threatening to bomb Serbia with NATO air strikes, which compelled Milosevic in October 1998 to

---

Box 19.2 **Major Humanitarian Military Interventions**

(Chronologically, by country and initial year of intervention)

Iraq, 1991

US-led coalition delivers aid to ethnic Kurds and enforces no-fly zone to prevent attacks by Iraqi air forces.

Somalia, 1992

UN and US interventions protect aid deliveries and unsuccessfully attempt nation-building, leading to the killing of peacekeepers.

Bosnia, 1992

UN, NATO, and US protect aid deliveries, bomb Serb forces for attacking civilians, and facilitate military aid to opposing ethnic groups, eventually leading to peace.

Kosovo, 1999

NATO bombs Serbia for attacking civilians, leading initially to increased violence against ethnic Albanians, then withdrawal of Serb forces, and finally revenge attacks against Serbs.

East Timor, 1999

Australia-led force establishes peace and facilitates the return of refugees in the wake of the independence referendum that triggered militia violence.

Sierra Leone, 2000

UK deploys troops to reinforce UN peacekeepers, enabling the defeat of rebels who had mutilated and killed civilians and violated peace accords.

DR Congo, 2003

French-led deployment reinforces UN peacekeepers, reducing the tribal fighting in eastern DR Congo that had displaced and killed thousands of civilians.

Darfur, 2004

African Union deploys monitors and peacekeepers who protect some civilians in refugee camps but fail to end the violence.

withdraw many Serbian forces and permit international monitors. But the ethnic Albanian rebels renewed attacks, reigniting war that again displaced civilians. The United States then drafted a peace agreement that promised Kosovo an independence referendum after three years, and demanded in February 1999 that Milosevic sign it or face NATO attack. This time, Milosevic refused, so NATO commenced bombing in late March 1999. Serbian forces responded by quickly expelling some 850,000 ethnic Albanians from Kosovo, approximately half their population in the province, and killing about 10,000. After eleven weeks of NATO bombing, Milosevic relented, signing a peace agreement to remove all his forces from Kosovo and to permit international peacekeepers. As the ethnic Albanian refugees returned, they forcibly displaced some 100,000 Serbs, approximately half their population in the province, and killed hundreds more, despite the presence of peacekeepers. Proponents of the intervention argue that it prevented even more Serb violence against Albanian civilians, while critics respond that it backfired, amplifying such violence and failing to prevent vengeance against Serb civilians.

Failure to Intervene

The failure to intervene has been harshly criticized in several recent cases of large-scale violence against civilians. In Rwanda, ethnic Tutsi rebels invaded in 1990 and fought for three years against a government controlled by members of the ethnic Hutu majority. In 1993, a peace agreement permitted the deployment of 2,500 UN peacekeepers. But in April 1994, the Hutu president was assassinated, and Hutu extremists immediately launched a genocidal campaign that killed half a million Tutsi (three-quarters of their population in the country) in just three months. Tens of thousands of Hutu were also killed. Most UN peacekeepers were withdrawn upon the renewal of violence, although 500 remained and protected several thousand civilians. The UN authorized a humanitarian military intervention one month later, in May 1994, but international reinforcements did not arrive in Rwanda until late June 1994, by which time the genocide was virtually over. In retrospect, many advocates of intervention have claimed that a quick UN deployment could have prevented the genocide, although this is disputed (Kuperman, 2001), as explained below.

In Sudan's northwest region of Darfur, militant members of African tribes launched a rebellion in 2003, complaining of neglect and discrimination by the Arab-dominated regime in Khartoum. Sudan's government retaliated with army deployments, indiscriminate air strikes, and the arming of local Arab militias, who conducted a scorched earth counter-insurgency against African villages. These attacks displaced two million civilians, resulting in tens of thousands of deaths. In 2004, the *African Union* (AU) authorized a small military intervention to monitor the situation and to facilitate humanitarian aid—a force that grew to 7,000 troops over the next three years. Violence diminished, but most of the affected civilians remained displaced, vulnerable, and dependent on humanitarian aid. In 2007, the United Nations authorized a larger, hybrid UN–AU force of 26,000 troops and police, but, as of late 2008, less than a quarter of the extra personnel had deployed, owing to the reluctance of potential troop contributors and the opposition of Sudan to certain contingents. Advocates of intervention urged the international community to deploy forces even without Sudan's permission, but sceptics feared that this could exacerbate the violence.

KEY POINTS

The norm of sovereignty was adopted in 1648 to promote peace by prohibiting war over domestic matters.

The UN Charter of 1945 reiterates non-interference in internal affairs.

Some individual human rights trump state sovereignty under the Genocide Convention and the responsibility to protect.

After the Cold War, humanitarian military intervention became more common, triggering increases in spending and a proliferation of humanitarian NGOs.

In Iraq, starting in 1991, humanitarian intervention also aided the self-determination movement of Kurds by altering the balance of power within the country.

In Somalia, starting in 1992, intervention alleviated the immediate humanitarian emergency but failed to address the root causes of continuing civilian suffering.

In Serbia, starting in 1998, intervention eventually ended the war in Kosovo but initially amplified the violence against its civilians.

In Rwanda and Sudan's Darfur region, the absence of forceful intervention has been harshly criticized by some NGOs.

Obstacles to Effectiveness

Several factors can impede timely humanitarian intervention in civil conflicts. Perhaps most obvious is the lack of *political will* by potential interveners, as discussed by Samantha Power (2002) in her book *A Problem from Hell*. She argues that powerful states could intervene fairly easily, including with military force, to prevent genocide but do not because they give low priority to humanitarian concerns in comparison to their traditional national interests of security and prosperity. Undoubtedly, states do relegate humanitarian concerns to a lower priority and this is one reason why they sometimes fail to intervene, or do so belatedly and inadequately, as in Rwanda and Darfur.

But there also are practical obstacles to a timely response, as discussed in my book, *The Limits of Humanitarian Intervention: Genocide in Rwanda* (Kuperman, 2001). This work identifies three common obstacles to effective intervention: the rapid pace of violence against civilians; the delay in accurate information reaching potential interveners; and the logistical hurdles to deploying an adequate force. In Rwanda, for example, I found that most of the Tutsi victims were killed in the first three weeks, but even regional experts did not realize what was happening for two weeks, while it would have required more than a month to deploy forces urgently by air to stop the genocide. Thus, even if potential interveners had possessed the political will, they could not have intervened quickly enough to prevent most of the genocide.

These obstacles to timely intervention are not universal but are common in man-made humanitarian crises. For example, violence against civilians has often been very quick: Croatia in 1995, where more than 100,000 ethnic Serbs were expelled from the Krajina region in less than a week; Kosovo in 1999, where most of the targeted ethnic Albanians were expelled in less than two weeks; and East Timor in 1999, where most of the infrastructure was destroyed and most of the population displaced in less than a week. In Darfur, the period of peak violence against civilians lasted considerably longer, perhaps a year, but it was not widely reported in Western media until spring 2004, by which time most of the potential displacement and killing had already taken place.

The deployment of intervention forces also confronts certain physical limitations that cannot be overcome by political will. Transporting forces by sea from Western military bases to conflict zones typically requires at least a month to load, travel, and unload. Air transport is quicker for transporting initial intervention forces, but another month or more is required to deploy essential weapons, equipment, and supplies by air because of logistical obstacles such as the small payload of transport aircraft, the limited throughput capacity of regional airfields, and the considerable mass of modern military forces. Therefore, even if humanitarian advocates could generate sufficient political will for military intervention, the forces would often arrive too late to protect most at-risk civilians. If humanitarians actually want to avert civilian suffering, they need to contemplate other, less forceful strategies.

KEY POINTS

Timely military intervention can be inhibited by a lack of political will among powerful states that prioritize traditional interests, such as their own security and prosperity.

Practical obstacles also inhibit timely intervention.

Large-scale violence against civilians is often perpetrated very quickly, sometimes within a week.

Due to delays in obtaining accurate information, violence may be mostly completed before Western media or intelligence agencies report it.

Deploying equipped military forces for humanitarian intervention typically requires at least a month, whether by air or by sea.

Even with sufficient political will, it may be impossible to deploy military forces in time to protect most at-risk civilians.

Humanitarians should expand their focus to include other, non-military strategies that can avert civilian suffering.

Unintended Consequences

Humanitarian intervention can have a wide range of unintended consequences contrary to its intent of protecting civilians. These perverse consequences sometimes arise simply from the delivery of subsistence commodities, as documented by John Prendergast (1996), Alex de Waal (1998), Mary Anderson (1999), and Fiona Terry (2002). Since militants often intermingle with civilians in places such as refugee camps, humanitarian aid may provide sustenance to rebels, enabling them to fight longer. The camps may inhibit reintegration too, thereby perpetuating grievance and mobilization that prolong or renew war. Combatants may also intercept aid and resell it, or charge a tax for its safe delivery, acquiring funds for their war effort. In some cases, combatants may even fight each other to control the delivery of aid, so humanitarian assistance unintentionally creates extra incentive for war.

Humanitarian aid can also undermine local economies and governance in several ways. First, the provision of free assistance may make it impossible for local farmers and businessmen to sell their goods, hindering economic development and potentially compelling them to turn to war to make a living. International aid organizations also siphon off local talent by employing skilled individuals as translators, drivers, and office workers, diminishing the human capital necessary for domestic entrepreneurship and good government. Moreover, so long as essential social services

are provided by external actors, local government may be deprived of the legitimacy that is essential for successful peace-building. Finally, because humanitarian NGOs engage in fierce competition to win government contracts, they may concentrate more on the rapid delivery of aid than on preventing such unintended consequences.

Military force on humanitarian grounds may also backfire. Richard Betts (1994) observes that military intervention can vary in two ways—being either biased or impartial, and either limited or overwhelming—which yields four potential combinations. One effective combination is limited–biased intervention on behalf of the stronger party, enabling it to attain victory and thereby end the violence. Two other effective combinations are overwhelming intervention in either a biased or impartial manner, so that a powerful intervener simply imposes a settlement. But, unfortunately, the typical combination in humanitarian military intervention is limited–impartial, says Betts, which assists the weaker party just enough to prolong the fighting but not to end it (see Table 19.1). Similarly, Edward Luttwak (1999) has noted that well-intentioned intervention backfires by prolonging war and the resulting humanitarian suffering. The better way to promote stability and humanitarianism, he argues, is not to intervene but instead to let the war burn out more quickly by permitting the victory of the stronger side.

TABLE 19.1 Four strategies for humanitarian military intervention.

	Limited force	Overwhelming force
Impartial	Most common. Saves lives in short-term, but may prolong war and resultant humanitarian suffering. **(Bosnia: UN peacekeepers, 1992–1995)**	Rare. Can end violence quickly, but at cost of major military commitment and entanglement in renewed violence if perceived as non-neutral. **(Somalia: US peacekeepers, 1992–1995)**
Biased	Less common. Works faster if biased towards stronger party. Or can end violence gradually by helping weaker side to win, but at risk of short-term backlash against civilians. **(Kosovo: NATO bombing of Yugoslavia, 1999)**	Rare. Can end violence by quickly helping one side to win, but at costs of major military commitment and loss of neutrality. **(Iraq: US-led intervention and no-fly zone in Kurd region, 1991–2003)**

Adapted from Betts (1994).

Moral Hazard

My own research warns of a systemic *moral hazard* problem whereby the responsibility to protect may perversely increase the human suffering that it intends to alleviate (Crawford and Kuperman, 2006; Kuperman, 2008). The root of the problem is that such civilian suffering often stems from state retaliation against a sub-state group for rebellion (such as armed secession) by some of its members. Humanitarian intervention not only protects at-risk civilians but often facilitates, intentionally or not, the political objectives of the rebels. The expectation of intervention can therefore encourage rebellion by lowering its anticipated cost and increasing its likelihood of success. Some militants even deliberately provoke state retaliation against civilians in order to attract intervention. Although humanitarian intervention may help rebels attain their political goals, it usually is too late or inadequate to avert retaliation against civilians. Thus, the responsibility to protect resembles an imperfect insurance policy against genocidal violence. It creates moral hazard that encourages the excessively risky or fraudulent behaviour of rebellion by members of groups that are vulnerable to retaliation, but it cannot fully protect the group's civilians against the violent backlash. As a result, the emerging norm of humanitarian intervention may cause some civilian suffering that otherwise would not occur. The most commonly cited examples of the moral hazard of humanitarian intervention are Kosovo, Darfur, and Bosnia—the last of which is detailed in the following section.

The moral hazard problem can arise from any international action that is primarily motivated by the humanitarian desire to protect civilian targets of state violence but which also helps rebels. The spectrum of such action is wide, ranging from low-cost measures that respect traditional state sovereignty to high-cost ones that impinge on it, including: rhetorical condemnation, threats or imposition of economic sanctions, recognizing the independence of secessionist entities, air strikes on military or economic assets, military assistance to or coordination with rebels perceived as defending at-risk civilians, consensual deployment of peacekeepers, and non-consensual deployment of troops for peace enforcement. Possible ways to overcome the moral hazard problem are discussed in the conclusion of this chapter.

KEY POINTS

Humanitarian provision of subsistence commodities may exacerbate violence if it sustains combatants, is stolen by them and sold, or becomes the object of fighting.

Such purely humanitarian aid may also undermine local economies and governance by making redundant the roles of farmers, businessmen, and government institutions.

International aid organizations hire away the most skilled in the local population, reducing their potential contribution to entrepreneurship and government.

Humanitarian NGOs often focus on winning contracts and delivering aid, rather than preventing unintended consequences.

Humanitarian military intervention is typically limited and impartial, which bolsters the weaker party just enough to prolong fighting and civilian suffering.

'Moral hazard' arises because humanitarian intervention may help rebels attain their political goals, thereby encouraging rebellion that provokes violence against civilians.

Moral hazard can stem from any international action, motivated by the humanitarian desire to protect civilian targets of state violence, if it also helps rebels.

Case Study: Bosnia

The dynamics of humanitarian intervention are well illustrated by Bosnia's war of 1992–1995. This war stemmed from the break-up of Yugoslavia—a formerly stable, communist country that had been the most prosperous in Eastern Europe from the Second World War until the late 1980s. The demise of Yugoslavia had multiple causes. Its population comprised multiple ethnic groups, several of which had histories of large-

FIGURE 19.1 Ethnic demography of pre-war Yugoslavia, 1991.

Source: Adapted from 'The Former Yugoslavia: A Map Folio' (1992, US Central Intelligence Agency). Available at http://www.lib.utexas.edu/maps/europe/yugoslav.jpg.

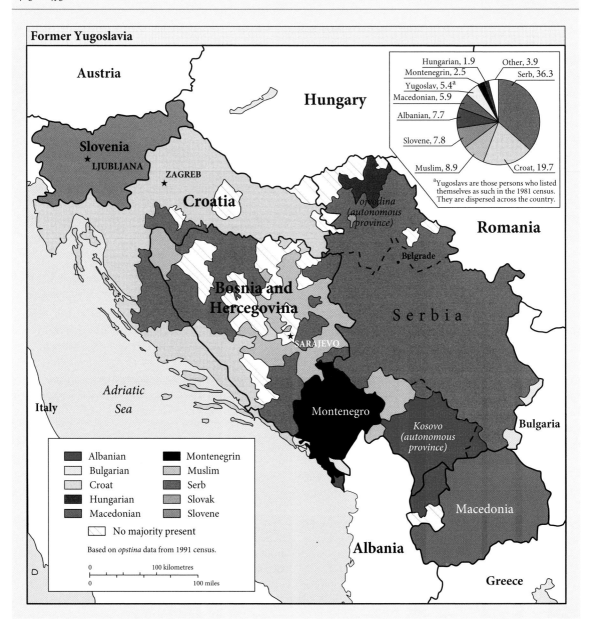

scale violence against each other. The country was divided territorially, mainly along ethnic lines, into six autonomous republics—Bosnia, Croatia, Macedonia, Montenegro, Serbia, and Slovenia—and two autonomous Serbian provinces, Kosovo and Vojvodina (see Fig. 19.1). Its leader after the Second World War, Marshal Josip Broz Tito, was able to suppress ethnic rivalries, but he died in 1980. Economic decline during the 1980s exacerbated tensions, especially among the richer republics of Slovenia and Croatia, which resented the drain of the poorer ones. The fall of the Berlin Wall in the late 1980s inspired democratization in Yugoslavia that revived nationalist tendencies. Serbia's leader Slobodan Milosevic accused ethnic Albanians in Kosovo of discriminating against ethnic Serbs, revoked the province's autonomy, and instituted a police state. This fostered secessionism in Slovenia and Croatia, the latter of which also adopted nationalist constitutional reforms that frightened its ethnic Serb minority. Both of these republics seceded from Yugoslavia in June 1991. The Serb-dominated Yugoslav army fought a short, unsuccessful war in Slovenia, where there were few Serbs. But in Croatia the Yugoslav army and Serb paramilitaries fought a bloody six-month war to retain control of Serb-populated territories and expel other ethnic groups. The war in Croatia killed thousands and displaced hundreds of thousands.

Bosnia remained largely peaceful during this time, but soon confronted a fateful decision. Its population comprised three main ethnic groups: Muslims (> 40%), Serbs (> 30%), and Croats (< 20%). Serbs ideally wanted Bosnia to stay part of Yugoslavia, but, if Bosnia were to become independent, they insisted it first be divided internally along ethnic lines into autonomous cantons, so that Serbs could rule areas where they predominated. The Muslims, sometimes known as 'Bosniaks', were the largest group and wanted Bosnia to become independent as a unitary state without ethnic division. Croats chose to ally temporarily with the Muslims in favour of independence, but secretly planned for their areas to be annexed by neighbouring Croatia.

Some Muslim leaders were concerned by the prospect of war if Bosnia declared independence, so in August 1991 they explored a deal to remain within Yugoslavia, but soon rejected it due to popular Muslim opposition. The Serbs reiterated that they would not accept peacefully the independence of a unitary Bosnia, and the Yugoslav army deployed to Bosnia its Serb forces originally from the republic. At the end of February 1992, Muslim and Croat leaders insisted on holding a referendum on independence, which their ethnic groups approved overwhelmingly, while virtually all Serbs boycotted.

Preventive Diplomacy Backfires

International diplomacy toward Bosnia was driven heavily by the humanitarian desire to avoid another war like the recent one in Croatia. The lead negotiator of the European Community (EC), Portuguese diplomat Jose Cutileiro, insisted that Bosnia's independence should not be recognized until the three groups agreed to an internal territorial division along ethnic lines. Briefly, leaders of the three groups agreed to such a plan in February 1992, based on a patchwork of non-contiguous ethnic cantons, and Cutileiro believed that war had been averted. But US diplomats argued that human rights and humanitarian interests could be better protected by recognizing the independence of a unitary Bosnia, to deter the Serbs from resorting to violence. After the United States convinced European officials to recognize Bosnia even without an agreement on internal ethnic division, the Muslims and Croats withdrew their approval for the Cutileiro plan. This exemplifies moral hazard: the United States intended to deter Serb violence, but instead emboldened the Muslims and Croats to reject a compromise and declare independence of a unitary Bosnia, despite Serb warnings that this would provoke war.

The decision by the United States and the EC to recognize the independence of a unitary Bosnia on 6–7 April 1992 failed to deter the Serbs as hoped and instead spurred them to violence, as they had warned. The Yugoslav army quickly seized control of territory, while Serb paramilitary groups engaged in killings, rapes, and forced expulsions (ethnic cleansing) to remove non-Serbs from Serb-dominated and ethnically mixed areas. Within three months, Serb forces controlled 70% of Bosnia and imposed a siege on the capital Sarajevo, attempting to compel the surrender of the Muslim and Croat leaders and the new Bosnian army that had been cobbled together from Muslim militias. By the end of June, 10,000 Muslim civilians had been killed, hundreds of thousands of Bosnians had been displaced, and Serb forces had established camps in which suspected militants were interrogated, tortured, or killed, and women were raped. The war, lasting three and a half years, ultimately killed 97,000 Bosnians—including 64,000 Muslims, 25,000 Serbs, and 8,000 Croats. Among these were 40,000 civilian victims, of whom 33,000 (82 per cent) were Muslim. The war and the forced expulsions by each ethnic group caused the displacement of two million Bosnians, representing half the population.

Humanitarian intervention formally began in June 1992, when the UN Security Council voted to reopen

Sarajevo airport for humanitarian deliveries and French president Francois Mitterand flew in to break the siege. The UN peacekeeping mission for the former Yugoslavia, originally created for Croatia in early 1992, was now expanded to ensure the delivery of aid to Sarajevo and (as of September 1992) the rest of Bosnia. For the next three years, the main focus of UN troops in Bosnia was assuring the delivery of humanitarian aid to those suffering deprivation due to the fighting. Serb forces continued to surround Sarajevo (and other Muslim enclaves) and attack them with artillery and sniper fire, but they permitted sufficient aid deliveries to alleviate humanitarian suffering, which also enabled the Bosnian army to fight on. The Serbs apparently hoped to preclude more decisive intervention against themselves by permitting the humanitarian deliveries. At the time, the United Nations maintained an arms embargo on the former Yugoslavia that perpetuated the Serb superiority in heavy weapons. As Betts (1994) argues, this 'limited impartial' humanitarian military intervention helped the weaker Muslims just enough to continue fighting but not to prevail, and so had the unintended effect of perpetuating the war and its consequent humanitarian suffering, albeit mitigated by the provision of aid.

Forceful Intervention

The UN and NATO tried to use military threats and force, and diplomatic pressure, to prevent or deter the Bosnian Serbs and their supporters in Yugoslavia from continuing the war and endangering civilians. In May 1992, the UN expanded its limited arms embargo on combatants to a comprehensive arms embargo on Yugoslavia's two remaining republics, Serbia and Montenegro, on the grounds that they supported the Bosnian Serbs. In November 1992, NATO also began enforcing a UN-authorized naval blockade on these two republics. The sanctions compelled Serbia's leader Milosevic to reduce military aid to the Bosnian Serbs to pressure them to make peace, but for domestic political reasons he could not cut them off entirely, so they refused to relent. This demonstrates that sanctions as a coercive tool of humanitarian intervention are not as toothless as some detractors claim, but neither can they force officials to take actions tantamount to political suicide.

In March 1993, the United Nations imposed a no-fly zone over Bosnia, and two months later authorized NATO air patrols to shoot down violators—both steps clearly targeted against Serbs, given that the Bosnian government lacked military aircraft. In April and May 1993, the UN Security Council also declared safe areas in six Bosnian Muslim enclaves: Bihac, Gorazde, Sarajevo, Srebrenica, Tuzla, and Zepa (see Fig. 19.2). This meant that Serb forces were prohibited from attacking these cities that they surrounded, even though Muslim forces used the cities as bases for attacks against Serbs. Both the no-fly zone and the safe areas illustrate how ostensibly impartial humanitarian intervention to protect civilians often is not neutral because it alters the balance of military power.

By 1993, the Muslim–Croat alliance had fractured, so that the most intense fighting and targeting of civilians during the summer was between these erstwhile allies. The United States still sought to roll back previous Serb gains in Bosnia, which required repairing the Muslim–Croat alliance. Through intense diplomacy and pledges of military assistance, the United States succeeded in March 1994 in forging the Washington Agreement: a new alliance between Bosnia's Muslims and Croats, and neighbouring Croatia. Retired US military officers began training the Croatian Army, and the United States stopped enforcing the arms embargo against Croatia, in return for it transferring a portion of imported weapons to Bosnia's Muslims and Croats. Such steps were all but certain to fuel renewed fighting, and, indeed, were intended to, revealing that the human rights imperative of reversing aggression and displacement took precedence over the humanitarian imperative of minimizing future civilian suffering.

Escalation of Intervention

Starting in 1994, NATO threatened and employed a variety of air strikes against the Serbs on humanitarian grounds, authorized initially under the previous year's UN Resolution 836 that called for 'all necessary measures, through the use of air power, in and around the safe areas'. In January, NATO threatened to bomb Serb forces near Sarajevo, compelling them to turn over heavy weapons to UN peacekeepers and withdraw further from the city. In February, NATO's governing council declared that it would utilize air strikes

FIGURE 19.2 Ethnic cleansing and 'safe areas' in Bosnia, 1994.

Source: Adapted from *Balkan Battlegrounds: A Military History of the Yugoslav Conflict 1990–1995* (2002–2003, Washington, DC: Central Intelligence Agency). Available at http://commons.wikimedia.org/wiki/Image:Bosnia_areas_of_control_Sep_94.jpg.

to enforce a heavy-weapon exclusion zone of 20 kilometres (12 miles) around Sarajevo. In March, NATO launched close-air-support strikes in support of UN peacekeepers confronting Serb forces. In April, NATO bombed Serb forces surrounding Gorazde, compelling them to withdraw and permit the entry of UN peacekeepers. In August, NATO bombed Serb forces in retaliation for retaking weapons from UN custody, which persuaded the Serbs to return the weapons. In September, NATO bombed Serb forces for violating the

Sarajevo exclusion zone. In November, the Muslim-led Bosnian army launched an offensive from the Bihac safe area, Serb forces counter-attacked, and NATO responded by bombing a Serb-controlled air base in Croatia. Throughout 1994, these small-scale air strikes succeeded at compelling the Serbs to permit humanitarian deliveries and not to crush the safe areas that they surrounded, but could not end the war or compel Serb forces to surrender territory. This demonstrates the limits of small-scale air strikes as a tool of humanitarian intervention, at least in the absence of coordination with capable ground forces. Advocates of more robust military intervention against the Serbs derided the 1994 air strikes as mere 'pinpricks'.

The moral hazard arising from anticipated humanitarian intervention also exacerbated the fighting. Bosnia's Muslim-controlled government and army repeatedly resisted ceasefires, even though the main victims of continued fighting were fellow Muslims, because of the expectation that such suffering would attract humanitarian military intervention sufficient to help them win the war. The UN's first commander of peacekeepers in Bosnia, Canadian General Lewis MacKenzie (1993, pp. 159, 308), declared that the Muslim-led 'Bosnian Presidency was committed to coercing the international community into intervening militarily.' A successor, British General Michael Rose (1998, p. 141), likewise reported that the Muslims rejected ceasefires because 'if the Bosnian Army attacked and lost, the resulting images of war and suffering guaranteed support in the West for the "victim State".' Even James Gow (1997, p. 96), an academic overtly sympathetic to the Muslims, concedes that the Bosnian army broke ceasefires 'in the hope of provoking a U.S. intervention'. A senior Bosnian Muslim official, Omer Behmen, later admitted that the strategy had been to 'put up a fight for long enough to bring in the international community' (Kuperman, 2008). If not for this expectation of humanitarian military intervention, the Muslims might well have agreed to an early ceasefire, truncating the war and the resultant civilian suffering.

Peace Plans Rejected

Diplomatic efforts failed for three years to end the war because the proposed peace deals did not adequately reflect the military facts on the ground. In January 1993, the UN and the EC proposed the Vance–Owen peace plan: an internal division of Bosnia into a patchwork of ethnic cantons. This was similar to the pre-war Cutileiro plan, which had been proposed by the EC and accepted by the Serbs but rejected by the Muslims, the Croats, and the United States. During the first months of 1993, the Vance–Owen plan overcame initial resistance from the United States, Bosnia's Muslims and Croats, and Serbia's leader Slobodan Milosevic. In spring 1993, however, Bosnia's Serbs rejected the proposal on grounds that the onset of war meant that, for security reasons, they now required a single contiguous Serb territory, not a patchwork.

The second diplomatic attempt by the UN and the EC, in August 1993, was the Owen–Stoltenberg plan, which responded to the Serbs' complaint by granting them a single, contiguous territory within 52 per cent of the republic, dividing the rest into Muslim and Croat zones. This proposal was initially opposed by the Muslims, on grounds that it represented an ethnic 'partition' of Bosnia, and later by the Serbs who were loath to give back so much of the 70 per cent of the republic's territory that they still controlled militarily.

The third diplomatic effort was sponsored by a new transatlantic coalition, the 'Contact Group', initially including the United States, Russia, France, Britain, and Germany. Its July 1994 peace plan built on the renewed Croat–Muslim alliance by proposing a two-way partition of Bosnia into a contiguous Serb entity, comprising 49 per cent of the republic, and a Muslim–Croat entity in the remainder. But the Serbs again refused to surrender peacefully the territory that they had captured in war.

A Double-Edged Sword

The double-edged nature of humanitarian military intervention is well illustrated by the events of 1995. Since the previous year, the United States had facilitated the arming of Croatia and Bosnia's Muslim–Croat alliance to reverse the military advantage of the Serbs and thereby compel them to surrender territory and end the war. In May 1995, Croatia demonstrated its newfound strength by recapturing western Slavonia, an area of its country that since 1991 had been controlled by Serbs, who now fled in terror, creating a new refugee crisis.

Bosnia's Serb leaders realized that humanitarian intervention had tilted the military balance against them—via aid, sanctions, air strikes, the no-fly zone, and especially the arming and training of their Croat and Muslim adversaries—so they moved to consolidate their territorial gains. For three years, the Serbs had surrounded, but not captured, the Muslim enclaves of eastern Bosnia, designated as safe areas by the UN in 1993, because they feared triggering a more robust humanitarian military intervention. But now such intervention was upon them anyway, so they were less deterred. In May 1995, Serb forces violated the Sarajevo exclusion zone, prompting NATO air strikes, to which the Serbs responded by shelling safe areas and seizing 370 UN peacekeepers as hostages. Even more consequentially, in July 1995, Bosnian Serb forces seized the safe areas of Srebrenica and Zepa. In Srebrenica, Serb forces killed an estimated 8,000 Muslim men—the single largest crime of the war—in a savage revenge for the Muslims previously having used the safe area as a base for attacks. A battalion of Dutch UN peacekeepers was present in Srebrenica, but chose not to confront the better-armed Serb forces. This illustrates the danger of attempting to deter humanitarian crimes with only air power and under-equipped ground forces, which offer a false sense of security that actually may increase the vulnerability of the populace. The events also demonstrate that, when humanitarian intervention is not neutral, it can provoke a violent backlash from those who perceive the interveners as being biased against them.

Decisive Intervention

The Srebrenica massacre and the seizure of UN hostages galvanized international support for more robust humanitarian military intervention against the Serbs. UN peacekeepers were consolidated in defensible areas to reduce their vulnerability, and a NATO rapid-reaction force was deployed to Mt Igman near Sarajevo. Ironically, the next major war crime in the region was committed not by Serbs but by Croatia's army, which in August 1995 seized control of its country's main Serb enclave, Krajina, and expelled more than 100,000 Serbs. This represented another example of the unintended consequences of humanitarian intervention: military aid intended to help the Croats and Muslims rectify one

set of humanitarian offences inadvertently facilitated revenge crimes. The United States did not intervene against the Croatian troops—indeed, it had helped to arm and train them—which spurred criticism by the Serbs of a double standard. The Croatian army then proceeded to assist Bosnia's Croat and Muslim forces to reverse Serb gains in western Bosnia, causing further displacement of civilians.

The final escalation of humanitarian military intervention came in late August 1995, in response to an alleged Serb attack on a marketplace in Sarajevo. The next day, NATO initiated Operation Deliberate Force, a two-week bombing campaign against Serb military targets in Bosnia. The air strikes facilitated a renewed Croat–Muslim offensive in western Bosnia, which rapidly diminished Serb control of the republic's territory from 70 per cent to 50 per cent or less. A ceasefire was agreed in October, and the following month the United States convened a peace conference in Dayton, Ohio. The Dayton peace accords, modelled on the Contact Group plan, were initialled in November and then signed in Paris in December 1995. The accords divided Bosnia internally into a contiguous 'Serb Republic' of 49 per cent, a contiguous Muslim–Croat Federation of 51 per cent, and a sliver of land in the north whose sovereignty was still to be determined. Bosnia's Serb leaders, who had refused the offer of 49 per cent of the republic when they controlled much more, now willingly accepted it in the face of abject retreat. Operation Deliberate Force illustrates that air power can be an effective tool of humanitarian intervention, when coordinated with sufficient numbers of capable ground forces.

Looking back over the entire episode, Bosnia demonstrates several dilemmas of humanitarian intervention. While fighting persisted, the provision of subsistence commodities reduced civilian suffering. But such aid also enabled the Muslims to break the siege of Sarajevo in summer 1992, and thereby perpetuated a war that might otherwise have ended quickly. The militarization of humanitarian intervention in Bosnia had even more complex consequences. Prior to the war, expectations of such intervention convinced the Muslim leadership to reject the Cutileiro plan and declare the independence of Bosnia as a unitary state, despite Serb threats to respond with violence, as soon occurred. After the fighting started, the Muslim leadership resisted ceasefires, despite fellow Muslims being the main victims of war, because they hoped that humanitarian suffering would attract military intervention on their behalf. These events demonstrate that the prospect of intervention contributed to both the outbreak and perpetuation of war. Military intervention—including weapons supply, training, a no-fly zone, and air strikes—gradually enabled the Muslims and Croats to reverse Serb military gains. But, by changing the balance of power, such intervention also unintentionally spurred humanitarian crimes, including the ethnic cleansing by Croatia of Serbs in Krajina and the slaughter by Serb forces of Muslims in Srebrenica. Overall, it is difficult to determine whether humanitarian intervention did more good than harm in Bosnia. But the experience does suggest ways to improve humanitarian intervention, which are discussed in this chapter's final section.

KEY POINTS	
Bosnia's war started because of distrust and disagreement among its three main ethnic groups. Serbs wanted Bosnia either to stay in Yugoslavia or to be divided internally along ethnic lines prior to independence. Muslims and Croats wanted Bosnia to become independent without internal ethnic division.	Economic sanctions compelled Serbian leader Slobodan Milosevic to reduce military aid to Bosnia's Serbs, but not to terminate it because he faced domestic pressure to support fellow Serbs.
When the Muslims and Croats declared Bosnia independent as a unitary state, Serb forces responded by quickly capturing 70 per cent of Bosnia's territory and killing, expelling, or raping many non-Serbs.	Non-neutral military intervention enabled the Croats and Muslims to reverse territorial losses and return to their homes, but also led to the ethnic cleansing of Croatia's Serbs and the massacre of Srebrenica's Muslims. These events illustrate the trade-off between promoting human rights and humanitarian objectives.
Humanitarian intervention alleviated civilian suffering but also helped perpetuate a war that eventually killed 97,000 Bosnians—including 40,000 civilians—and displaced two million.	Limited humanitarian military intervention—including air strikes, no-fly zones, and small deployments of peacekeepers—proved inadequate to guarantee the protection of civilians, as demonstrated in Srebrenica.
Muslim leaders rejected ceasefires because they expected the suffering of their own civilians to attract humanitarian military intervention that would help them win the war—which illustrates the moral hazard of humanitarian intervention.	Proposed peace plans failed for three years to end the war because they did not reflect the military facts on the ground, whereas the Dayton Accords succeeded by recognizing those facts, as they had been altered by intervention.

Conclusion

Some advocates of forceful intervention claim that it can simultaneously promote humanitarian and human rights objectives. In reality, there often is a trade-off between the two. This is most obvious for military intervention in support of 'freedom fighters'—those militants who claim to be fighting for their group's human rights, as in Bosnia. Such intervention unfortunately encourages the launching and perpetuation of rebellion or armed secession, which often provokes states to retaliate in a manner that inflicts suffering on the group's civilians. Forceful intervention to promote human rights thus often exacerbates humanitarian suffering. In theory, a timely and robust military intervention might achieve both objectives, but it is typically impossible to overcome the political and practical obstacles to such action.

Fortunately, this dilemma can be overcome through less forceful and more precise intervention methods. Relief aid should be delivered in ways that benefit mainly civilians—for example, by distributing it at refugee camps that are policed to exclude rebels, or at least their weapons. Human rights can be supported by intervening diplomatically and economically on behalf of non-violent protest groups—for example, by offering trade and aid to states that address the legitimate grievances of such resistance movements. Threats of forceful intervention should be reserved for cases in which states either attack non-violent groups or respond disproportionately to rebellion by deliberately targeting civilians. Such an enlightened approach, discouraging sub-state groups from rebelling while raising the incentives for states to liberalize, has the potential to promote both humanitarian and human rights objectives.

These lessons are illustrated by further investigation into the case of Kosovo (Kuperman, 2008). Starting in 1989, Serbia revoked the autonomy of this province, disenfranchised the local ethnic Albanian majority, banned public education in the Albanian language, dismissed most ethnic Albanian professionals from their jobs, and instituted repressive police patrols—a widespread and systematic violation of human rights. For the next eight years, the ethnic Albanians resisted by non-violent means, which provided an ideal opportunity for the international community to use diplomatic sticks and carrots to persuade Serbia to restore human rights, without risking a genocidal backlash because Serbia faced no violent opposition in the province. Analogous non-violent movements, typically benefiting from international support, have succeeded in promoting human rights in many countries, including India, the United States, South Africa, the Philippines, Indonesia, Serbia, Ukraine, and Lebanon.

Unfortunately, the international community devoted insufficient support to Kosovo's non-violent, human rights movement. As a result, this pacifist resistance eventually gave way in 1997 to a rebellion by militant ethnic Albanians, which provoked a violent counter-insurgency by Serbian forces that also endangered Albanian civilians. Interveners still might have mitigated violence if they had targeted humanitarian aid mainly to the affected civilians. Instead, the United States coordinated with the rebels and threatened to attack Serbia, and then NATO followed through on that threat—which only fuelled the Albanian rebellion, exacerbated Serbian retaliation, and magnified several-fold the humanitarian suffering.

This case demonstrates that, in order to promote both human rights and humanitarianism, the international community should focus its leverage to persuade oppressive states to meet the legitimate demands of non-violent groups. Failing that, if a rebellion breaks out, intervention should be aimed at helping civilians, not rebels, to avoid exacerbating rebellion and the resulting backlash against civilians.

The good news is that it is possible to simultaneously promote human rights and humanitarianism. The cautionary note is that, unless intervention is properly designed to avoid rewarding rebels, the promotion of one of these admirable goals could well undermine the other.

QUESTIONS

INDIVIDUAL STUDY QUESTIONS

1. What is the traditional definition of humanitarian intervention, and how and why has it changed since the end of WWII?

2. What is the difference between humanitarian intervention and the promotion of human rights?

3. What is the responsibility to protect, and how does it differ from the traditional norm of sovereignty?

4. What is the difference between impartiality and neutrality?

5. How was military force used in humanitarian intervention in Iraq, Somalia, and Kosovo, and in what cases was it conspicuously absent?

6. Why did war break out in Bosnia?

7. What were the military aspects of humanitarian intervention in Bosnia?

GROUP DISCUSSION QUESTIONS

1. When is humanitarian intervention compatible with the promotion of human rights, and when are they in tension?

2. What are the obstacles to effective humanitarian military intervention?

3. How and why does humanitarian intervention sometimes backfire, and what is the 'moral hazard' problem?

4. How did humanitarian intervention both reduce and increase civilian suffering in Bosnia?

5. What steps should be taken to improve humanitarian intervention?

FURTHER READING

Anderson, M. (1999). *Do No Harm: How Aid Can Support Peace—Or War*. Boulder, CO: Lynne Rienner.
A simple guide for would-be humanitarians.

Betts, R. (1994). The delusion of impartial intervention. *Foreign Affairs*, **73**/6, 20–33.
An argument for either taking sides or staying out.

Burg, S. and **Shoup**, P. (1999). *The War in Bosnia-Herzegovina*. New York: M. E. Sharpe.
The quintessential account of this case.

Crawford, T. and **Kuperman**, A. (eds) (2006). *Gambling on Humanitarian Intervention: Moral Hazard, Rebellion and Civil War*. New York: Routledge.
Scholars debate the moral hazard hypothesis, especially regarding Kosovo.

de Waal, A. (1998). *Famine Crimes; Politics and the Disaster Relief Industry in Africa*. Bloomington, IN: Indiana University Press.
Explains how and why humanitarian NGOs veer off course.

Kuperman, A. (2001). *The Limits of Humanitarian Intervention: Genocide in Rwanda*. Washington, DC: Brookings Institution Press.
Explains why political will is not the only obstacle to timely and effective intervention.

Kuperman, A. (2008). The moral hazard of humanitarian intervention: Lessons from the Balkans. *International Studies Quarterly*, **52**/1, 49–80.
Shows how expectations of intervention helped trigger and perpetuate violence in Bosnia and Kosovo.

Posen, B. (1996). Military responses to refugee disasters. *International Security*, **21**/1, 72–111.
A useful typology of intervention scenarios.

Prendergast, J. (1996). *Frontline Diplomacy: Humanitarian Aid and Conflict in Africa*. Boulder, CO: Lynne Rienner.
An early account of unintended consequences.

Terry, F. (2002). *Condemned to Repeat: The Paradox of Humanitarian Action*. Ithaca, NY: Cornell University Press.
Warns that humanitarian aid can lead to the militarization of refugee camps.

WEB LINKS

http://www.globalhumanitarianassistance.org Website for Global Humanitarian Assistance.

http://www.crisisgroup.org Website for the International Crisis Group.

http://www.nato.int/docu/handbook/2001/hb050102.htm Provides details of NATO Intervention in Bosnia.

http://www.un.org/Depts/dpko/dpko/co_mission/unprofor.htm Provides details of UN Intervention in Bosnia.

NOTE

1. See http://www.globalhumanitarianassistance.org/pdfdownloads/total%20humanitarian%20assistan
   ce%201990-2006.pdf.

ONLINE RESOURCE CENTRE

Visit the Online Resource Centre that accompanies this book for updates and a range of other
resources:

http://www.oxfordtextbooks.co.uk/orc/goodhart/

Transitional Justice

Joanna R. Quinn

Chapter Contents

Reader's Guide

In the months and years after atrocities such as genocide, disappearances, torture, civil conflict, and other gross violations of human rights have taken place, states are left with a puzzling and often difficult question: What to do with the perpetrators of such acts of violence? Such conflict leaves physical scars, evident in the destruction of hospitals and schools, for example. But it also leaves deep and lasting social scars. Transitional justice considers the social implications of this kind of brutal conflict. It is concerned with how to rebuild societies in the period after human rights violations, and with how such societies, and individuals within those societies, should be held to account for their actions. It is this past violation of human rights that forms the basis of transitional justice, and is the impetus that pushes the processes of transitional justice forward. How to deal appropriately with these kinds of past human rights violations makes the processes of transitional justice quite controversial.

Introduction

The idea that states can and should deal with the perpetrators of violent crime during a period of civil conflict, or repressive or authoritarian rule, is relatively new. For many years, leaders of rebel groups and states were simply left alone, without consideration of punishment, or having to 'pay' for their deeds. And so tyrants, such as Idi Amin of Uganda or Jean-Claude 'Baby Doc' Duvalier of Haiti, simply left their own countries, moved to countries that were willing to house them, and faded into obscurity. It was only in the 1990s that scholars and practitioners began to sort out how to deal with violent histories.

At that time, of course, there were many situations of violence and conflict underway, or just ending. (See Box 20.1.) Private property had been confiscated and secret government files maintained in former Soviet-bloc countries in Eastern Europe. The genocides of Rwanda and Bosnia were taking place. Bloody civil conflicts continued in countries such as Somalia, Sierra Leone, Liberia, Haiti, and Guatemala. Yet the perpetrators of even the most egregious human rights violations went free.

It was becoming clear that someone should be made to answer for such horrible crimes. Still, just who should be held to account, and for what, posed a dilemma. Should every single person who had committed a crime be punished and sent to jail? Should only the 'big fish', officials and officers of the former regime, be brought to trial? Or should those lower down the chain of command, the 'small fry', also be tried? Who should carry out such prosecutions? Should governments

and their bureaucracies be 'purged' of officials who had helped to carry out such awful acts? How should victims be rehabilitated for the abuses and injuries, both emotional and physical, that they have suffered? Should victims themselves be acknowledged for their suffering? Transitional justice, as it has come to be called, deals with all of these questions, and more.

These issues are intrinsically linked with the study of human rights for several reasons. First, the mechanisms of transitional justice deal explicitly with the gross human rights violations that have been committed. Second, transitional justice itself is an important tool for ending the cycle of impunity, and the kind of immunity from prosecution that is prevalent in states where the history of human rights abuses is in the not-so-distant past; justice itself is deeply related to human rights. Third, the mechanisms being utilized in the pursuit of transitional justice are increasingly established, sanctioned, or funded by parts of the United Nations—the main international organ concerned with the protection of human rights.

The task, therefore, that confronts societies aiming toward transition from authoritarian or repressive regimes to democracy, or from conflict to peace, is daunting. Where to start? Obviously, changes need to take place in virtually every sector, and at virtually every level. Often, reforms are required in sectors including security, economics, health care, education, and infrastructure. Transitional justice focuses specifically on reforms to the justice sector, working toward the re-establishment of the rule of law and assisting in the rebuilding of the system of courts that is required in a functioning, democratic society.

Even so, it can be difficult for transitional societies to come to an agreement about just what this means, or how it will be carried out. One worry, of course, is that decisions about who should be punished will be made by the victorious party, and will not necessarily address the concerns of the population as a whole. In post-apartheid South Africa, for example, white supporters of the defeated National Party worried that they would be attacked by the newly-victorious (and mostly black) African National Congress. A second worry is that, in the negotiation of peace settlements, or the handing-over of power from one regime to the next, the

---

Box 20.1 What are Some Situations that could Benefit from Mechanisms of Transitional Justice?

- Genocide.
- Civil conflict.
- Racism.
- Forced slavery.
- Community violence.
- Man-made famine.
- Gross violations of human rights.

perpetrators of heinous crimes will be given some kind of amnesty, or immunity from prosecution. In Chile, for example, General Pinochet simply granted himself and his accomplices lifetime immunity, insulating himself and them from possible criminal charges. Third, the capacity of the legal system may have been badly compromised during the conflict, and/or may find itself unable to cope with the large numbers of prosecutions that will be required. More than 120,000 people were identified as perpetrators of the Rwandan genocide, for example, which placed an enormous burden on the court system there; it was estimated that it would take nearly 180 years to prosecute all of them. And in Cambodia, the court system was weak to begin with. It has been reported that more than 80 per cent of judges there did not hold law degrees, and many of those had never received formal education at all, let alone legal training.

No one solution will ever be acceptable to everyone. For victims of heinous crimes, no remedy can ever be enough. No court sentence can restore a missing limb.

No amount of money will bring back a dead child. Similarly, for perpetrators—such as Nazi officers—whose actions were taken in an environment that condoned, rather than condemned, them, it may be difficult for society to try them. Still, common morality dictates that something must be done.

As the idea of coming to terms with past abuses has unfolded into practical application, different ways of dealing with both victims and perpetrators have developed (see Box 20.2). The types of mechanisms that states adopt tend to reflect the circumstances that arise from the particular crimes committed, and the social and political conditions that follow. They also correspond to particular ideas about how and why justice must be done, and must be seen to be done. Martha Minow (1998) has characterized these approaches into three distinct *paradigms* (philosophical or theoretical framework): retributive, restorative, and reparative justice. This typology is useful as a means of both explaining and understanding the different ways of approaching transitional justice.

Retributive Justice

Retributive justice is the kind of 'justice' that those in the 'West' are used to thinking about. In this paradigm, justice equates with legal prosecutions and the rule of law. This includes the kinds of court proceedings and sentencing that are common throughout much of the world today, all of which are based on the notion

---

Box 20.2 **Three Different Approaches to Transitional Justice**

Retributive Justice

Goal: to correct the perpetrator by means of prosecution and punishment.
Usual mechanisms: trials, tribunals.
Sample case: Cambodia: Extraordinary Chambers in the Courts of Cambodia established in 2001 by the Cambodian National Assembly to create a court to try serious crimes committed during the Khmer Rouge regime, 1975–1979.

Restorative Justice

Goal: to restore the dignity of the victim, to restore the perpetrator back into society.
Usual mechanisms: truth commissions, healing circles.
Sample case: Guatemala: Commission for Historical Clarification (*Comisión para el Esclarecimiento Histórico*) established in 1994, during negotiations between the Guatemalan Government and leftist rebels under the Oslo Accord process, which ended more than thirty-five years of violence.

Reparative Justice

Goal: to repair the injury suffered by victims.
Usual mechanisms: restitution, apology.
Sample case: United States: $20,000 was awarded by Congress in 1988 to each American of Japanese ancestry who had been forcibly removed and detained in internment camps located throughout the country during the Second World War.

Adapted from Minow (1998).

of retribution or punishment for crimes committed. Typically, a trial involves a person charged with the commission of a crime being brought before an arbitrator, if not a panel of his peers, whereupon his guilt and subsequent penalty is determined.

The rationale behind retributive justice is at least fourfold. First, if a person has done something wrong, those actions need to be publicly acknowledged. During the process of a trial, details about specific crimes committed are openly discussed, often being revealed for the first time. Second, he needs to be punished for his actions. The objective of punishment is both to remove the perpetrator from the circumstances in which he committed the crime and to rehabilitate him before his release into the community. Third, by disciplining someone for his actions, there is a wider, educative effect for the public. That is, if others see that someone is being punished for committing particular crimes, then they will be deterred from committing the same crimes. And fourth, the ability to conduct a trial demonstrates and reinforces that the justice system is both capable of carrying out retributive actions, and is viable as an institution. If a trial takes place, it must be the case that the justice system is fully-functioning, and able to transmit the full authority of the law of the land.

National Trials

And so, a number of societies in transition have opted to utilize mechanisms of retributive justice, mostly in the form of trials, to deal with the perpetrators of past crime. In most parts of the world, this is the remedy that would be expected. Under normal circumstances, in fact, it is the main forum for such resolution.

Such was the case in Greece, which experienced a *coup d'état* (violent overthrow) by a military *junta* (pronounced HOON-ta) in April 1967. The constitution was suspended and martial law was declared. The following two main incidents are associated with the regime's brutality. In 1973, thousands of students were arrested, injured, or killed in a violent protest at the Athens Polytechnic. And in 1974, the military dictatorship invaded the island of Cyprus, launching a bloody coup on its population. The coup continued until July 1974, when, through negotiations with the coup leaders, the deposed prime minister returned to power and restored order. In a series of trials held throughout 1975, more than 150 top officials were condemned for their actions. Many thousands of others were stripped of governmental and administrative positions—an attempt to 'dejuntify' the country in the aftermath of the coup.

International Justice

Sometimes, however, the national court system is unwilling to carry out these kinds of prosecutions. Furthermore, it may be unable to do so. In these cases, the international community has stepped in to assist with these prosecutions. Such trials began with the post-War Nuremberg Trials and Tokyo Tribunal, which were appointed to deal with Nazi war crimes and the crimes of Japanese officials. Thus began the development of the system of international criminal law (see Box 20.3). Previously, any and all laws had existed only at the national/state level (see Chapter 2).

It was several decades, however, until further international criminal legal avenues were pursued. The international community showed little interest in the prosecution of perpetrators of mass atrocities, genocide, and war crimes. In the 1990s, a number of international courts and tribunals were established, in conjunction with the United Nations Security Council. These included the International Criminal Tribunal for the Former Yugoslavia (ICTY) and the International Criminal Tribunal for Rwanda (ICTR), both established on an *ad hoc* basis to try cases pertaining to the genocides, war crimes, and other atrocities that took place in those countries. Most recently, the International Criminal Court (ICC), a permanent court with more or less international jurisdiction, was established to try such cases.

One other option in the international arena is that various individual states can step in and conduct trials of those people who have committed criminal acts in another country. Such cases are tried under the international legal principle of universal jurisdiction, which, until the late 1990s, had rarely been used. Universal jurisdiction is claimed on the grounds that the crime committed is considered to be a crime against all, and therefore any state may claim criminal jurisdiction. The idea, then, is that those people who have committed crimes may be tried in a country other than their own, regardless of nationality, country of residence, or any other relation with the prosecuting country, even

Box 20.3 **Timeline of Modern International Mechanisms of Transitional Justice**

1945 *Nuremberg Trials* **established by victorious Allies in post-War Germany**

- Tribunal located in Nuremberg, Germany.
- Four justices and four alternates from the four Allied countries adjudicated cases.
- Charges of crimes against peace, crimes against humanity laid—crimes that did not exist at the time of commission.
- More than 200 Nazi officials tried, excluding most senior decision makers.

1946 *Tokyo Trial* **established by victorious Allies in post-War Japan**

- Tribunal located in Tokyo, Japan.
- Eleven justices from ten countries adjudicated cases.
- Charges of crimes against peace, crimes against humanity, and conventional war crimes.
- Twenty-eight top Japanese officials tried.

1993 *International Criminal Tribunal for the Former Yugoslavia* **(ICTY) established by the UN Security Council to try top officials from the conflict in the Balkans**

- Tribunal located in The Hague, Netherlands.
- Sixteen justices elected to four-year terms by the UN General Assembly, and twelve *ad litem* justices (appointed only for specific cases) adjudicated cases.
- Charges included grave breaches of Geneva Conventions and Protocols, violations of laws of war, genocide, and crimes against humanity.
- Most 'big fish' eluded capture and escaped prosecution.
- Tribunal intended as *ad hoc* or temporary, to be disbanded when mandate met.

1994 *International Criminal Tribunal for Rwanda* **(ICTR) established by the UN Security Council to try high-ranking** *génocidaires* **from the 1994 genocide**

- Tribunal located in Arusha, Tanzania.
- Sixteen justices elected to four-year terms by the UN General Assembly, and nine *ad litem* justices (appointed only for specific cases) adjudicated cases.
- Charges included genocide, crimes against humanity, and violations of the Geneva Conventions and Protocols.
- Modelled after the ICTY; tribunal intended as *ad hoc.*

2002 *Special Court for Sierra Leone* **(SCSL) established between the United Nations and Sierra Leone as the first hybrid national/international tribunal to try criminals from Sierra Leone's brutal civil war**

- Tribunal located in Freetown, Sierra Leone (except Taylor, who was tried in The Hague under SCSL auspices).
- Eleven judges appointed from ten countries, from across Africa and the West.
- Charges included war crimes and crimes against humanity committed within Sierra Leone.
- 'Big fish' including Charles Taylor charged, detained, and tried.

2002 *International Criminal Court* **(ICC) established by states parties to the Rome Statute**

- Tribunal located in The Hague, Netherlands.
- Eighteen justices elected from Assembly of States Parties adjudicated cases.
- Charges included crimes of aggression, genocide, and war crimes.[1]
- ICC intended as permanent tribunal.

though their crimes have been committed outside the boundaries of the prosecuting state.

The case of Rwanda illustrates how retributive justice can be applied by the international community when a state itself is unwilling or unable to prosecute those responsible for criminal violations. Between early April and mid-July 1994, a genocide was carried out in Rwanda in which more than 800,000 mostly Tutsi Rwandan citizens were brutally murdered by mostly Hutu citizens. When the genocide came to an end, more than 120,000 Rwandans stood accused of the commission of these crimes. The justice system, as it then existed, was simply unable to deal with such an extreme number of cases. Two separate international mechanisms, along with an intricate national system of *gacaca* (pronounced ga-CHA-cha) courts, were established to try these accused. The international mechanisms are described below.

International trials: tribunals

The first is the International Criminal Tribunal for Rwanda (ICTR), which was established in 1994 by the United Nations Security Council to prosecute those responsible for genocide and other serious violations of international humanitarian law committed in the territory of Rwanda in 1994. Although it has jurisdiction over any and all crimes committed during the genocide, the ICTR was really intended as a mechanism to try only those charged with the greatest offences—those charged with lesser offences were to be tried by the *gacaca* courts. The international community recognized the need to strengthen African institutions, and to demonstrate that it had held at least the 'big fish' responsible, in an attempt to show other leaders around the world that they could not hope to get away with such crimes. The idea behind the court was that it would try a finite number of cases and then be disbanded.

International trials: universal jurisdiction

The second international mechanism being used in pursuit of retributive justice for crimes committed during the Rwandan genocide is the trial of *génocidaires*

by courts of, and located in, other countries, using the principle of universal jurisdiction. Belgium was the first country to try Rwandan *génocidaires* in its civilian courts, based on a law of universal jurisdiction passed in 1993. In 2001, four Rwandans were charged, convicted, and sentenced under the Belgian criminal justice system for crimes that they had committed in Rwanda. Canada, France, and Switzerland have also tried Rwandan genocide cases. Many other states are reluctant to do so.

KEY POINTS
Retributive justice generally involves the indictment, trial, and punishment of the perpetrators of crimes.
Trials for the perpetrators of crimes may be carried out by national courts.
Retributive justice may also be carried out by international tribunals.
Courts around the world have begun to try the perpetrators of crimes in other countries under the principle of international law known as *universal jurisdiction*.

Restorative Justice

Restorative justice may be a foreign concept to those who have grown up with the idea of retributive justice described above. In this paradigm, justice is about restoring both the victim and perpetrator of crimes back into harmony with the community. Restorative processes always seek to dignify and empower victims. And so, unlike retributive mechanisms such as court cases, which tend to focus only on the perpetrator, victims often play a central role in restorative processes. Ideally, the victim is also empowered through restorative processes. The wider community, too, is often a participant in restorative processes.

Restorative mechanisms may take many forms. A number of these are, and have been, actively used in the West and elsewhere, either instead of, or alongside, retributive mechanisms. In New Zealand, Family Group Conferences, based on traditional Maori principles,

including teaching, settlement, and community restoration, are used in conjunction with the court system. In many parts of Canada, aboriginal communities use healing circles instead of the courts to deal with community members who have committed crimes against the community. Ceremonies to 'cool the heart[s]' of former child soldiers upon their return to their home communities in Sierra Leone are commonplace.

Truth Commissions

In pursuit of justice in transitional communities, one of the most commonly used restorative mechanisms has been the truth commission. Truth commissions are bodies established to look at widespread human rights violations that took place during a specified period of time, on a temporary basis, by the state, often in conjunction with opposition forces and/or the involvement of the international community. While no two truth commissions ever look or function in exactly the same way, their aim, generally, is to inquire into past events (see Box 20.4). Often, the inquiry includes the collection of details from victims by means of questionnaires and sometimes by means of public testimony. In almost every case, each truth commission also produces a report that contains detailed or summary accounts of exactly what has taken place. In most cases, these reports are widely publicized. In Argentina, for example, the report published by the National Commission on the Disappeared, entitled *Nunca Más* (*Never Again*), has become one of the best-selling books of all time in that country. There have been approximately twenty-six truth commissions established around the world since 1974. The majority of these have been held in Africa and Latin America, although commissions have also been established in Asia and Europe.

The benefits of truth commissions over retributive mechanisms have been hotly debated. First, truth commissions have a much broader focus than trials. While the scope of a trial is often limited to the actions of one perpetrator, truth commissions focus on widespread abuses perpetrated by any number of individuals and on the suffering endured by hundreds, or more likely thousands, of victims. Second, truth commissions can have an educative effect through the public broadcasting of public hearings and testimony or through the publication and dissemination of the final report. Such measures might be the first opportunity that people have to hear about what happened in their own country. Third, truth commissions are not a 'one-size-fits-all' approach. Truth commissions may choose to focus on truth or they may choose to focus on reconciliation, as identified by the people of a particular country. They are also able to tailor their activities to suit the circumstances of the particular country in which they operate. Fourth, truth commissions are often seen as a less costly alternative to retributive approaches. Because truth commissions require far less in terms of infrastructure, personnel, and other expenses generally associated with a trial, for example, their expenses are considerably lower. The South African Truth and Reconciliation Commission, for example, had a total budget, for all five years of its operation, of 196 million Rand (approximately US $25 million)—a substantially smaller sum than the ICTR, as discussed above.

National implementation

Truth commissions are generally established and run by the *national government*, as happened in Chile. In 1973, the Government of democratically elected President Allende was overthrown by General Augusto Pinochet in a brutal and repressive military coup. More than 3,000 people were killed, and many more were injured. When the subsequent Government came to power in 1990, a truth commission was established. The *Comisión Nacional para la Verdad y Reconciliación* (National Commission on Truth and Reconciliation) worked for a period of nine months. During that time, the Commission received evidence from victims and their families in 3,400 cases, considered such evidence, and finally prepared a report. Testimony was heard, evidence gathered, and decisions made; in the end, all of the evidence was referred to the courts, except for the testimony of those who had been granted a blanket amnesty.

International involvement

In other cases, however, truth commissions are implemented and/or run by the *international community*. The involvement of the international community may come as a result of one or a combination of several factors. First, the national government may be too fragile to carry out such investigations on its own. The involvement of the international community gives legitimacy to the national regime, and the support that the international community can provide often strengthens the process immeasurably. Second, the financial resources of the national government may be too depleted for it to be able to carry out a truth commission on its own. Third, other resources within society, including members of the judicial community, or basic infrastructure needs, may be similarly depleted. The international community can provide for these needs. Fourth, there is enormous expertise in matters concerning truth commissions in the international community, which may be lacking at the national level. The inclusion of personnel from the international community can provide such expertise. Finally, the conditions to bring about the truth commission may have been negotiated between opposing parties under international supervision. The presence of members of the international community can keep disagreements between rival parties that are meant to be working together on the truth commission from flaring up and derailing the process.

Box 20.4 **Where have Truth Commissions been Established?**

Uganda	Commission of Inquiry into the Disappearance of People in Uganda Since the 25th January 1971 (1974)
Bolivia	*Comisión Nacional de Investigación de Desaparecidos** (1982–1984) (National Commission of Inquiry into Disappearances)
Argentina	*Comisión Nacional para ka Desaparición de Personas* (1983–1984) (National Commission on the Disappearance of Persons)
Uruguay	*Comisión Investigadora sobre la Situación de Personas Desaparecidos y Hechos que la Motivaron* (1985) (Investigative Commission on the Situation of Disappeared People and Its Causes)
Zimbabwe	Commission of Inquiry (1985)
Uganda	Commission of Inquiry into Violations of Human Rights (1986–1994)
Nepal	Commission of Inquiry to Locate the Persons Disappeared during the Panchayet Period (1990–1991)
Chile	*Comisión Nacional para la Verdad y Reconciliación* (1990–1991) (National Commission on Truth and Reconciliation)
Chad	*Commission d'Enquête sur les Crimes et Détournements Commis par l'Ex-Président Habré, ses co-Auteurs et/ou Complices* (1991–1992) (Commission of Inquiry on the Crimes and Misappropriations Committed by the Ex-President Habré, His Accomplices and/or Accessories)
South Africa	Commission of Enquiry into Complaints by Former African National Congress (ANC) Prisoners and Detainees (1992)
Germany	*Enquete Kommission Aufarbeitung von Geschichte und Folgen der SED-Diktatur in Deutschland* (1992–1994) (Commission of Inquiry for the Assessment of History and Consequences of the SED Dictatorship in Germany)
El Salvador	*Comisión de la Verdad para El Salvador* (1992–1993) (Commission on the Truth for El Salvador)
South Africa	Commission of Enquiry into Certain Allegations of Cruelty and Human Rights Abuse against ANC Prisoners and Detainees by ANC Members (1979–1991)
Sri Lanka	Commissions of Inquiry into the Involuntary Removal or Disappearance of Persons (1988–1994)
Haiti	*Commission nationale de vérité et de justice* (1991–1994) (National Commission of Truth and Justice)
Burundi	International Commission of Inquiry (1995–1996)
South Africa	Truth and Reconciliation Commission (1995–2000)
Ecuador	*Comisión de la Verdad et Justicia* (1996–1997) (Truth and Justice Commission)
Guatemala	*Comisión para el Esclarecimiento Histórico* (1997–1999) (Commission for Historical Clarification)
Nigeria	Commission of Inquiry for the Investigation of Human Rights Violations (1999–2000)
Sierra Leone	Truth and Reconciliation Commission (2000–2004)
Serbia	Yugoslav Truth and Reconciliation Commission* (2001–2003)
Peru	*Comisión de la Verdad y Reconciliación* (2003) (Truth and Reconciliation Commission)
Morocco	*Instance Équité et Réconciliation* (2004–2005) (Fairness and Reconciliation Commission)
Ghana	National Reconciliation Commission (2004–2005)
Timor-Leste	Commission for Reception, Truth, and Reconciliation (2005)
Liberia	Truth and Reconciliation Commission (2006–2008)

*Unable to complete its work; disbanded without producing a report.

Adapted from Hayner (2001).

The international community was very much integrated in the Haitian truth commission. President Jean-Bertrand Aristide was elected President of Haiti in 1990, but he was forced into exile in 1991 when a coup led by Raoul Cédras erupted. From 1991 to 1994, the military regime waged a campaign of torture against Aristide's supporters. In October 1994, after the US brokered an agreement between Aristide and Cédras, Aristide was returned to power, and appointed the *Commission nationale de vérité et de justice* (National Commission of Truth and Justice) in 1995. The idea for a Haitian truth commission and much of the work toward it was initiated and influenced by the Haitian diaspora community abroad. The Haitian commission was carried out by the Organization of American States (OAS) and the United Nations Permanent Mission to Haiti (*International Civilian Mission in Haiti*). In the end, four of the appointed commissioners were Haitian nationals, all of whom had then been living in exile. The three others were representatives of the international community, from Bahamas, Barbados, and Senegal. The Commission presented its final report in December 1995, as Aristide was again forced out of power—this time because of the terms of the Constitution.

KEY POINTS
Restorative justice is meant to restore the victim and perpetrator back into the community.
In pursuit of restorative justice, truth commissions have been the main mechanism utilized.
Truth commissions can be implemented and run by the national government.
Sometimes truth commissions are implemented and run by the international community in conjunction with, or in support of, the national government.

Reparative Justice

Reparative justice is a different kind of justice again from either retributive or restorative justice. The reparative paradigm is concerned with making right the things that went wrong. At its root is the idea of *repair*. The goal, therefore, is to provide a remedy for the suffering and loss that have occurred.

Apology

Reparative justice can take place in one of two ways, or it can contain a mixture of both. The first method of repairing the past is by issuing an *apology*. That is, the perpetrator himself can simply say sorry for what has taken place. Or, if sufficient time has passed that the perpetrator himself is no longer able to apologize—for instance, if generations have passed since the abuses were carried out and the perpetrator has died—then a representative of the perpetrator may apologize on his behalf. The Government of Canada, for example, apologized in 1992 for the hanging of Métis leader Louis Riel in 1885 for his role in the Northwest Rebellion. None of the elected officials who had been responsible for the decision to hang Riel in 1885 were still alive. Yet the modern-day Government took the initiative, as representatives of that regime, to issue a formal apology for the previous Government's actions.

The benefits of an apology are many. First, the wrong that the victim has suffered is acknowledged by the perpetrator. This kind of acknowledgement, that is publicly admitting to and accepting a knowledge of the events that have taken place, can allow the victim to move forward, and to begin to 'let go' of the wrong she has suffered. Second, and closely related to the first, is that an apology can lessen the bitterness that the victim feels. This is not to say that she will necessarily become suddenly freed of the loss, or will forget it entirely. Rather, an apology can reduce feelings of anger and hurt. Third, the victim may feel a sense of vindication at being recognized, finally, as being right. Fourth, the trauma of the incident may also be diminished.

Obviously, the hurts that a victim feels will not magically disappear simply because an apology is made. This is particularly the case if the victim feels that the apology is in any way insincere, or if she feels that the apology giver has not got the authority to issue a meaningful apology. An apology is not a panacea. But it does go some way toward repairing the damage that has been inflicted.

For example, the Government of Australia offered an apology for past wrongs to the Aboriginal people who live there. Between 1915 and 1969, thousands of Aboriginal children were forcibly removed from their parents and given to white families or institutions to raise. As a lasting outcome, Aboriginal people in Australia remain the country's poorest and most disadvantaged group. An inquiry into these policies was held in 1997, and a report was released. The following year, a National Sorry Day was instituted, to acknowledge the wrong that had been done. In 2008, the new Prime Minister, Paul Rudd, issued a formal apology. The apology was issued instead of the billion-dollar nationwide compensation package that Aboriginal campaigners had been calling for.

Restitution

The second method of repair is restitution. Restitution can be defined as a token paid in compensation for loss or injury. The idea behind this kind of compensation is similar to the awards offered by civil courts when, for example, a child is killed through an act of negligence. No one can be sure what that child's life might have been worth, yet a sum of money is awarded as payment or repair for the harm that was caused. This is the kind of repair that the Aboriginal community in Australia had been calling for.

To be sure, the idea of compensation is not completely adequate. No amount of money can ever fully compensate someone for loss or damage suffered, and no 'wrong' can be righted with the payment of money. Yet restitution has been utilized by a number of countries in an attempt to right the wrongs that were perpetrated. In Canada, for example, after the attack on Pearl Harbor in 1941, more than 20,000 Canadian citizens of Japanese ancestry, many of whom had lived in Canada for several generations and had Canadian citizenship, were suspected of aiding Japanese authorities in military espionage activities. These Canadian citizens were placed in internment camps, many of the men were taken to work camps, and homes, fishing boats, and other property were seized by the Government and sold without the permission of their rightful owners. At the end of the war, in 1945, these Canadians of Japanese ancestry were released from the camps, but were banned for the next five years from living near the coast. They were unable to reclaim much of their property. In 1950, the Bird Commission awarded $1.3 million in claims to 1,434 Japanese Canadians, based solely on claims for lost property. More than half a century later, in 1988, the Government awarded CAD $21,000 to each Canadian of Japanese ancestry who had been interned, under the *Japanese Canadian Redress Agreement*.

KEY POINTS
Reparative justice focuses on repairing suffering and loss.
One key method of bringing about reparation is by issuing an apology.
Another way of effecting reparation is by awarding compensation or restitution.

Putting Transitional Justice into Practice

These three paradigms of transitional justice represent three different visions of how a society can and should be rebuilt in a period of transition. Retributive justice focuses on holding perpetrators of crimes accountable for their actions. Restorative justice focuses on uncovering the truth about past crimes, focusing not only on the perpetrators, but also on the victims of criminal activities. Reparative justice focuses on making things right, whether by means of an apology, or by giving a token amount of money, or by replacing what was lost.

It is clear that there are both benefits and shortcomings to each of these approaches.

The number of mechanisms employed in the pursuit of transitional justice has grown considerably since the mid-1980s. And with every new attempt, knowledge about how to best carry out such efforts has grown too. Lessons can be learned from past attempts that can inform how new mechanisms will be set up.

In 2004, then-United Nations Secretary General Kofi Annan addressed the subject of transitional justice. One of the things that he stressed the most was the need for these mechanisms to work together:

> The international community must see transitional justice in a way that extends well beyond courts and tribunals. The challenges of post-conflict environments necessitate an approach that balances a variety of goals, including the pursuit of accountability, truth and reparation, the preservation of peace and the building of democracy and the rule of law ... Where transitional justice is required, strategies must be holistic, incorporating integrated attention to individual prosecutions, reparations, truth-seeking, institutional reform, vetting and dismissals, or an appropriately conceived combination thereof. The United Nations must consider through advance planning and consultation how different transitional justice mechanisms will interact to ensure that they do not conflict with one another. It is now generally recognized, for example, that truth commissions can positively complement criminal tribunals. (UN Secretary-General, 2004, p. 9)

Indeed, a number of transitional justice mechanisms have been established with just this in mind. One of the biggest needs is for some combination of all of the objectives of the three different paradigms (retributive, restorative, reparative) to be fulfilled. In some cases, one mechanism can fulfil more than one of these objectives on its own. The South African Truth and Reconciliation Commission, for example, was established with three distinct objectives, reflected in the three different Committees into which it was divided: gross violations of human rights, amnesty, and reparations.

In other cases, more than one mechanism must be employed in order to satisfy the objectives of the three paradigms. For example, in Sierra Leone, the Truth and Reconciliation Commission and the Special Court for Sierra Leone were established, and ran, concurrently. While this caused practical problems, such as the sharing of evidence and sheer amount of resources and capital required to carry out both projects simultaneously, the various needs of the population could be more adequately addressed.

However it works, in the aftermath of violent conflict and human rights abuses, societies in transition have a real need to overcome the social implications of past conflict. Obviously, not every situation will require the same kind of solution. Moreover, not every society will have the same ideas about what must be done. But it is the case that reforms in the justice sector can go a long way toward helping societies move forward. And these reforms help, overall, to strengthen a country's chances at a successful transition toward peace and democracy.

KEY POINTS
The number of mechanisms of transitional justice at work has grown.
Mechanisms can work alone or in tandem.
Where more than one mechanism is in use, they must work together.

Case Study: Uganda

The country of Uganda has experienced a high level of human rights abuses at the hands of the state since independence from Britain in 1962. From 1971 onward, the country experienced a series of coups, which culminated in a concentration of power in the head of state. Under Milton Obote, the country's first post-colonial Prime Minister, a number of groups carried out riots and armed attacks in protest against his accession to power (Berg-Schlosser and Siegler, 1990, p. 196).

In 1971, Obote was overthrown by his top general, Idi Amin, who carried out a systematic reign of terror, murdering anyone he considered to stand in his way

(Wright, 1996, p. 306). The military and paramilitary mechanisms of the state conducted brutal campaigns of torture (Khiddu-Makubuya, 1989, pp. 141–157). It is conservatively estimated that between 300,000 and 500,000 people were killed during this period (Briggs, 1998, p. 23). In 1979, Amin's forces were defeated by forces including those of Obote, of future president Yoweri Museveni, and of neighbouring Tanzania. Amin fled to exile in Libya (Ofcansky, 1996, p. 47). Interim Governments were appointed in 1979 and 1980.

As the result of rigged elections in 1980, Obote returned to power. He remained until 1985, when he was again overthrown by a faction of the Ugandan military. During this period, human rights abuses sky-rocketed as the paramilitary forces of the state carried out campaigns of torture, rape, and rampant looting (Khiddu-Makubuya 1989, p. 153). It is estimated that approximately 300,000 (*Uganda*, 1998, p. 53) to 500,000[2] people were killed, many of them within a small geographic area known as the Luweero Triangle. Obote fled into exile in Zambia (Museveni, 1997, p. 166). A military council ruled for six months, until it, too, was overthrown.

The current President, Yoweri Museveni, and the National Resistance Army (NRA; now National Resistance Movement, NRM) seized power by means of military force in January 1986. He, too, has ruled with an iron fist. As with his predecessors, Museveni has faced considerable opposition from many of the fifty-six different ethnic groups throughout the country. Between 1986 and 2008, Museveni faced more than twenty-seven armed insurgencies.[3]

One of the most violent has been carried out by the Lord's Resistance Army (LRA), a rebel group led by Joseph Kony. The LRA has perpetrated thousands of human rights abuses against the population of northern Uganda in its bid to defeat Museveni and take control of the country. Their fighting has spilled over to areas including the greater north and east of the country. An estimated 30,000 children have been abducted for use as child soldiers and sex slaves. Many thousands of women have been raped and gang-raped. And thousands of others have been tortured, many with lips, noses, and ears sliced off. At least 1.8 million people, which represents 80 per cent of the population of northern Uganda, have been forced, over the years, to flee to camps for **internally displaced persons** (IDPs)—and many have now been in the camps for twenty years or more. The fighting and rebel raids have tapered off during periods when peace talks are taking place, and at other times have become increasingly violent. One study reported that 79 per cent of community members reported having witnessed torture, 40 per cent had witnessed killing, and five per cent had been forced to physically harm another (Allen, 2005, p. 24).

This conflict, although distinct from many of the other conflicts that have taken place, is in many ways representative of the manner in which discord has manifest itself in the country. The scope of abuse, and the devastation of communities, is similar to many of the other conflicts that have seized Uganda. And so Uganda finds itself beleaguered by conflict, with many of the resulting problems untreated and questions unanswered—even though it has attempted, at different times and in different ways, to deal with the perpetrators of such conflicts.

Truth Commission

When Museveni and the NRM came to power in 1986, one of their programmes involved the creation of a truth commission. The role of the 1986 Commission was to inquire into 'the causes and circumstances' surrounding mass murders, arbitrary arrests, the role of law enforcement agents and the state security agencies, and discrimination that occurred between 1962 and January 1986, when Museveni and the NRM assumed power. It was also meant to suggest ways of preventing such abuses from reoccurring (Republic of Uganda, 1994, pp. 3–4). The Commission was also expected to determine the role of various state institutions in both perpetrating and hiding gross human rights violations. The Commission collected testimony from thousands of victims and witnesses, and, in the end, 608 witnesses appeared before the Commissioners at public hearings. Its final report is 720 pages in length.

In actuality, however, the Commission was able to accomplish very little. It faced a considerable number of constraints that ultimately proved its undoing. The Commission was beset by a number of institutional failures. These included a lack of capacity to be able to carry out the kinds of investigations and referrals to prosecution that it was meant to have undertaken. Its mandate, for example, was simply too vast: to investigate *all* human rights abuses committed between 1962 and 1986 would have required more than that with which the Commission was invested. And there was a dearth of hard evidence, either because that evidence was never preserved, or because it went missing (whether innocently or nefariously) in the intervening years. The passing of time also affected the ability of witnesses to testify, as those who might have provided important information either forgot crucial details or died before the opportunity arose. Funding, too, was a problem for the Commission, since it was never adequately funded or resourced by the Government. This affected everything from the Commission's ability to pay the commissioners and other staff, to their need for basic items such as file folders, pens, and petrol. In the end, funding came from international non-governmental organizations (NGOs) to enable the Commission to complete its work and publish the final report. Similarly, the Commission suffered from a general lack of political will to galvanize the process. Most citizens were too sceptical of the process to become involved; these people, who had been abused at the hands of their Governments for the better part of forty years, were not in a position to trust that this Government-initiated process might be beneficial for them. Likewise, the Government itself backed away from the work of the Commission almost before it started, and its officials, such as the Criminal Investigations Division and the Director of Public Prosecutions, which were supposed to have collected evidence and used it to prepare for prosecutions of perpetrators, failed to fulfil these responsibilities.

In the end, the work of the Commission was negligible. It touched only a marginal segment of the population in any real way. As a testament to the ineffectual performance of the Commission, all of its documents now reside in a locked, bug-infested closet, forgotten by everyone.

Amnesty Act

With the number of armed conflicts and the amount of bush warfare that has paralysed the country since 1962, it is not surprising that there are thousands of former rebel soldiers who face prosecution. This is especially relevant to the ongoing conflict in northern Uganda, in which thousands of people, including children, have been abducted into the rebel forces and made to commit heinous crimes. The people of Uganda, therefore, 'conceived [of an amnesty] as a tool for ending conflict . . . a significant step towards ending the conflict in the north and working towards a process of national reconciliation' (Hovil and Lomo, 2005, p. 6).

After a significant amount of persuasion of Government officials, particularly those in northern Uganda, in November 1999, the Government of Uganda passed an Amnesty Act, which was enacted in January 2000. The Act offers amnesty to anyone who has 'engaged in or is

engaging in war or armed rebellion against the government of the Republic of Uganda' (Republic of Uganda, 2000, II.3.i). By 2006, the Amnesty Commission had received more than 20,000 applications for amnesty.

The people of Uganda are deeply divided about whether those who have committed serious crimes should be punished for them. On the one hand, there is substantial support for the prosecution of those such as Joseph Kony, the leader of the LRA. There is little question among the population, particularly in the north, that Kony should simply go free. On the other hand, however, there is widespread concern that those who have been forced to commit such atrocities might also be held responsible—including those children and adults who were forcibly abducted by the LRA. For these, there is substantially less clarity about the issue of amnesty. Only one point garners consensus: the conflict must be stopped.

The Government of Uganda has waffled on the issue. Within the Parliament and the State House, there is at best

> ambiguous support for the amnesty process: numerous informants questioned whether or not the government was really serious about the Amnesty. Indeed, since its enactment, the government has never presented a consistent position on the Amnesty. … One elderly man in Kitgum articulated a commonly held view: 'Parliament said [the Amnesty Act] was ok, but the president himself didn't want it. This is no secret.' (Hovil and Lomo, 2005, p. 18)

In April 2006, the Government passed the Amnesty Amendment Bill (2003) to enable the Minister of Internal Affairs, with Parliamentary approval, to prevent specific people, most notably the LRA, from being granted amnesty.

International Criminal Court

Another piece of the 'justice' puzzle in Uganda has come in the form of the International Criminal Court (ICC). In what has been seen as a further indication of Museveni's dissatisfaction with the Amnesty Act, he formally requested an investigation by the ICC into the actions of the Lord's Resistance Army in northern Uganda in December 2003. This cast a more ominous shadow over the existing amnesty process. The Chief Prosecutor issued warrants for the arrest of Joseph Kony and four other senior members of the LRA,[4] making Uganda the first case to be examined by the Court. Individually, each of the five warrants details the atrocities attributed to the LRA, and to each of the five men, including more than 2,200 killings and 3,200 abductions in over 820 attacks. Kony, for example, is charged with 12 counts of crimes against humanity and 21 counts of war crimes.

Yet here, too, opinion is divided. The same justice versus peace debate rages on regarding the role of the ICC. International agencies have, for the most part, been very supportive of the role played by the ICC. On the ground, however, sentiments are mixed. Many Ugandans see the ICC as a troublesome intruder that threatens to take away any chance that they have for peace and a resolution of the conflict through negotiation with the rebels. For Kony and his men are unlikely to surrender in the face of such daunting warrants. Others seem relieved for the international community, finally,

to have become involved, when it has been clear that the Government of Uganda had no will to prosecute.

At the time of writing, the case of Uganda at the ICC was still active. Yet the warrants had not been executed, and little further action had been taken.

KEY POINTS
Protracted civil conflict has plagued Uganda since 1962.
Uganda's truth commission (1986–1994) failed to adequately acknowledge past events.
The Amnesty Act (2000) has been divisive, as people debate who should be punished, and how.
The warrants issued by the International Criminal Court have been equally divisive.

Conclusion

The case of Uganda aptly illustrates the difficulty that exists in putting into practice any form of 'justice' through the paradigms of retributive, restorative, and reparative justice discussed above, and resolving the social implications of prolonged violent conflict. What seems, on paper, a reasonable solution to a difficult problem, is often no match for the complexity of situations on the ground, or the complicated effects of human rights abuses. Scholars and practitioners of transitional justice are only now beginning to comprehend the manner in which such mechanisms can and should promote greater goals such as peace and democracy, and how these relate to and interact with other concurrent processes of transition, such as economic development, or the demobilization and disarmament of combatants, that are also likely to be underway.

The field of transitional justice is rife with debate about how these different paradigms fit together. Indeed, some have argued that without the rule of law,

as demonstrated by a rigorous use of retributive mechanisms, there simply is no justice, and that the restorative and reparative paradigms are neither fully right nor adequate. Others claim that the latter two approaches are merely a second best option, sufficient for use only when all else fails. Yet many contend that each of these approaches is sufficient, in and of itself, to bring about the desired outcome: the rebuilding of a society after human rights violations.

What is clear is that the three paradigms, and the institutions that operate within them, aim toward the same goals. Their methods and rationale, of course, differ greatly. But, in the end, it is entirely possible that the paradigms are themselves concordant pieces of a holistic process of justice. In the years to come, as transitional justice is applied through all three of its paradigms, in different cases and at different times, it will become more apparent whether this is, in fact, the case.

QUESTIONS

INDIVIDUAL STUDY QUESTIONS

1. What is transitional justice?
2. What is the main goal of retributive justice?
3. What is universal jurisdiction?
4. How does restorative justice differ from retributive justice?
5. What is a truth commission?

GROUP DISCUSSION QUESTIONS

1. Should these three different types of justice always work alone?
2. Is there any benefit to a society as a whole in avoiding retributive punishment?
3. Is there a role for amnesty in encouraging societal participation in restorative processes?
4. What should the responsibility of government be in apology or restitution? Should there be a statute of limitations on this responsibility?

FURTHER READING

Elster, J. (ed.) (2006). *Retribution and Reparation in the Transition to Democracy*. New York: Cambridge University Press.
Elster provides an in-depth treatment of a number of cases from the early stages of retroactive accountability for crimes of war that have taken place in the twentieth century. Elster also offers overviews of the history of the practice of transitional justice that neatly conceptualize the mechanisms and processes that are used.

Hayner, P. (2001). *Unspeakable Truths*. New York: Routledge.
Hayner deals with the need for and utility of truth commissions as a means of reckoning with past crimes. She provides a number of case studies, and a deep look at restorative justice.

Kritz, N. J. (ed.) (1995). *Transitional Justice: How Emerging Democracies Reckon with Former Regimes*. Washington, DC: United States Institute of Peace Press.
Kritz's three volumes look at the nuts and bolts of transitional justice, from theory (Vol. 1) to country studies (Vol. 2) to legal documentation (Vol. 3).

Minow, M. (1998). *Between Vengeance and Forgiveness: Facing History after Genocide and Mass Violence*. Boston, MA: Beacon Press.
Minow unpacks the three paradigms of transitional justice, and presents a thoughtful discussion of the positive and negative impacts of each.

Parliament of Australia (2008). Apology to Australia's Indigenous peoples. *House Hansard*. 13 February. http:// www.aph.gov.au/House/Rudd_Speech.pdf.
The full text of MP Kevin Rudd's apology to Australia's Indigenous population can be found here.

Quinn, J. and **Freeman**, M. (2003). Lessons learned: Practical lessons gleaned from inside the truth commissions of Guatemala and South Africa. *Human Rights Quarterly*, **25**/4, 1117–1149.
Using primary documents and information obtained by staff from the truth commissions in South Africa and Guatemala, Quinn and Freeman discuss the practical difficulties encountered by truth commissions.

Rotberg, R. I. and **Thompson**, D. (eds) (2000). *Truth v. Justice*. Princeton, NJ: Princeton University Press.
Rotberg and Thompson provide a collection of essays that deal with the essential paradox that paralysed transitional justice in its early years: is truth more important than justice?

Stover, E. and **Weinstein**, H. M. (eds) (2004). *My Neighbour, My Enemy: Justice and Community in the Aftermath of Mass Atrocity*. Cambridge: Cambridge University Press.
The essays provided in this book edited by Stover and Weinstein examine various responses to atrocity in Rwanda and the former Yugoslavia.

WEB LINKS

http://www.icc-cpi.int The website of the International Criminal Court contains details of each of the cases presently before the Court, as well as documents including the Rome Statute.

http://www.ictj.org The International Center for Transitional Justice is an NGO that works in countries around the world, helping to develop transitional justice solutions in post-conflict societies.

http://ijtj.oxfordjournals.org/ The International Journal for Transitional Justice publishes academic articles dealing with the topic of transitional justice.

http://www.usip.org/library/truth.html The website of the United States Institute of Peace has a collection of primary documents from a number of truth commissions.

NOTES

1. The Rome Statute of the International Criminal Court also specifies that the Court will try crimes of aggression. At the time of writing, however, such crimes remain undefined.

2. Confidential interview with Abdul Nadduli, District Commissioner, Luweero District, by the author on 17 November 2004, Luweero Town, Uganda.

3. These include rebellions by Action Restore Peace, Allied Democratic Forces, Apac rebellion, Citizen Army for Multiparty Politics, Force Obote Back, Former Uganda National Army, Holy Spirit Movement, Lord's Army, Lord's Resistance Army, National Federal Army, National Union for the Liberation of Uganda, Ninth October Movement, People's Redemption Army, Uganda Christian Democratic Army, Uganda Federal Democratic Front, Uganda Freedom Movement, Ugandan National Democratic Army, Uganda National Federal Army, Ugandan National Liberation Front, Ugandan National Rescue Fronts I and II, Ugandan People's Army, Ugandan People's Democratic Army, Uganda Salvation Army, and West Nile Bank Front (Hovil and Lomo, 2004, p. 4; 2005, p. 6).

4. At the time of writing, none of these warrants has been executed.

ONLINE RESOURCE CENTRE

Visit the Online Resource Centre that accompanies this book for updates and a range of other resources:

http://www.oxfordtextbooks.co.uk/orc/goodhart/

Conclusion: The Future of Human Rights

Michael Goodhart

Chapter Contents

Reader's Guide

This chapter looks to the future of human rights, exploring some of the key trends, obstacles, and possibilities discernible in their contemporary politics and practice. The first section focuses on the defence of human rights against three broad sets of challenges arising from ecological crisis, the 'war on terror', and from various global fundamentalisms. The second section discusses areas where the extension of human rights promises to be controversial, including social and economic rights, rights of lesbian, gay, bisexual, transgender, intersex, and queer (LGBTIQ) people, genetic rights, and 'rights beyond humanity'. The final section considers how human rights might be (more) effectively realized in the future, highlighting institutional, moral, and political factors that will determine their success or decline.

Introduction

This chapter considers the future of human rights. It offers projections (not predictions) about the likely shape and direction of human rights politics and practice in coming years. So, it does not provide a review or summation of the foregoing chapters—which are anyway too rich and diverse to be summarized neatly. The lessons and insights of those chapters, however, inform the discussion that follows.

One lesson that emerges quite clearly is that there is nothing inevitable about human rights. They are constantly objects of political contestation, never settled or secure. Many people's rights are unfulfilled, many people are inadequately protected by the existing human rights

framework, and often the discourse of human rights is manipulated to serve profit or power. Yet human rights remain integral to progressive politics all over the world, and the aspiration inherent in the idea of human rights remains vital and inspiring. This remarkable resilience stems from the broad and continuing appeal of the promise that human rights offer of a decent, dignified life free from domination and oppression.

The following discussion of the defence, extension, and achievement of human rights can be read as a reflection on the prospects of that promise in light of the challenges and opportunities discernible at the start of the twenty-first century.

Defending Human Rights

By 'defending' human rights I have in mind something more than the daily struggles to secure rights and the ongoing task of creating the laws, policies, and institutions needed to respect, protect, and fulfil them—although these are obviously of the utmost importance. By defending them I also mean defending the *idea* of human rights, the human rights paradigm or discourse, from broad, significant challenges to its legitimacy and viability.

In the second half of the twentieth century the primary challenges to human rights were cultural relativism and the Cold War. The philosophical concern that human rights were a Western construct unsuited for many people and societies in the developing world contributed to sometimes quite legitimate fears of neo-imperialism, fears often stoked by the proxy wars and support for brutal authoritarian regimes that typified the politics of superpower rivalry. With the collapse of communism, however, these threats receded. Human rights networks played a key role in challenging military regimes in Latin America (Keck and Sikkink, 1998; Risse and Sikkink, 1999) and in hastening the end of the Cold War in Eastern Europe (Thomas, 2001). This helped to create a political and discursive opening into which human rights emerged as the primary standard of legitimacy and dominant normative discourse in

global politics—a status reflected in the Vienna Declaration's affirmation of their universality.

This is not to say that the period from the collapse of the Berlin Wall on 9 November 1989 to the terrorist attacks of 11 September 2001—the period Thomas Risse has neatly called '11/9 to 9/11'[1]—was some sort of human rights utopia. The 1990s witnessed some of the most egregious human rights violations in memory as violence and genocide erupted in the Congo, Rwanda, and the former Yugoslavia, to name just a few. On the other hand, the 'third wave' of democratization (Huntington, 1991) meant that more regimes than ever before were democratic, itself a major, if imperfect, human rights advance (see Chapter 8).

Of the major threats facing human rights today, three stand out: ecological challenges, the 'war on terror', and the global rise of fundamentalisms. All three are related to the disparate collection of processes known as globalization. The following sections briefly address each of these threats.

Ecological Challenges

The degradation of the environment poses serious challenges to humanity and to human rights. As John

Barry and Kerri Woods explain in Chapter 18, 'environmental degradation and the depletion of resources such as oil and clean water have been a cause of or contributory factor in violent conflict in many parts of the world.' In addition, 'access to clean air and water is crucial for human life . . . [and] sustainable access to a sufficient quantity and quality of food is dependent on the environment in important ways and can clearly be regarded as crucial to human security and to the fulfilment of human rights.' Finally, 'human security is threatened when people are removed from their land because of environmental threats' (see Chapter 14 on the issues facing forced migrants and internally displaced persons). All of these problems would predictably worsen under many of the plausible scenarios projected in connection with future climate change.

Thus the question that Barry and Woods pose regarding the potential compatibility of human rights and sustainability looms large at the dawn of the twenty-first century, as the potential for intense struggles over increasingly scarce land and resources represents a challenge to the viability of human rights. Perhaps technological advances and changes in attitudes and lifestyles will combine to alleviate the worst of the unfolding ecological crisis. Yet in a worst-case scenario it is hard to see how human rights would withstand the often vicious imperative of bare survival. This is a pragmatic rather than a pessimistic assessment, one that underscores the urgency of finding sustainable solutions to the Earth's ecological challenges that facilitate the ongoing respect for and protection and fulfilment of human rights.

The 'War on Terror'

A second major threat to human rights originates in the 'war on terror' launched by the USA after the 11 September 2001 terrorist attacks and widely adopted (or co-opted) by other states since. This threat has several components. One is the use of extreme measures—unlimited detention, harsh interrogation and torture, the restriction of important civil liberties, warrantless domestic surveillance, and so on—as part of the effort to prevent further terrorist attacks and to disrupt terrorist networks. These measures, which have been adopted prominently but by no means exclusively by the USA, directly threaten or violate the rights of those unjustly detained, tortured, or spied upon, and they pose a wider challenge to human rights norms.

There is nothing wrong in principle with aggressive action against terrorism—in fact, reducing and preventing terrorism is essential to the protection of human rights, as terrorist tactics themselves involve significant violations of the rights of victims. The problem is with the wider discourse in which these policies have been rationalized, a discourse that bears striking similarities to the Cold War national security doctrines described in Chapter 5. This discourse depicts human rights as obstacles to the effective prevention of terrorist attacks and justifies their violation as a necessary part of providing security. Human rights become protections for terrorists; at the same time, anyone suspected of being a terrorist, in this view, forfeits his or her claim to human rights protections.

Besides licensing their direct violation, this approach has three worrying longer-term consequences for human rights. The first is the general expansion and justification of state power. The role of states as the main protectors and simultaneously the major violators of human rights has always required a careful balance between adequate state power to protect rights and effective checks and limits on that power. In the 'war on terror' we risk getting that balance dangerously wrong. The second consequence is that the 'war on terror' has become a convenient rationalization for the persecution of minorities (the Uighurs in western China, who became 'terrorists' after 9/11) and political dissenters (in Central Asia) and the prosecution of dubious wars (the US-led invasion of Iraq, Russia's destruction of Chechnya). Once the terrorist label is applied, human rights considerations go by the wayside with far too few questions asked. Such behaviour also revivifies concerns that human rights are merely ideological cover for the imperialistic impulses of powerful states.

This ties directly in to the third consequence of the 'war on terror': the erosion of the global human rights discourse. Since the early 1990s, human rights have been the dominant normative idea in world politics. This status, while no panacea, facilitated significant development of international human rights law and the consensus supporting it. It created the political space in which the global community could undertake more robust humanitarian intervention (see Chapter 19); it saw the incorporation of human rights into the development policies of the United Nations (see Chapter 10) and many international financial institutions such as the World Bank as well as the recognition that multinational corporations should also be held to high human rights standards. Perhaps, most fundamentally, the predominance of the human rights discourse contributed to a global political climate that made it impossible for states or international actors to violate or ignore human rights with impunity, thanks in large part to the effective mobilization of civil society actors in global politics (see Chapter 9)—a development directly threatened by heightened state secrecy and by paranoid monitoring of such 'security threats' as anti-war and civil liberties groups. If the security paradigm should displace human rights or even become a permanent rival to it, then we are likely to see the return to a Cold-War style of politics in which human rights considerations are regularly trumped by other concerns and in which further progress is difficult or impossible to achieve. Such a reversion is already noticeable in foreign and domestic policy in the United States and in parts of the EU.

Global Fundamentalisms

A third significant challenge to human rights in the twenty-first century is the global rise of various fundamentalisms. *Fundamentalism* is a devout and unshakable belief in some orthodoxy—be it sacred, cultural, or political. The term is most commonly used in describing religious devotees who have an unquestioning faith in the infallibility of certain texts or doctrines, but it equally well describes strident nationalist or ethnic supremacist beliefs and various forms of political or economic dogmatism.

Fundamentalism of all kinds has been on the rise in recent years. We see this in the ascendancy of religious–political fundamentalism, perhaps especially among certain Christian and Muslim groups (but not exclusively there). We see it in the tribal and ethnic politics of genocide (see Chapter 16) that tear apart states all over the world. We see it in the neoliberal orthodoxy represented in the Washington Consensus, which reveres a particular set of 'free market' policies as essential to prosperity (see Chapter 11) and constitutive of freedom.

The reasons for this increase in fundamentalism are certainly complex, but it is crucial to understand it in part—as Barber (1995) was one of the first to argue—as a response to the pressures and uncertainties created by globalization. Rapid change brings heightened uncertainty, which can in turn increase the appeal of

traditional forms of identity even as it intensifies them.

Fundamentalism threatens human rights because it often conflicts with the individualism, humanism, and rationalism that animate modern human rights thinking (see the Introduction). Views that place the needs and values of the community above those of the individual, divine will over human freedom, or ideology over facts and reason will almost certainly be in tension with at least some human rights. And if, as Rorty (1993) and others have argued, the chief obstacle to the greater realization of human rights lies in expanding the category of persons we consider and treat as *human*, it is easy to see how growing fundamentalism, which by its very nature excludes (irrationalizes, dehumanizes) non-believers, threatens human rights. This can easily be obscured by the contemporary tendency to try to enhance the appeal of human rights by locating them in all cultures and belief systems. These efforts, while well intentioned, miss the point that human rights challenge traditional hierarchy and power structures by design.

In contemporary discourse the noun 'fundamentalism' is associated almost exclusively with the adjective 'religious'. Yet market fundamentalism is perhaps the most worrying of all, as it drives a particular model of globalization that threatens people's security by prioritizing economic growth above all else while fetishizing policies that limit states' ability to provide programmes and assistance to ease the transition. Market fundamentalism poses a direct threat to human rights: the dogmatic insistence on austerity policies and a small public sector make it extremely difficult for all countries—rich or developing—to provide adequate protections for a wide range of rights, from education and welfare rights to civil liberties such as a functioning judiciary and electoral arrangements. Yet this type of fundamentalism is also dangerous because, as Barber argues, it is a key contributor to the growth of other forms of fundamentalism that threaten human rights around the world. Unlike its religious cousins, market fundamentalism masquerades as 'sound economics'—despite its evident human costs. People who would be reflexively sceptical of other forms of dogmatism nonetheless place unquestioning faith in the policy pronouncements of economists and policy makers, the self-styled 'gurus' of the neoliberal creed. This critique should not be mistaken for a facile denunciation of capitalism; it is rather to emphasize the large gulf between a model of capitalism geared toward fulfilling human rights and one enslaved to the idols of profit and efficiency.

Extending Human Rights

The dominance of human rights and their centrality to progressive politics means that human rights politics is constantly expanding. Marginalized or oppressed groups find in human rights a framework for articulating and advancing their claims. Utilizing this framework makes strategic sense given the pre-eminence and unparalleled legitimacy of human rights on the world stage. The idea of extending human rights can refer to their application in new 'domains'—such as genetic rights and what I shall call 'rights beyond humanity'— as well as to their application to more people or in more conditions. This latter extension might seem redundant given that human rights purport to be 'universal', but as the experience with women's rights shows plainly, genuine inclusivity requires the ongoing re-evaluation and redefinition of rights and expansion of the rights framework. One way to think about the extension of human rights, then, is as part of an ongoing endeavour to realize and express their universality in law, policy, and institutions.

Some critics worry that the ongoing extension of human rights threatens to overburden the concept: in their view, if there is a human right to every good thing, the distinctive power and appeal of human rights claims will be severely depleted. This is a legitimate concern, but one that nothing can be done about. As successes help to expand the human rights framework, their appeal becomes greater, inviting more attempts to push in new directions. If there are diminishing returns to human rights politics, where they begin and how severe they will be can only be determined in practice. It is not as if some decision—by scholars, diplomats, lawyers, or government officials—could draw a line or fix a limit to human rights claims and aspirations.

This section briefly highlights several areas in which human rights politics and practice are either presently expanding or seem likely to expand in the near future.

Social and Economic Rights

Social and economic rights are not new. They were articulated in the Universal Declaration of Human Rights (UDHR) and codified into international law through the International Covenant on Economic, Social and Cultural Rights (ICESCR) at the same time as civil and political rights. Yet the perception—born of academic debates and Cold War and neoliberal rhetoric—remains that Western countries are opposed to social and economic rights (Whelan and Donnelly, 2007). As a rule, social and economic rights are better protected in the West than elsewhere; this reflects, in part, the West's greater wealth but also its long-standing commitment to social welfare and insurance policies that—while far from perfect—remain historically and comparatively very generous (see Whelan and Donnelly, 2007).

In a global context, and against the backdrop of economic globalization, social and economic rights— including the right to development—seem poised to become a much more prominent site of contestation. The Cold War's end has helped to create more political and discursive space for social and economic rights, and the particular challenges to human security and well-being created by neoliberal globalization have pushed questions about poverty and development to the forefront of the world's political agenda. Increasingly, scholars and activists are paying attention to the Limburg Principles on the Implementation of the International Covenant on Economic, Social and Cultural Rights (1986) and the subsequent Maastricht Guidelines on Violations of Economic, Social, and Cultural Rights[2] as they seek ways better to institutionalize and protect social and economic rights.

Growing concern about the activities of transnational corporations led the UN Commission on Human Rights (Resn 2005/69) to ask the Secretary General to appoint a special representative on the issue of human rights and transnational corporations (TNCs) and other business enterprises. He complied, and the mandate for this special representative, John Ruggie of the USA, includes identifying and clarifying standards of corporate responsibility and accountability for human rights and elaborating on states' role in regulating and adjudicating the activities of TNCs in the human rights domain.[3] At the same time, non-governmental organizations (NGOs) and social movement networks committed to fighting for economic justice are making use of arenas such as the World Social Forum to help to ensure that social and economic rights command greater attention.

LGBTIQ Rights

Many people's human rights are violated because of their sexual identities. Lesbian, gay, bisexual, transgender, intersex, and queer (LGBTIQ) people frequently endure harassment, discrimination, abuse, and degrading treatment; many are denied full rights of citizenship and are subjected to arrest and criminal punishment; some endure torture and murder. The denial and violation of human rights on the basis of sexual identity really reflects a denial of the humanity of LGBTIQ people (see Rorty, 1993). This denial, driven by prejudice and fear, often manifests in the criminalization of certain sexual behaviours and in the denial of full civil and legal protection for LGBTIQ people.

International human rights instruments do not explicitly mention sexual orientation or gender identity (Amnesty International, 2008b). Still, a broad interpretation of international law encompasses the rights of LGBTIQ people around the world under the rights to privacy, equality, and freedom from discrimination. Moreover, the rights to life, liberty, security of the person, asylum, freedom from arbitrary arrest, and peaceful assembly and association have been used in successful litigation and casework involving LGBTIQ people (Amnesty International, 2008b). Achieving explicit recognition and protection of LGBTIQ rights at the international level is likely to prove difficult for some time to come, as the prejudices against people with different sexual identities are deeply culturally embedded and reinforced by fundamentalist strains of traditional religions.

As in other instances where particular groups or categories of persons are systematically denied human rights, some members of those groups doubt whether the human rights framework is adequate to provide protection for their needs and to ensure their dignity and security. Yet it might be precisely in cases where a group is particularly feared or despised that the human rights framework, with its stress on commonality and our shared humanity, might be most valuable. It remains to be seen how, and how effectively, the human rights framework might be used in struggles for greater national and international recognition and protection of LGBTIQ rights.

Genetic Rights

The science of the human genome has advanced quite rapidly and remarkably in recent years. It is now possible to locate genetic markers that signal predisposition toward certain diseases or other medical conditions. Some studies have also identified genetic predispositions toward criminal or anti-social behaviour (for an overview see Ishikawa and Raine, 2004).

As the amount and variety of genetic information available increases, more conflict is likely to emerge around control of that information. It is easy to imagine genetic information being bought and sold for marketing purposes or used by governments or corporations in ways that could violate privacy and security of the person or discriminate against some individuals. In addition, there are serious and difficult ethical questions connected to the manipulation of genetic material and to genetic engineering (see below). It seems likely that, as these technological advances continue, human rights concerning the control and use of genetic information will evolve rapidly.

Rights Beyond Humanity

This section concludes with a topic that might seem more suited to science fiction than a textbook on human rights, but it is a serious topic that deserves mention: the human rights implications of rapidly developing technologies including cloning, artificial intelligence, and genetic engineering. These so-called human enhancement technologies raise serious moral and political questions about who or what counts as human and which rights belong to what or whom. How to address such 'trans-human' technologies and their products (Hughes, 2004) will be an important issue in the field of human rights—just as questions about where to draw the line between humans and animals have been since the eighteenth century (see Goodin *et al.*, 1997).

If the possibility seems distant or far-fetched, consider the debates already swirling around assisted suicide, withdrawal of life support, sex selection, and other forms of genetic engineering, or the ethics of embryonic stem cell research (Hughes, 2004). These are the tip of a much larger iceberg of issues likely to surface sooner than we think. While some very sophisticated thinking on these questions has been done by science fiction writers, the human rights community has not so far engaged with them in any serious way. It is time to do so, paying special attention to the arguments previously and presently used to deny rights to women, to gays, lesbians, bisexuals, and transgender people, and to others.

Achieving Human Rights

The promise of a better, more dignified life lies at the heart of human rights' enduring appeal. For this reason, the challenge of actually achieving human rights—securing their enjoyment—is of crucial importance. Achieving human rights is a complex task with important institutional, moral, and political dimensions. The task is complicated by the lingering tension between state sovereignty and international action in the sphere of human rights.

Institutions

Institutions are obviously crucial to achieving human rights, both at the national and international levels. Nationally, these institutions include effective laws, policies, and programmes implementing human rights, as well as the development of responsive and accountable representative institutions and an independent judiciary (see Chapters 5 and 8). Many states are also beginning to utilize independent national human rights institutions (see Chapter 2) to provide crucial monitoring, accountability, and policy tasks.

It is often overlooked, however, that *every* governmental institution, *every* bureau and service provider, has a role to play in achieving human rights. It remains commonplace to think that specialized human rights laws and agencies will suffice to ensure that human rights are broadly respected. But unless transportation departments, schools, welfare programmes, statistical agencies, and others all make human rights a priority in their policies and functions, full realization of human rights will be difficult to achieve. The goal is not merely accountability and justice after the fact, but a society in which human rights are respected, protected, and fulfilled as a matter of course. To achieve this ambitious aim requires a thoroughgoing integration of human rights norms and priorities into governmental institutions of every kind at every level.

Turning to international institutions, it is important to stress that, while UN institutions are often over-emphasized relative to their importance in securing people's rights on the ground (see Chapter 6), in our highly interconnected world, national institutions alone are inadequate. The threats to human rights and the actors who violate them do not respect borders or boundaries. Many states lack the resources, the capacity, or the will to protect their citizens' human rights. International institutions are thus also essential for achieving human rights. Regional and UN-based institutions play a very large role in agenda setting, in monitoring and implementation, and, increasingly, in enforcement of human rights protections. All of these functions must be strengthened and democratized.

Strengthening international human rights institutions

Several recent developments reflect the strengthening of the international human rights regime. One is the creation of the International Criminal Court (ICC; see Chapter 9), with its jurisdiction over a broad range of war crimes and crimes against humanity and its global reach. While it is too soon to say how effective the Court will be as an agent of justice and in deterring future abuses of power, its very existence reflects a growing recognition of the international legal status of persons and of the need for global approaches to human rights violations. The creation of the UN's new Human Rights Council, while also too recent to assess with confidence, similarly signifies an important development insofar as it recognizes human rights practices within states as an explicitly international concern meriting UN attention.

Another important development in international human rights enforcement is the increasing recognition and use of universal jurisdiction. Although universal jurisdiction is exercised by states, the idea that certain crimes and human rights violations are sufficiently grave to be tried anywhere is another powerful indication of the growing moral and legal status of human rights in international politics.

Every bit as important in achieving human rights is the creation of better funded and more effective development and poverty-reduction agencies, programmes to help states develop the technical capacity they need to better protect human rights at home, and greater international cooperation on issues ranging from forced migration to sexual trafficking and climate change. While some such efforts are possible and indeed ongoing through the UN, regional approaches might well prove valuable in future, in part because of their (relative) insulation against worries about human rights as part of an imperialistic policy toward developing countries and because of lingering cultural concerns about the application of global human rights in particular contexts.

Democratizing international human rights

In Chapter 7, David Chandler argues that human rights represents and risks furthering a hollowing-out of traditional politics, that human rights can have depoliticizing effects. This is an important worry—not least because functioning democratic regimes at the national level are the best guarantors of human rights. This is one reason why the democratization of states is an indispensable part of any global human rights agenda, for it is only in the context of a democratic political regime that human rights can become the normative basis for a substantive politics of freedom and equality.

By democratizing international human rights I have in mind something like the processes touched on in the previous section: the recognition of individuals' legal status in international law and an explicit engagement with difficult questions about how to balance sovereignty and human rights in global politics. But democratization must also include the *politicization* of global human rights, their entrenchment in global institutions that are political in the democratic sense: responsive, accountable, and open to and welcoming of contestation. Indeed, unless all human rights institutions are democratic in this sense, then their institutionalization risks securing power rather than

providing mechanisms through which to tame and challenge it (see Chapter 6).

There is a real danger that through incessant invocation human rights will tend to trump, evade, or 'transcend' politics. This would be a shame and a mistake. Human rights have, from the beginning, been political claims; their force derives not from their truth, but from their appeal—from the appeal of the kind of politics they represent. It would be ironic, then, if human rights led to depoliticization—especially globally, where they are at present the closest thing to a political discourse that exists. It is an open question as to whether human rights can become a political basis for, or vehicle of, a global politics truly worthy of the name, but at present there seem to be no other plausible candidates.

Moral and Political Considerations

Creating the kinds of institutions needed to achieve human rights depends on creating the moral and political will to make human rights a priority. The duty to refrain from directly violating human rights is fairly straightforward—at least in theory. Yet it is not enough to ensure that human rights are achieved. The duty to refrain is far too narrow a moral basis for realizing the promise of Article 28 of the UDHR: 'Everyone is entitled to a social and international order in which the rights and freedoms set forth in this Declaration can be fully realized.'

Some scholars have begun to frame questions of global justice as human rights questions. The work of philosopher Thomas Pogge (2000) is perhaps the best example of this. He maintains that global justice should be conceived in large part as the creation and maintenance of a global order that realizes the promise of Article 28. Others have begun paying greater attention to the notion of *extraterritorial obligations*, the moral and legal duties of states to respect, protect, and fulfil the rights not just of their own citizens, but of people everywhere (Gibney and Skogly, 2009). This and other work clarifying the nature of global moral responsibility for human rights is incredibly valuable and timely, and more of it is needed.

Equally important, however, is the consideration of how to translate moral imperatives into political action. Making human rights a political priority, nationally or internationally, requires more than simply sound arguments. It requires the mobilization of a broad coalition in support of human rights. Human rights struggles have traditionally been led by those enduring abuses of their rights and their allies, or by small, dedicated groups of individuals intensely concerned with particular issues. Whether and how a broad-based human rights coalition might be established is one of the most important practical challenges facing the human rights movement today.

To talk about the normative thrust and appeal of human rights does not mean denying their socially constructed nature (see Chapters 6 and 13). While many normative accounts of human rights do *reify* human rights—treat them as having an independent existence 'out there' in the moral universe—the kind of human rights politics envisioned here recognizes their social construction explicitly. It does so by highlighting the need to create political coalitions to support human rights and to embed them in democratic political institutions. The normative appeal of human rights is itself an inter-subjective or socially constructed fact that shapes the social life of rights every bit as much as other social facts do.

Conclusion

Human rights face numerous political and practical challenges in the twenty-first century, ranging from the threats posed by ecological crisis, the 'war on terror', and the rise of global fundamentalisms to the changing needs and demands of human beings. Achieving human rights in light of these challenges will require not only the development of more effective national and international institutions, but also of the moral and political will to support them—of a global politics of human rights. Whether the kind of solidarity that a worldwide human rights movement requires is possible and sustainable is the paramount question concerning the future of human rights.

NOTES

1. Der Derian (2003) attributes the phrase to Thomas Risse.

2. Maastricht Guidelines on Violations of Economic, Social, and Cultural Rights, Maastricht, 22–26 January 1997. http://www.escr-net.org/resources_more/resources_more_show.htm?doc_id=425803.

3. See the reports issued in 2006, 2007, and 2008 at http://www2.ohchr.org/english/issues/trans_corporations/reports.htm.

ONLINE RESOURCE CENTRE

 Visit the Online Resource Centre that accompanies this book for updates and a range of other resources:

http://www.oxfordtextbooks.co.uk/orc/goodhart/

Appendix 1

Universal Declaration of Human Rights

Adopted and proclaimed by General Assembly resolution 217A (III) of 10 December 1948.

Preamble

Whereas recognition of the inherent dignity and of the equal and inalienable rights of all members of the human family is the foundation of freedom, justice and peace in the world,

Whereas disregard and contempt for human rights have resulted in barbarous acts which have outraged the conscience of mankind, and the advent of a world in which human beings shall enjoy freedom of speech and belief and freedom from fear and want has been proclaimed as the highest aspiration of the common people,

Whereas it is essential, if man is not to be compelled to have recourse, as a last resort, to rebellion against tyranny and oppression, that human rights should be protected by the rule of law,

Whereas it is essential to promote the development of friendly relations between nations,

Whereas the peoples of the United Nations have in the Charter reaffirmed their faith in fundamental human rights, in the dignity and worth of the human person and in the equal rights of men and women and have determined to promote social progress and better standards of life in larger freedom,

Whereas Member States have pledged themselves to achieve, in co-operation with the United Nations, the promotion of universal respect for and observance of human rights and fundamental freedoms,

Whereas a common understanding of these rights and freedoms is of the greatest importance for the full realization of this pledge,

Now, Therefore THE GENERAL ASSEMBLY proclaims THIS UNIVERSAL DECLARATION OF HUMAN RIGHTS as a common standard of achievement for all peoples and all nations, to the end that every individual and every organ of society, keeping this Declaration constantly in mind, shall strive by teaching and education to promote respect for these rights and freedoms and by progressive measures, national and international, to secure their universal and effective recognition and observance, both among the peoples of Member States themselves and among the peoples of territories under their jurisdiction.

Article 1

All human beings are born free and equal in dignity and rights. They are endowed with reason and conscience and should act towards one another in a spirit of brotherhood.

Article 2

Everyone is entitled to all the rights and freedoms set forth in this Declaration, without distinction of any kind, such as race, colour, sex, language, religion, political or other opinion, national or social origin, property, birth or other status. Furthermore, no distinction shall be made on the basis of the political, jurisdictional or international status of the country or territory to which a person belongs, whether it be independent, trust, non-self-governing or under any other limitation of sovereignty.

Article 3

Everyone has the right to life, liberty and security of person.

Article 4

No one shall be held in slavery or servitude; slavery and the slave trade shall be prohibited in all their forms.

Article 5

No one shall be subjected to torture or to cruel, inhuman or degrading treatment or punishment.

Article 6

Everyone has the right to recognition everywhere as a person before the law.

Article 7

All are equal before the law and are entitled without any discrimination to equal protection of the law. All are entitled to equal protection against any discrimination in violation of this Declaration and against any incitement to such discrimination.

Article 8

Everyone has the right to an effective remedy by the competent national tribunals for acts violating the fundamental rights granted him by the constitution or by law.

Article 9

No one shall be subjected to arbitrary arrest, detention or exile.

Article 10

Everyone is entitled in full equality to a fair and public hearing by an independent and impartial tribunal, in the determination of his rights and obligations and of any criminal charge against him.

Article 11

(1) Everyone charged with a penal offence has the right to be presumed innocent until proved guilty according to law in a public trial at which he has had all the guarantees necessary for his defence.

(2) No one shall be held guilty of any penal offence on account of any act or omission which did not constitute a penal offence, under national or international law, at the time when it was committed. Nor shall a heavier penalty be imposed than the one that was applicable at the time the penal offence was committed.

Article 12

No one shall be subjected to arbitrary interference with his privacy, family, home or correspondence, nor to attacks upon his honour and reputation. Everyone has the right to the protection of the law against such interference or attacks.

Article 13

(1) Everyone has the right to freedom of movement and residence within the borders of each state.

(2) Everyone has the right to leave any country, including his own, and to return to his country.

Article 14

(1) Everyone has the right to seek and to enjoy in other countries asylum from persecution.

(2) This right may not be invoked in the case of prosecutions genuinely arising from non-political crimes or from acts contrary to the purposes and principles of the United Nations.

Article 15

(1) Everyone has the right to a nationality.

(2) No one shall be arbitrarily deprived of his nationality nor denied the right to change his nationality.

Article 16

(1) Men and women of full age, without any limitation due to race, nationality or religion, have the right to marry and to found a family. They are entitled to equal rights as to marriage, during marriage and at its dissolution.

(2) Marriage shall be entered into only with the free and full consent of the intending spouses.

(3) The family is the natural and fundamental group unit of society and is entitled to protection by society and the State.

Article 17

(1) Everyone has the right to own property alone as well as in association with others.

(2) No one shall be arbitrarily deprived of his property.

Article 18

Everyone has the right to freedom of thought, conscience and religion; this right includes freedom to change his religion or belief, and freedom, either alone or in community with others and in public or private, to manifest his religion or belief in teaching, practice, worship and observance.

Article 19

Everyone has the right to freedom of opinion and expression; this right includes freedom to hold opinions without interference and to seek, receive and impart information and ideas through any media and regardless of frontiers.

Article 20

(1) Everyone has the right to freedom of peaceful assembly and association.

(2) No one may be compelled to belong to an association.

Article 21

(1) Everyone has the right to take part in the government of his country, directly or through freely chosen representatives.

(2) Everyone has the right of equal access to public service in his country.

(3) The will of the people shall be the basis of the authority of government; this will shall be expressed in periodic and genuine elections which shall be by universal and equal suffrage and shall be held by secret vote or by equivalent free voting procedures.

Article 22

Everyone, as a member of society, has the right to social security and is entitled to realization, through national effort and international co-operation and in accordance with the organization and resources of each State, of the economic, social and cultural rights indispensable for his dignity and the free development of his personality.

Article 23

(1) Everyone has the right to work, to free choice of employment, to just and favourable conditions of work and to protection against unemployment.

(2) Everyone, without any discrimination, has the right to equal pay for equal work.

(3) Everyone who works has the right to just and favourable remuneration ensuring for himself and his family an existence worthy of human dignity, and supplemented, if necessary, by other means of social protection.

(4) Everyone has the right to form and to join trade unions for the protection of his interests.

Article 24

Everyone has the right to rest and leisure, including reasonable limitation of working hours and periodic holidays with pay.

Article 25

(1) Everyone has the right to a standard of living adequate for the health and well-being of himself and of his family, including food, clothing, housing and medical care and necessary social services, and the right to security in the event of unemployment, sickness, disability, widowhood, old age or other lack of livelihood in circumstances beyond his control.

(2) Motherhood and childhood are entitled to special care and assistance. All children, whether born in or out of wedlock, shall enjoy the same social protection.

Article 26

(1) Everyone has the right to education. Education shall be free, at least in the elementary and fundamental stages. Elementary education shall be compulsory. Technical and professional education shall be made generally available and higher education shall be equally accessible to all on the basis of merit.

(2) Education shall be directed to the full development of the human personality and to the strengthening of respect for human rights and fundamental freedoms. It shall promote understanding, tolerance and friendship among all nations, racial or religious groups, and shall further the activities of the United Nations for the maintenance of peace.

(3) Parents have a prior right to choose the kind of education that shall be given to their children.

Article 27

(1) Everyone has the right freely to participate in the cultural life of the community, to enjoy the arts and to share in scientific advancement and its benefits.

(2) Everyone has the right to the protection of the moral and material interests resulting from any scientific, literary or artistic production of which he is the author.

Article 28

Everyone is entitled to a social and international order in which the rights and freedoms set forth in this Declaration can be fully realized.

Article 29

(1) Everyone has duties to the community in which alone the free and full development of his personality is possible.

(2) In the exercise of his rights and freedoms, everyone shall be subject only to such limitations as are determined by law solely for the purpose of securing due recognition and respect for the rights and freedoms of others and of meeting the just requirements of morality, public order and the general welfare in a democratic society.

(3) These rights and freedoms may in no case be exercised contrary to the purposes and principles of the United Nations.

Article 30

Nothing in this Declaration may be interpreted as implying for any State, group or person any right to engage in any activity or to perform any act aimed at the destruction of any of the rights and freedoms set forth herein.

Appendix 2

International Covenant on Civil and Political Rights

Adopted and opened for signature, ratification and accession by General Assembly resolution 2200A (XXI) of 16 December 1966
entry into force 23 March 1976, in accordance with Article 49

Preamble
The States Parties to the present Covenant,

Considering that, in accordance with the principles proclaimed in the Charter of the United Nations, recognition of the inherent dignity and of the equal and inalienable rights of all members of the human family is the foundation of freedom, justice and peace in the world,

Recognizing that these rights derive from the inherent dignity of the human person,

Recognizing that, in accordance with the Universal Declaration of Human Rights, the ideal of free human beings enjoying civil and political freedom and freedom from fear and want can only be achieved if conditions are created whereby everyone may enjoy his civil and political rights, as well as his economic, social and cultural rights,

Considering the obligation of States under the Charter of the United Nations to promote universal respect for, and observance of, human rights and freedoms,

Realizing that the individual, having duties to other individuals and to the community to which he belongs, is under a responsibility to strive for the promotion and observance of the rights recognized in the present Covenant,

Agree upon the following articles:

PART I

Article 1
1. All peoples have the right of self-determination. By virtue of that right they freely determine their political status and freely pursue their economic, social and cultural development.

2. All peoples may, for their own ends, freely dispose of their natural wealth and resources without prejudice to any obligations arising out of international economic co-operation, based upon the principle of mutual benefit, and international law. In no case may a people be deprived of its own means of subsistence.

3. The States Parties to the present Covenant, including those having responsibility for the administration of Non-Self-Governing and Trust Territories, shall promote the realization of the right of self-determination, and shall respect that right, in conformity with the provisions of the Charter of the United Nations.

PART II

Article 2

1. Each State Party to the present Covenant undertakes to respect and to ensure to all individuals within its territory and subject to its jurisdiction the rights recognized in the present Covenant, without distinction of any kind, such as race, colour, sex, language, religion, political or other opinion, national or social origin, property, birth or other status.

2. Where not already provided for by existing legislative or other measures, each State Party to the present Covenant undertakes to take the necessary steps, in accordance with its constitutional processes and with the provisions of the present Covenant, to adopt such laws or other measures as may be necessary to give effect to the rights recognized in the present Covenant.

3. Each State Party to the present Covenant undertakes:

(a) To ensure that any person whose rights or freedoms as herein recognized are violated shall have an effective remedy, notwithstanding that the violation has been committed by persons acting in an official capacity;

(b) To ensure that any person claiming such a remedy shall have his right thereto determined by competent judicial, administrative or legislative authorities, or by any other competent authority provided for by the legal system of the State, and to develop the possibilities of judicial remedy;

(c) To ensure that the competent authorities shall enforce such remedies when granted.

Article 3

The States Parties to the present Covenant undertake to ensure the equal right of men and women to the enjoyment of all civil and political rights set forth in the present Covenant.

Article 4

1. In time of public emergency which threatens the life of the nation and the existence of which is officially proclaimed, the States Parties to the present Covenant may take measures derogating from their obligations under the present Covenant to the extent strictly required by the exigencies of the situation, provided that such measures are not inconsistent with their other obligations under international law and do not involve discrimination solely on the ground of race, colour, sex, language, religion or social origin.

2. No derogation from articles 6, 7, 8 (paragraphs I and 2), 11, 15, 16 and 18 may be made under this provision.

3. Any State Party to the present Covenant availing itself of the right of derogation shall immediately inform the other States Parties to the present Covenant, through the intermediary of the Secretary-General of the United Nations, of the provisions from which it has derogated and of the reasons by which it was actuated. A further communication shall be made, through the same intermediary, on the date on which it terminates such derogation.

Article 5

1. Nothing in the present Covenant may be interpreted as implying for any State, group or person any right to engage in any activity or perform any act aimed at the

destruction of any of the rights and freedoms recognized herein or at their limitation to a greater extent than is provided for in the present Covenant.

2. There shall be no restriction upon or derogation from any of the fundamental human rights recognized or existing in any State Party to the present Covenant pursuant to law, conventions, regulations or custom on the pretext that the present Covenant does not recognize such rights or that it recognizes them to a lesser extent.

PART III

Article 6

1. Every human being has the inherent right to life. This right shall be protected by law. No one shall be arbitrarily deprived of his life.

2. In countries which have not abolished the death penalty, sentence of death may be imposed only for the most serious crimes in accordance with the law in force at the time of the commission of the crime and not contrary to the provisions of the present Covenant and to the Convention on the Prevention and Punishment of the Crime of Genocide. This penalty can only be carried out pursuant to a final judgement rendered by a competent court.

3. When deprivation of life constitutes the crime of genocide, it is understood that nothing in this article shall authorize any State Party to the present Covenant to derogate in any way from any obligation assumed under the provisions of the Convention on the Prevention and Punishment of the Crime of Genocide.

4. Anyone sentenced to death shall have the right to seek pardon or commutation of the sentence. Amnesty, pardon or commutation of the sentence of death may be granted in all cases.

5. Sentence of death shall not be imposed for crimes committed by persons below eighteen years of age and shall not be carried out on pregnant women.

6. Nothing in this article shall be invoked to delay or to prevent the abolition of capital punishment by any State Party to the present Covenant.

Article 7

No one shall be subjected to torture or to cruel, inhuman or degrading treatment or punishment. In particular, no one shall be subjected without his free consent to medical or scientific experimentation.

Article 8

1. No one shall be held in slavery; slavery and the slave-trade in all their forms shall be prohibited.

2. No one shall be held in servitude.

3.

(a) No one shall be required to perform forced or compulsory labour;

(b) Paragraph 3 (a) shall not be held to preclude, in countries where imprisonment with hard labour may be imposed as a punishment for a crime, the performance of hard labour in pursuance of a sentence to such punishment by a competent court;

(c) For the purpose of this paragraph the term 'forced or compulsory labour' shall not include:

(i) Any work or service, not referred to in subparagraph (b), normally required of a person who is under detention in consequence of a lawful order of a court, or of a person during conditional release from such detention;

(ii) Any service of a military character and, in countries where conscientious objection is recognized, any national service required by law of conscientious objectors;

(iii) Any service exacted in cases of emergency or calamity threatening the life or well-being of the community;

(iv) Any work or service which forms part of normal civil obligations.

Article 9

1. Everyone has the right to liberty and security of person. No one shall be subjected to arbitrary arrest or detention. No one shall be deprived of his liberty except on such grounds and in accordance with such procedure as are established by law.

2. Anyone who is arrested shall be informed, at the time of arrest, of the reasons for his arrest and shall be promptly informed of any charges against him.

3. Anyone arrested or detained on a criminal charge shall be brought promptly before a judge or other officer authorized by law to exercise judicial power and shall be entitled to trial within a reasonable time or to release. It shall not be the general rule that persons awaiting trial shall be detained in custody, but release may be subject to guarantees to appear for trial, at any other stage of the judicial proceedings, and, should occasion arise, for execution of the judgement.

4. Anyone who is deprived of his liberty by arrest or detention shall be entitled to take proceedings before a court, in order that that court may decide without delay on the lawfulness of his detention and order his release if the detention is not lawful.

5. Anyone who has been the victim of unlawful arrest or detention shall have an enforceable right to compensation.

Article 10

1. All persons deprived of their liberty shall be treated with humanity and with respect for the inherent dignity of the human person.

2.

(a) Accused persons shall, save in exceptional circumstances, be segregated from convicted persons and shall be subject to separate treatment appropriate to their status as unconvicted persons;

(b) Accused juvenile persons shall be separated from adults and brought as speedily as possible for adjudication.

3. The penitentiary system shall comprise treatment of prisoners the essential aim of which shall be their reformation and social rehabilitation. Juvenile offenders shall be segregated from adults and be accorded treatment appropriate to their age and legal status.

Article 11

No one shall be imprisoned merely on the ground of inability to fulfil a contractual obligation.

Article 12

1. Everyone lawfully within the territory of a State shall, within that territory, have the right to liberty of movement and freedom to choose his residence.

2. Everyone shall be free to leave any country, including his own.

3. The above-mentioned rights shall not be subject to any restrictions except those which are provided by law, are necessary to protect national security, public order

(ordre public), public health or morals or the rights and freedoms of others, and are consistent with the other rights recognized in the present Covenant.

4. No one shall be arbitrarily deprived of the right to enter his own country.

Article 13

An alien lawfully in the territory of a State Party to the present Covenant may be expelled therefrom only in pursuance of a decision reached in accordance with law and shall, except where compelling reasons of national security otherwise require, be allowed to submit the reasons against his expulsion and to have his case reviewed by, and be represented for the purpose before, the competent authority or a person or persons especially designated by the competent authority.

Article 14

1. All persons shall be equal before the courts and tribunals. In the determination of any criminal charge against him, or of his rights and obligations in a suit at law, everyone shall be entitled to a fair and public hearing by a competent, independent and impartial tribunal established by law. The press and the public may be excluded from all or part of a trial for reasons of morals, public order (ordre public) or national security in a democratic society, or when the interest of the private lives of the parties so requires, or to the extent strictly necessary in the opinion of the court in special circumstances where publicity would prejudice the interests of justice; but any judgement rendered in a criminal case or in a suit at law shall be made public except where the interest of juvenile persons otherwise requires or the proceedings concern matrimonial disputes or the guardianship of children.

2. Everyone charged with a criminal offence shall have the right to be presumed innocent until proved guilty according to law.

3. In the determination of any criminal charge against him, everyone shall be entitled to the following minimum guarantees, in full equality: (a) To be informed promptly and in detail in a language which he understands of the nature and cause of the charge against him;

(b) To have adequate time and facilities for the preparation of his defence and to communicate with counsel of his own choosing;

(c) To be tried without undue delay;

(d) To be tried in his presence, and to defend himself in person or through legal assistance of his own choosing; to be informed, if he does not have legal assistance, of this right; and to have legal assistance assigned to him, in any case where the interests of justice so require, and without payment by him in any such case if he does not have sufficient means to pay for it;

(e) To examine, or have examined, the witnesses against him and to obtain the attendance and examination of witnesses on his behalf under the same conditions as witnesses against him;

(f) To have the free assistance of an interpreter if he cannot understand or speak the language used in court;

(g) Not to be compelled to testify against himself or to confess guilt.

4. In the case of juvenile persons, the procedure shall be such as will take account of their age and the desirability of promoting their rehabilitation.

5. Everyone convicted of a crime shall have the right to his conviction and sentence being reviewed by a higher tribunal according to law.

6. When a person has by a final decision been convicted of a criminal offence and when subsequently his conviction has been reversed or he has been pardoned on the ground that a new or newly discovered fact shows conclusively that there has been a miscarriage of justice, the person who has suffered punishment as a result of such conviction shall be compensated according to law, unless it is proved that the non-disclosure of the unknown fact in time is wholly or partly attributable to him.

7. No one shall be liable to be tried or punished again for an offence for which he has already been finally convicted or acquitted in accordance with the law and penal procedure of each country.

Article 15

1. No one shall be held guilty of any criminal offence on account of any act or omission which did not constitute a criminal offence, under national or international law, at the time when it was committed. Nor shall a heavier penalty be imposed than the one that was applicable at the time when the criminal offence was committed. If, subsequent to the commission of the offence, provision is made by law for the imposition of the lighter penalty, the offender shall benefit thereby.

2. Nothing in this article shall prejudice the trial and punishment of any person for any act or omission which, at the time when it was committed, was criminal according to the general principles of law recognized by the community of nations.

Article 16

Everyone shall have the right to recognition everywhere as a person before the law.

Article 17

1. No one shall be subjected to arbitrary or unlawful interference with his privacy, family, or correspondence, nor to unlawful attacks on his honour and reputation.

2. Everyone has the right to the protection of the law against such interference or attacks.

Article 18

1. Everyone shall have the right to freedom of thought, conscience and religion. This right shall include freedom to have or to adopt a religion or belief of his choice, and freedom, either individually or in community with others and in public or private, to manifest his religion or belief in worship, observance, practice and teaching.

2. No one shall be subject to coercion which would impair his freedom to have or to adopt a religion or belief of his choice.

3. Freedom to manifest one's religion or beliefs may be subject only to such limitations as are prescribed by law and are necessary to protect public safety, order, health, or morals or the fundamental rights and freedoms of others.

4. The States Parties to the present Covenant undertake to have respect for the liberty of parents and, when applicable, legal guardians to ensure the religious and moral education of their children in conformity with their own convictions.

Article 19

1. Everyone shall have the right to hold opinions without interference.

2. Everyone shall have the right to freedom of expression; this right shall include freedom to seek, receive and impart information and ideas of all kinds, regardless of frontiers, either orally, in writing or in print, in the form of art, or through any other media of his choice.

3. The exercise of the rights provided for in paragraph 2 of this article carries with it special duties and responsibilities. It may therefore be subject to certain restrictions, but these shall only be such as are provided by law and are necessary:

(a) For respect of the rights or reputations of others;

(b) For the protection of national security or of public order (ordre public), or of public health or morals.

Article 20

1. Any propaganda for war shall be prohibited by law.

2. Any advocacy of national, racial or religious hatred that constitutes incitement to discrimination, hostility or violence shall be prohibited by law.

Article 21

The right of peaceful assembly shall be recognized. No restrictions may be placed on the exercise of this right other than those imposed in conformity with the law and which are necessary in a democratic society in the interests of national security or public safety, public order (ordre public), the protection of public health or morals or the protection of the rights and freedoms of others.

Article 22

1. Everyone shall have the right to freedom of association with others, including the right to form and join trade unions for the protection of his interests.

2. No restrictions may be placed on the exercise of this right other than those which are prescribed by law and which are necessary in a democratic society in the interests of national security or public safety, public order (ordre public), the protection of public health or morals or the protection of the rights and freedoms of others. This article shall not prevent the imposition of lawful restrictions on members of the armed forces and of the police in their exercise of this right.

3. Nothing in this article shall authorize States Parties to the International Labour Organisation Convention of 1948 concerning Freedom of Association and Protection of the Right to Organize to take legislative measures which would prejudice, or to apply the law in such a manner as to prejudice, the guarantees provided for in that Convention.

Article 23

1. The family is the natural and fundamental group unit of society and is entitled to protection by society and the State.

2. The right of men and women of marriageable age to marry and to found a family shall be recognized.

3. No marriage shall be entered into without the free and full consent of the intending spouses.

4. States Parties to the present Covenant shall take appropriate steps to ensure equality of rights and responsibilities of spouses as to marriage, during marriage and at its dissolution. In the case of dissolution, provision shall be made for the necessary protection of any children.

Article 24

1. Every child shall have, without any discrimination as to race, colour, sex, language, religion, national or social origin, property or birth, the right to such measures of protection as are required by his status as a minor, on the part of his family, society and the State.

2. Every child shall be registered immediately after birth and shall have a name.

3. Every child has the right to acquire a nationality.

Article 25

Every citizen shall have the right and the opportunity, without any of the distinctions mentioned in article 2 and without unreasonable restrictions:

(a) To take part in the conduct of public affairs, directly or through freely chosen representatives;

(b) To vote and to be elected at genuine periodic elections which shall be by universal and equal suffrage and shall be held by secret ballot, guaranteeing the free expression of the will of the electors;

(c) To have access, on general terms of equality, to public service in his country.

Article 26

All persons are equal before the law and are entitled without any discrimination to the equal protection of the law. In this respect, the law shall prohibit any discrimination and guarantee to all persons equal and effective protection against discrimination on any ground such as race, colour, sex, language, religion, political or other opinion, national or social origin, property, birth or other status.

Article 27

In those States in which ethnic, religious or linguistic minorities exist, persons belonging to such minorities shall not be denied the right, in community with the other members of their group, to enjoy their own culture, to profess and practise their own religion, or to use their own language.

PART IV

Article 28

1. There shall be established a Human Rights Committee (hereafter referred to in the present Covenant as the Committee). It shall consist of eighteen members and shall carry out the functions hereinafter provided.

2. The Committee shall be composed of nationals of the States Parties to the present Covenant who shall be persons of high moral character and recognized competence in the field of human rights, consideration being given to the usefulness of the participation of some persons having legal experience.

3. The members of the Committee shall be elected and shall serve in their personal capacity.

Article 29

1. The members of the Committee shall be elected by secret ballot from a list of persons possessing the qualifications prescribed in article 28 and nominated for the purpose by the States Parties to the present Covenant.

2. Each State Party to the present Covenant may nominate not more than two persons. These persons shall be nationals of the nominating State.

3. A person shall be eligible for renomination.

Article 30

1. The initial election shall be held no later than six months after the date of the entry into force of the present Covenant.

2. At least four months before the date of each election to the Committee, other than an election to fill a vacancy declared in accordance with article 34, the Secretary-General of the United Nations shall address a written invitation to the States Parties to the present Covenant to submit their nominations for membership of the Committee within three months.

3. The Secretary-General of the United Nations shall prepare a list in alphabetical order of all the persons thus nominated, with an indication of the States Parties which have nominated them, and shall submit it to the States Parties to the present Covenant no later than one month before the date of each election.

4. Elections of the members of the Committee shall be held at a meeting of the States Parties to the present Covenant convened by the Secretary General of the United Nations at the Headquarters of the United Nations. At that meeting, for which two thirds of the States Parties to the present Covenant shall constitute a quorum, the persons elected to the Committee shall be those nominees who obtain the largest number of votes and an absolute majority of the votes of the representatives of States Parties present and voting.

Article 31

1. The Committee may not include more than one national of the same State.

2. In the election of the Committee, consideration shall be given to equitable geographical distribution of membership and to the representation of the different forms of civilization and of the principal legal systems.

Article 32

1. The members of the Committee shall be elected for a term of four years. They shall be eligible for re-election if renominated. However, the terms of nine of the members elected at the first election shall expire at the end of two years; immediately after the first election, the names of these nine members shall be chosen by lot by the Chairman of the meeting referred to in article 30, paragraph 4.

2. Elections at the expiry of office shall be held in accordance with the preceding articles of this part of the present Covenant.

Article 33

1. If, in the unanimous opinion of the other members, a member of the Committee has ceased to carry out his functions for any cause other than absence of a temporary character, the Chairman of the Committee shall notify the Secretary-General of the United Nations, who shall then declare the seat of that member to be vacant.

2. In the event of the death or the resignation of a member of the Committee, the Chairman shall immediately notify the Secretary-General of the United Nations, who shall declare the seat vacant from the date of death or the date on which the resignation takes effect.

Article 34

1. When a vacancy is declared in accordance with article 33 and if the term of office of the member to be replaced does not expire within six months of the declaration of the vacancy, the Secretary-General of the United Nations shall notify each of the States Parties to the present Covenant, which may within two months submit nominations in accordance with article 29 for the purpose of filling the vacancy.

2. The Secretary-General of the United Nations shall prepare a list in alphabetical order of the persons thus nominated and shall submit it to the States Parties to the present Covenant. The election to fill the vacancy shall then take place in accordance with the relevant provisions of this part of the present Covenant.

3. A member of the Committee elected to fill a vacancy declared in accordance with article 33 shall hold office for the remainder of the term of the member who vacated the seat on the Committee under the provisions of that article.

Article 35

The members of the Committee shall, with the approval of the General Assembly of the United Nations, receive emoluments from United Nations resources on such terms and conditions as the General Assembly may decide, having regard to the importance of the Committee's responsibilities.

Article 36

The Secretary-General of the United Nations shall provide the necessary staff and facilities for the effective performance of the functions of the Committee under the present Covenant.

Article 37

1. The Secretary-General of the United Nations shall convene the initial meeting of the Committee at the Headquarters of the United Nations.

2. After its initial meeting, the Committee shall meet at such times as shall be provided in its rules of procedure.

3. The Committee shall normally meet at the Headquarters of the United Nations or at the United Nations Office at Geneva.

Article 38

Every member of the Committee shall, before taking up his duties, make a solemn declaration in open committee that he will perform his functions impartially and conscientiously.

Article 39

1. The Committee shall elect its officers for a term of two years. They may be re-elected.

2. The Committee shall establish its own rules of procedure, but these rules shall provide, inter alia, that:

(a) Twelve members shall constitute a quorum;

(b) Decisions of the Committee shall be made by a majority vote of the members present.

Article 40

1. The States Parties to the present Covenant undertake to submit reports on the measures they have adopted which give effect to the rights recognized herein and on the progress made in the enjoyment of those rights: (a) Within one year of the entry into force of the present Covenant for the States Parties concerned;

(b) Thereafter whenever the Committee so requests.

2. All reports shall be submitted to the Secretary-General of the United Nations, who shall transmit them to the Committee for consideration. Reports shall indicate the factors and difficulties, if any, affecting the implementation of the present Covenant.

3. The Secretary-General of the United Nations may, after consultation with the Committee, transmit to the specialized agencies concerned copies of such parts of the reports as may fall within their field of competence.

4. The Committee shall study the reports submitted by the States Parties to the present Covenant. It shall transmit its reports, and such general comments as it may consider appropriate, to the States Parties. The Committee may also transmit to the Economic and Social Council these comments along with the copies of the reports it has received from States Parties to the present Covenant.

5. The States Parties to the present Covenant may submit to the Committee observations on any comments that may be made in accordance with paragraph 4 of this article.

Article 41

1. A State Party to the present Covenant may at any time declare under this article that it recognizes the competence of the Committee to receive and consider communications to the effect that a State Party claims that another State Party is not fulfilling its obligations under the present Covenant. Communications under this article may be received and considered only if submitted by a State Party which has made a declaration recognizing in regard to itself the competence of the Committee. No communication shall be received by the Committee if it concerns a State Party which has not made such a declaration. Communications received under this article shall be dealt with in accordance with the following procedure:

(a) If a State Party to the present Covenant considers that another State Party is not giving effect to the provisions of the present Covenant, it may, by written communication, bring the matter to the attention of that State Party. Within three months after the receipt of the communication the receiving State shall afford the State which sent the communication an explanation, or any other statement in writing clarifying the matter which should include, to the extent possible and pertinent, reference to domestic procedures and remedies taken, pending, or available in the matter;

(b) If the matter is not adjusted to the satisfaction of both States Parties concerned within six months after the receipt by the receiving State of the initial communication, either State shall have the right to refer the matter to the Committee, by notice given to the Committee and to the other State;

(c) The Committee shall deal with a matter referred to it only after it has ascertained that all available domestic remedies have been invoked and exhausted in the matter, in conformity with the generally recognized principles of international law. This shall not be the rule where the application of the remedies is unreasonably prolonged;

(d) The Committee shall hold closed meetings when examining communications under this article;

(e) Subject to the provisions of subparagraph (c), the Committee shall make available its good offices to the States Parties concerned with a view to a friendly solution of the matter on the basis of respect for human rights and fundamental freedoms as recognized in the present Covenant;

(f) In any matter referred to it, the Committee may call upon the States Parties concerned, referred to in subparagraph (b), to supply any relevant information;

(g) The States Parties concerned, referred to in subparagraph (b), shall have the right to be represented when the matter is being considered in the Committee and to make submissions orally and/or in writing;

(h) The Committee shall, within twelve months after the date of receipt of notice under subparagraph (b), submit a report:

(i) If a solution within the terms of subparagraph (e) is reached, the Committee shall confine its report to a brief statement of the facts and of the solution reached;

(ii) If a solution within the terms of subparagraph (e) is not reached, the Committee shall confine its report to a brief statement of the facts; the written submissions and record of the oral submissions made by the States Parties concerned shall be attached to the report. In every matter, the report shall be communicated to the States Parties concerned.

2. The provisions of this article shall come into force when ten States Parties to the present Covenant have made declarations under paragraph I of this article. Such declarations shall be deposited by the States Parties with the Secretary-General of the United Nations, who shall transmit copies thereof to the other States Parties. A declaration may be withdrawn at any time by notification to the Secretary-General. Such a withdrawal shall not prejudice the consideration of any matter which is the subject of a communication already transmitted under this article; no further communication by any State Party shall be received after the notification of withdrawal of the declaration has been received by the Secretary-General, unless the State Party concerned has made a new declaration.

Article 42

1.

(a) If a matter referred to the Committee in accordance with article 41 is not resolved to the satisfaction of the States Parties concerned, the Committee may, with the prior consent of the States Parties concerned, appoint an ad hoc Conciliation Commission (hereinafter referred to as the Commission). The good offices of the Commission shall be made available to the States Parties concerned with a view to an amicable solution of the matter on the basis of respect for the present Covenant;

(b) The Commission shall consist of five persons acceptable to the States Parties concerned. If the States Parties concerned fail to reach agreement within three months on all or part of the composition of the Commission, the members of the Commission concerning whom no agreement has been reached shall be elected by secret ballot by a two-thirds majority vote of the Committee from among its members.

2. The members of the Commission shall serve in their personal capacity. They shall not be nationals of the States Parties concerned, or of a State not Party to the present Covenant, or of a State Party which has not made a declaration under article 41.

3. The Commission shall elect its own Chairman and adopt its own rules of procedure.

4. The meetings of the Commission shall normally be held at the Headquarters of the United Nations or at the United Nations Office at Geneva. However, they may be held at such other convenient places as the Commission may determine in consultation with the Secretary-General of the United Nations and the States Parties concerned.

5. The secretariat provided in accordance with article 36 shall also service the commissions appointed under this article.

6. The information received and collated by the Committee shall be made available to the Commission and the Commission may call upon the States Parties concerned to supply any other relevant information.

7. When the Commission has fully considered the matter, but in any event not later than twelve months after having been seized of the matter, it shall submit to the Chairman of the Committee a report for communication to the States Parties concerned:

(a) If the Commission is unable to complete its consideration of the matter within twelve months, it shall confine its report to a brief statement of the status of its consideration of the matter;

(b) If an amicable solution to the matter on tie [sic] basis of respect for human rights as recognized in the present Covenant is reached, the Commission shall confine its report to a brief statement of the facts and of the solution reached;

(c) If a solution within the terms of subparagraph (b) is not reached, the Commission's report shall embody its findings on all questions of fact relevant to the issues between the States Parties concerned, and its views on the possibilities of an amicable solution of the matter. This report shall also contain the written submissions and a record of the oral submissions made by the States Parties concerned;

(d) If the Commission's report is submitted under subparagraph (c), the States Parties concerned shall, within three months of the receipt of the report, notify the Chairman of the Committee whether or not they accept the contents of the report of the Commission.

8. The provisions of this article are without prejudice to the responsibilities of the Committee under article 41.

9. The States Parties concerned shall share equally all the expenses of the members of the Commission in accordance with estimates to be provided by the Secretary-General of the United Nations.

10. The Secretary-General of the United Nations shall be empowered to pay the expenses of the members of the Commission, if necessary, before reimbursement by the States Parties concerned, in accordance with paragraph 9 of this article.

Article 43
The members of the Committee, and of the ad hoc conciliation commissions which may be appointed under article 42, shall be entitled to the facilities, privileges and immunities of experts on mission for the United Nations as laid down in the relevant sections of the Convention on the Privileges and Immunities of the United Nations.

Article 44
The provisions for the implementation of the present Covenant shall apply without prejudice to the procedures prescribed in the field of human rights by or under the constituent instruments and the conventions of the United Nations and of the specialized agencies and shall not prevent the States Parties to the present Covenant from having recourse to other procedures for settling a dispute in accordance with general or special international agreements in force between them.

Article 45
The Committee shall submit to the General Assembly of the United Nations, through the Economic and Social Council, an annual report on its activities.

PART V

Article 46
Nothing in the present Covenant shall be interpreted as impairing the provisions of the Charter of the United Nations and of the constitutions of the specialized

agencies which define the respective responsibilities of the various organs of the United Nations and of the specialized agencies in regard to the matters dealt with in the present Covenant.

Article 47
Nothing in the present Covenant shall be interpreted as impairing the inherent right of all peoples to enjoy and utilize fully and freely their natural wealth and resources.

PART VI

Article 48
1. The present Covenant is open for signature by any State Member of the United Nations or member of any of its specialized agencies, by any State Party to the Statute of the International Court of Justice, and by any other State which has been invited by the General Assembly of the United Nations to become a Party to the present Covenant.

2. The present Covenant is subject to ratification. Instruments of ratification shall be deposited with the Secretary-General of the United Nations.

3. The present Covenant shall be open to accession by any State referred to in paragraph 1 of this article.

4. Accession shall be effected by the deposit of an instrument of accession with the Secretary-General of the United Nations.

5. The Secretary-General of the United Nations shall inform all States which have signed this Covenant or acceded to it of the deposit of each instrument of ratification or accession.

Article 49
1. The present Covenant shall enter into force three months after the date of the deposit with the Secretary-General of the United Nations of the thirty-fifth instrument of ratification or instrument of accession.

2. For each State ratifying the present Covenant or acceding to it after the deposit of the thirty-fifth instrument of ratification or instrument of accession, the present Covenant shall enter into force three months after the date of the deposit of its own instrument of ratification or instrument of accession.

Article 50
The provisions of the present Covenant shall extend to all parts of federal States without any limitations or exceptions.

Article 51
1. Any State Party to the present Covenant may propose an amendment and file it with the Secretary-General of the United Nations. The Secretary-General of the United Nations shall thereupon communicate any proposed amendments to the States Parties to the present Covenant with a request that they notify him whether they favour a conference of States Parties for the purpose of considering and voting upon the proposals. In the event that at least one third of the States Parties favours such a conference, the Secretary-General shall convene the conference under the auspices of the United Nations. Any amendment adopted by a majority of the States Parties present and voting at the conference shall be submitted to the General Assembly of the United Nations for approval.

2. Amendments shall come into force when they have been approved by the General Assembly of the United Nations and accepted by a two-thirds majority of the States Parties to the present Covenant in accordance with their respective constitutional processes.

3. When amendments come into force, they shall be binding on those States Parties which have accepted them, other States Parties still being bound by the provisions of the present Covenant and any earlier amendment which they have accepted.

Article 52

1. Irrespective of the notifications made under article 48, paragraph 5, the Secretary-General of the United Nations shall inform all States referred to in paragraph I of the same article of the following particulars:

(a) Signatures, ratifications and accessions under article 48;

(b) The date of the entry into force of the present Covenant under article 49 and the date of the entry into force of any amendments under article 51.

Article 53

1. The present Covenant, of which the Chinese, English, French, Russian and Spanish texts are equally authentic, shall be deposited in the archives of the United Nations.

2. The Secretary-General of the United Nations shall transmit certified copies of the present Covenant to all States referred to in article 48.

Appendix 3

International Covenant on Economic, Social and Cultural Rights

Adopted and opened for signature, ratification and accession by General Assembly resolution 2200A (XXI) of 16 December 1966
entry into force 3 January 1976, in accordance with article 27

Preamble

The States Parties to the present Covenant,

Considering that, in accordance with the principles proclaimed in the Charter of the United Nations, recognition of the inherent dignity and of the equal and inalienable rights of all members of the human family is the foundation of freedom, justice and peace in the world,

Recognizing that these rights derive from the inherent dignity of the human person,

Recognizing that, in accordance with the Universal Declaration of Human Rights, the ideal of free human beings enjoying freedom from fear and want can only be achieved if conditions are created whereby everyone may enjoy his economic, social and cultural rights, as well as his civil and political rights,

Considering the obligation of States under the Charter of the United Nations to promote universal respect for, and observance of, human rights and freedoms,

Realizing that the individual, having duties to other individuals and to the community to which he belongs, is under a responsibility to strive for the promotion and observance of the rights recognized in the present Covenant,

Agree upon the following articles:

PART I

Article 1

1. All peoples have the right of self-determination. By virtue of that right they freely determine their political status and freely pursue their economic, social and cultural development.

2. All peoples may, for their own ends, freely dispose of their natural wealth and resources without prejudice to any obligations arising out of international economic co-operation, based upon the principle of mutual benefit, and international law. In no case may a people be deprived of its own means of subsistence.

3. The States Parties to the present Covenant, including those having responsibility for the administration of Non-Self-Governing and Trust Territories, shall promote the realization of the right of self-determination, and shall respect that right, in conformity with the provisions of the Charter of the United Nations.

PART II

Article 2

1. Each State Party to the present Covenant undertakes to take steps, individually and through international assistance and co-operation, especially economic and technical, to the maximum of its available resources, with a view to achieving progressively the full realization of the rights recognized in the present Covenant by all appropriate means, including particularly the adoption of legislative measures.

2. The States Parties to the present Covenant undertake to guarantee that the rights enunciated in the present Covenant will be exercised without discrimination of any kind as to race, colour, sex, language, religion, political or other opinion, national or social origin, property, birth or other status.

3. Developing countries, with due regard to human rights and their national economy, may determine to what extent they would guarantee the economic rights recognized in the present Covenant to non-nationals.

Article 3

The States Parties to the present Covenant undertake to ensure the equal right of men and women to the enjoyment of all economic, social and cultural rights set forth in the present Covenant.

Article 4

The States Parties to the present Covenant recognize that, in the enjoyment of those rights provided by the State in conformity with the present Covenant, the State may subject such rights only to such limitations as are determined by law only in so far as this may be compatible with the nature of these rights and solely for the purpose of promoting the general welfare in a democratic society.

Article 5

1. Nothing in the present Covenant may be interpreted as implying for any State, group or person any right to engage in any activity or to perform any act aimed at the destruction of any of the rights or freedoms recognized herein, or at their limitation to a greater extent than is provided for in the present Covenant.

2. No restriction upon or derogation from any of the fundamental human rights recognized or existing in any country in virtue of law, conventions, regulations or custom shall be admitted on the pretext that the present Covenant does not recognize such rights or that it recognizes them to a lesser extent.

PART III

Article 6

1. The States Parties to the present Covenant recognize the right to work, which includes the right of everyone to the opportunity to gain his living by work which he freely chooses or accepts, and will take appropriate steps to safeguard this right.

2. The steps to be taken by a State Party to the present Covenant to achieve the full realization of this right shall include technical and vocational guidance and training programmes, policies and techniques to achieve steady economic, social and cultural development and full and productive employment under conditions safeguarding fundamental political and economic freedoms to the individual.

Article 7

The States Parties to the present Covenant recognize the right of everyone to the enjoyment of just and favourable conditions of work which ensure, in particular:

(a) Remuneration which provides all workers, as a minimum, with:

(i) Fair wages and equal remuneration for work of equal value without distinction of any kind, in particular women being guaranteed conditions of work not inferior to those enjoyed by men, with equal pay for equal work;

(ii) A decent living for themselves and their families in accordance with the provisions of the present Covenant;

(b) Safe and healthy working conditions;

(c) Equal opportunity for everyone to be promoted in his employment to an appropriate higher level, subject to no considerations other than those of seniority and competence;

(d) Rest, leisure and reasonable limitation of working hours and periodic holidays with pay, as well as remuneration for public holidays.

Article 8

1. The States Parties to the present Covenant undertake to ensure:

(a) The right of everyone to form trade unions and join the trade union of his choice, subject only to the rules of the organization concerned, for the promotion and protection of his economic and social interests. No restrictions may be placed on the exercise of this right other than those prescribed by law and which are necessary in a democratic society in the interests of national security or public order or for the protection of the rights and freedoms of others;

(b) The right of trade unions to establish national federations or confederations and the right of the latter to form or join international trade-union organizations;

(c) The right of trade unions to function freely subject to no limitations other than those prescribed by law and which are necessary in a democratic society in the interests of national security or public order or for the protection of the rights and freedoms of others;

(d) The right to strike, provided that it is exercised in conformity with the laws of the particular country.

2. This article shall not prevent the imposition of lawful restrictions on the exercise of these rights by members of the armed forces or of the police or of the administration of the State.

3. Nothing in this article shall authorize States Parties to the International Labour Organisation Convention of 1948 concerning Freedom of Association and Protection of the Right to Organize to take legislative measures which would prejudice, or apply the law in such a manner as would prejudice, the guarantees provided for in that Convention.

Article 9

The States Parties to the present Covenant recognize the right of everyone to social security, including social insurance.

Article 10

The States Parties to the present Covenant recognize that:

1. The widest possible protection and assistance should be accorded to the family, which is the natural and fundamental group unit of society, particularly for its

establishment and while it is responsible for the care and education of dependent children. Marriage must be entered into with the free consent of the intending spouses.

2. Special protection should be accorded to mothers during a reasonable period before and after childbirth. During such period working mothers should be accorded paid leave or leave with adequate social security benefits.

3. Special measures of protection and assistance should be taken on behalf of all children and young persons without any discrimination for reasons of parentage or other conditions. Children and young persons should be protected from economic and social exploitation. Their employment in work harmful to their morals or health or dangerous to life or likely to hamper their normal development should be punishable by law. States should also set age limits below which the paid employment of child labour should be prohibited and punishable by law.

Article 11

1. The States Parties to the present Covenant recognize the right of everyone to an adequate standard of living for himself and his family, including adequate food, clothing and housing, and to the continuous improvement of living conditions. The States Parties will take appropriate steps to ensure the realization of this right, recognizing to this effect the essential importance of international co-operation based on free consent.

2. The States Parties to the present Covenant, recognizing the fundamental right of everyone to be free from hunger, shall take, individually and through international co-operation, the measures, including specific programmes, which are needed:

(a) To improve methods of production, conservation and distribution of food by making full use of technical and scientific knowledge, by disseminating knowledge of the principles of nutrition and by developing or reforming agrarian systems in such a way as to achieve the most efficient development and utilization of natural resources;

(b) Taking into account the problems of both food-importing and food-exporting countries, to ensure an equitable distribution of world food supplies in relation to need.

Article 12

1. The States Parties to the present Covenant recognize the right of everyone to the enjoyment of the highest attainable standard of physical and mental health.

2. The steps to be taken by the States Parties to the present Covenant to achieve the full realization of this right shall include those necessary for:

(a) The provision for the reduction of the stillbirth-rate and of infant mortality and for the healthy development of the child;

(b) The improvement of all aspects of environmental and industrial hygiene;

(c) The prevention, treatment and control of epidemic, endemic, occupational and other diseases;

(d) The creation of conditions which would assure to all medical service and medical attention in the event of sickness.

Article 13

1. The States Parties to the present Covenant recognize the right of everyone to education. They agree that education shall be directed to the full development of the human personality and the sense of its dignity, and shall strengthen the respect for

human rights and fundamental freedoms. They further agree that education shall enable all persons to participate effectively in a free society, promote understanding, tolerance and friendship among all nations and all racial, ethnic or religious groups, and further the activities of the United Nations for the maintenance of peace.

2. The States Parties to the present Covenant recognize that, with a view to achieving the full realization of this right:

(a) Primary education shall be compulsory and available free to all;

(b) Secondary education in its different forms, including technical and vocational secondary education, shall be made generally available and accessible to all by every appropriate means, and in particular by the progressive introduction of free education;

(c) Higher education shall be made equally accessible to all, on the basis of capacity, by every appropriate means, and in particular by the progressive introduction of free education;

(d) Fundamental education shall be encouraged or intensified as far as possible for those persons who have not received or completed the whole period of their primary education;

(e) The development of a system of schools at all levels shall be actively pursued, an adequate fellowship system shall be established, and the material conditions of teaching staff shall be continuously improved.

3. The States Parties to the present Covenant undertake to have respect for the liberty of parents and, when applicable, legal guardians to choose for their children schools, other than those established by the public authorities, which conform to such minimum educational standards as may be laid down or approved by the State and to ensure the religious and moral education of their children in conformity with their own convictions.

4. No part of this article shall be construed so as to interfere with the liberty of individuals and bodies to establish and direct educational institutions, subject always to the observance of the principles set forth in paragraph I of this article and to the requirement that the education given in such institutions shall conform to such minimum standards as may be laid down by the State.

Article 14

Each State Party to the present Covenant which, at the time of becoming a Party, has not been able to secure in its metropolitan territory or other territories under its jurisdiction compulsory primary education, free of charge, undertakes, within two years, to work out and adopt a detailed plan of action for the progressive implementation, within a reasonable number of years, to be fixed in the plan, of the principle of compulsory education free of charge for all.

Article 15

1. The States Parties to the present Covenant recognize the right of everyone:

(a) To take part in cultural life;

(b) To enjoy the benefits of scientific progress and its applications;

(c) To benefit from the protection of the moral and material interests resulting from any scientific, literary or artistic production of which he is the author.

2. The steps to be taken by the States Parties to the present Covenant to achieve the full realization of this right shall include those necessary for the conservation, the development and the diffusion of science and culture.

3. The States Parties to the present Covenant undertake to respect the freedom indispensable for scientific research and creative activity.

4. The States Parties to the present Covenant recognize the benefits to be derived from the encouragement and development of international contacts and co-operation in the scientific and cultural fields.

PART IV

Article 16

1. The States Parties to the present Covenant undertake to submit in conformity with this part of the Covenant reports on the measures which they have adopted and the progress made in achieving the observance of the rights recognized herein.

2.

(a) All reports shall be submitted to the Secretary-General of the United Nations, who shall transmit copies to the Economic and Social Council for consideration in accordance with the provisions of the present Covenant;

(b) The Secretary-General of the United Nations shall also transmit to the specialized agencies copies of the reports, or any relevant parts therefrom, from States Parties to the present Covenant which are also members of these specialized agencies in so far as these reports, or parts therefrom, relate to any matters which fall within the responsibilities of the said agencies in accordance with their constitutional instruments.

Article 17

1. The States Parties to the present Covenant shall furnish their reports in stages, in accordance with a programme to be established by the Economic and Social Council within one year of the entry into force of the present Covenant after consultation with the States Parties and the specialized agencies concerned.

2. Reports may indicate factors and difficulties affecting the degree of fulfilment of obligations under the present Covenant.

3. Where relevant information has previously been furnished to the United Nations or to any specialized agency by any State Party to the present Covenant, it will not be necessary to reproduce that information, but a precise reference to the information so furnished will suffice.

Article 18

Pursuant to its responsibilities under the Charter of the United Nations in the field of human rights and fundamental freedoms, the Economic and Social Council may make arrangements with the specialized agencies in respect of their reporting to it on the progress made in achieving the observance of the provisions of the present Covenant falling within the scope of their activities. These reports may include particulars of decisions and recommendations on such implementation adopted by their competent organs.

Article 19

The Economic and Social Council may transmit to the Commission on Human Rights for study and general recommendation or, as appropriate, for information the reports concerning human rights submitted by States in accordance with articles 16 and 17, and those concerning human rights submitted by the specialized agencies in accordance with article 18.

Article 20

The States Parties to the present Covenant and the specialized agencies concerned may submit comments to the Economic and Social Council on any general recommendation under article 19 or reference to such general recommendation in any report of the Commission on Human Rights or any documentation referred to therein.

Article 21

The Economic and Social Council may submit from time to time to the General Assembly reports with recommendations of a general nature and a summary of the information received from the States Parties to the present Covenant and the specialized agencies on the measures taken and the progress made in achieving general observance of the rights recognized in the present Covenant.

Article 22

The Economic and Social Council may bring to the attention of other organs of the United Nations, their subsidiary organs and specialized agencies concerned with furnishing technical assistance any matters arising out of the reports referred to in this part of the present Covenant which may assist such bodies in deciding, each within its field of competence, on the advisability of international measures likely to contribute to the effective progressive implementation of the present Covenant.

Article 23

The States Parties to the present Covenant agree that international action for the achievement of the rights recognized in the present Covenant includes such methods as the conclusion of conventions, the adoption of recommendations, the furnishing of technical assistance and the holding of regional meetings and technical meetings for the purpose of consultation and study organized in conjunction with the Governments concerned.

Article 24

Nothing in the present Covenant shall be interpreted as impairing the provisions of the Charter of the United Nations and of the constitutions of the specialized agencies which define the respective responsibilities of the various organs of the United Nations and of the specialized agencies in regard to the matters dealt with in the present Covenant.

Article 25

Nothing in the present Covenant shall be interpreted as impairing the inherent right of all peoples to enjoy and utilize fully and freely their natural wealth and resources.

PART V

Article 26

1. The present Covenant is open for signature by any State Member of the United Nations or member of any of its specialized agencies, by any State Party to the Statute of the International Court of Justice, and by any other State which has been invited by the General Assembly of the United Nations to become a party to the present Covenant.

2. The present Covenant is subject to ratification. Instruments of ratification shall be deposited with the Secretary-General of the United Nations.

3. The present Covenant shall be open to accession by any State referred to in paragraph 1 of this article.

4. Accession shall be effected by the deposit of an instrument of accession with the Secretary-General of the United Nations.

5. The Secretary-General of the United Nations shall inform all States which have signed the present Covenant or acceded to it of the deposit of each instrument of ratification or accession.

Article 27

1. The present Covenant shall enter into force three months after the date of the deposit with the Secretary-General of the United Nations of the thirty-fifth instrument of ratification or instrument of accession.

2. For each State ratifying the present Covenant or acceding to it after the deposit of the thirty-fifth instrument of ratification or instrument of accession, the present Covenant shall enter into force three months after the date of the deposit of its own instrument of ratification or instrument of accession.

Article 28

The provisions of the present Covenant shall extend to all parts of federal States without any limitations or exceptions.

Article 29

1. Any State Party to the present Covenant may propose an amendment and file it with the Secretary-General of the United Nations. The Secretary-General shall thereupon communicate any proposed amendments to the States Parties to the present Covenant with a request that they notify him whether they favour a conference of States Parties for the purpose of considering and voting upon the proposals. In the event that at least one third of the States Parties favours such a conference, the Secretary-General shall convene the conference under the auspices of the United Nations. Any amendment adopted by a majority of the States Parties present and voting at the conference shall be submitted to the General Assembly of the United Nations for approval.

2. Amendments shall come into force when they have been approved by the General Assembly of the United Nations and accepted by a two-thirds majority of the States Parties to the present Covenant in accordance with their respective constitutional processes.

3. When amendments come into force they shall be binding on those States Parties which have accepted them, other States Parties still being bound by the provisions of the present Covenant and any earlier amendment which they have accepted.

Article 30

Irrespective of the notifications made under article 26, paragraph 5, the Secretary-General of the United Nations shall inform all States referred to in paragraph I of the same article of the following particulars:

(a) Signatures, ratifications and accessions under article 26;

(b) The date of the entry into force of the present Covenant under article 27 and the date of the entry into force of any amendments under article 29.

Article 31

1. The present Covenant, of which the Chinese, English, French, Russian and Spanish texts are equally authentic, shall be deposited in the archives of the United Nations.

2. The Secretary-General of the United Nations shall transmit certified copies of the present Covenant to all States referred to in article 26.

Abrogation of rights The failure to honour rights.

Accession or accretion The acquisition of territory that has emerged from the action of the forces of nature.

Alien Torts Claims Act (ATCA) An act of the US Congress passed in 1789 that provides jurisdiction in federal courts over lawsuits by aliens for torts committed either in violation of international law or of treaties to which the United States is a party. It has been used successfully by torture victims and their families to bring civil suits against torturers residing in the United States.

Amnesty Immunity from prosecution, often granted through legislation as part of a peace agreement.

Amnesty International One of the world's principal human rights organizations. It was founded in 1961 with international headquarters in London. Amnesty International is a non-aligned organization that reports on human rights violations and works for political prisoners in all regions of the world. It is represented at the United Nations and other international bodies.

Asylum seeker An individual who is seeking international protection. In countries with individualized procedures, an asylum seeker is someone whose claim has not yet been finally decided on by the country in which the claim is submitted.

Autonomy/autonomist Autonomy refers to self-government.

Behavioural revolution The period of development in political science starting in the late 1930s that sought to provide an objective, quantified approach to explaining and predicting political behaviour. This period of development is associated with the rise of the behavioural sciences, which were modelled after the natural sciences.

Bilateral treaty A **treaty** concluded between two parties only.

Biopolitical Regulation based on the needs of the population rather than the needs of the ruler or government. The concept derives from the work of Foucault, who counter-poses biopolitical regulation based on the public needs of the society to pre-modern rule purely in the personal needs of the Prince (see, for example, Foucault, 2003, 2007).

Bretton Woods institutions The Bretton Woods institutions are the **World Bank** and the **International Monetary Fund** (IMF). They were set up at a meeting of forty-three countries in Bretton Woods, New Hampshire, USA in July 1944. Their aims were to help rebuild the shattered post-War world economy and to promote international economic cooperation. The original Bretton Woods agreement also included plans for an International Trade Organization (ITO), but these lay dormant until the **World Trade Organization** (WTO) was created in the early 1990s. The creation of the World Bank and the IMF came at the end of the Second World War as a central feature of a multilateral framework established to overcome the destabilizing effects of the previous global economic depression and trade battles.

Brown* v. *Board of Education of Topeka, Kansas The landmark 1954 ruling by the US Supreme Court that overturned previously restrictive laws segregating blacks and whites in public schools. The ruling mandated that separating blacks and subjecting them to systematically poorer learning environments amounted to a denial of equal educational opportunities.

Capacity gap A capacity gap refers to where there is alleged to be an inability on the part of rights holders to act on their own behalf. An external agent steps in to act in their interest and, in doing so, often claims to enhance their capabilities or to empower them.

Cartagena Declaration of 1984 The Declaration adopted by a colloquium of experts from the Americas in November 1984. The Declaration enlarges the 1951 Convention definition of refugees to include 'persons who have fled their country because their lives, safety or freedom have been threatened by generalized violence, foreign aggression, internal conflicts, massive violation of human rights or other circumstances which have seriously disturbed public order.'

Cession The acquisition of the territory of another state through a treaty.

Child soldiers Children who have been recruited (usually forcibly) by non-state actors for military or forced labour purposes.

Citizenship Citizenship generally refers to the rights and duties of the member of a nation state or city. The work of sociologist T. H. Marshall is seen as a necessary starting point for understanding the modern concept sociologically. He defined citizenship as a status enjoyed by a person who is a full member of a community. It has three components: civil citizenship, which encapsulates individual freedoms; political citizenship, which grants rights to participation in the political process; and social citizenship, which grants rights to enjoy an appropriate standard of living.

Civil Rights Act The seminal law passed by the US Congress in 1964 banning segregation in employment, public schools, and public places.

Civil society Civil society refers to the arena of un-coerced collective action around shared interests, purposes, and values. In theory, its institutional forms are distinct from those of the state, family, and market, though in practice the boundaries are often blurred. Civil societies are populated by a network of social institutions and practices that play an important role in the functioning of democratic societies, comprising groups such as registered charities, community groups, women's organizations, faith-based organizations, professional associations, trade unions, self-help groups, business associations, coalitions, and advocacy groups.

Classical sociology It was not until the nineteenth century, in the aftermath of the industrial revolution, that a concern with 'society' emerged as an object of scholarly inquiry. Cumulatively, the writings of Marx, Durkheim, and Weber during that period are seen as broadly constituting 'classical sociology'.

Coding The practice of assigning a numerical score to a piece of empirical information. In the field of human rights, coding involves assigning scores to countries for the degree to which they protect different types of human rights, as well as coding treaty ratification and the filing of reservations.

Cold War The period of superpower rivalry between the USA and the USSR from the late 1940s to 1991. The idea of 'cold' war indicates that the two never fought directly, despite a massive arms race and numerous 'hot' proxy wars around the globe. The Cold War reflected traditional great power rivalry, as well as an ideological clash between communism (USSR and allies) and liberal democracy and capitalism (USA and allies). Human rights were one of the key ideological dividing lines in this conflict.

Collective sympathy Bryan Turner uses the concept to partly explain the emergence of human rights norms, the argument being that 'human beings will want their rights to be recognized *because they see in the plight of others their own (possible) misery.*'

Commission on Human Rights A functional body within the United Nations dealing with human rights concerns from 1946 to 2006. It was a subsidiary of the UN Economic and Social Council, though it also worked closely with the Office of the High Commissioner for Human Rights after 1993. Its main functions were to promote human rights, to hear complaints, and to investigate violations. The Commission was widely criticized as ineffective and was replaced in 2006 by the **Human Rights Council**.

Comparative politics The systematic study of domestic politics, or politics within countries. When applied to human rights, comparative politics helps to explain why states practice repression, how societal groups contribute to reforms, and the role of domestic institutions—from democracy to national courts—in changing human rights practices.

Conceptual Dealing with ideas or concepts, or having to do with the structure and coherence of ideas and arguments.

Conquest The acquisition of territory by the victor in a war.

Consequentialism/consequentialist approach to ethics The consequentialist approach to ethics is the notion that we ought to judge the moral worth of an act by its consequences (sometimes expressed simply as 'the ends justify the means'). **Utilitarianism** is one form of consequentialism.

Conservatism A political philosophy/ideology emphasizing the organic emergence of society out of historical times. It rejects attempts to radically remould society or human nature, emphasizes continuity and incremental change, and has a generally sceptical outlook toward the claim of either reason or government that the human condition can be morally or substantively improved.

Constructivism A theoretical approach to international relations that emphasizes the role of ideas, rules, norms, discourses, identities, and social relations in the generation of social life. Constructivism conceptualizes actors as being embedded in socially constructed institutional contexts, which are constitutive of actors' identities and interests and can be changed in interaction (see also **social constructionism**).

Contracting states (high contracting parties/state parties) Contracting states are states that have agreed to be bound to a **treaty** through signature, ratification, accession, or succession.

Convention Against Torture and Other Cruel, Inhuman, or Degrading Treatment or Punishment (CAT) The principal international treaty outlawing torture and governing the responsibilities with regard to the torture of **states parties**. It entered into force in 1987 and has been ratified by more than 140 countries.

Convention on the Punishment and Prevention of the Crime of Genocide (Genocide Convention) The 1948 international treaty that codifies the crime of **genocide** and obligates state parties to punish and prevent genocide. The treaty came into force in 1951 and is widely accepted around the world today.

Convention Relating to the Status of Refugees This convention established the most widely applicable framework for the protection of refugees. The Convention was adopted in July 1951 and entered into force in April 1954. Article 1 of the Convention limits its scope to 'events occurring before 1 January 1951', but this restriction was removed by the 1967 Protocol relating to the Status of Refugees. The convention has over 150 state signatories.

Council of Europe International organization founded in 1949 that seeks to promote democracy and human rights throughout Europe. The main instrument guiding the Council's work is the Convention for the Protection of Human Rights and Fundamental Freedoms (European Convention on Human Rights), which came into force in 1953. The **European Court of Human Rights** is the primary enforcement mechanism of the Convention. The Council presently has forty-seven members. See http://www.coe .int/T/e/Com/about_coe/.

Crime against humanity A deliberate widespread or systematic attack on civilians, including murder, forced deportation, enslavement, imprisonment, torture, rape, or persecution. On the spectrum of humanitarian offences, it is more extreme than a war crime but less extreme than genocide, which requires the intent to destroy a group in whole or in part.

Critique The praise or criticism of an idea, law, institution, policy, practice, etc. Critique can be based on, among others, **conceptual**, **empirical**, or **normative** concerns or perspectives.

Cultural relativism A view that holds that, because all truths are relative, cultures cannot be compared on moral or other normative grounds. In connection with human rights, it is the idea that human rights standards are Western and therefore inapplicable or inappropriate outside the West.

Customary international law State practice binding on states due to a period of uniform practice based on a sense of legal obligation.

Declaration A statement made by a state when agreeing to a **treaty**, which may or may not have legal effect. Also refers to an instrument adopted by international organizations that indicates or expresses international opinion but, unless otherwise stated in the organization's constituent instrument, is not legally binding.

Democratic deficit A democratic deficit occurs when decisions, particularly decisions by organizations ostensibly committed to democratic values, are taken without sufficient input from the citizens affected by them. Initially coined to refer to the insufficient impact of European citizens on decisions taken by the European Union, it has come to refer more broadly to the way in which different forms of globalization affect the capacity of citizens to make autonomous decisions in a national or sub-national democratic setting.

Deontological approach to ethics The notion that acts are considered intrinsically good or bad without reference to their consequences.

Dependent variable In a quantitative analysis, the dependent variable is the variable whose variation we seek to explain.

Deportation The forcible removal of an immigrant or asylum seeker to another country.

Derogation The suspension of a state's obligation to respect certain human rights during a time of national emergency; it is an emergency power of limited duration.

Detention The practice of holding a person claiming asylum while processing her or his application.

Diaspora The dispersion of a community of people of a particular ethnic, religious, or national group from its original homeland through emigration, persecution, economics, politics, or enslavement. Also refers to the members of the community living outside the original homeland who keep in close contact with their homeland and are frequently politically active.

Disaggregate/disaggregation An effort to break larger analytic units into smaller ones for the purposes of more careful analysis. For instance, one might look at states rather than the federal government in federal polities or at different branches of government rather than government as a whole.

Disappearance The forcible detention or abduction of people by the government (or with its consent), followed by a refusal to disclose their whereabouts.

Doctrine of necessity This refers to the notion that one harmful act may be justifiable to prevent a second, far more harmful act.

Earmarking Earmarking occurs when a donor state places conditions on the use of aid funds for a specific programme, country, or purpose.

Ecocide The killing of ecosystems, including planet Earth.

Ecological footprint The ecological footprint is a measure of human demand on the Earth's ecosystems and natural resources. Ecological footprint estimates the amount of biologically productive land and sea area needed to regenerate the resources a human population consumes and to absorb and render harmless the corresponding waste, given prevailing technology and current understanding. For example, if everyone in the world was to live the lifestyle of an average American, we would need five planet Earths.

Economic migrants Economic migrants are persons who leave their countries purely for economic reasons or in order to seek material improvements in their livelihood. Economic migrants do not fall within the criteria for refugee status and are therefore not entitled to benefit from international refugee protection.

Empirical Empirical refers to 'what is'. Empirical studies deal with data and information about the real world, gleaned from the real world. Empirical studies seek to describe or observe what is actually going on and to explain what accounts for the patterns and relationships in our observations or predicts what is likely to occur. Contrast this with **normative**.

Empirical ethnographic methodology This refers to the close relationships and sensory experiences utilized in the observation of social groups, in the attempt to describe and explain social phenomena, and in the subsequent production of a written record thereof.

Empowerment rights Empowerment rights are a subset of internationally recognized human rights that includes rights such as workers' rights and the rights to open and free political participation, movement, religion, and a free media, among others.

Encampment The practice of placing refugees in camps in host countries where they are protected and assisted by international organizations or host governments.

Enlightenment The European Enlightenment, also known as the Age of Reason, is usually said to have started between 1660 and 1685, and to have ended with the French Revolution. The Enlightenment philosophers believed in progress through human reason and were critical of superstition and religion, along with monarchical and aristocratic forms of political authority.

Environmental Kuznets curve (EKC) This is the idea that, after passing a threshold, economic growth 'outgrows' negative environmental pollution. Advocates of the EKC claim that economic growth is a benefit to the environment. Critics challenge the supporting evidence and argue that, where higher income/wealth levels are associated with improved environmental protection, this often results from wealthy nations 'exporting' polluting manufacturing to other parts of the world.

Equivalence principle of good governance The principle that stakeholders should have voice equivalent to that of decision makers in matters impacting directly upon their life chances and life choices.

Essentialism/essentialist The attribution of a behaviour or practice to human nature or to natural human tendencies, either generally or specifically in connection with a particular class or group of people. For instance, human rights violations might be attributed to human evil or animosities between social groups or to specific social or cultural factors. Consequently, this view can be deeply pessimistic about the prospects for human rights reform.

Ethnic cleansing The forced displacement of civilians based on their ethnicity, typically employing threats, fire, rape, or killing. Ethnic cleansing can sometimes constitute **genocide**.

Ethnocide The destruction of the culture and distinct identity of an ethnic group, sometimes described as cultural genocide.

Ethnography Ethnography (Greek ἔθνος *ethno*: people and γράφειν *graphein*: writing) is a type of research writing that uses fieldwork to generate data and facilitate the study of human societies. Anthropology and sociology, especially the constructivist and relativist paradigms, rely heavily on ethnographic research.

Eugenics An ideology based on a hierarchy of races of people that informed nineteenth- and twentieth-century 'scientific' racism.

European Court of Human Rights The primary enforcement mechanism of the Convention for the Protection of Human Rights and Fundamental Freedoms (European Convention on Human Rights), which came into force in 1953 (see **Council of Europe**). It is widely recognized as being the most evolved supranational mechanism for human rights enforcement. The Court took on its present form through changes implemented with Protocol No. 11 to the Convention, which came into force in 1998. See http://www.echr.coe.int/echr/.

Exclusionary ideologies Exclusionary ideologies define the conditions under which it is appropriate to repress certain categories of people. Examples include national security doctrines and broader ideologies of discrimination, targeting people on the basis of political orientation or social identity. Exclusionary ideologies are a fundamental source of state repression.

Executive Committee (UNHCR) The Executive Committee is charged with approving the UNHCR's assistance programmes, advising the High Commissioner on the exercise of his/her functions, and overseeing the Office's finances and administration. The Executive Committee is composed of representatives of seventy states with a demonstrated interest in refugee issues. Other states may attend, along with intergovernmental organizations and non-governmental organizations as observers.

Externalities Externalities are the costs or benefits of a decision or policy to third parties—often, although not necessarily, from the use of a public good. A negative externality is one where the producer of a product does not bear all of the costs. Manufacturing that causes air pollution or environmental degradation imposes costs on others when making use of public air that are not borne by the polluter nor reflected in the price of the good.

Failed and fragile states A failed state is one that has collapsed or is near collapse and cannot provide for its citizens without substantial external support. A fragile state has weak institutions and capacities and is in danger of failing.

First generation rights Civil and political rights that protect the interests and negative liberties of the individual against the power and encroachment of states, such as freedom of speech, religion, and association, rights to a fair trial, and voting rights, among others. The idea of generations of rights is controversial historically and conceptually. So-called first generation rights are codified in the UN's **International Covenant on Civil and Political Rights**.

Foreign direct investment (FDI) The investment a corporation or business makes outside its home country—either the construction of plants or acquiring of a controlling interest (more than 10 per cent of outstanding stock) in an existing overseas company. FDI is a central part of the **neoliberal** model of economic **globalization**, which encourages governments to lower corporate tax rates and provide other incentives to attract foreign investment capital.

Foundationalism/foundationalist Foundationalism is the view that any theory or principle must be justified by reference to more basic or foundational beliefs, which are held to be self-evident or self-justifying. Thus, a foundationalist position is one that relies on an apparently self-evident claim, e.g., 'Human frailty is a universal experience of human existence' (Turner, 1993, p. 505; Turner and Rojek, 2001, p. 110).

Freedom Riders Freedom Riders were a group of activists, generally from the northern USA, who travelled to the south in an effort to challenge discriminatory laws mandating segregation in public transportation across state lines.

***Gacaca* courts** Literally translated as 'justice on the grass', the *gacaca* courts were established after the 1994 Rwandan genocide using a traditional model. Local courts were established to try perpetrators of the Rwandan genocide for crimes that were divided into four categories, based on the seriousness of the offence; judges were elected by the local community to adjudicate these trials.

Geneva Conventions and Protocols The Geneva Conventions are four treaties, the first of which was adopted at an international conference in 1864, that set international legal standards regarding humanitarian matters, especially concerning the treatment of non-combatants and prisoners of war during wartime. The Geneva Conventions are the foundation of modern humanitarian law and have since been expanded.

Gender Empowerment Measure (GEM) Created and published by the United Nations Development Programme's Human Development Reports, the GEM aims to measure disparity in empowerment by gender. It is a composite index that includes three basic dimensions of empowerment— economic participation and decision making, political participation, and decision making and power over economic resources.

Gender-related Development Index (GDI) Created and published by the United Nations Development Programme's Human Development Reports, GDI is a composite index that measures human development in the same dimensions as the human development index (HDI), while adjusting for gender inequality in those basic dimensions. Its coverage is limited to 136 countries and areas for which the HDI rank was recalculated.

Genocide Genocide, as defined by the 1948 UN **Convention on the Punishment and Prevention of the Crime of Genocide**, is a crime under international law comprising acts 'committed with intent to destroy, in whole or in part, a national, ethnical, racial or religious group, as such.'

Genocide Convention See **Convention on the Punishment and Prevention of the Crime of Genocide**.

Global civil society (GCS) The sphere of ideas, institutions, organizations, networks, and individuals operating beyond the confines of national societies, polities, and economies; it is the international analogue of **civil society**. The term also carries **normative** connotations of belonging to a global imagined community, belief in human rights, global social justice, and/ or shared responsibility for the environment. However, not all groups operating within the domain of GCS share these normative views.

Globalization Globalization is a historical process that links distant communities and expands the reach of power relations across regions and continents. It involves a shift in social relations and interaction from more local to more global levels. Popularly the term is often used to describe an integrated world economy and society. *Economic* globalization can refer generally to an increase in the worldwide flow of goods, services, labour, and capital or specifically to the implementation of **neoliberal** economic policy reforms.

Governance Governance refers to 'state-like' activity. It is used particularly in reference to the evolving global system of formal and informal political coordination among states and intergovernmental organizations and non-state actors seeking to realize common purposes or resolve collective problems through the making and implementation of global or trans-national norms, rules, programmes, and policies.

Hague Conventions The Hague Conventions are two international **treaties** negotiated in 1899 and 1907 governing the conduct of war itself, the weapons that may and may not be employed under international law, and the definition of war crimes.

Harmonization The process by which domestic laws and rules are aligned with international standards. States are obligated to alter domestic laws, rules, and regulations that conflict with international human rights norms. Harmonization is essential if human rights reforms are to be sustainable.

Helsinki Accords/Agreement Accords signed in 1975 by the United States, Canada, the Soviet Union, and most European states including Turkey. It was the Final Act of the Conference on Security and Cooperation in Europe. The Agreement was seen as a major step in reducing **Cold War** tensions through the recognition of the territorial integrity of Eastern bloc states; its human rights provisions later became the basis for **civil society**-based challenges to Soviet rule.

Helsinki committees **Non-governmental organizations** formed during the **Cold War** within Eastern European countries to promote human rights. These committees date to the 1975 Helsinki Accords, which inserted human rights issues into East–West relations. Some credit the committees, and the transnational linkages they forged, with ending the Cold War.

Human Development Index (HDI) An aggregate index combining normalized measures of life expectancy, literacy, education, and gross domestic product per capita for countries worldwide. It has become a standard means of measuring human development, a concept that refers to the process of widening the options of individuals, giving them greater opportunities for education, health care, income, employment, etc. The HDI is published annually in the United Nations Development Programme's Human Development Reports.

Human development/capability approach (HD/CA) A development approach framed in Amartya Sen's concept of development as capability expansion (Sen, 1989) or freedom (Sen, 1999). Development is defined by its ends or purpose: expanding capabilities that individuals have to lead lives they value; or alternatively, expanding choices that people have in their lives. As a development approach, HD/CA emphasizes the creation of an enabling environment for pursuing these ends. Economic growth is only one such means.

Human Dimension Mechanism Organization for Security and Cooperation in Europe (OSCE) procedure that allows member states to raise issues of human rights concern with other members. The Moscow Mechanism (established at the last meeting of the Conference on the Human Dimension in Moscow in 1991) provides for the additional possibility for participating states to establish *ad hoc* missions of independent experts to assist in the resolution of a specific human dimension problem either on their own territory or in other OSCE participating states.

Human Poverty Index (HPI) Created and published by the United Nations Development Programme's Human Development Reports, to measure the level of poverty by focusing on human lives, the HPI is a composite index that complements the human development index. HPI-1 for developing countries includes deprivations in the three basic dimensions captured in the human development index—a long and healthy life, knowledge, and a decent standard of living. HPI-2 for selected high-income Organization for Economic Co-operation and Development (OECD) countries includes social exclusion, in addition to the three dimensions included in HPI-1. HPI-2 uses indicators and threshold levels more appropriate to high-income OECD societies.

Human rights-based approach to development (HRBA) HRBA is a discourse in the development field. OHCHR (2006) defines it as 'a conceptual framework for the process of human development that is normatively based on international human rights standards and operationally directed at promoting and protecting human rights. It seeks to analyse inequalities which lie at the heart of development problems and redress discriminatory practices and unjust distributions of power that impede development progress.'

Human Rights Council (HRC) The UN human rights body established by General Assembly Resolution 60/251 in 2006. The Council replaced the **Commission on Human Rights**.

Human Rights Watch (HRW) One of the world's principal international human rights organizations with headquarters in New York City. Founded in 1978 under the name Helsinki Watch to monitor the former Soviet Union's compliance with the **Helsinki Accords**. As the organization grew, it formed other watch committees to cover other regions of the world. In 1988, all of the committees were united under one umbrella to form Human Rights Watch. HRW conducts research and advocacy on a wide range of human rights issues around the world and is represented at the United Nations and other international bodies.

Humanitarian intervention Originally defined as the provision of vital materials (food, water, shelter, and medical care) to at-risk civilians in conflict areas. It now also includes any international action—economic, diplomatic, or military—motivated primarily by the humanitarian desire to protect civilian targets of violence.

Humanitarian law Refers both to laws, such as the **Geneva Conventions and Protocols**, governing the conduct of war (in Latin, *jus in bello*), and laws concerning the circumstances under which war is justified (in Latin, *jus ad bellum*). Sometimes called the 'laws of war'.

Impartiality State of not favouring any side or position. In discussions of humanitarian assistance, impartiality means providing aid solely on the basis of need, without consideration of the political or military allegiance of the recipient or the effect on a conflict's balance of power. Compare with **neutrality**.

Impunity Exemption from punishment. Often refers specifically to the status of known human rights violators who are not prosecuted or otherwise brought to justice.

Inclusiveness and subsidiarity principle of good governance That those whose life chances and life choices are most affected by actions and decisions should have the greatest say in deliberations concerning these.

Independent variable In a quantitative analysis, this is a variable used to explain variation in the **dependent variable**. For example, altitude is one independent variable that could be used to explain variations in the time it takes for water to boil (the dependent variable) in different places around the world.

Indivisibility The principle that each and every human right is inherent to the dignity of every human person. Consequently, they all have equal status as rights and cannot be ranked in a hierarchy of importance. This is an important principle in many debates, as some argue that civil and political rights are more significant than economic and social rights, or vice versa.

Interdiction The practice of intercepting refugees and asylum seekers before they cross the border of the country in which they intend to seek asylum.

Internally displaced person (IDP) An individual who has been forced or obliged to flee from the individual's home or place of habitual residence as a result of, or in order to seek safety and protection from, the effects of armed conflicts, situations of generalized violence, violations of human rights, or natural or human-made disasters, and who has not crossed an internationally recognized state border.

International Committee of the Red Cross (ICRC)
Prototypical humanitarian organization, founded in 1863 at the international conference that also gave rise to the original version of the **Geneva Conventions and Protocols**. The ICRC eschews political criticism of states in order to maintain access to provide humanitarian relief.

International Court of Justice (ICJ or World Court) The principal judicial organ of the United Nations. The only permanent international court with competence to hear inter-state disputes (brought with the consent of both parties).

International Covenant on Civil and Political Rights (ICCPR) One of the 'twin covenants' that forms the backbone of the International Bill of Rights. The ICCPR tabulates in a legally binding form the first half of the rights and freedoms enshrined in the **Universal Declaration of Human Rights**.

International Covenant on Economic, Social and Cultural Rights (ICESCR) One of the 'twin covenants' that forms the backbone of the International Bill of Rights. The ICESCR tabulates in a legally binding form the second half of the rights and freedoms enshrined in the **Universal Declaration of Human Rights**.

International Criminal Court (ICC) Permanent court created by the Rome Treaty (1998) and established in 2002 with jurisdiction to prosecute individuals who have allegedly perpetrated crimes listed in the 1998 Statute of the International Criminal Court. Cases can be referred to the Office of the Prosecutor by the state itself (e.g. Uganda) or by the Security Council (e.g. Sudan).

International Criminal Tribunal for Rwanda (ICTR) The United Nations *ad hoc* tribunal established to prosecute the major planners of the 1994 genocide in Rwanda. The court is based in Arusha, Tanzania.

International Criminal Tribunal for the former Yugoslavia (ICTY) The United Nations *ad hoc* tribunal established to prosecute war crimes committed in the former Yugoslavia. The court is based in The Hague, the Netherlands.

International Labor Organization (ILO) International organization established in 1919; now a specialized agency of the United Nations, with primary responsibility for addressing issues of workers rights and social justice. The ILO adopts many treaties and recommendations on labour and related matters.

International Monetary Fund (IMF) One of the **Bretton Woods institutions** established in 1944 to provide short-term financial help to countries seeking to stabilize exchange rates or improve balance of payments difficulties. Since the 1980s, the IMF has become progressively more involved in the economic decision making of nations through the **structural adjustment programmes** associated with its loans.

Law of coercive response This law asserts that states will respond to armed threats and social dissent with coercion or repression. There is overwhelming statistical evidence for this proposition, and hence its law-like status. The response occurs because all states are keen to retain power and will forcefully resist challenges to their authority.

League of Nations An international organization created after the First World War by the Treaty of Versailles. Its goal was to prevent war from happening again. It had some success in the 1920s, but was ultimately unable to withstand the aggression of the Axis powers in the 1930s. After the Second World War it was replaced by the United Nations.

Legal positivism The view that the law is separate from considerations of morality or justice. On this view the law does not gain its legitimacy from the natural law or other ethical considerations, but from being enacted by an appropriate institutional authority.

Liberalism A political philosophy/ideology emphasizing humans' rational capacities, the role of individuals in shaping social life, the harmony of individuals' rights, freedoms, and interests, market economics (in either classical liberal or welfare liberal strands), and democratic government (conceived often as limited government). Freedom or liberty is the primary value that should be instantiated in society and protected by government, in the liberal view; all individuals are equal, and their rights are to be protected equally under the **rule of law**. In international relations theory the term is associated with a variety of approaches that emphasize the role of democratic states in generating cooperation internationally as well as the role of international institutions in generating cooperation between states.

Like-minded group A like-minded group is an informal coalition of states who coalesce around a joint position in a particular international forum. In the field of human rights, this has traditionally referred to a group of small Western powers, including Canada, the Netherlands, and the Scandinavian countries, committed to furthering human rights issues in the United Nations. In the negotiations on the **International Criminal Court** the like-minded group grew from this base to encompass a much larger group of states in favour of a strong, independent Court, including most European, African, and Latin American states. But, most recently, in the context of the **Human Rights Council**, the term 'like-minded group' has been used conversely to refer to a group of states committed to privileging national sovereignty over human rights.

Limburg Principles on the Implementation of the International Covenant on Economic, Social and Cultural Rights A set of 103 principles drawn up by a group of distinguished experts in international law who convened in the province of Limburg (the Netherlands) in 1986 to elucidate the nature and scope of the obligations of **states parties** to the **International Covenant on Economic, Social and Cultural Rights**. They were supplemented a decade later with the

Maastricht Guidelines on Violations of Economic, Social and Cultural Rights.

Millennium Declaration (MD) **Declaration** made by heads of state convened at the 2000 Millennium Summit committing their nations to 'doing their utmost' for global development. The MD vowed to overcome poverty and achieve peace, human rights, democracy, and environmental sustainability while respecting the principles of equality and solidarity. It also set out specific goals and targets for development, which were further elaborated in the **Millennium Development Goals**.

Millennium Development Goals (MDGs) A set of eight goals, eighteen associated targets, and forty-eight progress indicators for development, subsequent to the 2000 **Millennium Declaration**. The MDGs address seven key dimensions of poverty: hunger, primary education, gender equality and empowerment of women, maternal mortality, child mortality, HIV/AIDS and other major diseases, and environmental sustainability. The eighth goal calls for stronger global partnerships and cooperation on development.

Moral hazard of humanitarian intervention A perverse dynamic in which the emerging norm of intervention to protect at-risk civilians, or **Responsibility to Protect**, has the unintentional consequence of encouraging rebellion that provokes state retaliation against civilians.

Multilateral treaty **Treaty** concluded between more than two parties or a treaty concluded by two parties but open to a larger group of states to ratify.

Multinational corporation (MNC) A corporation that does business and/or has branches in more than one country (sometimes also referred to as a transnational corporation or TNC).

Naming and shaming Closely related strategies used by human rights activists. Groups document and disseminate evidence of human rights violations with the aim of shaming or embarrassing governments into complying.

National human rights institutions Governmental agencies designed to promote and protect international human rights norms domestically. These institutions have proliferated worldwide since the early 1990s, and they now exist in over 100 countries. They are commonly tasked with collecting and investigating human rights complaints, issuing recommendations, and engaging in human rights education.

National security doctrines **Exclusionary ideologies** that legitimate the state's use of coercion to contain social instability and guarantee national security. Influential during the **Cold War**, as well as in today's global 'war on terror', national security doctrines provide a rationale for why it is acceptable and even necessary to respond to societal challenges with repression.

Natural law A moral law or code that is supposedly objective because it is built into the cosmos. Natural law has pre-Christian antecedents, but it was the Christian version that provided the theoretical backdrop to the emergence of the **rights of man** and modern human rights.

Natural rights Rights based on the **natural law** and justified in the first age of rights through ideas from Christian theology. As this theology lost favour among philosophers, natural rights were argued to emerge out of our basic humanity, rather than out of God's natural law. But philosophers then disagreed about how such rights should be understood to emerge out of our humanity.

Neoliberal/neoliberalism Neoliberalism is an ideology that defines freedom primarily in terms of the operation of markets with minimal government regulation and the protection of capital from taxation, expropriation, or social responsibilities. Neoliberals hold that the 'free market' leads to the greatest possible degree of freedom and prosperity for everyone. The main tenets of neoliberalism include trade liberalization, deregulation, elimination of or drastic reduction in public spending, and securing of property rights. Policies implementing these aims are said by proponents to increase economic growth by reducing the role of the state in the economy. Critics claim that neoliberalism is a way of reinforcing Western hegemony.

Neutrality A status of ensuring that one's intervention does not affect the balance of things. In discussions of humanitarian intervention, neutral assistance is assistance that does not alter the balance of power between warring parties. Compare with **impartiality**.

New International Economic Order (NIEO) A set of proposals advanced by developing countries in the 1970s to make the global economic system more fair. These proposals included more trade, tariff reform, increased development assistance, and changes to a system of global economic decision making that was viewed as favouring the rich countries.

No-fly zone Intervention to patrol the skies and shoot down any unauthorized military aircraft, often in support of humanitarian intervention, as in parts of Iraq from 1991–2003 and Bosnia from 1993–1995.

Non-governmental organizations (NGOs) Legally constituted, private, not-for-profit organizations that, in the field of human rights, work on advocacy campaigns, develop and set international human rights standards, monitor human rights violations, and provide service delivery primarily in developing countries. Many are active in **global civil society**.

Non-materialist Non-materialist explanations emphasize the role of ideas, norms, and identities (i.e. ideational factors in human events). They focus less on the calculations and concrete interests that underlie the decision to repress, for example, than on the exclusionary ideologies that render repression appropriate in the first place.

Non-refoulement *Refoulement* is the removal of a person to a territory or frontier of a territory where the person's life or freedom would be threatened on account of the person's race, religion, nationality, membership of a particular social group, or political opinions. The duty of *non-refoulement* or not returning such individuals at risk is a part of **customary international law** and is therefore binding on all states whether or not they are parties to the **Convention Relating to the Status of Refugees**.

Non-state actors Refers to all actors at the international level who are not states, e.g. terror groups, **multinational corporations**, **non-governmental organizations**, private security contractors, etc.

Normative Normative refers to what ought to be. Normative studies address moral, conceptual, and philosophical questions and are concerned with clarifying and justifying concepts and making moral arguments and **critiques**. Contrast with **empirical**.

Nuremberg Trials/Nuremberg Tribunal (International Military Tribunal (IMT) at Nuremberg) A series of trials held in Nuremberg, Germany by the Allies following the end of the Second World War. These trials prosecuted captured German leaders for crimes against peace, war crimes, and crimes against humanity. (Similar trials were held in Tokyo before the International Military Tribunal for the Far East.) In the most famous trial, nineteen high-ranking German defendants were found guilty in 1946. The court was the first international criminal tribunal of its kind, and is today seen as a precedent for the United Nations *ad hoc* criminal tribunals and the **International Criminal Court**.

OAU Convention Governing Specific Aspects of Refugee Problems in Africa This regional complement to the 1951 Convention provides for a broader refugee definition. Adopted in 1969, the OAU Convention stipulates that the term 'refugee' also 'applies to those fleeing from external aggression, occupation, foreign domination or events seriously disturbing public order in either part or whole of the country of origin'.

Occupation The acquisition of territory that is not under the power of another sovereign state.

Offshore processing The practice of processing claims of asylum seekers outside the country that they are bound for.

Palermo Protocol The Protocol to Prevent, Suppress, and Punish Trafficking in Persons, especially Women and Children. The Palermo Protocol supplemented the UN Convention against Transnational Organized Crime; it was signed in Palermo, Italy in 2000 and provided a contemporary definition of human trafficking that encompassed trafficking for labour and sexual exploitation.

Philosophes A term used to describe those thinkers and authors who were active and influential during the period of the European Enlightenment.

Physical integrity rights/violations A subset of internationally recognized human rights that typically includes the rights to protection from execution, torture, **disappearance**, or political imprisonment. Physical integrity violations, commonly known as state repression or coercion, consist of the use or threatened use of violence by the state and its agents to violate physical integrity rights.

Physical Quality of Life Index (PQLI) Index measuring the quality of life or overall well-being of a country. The index is a single number derived from the basic literacy rate, infant mortality, and life expectancy at age one. It has in many ways been displaced by the use of the **Human Development Index**, but in some studies has been used by political scientists as a measure of 'subsistence' rights.

Polity index This is a data collection effort pioneered by Ted Gurr that attempts to measure diverse political characteristics of governmental authority on a range of indicators. It focuses on governing institutions rather than discreet and mutually exclusive forms of governance. The index conceives of governmental authority on a spectrum ranging from fully institutionalized autocracy to fully institutionalized democracy using a 21-point scale. The index is used to identify three regime types: autocracies (scores of –10 to –6), 'anocracies' (–5 to +5, plus special values), and democracies (+6 to +10).

Portfolio investment The purchase of stocks and bonds totalling less than 10 per cent of the outstanding stock in foreign firms.

Poverty Reduction Strategy Papers (PRSPs) Policy frameworks for poverty reduction prepared by governments of low-income countries to mobilize donor support. Elaborate documents of several hundred pages, they analyse the causes of poverty and set strategic priorities and define action plans for economic growth and poverty reduction. They are underpinned by a framework of macroeconomic policies intended to maintain stability.

Prescription The acquisition of territory based on its effective possession over a period of time.

Proletariat A term used in Marxist theory to refer to those who are wage or salary workers. They are people who do not have ownership of the means of production, that is, who are not part of the ruling capitalist class (the bourgeoisie).

Qualitative/qualitative studies Qualitative studies are **empirical** studies that rely on the analysis and interpretation of data in ways that do not involve statistical techniques. These studies often utilize an in-depth case analysis of a particular country, region, or reference group; evidence might include interviews, assessments of historical data, etc.

Quantitative/quantitative studies Quantitative studies are **empirical** research studies that rely on statistical techniques for the analysis and interpretation of data (typically, *regression analysis*—a technique for determining the nature and strength of the relationship between a **dependent variable** and one or more **independent variables**). In the human rights field, quantitative methods examine a number of countries together over a period of time in the search for generalizations that can be made from these countries' collective experiences—for instance, to explain state repression or treaty ratification.

Ratification Practice of agreeing to the terms of a **treaty** (in accordance with constitutional national law) to enable it to be enforced.

Realism A school of thought about international relations that emphasizes the nature of the international system as competitive and 'anarchic' (without a world authority able to compel states to act in any given way), and which therefore requires individual states to protect their interests through military means if required. For realists, international law and institutions exert almost no constraining effect on the conduct of states. Instead, their behaviour is animated by the unrelenting pursuit of the national interest.

Realpolitik Term used to describe state policies that concern themselves solely with the pursuit of the national interest.

Refugee determination process The process carried out by the UN High Commissioner for Refugees or state governments to determine whether or not a person is a genuine refugee according to international legal refugee instruments.

Regimes Institutions, principles, norms, rules, and decision-making procedures around which actors' expectations converge in international relations. The international human rights regime comprises the UN system, relevant international law, and so on.

Reparations A range of remedies available for a breach of international law; term used variously to denote monetary compensation (narrow definition) or to include non-monetary damages (broader definition).

Reparative justice Justice that makes right the things that have gone wrong by provision of a remedy (such as **reparations** or **restitution**) for the suffering and loss that have occurred; comes from the notion of 'repair'.

Reservation A unilateral exemption from specified parts of a **treaty** by a **states party**, usually submitted on ratification.

Resettlement The transfer of refugees from the country in which they have sought asylum to another state that has agreed to admit them.

Responsibility to Protect A principle endorsed by the UN in 2005 that recognizes all states' responsibility to protect their own citizens. When a state is unable or unwilling to provide this protection the responsibility is transferred to the international community, licensing **humanitarian intervention**.

Restitution A token paid in compensation for loss or injury.

Restorative justice A process whereby both the victim and perpetrator of a crime are brought back into harmony with the community.

Retributive justice The dispensing of sanctions (imprisonment, monetary fine) in punishment for a crime committed by an individual.

Returnees Persons who are of concern to the UN High Commissioner for Refugees when outside of their country of origin and who remain so for a limited period after returning to their country of origin.

Right to development (RTD) As defined by the Special Rapporteur on the Right to Development, it is a right to a particular kind of development that would set the necessary conditions for the fulfilment of human rights. The rights in the Declaration include: full sovereignty over natural resources; self-determination; popular participation in development; equality of opportunity; and, the creation of favourable conditions for the enjoyment of other civil, political, economic, social, and cultural rights.

Rights of man The term used by **Enlightenment** thinkers to refer to the **natural rights** that they wrote into the early rights declarations and associated literature; in its modernized form, it refers to human rights.

Rule of law The principle in which state authorities, including the courts, apply legal standards fairly across cases, rather than arbitrarily or in response to political calculations. State accountability is an essential aspect of any rule-of-law system. Human rights protection, in turn, requires strong rule of law.

Safe areas Enclaves declared off-limits to attacks during war. A tactic of **humanitarian intervention** to protect civilians, but controversial when such areas are misused as rebel bases. In Bosnia, in July 1995, UN peacekeepers failed to prevent Serb forces from capturing the safe area of Srebrenica and slaughtering 8,000 Muslims.

Second generation rights Rights recognizing that certain basic goods should be equally available to all people, such as basic levels of economic subsistence, education, work, housing, and health care. These rights are often called positive rights because they require rights providers to act, rather than to refrain from interfering. The idea of generations of rights is controversial historically and conceptually. So-called second generation rights are codified in the UN's **International Covenant on Economic, Social and Cultural Rights**.

Self-determination The right to choice of one's own acts, free from external compulsion; in connection with human rights, the freedom of the people in a given territory to freely determine their own political arrangements. In the context of Indigenous peoples, it refers to the right to govern according to the wishes of the group, which is seen as a remedial political right of distinct dispossessed 'peoples' and 'nations', in contrast to the individual citizenship rights, or limited rights to land occupation, conferred on them by colonial nation states.

Social constructionism A theoretical approach emphasizing the socially created nature of social life and 'reality'. When the approach is turned to human rights, it views them as social inventions and, invariably, the product of the balance of power between social actors at a particular point in history and in a particular social context.

Social movements   Networks of people in **civil society** who organize efforts to bring or resist change, today often using the language of human rights. Social movements frequently have a significant say in institutionalizing rights.

Social structure   This refers to the ordered interrelationships between elements of society, such as the different forms of kinship and legal, religious, economic, political, and other institutions of a society.

Socialism   A political philosophy/ideology that enjoins wholesale change in the structures of society so that the means of production are owned by the workers or **proletariat** rather than by elite capitalist classes, so that the productive power of society is used for the common good, not merely in the interests of a few. Marxists and Communists are socialists who seek radical change to society by altering its economic base, and have historically pursued revolutionary politics to this end.

Soft law   Instruments that are not, strictly speaking, legally binding but that nevertheless may influence state behaviour, e.g. a **declaration**.

Sovereign immunity   The legal principle that a head of government is immune from prosecution for acts committed in his official role as sovereign (as opposed to acts committed in pursuit of his own private interests). It is generally understood that, while a head of state could be prosecuted for such things as personal corruption or murder of a spouse, he/she could not be prosecuted for the consequences of state policies.

Sovereignty   Legal or constitutional independence of a territorial state, entailing the right to govern and control the identified territory and legal and political jurisdiction within that territory without external interference. The concept is conventionally dated to the 1648 Peace of Westphalia, which established a norm of non-interference that was codified in the 1945 UN Charter and is—or was until quite recently—sacrosanct in international law. Sovereignty today is increasingly understood as the shared exercise of public power and authority between national, regional, and global authorities.

Spiral model of human rights change   This describes the process by which international norms gradually influence domestic-level human rights changes. The assumption is that states, in responding to human rights pressures, will initially deny abuses, then begin making small concessions, move to more concrete if still sometimes cosmetic reforms, and eventually—in some cases—alter their behaviour so that it is consistent with internationally recognized human rights norms.

Stateless persons   Persons who are not considered as nationals by any state under the operation of its law, including persons whose nationality is not established.

States parties   See **contracting states**.

Stolen generations   Aboriginal or part-Aboriginal children in Australia whom authorities forcibly removed from their families and culture. This policy of forcible removal continued into the 1960s. An official inquiry described the practice as genocidal. One of the first acts of the Rudd Labour Government in Australia was to make a public apology to the stolen generations and their families on 13 February 2008.

Structural adjustment policies/programmes (SAPs)   Lending policies of the **International Monetary Fund** and the **World Bank** that are designed to promote economic efficiency and growth in developing countries by minimizing the role of the state in the economy. These policies or programmes take the form of conditions attached to loans and promote a range of **neoliberal** policies.

Sustainable development   A form of development in which meeting the needs and rights of the present generation is not achieved at the expense of the needs and rights of future generations. It is often expressed as a form of 'triple bottom line' development that encompasses social, environmental, and economic bottom lines, rather than focusing simply on economic growth. Sustainable development prioritizes social inclusion and social justice and respect for critical ecological systems.

Terra nullius   Latin for 'land of no one'. Colonizing states (especially the British in Australia) conflated the interpretation 'land of no occupying sovereign' with the interpretation 'land without inhabitants with legal personality recognized by civilized nations' to arrive at the meaning 'uninhabited land'.

Third generation rights   Rights concerned with the rights of minority groups such as women, Indigenous peoples, linguistic and cultural minorities, and people of diverse sexualities, as well as environmental rights and the **right to development**. The idea of generations of rights is controversial historically and conceptually. This category of rights is not well institutionalized.

Torture warrant   Refers to a proposed legal order that could be issued by a judge sanctioning the torture of one or more specified individuals.

Trafficking   The organized transportation of contraband from one country to another for profit. *Human* trafficking involves the recruitment and transportation of people and/or their exploitation in work and employment. Human trafficking often involves the use of coercion and/or deception throughout, or at some stage in, the process.

Trafficking Victims Protection Act (TVPA)   A progressive law defining human trafficking passed by the United States Congress and signed by President Bill Clinton in 2000.

The TVPA established the norms of the 3Ps: prevention of trafficking, protection of victims, and prosecution of traffickers. The TVPA is both a domestic tool to address trafficking and a foreign policy tool to pressure other governments to address trafficking.

Transitional justice A process of helping societies deal with the difficult questions of justice that arise as a society moves from war to peace, or from a repressive or authoritarian regime to democracy. It focuses particularly on social, political, and economic institutions and on addressing past wrongs and on roles for former combatants. It may be carried out by means of **retributive**, **restorative**, or **reparative justice** or some combination of these.

Treaty Binding written agreement concluded between states.

Truth commission A mechanism established to uncover the truth about past events, often part of a programme of **transitional justice**.

UN Development Programme (UNDP) The United Nations' global development network, which provides assistance, advice, and resources to developing countries. The UNDP has a presence in 166 countries and has special programmes on democratic governance, poverty reduction, crisis prevention and recovery, environment and energy, and HIV-AIDS.

UN High Commissioner for Refugees (UNHCR) The UNHCR, established on 14 December 1950, is a UN agency mandated to protect and assist refugees at the request of a government or the UN itself. It assists in finding solutions to the plight of refugees, primarily in their return to their home countries or in their resettlement to other countries. The UNHCR is headquartered in Geneva and has offices in over 100 countries worldwide.

UN Peacebuilding Commission Established in 2007 as an intergovernmental advisory body of the UN that supports peace efforts in countries emerging from conflict.

UN Relief and Works Agency for Palestine Refugees in the Near East Founded in 1948, the UNRWA is the UN agency that provides assistance to millions of Palestinian refugees throughout the Middle East.

Universal Declaration of Human Rights (UDHR) Landmark **declaration** adopted and proclaimed by the General Assembly of the United Nations on 10 December 1948, it marks the dawn of the modern age of human rights. Its thirty articles outline a wide range of civil, cultural, economic, political, and social rights, rights subsequently codified in international law through the **International Covenant on Civil and Political Rights** and the **International Covenant on Economic, Social and Cultural Rights**. The UDHR establishes 'a common standard of achievement for all peoples and all nations, to the end that every individual and every organ of society' shall strive to ensure 'their universal and effective recognition and observance'.

Universal jurisdiction The legal doctrine that certain crimes are so grave that any/all states may prosecute individuals allegedly perpetrating these crimes, irrespective of the existence of any connection to the state seeking to prosecute. Crimes claimed to fall within this jurisdiction include genocide, slavery, and war crimes.

Utilitarianism A political philosophy/ideology of the **Enlightenment**, pioneered by Jeremy Bentham. It is a **consequentialist** theory holding (in simplified form) that an act is morally justified if and only if it leads to the greatest good for the greatest number.

Vienna Declaration A human rights **declaration** issued by the **Vienna World Conference on Human Rights** in 1993; it reaffirmed the universality of human rights and their indivisibility and interdependence.

Vienna Process The negotiations leading to the Protocol to Prevent, Suppress, and Punish Trafficking in Persons, especially Women and Children (see **Palermo Protocol**), conducted in Vienna, Austria. The Vienna Process was marked by highly contentious debates between abolitionist feminists, who believe that all forms of prostitution are exploitive and thus forms of trafficking, and human rights feminists, who believe that only forced prostitution should be considered a form of trafficking.

Vienna World Conference on Human Rights (Vienna Conference) A ground-breaking global conference held in 1993. It charted the course of post-Cold War human rights policy. Among other issues, it emphasized the importance of embedding international human rights standards in domestic structures, including legal systems, national human rights institutions, non-governmental organizations, and the media.

Violations approach An approach to measuring human rights that focuses on the violation of particular rights, allowing for an enumeration of violations or a **coding** of country performance on a standardized scale.

Voting Rights Act Landmark 1965 legislation passed by the US Congress outlawing discriminatory electoral practices throughout the United States.

War crime A violation of the laws or customs of war, including targeting civilians for murder, ill-treatment, or forced deportation. See **Geneva Conventions and Protocols**.

White slavery Term used at the turn of the twentieth century to describe the abduction of white girls and women in Western Europe and the United States, who were forced into prostitution in their home countries or trafficked to other countries. Most scholars now believe that the scope of the white slave trade was much smaller than suggested by the hype in the media.

World Bank One of the **Bretton Woods institutions** established in 1944 to provide economic assistance to the reconstruction of Europe after the Second World War. Today it is the leading public development institution in the world, providing long-term loans to governments for development projects.

World Social Forum (WSF) First held in 2001 in the Brazilian city of Porto Alegre as a response by critics of economic globalization to the World Economic Forum, a meeting of political and economic elites held annually in Davos, Switzerland. The WSF defines itself as 'an open meeting place for reflective thinking, democratic debate of ideas, formulation of proposals, free exchange of experiences and interlinking for effective action, by groups and movements of civil society that are opposed to neo-liberalism and to domination of the world by capital and any form of imperialism, and are committed to building a planetary society directed towards fruitful relationships among Mankind and between it and the Earth.'

World Trade Organization (WTO) Intergovernmental organization that sets the rules governing global trade and provides a mechanism for the settlement of trade-related disputes. The WTO was established in 1994; it grew out of the Uruguay round of negotiations under the framework of the General Agreement on Tariffs and Trade (GATT). The original **Bretton Woods institutions** were to have included an International Trade Organization (ITO), but these plans were never realized. Critics complain about the WTO's **neoliberal** agenda.

References

AAA (American Anthropological Association) (1947). Statement of human rights. *American Anthropologist*, **49**/4, 539–543.

Aaronson, S. and Zimmerman, J. (2006). Fair trade? How Oxfam presented a systemic approach to poverty, development, human rights, and trade. *Human Rights Quarterly*, **28**/4, 998–1030.

Abouharb, R. and Cingranelli, D. (2006). The human rights effects of World Bank structural adjustment. *International Studies Quarterly*, **50**/2, 233–262.

Adcock, R. and Collier, D. (2001). Measurement validity: A shared standard for qualitative and quantitative research. *American Political Science Review*, **95**/3, 529–546.

Agamben, G. (2005). *State of Exception*. Chicago, IL: University of Chicago Press.

AHRC (Asian Human Rights Commission) (2003). Electricity for development vs. displacement of people. http://www.ahrchk.net/ua/mainfile.php/2003/498/.

Akinci, B. (2006). Turkey faces hazelnut crisis as growers protest prices. *Turkish Daily News*, 15 August.

Alderson, A. S. (2004). Explaining the upswing in direct investment: A test of mainstream and heterodox theories of globalization. *Social Forces*, **83**/1, 81–122.

Alfredsson, G. (2005). Minorities, Indigenous and tribal peoples: Definitions of terms as a matter of international law. *Minorities, Peoples and Self-Determination—Essays in Honour of Patrick Thornberry* (ed. N. Ghanea and A. Xanthaki). Leiden: Martinus Nijhoff.

Allen, B. (1996). *Rape Warfare: The Hidden Genocide in Bosnia-Herzegovina and Croatia*. Minneapolis, MN: University of Minnesota Press.

Allen, T. (2005). *War and Justice in Northern Uganda: An Assessment of the International Criminal Court's Intervention*. London: Crisis States Research Centre, Development Studies Institute, London School of Economics.

Alston, P. (1997). Effective functioning of bodies established pursuant to United Nations human rights instruments—final report on enhancing the long-term effectiveness of the United Nations human rights treaty system. UN Doc. E/CN.4/1997/74.

_____ (2005). Ships passing in the night: The current state of the human rights and development debate seen through the lens of the millennium development goals. *Human Rights Quarterly*, **27**/3, 755–829.

Amnesty International (2005). *Human Rights for Human Dignity: A Primer on Economic, Social and Cultural Rights*. http://www.amnesty.org/en/library/asset/POL34/009/2005/en/dom-POL340092005en.html.

_____ (2008a). Ask Amnesty: Torture. http://www.amnestyusa.org/askamnesty/torture200112.html.

_____ (2008b). Human rights and the rights of lesbian, gay, bisexual and transgender people. http://www.amnestyusa.org/lgbt-human-rights/about-lgbt-human-rights/page.do?id=1106573&n1=3&n2=36&n3=1123.

Anaya, J. (2004). *Indigenous Peoples in International Law* (2nd edn). Oxford: Oxford University Press.

Anderson, B. and O'Connell Davidson, J. (2002). *Trafficking—A Demand Led Problem?* Washington, DC: Save the Children.

Anderson, C. J., Paskeviciute, A., Sandovici, M. E., and Tverdova, Y. V. (2005). In the eye of the beholder?: The foundations of subjective human rights conditions in east–central Europe. *Comparative Political Studies*, **38**/7 (September), 771–798.

Anderson, M. (1999). *Do No Harm: How Aid Can Support Peace—Or War*. Boulder, CO: Lynne Rienner.

Andersson, J. O. and Lindroth, M. (2001). Ecologically unsustainable trade. *Ecological Economics*, **37**, 113–122.

Andreassen, B. A. and Marks, S. P. (eds) (2006). *Development as a Human Right: Legal, Political and Economic Dimensions*. Cambridge, MA: Harvard School of Public Health. Distributed by Harvard University Press.

Anheier, H., Glasius, M., and Kaldor, M. (2001). Introducing global civil society. *Global Civil Society* (ed. H. Anheier, M. Glasius, and M. Kaldor). Oxford: Oxford University Press.

Annan, K. (2002). Strengthening of the United Nations: An agenda for further change. UN Doc. A/57/387.

_____ (2005). In larger freedom: Towards development, security and human rights for all. UN Doc. A/59/2005.

Apodaca, C. (2001). Global economic patterns and personal integrity rights after the Cold War. *International Studies Quarterly*, **45**/4, 587–602.

_____ (2002). The globalization of capital in east and southeast Asia. *Asian Survey*, **42**/6, 883–905.

Arbour, L. (2007). Foreword. *Frequently Asked Questions on a Human Rights-Based Approach to Development Cooperation*. Geneva: Office of the United Nations High Commissioner for Human Rights.

Arendt, H. (1959). *The Human Condition*. New York: Doubleday.

_____ (1969). Reflections on violence. *New York Review of Books*, 27 February.

_____ (1973). *The Origins of Totalitarianism* (new edn). New York: Harvest.

Ariès, P. (1962). *Centuries of Childhood*. London: Cape.

Arnold, D. and Hartman, L. (2006). Workers rights and low wage industrialization: How to avoid sweatshops. *Human Rights Quarterly*, **28**/3, 676–700.

Asiedu, E. (2002). On the determinants of foreign direct investment to developing countries: Is Africa different? *World Development*, **30**/1, 107–119.

Askin, K. (2006). Prosecuting gender crimes committed in Darfur: Holding leaders accountable for sexual violence. *Genocide in Darfur: Investigating the Atrocities in the Sudan* (ed. S. Totten and E. Markusen). New York: Routledge.

Atkinson, K. (1989). The torturer's tale. *Toronto Life*, March.

Badiou, A. (2001). *Ethics: An Essay on the Understanding of Evil*. London: Verso.

Bales, K. and Lize, S. (2005). *Trafficking in Persons in the United States*. Washington, DC: National Institute of Justice.

Ball, P. B. (2000). The Guatemalan Commission for Historical Clarification: Generating analytical reports; inter-sample analysis. *Making the Case: Investigating Large Scale Human Rights Violations Using Information Systems and Data Analysis* (ed. P. B. Ball, H. F. Spirer, and L. Spirer). Washington, DC: American Association for the Advancement of Science.

_____, Kobrak, P., and Spirer, H. (1999). *State Violence in Guatemala, 1960–1996: A Quantitative Reflection*. Washington, DC: American Association for the Advancement of Science.

_____, Spirer, H. F., and Spirer, L. (eds) (2000). *Making the Case: Investigating Large Scale Human Rights Violations Using Information Systems and Data Analysis*. Washington, DC: American Association for the Advancement of Science.

_____, Betts, W., Scheuren, F., Dudukovich, J., and Asher, J. (2002). Killings and refugee flow in Kosovo March–June 1999: A report to the International Criminal Tribunal for the Former Yugoslavia, 3 January. Washington, DC: American Association for the Advancement of Science, American Bar Association.

_____, Asher, J., Sulmont, D., and Manrique, D. (2003). *How Many Peruvians have Died?* Washington, DC: American Association for the Advancement of Science.

Ban, K. (2007). Leadership and climate change. UN Secretary General, press article, 23 September. http://www.un.org/sg/press_article_climate.shtml.

Bandelj, N. (2002). Embedded economies: Social relations as determinants of foreign direct investment in central and eastern Europe. *Social Forces*, **81**/2, 411–444.

Bar-On, A. (1996). Criminalising survival: Images and reality of street children. *Journal of Social Policy*, **26**/1, 63–78.

Barbalet, J. M. (1988). *Citizenship: Rights, Struggle and Class Inequality*. Milton Keynes: Open University Press.

Barber, B. (1995). *Jihad vs. McWorld*. New York: Ballantine Books.

Barnett, H. G. (1948). On science and human rights. *American Anthropologist*, **50**/2, 352–355.

Barnett, M. (2002). *Eyewitness to a Genocide: The United Nations and Rwanda*. Ithaca, NY: Cornell University Press.

_____ (2008). Duties beyond borders. *Foreign Policy: Theories, Actors, Cases* (ed. S. Smith, A. Hadfield, and T. Dunne). Oxford: Oxford University Press.

Barry, J. (1999). *Rethinking Green Politics: Nature, Virtue and Progress*. London: Sage.

_____ (2004). Ecological modernisation. *Debating the Earth* (2nd edn) (ed. J. Dryzek and D. Schlosberg). Oxford: Oxford University Press.

Barry, K. (1979). *Female Sexual Slavery*. New York: New York University Press.

Baxi, U. (2006). *The Future of Human Rights*. Oxford: Oxford University Press.

Bayefsky, A. (1996). The UN human rights treaties: Facing the implementation crisis. Committee on International Human Rights Law and Practice report. International Law Association.

_____ (2001). *The UN Human Rights Treaty System: Universality at the Crossroads*. The Hague: Kluwer.

Beckerman, W. (2001). *Justice, Posterity, and the Environment*. Oxford: Oxford University Press.

Bedont, B. and Hall Martinez, K. (1999). Ending impunity for gender crimes under the International Criminal Court. *Brown Journal of World Affairs*, **6**/1, 65–85.

Beetham, D. (1994). *Defining and Measuring Democracy*. Beverly Hills, CA: Sage Publications.

_____ (2006). The right to development and its corresponding obligations. *Development as a Human Right, Legal, Political and Economic Dimensions* (ed. B. A. Andreassen and S. P. Marks). Boston, MA: Harvard School of Public Health. Distributed by Harvard University Press.

Belknap, M. (1987). *Federal Law and Southern Order: Racial Violence and Constitutional Conflict in the Post-Brown South*. Athens, GA: University of Georgia Press.

Bell, E. (1910). *Fighting the Traffic in Young Girls or the War on the White Slave Trade*. Chicago, IL: G. S. Ball.

Benedict, R. (1961). *Patterns of Culture*. London: Routledge.

Benhabib, S. (2002). *The Claims of Culture, Equality and Diversity in the Global Era*. Princeton, NJ: Princeton University Press.

Bentham, J. (1843). Anarchical fallacies. *The Complete Works of Jeremy Bentham*, Vol. II (ed. J. Bowring). Edinburgh: William Tait.

Berg-Schlosser, D. and Siegler, R. (1990). *Political Stability and Development: A Comparative Analysis of Kenya, Tanzania and Uganda*. Boulder, CO: Lynne Rienner.

Berger, P., Berger, B., and Keller, H. (1974). *The Homeless Mind: Modernization and Consciousness*. Harmondsworth: Penguin.

Bernstein, R. (2003). Kidnapping has Germans debating police torture. *The New York Times*, 10 April.

Betts, R. (1994). The delusion of impartial intervention. *Foreign Affairs*, **73**/6, 20–33.

Bhagwati, J. (2004). *In Defense of Globalization*. Oxford: Oxford University Press.

Biersteker, T. J. (1978). *Distortion or Development*. Cambridge, MA: MIT Press.

Bissio, R. (2003). *Civil Society and the MDGs*. Montevideo: Instituto del Tercer Mundo.

Black, M. (1996). *Children First: The Story of UNICEF*. Oxford: Oxford University Press.

Black, R. (2001). Environmental refugees: Myth or reality? UNHCR working paper no. 34. http://www.unhcr.org/research/RESEARCH/3ae6a0d00.pdf.

Blackstone, W. (1765–1769). *Commentaries on the Laws of England*. Oxford: Clarendon Press. http://avalon.law.yale.edu/subject_menus/blackstone.asp (New Haven, CT: Yale University, Lillian Goldman Law Library, The Avalon Project).

Bloed, A. (1993). Monitoring the CSCE human dimension: In search of its effectiveness. *Monitoring Human Rights in Europe* (ed. A. Bloed, A. L. Leicht, M. Nowak, and A. Rosas). London: Martinus Nijhoff.

Bob, C. (2005). *The Marketing of Rebellion: Insurgents, Media and International Activism*. New York: Cambridge University Press.

Bobbio, N. (1999). *The Age of Rights*. Oxford: Polity.

Boekle, H. (1995). Western states, the UN Commission on Human Rights, and the '1235' procedure: The question of bias revisited. *Netherlands Quarterly of Human Rights*, **13**/4, 367–402.

Bollen, K. A. (1992). Political rights and political liberties in nations: An evaluation of rights measures, 1950 to 1984. *Human Rights and Statistics: Getting the Record Straight* (ed. T. B. Jabine and R. P. Claude). Philadelphia, PA: University of Pennsylvania Press.

Bos, A. (1999). The International Criminal Court: Recent developments. *Reflections on the International Criminal Court: Essays in Honour of Adriaan Bos* (ed. H. A. M. von Hebel, J. G. Lammers, and J. Schukking). The Hague: T. M. C. Asser.

Bosselmann, K. (2001). Human rights and the environment: Redefining fundamental principles? *Governing for the Environment: Global Problems, Ethics and Democracy* (ed. B. Gleeson and N. Low). Basingstoke: Palgrave.

Boudreau, V. (2004). *Resisting Dictatorship: Repression and Protest in Southeast Asia*. New York: Cambridge University Press.

Boyden, J. (1990). Childhood and the policy makers: A comparative perspective on the globalization of childhood. *Constructing and Reconstructing Childhood: Contemporary Issues in the Sociological Study of Childhood* (ed. A. James and A. Prout). London: Falmer.

_____ (1994). Children's experience of conflict related emergencies: Some implications for relief policy and practise. *Disasters*, **18**/3, 254–267.

_____ (1997). Childhood and policy makers: A comparative perspective on the globalization of childhood. *Constructing and Reconstructing Childhood: Contemporary Issues in the Sociological Study of Childhood* (2nd edn) (ed. A. James and A. Prout). London: Falmer.

Boyle, K. (1995). Stock-taking on human rights: The World Conference on Human Rights, Vienna 1993. *Political Studies*, **43**/Special issue, 79–95.

Brandt Commission (or Independent Commission on International Development Issues) (1980). *North–South: A Programme for Survival*. London: Pan Books.

Brett, R. (1993). The human dimension of the CSCE and the CSCE response to minorities. *The CSCE in the 1990s: Constructing European Security and Cooperation* (ed. M. R. Lucas). Baden-Baden: Nomos Verlagsgesellschaft.

Briggs, P. (1998). *Uganda*. Old Saybrook, CT: Globe Pequot.

Bristow, E. J. (1977). *Vice and Vigilance: Purity Movements in Britain Since 1700*. Dublin: Gill and Macmillan.

Brockett, C. (2005). *Political Movements and Violence in Central America*. Cambridge: Cambridge University Press.

Brookings-Bern Project on Internal Displacement (2007). Disaster risk reduction: A front line defense against climate change and displacement. http://www.brookings.edu/reports/2007/1010_disaster_risk_reduction.aspx.

_____ (2008). Human rights and natural disasters: Operational guidelines and field manual on human rights protection in situations of natural disaster. http://www.brookings.edu/reports/2008/spring_natural_disasters.aspx.

Brown, C. (2007). From humanized war to humanitarian intervention: Carl Schmitt's critique of the just war tradition. *The International Political Thought of Carl Schmitt: Terror, Liberal War and the Crisis of Global Order* (ed. L. Odysseos and F. Petito). London: Routledge.

Brown Thompson, K. (2002). Women's rights are human rights. *Restructuring World Politics* (ed. S. Khagram, J. Riker, and K. Sikkink). Minneapolis, MN: University of Minnesota Press.

Bryant, R. L. and Bailey, S. (1997). *Third World Political Ecology*. London: Routledge.

Budiardjo, C. and L. S. Liong (1984). *The War Against East Timor*. London: Zed Books.

Bueno de Mesquita, B., Downs, G. W., Smith, A., and Cherif, F. M. (2005). Thinking inside the box: A closer look at democracy and human rights. *International Studies Quarterly*, **49**/3, 439–457.

Burgers, J. (1992). The road to San Francisco: The revival of the human rights idea in the twentieth century. *Human Rights Quarterly*, **14**/4, 447–477.

Burgoon, B. (2001). Globalization and welfare compensation: Disentangling the ties that bind. *International Organization*, **55**/3, 509–551.

Burke, E. ([1790] 1971). *Reflections on the Revolution in France*. London: Dent.

Burkhart, R. E. (2002). The capitalist political economy and human rights: Cross-national evidence. *The Social Science Journal*, **39**/2, 155–170.

_____ and Lewis-Beck, M. (1994). Comparative democracy— the economic-development thesis. *American Political Science Review*, **88**/4, 903–910.

Burman, E. (1994). Innocents abroad: Western fantasies of childhood and the iconography of emergencies. *Disasters*, **18**/3, 238–253.

_____ (1995). Developing differences: Gender, childhood and economic development. *Children and Society*, **9**/3, 121–142.

Bybee, J. S. (2005). Standards of conduct for interrogation under 18 U.S.C.—1 August 2002. *The Torture Papers: The Road to Abu Ghraib* (ed. K. J. Greenberg and J. Datel). Cambridge: Cambridge University Press.

C-FAM (1998). Catholic, Muslim nations unite against 'enforced pregnancy' and 'gender justice'. *Friday Fax*, **1**/39.

Camp Keith, L. (1999). The United Nations International Covenant on Civil and Political Rights: Does it make a difference in human rights behavior? *Journal of Peace Research*, **36**/1, 95–118.

_____ (2002). Constitutional provisions for individual human rights (1977–1996): Are they more than mere 'window dressing'? *Political Research Quarterly*, **55**/1, 111–143.

Capotorti, F. (1977). Study on the rights of persons belonging to ethnic, religious and linguistic minorities. UN Doc. E/CN.4/Sub.2/384/Add.1–7.

Cardenas, S. (2007). *Conflict and Compliance: State Responses to International Human Rights Pressure*. Philadelphia, PA: University of Pennsylvania Press.

_____ (to appear). *Chains of Justice: The Global Rise of National Human Rights Institutions*. Philadelphia, PA: University of Pennsylvania Press.

Carey, C. and Poe, S. (eds) (2004). *Understanding Human Rights Violations: New Systematic Studies*. Aldershot: Ashgate.

Carothers, T. (2002). The end of the transition paradigm. *Journal of Democracy*, **13**/1, 5–21.

Carr, E. H. (1946). *The Twenty Years Crisis, 1919–1939: An Introduction to the Study of International Relations* (revised edn). London: Macmillan.

Carter, P. (2005). Taxonomy of torture. *Slate*, 26 May. http://slate.com/features/whatistorture/Taxonomy.html.

Cassesse, A. (2003). *International Criminal Law*. Oxford: Oxford University Press.

Castellino, J. (2005). Conceptual difficulties and the right to indigenous self-determination. *Minorities, Peoples and Self-Determination—Essays in Honour of Patrick Thornberry* (ed. N. Ghanea and A. Xanthaki). Leiden: Martinus Nijhoff.

Chandler, D. (2001). The road to military humanitarianism: How the human rights NGOs shaped a new humanitarian agenda. *Human Rights Quarterly*, **23**/3, 678–700.

_____ (2003). New rights for old? Cosmopolitan citizenship and the critique of state sovereignty. *Political Studies*, **51**/2, 339–356.

_____ (2006). *Empire in Denial: The Politics of State-Building*. London: Pluto.

_____ (2007a). Hollow hegemony: Theorising the shift from interest-based to value-based international policy-making. *Millennium: Journal of International Studies*, **35**/3, 703–723.

_____ (2007b). The security-development nexus and the rise of 'anti-foreign policy'. *Journal of International Relations and Development*, **10**/4, 362–386.

_____ (2008). The revival of Carl Schmitt in international relations: The last refuge of critical theorists? *Millennium: Journal of International Studies*, **37**/1, 27–48.

Chapman, A. (1996). A 'violations approach' for monitoring the International Covenant on Economic, Social, and Cultural Rights. *Human Rights Quarterly*, **18**/1, 23–66.

Cheng, L. (1999). Globalization and women's paid labour in Asia. *International Social Science Journal*, **52**/160, 217–228.

Chesterman, S. (2002). East Timor in transition: Self-determination, state-building and the United Nations. *International Peacekeeping*, **9**/1, 45–76.

Chrétien, J. P. (2003). *The Great Lakes of Africa: Two Thousand Years of History* (trans. S. Straus). New York: Zone Books.

Chuang, J. (2006a). The United States as global sheriff: Using unilateral sanctions to combat trafficking. *Michigan Journal of International Law*, **27**/2, 437–494.

Cingranelli, D. L. and Richards, D. L. (2007). Measuring government effort to respect economic and social human rights: A peer benchmark. *Economic Rights: Conceptual, Measurement, and Policy Issues* (ed. S. Hertel and L. Minkler). Cambridge: Cambridge University Press.

_____ and Richards, D. L. (2008). The Cingranelli–Richards (CIRI) human rights data project. www.humanrightsdata.org.

Clark, A. M. (2001). *Diplomacy of Conscience: Amnesty International and Changing Human Rights Norms*. Princeton, NJ: Princeton University Press.

Claude, R. P. (1976). The classical model of human rights development. *Comparative Human Rights* (ed. R. P. Claude). Baltimore, MD: Johns Hopkins University Press.

_____ (1983). The case of Joelito Filartiga and the clinic of hope. *Human Rights Quarterly*, **5**/3, 275–295.

_____ and Jabine, T. B. (1992). Exploring human rights issues with statistics. *Human Rights and Statistics: Getting the Record Straight* (ed. T. B. Jabine and R. P. Claude). Philadelphia, PA: University of Pennsylvania Press.

Coetzee, J. M. (1982). *Waiting for the Barbarians*. New York: Penguin.

Cohen, R. and Rai, S. (eds) (2000). *Global Social Movements*. London: Athlone.

Cohn, T. (2003). *Global Political Economy* (2nd edn). New York: Addison Wesley and Longman, Inc.

COI (Commission of Inquiry) (2005). Report of the International Commission of Inquiry on Darfur to the United Nations Secretary-General. Geneva, 25 January.

Cole, M. (2000). *Trade Liberalisation, Economic Growth and the Environment*. London: Edward Elgar.

Collins, K. (2007). Thai men sue N. C. contractor. *News and Observer*, 10 March.

Colonomos, A. and Santiso, J. (2005). Viva la France! French multinationals and human rights. *Human Rights Quarterly*, **27**/4, 1307–1345.

Comte, A. (1896). *The Positive Philosophy*. London: George Bell. Republished Batoche Books Kitchner (2000) at http://socserv2.mcmaster.ca/~econ/ugcm/3ll3/comte/Philosophy2.pdf.

Conference on Security and Cooperation in Europe, Final Act (1975). Helsinki, 1 August. http://www.osce.org/documents/mcs/1975/08/4044_en.pdf.

Conisbee, M. and Simms, A. (2003). *Environmental Refugees: The Case for Recognition*. London: new economics foundation. http://www.neweconomics.org/gen/z_sys_PublicationDetail.aspx?pid=159.

Connelly, M. T. (1980). *The Response to Prostitution in the Progressive Era*. Chapel Hill, NC: University of North Carolina.

Copelon, R. (1994). Intimate terror: Understanding domestic violence as torture. *Human Rights of Women: National and International Perspectives* (ed. R. J. Cook). Philadelphia, PA: University of Pennsylvania Press.

Corbin, A. (1990). *Women for Hire: Prostitution and Sexuality in France After 1850* (trans. A. Sheridan). Cambridge, MA: Harvard University Press.

Cornia, G. A., Jolly, R., and Stewart, F. (1987). *Adjustment With a Human Face, Volume 1: Protecting the Vulnerable and Promoting Growth*. Oxford: Oxford University Press.

Courthoys, A. and Docker, J. (2008). Defining genocide. *The Historiography of Genocide* (ed. D. Stone). London: Palgrave Macmillan.

Cowan, J. K., Dembour, M. B., and Wilson, R. A. (eds) (2001). *Culture and Rights: Anthropological Perspectives*. Cambridge: Cambridge University Press.

Cowell, A. (2000). A call to put social issues on the corporate agenda. *The New York Times*, 6 April.

Cox, R. (1996). *Shaping Childhood: Themes of Uncertainty in the History of Adult–Child Relationships*. London: Routledge.

Crawford, T. and Kuperman, A. (eds) (2006). *Gambling on Humanitarian Intervention: Moral Hazard, Rebellion and Civil War*. New York: Routledge.

Crelinsten, R. (2005). How to make a torturer. *Index on Censorship*, **34**/1, 72–77.

Crenshaw, E. (1991). Foreign investment as a dependent variable: Determinants of foreign investment and capital penetration in developing nations, 1967–1978. *Social Forces*, **69**/4, 1169–1182.

CSDH (Commission on Social Determinants of Health) (2007). Social determinants and indigenous health: The international experience and its policy implications. http://www.who.int/social_determinants/resources/indigenous_health_adelaide_report_07.pdf.

Cunningham, H. (1995). *Children and Childhood in Western Society Since 1500*. London: Longman.

Daes, E. and Eide, A. (2000). Working paper on the relationship and distinction between the rights of persons belonging to minorities and those of Indigenous peoples. UN Doc. E/CN.4/Sub.2/2000/10. http://www.unhchr.ch/huridocda/huridoca.nsf/0/e2bb9e4b569ae37fc12569290050ae93?OpenDocument.

Dahl, R. A. (1966). *Political Opposition in Western Democracies*. New Haven, CT: Yale University Press.

_____ (1971). *Polyarchy: Participation and Opposition*. New Haven, CT: Yale University Press.

Dallaire, R. with Beardsley, B. (2003). *Shake Hands with the Devil: The Failure of Humanity in Rwanda*. Toronto: Random House Canada.

Dallin, A. and Breslauer, G. (1970). *Political Terror in Communist Systems*. Stanford, CA: Stanford University Press.

Daly, M. (2007). *Darfur's Sorrow: A History of Destruction and Genocide*. New York: Cambridge University Press.

Danner, M. (2004). *Torture and Truth, America, Abu Ghraib and the War on Terror*. New York: New York Review of Books.

Darrow, M. and Tomas, A. (2005). Power, capture and conflict: A call for human rights accountability in development cooperation. *Human Rights Quarterly*, **27**/2, 471–538.

Dassin, J. (ed.) (1986). *Torture in Brazil: A Report by the Archdiocese of Sao Paulo*. New York: Vintage.

Davenport, C. (1995). Multi-dimensional threat perception and state repression: An inquiry into why states apply negative sanctions. *American Journal of Political Science*, **39**/3, 683–713.

_____ (1996). 'Constitutional promises' and repressive reality: A cross-national time-series investigation of why political and civil liberties are suppressed. *Journal of Politics*, **58**/3: 627–654.

_____ (1997). From ballots to bullets: An empirical assessment of how national elections influence state uses of political repression. *Electoral Studies*, **16**/4, 517–540.

_____ (1999). Human rights and the democratic proposition. *Journal of Conflict Resolution*, **43**/1, 92–116.

_____ (ed.) (2000). *Paths to State Repression: Human Rights Violations and Contentious Politics*. Boulder, CO: Rowman and Littlefield.

_____ (2004). The promise of democratic pacification: An empirical assessment. *International Studies Quarterly*, **48**/3, 539–560.

_____ (2007a). *State Repression and the Domestic Democratic Peace*. New York: Cambridge University Press.

_____ (2007b). State repression and political order. *Annual Review of Political Science*, **10**, 1–23.

_____ and Armstrong II, D. A. (2004). Democracy and the violation of human rights: A statistical analysis from 1976–1996. *American Journal of Political Science*, **48**/3, 538–554.

_____ and Stam, A. (2003). Mass killing and the oases of humanity: Understanding Rwandan genocide and resistance. National Science Foundation (SES-0321518), Spring.

_____, Johnston, H., and Mueller, C. (eds) (2005). *Repression and Mobilization*. Minneapolis, MN: University of Minnesota Press.

_____, Moore, W., and Armstrong II, D. A. (2008). Waterboarding and democracy: Understanding torture and domestic threats. Manuscript.

David, F. (1999). New threats or old stereotypes: The revival of 'trafficking' as a discourse. History of Crime, Policing and Punishment Conference, Australian Institute of Criminology in conjunction with Charles Stuart University, Canberra, 9–10 December. http://www.aic.gov.au/conferences/hcpp/david.pdf.

Davis, M. (2008). Unforgivable behavior, inadmissible evidence. *The New York Times*, 17 February.

de Waal, A. (1998). *Famine Crimes: Politics and the Disaster Relief Industry in Africa*. Bloomington, IN: Indiana University Press.

de-Shalit, A. (1995). *Why Posterity Matters*. London: Routledge.

_____ (2001). Ten commandments of how to fail in an environmental campaign. *Political Theory and the Environment: A Reassessment* (ed. M. Humphrey). London: Frank Cass.

Deng, F. (1995). *War of Visions: Conflict of Identities in the Sudan*. Washington, DC: Brookings Institution Press.

_____, Kimaro, S., Lyons, T., Rothchild, D., and Zartman, I. W. (1996). *Sovereignty as Responsibility: Conflict Management in Africa*. Washington, DC: Brookings Institution Press.

Der Derian, J. (2003). The question of information technology in international relations. *Millennium: Journal of International Studies*, **32**/3, 441–456.

Dershowitz, A. (2002). *Why Terrorism Works: Understanding the Threat, Responding to the Challenge*. New Haven, CT: Yale University Press.

_____ (2004). Torture warrant: A response to Professor Strauss. *New York Law School Law Review*, **48**/1, 275–294.

Des Forges, A. (1999). *Leave None to Tell the Story: Genocide in Rwanda*. New York: Human Rights Watch.

Devetak, R. (2007). Between Kant and Pufendorf: Humanitarian intervention, statist anti-cosmopolitanism and critical international theory. *Review of International Studies*, **33**/Special issue, 51–174.

Diamond, L. (2002). Thinking about hybrid regimes. *Journal of Democracy*, **13**/2, 21–35.

_____ (2008). *The Spirit of Democracy: The Struggle to Build Free Societies Throughout the World*. New York: Times Books.

Dicke, W. and Holland, F. (eds) (2007). Water: A global contestation. *Global Civil Society 2006/7* (ed. M. Kaldor et al.). London: Sage.

Diebold, J. (1974). Why be scared of them. *Foreign Policy*, **3**, 79–95.

Doezema, J. (2000). Loose women or lost women? The re-emergence of the myth of white slavery in contemporary discourses of trafficking in women. *Gender Issues*, **18**/1, 23–50.

_____ (2002). Who gets to choose? Coercion, consent and the UN trafficking protocol. *Gender and Development*, **10**/1, 20–27.

Donnelly, J. (1989). *Universal Human Rights in Theory and Practice*. Ithaca, NY: Cornell University Press.

_____ (2003). *Universal Human Rights in Theory and Practice* (2nd edn). Ithaca, NY: Cornell University Press.

_____ (2006). *International Human Rights* (3rd edn). Boulder, CO: Westview.

Donner, F. J. (1990). *Protectors of Privilege: Red Squads and Police Repression in Urban America*. Berkeley, CA: University of California Press.

Douzinas, C. (2007). *Human Rights and Empire: The Political Philosophy of Cosmopolitanism*. London: Routledge Cavendish.

Doyle, T. (1998). Sustainable development and Agenda 21: The secular bible of global free markets and pluralist democracy. *Third World Quarterly*, **19**/4, 771–786.

Dryzek, J. (1987). *Rational Ecology: Environment and Political Economy*. London: Wiley Blackwell.

DuBois, P. (1991). *Torture and Truth*. London: Routledge.

Duffield, M. (2007). *Development, Security and Unending War: Governing the World of Peoples*. Cambridge: Polity.

Dunn, J. S. (1983). *Timor: A People Betrayed*. Milton, Queensland: Jacaranda.

Duvall, R. and Stohl, M. (1988). Governance by terror. *The Politics of Terrorism* (ed. M. Stohl). New York: M. Dekker.

Dworkin, R. (1977). *Taking Rights Seriously*. Cambridge, MA: Harvard University Press.

Dyer, A. S. (1880). *The European Slave Trade in English Girls: A Narrative of Facts*. London: Dyer Brothers.

Eckersley, R. (1996). Greening liberal democracy: The rights discourse revisited. *Democracy and Green Political Thought: Sustainability, Rights and Citizenship* (ed. B. Doherty and M. de Geus). London: Routledge.

Eckholm, E. (2003). Tide of China's migrants: Flowing to boom or bust? *New York Times*, 29 July.

Ecuador (2004). International trade, health, and children's rights. 3D country briefing. September. http://www.3dthree.org/pdf_3D/3DCRCEcuadorBrief_Sept04.pdf.

Edmundson, W. A. (2004). *An Introduction to Rights*. Cambridge: Cambridge University Press.

Edwards, M. (2003). NGO legitimacy: Voice or vote? *BOND Networker*, February.

_____ and Gaventa, J. (eds) (2001). *Global Citizen Action*. London: Earthscan.

Edwards, S. (1990). Capital flows, foreign direct investment and debt. NBER working paper no. 3497. Cambridge, MA: NBER.

Eide, A. (2006). Human rights based development in an age of economic globalization. *Development as a Human Right: Legal, Political, and Economic Dimensions* (ed. B. A. Andreassen and S. P. Marks). Cambridge, MA: Harvard School of Public Health. Distributed by Harvard University Press .

Ekins, P. (2000). *Economic Growth and Environmental Sustainability: The Prospects for Green Growth*. London: Routledge.

Elazar, D. J. (1972). *American Federalism: A View from the States* (2nd edn). New York: Thomas Y. Crowell.

Elson, D. (2006). *Budgeting for Women's Rights: Monitoring Government Budgets for Compliance with CEDAW*. New York: UNIFEM.

Emmerij, L., Jolly, R., and Weiss, T. (2001). *Ahead of the Curve? UN Ideas and Global Challenges*. Bloomington, IN: Indiana University Press.

Escobar, A. (1997). The making and unmaking of the Third World. *The Post-Development Reader* (ed. M. Rahnema with V. Bawtree). London: Zed Books.

Etzioni, A. (2006). Sovereignty as responsibility. *Orbis*, **50**/1, 71–85.

Evans, G. (2007). The responsibility to protect: Creating and implementing a new international norm. Address by Gareth Evans, President, International Crisis Group, to Human Rights Law Resource Centre, Melbourne, 13 August 2007

and to Community Legal Centres and Lawyers for Human Rights, Sydney, 28 August 2007.

_____ (2008). State sovereignty was a licence to kill. Interview with Gareth Evans. *SEF News (Stiftung Entwicklung und Frieden)*, Spring.

Evans, J. (1998). Pro-lifers win limits on new UN criminal court. *The Interim*, August.

Evans, T. (1996). *US Hegemony and the Project of Universal Human Rights*. Basingstoke: Macmillan.

_____ (ed.) (1998). *Human Rights Fifty Years On: An Appraisal*. Manchester: Manchester University Press.

Falk, R. (2000). *Human Rights Horizons*. London: Routledge.

Fanon, F. (2004). *The Wretched of the Earth*. New York: Grove.

Farrior, S. (1997). The international law on trafficking in women and children for prostitution: Making it live up to its potential. *Harvard Human Rights Journal*, **10**, 213–255.

Federle, K. (1994). Rights flow downhill. *International Journal of Children's Rights*, **2**, 343–376.

Fein, H. (1979). *Accounting for Genocide: National Responses and Jewish Victimization During the Holocaust*. Chicago, IL: University of Chicago Press.

_____ (1995). More murder in the middle: Life-integrity violations and democracy in the world, 1987. *Human Rights Quarterly*, **17**/1, 170–191.

Feith, H. (1992). East Timor: The opening up, the crackdown and the possibility of a durable settlement. *Indonesia Assessment 1992: Political Perspectives on the 1990s* (ed. H. Crouch and H. Hill). Political and Social Change Monograph, No. 17. Canberra: Department of Political and Social Change, Research School of Pacific Studies, Australian National University.

Felner, E. (2005). Torture and terrorism: Painful lessons from Israel. *Torture: Does it Make Us Safer? Is it Ever OK?* (ed. K. Roth and M. Worden). New York: New Press/Human Rights Watch.

Fields, A. B. (2003). *Rethinking Human Rights for the New Millennium*. New York: Palgrave Macmillan.

Fisher, T. (1997). *Prostitution and the Victorians*. New York: St Martins.

Flint, J. and de Waal, A. (2008). *Darfur: A New History of a Long War, Revised and Updated*. London: Zed Books.

Florini, A. M. (ed.) (2000). *The Third Force: The Rise of Transnational Civil Society*. Tokyo: Japan Center for International Exchange and Washington, DC: Carnegie Endowment for Peace.

Foot, R. (2000). *Rights Beyond Borders: The Global Community and the Struggle Over Human Rights in China*. Oxford: Oxford University Press.

Forest Peoples Programme & Tebtebba Foundation (2006). Peoples' rights, extractive industries and transnational and other business enterprises. http://www.business-humanrights.org/Documents/Forest-Peoples-Tebtebba-submission-to-SRSG-re-indigenous-rights-29-Dec-2006.pdf.

Forsyth, D. (2006). *Human Rights in International Relations* (2nd edn). Cambridge: Cambridge University Press.

Forum Social Mundial (World Social Forum) (2005). Programmacao (Programme) 29 30 31.

Foster, J. (2002). *The Millennium Declaration: Engaging Civil Society Organisations*. New York: World Federation of United Nations Associations. http://www.wfuna.org.

Foucault, M. (1977). *Discipline and Punish: The Birth of the Prison*. New York: Pantheon.

_____ (2003). '*Society Must be Defended': Lectures at the Collège de France 1975–1976*. London: Allen Lane/Penguin.

_____ (2007). *Security, Territory, Population: Lectures at the Collège de France 1977–1978*. Basingstoke: Palgrave.

Foweraker, J. and Landman, T. (1997). *Citizenship Rights and Social Movements: A Comparative and Statistical Analysis*. Oxford: Oxford University Press.

Fox, F. (2001). New humanitarianism: Does it provide a moral banner for the 21st century? *Disasters*, **25**/4, 275–289.

Francis, R. (2005). *Judge Sewall's Apology: The Salem Witch Trials and the Forming of an American Conscience*. New York: Harper Collins.

Franck, T. M. (1984). Of gnats and camels: Is there a double standard at the United Nations? *American Journal of International Law*, **78**/4, 811–833.

_____ (2000). Legitimacy of the democratic entitlement. *Democratic Governance and International Law* (ed. G. H. Fox and B. R. Roth). Cambridge: Cambridge University Press.

Frank, A. G. (1970). *Latin America: Underdevelopment or Revolution: Essays on the Development of Underdevelopment and the Immediate Enemy*. New York: Monthly Review Press.

_____ (1971). *Capitalism and Underdevelopment in Latin America: Historical Studies of Chile and Brazil*. Harmondsworth: Penguin.

Frankel, J. and P. Romer. (1999). Does trade cause growth? *American Economic Review*, **89**/3, 379–399.

Franklin, B. (ed.) (1995). *The Handbook of Children's Rights*. London: Routledge.

Freeman, M. (1997). *The Moral Status of Children: Essays on the Rights of the Child*. The Hague: Martinus Nijhoff.

_____ (2001). Is a political science of human rights possible? *The Netherlands Quarterly of Human Rights*, **19**/2, 121–137.

_____ (2002). *Human Rights: An Interdisciplinary Approach*. Cambridge: Polity.

Frenkel, S. and Kuruvilla, S. (2002). Logics of action, globalization, and changing employment relations in China, India, Malaysia, and the Phillipines. *Industrial and Labor Relations Review*, **55**/3, 387–412.

Friedman, M. (1962). *Capitalism and Freedom*. Chicago, IL: Chicago University Press.

Friends of River Narmada (2008). Introduction. http://www.narmada.org/introduction.html.

Fukuda-Parr, S. (2005). Millennium development goals: Why they matter. *Global Governance*, **10**/3, 395–402.

_____ (2006). Millennium development goal 8—international human rights obligations? *Human Rights Quarterly*, **28**/4, 966–997.

_____ (2008a). Human rights and development. *Social Welfare, Moral Philosophy and Development: Essays in Honour of Amartya Sen's Seventy Fifth Birthday* (ed. K. Basu and R. Kanbur). Oxford: Oxford University Press.

_____ (2008b). Are internationally agreed development goals (IADGs) being implemented in national development strategies and aid programmes? A review of poverty reduction strategy papers (PRSPs) and development cooperation policy statements. Background papers for the 2008 Development Cooperation Forum, Mainstreaming of IADGs. New York: UN Department for Economic and Social Affairs. http://www.un.org/ecosoc/docs/pdfs/Mainstreaming_of_IADGs.pdf.

Fukuyama, F. (1992). *The End of History and the Last Man*. London: Hamish Hamilton.

Furedi, F. (1997). *Population and Development: A Critical Introduction*. Cambridge: Polity.

Galbraith, J. K. (1964). *Economic Development*. Cambridge, MA: Harvard University Press.

_____ (1977). *The Nature of Mass Poverty*. Cambridge, MA: Harvard University Press.

Gallie, W. B. (1956). Essentially contested concepts. *Proceedings of the Aristotelian Society*, **51**, 167–198.

Gandhi, M. (1997). The quest for simplicity: 'My idea of Swaraj'. *The Post-Development Reader* (ed. M Rahnema with V. Bawtree). London: Zed Books.

Garrett, G. (1995). Capital mobility, trade, and the domestic politics of economic policy. *International Organization*, **49**/4, 657–687.

_____ (1998). *Partisan Politics in the Global Economy*. Cambridge: Cambridge University Press.

Gartner, S. and Regan, P. (1996). Threat and repression: The non-linear relationship between government and opposition violence. *Journal of Peace Research*, **33**/3, 273–287.

Gastanaga, V. and Nugent, J. B. (1998). Host country reforms and FDI inflows: How much difference do they make? *World Development*, **26**/7, 1299–1314.

Gastil, R. D. (1978). *Freedom in the World: Political Rights and Civil Liberties, 1978*. Boston, MA: G. K. Hall.

_____ (1980). *Freedom in the World: Political Rights and Civil Liberties*. Westport, CT: Greenwood.

_____ (1988). *Freedom in the World: Political and Civil Liberties, 1986–1987*. New York: Freedom House.

Gastil, R. D. (1990). The comparative survey of freedom: Experiences and suggestions. *Studies in Comparative International Development*, **25**/1, 25–50.

Gelleny, R. and McCoy, M. (2001). Globalization and government policy independence: The issue of taxation. *Political Research Quarterly*, **54**/3, 509–530.

General Assembly (1993). Resolution 43/134 endorsing the Paris Principles on National Human Rights Institutions. UN Doc. A/RES/48/134.

Gewirth, A. (1996). *The Community of Rights*. Chicago, IL: University of Chicago Press.

Ghani, A., Lockhart, C., and Carnahan, M. (2005). Closing the sovereignty gap: An approach to state-building. Overseas Development Institute working paper no. 253, September. http://www.odi.org.uk/Publications/working_papers/wp253.pdf.

Gibbons, E. (2006). The convention on the rights of the child and implementation of economic, social and cultural rights in Latin America. *Los Derechos Economicos, Sociales y Culturales en America Latina* (ed. A. Yamin). Ottawa: IDRC and Plaza y Valdes. http://www.idrc.ca/en/ev-100733-201-1-DO_TOPIC.html. Spanish original.

Gibney, M. and Skogly, S. (2009). *Extraterritorial Human Rights Obligations*. Philadelphia, PA: University of Pennsylvania Press. In press.

_____ and Stohl, M. (1998). Human rights and US refugee policy. *Open Borders? Closed Societies?: The Ethical and Political Issues* (ed. M. Gibney). Westport, CT: Greenwood.

Gibson, M. (1986). *Prostitution and the State in Italy, 1860–1915*. New Brunswick, NJ: Rutgers University Press.

Gilpin, R. (2001). *Global Political Economy*. Princeton, NJ: Princeton University Press.

Glasius, M. (1999a). *Foreign policy on human rights: Its influence on Indonesia under Soeharto*. Antwerp: Intersentia.

_____ (1999b). For the people, without the people: Lessons from the Timor tragedy. *Netherlands Quarterly on Human Rights*, **17**/4, 385–387.

_____ (2006). *The International Criminal Court: A Global Civil Society Achievement*. London: Routledge.

_____ (2007). Pipedream or panacea? Global civil society and economic and social rights. *Global Civil Society* (ed. H. Anheier, M. Glasius, and M. Kaldor). Oxford: Oxford University Press.

Gleditsch, N. P., Wallensteen, P., Eriksson, M., Sollenberg, M., and Strand, H. (2002). Armed conflict 1946–2001: A new dataset. *Journal of Peace Research*, **39**/5, 615–637. Data available at http://www.prio.no/jpr/datasets.asp.

Glucksmann, M. (2006). Developing an economic sociology of care and rights. *Rights: Sociological Perspectives* (ed. L. Morris). London: Routledge.

Goldstein, R. J. (1978). *Political Repression in Modern America: From 1870 to the Present*. Cambridge: Schenkman Publishing.

Golston, J. C. (1993). Ritual abuse: Raising hell in psychotherapy: The political, military and multigenerational training of torturers: Violent initiation and the role of traumatic dissociation. *Treating Abuse Today*, **3**/6, 12–19.

Goodale, M. (2006a). Introduction. In 'In focus: Anthropology and human rights in a new key'. *American Anthropologist*, **108**/1, 1–8.

_____ (2006b). Ethical theory as social practice. *American Anthropologist*, **108**/1, 25–37.

_____ (2008). *Human Rights: An Anthropological Reader*. Blackwell Readers in Anthropology. Chichester: Blackwell.

Goodhart, M. (2005). *Democracy as Human Rights: Freedom and Equality in the Age of Globalization*. New York: Routledge.

Goodin, R. E., Pateman, C., and Pateman, R. (1997). Simian sovereignty. *Political Theory*, **25**/6, 821–849.

Gorbachev, M. (1989). Speech reproduced in *Current Digest of the Soviet Press*, **41**/46, 13 December.

Gould, C. C. (2004). *Globalizing Democracy and Human Rights*. Cambridge: Cambridge University Press.

Gow, J. (1997). *Triumph of the Lack of Will*. New York: Columbia University Press.

Gray, M. M., Kittilson, M. C., and Sandholtz, W. (2006). Women and globalization: A study of 180 nations, 1975–2000. *International Organization*, **60**/2, 293–333.

Gready, P. and Ensor, J. (eds) (2005). *Reinventing Development? Translating Rights-Based Approaches from Theory into Practice*. London: Zed Books.

Green, M. (2001). What we talk about when we talk about indicators: Current approaches to human rights measurement. *Human Rights Quarterly*, **23**/4, 1062–1097.

Greenberg K. J. and Datel, J. (eds) (2005). *The Torture Papers: The Road to Abu Ghraib*. Cambridge: Cambridge University Press.

Greer, D. (1935). *The Incidence of Terror During the French Revolution: A Statistical Interpretation*. Cambridge, MA: Harvard University Press.

Greig, A., Hume, D., and Turner, M. (2007). *Challenging Global Inequality: Development Theory and Practice in the 21st Century*. New York: Palgrave Macmillan.

Grittner, F. K. (1990). *White Slavery: Myth, Ideology and American Law*. New York: Garland.

Gross, O. (2004). The prohibition on torture and the limits of the law. *Torture: A Collection* (ed. S. Levinson). Oxford: Oxford University Press.

Guibernau, M. (1999). *Nations Without States: Political Communities in a Global Age*. Cambridge: Polity.

Guinier, L. (1994). *The Tyranny of the Majority: Fundamental Fairness in Representative Democracy*. New York: Free Press.

Gunning, I. (1992). Arrogant perception, world-travelling, and multicultural feminism: The case of female genital surgeries. *Columbia Human Rights Law Review*, **23**/2, 189–248.

Gurr, T. R. (1970). *Why Men Rebel*. Princeton, NJ: Princeton University Press.

_____ (1974). Persistence and change in political systems, 1800–1971. *American Political Science Review*, **68**/4, 1482–1504.

_____ (1986). The political origins of state violence and terror: A theoretical analysis. *Government Violence and Repression: An Agenda for Research* (ed. M. Stohl and G. A. Lopez). New York: Greenwood.

Guzmán, D., Guberek, T., Hoover, A., and Ball, P. (2007). Missing people in Casanare. Palo Alto, CA: The Benetech Initiative. http://www.hrdag.org/resources/publications/casanare-missing-report.pdf.

Haakonssen, K. (1991). From natural law to the rights of man: A European perspective on American debates. *A Culture of Rights: The Bill of Rights in Philosophy, Politics and Law—1791 and 1991* (ed. M. J. Lacey and K. Haakonssen). Cambridge: Woodrow Wilson International Center for Scholars and Cambridge University Press.

Haas, P. M. (1992). Introduction: Epistemic communities and international policy coordination. *Knowledge, Power and International Policy Coordination* (ed. P. M. Haas). Columbia, SC: University of South Carolina Press.

Habermas, J. (1996). *Between Facts and Norms: Contributions to a Discourse Theory of Law and Democracy*. Cambridge, MA: MIT Press.

_____ (1999). Bestialität and Humanität. *Die Zeit*, 29 April.

Hafner-Burton, E. M. (2005). Right or robust? The sensitive nature of repression to globalization. *Journal of Peace Research*, **42**/6, 679–698.

_____ (to appear). *Coercing Human Rights: Why Preferential Trade Agreements Regulate Repression*. Ithaca, NY: Cornell University Press.

_____ and Tsutsui, K. (2005). Human rights in a globalizing world: The paradox of empty promises. *American Journal of Sociology*, **110**/5, 1373–1411.

_____ _____ (2007). Justice lost! The failure of international human rights law to matter where needed most. *Journal of Peace Research*, **44**/4, 407–425.

Hancock, J. (2003). *Environmental Human Rights: Power, Ethics and Law*. London: Ashgate.

Haney, C., Banks, W. C., and Zimbardo, P. G. (1973). Interpersonal dynamics in a simulated prison. *International Journal of Criminology and Penology*, **1**, 69–97.

Hannum, H. (1990). *Autonomy, Sovereignty and Self-Determination*. Philadelphia, PA: University of Pennsylvania Press.

Hanson, M. (1994). Democratisation and norm creation in Europe. *Adelphi Paper*, **284** (International Institute for Strategic Studies/Brasseys), January.

Haq, Mahbub ul (1995). *Reflections on Human Development*. New York: Oxford University Press.

Hardin, G. (1977). *The Limits to Altruism*. Indianapolis, IN: Indiana University Press.

Hardt, M. and Negri, A. (2001). *Empire*. New York: Harvard University Press.

Harff, B. (2003). No lessons learned from the Holocaust? Assessing risks of genocide and political mass murder since 1955. *American Political Science Review*, **97**/1, 57–73.

Haritos-Fatouros, M. (1988). The official torturer: A learning model for obedience to the authority of violence. *Journal of Applied Social Psychology*, **18**/13, 1107–1120.

Harrison, A. and Scorse, J. (2003). Globalization's impact on compliance with labor standards. *Brookings Trade Forum*, 45–82.

Harrison, G. (2004). *The World Bank and Africa: The Construction of Governance States*. London: Routledge.

Hart, J. (2006). Saving children: What role for anthropology? *Anthropology Today*, **22**/1, 5–8.

Hasselback, D. (2001). Lundins search for the big score. *Financial Post*, 22 June.

Hathaway, O. (2002). Do treaties make a difference? Human rights treaties and the problem of compliance. *Yale Law Journal*, **111**/8, 1932–2042.

_____ (2007). Why do countries commit to human rights treaties? *Journal of Conflict Resolution*, **51**/4, 588–621.

Hauser, P. (ed.) (1961). *Urbanization in Latin America*. New York: Columbia University Press.

Hayner, P. (2001). *Unspeakable Truths*. New York: Routledge.

_____ (2002). *Unspeakable Truths: Facing the Challenges of Truth Commissions*. New York: Routledge.

Hayward, T. (2005). *Constitutional Environmental Rights*. Oxford: Oxford University Press.

Hechter, M. (2000). *Containing Nationalism*. Oxford: Oxford University Press.

Held, D. (1995). *Democracy and the Global Order: From the Modern State to Cosmopolitan Governance*. Cambridge: Polity.

_____ (1996). *Models of Democracy*. Stanford, CA: Stanford University Press.

_____ (2004). *Global Covenant: The Social Democratic Alternative to the Washington Consensus*. Cambridge: Polity.

_____ (2005). Democratic accountability and political effectiveness from a cosmopolitan perspective. *Global Governance and Public Accountability* (ed. D. Held and M. Koenig-Archibugi). Oxford: Blackwell Publishing.

Hempel, C. G. H. (1966). *The Philosophy of Natural Science*. Engelwood Cliffs, NJ: Prentice Hall.

Henderson, C. W. (1991). Conditions affecting the use of political repression. *Journal of Conflict Resolution*, **35**/1, 120–142.

_____ (1993). Population pressures and political repression. *Social Science Quarterly*, **74**/2, 322–333.

Henkin, L. (1981). International Human Rights as 'Rights'. *Human Rights* (ed. J. R. Pennock and J. W. Chapman). New York: New York University Press.

Hertel, S. (2006). *Unexpected Power: Conflict and Change among Transnational Activists*. Ithaca, NY: Cornell University Press.

_____ and Minkler, L. (eds) (2007). *Economic Rights: Conceptual, Measurement, and Policy Issues*. Cambridge: Cambridge University Press.

Hibbs, D. A. (1973). *Mass Political Violence: A Cross-National Causal Analysis*. New York: Wiley.

Hill, K. (1994). *Democracy in the Fifty States*. Lincoln, NE: University of Nebraska Press.

Hirano, K. (2007). Government not persuaded—Ainu hope U.N. move aids indigenous status quest. *The Japan Times*, 13 October. http://search.japantimes.co.jp/cgi-bin/nn20071013f1.html.

Hobbes, T. (1968). *Leviathan*. New York: Penguin.

Hochschild, A. (1998). *King Leopold's Ghost: A Story of Greed, Terror, and Heroism in Colonial Africa*. New York: Houghton Mifflin.

Holmes, S. and Sunstein, C. R. (1999). *The Cost of Rights: Why Liberty Depends on Taxes*. New York: W. W. Norton.

Horowitz, I. (1976). *Genocide: State Power and Mass Murder*. New Brunswick, NJ: Transaction Publishers.

_____ (1997). *Taking Lives: Genocide and State Power*. New Brunswick, NJ: Transaction Publishers.

Hovil, L. and Lomo, Z. (2004). Working paper 11: Behind the violence: Causes, consequences and the search for solutions to the war in northern Uganda. Kampala: Refugee Law Project.

_____ _____ (2005). Working paper 15: Whose justice? Perceptions of Uganda's Amnesty Act 2000: The potential for conflict resolution and long-term reconciliation. Kampala: Refugee Law Project.

Howard, R. (1986). *Human Rights in Commonwealth Africa*. New Jersey: Rowman & Littlefield.

Howard-Hassmann, R. (2005). The second great transformation: Human rights leapfrogging in the era of globalization. *Human Rights Quarterly*, **27**/1, 1–40.

Howell, J. and Pearce, J. (2001). *Civil Society and Development: A Critical Exploration*. Boulder, CO: Lynne Rienner.

HRCA (Human Rights Council of Australia) (1995). *The Right Way to Development: Human Rights Approach to Development Assistance*. Melbourne: HRCA.

HRW (Human Rights Watch) (1999). Human rights trump sovereignty in 1999: Crimes against humanity provoke international action. 9 December. http://www.hrw.org/english/docs/1999/12/09/global8916.htm.

Hughes, J. (2004). *Citizen Cyborg: Why Democratic Societies Must Respond to the Redesigned Human of the Future*. Boulder, CO: Westview.

Human Rights Committee (1994). General comment 24 on issues relating to reservations made upon ratification or accession to the Covenant or the Optional Protocols thereto, or in relation to declarations under article 41 of the Covenant. New York: United Nations.

Human security report (2005). Vancouver: Human Security Centre. http://www.humansecurityreport.info/.

Humphrey, M. (2007). *Ecological Politics and Democratic Theory: The Challenge of the Deliberative Ideal*. London: Routledge.

Hunt, L. (2007). *Inventing Human Rights: A History*. New York: W. W. Norton.

Huntington, S. (1968). *Political Order in Changing Societies*. New Haven, CT: Yale University Press.

_____ (1991). *The Third Wave: Democratization in the Late Twentieth Century*. Norman, OK: University of Oklahoma Press.

Hyland, K. E. (2001). Protecting human victims of trafficking: An American framework. *Berkeley Women's Law Journal*, **16**, 29–71.

ICG (International Crisis Group) (2001). International criminal tribunal for Rwanda: Justice delayed. Africa report no. 30.

_____ (2007). Darfur's new security reality. Africa report no. 134.

ICISS (International Commission on Intervention and State Sovereignty) (2001). The Responsibility to Protect. Ottawa: International Development Research Centre. http://www.iciss.gc.ca/report-en.asp.

IFAD (undated). Indigenous peoples. Fact sheet at http://www.ifad.org/pub/factsheet/ip/e.pdf.

Ignatieff, M. (1998). *The Warrior's Honor: Ethnic War and the Modern Conscience*. New York: Chatto & Windus.

_____ (2001). *Human Rights as Politics and Idolatry*. Princeton, NJ: Princeton University Press.

_____ (2004). *The Lesser Evil: Political Ethics in an Age of Terror: Political Ethics in an Age of Terror*. Princeton, NJ: Princeton University Press.

IICK (Independent International Commission on Kosovo) (2000). *The Kosovo Report*. Oxford: Oxford University Press.

Ikenberry, J. (2001). *After Victory: Institutions, Strategic Restraint and the Rebuilding of Order After Major Wars*. Princeton, NJ: Princeton University Press.

Illich, I. (1997). Development as planned poverty. *The Post-Development Reader* (ed. M. Rahnema with V. Bawtree). London: Zed Books.

IMF (International Monetary Fund) (various years). Annual reports on exchange arrangements and exchange controls. Washington, DC: IMF.

International Military Tribunal at Nuremberg (1946). Nuremberg Trial proceedings. Vol. 1. Indictment: Count Three—War Crimes. http://avalon.law.yale.edu/imt/count3.asp.

Inglehart, R. (1997). *Modernization and Postmodernization: Cultural, Political and Economic Change in 43 Societies.* Princeton, NJ: Princeton University Press.

Ingram, J. and Freestone, D. (2006). Human rights and development. *Development Outreach*, October 2006. Washington, DC: World Bank Institute.

Inkeles, A. (1963). Social change and social character: The role of parental mediation. *Personality and Social Systems* (ed. N. Smelser and W. Smelser). New York: Wiley.

Institute for the Study of International Migration (ISIM) and Brookings-Bern Project (2008). Global database—guiding principles on internal displacement. http://www.idpguidingprinciples.org/.

The Interim (1998). ICC: Promise of justice or threat of tyranny? August.

International Working Group for Disease Monitoring and Forecasting (1995). Capture–recapture and multiple record systems estimation I: History and theoretical development. *American Journal of Epidemiology*, **142**/10, 1047–1058.

IPCC (2007). Fourth assessment report: Climate change 2007 synthesis report. http://www.ipcc.ch/ipccreports/ar4-syr.htm.

Irwin, M. A. (1996). 'White slavery' as metaphor: Anatomy of a moral panic. *Ex Post Facto: The History Journal*, **5**. https://sslvpn.pitt.edu/csis/papers/,DanaInfo=www.walnet.org+irwin-wslavery.html.

Ishay, M. R. (2004). *The History of Human Rights: From Ancient Times to the Globalization Era.* Berkeley, CA: University of California Press.

Ishikawa, S. S. and Raine, A. (2004). Behavioral genetics and crime. *The Neurobiology of Criminal Behavior* (ed. J. Glicksohn). Boston, MA: Kluwer.

Jabine, T. B. and Claude, R. P. (eds) (1992). *Human Rights and Statistics: Getting the Record Straight.* Philadelphia, PA: University of Pennsylvania Press.

Jabri, V. (2007). *War and the Transformation of Global Politics.* Basingstoke: Palgrave.

Jackson, R. (1990). *Quasi-States: Sovereignty, International Relations and the Third World.* Cambridge: Cambridge University Press.

Jahic, G. and Finckenauer, J. O. (2005). Representations and misrepresentations of human trafficking. *Trends in Organized Crime*, **8**/3, 24–40.

James, A. and Prout, A. (eds) (1990). *Constructing and Reconstructing Childhood: Contemporary Issues in the Sociological Study of Childhood.* London: Routledge.

_____ and Prout, A. (eds) (1997). *Constructing and Reconstructing Childhood: Contemporary Issues in the Sociological Study of Childhood* (2nd edn). London: Routledge.

Jolly, R. (1999). Human development and neoliberalism, paradigms compared. *Readings in Human Development* (ed. S. Fukuda-Parr and A. K. Shiva Kumar). New Delhi: Oxford University Press.

_____ (2004). Global goals: The United Nations experience. *Journal of Human Development*, **5**/1, 69–95.

Jones, B. (2001). *Peacemaking in Rwanda: The Dynamics of Failure.* Boulder, CO: Lynne Rienner.

Jones, P. (1999). Group rights and group oppression. *The Journal of Political Philosophy*, **7**/4, 353–377.

_____ (ed.) (2008). *Group Rights.* Aldershot: Ashgate.

Kaase, M. and Newton, K. (1995). *Beliefs in Government, Vol. V: Beliefs in Government.* Oxford: Oxford University Press.

Kaldor, M. (2003). *Global Civil Society: An Answer to War.* Cambridge: Polity.

Kalyvas, S. (2006). *The Logic of Violence in Civil War.* New York: Cambridge University Press.

Kamenka, E. (1978). The anatomy of an idea. *Human Rights* (ed. E. Kamenka and A. Erh-Soon Tay). Port Melbourne: Edward Arnold.

Kanbur, R. (2007). Attacking poverty: What is the value added of a human rights approach? http://www.people.cornell.edu/pages/sk145.

Kant, I. (1991). Perpetual peace: A philosophical sketch. *Political Writings* (ed. H. Reiss). Cambridge: Cambridge University Press.

_____ (2002). *Groundwork for the Metaphysics of Morals* (trans. A. W. Wood). New Haven, CT: Yale University Press.

Kanyongo, G. Y. (2005). Zimbabwe's public education system reforms: Successes and challenges. *International Education Journal*, **6**/1, 65–74.

Karklins, R. and Petersen, R. (1993). Decision calculus of protesters and regimes—eastern Europe 1989. *Journal of Politics*, **55**/3, 588–614.

Keck, M. E. and Sikkink, K. (1998). *Activists Beyond Borders: Advocacy Networks in International Politics.* Ithaca, NY: Cornell University Press.

Keller-Herzog, A. (1996). Globalization and gender—Development perspectives and interventions. Women in Development and Gender Equity Division Policy Branch. Canada: Canadian International Development Agency.

Kempadoo, K. (ed.) (2005a). *Trafficking and Prostitution Reconsidered.* Boulder, CO: Paradigm Publishers.

_____ (2005b). From moral panic to global justice: Changing perspectives on trafficking. *Trafficking and Prostitution Reconsidered* (ed. K. Kempadoo). Boulder, CO: Paradigm Publishers.

Kenen, P. B. (1994). *The International Economy* (3rd edn). Cambridge: Cambridge University Press.

Khiddu-Makubuya, E. (1989). Paramilitarism and human rights. *Conflict Resolution in Uganda* (ed. K. Rupesinghe). Oslo: International Peace Research Institute.

Kiernan, B. (2007). *Blood and Soil: A World History of Genocide and Extermination from Sparta to Darfur.* New Haven, CT: Yale University Press.

King, J. (2000). Exploring the ameliorating effects of democracy on political repression: Cross-national evidence. *Paths to State Repression: Human Rights Violations and Contentious Politics* (ed. C. Davenport). Boulder, CO: Rowman and Littlefield.

King, M. (1997). *A Better World for Children? Explorations in Morality and Authority*. London Routledge.

Kinley, D. and Joseph, S. (2002). Multinational corporations and human rights. *Alternative Law Journal*, **27**/1, 7–11.

Kirmayer, L. J., MacDonald, M. E., and Brass, G. M. (eds) (2001). The mental health of Indigenous peoples. Culture and Mental Health Research Unit report 10. Division of Social and Transcultural Psychiatry, McGill University, Montreal.

Kirsch, P. and Holmes, J. T. (1999). The birth of the International Criminal Court: The 1998 Rome conference. *Canadian Yearbook of International Law*, **36**, 3–39.

Klein, N. (2007). *The Shock Doctrine: The Rise of Disaster Capitalism*. New York: Metropolitan.

Korey, W. (1999). Human rights NGOs: The power of persuasion. *Ethics and International Affairs*, **13**, 151–174.

Kramer, P. (2008). The water cure. *The New Yorker*, 25 February.

Kramnick, I. (ed.) (1995). *The Portable Enlightenment Reader*. London: Penguin.

Krasner, S. (1999). *Sovereignty: Organized Hypocrisy*. Princeton, NJ: Princeton University Press.

Kraut, A. (1996). *Records of the Immigration and Naturalization Service. Series A: Subject Correspondence Files. Part 5: Prostitution and 'White Slavery,' 1902–1933*. Bethesda, MD: University Publications of America.

Kucera, D. (2001). The effects of core workers rights on labour costs and foreign direct investment: Evaluating the conventional wisdom. IILS working paper no. 130. International Labour Organization. http://ssrn.com/abstract=313079.

Kuper, A. (1999). *Culture: The Anthropologists' Account*. Cambridge, MA: Harvard University Press.

Kuper, L. (1981). *Genocide: Its Political Use in the Twentieth Century*. New Haven, CT: Yale University Press.

Kuperman, A. (2001). *The Limits of Humanitarian Intervention: Genocide in Rwanda*. Washington, DC: Brookings Institution Press.

_____ (2008). The moral hazard of humanitarian intervention: Lessons from the Balkans. *International Studies Quarterly*, **52**/1, 49–80.

Kymlicka, W. (1995). *Multicultural Citizenship: A Liberal Theory of Minority Rights*. Oxford: Oxford University Press.

_____ (2007). *Multicultural Odysseys*. Oxford: Oxford University Press.

Laïdi, Z. (1998). *A World Without Meaning: The Crisis of Meaning in International Relations*. London: Routledge.

Landau Commission Report (1989). *Israel Law Review*, **23**/2–3.

Landman, T. (2002). Comparative politics and human rights. *Human Rights Quarterly*, **24**/4, 890–923.

_____ (2004). Measuring human rights: Principle, practice, and policy. *Human Rights Quarterly*, **26**/4, 906–931.

_____ (2005a). Review article: The political science of human rights. *British Journal of Political Science*, **35**/3, 549–572.

_____ (2005b). *Protecting Human Rights: A Global Comparative Study*. Washington, DC: Georgetown University Press.

_____ (2006a). Holding the line: Human rights defenders in the age of terror. *British Journal of Politics and International Relations*, **8**, 123–147.

_____ (2006b). *Studying Human Rights*. London: Routledge.

_____ and Carvalho, E. (to appear). *Measuring Human Rights*. London: Routledge.

_____ and Häusermann, J. (2003). Map-making and analysis of the main international initiatives on developing indicators on democracy and good governance. Report for the Statistical Office of the Commission of the European Communities (EUROSTAT). Human Rights Centre, University of Essex.

Langbein, J. H. (1977). *Torture and the Law of Proof: Europe and England in the Ancien Régime*. Chicago, IL: University of Chicago Press.

Langlois, A. J. (2001). *The Politics of Justice and Human Rights*. Cambridge: Cambridge University Press.

_____ (2004). The elusive ontology of human rights. *Global Society*, **18**/3, 243–261.

Las Casas, B. de (1992). *The Devastation of the Indies: A Brief Account*. Baltimore, MD: Johns Hopkins University Press.

Laughland, J. (2007). *Travesty: The Trial of Slobodan Milosevic and the Corruption of International Justice*. London: Pluto.

Lauren, P. G. (1998). *The Evolution of International Human Rights: Visions Seen*. Philadelphia, PA: University of Pennsylvania Press.

Leader, N. (1998). Proliferating principles; or how to sup with the Devil without getting eaten. *Disasters*, **22**/4, 288–308.

League of Nations (1926). Slavery, Servitude, Forced Labour and Similar Institutions and Practices Convention of 1926 (Slavery Convention of 1926). 60 L.N.T.S. 253. Entered into force 9 March 1927.

Lemarchand, R. (1970). *Rwanda and Burundi*. London: Pall Mall.

Lemkin, R. (1944). *Axis Rule in Occupied Europe: Laws of Occupation, Analysis of Government, Proposals for Redress*. New York: Columbia.

_____ (1947). Genocide as a crime under international law. *American Journal of International Law*, **41**/1, 145–151.

Lerner, D. (1958). *The Passing of Traditional Society: Modernizing the Middle East*. Glencoe, IL: Free Press.

_____ (1967). Comparative analysis of processes of modernisation. *The City in Modern Africa* (ed. H. Miner). London: Pall Mall.

Lesch, A. (1998). *The Sudan: Contested National Identities*. Bloomington, IN: Indiana University Press.

Levene, M. (2005). *Genocide in the Age of the Nation State*. London: I. B. Tauris.

Levin, M. (1982). The case for torture. *Newsweek*, 7 June.

LeVine, R., Klein, N., and Owen, C. (1967). Father–child relationships and changing life-styles in Ibadan, Nigeria. *The City in Modern Africa* (ed. H. Miner). London: Pall Mall.

Levitsky, S. and Way, L. (2002). The rise of competitive authoritarianism. *Journal of Democracy*, **13**/2, 51–65.

Lewis, D. (2002). Civil society in African contexts: Reflections on the usefulness of a concept. *Development and Change*, **33**/4, 569–586.

Lewis, N. (1998). Human rights, law and democracy in an unfree world. *Human Rights Fifty Years On: An Appraisal* (ed. T. Evans). Manchester: Manchester University Press.

Li, Q. and Resnick, A. (2003). Reversal of fortunes: Democratic institutions and foreign direct investment inflows to developing countries. *International Organization*, **57**/1, 1–37.

Lichbach, M. I. (1995). *The Rebel's Dilemma*. Ann Arbor, MI: University of Michigan Press.

Life Advocate Magazine (1998). Rome conference ends without consensus, **13**/2, September/October.

Likosky, M. (2003). Mitigating human rights risks under state-financed and privatized infrastructure projects. *Indiana Journal of Global Legal Studies*, **10**/2, 65–85.

Lim, L. L. (ed.) (1998). *The Sex Sector*. Geneva: International Labour Office.

Linklater, A. (1998). *The Transformation of Political Community: Ethical Foundations of the Post-Westphalian Era*. Cambridge: Polity.

_____ (2007). *Critical Theory and World Politics: Sovereignty, Citizenship and Humanity*. Abingdon: Routledge.

Lipset, S. M. (1959). Some social requisites of democracy—Economic-development and political legitimacy. *American Political Science Review*, **53**/1, 69–105.

Lobe, J. (2003). Ending exceptionalism: New human rights network denounces selectivity in Bush Administration's human rights agenda. *Foreign Policy In Focus*, 11 December.

Locke, J. (1952). *The Second Treatise of Government* (ed. T. P. Peardon). Indianapolis, IN: Bobbs-Merrill.

_____ (1960). *Two Treatises of Government*. Cambridge: Cambridge University Press.

Loescher, G. (1999). Refugees: A global human rights and security crisis. *Human Rights in Global Politics* (ed. T. Dunne and N. Wheeler). Cambridge: Cambridge University Press.

_____ (2001). *UNHCR and World Politics*. Oxford: Oxford University Press.

Loescher, G. and Milner, J. (2006). Protracted refugee situations: The search for practical solutions. *The State of the World's Refugees: Human Displacement in the New Millennium*. Oxford: Oxford University Press.

_____, Betts, A., and Milner, J. (2008). *UNHCR: The Politics and Practice of Refugee Protection into the 21st Century*. London: Routledge.

Long, L. D. (2004). Anthropological perspectives on the trafficking of women for sexual exploitation. *International Migration*, **42**/1, 5–31.

Luttwak, E. (1999). Give war a chance. *Foreign Affairs*, **78**/4, 36–44.

Maastricht Guidelines on Violations of Economic, Social and Cultural Rights (1997). Maastricht, 22–26 January. http://www.escr-net.org/resources_more/resources_more_show.htm?doc_id=425803.

Macchi, M. with Oviedo, G., Gotheil, S., Cross, K., Boedhihartono, A., Wolfangel, C., and Howell, M. (2008). Indigenous and traditional peoples and climate change—Issues paper, March. Gland: IUCN. http://cmsdata.iucn.org/downloads/indigenous_peoples_climate_change.pdf.

MacKenzie, L. (1993). *Peacekeeper: The Road to Sarajevo*. Vancouver: Douglas & McIntyre.

Macklin, R. (1981). Can future generations correctly be said to have rights? *Responsibilities to Future Generations* (ed. E. Partridge). Buffalo, NY: Prometheus Books.

MacMahon, P. (2007). Parties reject call for legal smacking ban. *Scotsman*, 23 January.

Mamdani, M. (2001). *When Victims Become Killers: Colonialism, Nativism, and the Genocide in Rwanda*. Princeton, NJ: Princeton University Press.

Mander, J. (2003). Intrinsic negative effects of economic globalization on the environment. *Worlds Apart: Globalization and the Environment* (ed. J. G. Speth). London: Island.

Mann, M. (2005). *The Dark Side of Democracy: Explaining Ethnic Cleansing*. New York: Cambridge University Press.

Marcon, G. and Pianta, M. (2001). New wars, new peace movements. *Soundings: A Journal of Politics and Culture*, **17**, 11–24.

Marcuse, H. (1964). *One Dimensional Man: Studies in the Ideology of Advanced Industrial Society*. London: Routledge.

Marshall, M. G. and Jaggers, K. (2000). Polity IV Project: Political regime characteristics and transitions, 1800–1999. Data users manual.

Marshall, T. H. (1963). Citizenship and social class. *Sociology at the Crossroads and Other Essays*. London: Heinemann.

Martin, I. (2001). *Self-Determination in East Timor: The United Nations, the Ballot, and International Intervention*. Boulder, CO: Lynne Rienner.

Martinez, J. (2008). Antislavery courts and the dawn of international human rights law. *Yale Law Journal*, **117**/4, 550–641.

Martinez-Alier, J. (2003). Mining conflicts, environmental justice, and valuation. *Just Sustainabilities: Development in an Unequal World* (ed. J. Agyeman, R. D. Bullard, and B. Evans). London: Earthscan.

Martinez-Cobo, J. (1986). Study of the problem of discrimination against Indigenous populations. UN Doc. E/CN.4/Sub.2/1986/7 and Add. 1–4, paragraph 379. http://www.un.org/esa/socdev/unpfii/en/spdaip.html.

Marx, K. (1987). On 'the Jewish question'. *Nonsense Upon Stilts: Bentham, Burke and Marx on the Rights of Man* (ed. J. Waldron). London: Methuen.

_____ (1990). *Capital: A Critique of Political Economy*, Vol. I. London: Penguin.

Maviglia, M. A. (2002). Historical trauma and PTSD: The 'existential' versus the 'clinical'. http://www.psychiatryonline.it/ital/fromstates2e.htm.

Maxfield, S. (1998). Understanding the political implications of financial internationalization in emerging market countries. *World Development*, **26**/7, 1201–1219.

May, M. (2006). San Francisco is hub for trafficking for sexual exploitation. *San Francisco Chronicle*, 6 November.

McCamant, J. F. (1981). Social science and human rights. *International Organization*, **35**/3, 531–552.

McCorquodale, R. and Fairbrother, R. (1999). Globalization and human rights. *Human Rights Quarterly*, **21**/3, 735–766.

_____ (1994) Why children do have equal rights. *International Journal of Children's Rights*, **2**/3, 243–258.

Mead, M. (ed.) (1953). *Cultural Patterns and Technical Change*. Paris: UNESCO with the World Federation for Mental Health.

_____ (1956). *New Lives for Old: Cultural Transformation—Manus, 1928–1953*. New York: Mentor Books.

_____ (1966). *Culture, Health and Disease: Social and Cultural Influence on Health Programmes in Developing Countries*. London: Tavistock.

_____ and Wolfenstein, M. (1955). *Childhood in Contemporary Cultures*. Chicago, IL: Chicago University Press.

Mears, R. R. (1995). The impact of globalization on women and work in the Americas. Women's Rights Committee Inter-American Bar Association Conference, Quito, Ecuador.

Meijknecht, A. (2001). *Towards International Personality: The Position of Minorities and Indigenous Peoples in International Law*. Antwerp: Intersentia.

Melson, R. (1992). *Revolution and Genocide: On the Origins of the Armenian Genocide and the Holocaust*. Chicago, IL: University of Chicago Press.

Mendus, S. (1995). Human rights in political theory. *Political Studies*, **43**/Special issue, 10–24.

Merrills, J. G. (1996). Environmental protection and human rights: Conceptual aspects. *Human Rights Approaches to Environmental Protection* (ed. A. E. Boyle and M. R. Anderson). Oxford: Clarendon.

Merry, S.-E. (2005). *Human Rights and Gender Violence: Translating International Law into Local Justice*. Chicago, IL: University of Chicago Press.

_____ (2006). Transnational human rights and local activism: Mapping the middle. In 'In focus: Anthropology and human rights in a new key'. *American Anthropologist*, **108**/1, 38–51.

Meyer, W. H. (1996). Human rights and MNCs: Theory versus quantitative analysis. *Human Rights Quarterly*, **18**/2, 368–397.

_____ (1998). *Human Rights and International Political Economy in Third World Nations*. Westport, CT: Praeger.

Midlarsky, M. (2005). *The Killing Trap: Genocide in the Twentieth Century*. New York: Cambridge University Press.

Milgram, S. (1974). *Obedience to Authority: An Experimental View*. New York: Harper Collins.

Mill, J. S. (1972). On liberty. *John Stuart Mill: Utilitarianism, on Liberty, Considerations on Representative Government* (ed. H. B. Acton). London: Everyman.

_____ (1985). *On Liberty*. London: Penguin.

Miller, A. and Stewart, A. N. (1998). Report from the roundtable on the meaning of 'trafficking in persons': A human rights perspective. *Women's Rights Law Report*, **20**/1, 11–19.

Mills, C. W. (1997). *The Racial Contract*. Ithaca, NY: Cornell University Press.

Milner, W., Poe, S., and Leblang, D. (1999). Security rights, subsistence rights, and liberties: A theoretical survey of the empirical landscape. *Human Rights Quarterly*, **21**/2, 403–444.

Minogue, K. (1979). The history of the idea of human rights. *The Human Rights Reader* (ed. W. Laquer and B. Rubin). New York: New Amsterdam Library.

Minow, M. (1990). *Making All the Difference: Inclusion, Exclusion and American Law*. Ithaca, NY: Cornell University Press.

_____ (1998). *Between Vengeance and Forgiveness*. Boston, MA: Beacon.

Mitchell, C., Stohl, M., Carleton, D., and Lopez, G. (1986). State terrorism: Issues of concept and measurement. *Government Violence and Repression: An Agenda for Research* (ed. M. Stohl and G. Lopez). New York: Greenwood.

Mitchell, N. J. and McCormick, J. M. (1988). Economic and political explanations of human rights violations. *World Politics*, **40**/4, 476–498.

Moghadam, V. M. (1993). *Gender Dynamics of Restructuring in the Semi-Periphery*. WIDER Research for Action Series. New York: United Nations University.

Monshipouri, M., Welch, C., and Kennedy, E. (2003). Multinational corporations and the ethics of global responsibility: Problems and possibilities. *Human Rights Quarterly*, **25**/4, 965–989.

Moravscik, A. (2000). The origins of human rights regimes: Democratic delegation in postwar Europe. *International Organization*, **54**, 217–252.

Morgan, R. (2004). Advancing indigenous rights at the United Nations: Strategic framing and its impact on the normative development of international law. *Social and Legal Studies*, **13**/4, 481–500.

Morgenthau, H. (1948). *Politics Among Nations*. New York: Knopf.

Morris, L. (2006). Sociology and rights: An emergent field. *Rights: Sociological Perspectives* (ed. L. Morris). New York: Routledge.

Morsink, J. (2000). *The Universal Declaration of Human Rights: Origins, Drafting, and Intent*. Philadelphia, PA: University of Pennsylvania Press.

Muller, E. N. (1985). Income inequality, regime repressiveness, and political violence. *American Sociological Review*, **50**/1, 47–61.

Munck, G. and Verkuilen, J. (2002). Conceptualizing and measuring democracy: Evaluating alternative indices. *Comparative Political Studies*, **35**/1, 5–35.

Murray, P. (1951). *State Laws on Race and Color*. Athens, GA: University of Georgia Press.

Museveni, Y. K. (1997). *Sowing the Mustard Seed*. London: Macmillan.

Mutua, W. (1996). The ideology of human rights. *Virginia Journal of International Law*, **36**, 589–657.

Narayan, D. with Patel, R., Schafft, K., Radenmacher, A., and Koch-Schulte, S. (2000). *Voices of the Poor: Can Anyone Hear Us?* Oxford: Oxford University Press.

Neier, A. (2003). *Taking Liberties: Four Decades in the Struggle for Rights*. New York: Public Affairs.

Nell, V. (2006). Cruelty's rewards: The gratifications of perpetrators and spectators. *Behavioral and Brain Sciences*, **29**/3, 211–224.

Nelson, J. (1969). *Migrants, Urban Poverty, and Instability in Developing Nations*. Occasional Papers in International Affairs, 22. Cambridge, MA: Center for International Affairs, Harvard University.

Nelson, J. M. (1987). Political participation. *Understanding Political Development* (ed. M. Weiner and S. Huntington). London: Little, Brown.

Nelson, P. and Dorsey, E. (2003). At the nexus of human rights and development: New methods and strategies of global NGOs. *World Development*, **31**/12, 2013–2026.

Neumayer, E. (2004). The WTO and the environment: Its past record is better than critics believe, but the future outlook is bleak. *Global Environmental Politics*, **4**/3, 1–8.

_____ (2005). Do international human rights treaties improve respect for human rights? *Journal of Conflict Resolution*, **49**/6, 925–953.

new economics foundation (2006). *The UK Interdependence Report: How the World Sustains the Nation's Lifestyles and the Price it Pays*. London: new economics foundation.

Newbury, C. (1988). *The Cohesion of Oppression: Clientship and Ethnicity in Rwanda, 1860–1960*. New York: Columbia.

Nieuwenhuys, O. (2000). The household economy and the commercial exploitation of children's work: The case of Kerala. *The Exploited Child* (ed. B. Schlemmer). London: Zed Books.

_____ (2001). By the sweat of their brow? Street children, NGOs and children's rights in Addis Ababa. *Africa*, **71**/4, 539–557.

Niezen, R. (2003). *The Origins of Indigenism*. Berkeley, CA: University of California Press.

Nitzan, J. and Bichler, S. (2000). Capital accumulation: Breaking the dualism of 'economics' and 'politics'. *Global Political Economy: Contemporary Theories* (ed. R. Palan). London: Routledge.

North, D. (1990). *Institution, Institutional Change and Economic Performance*. Cambridge: Cambridge University Press.

Nussbaum, M. (1997). Capabilities and human rights. *Fordham Law Review 66*. Reprinted in Hayden, P. (ed.) (2001). *The Philosophy of Human Rights*. St Paul, MN: Paragon House.

_____ (2000). *Women and Human Development: The Capabilities Approach*. Cambridge: Cambridge University Press.

Nwankwo, E., Phillips, N., and Tracey, P. (2007). Social investment through community enterprise: The case of multinational corporations involvement in the development of Nigerian water resources. *Journal of Business Ethics*, **73**/1, 91–101.

O'Neill, J. (2007). *Markets, Deliberation and Environmental Value*. London: Routledge.

O'Neill, O. (1992). Children's rights and children's lives. *Children, Rights and the Law* (ed. P. Alston, S. Parker, and J. Seymour). Oxford: Clarendon.

OAU (Organisation of African Unity) (1990). African Charter on the Rights and Welfare of the Child. OAU Doc. CAB/LEG/24.9/49 (1990). Entered into force 29 November, 1999.

_____ (2000). Rwanda: The preventable genocide. The report of the International Panel of Eminent Personalities to investigate the 1994 genocide in Rwanda and the surrounding events. Presented by Sir Ketumile Masire. xxii, 318 S. Addis Ababa: Organization of African Unity/IPEP.

Obadan, M. (1982). Direct foreign investment in Nigeria: An empirical analysis. *African Studies Review*, **25**/1, 67–81.

Oberleitner, G. (2007). *Global Human Rights Institutions.* Cambridge: Polity.

ODI (2006). Human rights and poverty reduction: Realities, controversies and strategies. http://www.odi.org.uk/rights/Publications/Rights%20Meeting%20Series%20Publication%202006/intro_screen.pdf.

OECD (1996). *Shaping the 21st Century: The Contribution of Development Co-operation.* Paris: OECD.

OECD/DAC (Development Assistance Committee) (2007). Action-oriented paper on human rights and development. DCD/DAC(2007)15. Paris: OECD.

Ofcansky, T. P. (1996). *Uganda: Tarnished Pearl of Africa.* Boulder, CO: Westview.

OHCHR (Office of the High Commissioner for Human Rights) (1993). Fact sheet no. 19, National Institutions for the Promotion and Protection of Human Rights. http://www.unhchr.ch/html/menu6/2/fs19.htm.

_____ (2006). *Frequently Asked Questions on a Human Rights-Based Approach to Development Cooperation.* New York: United Nations. http://www.unhchr.org.

_____ (2007). Mary Robinson, United Nations High Commissioner for Human Rights (1997–2002). http://www.unhchr.ch/html/hchr/unhc.htm.

_____ (2008). *Claiming the Millennium Development Goals: A Human Rights Approach.* New York: United Nations.

Okin, S. M. (1999). Is multiculturalism bad for women? *Is Multiculturalism Bad for Women?* (ed. J. Cohen, M. Howard, and M. Nussbaum). Princeton, NJ: Princeton University Press.

Olson, M. (1993). Dictatorship, democracy and development. *American Political Science Review*, **87**/3, 567–576.

Oosterveld, V. L. (1999). The making of a gender-sensitive international criminal court. *International Law FORUM du droit international*, **1**/1, 38–41.

Ophuls, W. (1977). *Ecology and the Politics of Scarcity.* San Francisco, CA: Freeman.

Orbinski, J. (1999). Nobel lecture by James Orbinski, Médecins Sans Frontières, Oslo, 10 December. http://nobelprize.org/nobel_prizes/peace/laureates/1999/msf-lecture.html.

Orlin, T. S., Rosas, A., and Scheinin, M. (2000). *The Jurisprudence of Human Rights Law: A Comparative Approach.* Abo, Finland: Institute for Human Rights, Abo Akademi University.

Oxfam (2007). Close the gap: Solutions to the indigenous health crisis facing Australia. A policy briefing paper from the National Aboriginal Community Controlled Health Organisation and Oxfam Australia, April. http://www.ahmrc.org.au/Downloads/CTG.pdf.

Pace, W. R. (1999). The relationship between the International Criminal Court and non-governmental organizations. *Reflections on the International Criminal Court: Essays in Honour of Adriaan Bos* (ed. H. A. M. von Hebel, J. G. Lammers, and J. Schukking). The Hague: TMC Asser.

_____ and Thieroff, M. (1999). Participation of non-governmental organizations. *The International Criminal Court: The Making of the Rome Statute; Issues, Negotiations, Results* (ed. R. S. Lee). The Hague: Kluwer Law International.

Parry, M. L., Canziani, O. F., Palutikof, J. P., van der Linden, P. J., and Hanson, C. E. (eds) (2007). Cross-chapter case study. *Climate Change 2007: Impacts, Adaptation and Vulnerability. Contribution of Working Group II to the Fourth Assessment Report of the Intergovernmental Panel on Climate Change.* Cambridge: Cambridge University Press. http://www.ipcc.ch/pdf/assessment-report/ar4/wg2/ar4-wg2-xccc.pdf.

Parton, N. (1985). *The Politics of Child Abuse.* Basingstoke: Macmillan.

Partridge, E. (1990). On the rights of future generations. *Upstream/Downstream: Issues in Environmental Ethics* (ed. D. Scherer). Philadelphia, PA: Temple University Press.

Pateman, C. (1988). *The Sexual Contract.* Stanford, CA: Stanford University Press.

Pavlovic, Z. (2007). Are children's rights starting to damage human rights? Unpublished paper. Ljubljana.

Pearson, E. (2005). *The Mekong Challenge: Human Trafficking: Redefining Demand.* Bangkok: International Labour Office.

Pender, J. (2002). Relegitimising intervention: The World Bank and the voices of the poor. *Rethinking Human Rights: Critical Approaches to International Politics* (ed. D. Chandler). Basingstoke: Palgrave.

_____ (2007). Country ownership: The evasion of donor accountability. *Politics Without Sovereignty: A Critique of Contemporary International Relations* (ed. C. Bickerton, P. Cunliffe, and A. Gourevitich). London: Routledge.

Perry, M. (2000). *The Idea of Human Rights.* Oxford: Oxford University Press.

Peskin, V. (2008). *International Justice in Rwanda and the Balkans: Virtual Trials and the Struggle for State Cooperation.* New York: Cambridge University Press.

Picolotti, R. (2003). Agenda 21 and human rights: The right to participate. *Linking Human Rights and the Environment* (ed. R. Picolotti and J. D. Taillant). Tucson, AZ: University of Arizona Press.

Pieterse, M. (2004). Possibilities and pitfalls in the domestic enforcement of social rights: Contemplating the South African experience. *Human Rights Quarterly*, **26**/4, 882–905.

Piron, L.-H. (2005). Integrating human rights into development: A synthesis of donor approaches and experiences. London: ODI. Prepared for the OECD/DAC Network on Governance (GOVNET). http://www.odi.org.uk.

Platt, A. (1977). *The Child Savers: The Invention of Delinquency*. Chicago, IL: University of Chicago Press.

Plummer, K. (2006). Rights work: Constructing lesbian, gay and sexual rights in late modern times. *Rights: Sociological Perspectives* (ed. L. Morris). New York: Routledge.

Poe, S. and Tate, C. N. (1994). Repression of human rights to personal integrity in the 1980s: A global analysis. *American Political Science Review*, **88**/4, 853–872.

_____, Tate, C. N., and Camp Keith, L. (1999). Repression of the human right to personal integrity revisited: A global cross-national study covering the years 1976–1993. *International Studies Quarterly*, **43**/2, 291–313.

Pogge, T. W. (2000). The international significance of human rights. *The Journal of Ethics*, **4**/1–2, 45–69.

_____ (2002). *World Poverty and Human Rights*. Cambridge: Polity.

_____ (2007). Severe poverty as a human rights violation. *Freedom From Poverty as a Human Right: Who Owes What to the Very Poor?* (ed. T. W. Pogge). Oxford: Oxford University Press.

Pollis, A. and Schwab, P. (eds.) (2000). *Human Rights: New Perspectives, New Realities*. Boulder, CO: Lynne Rienner.

Power, S. (2002). *'A Problem from Hell': America and the Age of Genocide*. New York: Basic Books/London: Flamingo.

Prendergast, J. (1996). *Frontline Diplomacy: Humanitarian Aid and Conflict in Africa*. Boulder, CO: Lynne Rienner.

Prunier, G. (2005). *Darfur: An Ambiguous Genocide*. Ithaca, NY: Cornell University Press.

Przeworski, A. (2000). *Democracy and Development: Political Institutions and Well-Being in the World, 1950–1990*. Cambridge: Cambridge University Press.

_____ and Vreeland, J. R. (2000). The effects of IMF programs on economic growth. *The Journal of Development Economics*, **62**/2, 385–421.

Pupavac, V. (2001). Misanthropy without borders: The International Children's Rights Regime. *Disasters*, **25**/2, 95–115.

_____ (2002). The International Children's Rights Regime. *Rethinking Human Rights: Critical Approaches to International Politics* (ed. D. Chandler). Basingstoke: Palgrave.

_____ (2005). Human security and the rise of global therapeutic governance. *Conflict, Security and Development*, **5**/2, 161–181.

Putnam, R. (1994). *Making Democracy Work: Civic Traditions in Modern Italy*. Princeton, NJ: Princeton University Press.

Pye, L. W. and Verba, S. (eds) (1965). *Political Culture and Political Development*. Princeton, NJ: Princeton University Press.

Rahnema, M. with Bawtree, V. (eds) (1997). *The Post-Development Reader*. London: Zed Books.

Rawls, J. (1971). *A Theory of Justice*. Boston, MA: Harvard University Press/Oxford: Oxford University Press.

_____ (1973) *A Theory of Justice*. Oxford: Oxford University Press.

_____ (1993). *Political Liberalism*. New York: Columbia University Press.

_____ (1999). *The Laws of Peoples with 'The Idea of Public Reason Revisited'*. Cambridge, MA: Harvard University Press.

Raymond, J. G., D'Cunha, J., Ruhaini Dzuhayatin, S., Hynes, H. P., Ramirez Rodriguez, Z., and Santos, A. (2002). *A Comparative Study of Women Trafficked in the Migration Process*. Amherst, MA: Coalition Against Trafficking in Women.

Raz, J. (1986). *The Morality of Freedom*. Oxford: Oxford University Press.

REAL Women of Canada (1998). Canada courts disaster with World Court. *REALity Newsletter*, **16**/10, July/August.

Regan, P. and Henderson, E. (2002). Democracy, threats and political repression in developing countries: Are democracies internally less violent? *Third World Quarterly*, **23**/1, 119–136.

Rejali, D. (2007). *Torture and Democracy*. Princeton, NJ: Princeton University Press.

Republic of Uganda (2000). *Amnesty Act*. Kampala: Government of Uganda.

Reus-Smit, C. (2001). Human rights and the social construction of sovereignty. *Review of International Studies*, **27**/3, 519–538.

_____ and Price, R. (1998). Dangerous liaisons? Critical international theory and constructivism. *European Journal of International Relations*, **4**/3, 259–294.

Richards, D. L. (1999a). Perilous proxy: Human rights and the presence of national elections. *Social Science Quarterly*, **80**/4, 648–665.

_____ (1999b). *Death Takes a Holiday: National Elections, Political Parties and Government Respect for Human Rights*. Ph.D. Dissertation. State University of New York at Binghamton, NY: Department of Political Science.

_____ (2006). What do citizens mean when they say 'human rights'? A comparative examination of the formation of citizen attitudes about, and understandings of, human rights. 2006 Annual Meeting of the American Political Science Association, 30 August–3 September, Philadelphia, PA.

_____ (2007). Women's status and economic globalization. *International Studies Quarterly*, **51**/4, 855–876.

_____ and Gelleny, R. D. (2002). Is it a small world after all? Economic globalization and government respect for human rights in developing countries. *Coping With Globalization* (ed. S. Chan and J. R. Scarritt). London: Frank Cass.

Richards, D. L., Gelleny, R. D., and Sacko, D. H. (2001). Money with a mean streak? Foreign economic penetration and government respect for human rights in developing countries. *International Studies Quarterly*, **45**/2, 219–239.

Riles, A. (2000). *The Network Inside Out*. Ann Arbor, MI: University of Michigan Press.

Risse, T. and Sikkink, K. (1999). The socialization of international human rights norms into domestic practices: Introductions. *The Power of Human Rights: International Norms and Domestic Change* (ed. T. Risse, S. C. Ropp, and K. Sikkink). Cambridge: Cambridge University Press.

_____, Ropp, S. C., and Sikkink, K. (eds) (1999). *The Power of Human Rights: International Norms and Domestic Change*. Cambridge: Cambridge University Press.

Robinson, M. (2005). What rights can add to good development practice. *Human Rights and Development: Towards Mutual Reinforcement* (ed. P. Alston and M. Robinson). New York: Oxford University Press.

Rodriguez, H. (2004). A 'long walk to freedom' and democracy: Human rights, globalization, and social injustice. *Social Forces*, **83**/1, 391–412.

Rodrik, D. (1997). *Has Globalization Gone Too Far?* Washington, DC: Institute for International Economics.

Rorty, R. (1993). Human rights, rationality, and sentimentality. *On Human Rights: The Oxford Amnesty Lectures 1993* (ed. S. Shute and S. Hurley). New York: Basic Books.

Rose, M. (1998). *Fighting for Peace: Bosnia 1994*. London: Harvill.

Rosenau, J. (1997). *Along the Domestic–Foreign Frontier: Exploring Globalisation in a Turbulent World*. Cambridge: Cambridge University Press.

_____ (1998). Governance and democracy in a globalizing world. *Re-Imagining Political Community: Studies in Cosmopolitan Democracy* (ed. D. Archibugi, D. Held, and M. Köhler). Stanford, CA: Stanford University Press.

Rostow, W. W. (1960). *The Stages of Economic Growth: A Non-Communist Manifesto*. London: Cambridge University Press.

Roth, K. (2004a). Defending economic, social and cultural rights: Practical issues faced by an international human rights organization. *Human Rights Quarterly*, **26**/1, 63–73.

_____ (2004b). Response to Leonard S. Rubenstein. *Human Rights Quarterly*, **26**/4, 873–878.

Rubenstein, L. S. (2004a). How international human rights organizations can advance economic, social and cultural rights: A response to Kenneth Roth. *Human Rights Quarterly*, **26**/4, 845–865.

_____ (2004b). Response by Leonard S. Rubenstein. *Human Rights Quarterly*, **26**/4, 879–881.

Rubin, B. R. and Newberg, P. R. (1980). Statistical analysis for implementing human rights policy. *The Politics of Human Rights* (ed. P. R. Newberg). New York: New York University Press.

Rummel, R. (1994). *Death by Government*. New Brunswick, NJ: Transaction Publishers.

Ruzza, C. (2006). Human rights, anti-racism and EU advocacy coalitions. *Rights: Sociological Perspectives* (ed. L. Morris). New York: Routledge.

Sachs, A. and Peterson, J. A. (1995). Eco-justice: Linking human rights and the environment. *Worldwatch Paper*, **127**.

Sahlins, M. (1997). The original affluent society. *The Post-Development Reader* (M. Rahnema with V. Bawtree). London: Zed Books.

Saith, A. (2006). From universal values to millennium development goals: Lost in translation. *Development and Change*, **37**/6, 1167–1199.

Salick, J. and Byg, A. (eds) (2007). *Indigenous Peoples and Climate Change*. Oxford: Tyndall Centre for Climate Change Research, University of Oxford and Missouri Botanical Garden. http://www.tyndall.ac.uk/publications/Indigenouspeoples.pdf.

Samson, C. and Short, D. (2006). Sociology of Indigenous peoples rights. *Rights: Sociological Perspectives* (ed. L. Morris). New York: Routledge.

Sands, P. (2006). *Lawless World: Making and Breaking Global Rules*. London: Penguin.

Sanford, V. (2008). Si hubo genocidio en Guatemala! *The Historiography of Genocide* (ed. D. Stone). London: Palgrave Macmillan.

Sano, H. O. (2000). Development and human rights: The necessary, but partial integration of human rights and development. *Human Rights Quarterly*, **22**/3, 734–752.

Schabas, W. (2000). *Genocide in International Law: The Crimes of Crimes*. Cambridge: Cambridge University Press.

Scheinin, M. (2005). What are Indigenous peoples? *Minorities, Peoples and Self-Determination—Essays in Honour of Patrick Thornberry* (ed. N. Ghanea and A. Xanthaki). Leiden: Martinus Nijhoff.

Schmitt, C. (1996). *The Concept of the Political*. Chicago, IL: University of Chicago Press.

_____ (2003). *The Nomos of the Earth: In the International Law of the Jus Publicum Europaeum*. New York: Telos.

Schofield, K. (2007). Smacking vital as last resort, insist parents in 'growing up' study. *Scotsman*, 20 January.

Scholte, J. A. (2001). Civil society and democracy in global governance. CSGR working paper no. 65/01. Warwick University: Centre for the Study of Globalisation and Regionalisation.

Schoof, R. (2008). CIA Director: Agency used waterboarding. *The Seattle Times*, 6 February.

Schulz, W. (2003). *Tainted Legacy: 9/11 and the Ruin of Human Rights*. New York: Thunder's Mouth/Nation Books.

Schumacher, E. F. (1973). *Small is Beautiful: A Study of Economics as if People Matter*. London: Blond & Briggs.

Schwarz, A. (1994). *A Nation in Waiting: Indonesia in the 1990s*. Boulder, CO: Westview.

Seckinelgin, H. (2002). Time to stop and think: HIV/Aids, global civil society and people's politics. *Global Civil Society 2002* (ed. M. Glasius, M. Kaldor, and H. Anheier). Oxford: Oxford University Press.

Seligman, A. (1992). *The Idea of Civil Society*. New York: Free Press.

Sellars, K. (2002). *The Rise and Rise of Human Rights*. Stroud: Sutton.

Sémelin, J. (2007). *Purify and Destroy: The Political Uses of Massacre and Genocide* (trans. C. Schoch). New York: Columbia University Press.

Sen, A. K. (1981). *Poverty and Famines: An Essay on Entitlement and Deprivation*. Oxford: Clarendon.

_____ (1988). *The Standard of Living: The Tanner Lectures, Clare Hall, Cambridge, 1985*. Cambridge: Cambridge University Press.

_____ (1989). Development as capability expansion. *Journal of Development Planning*, **19**, 41–58. Reprinted in S. Fukuda-Parr and A. K. Shiva Kumar (eds) (2003), *Readings in Human Development*, Dehli: Oxford University Press.

_____ (1999). *Development as Freedom*. New York: Alfred Knopf Publishers.

_____ (2004). Elements of a theory of human rights. *Philosophy and Public Affairs*, **34**/4, 315–356.

_____ (2005). Human rights and capabilities. *Journal of Human Development*, **6**/2, 151–166.

_____ (2006). Human rights and development. *Development as a Human Right: Legal, Political, and Economic Dimensions* (ed. B. A. Andreassen and S. P. Marks). Cambridge, MA: Harvard School of Public Health. Distributed by Harvard University Press.

Sengupta, A. (2006). The human right to development. *Development as a Human Right, Legal, Political and Economic Dimensions* (ed. B. A. Andreassen and S. P. Marks). Boston, MA: Harvard School of Public Health. Distributed by Harvard University Press.

Shaw, M. (2000). *Theory of the Global State: Globality as an Unfinished Revolution*. New York: Cambridge University Press.

Shelton, D. (2000). Law, non-law and the problem of 'soft law'. *Commitment and Compliance: The Role of Non-Binding Norms in the International Legal System* (ed. D. Shelton). New York: Oxford University Press.

Shiva, V. (1999). Food rights, free trade, and fascism. *Globalizing Rights: The Oxford Amnesty Lectures 1999* (ed. M. Gibney). Oxford: Oxford University Press.

_____ (2003). The myths of globalisation exposed: Advancing towards living democracy. *Worlds Apart: Globalization and the Environment* (ed. J. G. Speth). London: Island.

Shor, E. (2008). Conflict, terrorism, and the socialization of human rights norms: The spiral model revisited. *Social Problems*, **55**, 117–138.

Short, D. (2007). The social construction of indigenous 'native title' land rights in Australia. *Current Sociology*, **55**/6, 857–876.

_____ (2008). *Reconciliation and Colonial Power: Indigenous Rights in Australia*. Aldershot: Ashgate.

Shue, H. (1980). *Basic Rights: Subsistence, Affluence, and U.S. Foreign Policy*. Princeton, NJ: Princeton University Press.

_____ (1996). *Basic Rights: Subsistence, Affluence and U.S. Foreign Policy* (2nd edn). Chichester: Princeton University Press.

Sikkink, K. (1993). The power of principled ideas: Human rights policies in the United States and western Europe. *Ideas and Foreign Policy: Beliefs, Institutions, and Political Change* (ed. J. Goldstein and R. O. Keohane). Ithaca, NY: Cornell University Press.

_____ (2004). *Mixed Signals: U.S. Human Rights Policy and Latin America*. Ithaca, NY: Cornell University Press.

Simms, A. (2005). *Ecological Debt: The Health of the Planet and the Wealth of Nations*. London: new economics foundation.

Simon, M. (1994). Hawks, doves and civil conflict dynamics: A 'strategic' action–reaction model. *International Interactions*, **19**/3, 213–239.

Simpson, G. (2004). *Great Powers and Outlaw States: Unequal Sovereigns in the International Legal Order*. Cambridge: Cambridge University Press.

Singer, P. (2006). The great ape debate. *Project Syndicate*, May. http://www.utilitarian.net/singer/by/200605--.htm.

Skogly, S. (1993). Structural adjustment and development: Human rights—an agenda for change. *Human Rights Quarterly*, **15**/4, 751–778.

Slaughter, A. M. (2004). *A New World Order*. Princeton, NJ: Princeton University Press.

Slyomovics, S. (2005). *The Performance of Human Rights in Morocco*. Philadelphia, PA: University of Pennsylvania Press.

Smith, J., Bolyard, M., and Ippolito, A. (1999). Human rights and the global economy: A response to Meyer. *Human Rights Quarterly*, **21**/1, 207–219.

_____, Chatfield, C., and Pagnucco, R. (eds) (1997). *Transnational Social Movements and World Politics: Solidarity Beyond the State*. Syracuse, NY: Syracuse University Press.

Solzhenitsyn, A. (1973). *The Gulag Archipelago: 1918–1956: An Experiment in Literary Investigation*. New York: Harper & Row.

Spar, D. (1998). The spotlight and the bottom line: How multinationals export human rights. *Foreign Affairs*, **77**/7, 7–12.

Speed, S. (2006). At the crossroads of human rights and anthropology: Toward a critically engaged activist research. In 'In focus: Anthropology and human rights in a new key. *American Anthropologist*, **108**/1, 66–76.

Spero, J. and Hart, J. (1997). *The Politics of International Relations* (5th edn). New York: St Martins.

Speth, J. G. (2003). Two perspectives on globalization and the environment. *Worlds Apart: Globalization and the Environment* (ed. J. G. Speth). Washington, DC: Island.

Spiliopoulo Akermark, S. (2005). The World Bank and Indigenous peoples. *Minorities, Peoples and Self-Determination—Essays in Honour of Patrick Thornberry* (ed. N. Ghanea and A. Xanthaki). Leiden: Martinus Nijhoff.

Stammers, N. (1999). Social movements and the social construction of human rights. *Human Rights Quarterly*, **21**/4, 980–1008.

Staub, E. (1989). *The Roots of Evil: The Origins of Genocide and Other Group Violence*. Cambridge: Cambridge University Press.

_____ (1990). The psychology and culture of torture and torturers. *Psychology and Torture* (ed. P. Suedfeld). New York: Hemisphere.

Stavenhagen, R. (2007). General considerations on the situation of human rights and fundamental freedoms of Indigenous peoples in Asia. UNPFII, Sixth Session, New York, 14–25 May. UN Doc. E/C.19/2007/CRP.11. http://www.tebtebba.org/tebtebba_files/unpf/pf6/6session_crp11_en.pdf.

Steains, C. (1999). Gender issues. *The International Criminal Court: The Making of the Rome Statute; Issues, Negotiations, Results* (ed. R. S. Lee). The Hague: Kluwer Law International.

Stern, N. (ed.) (2006). Stern review on the economics of climate change. http://www.hm-treasury.gov.uk/independent_reviews/stern_review_economics_climate_change/sternreview_index.cfm.

Steward, J. (1948). Comments on the statement on human rights. *American Anthropologist*, **50**/2, 351–352.

Stiglitz, J. (2002). *Globalization and its Discontents*. London: Allen Lane.

Straus, S. (2001). Contesting meanings and conflicting imperatives: A conceptual analysis of genocide. *Journal of Genocide Research*, **3**/3, 349–375.

_____ (2005). Darfur and the genocide debate. *Foreign Affairs*, **84**/1, 123–133.

_____ (2007). Second generation comparative research on genocide. *World Politics*, **59**/3, 476–501.

Sudan Divestment Task Force (2007). *Sudan Company Rankings 12/20/2007*. Washington, DC.

Supreme Court of Israel (1999). Judgment concerning the legality of the General Security Service's interrogation methods. 38 ILM 1471, 1488.

Tauli-Corpuz, V. and Lynge, A. (2008). Impact of climate change mitigation measures on Indigenous peoples and on their territories and lands. UNPFII, Seventh Session, New York, 21 April–2 May. UN Doc. E/C.19/2008/10. http://www.tebtebba.org/tebtebba_files/susdev/cc_energy/UNPFII_Climate_Rapporteurs_final.pdf.

_____ and Tamang, P. (2007). Oil palm and other commercial tree plantations, mono-cropping: Impacts on Indigenous peoples' land tenure and resource management systems and livelihoods. UNPFII, Sixth Session, New York, 14–25 May. UN Doc. E/C.19/2007/CRP.6. http://www.un.org/esa/socdev/unpfii/documents/6session_crp6.doc.

Taylor, C. (1994). *Multiculturalism and the Politics of Recognition*. Princeton, NJ: Princeton University Press.

Tearfund (2006). Feeling the heat. http://www.tearfund.org/webdocs/Website/News/Feeling%20the%20Heat%20Tearfund%20report.pdf.

Terry, F. (2002). *Condemned to Repeat: The Paradox of Humanitarian Action*. Ithaca, NY: Cornell University Press.

Thakur, R. (2002). Outlook: Intervention, sovereignty and the responsibility to protect. *Security Dialogue*, **33**/3, 323–340.

Thomas, D. C. (1999). The Helsinki accords and political change in eastern Europe. *The Power of Human Rights: International Norms and Domestic Change* (ed. T. Risse, S. C. Ropp, and K. Sikkink). Cambridge: Cambridge University Press.

_____ (2001). *The Helsinki Effect: International Norms, Human Rights, and the Demise of Communism*. Princeton, NJ: Princeton University Press.

Thornberry, P. (1991). *International Law and the Rights of Minorities*. Oxford: Clarendon.

_____ (2002). *Indigenous Peoples and International Law*. Manchester: Manchester University Press.

Tilly, C., Tilly, L., and Tilly, R. (1975). *The Rebellious Century 1830–1930*. Cambridge, MA: Harvard University Press.

Tomuschat, C. (2003). *Human Rights Between Idealism and Realism*. Oxford: Oxford University Press.

Totten, S. and Markusen, E. (2006). *Genocide in Darfur: Investigating the Atrocities in the Sudan*. New York: Routledge.

Tsebelis, G. (2002). *Veto Players: How Political Institutions Work*. Princeton, NJ: Princeton University Press.

Tuck, R. (1979). *Natural Rights Theories: Their Origin and Development*. Cambridge: Cambridge University Press.

Tuman, J. P. and Emmert, C. F. (2004). The political economy of U.S. foreign direct investment in Latin America: A reappraisal. *Latin American Research Review*, **39**/3, 9–28.

Turner, B. S. (1993). Outline of a theory of human rights. *Sociology*, **27**/3, 489–512.

_____ (1997) A neo-Hobbesian theory of human rights: A reply to Malcolm Waters. *Sociology* **31**/3, 565–571.

_____ (2006). *Vulnerability and Human Rights*. University Park, PA: The Pennsylvania State University Press.

_____ and Rojek, C. (2001). *Society and Culture: Principles of Scarcity and Solidarity*. London: Sage.

Uçarer, E. (1999). Trafficking in women: Alternate migration or modern slave trade. *Gender Politics in Global Governance* (ed. M. Meyer and E. Prugl). Lanham, MD: Roman and Littlefield.

Uganda (1998). Brooklyn, NY: Interlink Books.

UN Secretary General (2001). We the children: End-decade review of the follow-up to the World Summit for Children. New York: United Nations. http://www.unicef.org/specialsession/documentation/documents/a-s-27-3e.doc.

_____ (2004). Report of the Secretary General: The rule of law and transitional justice in conflict and post-conflict situations. S/2004/616.

_____ (2006). Secretary General study on violence against children. New York: United Nations. http://www.violencestudy.org/r25.

UNCTAD (2007). *Doing Business 2007*. New York: United Nations Publications.

UNDG (2003). The human rights based approach to development cooperation towards a common understanding among UN agencies. http://www.undg.org/archive_docs/6959-The_Human_Rights_Based_Approach_to_Development_Cooperation_Towards_a_Common_Understanding_among_UN.pdf.

UNDP (United Nations Development Program) (1990) *Human Development Report*. New York: Oxford University Press.

_____ (1999). *Human Development Report: Globalization with a Human Face*. Oxford: Oxford University Press.

_____ (2000). *Human Development Report: Human Rights*. New York: Oxford University Press.

_____ (2002). *Human Development Report: Deepening Democracy in a Fragmented World*. New York: Oxford University Press.

_____ (2003). *Human Development Report: MDGs: A Compact Among Nations to End Human Poverty*. New York: Oxford University Press.

_____ (2004). *Governance Indicators: A User's Guide*. Oslo: Oslo Governance Centre.

_____ (2006). *Indicators for Rights-Based Approaches to Development Programming: A User's Guide*. Oslo: Oslo Governance Centre.

_____ (2008). Fighting climate change: Human solidarity in a divided world. http://hdr.undp.org/en/reports/global/hdr2007-2008/.

UNECE (United Nations Economic Commission on Europe) (1998). Convention on access to information, public participation in decision-making and access to justice in environmental matters. http://www.unece.org/env/pp/documents/cep43e.pdf.

UNEP (United Nations Environment Program) (1992). The Rio declaration on environment and development. http://www.unep.org/Documents.Multilingual/Default.asp?DocumentID=78&ArticleID=1163.

UNESCO (1978). 1978 Study of the procedures which should be followed in the examination of cases and questions which might be submitted to UNESCO concerning the exercise of human rights in the spheres of its competence, in order to make its action more effective. Decision 104, EX/3.3.

UNHCR (2006). Colombia: Humanitarian emergency looms for indigenous communities. UNHCR Briefing Notes, 4 April. http://www.unhcr.org/cgi-bin/texis/vtx/news/opendoc.htm?tbl=NEWS&id=4432474c6.

UNICEF (undated). Introduction to the Convention on the Rights of the Child. Definition of key terms. http://www.unicef.org/crc/files/Definitions.pdf.

_____ (1963). *The Needs of Children*. New York: The Free Press of Glencoe.

_____ (1964). *Children of the Developing Countries*. London: William Clowes.

United Nations (1979). UN convention on the elimination of all forms of discrimination against women (CEDAW).

_____ (2004). A more secure world: Our shared responsibility. Report of the Secretary-General's High-level Panel on Threats, Challenges and Change, 3 December. http://www.un.org/secureworld/.

_____ (2005). Resolution adopted by the General Assembly. A/RES/60/1: World Summit Outcome, 24 October.

_____ (2006). Human rights council. GA Resn 60/251 at 2. UN Doc. A/RES/60/251. http://daccessdds.un.org/doc/UNDOC/GEN/N05/502/66/PDF/N0550266.pdf?OpenElement.

United Nations General Assembly (1989). UN convention on the rights of the child. General Assembly Resolution 44/25, 20 November.

_____ (2001) We the children: End-decade review of the follow-up to the World Summit for Children. Report of the Secretary-General. A/S-27/3, June. http://www.unicef.org/specialsession/documentation/archive.htm.

United States Code (2000). Code 22, §7101. *Trafficking Victims Protection Act of 2000*.

UNPFII (UN Permanent Forum for Indigenous Issues) (2006). Who are Indigenous peoples? http://www.un.org/esa/socdev/unpfii/documents/5session_factsheet1.pdf.

_____ (2008). Climate change, bio-cultural diversity and livelihoods of Indigenous peoples to be focus of UN forum. Press release, New York, 16 April. http://www.un.org/esa/socdev/unpfii/documents/Opening_%20PR_7th_Sess_PFII.pdf.

US Department of Justice (2007). Attorney General's annual report to Congress on U.S. Government activities to combat trafficking in persons fiscal year 2006. May. Washington, DC.

US Department of State (2006). Trafficking in persons report. Washington, DC. http://www.state.gov/g/tip/rls/tiprpt/2006/.

_____ (2008). Trafficking in persons report. Washington, DC. http://www.state.gov/g/tip/rls/tiprpt/2008/.

Uvin, P. (1998). *Aiding Violence: The Development Enterprise in Rwanda*. West Hartford, CT: Kumarian.

_____ (2004). *Human Rights and Development*. Bloomfield, CT: Kumarian.

_____ (2007). From the right to development to the rights based approach: How human rights entered development. *Development in Practice*, **17**/4–5, 598–604.

Valadez, J. (2000). *Deliberative Democracy, Political Legitimacy and Self-Determination in Multi-Cultural Societies*. Boulder, CO: Westview.

Valentino, B. (2004). *Final Solutions: Mass Killing and Genocide in the Twentieth Century*. Ithaca, NY: Cornell University Press.

_____, Huth, P., and Balch-Lindsay, D. (2004). 'Draining the sea': Mass killing and guerrilla warfare. *International Organization*, **58**, 375–407.

Van Bueren, G. (1995). *The International Law on the Rights of the Child*. Dordrecht: Martinus Nijhoff.

Vienna Declaration and Programme of Action (1993). Adopted by the World Conference on Human Rights, Vienna, 14–25 June. UN Doc. A/CONF.157/23. http://www.unhchr.ch/huridocda/huridoca.nsf/(Symbol)/A.CONF.157.23.En.

Village Voice (2001). The case against torture. 28 November–4 December.

Vincent, R. J. (1986). *Human Rights in International Relations*. Cambridge: Cambridge University Press.

Von Doussa, J., Corkery, A., and Chartres, R. (2008). Background paper: Human rights and climate change. Sydney: Human Rights and Equal Opportunities Commission. http://www.humanrights.gov.au/about/media/papers/index.html.

Vreeland, J. R. (2003). *The IMF and Economic Development*. Cambridge: Cambridge University Press.

_____ (2008). Political institutions and human rights: Why dictatorships enter into the United Nations Convention Against Torture. *International Organization*, **62**/1, 65–101.

Waldorf, L. (2006). Mass justice for mass atrocity: Rethinking local justice as transitional justice. *Temple Law Review*, **79**/1, 1–88.

Waldron, J. (1987). *Nonsense Upon Stilts: Bentham, Burke and Marx on the Rights of Man*. London: Methuen.

Walkowitz, J. R. (1980). *Prostitution and Victorian Society: Women, Class and the State*. Cambridge: Cambridge University Press.

Walter, E. V. (1969). *Terror and Resistance: A Study of Political Violence, with Case Studies of Some Primitive African Communities*. New York: Oxford University Press.

Walther, T. (1997). *The World Economy*. New York: Wiley.

Waters, M. (1996). Human rights and the universalisation of interests: Towards a social constructionist approach. *Sociology*, **30**/3, 593–600.

Watson, A. (2006). Children and international relations: A new site of knowledge? *Review of International Studies*, **32**/2, 237–250.

WCED (1987). Our common future. http://www.un-documents.net/ocf-ov.htm.

Webber, A. and Shirk, D. (2005). Hidden victims: Evaluating protections for undocumented victims of human trafficking. *Immigration Policy in Focus*, **4**/8. Washington, DC: Immigration Policy Center.

Weber, M. (1954). *Max Weber on Law in Economy and Society*. New York: Simon & Schuster.

_____ (1978). *Economy and Society*. Berkeley, CA: University of California Press.

_____ (2004). Politics as a vocation. *The Vocation Lectures* (ed. D. Owen). Indianapolis, IN: Hackett.

Weiner, M. (ed.) (1966). *Modernization: The Dynamics of Growth*. Washington, DC: Voice of America Forum Lectures.

Weitz, E. (2003). *Century of Genocide: Utopias of Race and Nation*. Princeton, NJ: Princeton University Press.

Wells, H. G. (1940). *The Rights of Man, or, What Are We Fighting For?* New York: Penguin.

Weschler, L. (1990). *A Miracle, a Universe: Settling Accounts with Torturers*. New York: Pantheon.

Whelan, D. J. and Donnelly, J. (2007). The West, economic and social rights, and the global human rights regime: Setting the record straight. *Human Rights Quarterly*, **29**/4, 908–949.

Whitcomb, C. (2002). The shadow war. *Gentlemen's Quarterly*, 22 September.

White, H. and Black, R. (eds) (2002). *Targeting Development: Critical Perspectives on Millennium Development Goals and International Development Targets*. London: Routledge.

Whiteley, P. (1999). The origins of social capital. *Social Capital and European Democracy* (ed. J. Van Deth, M. Maraffi, K. Newton, and P. Whiteley). London: Routledge.

_____ (2000). Economic growth and social capital. *Political Studies*, **48**, 443–466.

Wilkinson, S. (2004). *Votes and Violence: Electoral Competition and Ethnic Riots in India*. New York: Cambridge University Press.

Williams, R. (1963). *Culture and Society 1789–1950*. Harmondsworth: Penguin.

Wilson, R. A. (1997). Human rights culture and context: An introduction. *Human Rights, Culture and Context: Anthropological Perspectives* (ed. R. A. Wilson). London: Pluto.

_____ (2001). *The Politics of Truth and Reconciliation in South Africa: Legitimising the Post Apartheid State*. Cambridge: Cambridge University Press.

_____ (2006). 'Afterword' to 'Anthropology and human rights in a new key: The social life of human rights.' In 'In focus: Anthropology and human rights in a new key'. *American Anthropologist*, **108**/1, 38–51.

_____ and Mitchell, J. P. (eds) (2003). *Human Rights in Global Perspective: Anthropological Studies of Rights, Claims, and Entitlements*. London: Routledge.

Wood, E. J. (2000). *Forging Democracy from Below: Insurgent Transitions in South Africa and El Salvador*. Cambridge: Cambridge University Press.

Woodiwiss, A. (2005). *Human Rights*. New York: Routledge.

Woods, N. (2000). The political economy of globalization. *The Political Economy of Globalization* (ed. N. Woods). Basingstoke: Palgrave.

Woodward, C. V. (1951). *Origins of the New South, 1877–1913*. Baton Rouge, LA: Louisiana State University Press.

Worden, M. (2005). Torture spoken here: Ending global torture. *Torture: A Human Rights Perspective* (ed. K. Roth and M. Worden). New York: New Press/Human Rights Watch.

World Bank (2005). *World Development Indicators on CD-Rom*. Washington, DC: World Bank.

Wright, N. G. (1996). Uganda: History from 1971. *Encyclopedia of Africa South of the Sahara* (ed. J. Middleton). New York: Charles Scribner's Sons.

WSSD (2002). Report of the World Summit on Sustainable Development. http://www.unmillenniumproject.org/documents/131302_wssd_report_reissued.pdf.

WTO (World Trade Organisation) (2003). Implementation of paragraph 6 of the Doha Declaration on the TRIPS Agreement and Public Health Decision of the General Council of 30 August 2003. http://www.wto.org/english/tratop_e/trips_e/implem_para6_e.htm.

Zakaria, F. (2003). *The Future of Freedom: Illiberal Democracy at Home and Abroad*. New York: W. W. Norton.

Zanger, S. C. (2000). A global analysis of the effect of political regime changes on life integrity violations, 1977–1993. *Journal of Peace Research*, **37**/2, 213–233.

Ziegenhagen, E. A. (1986). *The Regulation of Political Conflict*. New York: Praeger.

Zolo, D. (2002). *Invoking Humanity: War, Law and Global Order*. London: Continuum.

Index